DARWIN

A NORTON CRITICAL EDITION

DARWIN

A NORTON CRITICAL EDITION

Edited by

PHILIP APPLEMAN

INDIANA UNIVERSITY

"It was characteristic of Darwin on his journeys
that when he saw a mountain he always tried to
climb it."   —Sir Gavin de Beer

W·W·NORTON & COMPANY·INC· *New York*

HERBERT J. MULLER, Indiana University, is the general editor of this and forthcoming Norton Critical Editions in the history of ideas.

Contents

Part IV: Darwin's Influence on Theological and Philosophical Thought

Part V: Darwin and Society

Part VI: Darwin and the Literary Mind

Part VII: Epilogue

Preface

The purpose of this anthology is to demonstrate some of the ways in which Darwin's work exercised an influence on the intellectual history, and on the day-to-day life, of modern man. To fulfill such a task at really satisfying length would of course require many volumes as large as this. Nevertheless, I hope that by excerpting primary materials and carefully selecting scholarly commentary, I have succeeded in drawing into one book the main outlines of this vast subject. Those who wish to explore further will find suggestions in the contents themselves and in the Selected Readings.

I want to thank those scholars who have advised me in various ways in planning this collection: Walter F. Cannon, Frederick B. Churchill, Sir Gavin de Beer, P. J. Gautrey, Donald Gray, George Levine, Bert James Loewenberg, William Madden, Herbert J. Muller, Morse Peckham, George Gaylord Simpson, and Michael Wolff. I should add that any faults in the book are mine alone.

I cannot release to the world so Victorian a product without an extra word of nostalgic gratitude to those extraordinarily fine gentlemen, my colleagues for years at *Victorian Studies,* to whom this work is dedicated. Nor is it by force of habit that I publicly thank yet again that able critic whose intelligence, and whose presence at breakfast, have alike been indispensable to me.

P.A.
Bloomington, Indiana
December, 1969

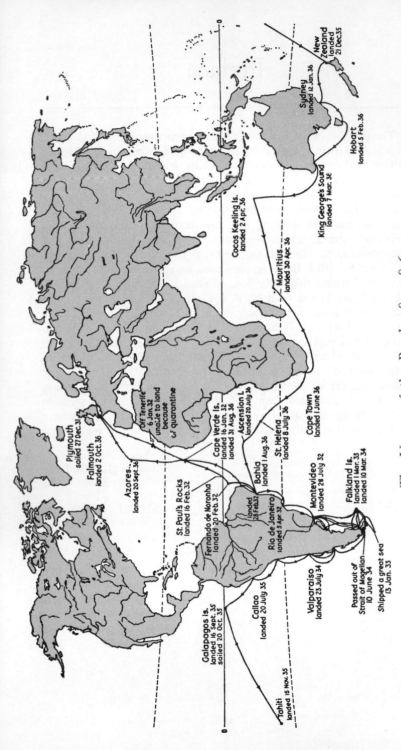

The Voyage of the *Beagle* 1831–1836

(The dates of Darwin's landings are not always those of the ship's arrival.)

New Zealand landed 21 Dec 35

Sydney landed 12 Jan. 36

Hobart landed 5 Feb. 36

King George's Sound landed 7 Mar. 36

Cocos Keeling Is. landed 2 Apr. 36

Mauritius landed 30 Apr. 36

Plymouth sailed 27 Dec.31

Falmouth landed 2 Oct. 36

Off Tenerife 6 Jan.32 unable to land because of quarantine

Azores landed 20 Sept.36

St. Paul's Rocks landed 16 Feb.32

Cape Verde Is. landed 16 Jan. 32 landed 31 Aug. 36

Ascension I. landed 20 July 36

Bahia landed 1 Aug. 36

St. Helena landed 8 July 36

Cape Town landed 1 June 36

Fernando de Noronha landed 20 Feb. 32

Rio de Janeiro landed 28 Feb. 32 landed 5 Apr. 32

Montevideo landed 28 July 32

Falkland Is. landed 1 Mar. 33 landed 10 Mar. 34

Galapagos Is. landed 16 Sept. 35 sailed 20 Oct. 35

Callao landed 20 July 35

Valparaiso landed 23 July 34

Passed out of Strait of Magellan 10 June 34

Shipped a great sea 13 Jan. 33

Tahiti landed 15 Nov. 35

Introduction

Charles Darwin's youth was unmarked by signs of genius. Born in 1809 into the well-to-do Darwin and Wedgwood clans (his mother was a Wedgwood, and Darwin himself was to marry another), he led a secure and carefree childhood, happy with his family, indifferent to books, responsive to nature. The son and grandson of impressively successful physicians, he eventually tried medical training himself, but found the studies dull and surgery (before anesthesia) too ghastly even to watch. So, for want of anything better, he followed the advice of his awesome father (6'2," 336 pounds, domineering in temperament) and studied for the ministry, taking his B.A. at Christ's College, Cambridge, in 1831.

Then a remarkable turn of events saved Darwin from a country parsonage. His science teacher at Cambridge, John Stevens Henslow, arranged for Darwin the invitation to be naturalist on H.M.S. *Beagle* during a long voyage of exploration. Despite his father's initial reluctance, Darwin got the position, and at the end of 1831 left England for a five-year voyage around the globe that turned out to be not only a crucial experience for Darwin himself, but a passage of consequence for the whole world.

The voyage of the *Beagle* made a scientist of Darwin—an industrious collector, a keen observer, a canny theorist—and it set him a momentous problem that he was to spend the next twenty years struggling with: the problem of the origin of species. By 1858, when another young naturalist, Alfred Russel Wallace, was himself pondering the same problem aboard yet another of Her Majesty's discovery ships, Darwin had collected enormous masses of detail relating to species and supporting his theory of natural selection. Faced, after decades of work, with the threat of being anticipated by Wallace's independent discoveries, Darwin quickly finished and published his great work, *The Origin of Species*, in 1859.

The effects of that publication were many and profound; hardly any kind of thought—scientific, philosophical, social, literary, historical—remained long unchanged by the implications of the *Origin*. That is what this anthology is about, and what is reviewed in the Epilogue.

Except for the voyage of the *Beagle*, however, Darwin's adventures were mostly intellectual, his life deliberately domestic. A chronic sufferer from a mysterious ailment, he had neither the strength nor the temperament for an active and public career; he remained secluded at his country house at Down, shunning the furious post-*Origin* controversies and leaving the defense of "Darwinism" to his more pugnacious friends. But always he worked. Good Victorian that he was, he worked as much every day as his strength permitted, and his industrious life was studded with solid contributions to science in articles, reviews, and books: *The Descent of Man* (1871), *The Expression of the Emotions* (1872), *The Formation of Vegetable Mould* (1881), and so on, and on.*

There was something paradoxical but eminently admirable about both Darwin's character and his devotion to his task. Intellectually he was a revolutionary, but the gentlest of revolutionaries. Spiritually he became an agnostic, but never a simple materialist; like many another Victorian agnostic, he exemplified in his life and work a high-minded benevolence not only toward his fellow men but for all creatures, and he continued always to write of the "grandeur" of "beautiful" and "wonderful" forms of life, and of men's high "destiny" in the future.

When he died in 1882, the man whose sacrilegious ideas had once been publicly assailed, from pulpit and periodical, by a multitude of "old ladies, of both sexes" (as T. H. Huxley called them) was buried, with the cordial acquiescence of the Dean, in Westminster Abbey—a few feet from the grave of the other immortal among British scientists, Sir Isaac Newton.

* See the Selected Readings at the end of this volume.

PART I

Scientific Opinion in the Early Nineteenth Century

As a record of a former state of things, I have retained in the foregoing paragraphs, and elsewhere, several sentences which imply that naturalists believe in the separate creation of each species; and I have been much censured for having thus expressed myself. But undoubtedly this was the general belief when the first edition of the present work appeared. I formerly spoke to very many naturalists on the subject of evolution, and never once met with any sympathetic agreement. It is probable that some did then believe in evolution, but they were either silent, or expressed themselves so ambiguously that it was not easy to understand their meaning. Now things are wholly changed, and almost every naturalist admits the great principle of evolution.

—Charles Darwin, 1872

He succeeded in putting the *whole* of past life into *every* aspect of *every* form of present life. In this respect Darwin has no precursor.

—Bert James Loewenberg, 1965

Introduction

SIR GAVIN DE BEER

Biology Before the *Beagle* (1964) †

* * * The subject of mutability of species had been taken up in speculative manner by a group of French philosophers including Montesquieu, Maupertuis, and Diderot. Basing themselves on certain facts such as the gradations that can be imagined between different species arranged in series, the appearance of new varieties of cultivated plants and domestic animals and of hereditary sports such as six-fingered men, the significance of monstrous births and imperfections of development, and the changes undergone by animals during their own life-histories, these thinkers concluded by deduction that species must have been mutable. Diderot even suggested that there was a prototype from which all living beings were descended and that the agent responsible for change was the age-old folk-belief that characters impressed on an organism during its life were transmitted by inheritance to the offspring. This, in his view, would account for the supposed perpetuation of the effects of use and disuse of organs, while the principle that if an animal experienced a need this need would provoke the formation of an organ that satisfied the need, accounted for the origin of such an organ.

In substantial agreement with these speculations was Erasmus Darwin, physician-philosopher-poet, whose work *Zoönomia or the Laws of Organic Life* was published in 1794. Like his French predecessors, Erasmus Darwin believed in the mutability of species because of the changes undergone by animals during embryonic development, particularly the metamorphoses of the caterpillar into the moth and the tadpole into the frog, because of the changes brought about by domestication and resulting from hybridization, because of the significance of monstrous births, and the similarity in plan of structure of vertebrate animals. He believed that the modification of species was brought about by the satisfaction of wants due to "lust, hunger, and danger," and as a result of "their own exertions in consequence of their desires and aversions, of their

† From Chapter 1 of *Charles Darwin: A Scientific Biography* (New York, 1964). Sir Gavin de Beer (b. 1899) was formerly director of the Natural History Department of the British Museum and professor of embryology at the University of London.

pleasures and pains, or of irritations, or of associations; and many of these acquired forms or propensities are transmitted to their posterity." He recognized the importance of adaptation of organisms to their environments in the struggle for existence, of protective coloration; of artificial selection and sexual selection in bringing about change; of cross-fertilization in maintaining vigor; of the significance of vestigial organs that were without function in their possessors but presupposed a former function; of monstrous births as disproof of the notion that the embryo is preformed in the germ; and of sports or mutations such as six-toed cats and rumpless fowls. But when it came to explaining how adaptations were produced in an organism, Erasmus Darwin had nothing to offer but "the power of acquiring new parts, attended with new propensities, directed by irritations, sensations, volitions, and associations; and thus possessing the faculties of continuing to improve by its own inherent activity, and of delivering down those improvements to its posterity, world without end."

Independently, although heir to the same speculative background, Jean-Baptiste de Lamarck came to conclusions very similar to those of Erasmus Darwin. A soldier of outstanding gallantry in the Seven Years War who had subsequently become fascinated by the luxuriance of plants in his garrison stations in the south of France, Lamarck abandoned the army as a profession and took up the study of natural history. In his book *Hydrogéologie* published in 1802 he opposed the "catastrophic" theories of geological causes then in vogue which required fantastic catastrophes to explain the state of the earth and, like James Hutton, advocated the uninterrupted continuity of past and present causes and effects. Lamarck recognized the unlimited amount of time required to account for the history of the earth, deduced the organic origin of sedimentary rocks, and pointed out the importance of fossils for the estimation of past changes of climate, valuable services to science, largely ignored even today.

It is for his *Philosophie zoologique* published in 1809 that Lamarck is remembered in the history of science. Confronted with the task of classifying the collections in the Paris Museum of Natural History, he experienced such difficulty in distinguishing between species and varieties of species that he concluded that there was no basic difference between them. He argued that if enough closely related species were studied together, differences between them could no longer be made out and they merged into one another. In fact this is not the case, because the barrier between species is always discernible even if very difficult to detect, but the appearance that species graded into one another led Lamarck to put forward a full theory of "transformism" or evolution, which he was the first to do, invoking descent of species during long periods of time from other species, so that the Animal Kingdom could be represented by a genealogy of branching lines, the last branch being that of man. Fossil organisms he thought had not become extinct but had been transmuted into their living descendants.

Lamarck accounted for evolution by means of the action of two factors. The first was a supposed tendency to perfection and to increased complexity, which he held responsible for the existence of the scale of beings from the simplest organisms at the bottom to man at the top. He regarded this concept as so self-evident as not to require proof, of which in fact it is incapable, being inaccessible to scientific investigation. It led him to suppose that as simple lowly organisms exist today without having been perfected or made complex, they must have arisen recently by spontaneous generation. Lamarck's second factor was introduced because the scale of beings is not a perfect series graded from the lowest to the highest but shows anomalies, deviations, and branchings from what it might and in his view would have been if the environment had not interfered. Like Diderot and Erasmus Darwin, Lamarck supposed that as a result of new needs experienced by the animal in its environment, its "inner feeling," comparable to Erasmus Darwin's "internal impulse" or "living force," set in motion bodily movements and instituted habits that produced new organs satisfying those needs, in other words, adapting the animal to its environment. These organs, and the effects of their use and disuse, he thought were then transmitted by heredity. As this explanation could not be applied to plants or to the lowest animals, Lamarck concluded that their evolution was conditioned by the direct effects of the environment. He was therefore unable to provide a unitary theory of evolution.

These views led contemporary scientists to reject them, and with them the theory of transmutation. Even Étienne Geoffroy-Saint-Hilaire, who accepted the transmutation of species, regretted that by his speculations Lamarck had compromised it. Scientists like Baron Georges Cuvier who rejected transmutation were even more opposed to Lamarck. It is, however, only fair to say that Lamarck has been treated with less than justice by history, for his name is associated with a hypothetic cause of evolution that he did not invent and that is unacceptable, whereas it was his genius in proposing a scheme of evolution that deserves commemoration in the term Lamarckism.

As a result of his extensive researches in comparative anatomy and paleontology published in 1812, Cuvier was struck by the fact that in the rocks of the Paris basin some strata contained fossils of marine animals, others fossils of fresh-water animals, and others again no fossils at all. From the apparently sudden appearance and equally sudden disappearance of these remains of bygone life, Cuvier concluded that catastrophes similar to the Biblical Flood had repeatedly destroyed life, and that after each catastrophe it had blossomed out afresh through successive creations and immigrations of such organisms as had escaped destruction because they had previously lived elsewhere on earth, out of reach of that particular catastrophe. There had therefore been extensive extinction of species, which was a new concept involving the abandonment of some objects of creation to their melancholy fate by the Supreme Being. It was not many years since John Wesley, in 1770, had written, "Death . . . is never permitted to destroy the most inconsiderable species," and Thomas Jefferson, referring to fossil bones of the American mastodon, which he refused to regard as extinct, wrote, "Such is the economy of nature, that no instance can be produced, of her having permitted any one race of her animals to become extinct; of her having formed any link in her great work, so weak as to be broken."

It was also obvious to Cuvier that after each "catastrophe" there was an advance in the complexity of life, so that each new wave of living beings showed a superiority of organization over their extinct predecessors. The younger the strata, the more fossils they contained belonging to animals similar to those living. A transcendental principle of progressionism had therefore to be invoked to account for this, since two reasons prevented him from accepting transmutation: the absence of any known intermediate forms, and the fact that organisms found in the oldest tombs of Egypt were identical with those still living and had therefore undergone no transmutation during the intervening period of time. Finally, Cuvier showed that the anatomical diversity exhibited by different groups of animals could not be accommodated on any single plan of structure undergoing progression from the simplest to the most complex. He therefore introduced the concept of four major groups or *embranchements* into which the Animal Kingdom was divided: Radiata (jellyfish, starfish), Articulata (worms, insects), Mollusca (snails, octopus), and Vertebrata. In other words, for the single scale of beings Cuvier substituted four plans of structure, which introduced the concept of divergence.

Another concept introduced by Cuvier was that of correlation of parts. His mastery of comparative anatomy enabled him to claim that "the smallest fragment of bone, even the most apparently insignificant apophysis, possesses a fixed and determinate character, relative to the class, order, genus and species of the animal to which it belonged; insomuch, that when we find merely the extremity of a well-preserved bone, we are able by careful examination, assisted by analogy and exact comparison, to determine the species to which it once belonged, as certainly as if we had the entire animal before us." * * *

Cuvier's principle of correlation was, in fact, based on his recognition of the fact and importance of adaptation; organs serve functions that adapt the organisms to their environments or conditions of existence, and in his view, as in that of many of his contemporaries, this fact of adaptation was evidence of purpose or of final causes: organisms had been created with their organs as they are in order that they might exploit their several ways of life and enjoy their environments. Teleology had been introduced into the details of anatomy and physiology.

To the geologist Charles Lyell, Cuvier's theories of catastrophism and progressionism were unacceptable, first because Lyell's observations and researches had convinced him that the geological agents that were to be seen operating in the present could, given sufficient time, have caused everything that had happened in the past history of the earth. This was the principle of uniformitarianism, first introduced by James Hutton in 1785 and developed independently by Lyell in his *Principles of Geology* (1830) to a point where it could not fail to prevail over the speculations of catastrophism. Lyell's objection to progressionism was due partly to its association with catastrophism and partly to his opinion that the paleontological evidence obtainable from the fossil record as known in his day was insufficient to support progressionism. Dicotyledonous plants, the highest types of the vegetable kingdom, had been found in coal measures of the Carboniferous period, and mammals in Secondary strata. Lyell therefore rejected progressionism and, with it, Lamarck's theory of transmutation, all the more because "if we look for some of those essential changes which would be required to lend even the semblance of a foundation for the theory of Lamarck, respecting the growth of new organs and the gradual obliteration of others, we find nothing of the kind." In his view, the theory lacked evidence, no intermediate forms were known, he thought it extravagant to claim that organisms could vary sufficiently to account for the differences between species, and the notion that when organs were needed they arose, removed the problem out of the realm of science into that of fanciful speculation. It must be added that Lamarck's inclusion of man in his scheme of evolution could not fail to disturb Lyell, for he was not yet prepared to contemplate unorthodox opinion where man was concerned, notwithstanding his scientific approach and rejection of scriptural interpretation in problems of geology. The result was that Lyell accepted the fact that species could become extinct, as a result of failure in the struggle for existence, and he knew that extinct species had been replaced by other species, but as to how this occurred and by what process fresh species originated, he had nothing to offer.

The problem of the origination of fresh species had, however, to be answered somehow, and the inability of the uniformitarian view to provide an answer drove its critics to adopt the only alternative known to them, namely miraculous interposition by the Creator. * * * The theory of evolution was tinged with political overtones that still persist. Then, they resulted in the writing of two books that had profound though unexpected effects on the future of natural history. On the sociological plane, a valiant attempt to stem the tide of the French ungodly was made by Thomas Robert Malthus with his *Essay on Population*, while on the theological side William Paley set out in his *Natural Theology* to prove that the study of natural history inevitably led to belief in a divine Creator.

* * * [Malthus] generalized the principle that "Population, when unchecked, increases in a geometrical ratio. Subsistence increases only in an arithmetical ratio. . . . I can see no way by which man can escape from the weight of this law which pervades all animate nature." Unwittingly, no doubt, Malthus here placed man on the same plane as the rest of the animal kingdom. Among plants and animals the growth of population was kept down by mortality due to "want of room and nourishment" and falling a prey to predators. In man, if in spite of famines and epidemics and the preventive checks imposed by reason, population nevertheless increased too fast, those of its members who could least afford the necessities of life were doomed to misery and death. On the other hand, if the checks to the increase in numbers of a population through delayed marriage and abstinence were artificial and too effective, there would be no competition or compulsion to work exerted on those whose livelihood depended on it, and the results would equally be misery from the effects of immorality, idleness, and sloth.

It followed, as H. N. Brailsford has pointed out, that all attempts to preserve life were contrary to the correct application of principle, charity was an economic sin, altruism "unscientific," and presumably the medical profession pursued an anti-social aim. Since the possibilities of variation, shown by cultivated plants and domestic animals, were in Malthus' view strictly limited, progress was impossible; attempts to achieve it as in the French Revolution were doomed to failure; and mankind could neither improve nor be perfected. Malthus' book was reprinted several times and the main lines of evidence on which his argument rested were on his own admission more and more undermined, but he nevertheless stuck to the sloganlike antithesis between geometrical and arithmetical rates of increase for growth of population and of subsistence. In this, Malthus performed a service to science, because most of those of his contemporaries who were aware of the struggle for existence in nature ran away from the horrors of tooth and claw and tried to veil it, minimize it, or moralize on the greater resulting happiness for the survivors. As will be seen, this aspect of Malthus' work had far-reaching effects.

Among Malthus' adherents was William Paley, who based his *Natural Theology* (1802) on the argument that a contrivance implies a contriver, just as a design implies a designer, and illustrated this analogy by means of a watch. Passing from horology to natural history he pointed out that the lens of the eye in fishes is more spherical than that of the eye of land vertebrates, which showed that each eye is *adapted* to the refractive index of the medium, water or air, in which the animal lives. "What plainer manifestation of design can there be than this instance?" he asked. The function of the iris diaphragm, accommodation for distance, the fact that the blind spots of the two eyes of an individual are not at conjugate points on the retina, that the eyebrow and eyelid protect the eye, all pointed to intelligent construction: "it is only by the display of contrivance, that the existence, the agency, the wisdom, of the Deity *could* be testified to his rational creatures." The same argument applied to the ear and to the function of all organs and tissues: down-feathers for warmth, flight-feathers for flight, webbed feet for progression in water, poison-fangs for defense in snakes, pouches for containing the young in marsupials, the long tongue of the woodpecker for catching grubs, the complicated life history of mistletoe. Some adaptations are even anticipatory, such as migration in birds, a contrivance to avoid and survive a cold season that has not yet arrived, or the foramen ovale and ductus arteriosus of the mammalian embryo, which enable it to switch instantly at birth from the intra-uterine to the aerial type of respiration and blood-circulation. All these were adaptations and Paley summed them up with the words: "The marks of *design* are too strong to be gotten over. Design must have had a designer. That designer must have been a person. That person is God." * * *

It is in the treatment of the problem of suffering that Paley had the greatest difficulty in making his case. "Pain, no doubt, and privations exist . . . Evil, no doubt, exists; but it is never, that we can perceive, the *object* of contrivance. Teeth are contrived to eat, not to ache." The "aches" caused in what teeth kill and eat are ignored, although the undeniable carnage of nature forces Paley to admit that "We cannot avoid the difficulty by saying that the effect was not intended. The only question open to us is whether it be ultimately evil. From the confessed and felt imperfection of our knowledge, we ought to presume that there may be consequences of this economy which are hidden from us," a form of argument that will be met again in very different circumstances. In an attempt to minimize the horror of the war of nature, he continues, "I believe the cases of bites which produce death in large animals (of stings I think there are none) to be very few."

Again, "Pain also itself is not without its *alleviations*. It may be violent and frequent; but it is seldom violent and long-continued; and its pauses and intermissions become positive pleasures. Of *mortal* diseases the great use is to reconcile us to death." In any case, by Malthus' principle, death is necessary to prevent overpopulation, and therefore beneficial. In compensation, "The Deity has super-added *pleasure* to animal sensations, beyond what was necessary for any purpose . . . it is a happy world after all." Then, as a parting shot, "The appearance of chance will always bear a proportion to the ignorance of the observer," with which Paley was confident that he had defended his religion and confounded the infidel. * * *

What Paley had, in fact, done was to provide a catalogue of adaptations that was shortly to come in very useful, and this is why it has been necessary to allot to Paley, as to Malthus, more space than would be justified by the intrinsic merits of their special pleading, masquerading as science. Furthermore, Paley's works, which were prescribed reading in British universities for many years, represent the prevailing points of view and attitudes of mind that had to be overcome by hard scientific evidence before the theory of evolution could be established, and, by an astonishing irony of history, his and Malthus' works unwittingly contributed more than any other publications to the establishment of that theory.

Such were the tides, currents, and backwaters of thought when on December 27, 1831 H.M.S. *Beagle* set sail from Plymouth.

Before Darwin: Conventional Scientific Opinion on the Fixity of Species

SIR CHARLES LYELL

Principles of Geology (1830–1833) †

* * *

Whether species have a real existence in nature

Before we can advance a step in our proposed inquiry, we must be able to define precisely the meaning which we attach to the term species. This is even more necessary in geology than in the ordinary studies of the naturalist; for they who deny that such a thing as a species exists, concede nevertheless that a botanist or zoologist may reason as if the specific character were constant, because they confine their observations to a brief period of time. Just as the geographer, in constructing his maps from century to century, may proceed as if the apparent places of the fixed stars remained absolutely the same, and as if no alteration were brought about by the precession of the equinoxes; so, it is said, in the organic world, the stability of a species may be taken as absolute, if we do not extend our views beyond the narrow period of human history; but let a

† Sir Charles Lyell (1797–1875) was a Fellow of the Royal Society and president of the British Association. His three-volume *Principles of Geology*, which went through eleven editions in his lifetime, illustrates by its continual accretions the progress of geology over half a century. The following passage, critical of Lamarck's theory of transformation, is from Volume II of the *Principles*, which Darwin received while aboard the *Beagle* in 1832.

Lyell's relationship with Darwin was a complex one. His "Uniformitarian" principle (the view that past changes in the earth's surface are to be accounted for by processes still in operation) was part of the underlying rationale for Darwin's work, and was an unorthodox geological opinion in the 1830's. Yet Lyell, though a friend of (and constant devil's advocate for) Darwin, could not bring himself to accept Darwin's theory until some years after the publication of the *Origin*.

The present text is from Volume II, Book III, Chapter 24, of the ninth edition of the *Principles* (1853), the last edition before the appearance of Darwin's book.

sufficient number of centuries elapse, to allow of important revolutions in climate, physical geography, and other circumstances, and the characters, say they, of the descendants of common parents may deviate indefinitely from their original type. * * *

Lamarck's arguments in favour of the transmutation of species

The name of species, observes Lamarck, has been usually applied to "every collection of similar individuals produced by other individuals like themselves." [1] This definition, he admits, is correct; because every living individual bears a very close resemblance to those from which it springs. But this is not all which is usually implied by the term species; for the majority of naturalists agree with Linnæus in supposing that all the individuals propagated from one stock have certain distinguishing characters in common, which will never vary, and which have remained the same since the creation of each species.

In order to shake this opinion, Lamarck enters upon the following line of argument:—The more we advance in the knowledge of the different organized bodies which cover the surface of the globe, the more our embarrassment increases, to determine what ought to be regarded as a species, and still more how to limit and distinguish genera. In proportion as our collections are enriched, we see almost every void filled up, and all our lines of separation effaced! we are reduced to arbitrary determinations, and are sometimes fain to seize upon the slight differences of mere varieties, in order to form characters for what we choose to call a species; and sometimes we are induced to pronounce individuals but slightly differing, and which others regard as true species, to be varieties.

The greater the abundance of natural objects assembled together, the more do we discover proofs that every thing passes by insensible shades into something else; that even the more remarkable differences are evanescent, and that nature has, for the most part, left us nothing at our disposal for establishing distinctions, save trifling, and, in some respects, puerile particularities. * * *

Every considerable alteration in the local circumstances in which each race of animals exists causes a change in their wants, and these new wants excite them to new actions and habits. These actions require the more frequent employer of some parts before but slightly exercised, and then greater development follows as a consequence of their more frequent use. Other organs no longer in use are impoverished and diminished in size, nay, are sometimes entirely annihilated, while in their place new parts are insensibly produced for the discharge of new functions.[2]

1. Lamarck, *Philosophie Zoologique,*   2. *Ibid.,* I, 234.
I, 54.

I must here interrupt the author's argument, by observing, that no positive fact is cited to exemplify the substitution of some *entirely new* sense, faculty, or organ, in the room of some other suppressed as useless. All the instances adduced go only to prove that the dimensions and strength of members and the perfection of certain attributes may, in a long succession of generations, be lessened and enfeebled by disuse; or, on the contrary, be matured and augmented by active exertion; just as we know that the power of scent is feeble in the greyhound, while its swiftness of pace and its acuteness of sight are remarkable—that the harrier and stag-hound, on the contrary, are comparatively slow in their movements, but excel in the sense of smelling.

It was necessary to point out to the reader this important chasm in the chain of evidence, because he might otherwise imagine that I had merely omitted the illustrations for the sake of brevity; but the plain truth is, that there were no examples to be found; and when Lamarck talks "of the efforts of internal sentiment," "the influence of subtle fluids," and "acts of organization," as causes whereby animals and plants may acquire *new organs*, he substitutes names for things; and, with a disregard to the strict rules of induction, resorts to fictions, as ideal as the "plastic virtue," and other phantoms of the geologists of the middle ages.

It is evident that, if some well-authenticated facts could have been adduced to establish one complete step in the process of transformation, such as the appearance, in individuals descending from a common stock, of a sense or organ entirely new, and a complete disappearance of some other enjoyed by their progenitors, time alone might then be supposed sufficient to bring about any amount of metamorphosis. The gratuitous assumption, therefore, of a point so vital to the theory of transmutation, was unpardonable on the part of its advocate.

But to proceed with the system: it being assumed as an undoubted fact, that a change of external circumstances may cause one organ to become entirely obsolete, and a new one to be developed, such as never before belonged to the species, the following proposition is announced, which, however staggering and absurd it may seem, is logically deduced from the assumed premises. It is not the organs, or, in other words, the nature and form of the parts of the body of an animal, which have given rise to its habits, and its particular faculties; but, on the contrary, its habits, its manner of living, and those of its progenitors, have in the course of time determined the form of its body, the number and condition of its organs—in short, the faculties which it enjoys. Thus otters, beavers, waterfowl, turtles, and frogs, were not made web-footed in order that they might swim; but their wants having attracted them to the water in search of prey, they stretched out the toes of their feet to strike the water and move rapidly along its surface. By the repeated stretching of their toes, the skin which united them at the base acquired a habit of extension, until, in the course of time, the broad membranes which now connect their extremities were formed.

In like manner, the antelope and the gazelle were not endowed with light agile forms, in order that they might escape by flight from carnivorous animals; but, having been exposed to the danger of being devoured by lions, tigers, and other beasts of prey, they were compelled to exert themselves in running with great celerity; a habit which, in the course of many generations, gave rise to the peculiar slenderness of their legs, and the agility and elegance of their forms. * * *

Lamarck's theory of the transformation of the orang-outang into the human species

Such is the machinery of the Lamarckian system; but the reader will hardly, perhaps, be able to form a perfect conception of so complicated a piece of mechanism, unless it is exhibited in motion, so that we may see in what manner it can work out, under the author's guidance, all the extraordinary effects which we behold in the present state of the animate creation. I have only space for exhibiting a small part of the entire process by which a complete metamorphosis is achieved, and shall therefore omit the mode by which, after a countless succession of generations, a small gelatinous body is transformed into an oak or an ape; passing on at once to the last grand step in the progressive scheme, by which the orang-outang, having been already evolved out of a monad, is made slowly to attain the attributes and dignity of man.

One of the races of quadrumanous animals which had reached the highest state of perfection, lost, by constraint of circumstances (concerning the exact nature of which tradition is unfortunately silent), the habit of climbing trees, and of hanging on by grasping the boughs with their feet as with hands. The individuals of this race being obliged, for a long series of generations, to use their feet exclusively for walking, and ceasing to employ their hands as feet, were transformed into bimanous animals, and what before were thumbs became mere toes, no separation being required when their feet were used solely for walking. Having acquired a habit of holding themselves upright, their legs and feet assumed, insensibly, a conformation fitted to support them in an erect attitude, till at last these animals could no longer go on all-fours without much inconvenience. * * *

Among other ideas which the natural *tendency to perfection* en-

gendered, the desire of ruling suggested itself, and this race succeeded at length in getting the better of the other animals, and
made themselves masters of all those spots on the surface of the
globe which best suited them. They drove out the animals which
approached nearest them in organization and intelligence, and
which were in a condition to dispute with them the good things of
this world, forcing them to take refuge in deserts, woods, and
wildernesses, where their multiplication was checked, and the progressive development of their faculties retarded; while, in the mean-
time, the dominant race spread itself in every direction, and lived in
large companies, where new wants were successively created, exciting them to industry, and gradually perfecting their means and
faculties.

In the supremacy and increased intelligence acquired by the
ruling race, we see an illustration of the natural tendency of the
organic world to grow more perfect; and, in their influence in
repressing the advance of others, an example of one of those disturbing causes before enumerated, that *force of external circumstances* which causes such wide chasms in the regular series of
animated being.

When the individuals of the dominant race became very numerous, their ideas greatly increased in number, and they felt the
necessity of communicating them to each other, and of augmenting
and varying the signs proper for the communication of ideas.
Meanwhile the inferior quadrumanous animals, although most of
them were gregarious, acquired no new ideas, being persecuted and
restless in the deserts, and obliged to fly and conceal themselves,
so that they conceived no new wants. Such ideas as they already
had remained unaltered, and they could dispense with the communication of the greater part of these. To make themselves,
therefore, understood by their fellows, required merely a few
movements of the body or limbs—whistling, and the uttering of
certain cries varied by the inflexions of the voice.

On the contrary, the individuals of the ascendant race, animated
with a desire of interchanging their ideas, which became more and
more numerous, were prompted to multiply the means of communication, and were no longer satisfied with mere pantomimic
signs, nor even with all the possible inflexions of the voice, but
made continual efforts to acquire the power of uttering articulate
sounds, employing a few at first, but afterwards varying and perfecting them according to the increase of their wants. The habitual
exercise of their throat, tongue, and lips, insensibly modified the
conformation of these organs, until they became fitted for the
faculty of speech.[3]

3. *Ibid.*, I, 356.

In effecting this mighty change, "the exigencies of the individuals were the sole agents; they gave rise to efforts, and the organs proper for articulating sounds were developed by their habitual employment." Hence, in this peculiar race, the origin of the admirable faculty of speech; hence also the diversity of languages, since the distance of places where the individuals composing the race established themselves soon favored the corruption of conventional signs.[4]

In conclusion, it may be proper to observe that the above sketch of the Lamarckian theory is no exaggerated picture, and those passages which have probably excited the greatest surprise in the mind of the reader are literal translations from the original.

SIR CHARLES BELL

The Hand: Its Mechanism and Vital Endowments as Evincing Design (1833) †

* * * In seeking assistance from the works of distinguished naturalists, we do not always find indications of that disposition of mind prevailing, which we should be apt to suppose was a necessary result of their peculiar studies. We do not discover that combination of genius with sound sense, which distinguished Cuvier, and has been the characteristic of all the great men of science. It is, above all, surprising with what perverse ingenuity some will seek to obscure the conception of a Divine Author, an intelligent, designing, and benevolent Being, and clinging to the greatest absurdities, will rather interpose the cold and inanimate influence of the mere "elements," in a manner to extinguish all feeling of dependence in our minds, and all emotions of gratitude.

Some will maintain that all the varieties in animated beings are merely the result of a change of circumstances influencing the original animal; that new organs have been produced by a desire, and consequent effort, of the animal, to stretch and mould itself into a shape suitable to the condition in which it is placed,—that,

---

4. *Ibid.*, I, 357.
† Sir Charles Bell (1774–1842), distinguished Scottish anatomist, held several important academic and medical posts in Britain and was well known for his important work on the nervous system. At the time he published this "Bridgewater Treatise," he was professor of surgery in the University of Edinburgh. The present text is from Chapter 6 of the 1837 printing of his Treatise. (Notice Darwin's reference to this work below, pp. 80–81 and 232.

The Bridgewater Treatises were a series of eight popularizing books written by eminent scientists and moralists in the 1830's to illustrate "the power, wisdom, and goodness of God as manifested in the Creation." The series, administered by the Royal Society, may be fairly taken to represent prevailing scientific opinion in the early nineteenth century.

as the leaves of a plant expand to light, or turn to the sun, or as the roots shoot to the appropriate soil, so do the exterior organs of animals grow and adapt themselves. We shall presently find that an opinion has prevailed that it is the organization of animals which has determined their propensities; but the philosophers of whom we are now speaking, imagine the contrary,—they conceive that, under the influence of new circumstances, organs have accommodated themselves, and assumed their particular forms.[1]

It must be here remarked that there are no instances of the production of new organs, by the union of individuals belonging to different species. Nor is there any foundation, in observation, for the opinion that a new species may be formed by the union of individuals of different families. But it is contended, that, although the species of animals have not changed in the last 5000 years, we do not know what may have been the effect of the revolutions in the globe before that time; that is, previous to the present condition of the world. On subjects of this nature, however, we must argue from what we know, and from what we see. * * *

These facts countenance the conclusion drawn from the comparative anatomy of the hand and arm—that with each new instrument, visible externally, there are a thousand internal relations established: the introduction of a new mechanical contrivance in the bones or joints, infers an alteration in every part of the skeleton; a corresponding arrangement of all the muscles; that the nervous filaments, laid intermediate between the instrument and the centre of life and motion, have an appropriate texture and distribution: and, finally, we shall discover, as we proceed, that new sources of activity must be created, in relation to the new organ, otherwise the part will hang an useless appendage.

It must now be apparent that nothing less than the Power which originally created, is equal to effect those changes on animals, which adapt them to their conditions: and that their organization is pre-

---

1. According to Lamarck, time, and favourable circumstances, are the means which *Nature* employs to give existence to all its productions. The circumstances alluded to, are climate, temperature, and the surrounding elements: as to the time, he allows no bounds. The bird which must seek its nourishment in the water, stretches its toes, and in time, the membranes extend between them, and the foot is perfected, as we see them in the duck. But the toes of the bird that perches on the branch have the points lengthened and hooked to embrace the twig. The bird which wades, and either cannot swim, or is unwilling to put its body in the water, extends its feet to obtain its food, and in time those feet and limbs are lengthened, so that the body is raised, as it were, on stilts. By a similar process of gradual development, he would persuade his readers, that the oranoutang has shortened his arms, lost his tail, and broadened his feet, and has taken the stature and bearing of a human being.

That a man, in jest, or in mere idleness, or to provoke discussion, should have given expression to such fancies, is probable: but that any one should have published them, as a serious introduction to a system of natural history, is, indeed, surprising. It is a miserable theory, to which we can only conceive a man driven by the shame, or fear, of being thought to harbour the belief of vulgar minds.—See the Système des Animaux sans Vertèbres: discours d'ouverture, p. 15.

determined; not consequent on the condition of the earth or of the surrounding elements. Neither can a property in the animal itself account for the changes which take place in the individual, any more than it can for the varieties in the species. Every thing declares the diversity of species to have its origin in distinct creations, and not to be owing to a process of gradual transition from some original type. Any other hypothesis than that of new creations of animals, suited to the successive changes in the inorganic matter of the globe—the condition of the water, atmosphere, and temperature—brings with it only an accumulation of difficulties. * * *

* * * It has been shown, that whether we take the animal body as a single machine, or embrace in the survey the successive creation of animals, conforming always to the improving condition of the earth, there is nothing like chance or irregularity in the composition of the system. In proportion indeed as we comprehend the principles of mechanics, or of hydraulics, as applicable to the animal machinery, we shall be satisfied of the perfection of the design. If anything appear disjointed or thrown in by chance, let the student mark that for contemplation and experiment, and most certainly, when it comes to be understood, other parts will receive the illumination, and the whole design stand more fully disclosed. * * *

WILLIAM BUCKLAND

Geology and Mineralogy Considered with Reference to Natural Theology (1836) †

* * * It has been stated in our Sixth Chapter, on primary stratified rocks, that Geology has rendered an important service to Natural Theology, in demonstrating by evidences peculiar to itself, that there was a time when none of the existing forms of organic beings had appeared upon our Planet, and that the doctrines of the derivation of living species either by *Development* and *Transmutation* [1] from other species, or by an *Eternal Succession* from preceding individuals of the same species, without any evidence of a Begin-

† William Buckland (1784–1856), Fellow of the Royal Society and twice president of the Geological Society, held a number of scientific posts at Oxford, as well as several clerical positions, including the Deanery of Westminster. The present text is from the Conclusion to the 1837 printing of Buckland's Bridgewater Treatise, which by 1858 went through three editions. 1. As a misunderstanding may arise in the minds of persons not familiar with the language of physiology, respecting the import of the word *Development*, it may be proper here to state, that in its primary sense, it is applied to express the organic changes which take place in the bodies of every animal and vegetable Being, from their embryo state, until they arrive at full maturity. In a more extended sense, the term is also applied to those progressive changes in fossil genera and species, which have followed one another during the deposition of the strata of the earth, in the course of

ning or prospect of an End, has no where been met by so full an answer, as that afforded by the phenomena, of fossil Organic Remains.

In the course of our enquiry, we have found abundant proofs, both of the Beginning and the End of several successive systems of animal and vegetable life; each compelling us to refer its origin to the direct agency of Creative Interference; "We conceive it undeniable, that we see, in the transition from an Earth peopled by one set of animals to the same Earth swarming with entirely new forms of organic life, a distinct manifestation of creative power transcending the operation of known laws of nature: and, it appears to us, that Geology has thus lighted a new lamp along the path of Natural Theology." [2]

Whatever alarm therefore may have been excited in the earlier stages of their development, the time is now arrived when Geological discoveries appear to be so far from disclosing any phenomena, that are not in harmony with the arguments supplied by other branches of physical Science, in proof of the existence and agency of One and the same all-wise and all-powerful Creator, that they add to the evidences of Natural Religion links of high importance that have confessedly been wanting, and are now filled up by facts which the investigation of the structure of the Earth has brought to light. * * *

SIR JOSEPH DALTON HOOKER

Flora Nova-Zelandiae (1853) †

* * * The arguments in favour of the permanence of specific characters in plants are:—

1. The fact that the amount of change produced by external causes does not warrant our assuming the contrary as a general

the gradual advancement of the grand system of Creation. The same term has been adopted by Lamarck, to express his hypothetical views of the derivation of existing species from preceding species, by successive *Transmutations* of one form of organization into another form, independent of the influence of any creative Agent. It is important that these distinctions should be rightly understood, lest the frequent application of the word *Development*, which occurs in the writings of modern physiologists, should lead to a false inference, that the use of this term implies an admission of the theory of *Transmutation* with which Lamarck has associated it.

2. British Critic, No. XVII. Jan. 1831,

p. 194.

† Sir Joseph Dalton Hooker (1817–1911), Fellow (and for five years president) of the Royal Society, shared with Darwin, Huxley, Wallace, and other Victorian naturalists the valuable experience of a long voyage of exploration. The fruits of his travels are three volumes under the general title, *The Botany of the Antarctic Voyage of H.M. Discovery Ships Erebus and Terror, in the Years 1839–1843*, of which the present text is from Chapter 2 of the Introductory Essay to Volume II. Hooker was an old friend and correspondent of Darwin's, but as this 1853 essay shows, he too was skeptical of Darwin's ideas.

law. Though there are many notorious cases in which cultivation and other causes produce changes of greater apparent value than specific characters generally possess, this happens in comparatively very few families, and only in such as are easily cultivated. In the whole range of the vegetable kingdom it is difficult to produce a change of specific value, however much we may alter conditions; it is much more difficult to prevent an induced variety from reverting to its original state, though we persevere in supplying the original conditions; and it is most difficult of all to reproduce a variety with similar materials and processes.[1]

2. In tracing widely dispersed species, the permanence with which they retain their characters strikes the most ordinary observer; and this, whether we take such plants as have been dispersed without the aid of man (as *Sonchus oleraceus, Callitriche,* and *Montia*) through all latitudes from England to New Zealand; or such as have within modern times followed the migrations of man (as *Poa annua, Phalaris Canariensis,* Dock, Clover, *Alsine media, Capsella bursa-pastoris,* and a host of others); or such as man transports with him, whether such temperate climate plants as the cerealia, fruits, and flowers of the garden or field, or such tropical forms as *Convolvulus Batatas* and yams, which were introduced into New Zealand by its earliest inhabitants;—all these, in whatever climate to which we may follow them, retain the impress of their kind, unchanged save in a trifling degree.

3. With comparatively few exceptions, plants are confined within well-marked limits, which, though often very wide, are sometimes as much the reverse; while the instances are rare of sporadic species, as such are called which are found in small numbers in widely sundered localities. These facts seem incompatible on the one hand with the theory of species spreading from many centres, and on the other with their varying indefinitely; for were it otherwise, sporadic distribution would be the rule, insular floras would not necessarily be peculiar, and similar climates would have similar, if not identical species, which is not the case.

4. A multitude of allied species of plants grow close together without any interchange of specific character; and there are instances of exceedingly closely allied plants keeping company under many

---

1. I am quite aware that this argument will be met by many instances of change produced in our garden plants: but, after all, the skill of the gardener is successfully exerted in but few cases upon the whole: out of more than twenty thousand species cultivated at one time or another in the Royal Gardens of Kew, how few there are which do not come up, not only true to their species, but even to the race or variety from which they spring; yet it would be difficult to suggest a more complete change than that from the Alps or Polar regions to Surrey, or from the free air of the tropics to the thoroughly artificial conditions of our hothouses. Plants do not accommodate themselves to these changes: either they have passive powers of resisting their effects to a greater or less degree, or they succumb to them.

modifications of climate, soil, and elevation, yet never losing their distinctive marks.

5. The individuals that inhabit the circumference of the area occupied by a species, are not found passing into other species, but ceasing more or less abruptly; their limits may meet or overlap those of one or more very similar species, when the individuals associate, but do not amalgamate.

6. One negative argument in favour of distribution from one centre only, is, that taking the broadest view of the dispersion of species, we find that the more extensive families [2] are more or less widely distributed, very much in proportion to the facilities they present for dispersion. Thus the most minute-spored Cryptogams [3] are the most widely dispersed of all organized nature; plants that resist the influence of climate best, range furthest; water-plants are more cosmopolite than land-plants, and inhabitants of salt, more than those of fresh water: the more equable and uniform is the climate of a tract of land, the more uniformly and widely will its plants be distributed.

7. The species of the lowest Orders are not only the most widely diffused, but their specific characters are not modified by the greatest changes of climate, however much their stature and luxuriance may vary. Fungi offer a remarkable instance of this: their microscopic spores are wafted in myriads through the air; the life of the individuals is often of very short duration, and many of them being as sensitive as insects to temperature and humidity, they are ephemeral in all senses; sometimes appearing only once in the same spot, and remaining but a few days, never to reappear within the observer's experience. The specific characters of many reside in the diameter, form, colour, and arrangement of their most minute organs, whose analysis demands a refinement of microscopic skill; yet the most accomplished and profound botanist in this Natural Order (who has favoured me with the descriptions of the New Zealand Fungi) fails to find the most trifling character by which to separate many New Zealand species from European.

8. The fact, now universally conceded by all intelligent horticulturists, that no plant has been acclimated in England within the experience of man, is a very suggestive one, though not conclusive; for it may be answered, that plants which cannot survive a sudden change, might a slow and progressive one. On the other hand, plants

---

2. This rule does not extend to the Natural Orders themselves. The *Compositæ*, whose facilities for dispersion are proverbial, are amongst the most local; and the same may be said of *Leguminosæ* and *Solaneæ*, whose seeds retain their vitality in a remarkable degree: a few of their species are remarkably cosmopolite, but the greater number have generally narrow ranges.

3. The fact (first communicated to me by the Rev. M. J. Berkeley) of the spores of Fungi having been found by Professor Ehrenberg mingled with the atmospheric dust that has fallen on ships far out at sea, is one of the most decisive proofs of this.

have powers of enduring change when self-propagated that they have not in our gardens; thus I find a great difference in the hardiness of individual species of several Himalayan plants,[4] depending upon the altitude at which they were gathered. In these cases the species is the same, and the parent individuals were not even varieties of one another, except so far as regards hardiness, in other words, the specific character remains unaltered in spite of the change of constitution, just as the climate of one part of the globe disagrees with the human race of another, and is even fatal to it.

Such are a few of the leading phenomena or facts that appear to me to give the greatest weight to the opinion that individuals of a species are all derived from one parent: for such arguments as the New Zealand Flora furnishes, I must refer my readers to the following chapter. I would again remind the student that the hasty adoption of any of these theories is not advisable: plants should be largely collected, and studied both in the living and dried states, and the result of their dissection noted, without reference to any speculations, which are too apt to lead the inquirer away from the rigorous investigation of details, from which alone truth can be elicited. When however the opportunity or necessity arises for combining results, and presenting them in that systematic form which can alone render them available for the purposes of science, it becomes necessary for the generalizer to proceed upon some determinate principle; and I cannot conclude this part of the subject better than by adopting the words of the most able of Transatlantic botanists, who is no less sound as a generalizer than profound in his knowledge of details:—"All classification and system in Natural History rests upon the fundamental idea of the original creation of certain forms, which have naturally been perpetuated unchanged, or with such changes only as we may conceive or prove to have arisen from varying physical influences, accidental circumstances, or from cultivation."[5] * * *

In the above speculative review of some of the causes which appear to affect the life and range of species in the vegetable kingdom, I have not touched upon one point, namely, that which concerns the original introduction of existing species of plants upon the earth. I have assumed that they have existed for ages in the forms they now retain, that assumption agreeing, in my opinion, with the facts elicited by a survey of all the phenomena they present, and, according to the most eminent zoologists, with those laws that

---

4. Thus some of the seedling Pines whose parents grew at 12,000 feet appear hardy, whilst those of the same species from 10,000 are tender. The common scarlet *Rhododendron* of Nepal and the North-west Himalaya is tender, but seedlings of the same species from Sikkim, whose parents grew at a greater elevation, have proved perfectly hardy.

5. Botanical Text-book, p. 303, by Professor Asa Gray, of Cambridge University, U.S.

govern animal life also; but there is nothing in what is assumed above, in favour of the antiquity of species and their wide distribution, that is inconsistent with any theory of their origin that the speculator may adopt. My object has not so much been to ascertain what may, or may not, have been the original condition of species, as to show that, granting more scope for variation than is generally allowed, still there are no unassailable grounds for concluding that they now vary so as to obliterate specific character; in other words, I have endeavoured to show that they are, for all practical purposes of progress in botanical science, to be regarded as permanently distinct creations, which have survived great geological changes, and which will either die out, or be destroyed, with their distinctive marks unchanged. * * *

LOUIS AGASSIZ

Essay on Classification (1857) †

* * *

Permanency of specific peculiarities in all organized beings

It was a great step in the progress of science when it was ascertained that species have fixed characters, and that they do not change in the course of time. But this fact, for which we are indebted to Cuvier,[1] has acquired a still greater importance since it has also been established, that even the most extraordinary changes in the mode of existence, and in the conditions under which animals are placed, have no more influence upon their essential characters than the lapse of time.

The facts bearing upon these two subjects are too well known to require special illustration. I will, therefore, allude only to a few points, to avoid even the possibility of a misapprehension of my statements. That animals of different geological periods differ specially, *en masse*, from those of preceding or following formations, is

† Louis Agassiz (1807–1873), Swiss-American naturalist famous for his work on fossil fishes and glacial movements, became professor of zoology at Harvard in 1848. The *Essay on Classification* was undertaken as an introduction to Agassiz's monumental *Contributions to the Natural History of the United States*. Despite the importance of his own scientific work, Agassiz could not accept the idea of the mutability of species and remained, throughout his life, one of its most vigorous and distinguished opponents.

The *Essay on Classification*, published in America in 1857, was brought out in London just a few months before Darwin's book. The present text is from Chapter 1, Section 15, of the London (1859) edition.

1. Cuvier, (G.), Recherches sur les ossements fossiles, etc., Nouv. édit.; Paris, 1821, 5 vols., 4to., fig. vol. i, sur l'Ibis, p. cxli.

a fact satisfactorily ascertained. Between two successive geological periods, then, changes have taken place among animals and plants. But none of those primordial forms of life which naturalists call species are known to have changed during any of these periods. It cannot be denied, that the species of different successive periods are supposed by some naturalists to derive their distinguishing features from changes which have taken place in those of preceding ages; but this is a mere supposition, supported neither by physiological nor by geological evidence; and the assumption that animals and plants change in a similar manner during one and the same period, is equally gratuitous. On the contrary, it is known, by the evidence furnished by the Egyptian monuments, and by the most careful comparison between animals found in the tombs of Egypt with living specimens of the same species obtained in the same country, that there is not the shadow of a difference between them for a period of about five thousand years. These comparisons, first instituted by Cuvier, have proved, that, as far as it has been possible to carry back the investigation, it does not afford the beginning of an evidence that species change in the course of time, if the comparisons be limited to the same great cosmic epoch. Geology only shows that at different periods [2] there have existed different species;

2. I trust no reader will be so ignorant of the facts here alluded to as to infer from the use of the word "period" for different eras and epochs of great length,—each of which is characterized by different animals,—that the differences these animals exhibit is in itself evidence of a change in the species. The question is, whether any changes take place during one or any of these periods. It is almost incredible how loosely some people will argue upon this point from a want of knowledge of the facts, even though they seem to reason logically. A distinguished physicist has recently taken up this subject of the immutability of species, and called in question the logic of those who uphold it. I will put his argument into as few words as possible, and show, I hope, that it does not touch the case. "Changes are observed from one geological period to another; species which do not exist at an earlier period are observed at a later period, while the former have disappeared; and, though each species may have possessed its peculiarities unchanged for a lapse of time, the fact that, when long periods are considered, all those of an earlier period are replaced by new ones at a later period, proves that species change in the end, provided a sufficiently long period of time is granted." I have nothing to object to the statement of facts, as far

as it goes, but I maintain that the conclusion is not logical. It is true that species are limited to particular geological epochs; and it is equally true, that, in all geological formations, those of successive periods are different one from the other. But because they so differ, does it follow that they have themselves changed and not been exchanged for, or replaced by, others? The length of time taken for the operation has nothing to do with the argument. Granting myriads of years for each period, no matter how many or how few, the question remains simply this: When the change takes place, does it take place spontaneously, under the action of physical agents, according to their law, or is it produced by the intervention of an agency not at work in that way before or afterwards? A comparison may explain my view more fully. Let a lover of the fine arts visit a museum arranged systematically, and in which the works of the different schools are placed in chronological order. As he passes from one room to another, he beholds changes as great as those which the palæontologist observes in passing from one system of rocks to another. But, because these works bear a closer resemblance as they belong to one or the other school or to periods following one another closely, would the critic be in any way justified in assuming that the earlier works have but no transition from those of a preceding into those of the following epoch has ever been noticed anywhere; and the question alluded to here is to be distinguished from that of the origin of the differences in the bulk of species belonging to two different geological eras. The question we are now examining involves only the fixity or mutability of species during one epoch, one era, one period, in the history of our globe. And nothing furnishes the slightest argument in favour of their mutability. On the contrary, every modern investigation [3] has gone only to confirm the results first obtained by Cuvier, and his views, that species are fixed. * * *

It is very prejudicial to the best interests of science to confound questions that are entirely different, merely for the sake of supporting a theory; and yet this is constantly done, whenever the question of the fixity of species is alluded to. A few more words upon this point, therefore, will not be out of place here.

I will not enter into a discussion upon the question, whether any species are found identically the same in two successive formations, as I have already examined it at full length elsewhere,[4] and it may be settled finally, one way or the other, without affecting the proposition now under consideration; for it is plain, that, if such identity could be proved, it would only show more satisfactorily how tenacious species are in their character, to continue to live through all the physical changes which have taken place between two successive geological periods. Again, such identity, once proved, would leave it still doubtful, whether their representatives in two successive epochs are descendants one of the other, as we have already strong

changed into those of a later period, or in denying that they are the works or artists living and active at the time of their production? The question about the immutability of species is identical with this supposed case. It is not because species have lasted for a longer or shorter time in past ages that naturalists consider them as immutable, but because, in the whole series of geological ages, taking the entire lapse of time which has passed since the first introduction of animals or plants upon earth, not the slightest evidence has yet been produced that species are actually transformed one into the other. We only know that they are different at different periods, as are works of art of different periods and of different schools; but, as long as we have no other data to reason upon than those which Geology has furnished to this day, it is as unphilosophical and illogical, because such differences exist, to assume that species do change, and have changed,—that is, are transformed, or have been transformed,—as it would be to maintain that works of art change in the course of time. We do not know how organized beings have originated, it is true; and no naturalist can be prepared to account for their appearance in the beginning, or for their difference in different periods; but enough is known to repudiate the assumption of their transmutation, as it does not explain the facts, and shuts out further attempts at proper investigations. See Baden Powell's Essays, quoted above, p. 412 et seq., and Essay 3rd, generally.
3. Kunth, Recherches sur les plantes trouvées dans les tombeaux égyptiens; Ann. des scien. nat., vol. viii, 1826, p. 411.
4. Agassiz (L.) Coquilles tertiaires réputées identiques avec les espèces vivantes; Nouv. Mém. de la Soc. Helv. des sc. nat., Neuchâtel, 1845, vol. 7, 4to., fig.—Agassiz (L.), Etudes critiques sur les Mollusques fossiles; Neuchâtel, 1831–45, 4to., fig.—Agassiz (L.), Monographies d'Echinodermes vivans et fossiles; Neuchâtel, 1838–42, 4 nos., 4to., fig.—Agassiz (L.), Recherches sur les Poissons fossiles; Neuchâtel, 1833–44, 5 vols., 4to., atlas, fol.

evidence in favour of the separate origin of the representatives of the same species in separate geographical areas. The case of closely allied but different species occurring in successive periods, yet limited respectively to their epochs, affords, in the course of time, a parallel to the case of closely allied, so-called, representative species occupying different areas in space, which no sound naturalist would now suppose to be derived one from the other. There is no more reason to suppose species equally allied, following one another in time, to be derived one from the other; and all that has been said in preceding paragraphs respecting the differences observed between species occurring in different geographical areas applies with the same force to species succeeding each other in the course of time.

When domesticated animals and cultivated plants are mentioned as furnishing evidence of the mutability of species, the circumstance is constantly overlooked, or passed over in silence, that the first point to be established respecting them, in order to justify any inference from them against the fixity of species, would be to show that each of them has originated from one common stock, which, far from being the case, is flatly contradicted by the positive knowledge we have that the varieties of several of them at least are owing to the entire amalgamation of different species.[5] The Egyptian monuments further show that many of these so-called varieties, which are supposed to be the product of time, are as old as any other animals which have been known to man. At all events, we have no tradition, no monumental evidence of the existence of any wild animal older than those which represent domesticated animals, already as different among themselves as they are now.[6] It is, therefore, quite possible that the different races of domesticated animals were originally distinct species, more or less mixed now, as the different races of men are. Moreover, neither domesticated animals, nor cultivated plants, nor the races of men, are the proper subjects for an investigation respecting the fixity or mutability of species, as all involve already the question at issue in the premises which are assumed in introducing them as evidence in the case. With reference to the different breeds of our domesticated animals, which are known to be produced by the management of man, as well as certain varieties of our cultivated plants, they must be well distinguished from permanent races, which, for aught we know, may be primordial; for breeds are the result of the fostering care of man: they are the product of the limited influence and control the human mind has over organized beings, and not the free product of mere physical agents. They show, therefore, that even the least important changes which may take place during one and the same cosmic

5. Our fowls, for instance.
6. Nott and Gliddon, Types of Mankind, p. 386.

period, among animals and plants, are controlled by an intellectual power, and do not result from the immediate action of physical causes.

So far, then, from disclosing the effects of physical agents, whatever changes are known to take place in the course of time among organized beings appear as the result of an intellectual power, and go therefore to substantiate the view, that all the differences observed among finite beings are ordained by the action of the Supreme Intellect, and not determined by physical causes. * * *

The "Forerunners" of Darwin

CHARLES DARWIN

An Historical Sketch of the Progress of Opinion on the Origin of Species, previously to the Publication of This Work (1861) †

I will here give a brief sketch of the progress of opinion on the Origin of Species. Until recently the great majority of naturalists believed that species were immutable productions, and had been separately created. This view has been ably maintained by many authors. Some few naturalists, on the other hand, have believed that species undergo modification and that the existing forms of life are the descendants by true generation of pre-existing forms. Passing over allusions to the subject in the classical writers,[1] the first author who in modern times has treated it in a scientific spirit was Buffon. But as his opinions fluctuated greatly at different periods, and as he does not enter on the causes or means of the transformation of species, I need not here enter on details.

Lamarck was the first man whose conclusions on the subject excited much attention. This justly celebrated naturalist first published his views in 1801; he much enlarged them in 1809 in his 'Philosophie Zoologique,' and subsequently, in 1815, in the Intro-

† This sketch was first added to the *Origin of Species* in the third edition (1861) and was supplemented in later editions. Darwin had been criticized from various quarters for giving insufficient credit to his "predecessors." Regarding this criticism, see Sir Gavin de Beer's Introduction to Darwin's Notebooks, pp. 72–73, below.

The present text is from the sixth edition of the *Origin*, the last in Darwin's lifetime.

1. Aristotle, in his 'Physicae Auscultationes' (lib. 2, cap. 8, s. 2), after remarking that rain does not fall in order to make the corn grow, any more than it falls to spoil the farmer's corn when threshed out of doors, applies the same argument to organisation; and adds (as translated by Mr. Clair Grece, who first ponited out the passage to me), "So what hinders the different parts [of the body] from having this merely accidental relation in nature? as the teeth, for example, grow by necessity, the front ones sharp, adapted for dividing, and the grinders flat, and serviceable for masticating the food; since they were not made for the sake of this, but it was the result of accident. And in like manner as to the other parts in which there appears to exist an adaptation to an end. Wheresoever, therefore, all things together (that is all the parts of one whole) happened like as if they were made for the sake of something, these were preserved, having been appropriately constituted by an internal spontaneity; and whatsoever things were not thus constituted, perished, and still perish." We here see the principle of natural selection shadowed forth, but how little Aristotle fully comprehended the principle, is shown by his remarks on the formation of the teeth.

duction to his 'Hist. Nat. des Animaux sans Vertèbres.' In these works he upholds the doctrine that all species, including man, are descended from other species. He first did the eminent service of arousing attention to the probability of all changes in the organic, as well as in the inorganic world, being the result of law, and not of miraculous interposition. Lamarck seems to have been chiefly led to his conclusion on the gradual change of species, by the difficulty of distinguishing species and varieties, by the almost perfect gradation of forms in certain groups, and by the analogy of domestic productions. With respect to the means of modification, he attributed something to the direct action of the physical conditions of life, something to the crossing of already existing forms, and much to use and disuse, that is, to the effects of habit. To this latter agency he seems to attribute all the beautiful adaptations in nature;—such as the long neck of the giraffe for browsing on the branches of trees. But he likewise believed in a law of progressive development; and as all the forms of life thus tend to progress, in order to account for the existence at the present day of simple productions, he maintains that such forms are now spontaneously generated.[2]

Geoffroy Saint-Hilaire, as is stated in his 'Life,' written by his son, suspected, as early as 1795, that what we call species are various degenerations of the same type. It was not until 1828 that he published his conviction that the same forms have not been perpetuated since the origin of all things. Geoffroy seems to have relied chiefly on the conditions of life, or the *'monde ambiant'* as the cause of change. He was cautious in drawing conclusions, and did not believe that existing species are now undergoing modification; and, as his son adds, "C'est donc un problème à réserver entièrement à l'avenir, supposé même que l'avenir doive avoir prise sur lui."

In 1813, Dr. W. C. Wells read before the Royal Society 'An Account of a White female, part of whose skin resembles that of a Negro'; but his paper was not published until his famous 'Two Essays upon Dew and Single Vision' appeared in 1818. In this paper he distinctly recognises the principle of natural selection, and this is

2. I have taken the date of the first publication of Lamarck from Isid. Geoffroy Saint-Hilaire's ('Hist. Nat. Générale,' tom. ii. p. 405, 1859) excellent history of opinion on this subject. In this work a full account is given of Buffon's conclusions on the same subject. It is curious how largely my grandfather, Dr. Erasmus Darwin, anticipated the views and erroneous grounds of opinion of Lamarck in his 'Zoonomia' (vol. i. pp. 500–510), published in 1794. According to Isid. Geoffroy there is no doubt that Goethe was an extreme partisan of similar views, as shown in the Introduction to a work written in 1794 and 1795, but not published till long afterwards: he has pointedly remarked ('Goethe als Naturforscher,' von Dr. Karl Meding, s. 34) that the future question for naturalists will be how, for instance, cattle got their horns, and not for what they are used. It is rather a singular instance of the manner in which similar views arise at about the same time, that Goethe in Germany, Dr. Darwin in England, and Geoffroy Saint-Hilaire (as we shall immediately see) in France, came to the same conclusion on the origin of species, in the years 1794–5.

the first recognition which has been indicated; but he applies it only to the races of man, and to certain characters alone. After remarking that Negroes and mulattoes enjoy an immunity from certain tropical diseases, he observes, firstly, that all animals tend to vary in some degree, and, secondly, that agriculturists improve their domesticated animals by selection; and then, he adds, but what is done in this latter case "by art, seems to be done with equal efficacy, though more slowly, by nature, in the formation of varieties of mankind, fitted for the country which they inhabit. Of the accidental varieties of man, which would occur among the first few and scattered inhabitants of the middle regions of Africa, some one would be better fitted than the others to bear the diseases of the country. This race would consequently multiply, while the others would decrease; not only from their inability to sustain the attacks of disease, but from their incapacity of contending with their more vigorous neighbours. The colour of this vigorous race I take for granted, from what has been already said, would be dark. But the same disposition to form varieties still existing, a darker and a darker race would in the course of time occur: and as the darkest would be the best fitted for the climate, this would at length become the most prevalent, if not the only race, in the particular country in which it had originated." He then extends these same views to the white inhabitants of colder climates. I am indebted to Mr. Rowley, of the United States, for having called my attention, through Mr. Brace, to the above passage in Dr. Wells' work.

The Hon. and Rev. W. Herbert, afterwards Dean of Manchester, in the fourth volume of the 'Horticultural Transactions,' 1882, and in his work on the 'Amaryllidaceæ' (1837, pp. 19, 339), declares that "horticultural experiments have established, beyond the possibility of refutation, that botanical species are only a higher and more permanent class of varieties." He extends the same view to animals. The Dean believes that single species of each genus were created in an originally highly plastic condition, and that these have produced, chiefly by intercrossing, but likewise by variation, all our existing species.

In 1826 Professor Grant, in the concluding paragraph in his well-known paper ('Edinburgh Philosophical Journal,' vol. xiv. p. 283) on the Spongilla, clearly declares his belief that species are descended from other species, and that they become improved in the course of modification. This same view was given in his 55th Lecture, published in the 'Lancet' in 1834.

In 1831 Mr. Patrick Matthew published his work on 'Naval Timber and Arboriculture,' in which he gives precisely the same view on the origin of species as that (presently to be alluded to) propounded by Mr. Wallace and myself in the 'Linnean Journal,' and as that enlarged in the present volume. Unfortunately the view was given by Mr. Matthew very briefly in scattered passages in an Appendix to a work on a different subject, so that it remained unnoticed until Mr. Matthew himself drew attention to it in the 'Gardener's Chronicle,' on April 7th, 1860. The differences of Mr. Matthew's view from mine are not of much importance: he seems to consider that the world was nearly depopulated at successive periods, and then re-stocked; and he gives as an alternative, that new forms may be generated "without the presence of any mould or germ of former aggregates." I am not sure that I understand some passages; but it seems that he attributes much influence to the direct action of the conditions of life. He clearly saw, however, the full force of the principle of natural selection.

The celebrated geologist and naturalist, Von Buch, in his excellent 'Description Physique des Isles Canaries' (1836, p. 147), clearly expresses his belief that varieties slowly become changed into permanent species, which are no longer capable of intercrossing.

Rafinesque, in his 'New Flora of North America,' published in 1836, wrote (p. 6) as follows:—"All species might have been varieties once, and many varieties are gradually becoming species by assuming constant and peculiar characters"; but farther on (p. 18) he adds, "except the original types or ancestors of the genus."

In 1843–44 Professor Haldeman ('Boston Journal of Nat. Hist. U. States,' vol. iv. p. 468) has ably given the arguments for and against the hypothesis of the development and modification of species: he seems to lean towards the side of change.

The 'Vestiges of Creation' appeared in 1844. In the tenth and much improved edition (1853) the anonymous author says (p. 155):—"The proposition determined on after much consideration is, that the several series of animated beings, from the simplest and oldest up to the highest and most recent, are, under the providence of God, the results, *first*, of an impulse which has been imparted to the forms of life, advancing them, in definite times, by generation, through grades of organisation terminating in the highest dicotyledons and vertebrata, these grades being few in number, and generally marked by intervals of organic character, which we find to be a practical difficulty in ascertaining affinities; *second*, of another impulse connected with the vital forces, tending, in the course of generations, to modify organic structures in accordance with external circumstances, as food, the nature of the habitat, and the meteoric agencies, these being the 'adaptations' of the natural theologian." The author apparently believes that organisation progresses by sudden leaps, but that the effects produced by the conditions of life are gradual. He argues with much force on general grounds that species are not immutable productions. But I cannot

see how the two supposed "impulses" account in a scientific sense
for the numerous and beautiful coadaptations which we see
throughout nature; I cannot see that we thus gain any insight how,
for instance, a woodpecker has become adapted to its peculiar habits of life. The work, from its powerful and brilliant style, though
displaying in the earlier editions little accurate knowledge and a
great want of scientific caution, immediately had a very wide circulation. In my opinion it has done excellent service in this country
in calling attention to the subject, in removing prejudice, and in
thus preparing the ground for the reception of analogous views.

In 1846 the veteran geologist M. J. d'Omalius d'Halloy published in an excellent though short paper ('Bulletins de l'Acad. Roy.
Bruxelles,' tom. xiii. p. 581) his opinion that it is more probable
that new species have been produced by descent with modification
than that they have been separately created: the author first promulgated this opinion in 1831.

Profesor Owen, in 1849 ('Nature of Limbs,' p. 86), wrote as follows:—"The archetypal idea was manifested in the flesh under
diverse such modifications, upon this planet, long prior to the
existence of those animal species that actually exemplify it. To what
natural laws or secondary causes the orderly succession and progression of such organic phenomena may have been committed, we, as
yet, are ignorant." In his Address to the British Association, in
1858, he speaks (p. li.) of "the axiom of the continuous operation
of creative power, or of the ordained becoming of living things."
Farther on (p. xc.), after referring to geographical distribution, he
adds, "These phenomena shake our confidence in the conclusion
that the Apteryx of New Zealand and the Red Grouse of England
were distinct creations in and for those islands respectively. Always,
also, it may be well to bear in mind that by the word 'creation'
the zoologist means 'a process he knows not what.' " He amplifies
this idea by adding that when such cases as that of the Red Grouse
are "enumerated by the zoologist as evidence of distinct creation
of the bird in and for such islands, he chiefly expresses that he
knows not how the Red Grouse came to be there, and there exclusively; signifying also, by this mode of expressing such ignorance,
his belief that both the bird and the islands owed their origin to a
great first Creative Cause." If we interpret these sentences given
in the same Address, one by the other, it appears that this eminent
philosopher felt in 1858 his confidence shaken that the Apteryx
and the Red Grouse first appeared in their respective homes, "he
knew not how," or by some process "he knew not what."

This Address was delivered after the papers by Mr. Wallace and
myself on the Origin of Species, presently to be referred to, had
been read before the Linnean Society. When the first edition of

this work was published, I was so completely deceived, as were many others, by such expressions as "the continuous operation of creative power," that I included Professor Owen with other palæontologists as being firmly convinced of the immutability of species; but it appears ('Anat. of Vertebrates,' vol. iii. p. 796) that this was on my part a preposterous error. In the last edition of this work I inferred, and the inference still seems to me perfectly just, from a passage beginning with the words "no doubt the type-form," &c. (Ibid. vol. i. p. xxxv.), that Professor Owen admitted that natural selection may have done something in the formation of a new species; but this it appears (Ibid. vol. iii. p. 798) is inaccurate and without evidence. I also gave some extracts from a correspondence between Professor Owen and the Editor of the 'London Review,' from which it appeared manifest to the Editor as well as myself, that Professor Owen claimed to have promulgated the theory of natural selection before I had done so; and I expressed my surprise and satisfaction at this announcement; but as far as it is possible to understand certain recently published passages (Ibid vol. iii. p. 798) I have either partially or wholly again fallen into error. It is consolatory to me that others find Professor Owen's controversial writings as difficult to understand and to reconcile with each other, as I do. As far as the mere enunciation of the principle of natural selection is concerned, it is quite immaterial whether or not Professor Owen preceded me, for both of us, as shown in this historical sketch, were long ago preceded by Dr. Wells and Mr. Matthew.

M. Isidore Geoffroy Saint-Hilaire, in his lectures delivered in 1850 (of which a Résumé appeared in the 'Revue et Mag. de Zoolog.,' Jan. 1851), briefly gives his reason for believing that specific characters "sont fixés, pour chaque espèce, tant qu'elle se perpétue au milieu des mêmes circonstances: ils se modifient, si les circonstances ambiantes viennent à changer." "En-résumé, *l'observation* des animaux sauvages démontre déjà la variabilité *limitée* des espèces. Les *expériences* sur les animaux sauvages, devenus domestiques, et sur les animaux domestiques redevenus sauvages, la démontrent plus clairement encore. Ces mêmes expériences prouvent, de plus, que les différences produites peuvent être de *valeur générique*." In his 'Hist. Nat. Générale' (tom. ii. p. 430, 1859) he amplifies analogous conclusions.

From a circular lately issued it appears that Dr. Freke, in 1851 ('Dublin Medical Press,' p. 322), propounded the doctrine that all organic beings have descended from one primordial form. His grounds of belief and treatment of the subject are wholly different from mine; but as Dr. Freke has now (1861) published his Essay on the 'Origin of Species by means of Organic Affinity,' the difficult attempt to give any idea of his views would be superfluous on my part.

Mr. Herbert Spencer, in an Essay (originally published in the 'Leader,' March, 1852, and republished in his 'Essays,' in 1858), has contrasted the theories of the Creation and the Development of organic beings with remarkable skill and force. He argues from the analogy of domestic productions, from the changes which the embryos of many species undergo, from the difficulty of distinguishing species and varieties, and from the principle of general gradation, that species have been modified; and he attributes the modification to the change of circumstances. The author (1855) has also treated Psychology on the principle of the necessary acquirement of each mental power and capacity by gradation.

In 1852 M. Naudin, a distinguished botanist, expressly stated, in an admirable paper on the Origin of Species ('Revue Horticole,' p. 102; since partly republished in the 'Nouvelles Archives du Muséum,' tom. i. p. 171), his belief that species are formed in an analogous manner as varieties are under cultivation; and the latter process he attributes to man's power of selection. But he does not show how selection acts under nature. He believes, like Dean Herbert, that species, when nascent, were more plastic than at present. He lays weight on what he calls the principle of finality, "puissance mystérieuse, indéterminée; fatalité pour les uns; pour les autres, volonté providentielle, dont l'action incessante sur les êtres vivants détermine, à toutes les époques de l'existence du monde, la forme, le volume, et la durée de chacun d'eux, en raison de sa destinée dans l'ordre de choses dont il fait partie. C'est cette puissance qui harmonise chaque membre à l'ensemble, en l'appropriant à la fonction qu'il doit remplir dans l'organisme général de la nature, fonction qui est pour lui sa raison d'être." [3]

In 1853 a celebrated geologist, Count Keyserling ('Bulletin de la Soc. Géolog.,' 2nd Ser., tom x. p. 357), suggested that as new diseases, supposed to have been caused by some miasma, have arisen and spread over the world, so at certain periods the germs of existing species may have been chemically affected by circumambient molecules of a particular nature, and thus have given rise to new forms.

3. From references in Bronn's 'Untersuchungen über die Entwickelungs-Gesetze,' it appears that the celebrated botanist and palaeontologist Unger published, in 1852, his belief that species undergo development and modification. Dalton, likewise, in Pander and Dalton's work on Fossil Sloths, expressed, in 1821, a similar belief. Similar views have, as is well known, been maintained by Oken in his mystical 'Natur-Philosophie.' From other references in Godron's work 'Sur l'Espèce,' it seems that Bory St. Vincent, Burdach, Poiret, and Fries, have all admitted that new species are continually being produced.

I may add, that of the thirty-four authors named in this Historical Sketch, who believe in the modification of species, or at least disbelieve in separate acts of creation, twenty-seven have written on special branches of natural history or geology.

In this same year, 1853, Dr. Schaaffhausen published an excellent pamphlet ('Verhand. des Naturhist. Vereins der Preuss. Rheinlands,' &c.), in which he maintains the development of organic forms on the earth. He infers that many species have kept true for long periods, whereas a few have become modified. The distinction of species he explains by the destruction of intermediate graduated forms. "Thus living plants and animals are not separated from the extinct by new creations, but are to be regarded as their descendants through continued reproduction."

A well-known French botanist, M. Lecoq, writes in 1854 (Etudes sur Géograph. Bot.,' tom. i. p. 250), "On voit que nos recherches sur la fixité ou la variation de l'espèce, nous conduisent directement aux idées émises, par deux hommes justement célèbres, Geoffroy Saint-Hilaire et Goethe." Some other passages scattered through M. Lecoq's large work, make it a little doubtful how far he extends his views on the modification of species.

The 'Philosophy of Creation' has been treated in a masterly manner by the Rev. Baden Powell, in his 'Essays on the Unity of Worlds,' 1855. Nothing can be more striking than the manner in which he shows that the introduction of new species is "a regular, not a casual phenomenon," or, as Sir John Herschel expresses it, "a natural in contr..distinction to a miraculous process."

The third volume of the 'Journal of the Linnean Society' contains papers, read July 1st, 1858, by Mr. Wallace and myself, in which, as stated in the introductory remarks to this volume, the theory of Natural Selection is promulgated by Mr. Wallace with admirable force and clearness.

Von Baer, towards whom all zoologists feel so profound a respect, expressed about the year 1859 (see Prof. Rudolph Wagner, 'Zoologisch-Anthropologische Untersuchungen,' 1861, s. 51) his conviction, chiefly grounded on the laws of geographical distribution, that forms now perfectly distinct have descended from a single parent-form.

In June, 1859, Professor Huxley gave a lecture before the Royal Institution on the 'Persistent Types of Animal Life.' Referring to such cases, he remarks, "It is difficult to comprehend the meaning of such facts as these, if we suppose that each species of animal and plant, or each great type of organisation, was formed and placed upon the surface of the globe at long intervals by a distinct act of creative power; and it is well to recollect that such an assumption is as unsupported by tradition or revelation as it is opposed to the general analogy of nature. If, on the other hand, we view 'Persistent Types' in relation to that hypothesis which supposes the species living at any time to be the result of the gradual modification of preexisting species, a hypothesis which, though unproven, and sadly damaged by some of its supporters, is yet the only one to which physiology lends any countenance; their existence would seem to show that the amount of modification which living beings have undergone during geological time is but very small in relation to the whole series of changes which they have suffered."

In December, 1859, Dr. Hooker published his 'Introduction to the Australian Flora.' In the first part of this great work he admits the truth of the descent and modification of species, and supports this doctrine by many original observations.

The first edition of this work was published on November 24th, 1859, and the second edition on January 7th, 1860.

MILTON MILLHAUSER

"In the Air" (1959) †

* * *

Evolution, then, was "in the air" in the years immediately preceding the publication of Vestiges [Robert Chambers, Vestiges of * * * Creation, 1844], in a number of specific senses. First, a fair number of scientists, from Buffon and Maupertius to Lamarck and Saint-Hilaire and Meckel, had given it the cachet of their approval; and while most of these were obscure enough, a few were of some importance in their fields or had taken pains to be noticed. Second, the idea had also attracted several nonscientific writers, ranging in influence and quality from Kant to Erasmus Darwin and Monboddo. Third, there had been of late a considerable accumulation of technical findings leading in the same direction, most strikingly in geology, embryology, and comparative anatomy. Fourth, a good many of the neutral and half-convinced were recording the hypothesis honestly enough, sometimes even in popular treatises, as at least a possibility. Fifth, these influences had rendered the idea sufficiently conspicuous that even hostile writers, when addressing an informed audience, were forced to deal seriously with it, thereby giving it a sort of disagreeable publicity of their own. (Herbert Spencer was first seriously interested in evolution by Lyell's refutation of it in the *Principles*.)

And, finally, there was a sixth, contributory influence, the weight of which cannot be estimated but can hardly have been negligible.

† From Chapter 3 of *Just before Darwin* (Middletown, Conn., 1959). Milton Millhauser (b. 1910) is professor of English at the University of Bridgeport.

The idea of development had entered the world and was touching other fields than biology; thinking in terms of growth and change was becoming a familiar habit of the age.

History, for instance, was never in much danger of neglecting change; but since the eighteenth century it had turned noticeably from an earlier habit of chronicle to tracing the development and transformation of institutions, or to emphasizing the uniqueness and organic unity of the societies out of which had sprung our own. (The Victorians tended sometimes to think of it as synonymous with "progress.") John Henry Newman, then still a Protestant, had introduced roughly comparable ideas into English theology (and, by one reviewer of *Vestiges*, was sharply criticized for so doing). A similar line was being followed by the German "higher critics," who regarded the sacred documents of theology as the products of tradition and subject to the processes of history. The historical novel, which tells us that our fathers' world was unlike our own, was an eighteenth-century invention and a nineteenth-century speciality; it was a typical outgrowth of the romantic spirit, which looks back, and traces continuity through change. Romantic psychology, under the influence of Rousseau, drove back the concept of growth and change into our own mental life; emphasizing the kinship of the youth's intellectual processes with those of the savage, it introduced a kind of "recapitulation" of its own. German philosophy had centered, from Lessing to Hegel, on the idea of "becoming"; Comtism, with its "three stages," might also be considered in a crude and elementary way a developmental system. Economics was still in 1844 the domain of absolute principles; but, if this is any comfort to the generalizing mind, it was not long to remain so. In 1848 two solemn theorizers, one British and empirical, one metaphysical and German, were to found a new type of forward-looking economic science, in which the socialism of the future —whether Mill's or Marx's—was to work itself into being out of the structure and process of contemporary society.

The sciences were also moving in this direction. Geology and embryology, those vigorous nineteenth-century growths, were both (aside from their connection with evolution) sciences of "becoming," which taught the mind to look on development as not magnification but change. Chemistry was investigating elements whose properties changed unpredictably when they were combined; it had also synthesized an organic substance, urea. G. J. Mulder, a Dutch physicist of the time, was merely the latest of a long line of "gradationists" who believed that the organic world shaded off into the inorganic, and that the nature of vital activity might be found in a study of the biochemical processes. (The great Schleiden himself had said that the growth of the cell was of the same order of phenomena with the growth of the crystal.) Even more mystifying was electricity, which also had been shown to have its obscure relations with life. From Mesmer and Galvani, this exciting notion had filtered down to reach a literary public; so generally metaphysical a thinker as S. T. Coleridge (not to speak of the "Vestigitarian") thought it worth his while to attempt to trace out, or at least to point to, a connection. Biology was still—in those far days—divided over the question whether life proceeded from a specifically "vital" or merely physical "principle"; any circumstance that favored the latter answer, any observation that extended the bounds and subtlety of the realm of matter, naturally encouraged that intellectual materialism which was the soil in which evolution flourished.

Of all the sciences that contributed incidentally or analogically to this effect, none was more potent over men's imaginations than astronomy. To the young man of the 1830's, the single most impressive contribution to astronomy since Newton was the nebular hypothesis. Suggested independently by Kant and Emanuel Swedenborg, elaborated by Laplace, buttressed by Comte's mathematics, and supported inferentially by the observations of the elder Herschel, it enjoyed throughout the first part of the century a tremendous vogue; it seemed to explain and fulfil the universe of simple laws and ordered forces that previous centuries had spread across the sky. Theoretical objections were early raised against it; but in the 1840's, though it had already been abandoned by most astronomers, it still exercised a powerful sway over the popular mind. The great Baron von Humboldt, who did not accept it, nevertheless afforded it a certain prominence, and his English reviewers treated it with respect.[1] The effect of this theory was much the same as that of uniformitarian geology: it set back infinitely far the date of any possible Creation, adding the aeons of the nebula to the aeons of the earth; and it disposed men's minds to think of their universe as *generated*, developed through successive stages and in accordance with mechanical laws, rather than created miraculously in virtually its present form. Even the observations that had recently shaken faith in the nebular hypothesis, "resolving" what had appeared to be diffuse masses of primitive matter into swarms of distant stars, were not calculated to buttress the old ways of thinking. The awe-inspiring reaches of interstellar space, the compounded infinitudes of galaxies and systems that the modern telescope was thus opening to men's gaze, militated with a terrible force against the notion that mankind, masters of certain circumscribed areas on the accidental satellite of a half-burnt-out star, could possibly have

1. The *Quarterly Review*, in 1845, obviously believes that Humboldt was on this account a follower of Erasmus Darwin, and that he was willing to ascribe the power of "indefinite development" to matter.

any special value—let alone a central and decisive position—in the whole stupendous scheme of things.

Here was a whole concatenation of influences, ranging from the direct and explicit to the vaguely suggestive and remote, some diffused through the entire intellectual atmosphere, others inaccessible except to the specialist, but all finally inclining the mind in the same general direction. Nevertheless, the force of these influences, as compared to that of clerical conservatism and the hostility of many eminent scientists to the very idea of evolution, was limited and slight. The mere habit of thinking developmentally (which had not yet filtered down effectively to the popular level) would be of trifling effect without the science; and among popular writers, it was precisely the technical studies that were least read and therefore least reflected. Science reached the public—the large public of which we are now speaking—through the Scriptural Geologist and the reconciling divine; through skilled expositors like Lyell and Whewell, both conservative on the issue of evolution; and through popular treatises, which tended, by and large, to assume a safe, conventional position. Biology was a difficult subject to follow, especially in its microscopic phases (geology, by contrast, was spread out across a vast specimen case that any healthy pedestrian Englishman could inspect at leisure); its more specialized findings and more questionable theories were not particularly well advertised. The sense of an impending crisis, which was beginning to be felt by men like Lyell and Whewell and the Scriptural Geologists—and by a few of their most discerning readers—was not generally shared. Buffon was read as a descriptive naturalist, Erasmus Darwin as a literary curiosity, and Lamarck not at all. There was a widespread interest in "natural history," and some in paleontology, which were both serviceable as far as they went; but theoretical biology, for all its recent strides, was virtually unknown.[2]

Thus the actual effect of the influences we have traced out was not to spread the idea broadcast, in however attenuated a form, but rather to trouble the minds of an informed few; and, beyond that, to prepare an atmosphere or temper of mind that—when at long last it did come irresistibly—might fit the theory of evolution into its place among the opinions of the age. Even the scientist, bound by his own prejudices or dubious of a rather sketchy demonstration, might require this sort of prodding and encouragement; how long it took for Lyell to come round! As for the general reader, even the rather studious and thoughtful one, he was being readied by forces he did not recognize for a revelation of which he did not dream.

2. That is, by popular writers on general subjects. Naturally, the physicians and other specialists were acquainted with it.

Meanwhile it was inevitable that the idea should occur at intervals to scattered thinkers, each of whom formed a little focus whence it radiated for a space; or that, to those who first encountered it in some slighting reference, it should have seemed less strange, less wholly unexpected, than it might have been without the work of preparation. We must draw a twofold distinction, which is also something—but not too much—of an oversimplification: between a specially informed small public and an only generally informed large one; between widespread but inconclusive influences such as geology and comparative anatomy, and narrowly restricted but powerfully suggestive ones such as biochemistry and embryology. Only then can we comprehend the paradox that evolution, when it came, struck an unprepared British audience as a profound moral shock; and that it still seemed in retrospect, to the Victorians themselves, to have been for a generation before 1859 "in the air." * * *

WALTER F. CANNON

The Bases of Darwin's Achievement: A Revaluation (1961) †

I

Young Charles Lyell, in his *Principles of Geology* of 1830–33, presented a view of the history of geology which has been a leading historiographical tradition ever since.[1] Lyell felt that the chief hindrance to the development of geology had been the pressure of religious ideas. Although he objected to non-scientists trying to force scientists to conform to extra-scientific ideas, he was more particularly concerned with the belief of some scientists themselves in religious ideas, which they then used to interpret their data. Progress could be obtained by rooting out these intruders and replacing them by truly scientific ideas—which, for Lyell, meant truly Uniformitarian ideas. This historiographical notion, extended to biology by Thomas Huxley and to cosmological thought in general by John Tyndall, has been a major method of interpreting the Darwinian debates ever since.[2] Perhaps most supporters of Darwinism

† *Victorian Studies*, V (1961), 109–134. Walter F. Cannon (b. 1925) is Curator of the History of Physics and Geoscience, Smithsonian Institution.

1. An earlier version of this paper was read to the joint meeting of the American Historical Association and the History of Science Society in Chicago, 29 December 1959.
2. Lyell, *Principles*, 2nd ed. (1832–33), I, 2–13, 69–70; T. H. Huxley, "On the Reception of the *Origin of Species*," in Charles Darwin, *Life and Letters*, ed. Francis Darwin (London, 1887), I, 544; John Tyndall, "The Belfast Address," *Fragments of Science* (London, 1904), II, 194–197.

have believed that Darwin threw religious (or metaphysical) ideas out of his area of biology and introduced the reign of scientific (or inductive methods.

My object in this paper is to disagree with this Lyellian tradition. I propose the following thesis instead: that the triumph of Darwinism is the triumph of a Christian way of picturing the world over the other ways available to scientists. I mean "available," of course, in the sense of William James' living hypotheses. An idea which may have occurred to an ancient Greek is not available in the nineteenth century unless it is one of the ways in which good contemporary scientists could present their findings. Similarly by "Christian" I mean an actually present body of thought believed by contemporary Christians (or some of them) to be Christian. I do not assert that all of the elements of this thought were originated by Christians. After all, the book of Genesis was not written by a Christian, according to the secular historian; and the same person may wish to trace the idea of Incarnation back to primitive religion. Nevertheless there is for the nineteenth-century Englishman only one living body of thought which contains belief both in Genesis and in Incarnation, and that collection of ideas is historically called Christian.

I suggest, then, that the Darwinian debates among the educated (for there are always obscurantists among scientists and in Christendom) are at bottom an argument as to whether or not to accept a secular version of a world described in Christian thought. The subsequent wrath of the Christians is not the wrath of those who have been beaten by an alien; it is wrath of those whose treasured possession has been stolen from them. Stolen—and then fitted out with an active mechanism, natural selection, whose properties are quite difficult to picture as dependent on a beneficent Deity. * * *

II

* * * Let us look at the world as pictured by Charles Lyell himself. Lyell sees two sets of forces fighting for mastery in the world, one made up of everything which makes the surface of the globe uneven—earthquakes, volcanoes, continental elevations, etc.—and the other made up of all the levelling forces—principally water, as in erosion, but also, for example, lightning. These sets of forces are so evenly balanced that neither can triumph. Lyell does *not* believe in a periodic system, one in which a great continent-building era is followed by a long continent-eroding era. If elevation is happening in one part of the globe, erosion is equally happening in another. How long has all this been going on? Indefinitely. Looking as far back as we can, we see nothing but this same system of contending

forces, here raising a mountain, there drowning part of a continent, without any plan or regular development at all.[3]

If we ask what of significance has happened in this expanse of time, the answer is, "Nothing." There have been no unique events. There have been no stages of growth. We have a system which is not exactly static; it is rather a system of indifference, of more or less meaningless fluctuations around an eternal mean. As one of Lyell's admirers put it, his is a theory in which "the thing that has been is the thing that is and shall be.[4]

Now we can explain why Lyell had to combat Lamarck's evolutionary theories and why he remained for thirty years the great opponent of all developmental ideas in biology as well as in geology. The opposition has been presented as a lapse of logic or failure of insight on Lyell's part by such interpreters of the history of science as Thomas Huxley, Arthur Lovejoy, and Charles Gillispie.[5] But Lyell's opposition was not a lapse; it was an obvious necessity if Lyell was to keep his universe free from Christianity. One thing that could be proved in 1830 was how closely living beings are adapted to their environment. Therefore, if you accepted the idea of development in biological history, the conclusion that there must have been a corresponding development in the geological environment would become almost impossible to avoid. And precisely this developmental thinking, Lyell believed, was the alien Christian tendency which had marred the whole history of geology prior to the work of James Hutton. It was to refute just such ideas that he had written his book in the first place.

Now we can understand why Darwin, when he revealed to his friends that he did believe in evolution, used such odd phrases as, "I know that this will make you despise me," and, "It is like confessing a murder." [6] It *was* murder; given his master Lyell's antievolutionary convictions, it was intellectual parricide. Darwin could learn of the conservative aspects of natural selection in weeding out failures from Lyell (or for that matter from Lucretius), but Lyell's

3. Lyell, *Principles*, I, 134, 192–193, 298, 544–553, esp. 547.
4. Lyell, *Principles*, II, 157; Gray, *Darwiniana*, p. 103.
5. Huxley, "Reception of the *Origin*," I, 544; Lovejoy, "The Argument for Organic Evolution Before the *Origin of Species*, 1830–1858," in *Forerunners of Darwin*, ed. B. Glass, O. Temkin, and W. Straus (Baltimore, 1959), p. 369; Gillispie, *Genesis and Geology* (Cambridge, Mass., 1951), p. 131. In contrast to these, see Reijier Hooykaas, *Natural Law and Divine Miracle* (Leiden, 1959), pp. 94–95, 100. I was not able to consult Hooykaas' book in preparing this paper, so that our numerous agreements may be taken as additional confirmation of the validity of our analysis.
6. Darwin, *Life and Letters*, I, 384, 437, and cf. the version of the latter, taken from the original, in Dupree, *Asa Gray*, pp. 244–245. These phrases have often been interpreted as Darwin's expressions of timidity in the face of theological orthodoxy; but why should Darwin be self-abusive about his lack of belief in private letters to scientific friends? And Darwin himself says that he was for some time "scientifically orthodox" before he saw how to explain adaptation in nature (Dupree, *Asa Gray*, p. 246).

universe had no room for its creative aspect.[7] Nor in a non-evolutionary world such as Lyell's is the origin of species a major problem. It was indeed Lyell's geological opponents, the Catastrophists, who spotlighted the problem of the origin of species in the 1830's, although their solutions might not satisfy a modern scientist.[8]

One final point concerns the nature of time in Lyell's world. Because Lyell insisted on an unlimited amount of time for geological speculation, he has sometimes been credited with a "historical" vision. But this, I think, is an incorrect use of the word "historical." An unlimited extent of meaningless time is not, I believe, the historian's view of time. Even if we avoid equating history with historicism and instead consider that our statements must apply to Book One of Thucydides, we can say that the historian is concerned with particular events set in a definite sequential relation, and time is significant because it is filled full of particular significant happenings. Lyell's world is no more historical than is an astronomical universe in which, for the sake of calculating orbits, the coordinate t may be as indefinitely large as the calculator desires. It is the significant happenings, and not the vast amount of Lyellian time, which make Darwin's universe historical (cf. Hooykaas, p. 144).

However this may be, at least we can say that Lyell's universe does specifically exclude significant development over time, and thus cannot be the basis of an evolutionary cosmography. * * *

At the period when young Charles Darwin was delighting in Paley's *Natural Theology* and *Evidences of Christianity* at Cambridge [9] and opening his first notebook on the transmutation of species, there was present in natural theology the following collection of concepts: 1. The essential randomness of raw nature; 2. The impotence of a "law of nature," which is only a statement of observed sequences; 3. The scientific naiveté of attributing to raw nature an inherent organizing power of its own; 4. Therefore the necessity for an external power to produce organization; 5. The universal adaptation of living beings to their environments; and therefore 6. The usefulness of *purpose* or *conditions of existence* as a fruitful concept in biology; 7. The usefulness of every organ to the individual and not to some other species—a corollary not of the previous points but of the goodness of God towards all of his creation; 8. The subservience of Malthusian superfecundity to the purposes of the system; 9. The historical nature of the past, which has developed from time zero in an irreversible process, but not in a single line, and not merely eventuating in man; 10. The progressive

7. Loren Eiseley, "Charles Darwin, Edward Blyth, and the Theory of Natural Selection," *Proceedings of the American Philosophical Society*, CIII (1959), 105.

8. See my article, "The Problem of Miracles in the 1830's," *Victorian Studies*, IV (1960), 8.
9. Darwin, *Autobiography*, p. 59; *Life and Letters*, II, 15.

nature of that development, a progress which is not metaphysically derived but is asserted empirically. * * *

The universe defined by these concepts is the same as Darwin's. In his theory, the general randomness of raw nature shows up specifically as the fortuitous variations among individuals. The external organizing power is that of natural selection, which functions to ensure that only those developments which have purpose will in the long run endure. Development is unique and irreversible; it is progressive only because the environment has been such as to permit more and more complex organisms to survive.[1] The defined universe is one in which, if species are considered to be stable organizations, the problem of investigating the secondary causes of their origin is a legitimate and indeed obvious one. And this investigation should produce results that can be correlated with the historical nature of the past.

The natural theologians had accepted a set of postulates which, they believed, relied upon the best scientific principles to show that the world is both purposeful and historical. They were shocked to find that the animate organization in this world could be explained by natural selection as easily as by reference to God, that indeed natural selection apparently must operate whether God does or not. This is what I mean by saying that Darwin "stole" the universe of the theologians from them. And it is because they were arguing in terms of the same universe that the Darwinians and the theologians could argue so heatedly. Between Darwin and, say, Agassiz there could be no real argument, for to accept one meant to reject the very idea of explanation of the other.

We can now see why it has been easy to represent the Darwinian debates as the clash of empirical methods and idealistic metaphysics simply by taking Owen or Agassiz as Darwin's chief philosophic opponents. The universe which Darwin has used, the universe of the natural theologians, contains several features found in British empiricism, in particular the notion of law as only constant conjunction. But this is not merely an empiricist's universe. Historically it is rather the theologian's answer to the secular or skeptical empiricists.

If what I have suggested so far is correct, then we can make a further judgment about Darwin's predecessors. I have said that in the universe of the natural theologians the problem of the origin of species should arise *if* species are considered as stable organizations, since all real examples of organization require explanation in

1. Theodosius Dobzhansky calls the evolutionary process "unique, unrepeatable, and irreversible" in the *American Scientist*, XLV (1957), 388. It cannot be too often emphasized that Darwinian evolution is not necessarily progressive and could become retrogressive if the environment should change so as to be definitely unfavorable for complex organisms.

that universe. Let us oppose Linnaeus to Buffon, Paley to Erasmus Darwin, and Cuvier to Lamarck. Then the true "predecessors" of Darwin are Linnaeus, Paley, and Cuvier; and the ideas of Buffon, Erasmus Darwin, and Lamarck, the "evolutionists" of the period before Charles Darwin, have little relevance for an understanding of Darwin's problem and his solution. It is those thinkers described by Arthur Lovejoy, who picture the world "as tied up in neat and orderly parcels" with "rigid categories and absolute antitheses," who set the stage for Darwin; whereas the departure from this tradition in the direction of a law of continuity and self-energized monads led only to the dead-end of Lamarck.[2] Darwin in his own context might appear to be a champion of continuity in his blurring of species differences, but this is true only in comparison to the extreme rigidity of structural (Owen) or Platonic (Agassiz) approaches which opposed him in 1859. Species must be considered as real entities before their origin could be of importance. As Zirkle observes, "A scientific theory of evolution became possible only after the stability of species had been established. Evolution demands that species change but it demands that they change in an orderly fashion."[3] * * *

CHARLES COULSTON GILLISPIE

Lamarck and Darwin in the History of Science (1959) †

* * * Having rejected Darwin's evolutionary principles, most of his opponents thought it worthwhile to impugn his originality. Among moralists Samuel Butler, and among scientists (though for different reasons) the French, put it about that Lamarck had had everything essential to an evolutionary biology. And * * * it would be difficult indeed to claim the fact of the evolutionary variation of species as a Darwinian discovery. It is true that Darwin disposed of a greater fund of species than had Lamarck. Moreover, the seating of the chronology of earth history in paleontological indices gave biologists by way of return the succession of species in geological time. It was for lack of this information that Lamarck had

2. Lovejoy, "Buffon and the Problem of Species," *Forerunners of Darwin*, pp. 90–91. I am assuming that, regardless of how the individual opinions of each changed, the total effect of Linnaeus' career was to emphasize the value of a fairly rigid classificatory system, and the effect of Buffon's career was to question most sharp-cut differences in nature. See especially Philip Darlington, Jr., "Darwin and Zoogeography," *Proc. Am. Phil. Soc.*, CIII (1959), 317; and the references in note 25, above.
3. "Species Before Darwin," *Proc. Am. Phil. Soc.*, CIII (1959), 643.
† From Chapter 10 of Bentley Glass *et al.*, *Forerunners of Darwin* (Baltimore, 1959). Charles Coulston Gillispie (b. 1918) is professor of the history of science at Princeton University.

had to establish his order in the scale of increasing morphological complexity.

It is to be doubted, however, whether the uniformitarian philosophy of Charles Lyell was as essential to Darwin's success as is usually said, or as I once said myself.[1] For Lamarck had been his own Lyell. His *Hydrogéologie* prepared the ground for his theory of evolution with a uniformitarian earth history as uncompromising as Lyell's, if not so well founded.[2] More generally, it might be argued—indeed, I do argue—that in the relative cogency with which the two theories organize actual biological information, Lamarck's presentation in the great *Histoire naturelle des animaux sans vertèbres* is the more interesting and elegant.[3] It is analytical and informs a systematic taxonomy, whereas Darwin simply amassed detail and pursued his argument through the accumulated observations in a naturalist's commonplace-book. To be single-minded and relentless is not necessarily to be systematic, and the merit of Darwin's approach must be sought elsewhere.

Nevertheless, despite the greater formal elegance of Lamarck's ultimate presentation, his theory failed to compel assent. It scarcely even won attention. Those most competent to judge, Lamarck's own scientific colleagues, treated his ventures into theory as the embarrassing aberrations of a gifted observer, to be passed over in silence. "I know full well," he once observed bitterly, "that very few will be interested in what I am going to propose, and that among those who do read this essay, the greater part will pretend to find in it only systems, only vague opinions, in no way founded in exact knowledge. They will say that: but they will not write it." [4] Cuvier and Lamarck were able to work together in actual taxonomy. But they could never agree on the structure of nature.

No such humiliating judgment of irrelevance awaited Darwin's theory. (Even though my argument is that Darwin's original contribution was the theory and not the evidence, I shall in the interests of economy perpetuate the injustice which makes Wallace's role in the history of science little more than an object lesson in the agonizing generosity of creative minds.) Huxley's description of his own reaction is well known. Once stated, the force of the concept leapt out at him like the pattern from the pieces of the puzzle of adaptation, so that all he could say to himself was, "How extremely stupid not to have thought of that." [5] The right answer, it presented itself in that combination of unexpectedness and irresistibility which has often been the hallmark of a truly new concept in

1. *Genesis and Geology* (Harvard University Press, Cambridge, 1951).
2. Paris, 1802.
3. Paris, 1815–1822.
4. *Recherches sur l'organisation des corps vivants* (Paris, 1802), p. 69.
5. Leonard Huxley, *Life and Letters of T. H. Huxley* (2 v., Appleton, New York, 1901), I, p. 183.

scientific history.

One sometimes reads, however, that the force of Darwin's ideas derived from their mechanistic character in an age which identified the scientific with the mechanistic. I cannot think this quite correct. The one thing Darwin did not, and could not, specify was the mechanism of variation or heredity. All he could do was postulate its naturalistic mode. Ultimately, of course, his hypothesis was vindicated by discoveries in genetics of a materialistic character. But that is quite another matter—the *bête-machine* belongs to the 18th century (or to the 20th), but not to the 19th. It was through no metaphor or analogy that Darwin prevailed. He prevailed because his work turned the study of the whole of living nature into an objective science. In the unlikely guise of a Victorian sermon on self-help in nature, on profit and loss, on progress through competition, there was clothed nothing less than a new natural philosophy, as new in its domain as Galileo's in physics. Darwin, indeed, abolished the distinction which had divided biology from physics at least since Newton, and which rested on the supposition (or defense) that the biologist must characteristically study the nature and the wisdom of the whole rather than the structure of the parts.

Lamarck, too, conveyed a philosophy of nature in his theory of the development of life, but it stands in the same relationship to Darwin's as does Hegel's historical dialectic to that of Marx. It is no compliment to Lamarck's own conception of his lifework, therefore, to make him out an unappreciated forerunner of Darwin. I recently asked a friend who is a biologist specializing in evolution what he and his colleagues understood by Lamarckism, and the first thing he said was the inheritance of acquired characteristics, and after that a lingering temptation in biology generally to indulge in an "Aristotelian vitalism." [6] Now vitalism and the mode of acquisition and transmission of variations were, indeed, the points on which scientific discussion of evolution turned in the later decades of the 19th century and before the establishment of modern genetics. And it is most natural that biologists should have looked upon Lamarck in the perspective of their science, which takes the shape of evolution from Darwin. But in doing so they have first missed and then misrepresented the point of Lamarck's work, which was neither Aristotelian nor vitalistic, and which instead was meant to establish, not simply the subordinate fact of transmutation, but a view of the world. For Lamarck's theory of evolution was the last

6. I wish to acknowledge the kindness of the colleague in question, Dr. Colin S. Pittendrigh, who explained to me very patiently various aspects of the outlook of modern evolutionists. Section V of this essay has specially profited from this discussion—though I should be distressed if any mistakes which remain were attributed to anyone but me.

attempt to make a science out of the instinct, as old as Heraclitos and deeply hostile to Aristotelian formalization, that the world is flux and process, and that science is to study, not the configurations of matter, nor the categories of form, but the manifestations of that activity which is ontologically fundamental as bodies in motion and species of being are not. * * *

Like the law of falling bodies, the theory of natural selection is so widely taken for granted that its magnitude is not on the face of it apparent. And rather than rehearse it once again, it may perhaps set Darwin off to better advantage to consider briefly what his theory did not do and what it forbade others to do. For Darwin's opponents—the serious ones, not the theologians, who were only pathetic—did not deny the fact of evolutionary variation. But they did want things from biology which science cannot give without ceasing to be science and becoming moral or social philosophy. And this perspective will make apparent the justice of the judgment which attributes to Darwin the importance for biology that Newton has for physics, so that his rather numbing humility becomes, not the attribute of inferiority, but only the quality fitted to a science in which observation plays a larger role than abstract formalization.

Both Newton and Darwin, to begin with, were criticized for ingratitude to their predecessors. This is not just a question of scholarly manners: once the theory—gravitation, natural selection —is repudiated, then what is left is the evidence—the inverse square relationship, the fact of variation—in which intellectual property might indeed be claimed for predecessors. But in both cases the theory was rejected, not as mistaken, but as meaningless. For Newton and Darwin had a way of simply accepting the phenomena as given. They excluded reason and purpose, according to this complaint, not in any dogmatic or positive fashion, but simply as an abdication of judgment. Thus, they prevented philosophy from coming to grips with science.

Fontenelle, for example, dismissed Newton's geometric manner of proof on the same grounds that led Darwin's critics to deny merit to the concept of fitness in the organism. These are not scientific demonstrations, say the critics. Nor can they be because they come out precisely even. They are simply tautologies which circle through the phenomena right back to their starting point. What is causation in Newton and what in Darwin?—only a formless sequence of results extending backward or outward endlessly into a metaphysical limbo. Newton purports to unite his system with the principle of gravity, and Darwin with the principle of natural selection. But if either is asked what causes gravity, or what causes the variations that are selected, he does not know. Nor did the theory depend upon his trying to say. Indeed, its success hinged precisely on dropping that question. * * *

So far as the intellectual and cultural significance of evolutionary theory is concerned, therefore, Darwin had no predecessor in Lamarck. Lamarck's theory of evolution belongs to the contracting and self-defeating history of subjective science, and Darwin's to the expanding and conquering history of objective science. In the concept of natural selection, Darwin put an end to the opposition between mechanism and organism through which the humane view of nature, ultimately the Greek view, had found refuge from Newton in biology. Lamarck's theory, on the other hand, originated as the transfer to natural history of that old view for which Lavoisier had made chemistry, the science of matter, uninhabitable. It is for this reason that Darwin was the orderer of biological science, as Newton was of physics and Galileo of mechanics. He was the first to frame objective concepts widely enough to embrace the whole range of phenomena studied by his science. And it may be worthwhile to consider the theory of natural selection analytically for a moment, in order to specify what were the elements of its success, and how it was that, schematically speaking, Darwinian evolutionary theory stands in the same relation to Lamarckian in the overall structure of the history of science as does Galilean to Aristotelian mechanics.

In mechanics, Galileo achieved objectivity by accepting motion as natural, and considering its quantity as something to be measured independently of the moving body. This he accomplished by treating time as a dimension, after which motion in physics is no longer taken as a substantial change. In Darwin—to begin drawing out the parallel—natural selection treats that sort of change which expresses itself in organic variation in the same way. Instead of explaining variation, he begins with it as a fundamental fact of nature. Variations are assumed to occur at random, requiring no further explanation and pre-supposing no causative agent for science to seek out. This is what opened the breach through which biology might follow physics into objectivity, because it introduced the distinction, which Darwin was the first to make, between the origin of variations and their preservation. Variations arise by chance. But they are preserved according as they work more or less effectively in objective circumstance. In Lamarck, on the other hand, the two problems are handled as a single question, which in effect is begged by its solution in the inheritance of acquired characteristics. Lamarck, therefore, could no more have distinguished the study of variations from the study of the organism as a whole than the impetus school could separate motion from the missile. * * *

PART II

A Selection of Darwin's Work

Darwin's *essential* achievement was the demonstration that the almost incredible variety of life, with all its complex and puzzling relations to its environment, was explicable in scientific terms.

—Julian Huxley, 1958

This second supposed cause of evolution was known as "the inheritance of acquired characters," a doctrine that had been accepted generally for well over two thousand years. Not until late in the nineteenth century was its validity questioned seriously. Then the critical experiments, designed to test its validity, gave negative results * * * and now the belief has been abandoned by all honest and critical biologists.

—Conway Zirkle, 1958

CHARLES DARWIN

Selected Letters (1832–1859) †

To R. W. Darwin

Bahia, or San Salvador, Brazils,[1] [February 8, 1832].
I find after the first page I have
been writing to my sisters.

My dear Father,

I am writing this on the 8th of February, one day's sail past St.
Jago (Cape de Verd), and intend taking the chance of meeting with
a homeward-bound vessel somewhere about the equator. The date,
however, will tell this whenever the opportunity occurs. I will now
begin from the day of leaving England, and give a short account of
our progress. We sailed, as you know, on the 27th of December, and
have been fortunate enough to have had from that time to the
present a fair and moderate breeze. It afterwards proved that we
had escaped a heavy gale in the Channel, another at Madeira, and
another on [the] Coast of Africa. But in escaping the gale, we felt
its consequences—a heavy sea. In the Bay of Biscay there was a
long and continuous swell, and the misery I endured from sea-sickness is far beyond what I ever guessed at. I believe you are curious
about it. I will give you all my dear-bought experience. Nobody
who has only been to sea for twenty-four hours has a right to say
that sea-sickness is even uncomfortable. The real misery only begins
when you are so exhausted that a little exertion makes a feeling of
faintness come on. I found nothing but lying in my hammock did
me any good. I must especially except your receipt of raisins, which
is the only food that the stomach will bear.

On the 4th of January we were not many miles from Madeira,
but as there was a heavy sea running, and the island lay to wind-
ward, it was not thought worth while to beat up to it. It afterwards
has turned out it was lucky we saved ourselves the trouble. I was
much too sick even to get up to see the distant outline. On the 6th,
in the evening, we sailed into the harbour of Santa Cruz. I now first
felt even moderately well, and I was picturing to myself all the delights of fresh fruits growing in beautiful valleys, and reading Humboldt's descriptions of the island's glorious views, when perhaps

† These letters indicate something of
Darwin's various preoccupations between the years 1832, aboard the
Beagle, and 1859, when the *Origin*
appeared. The text is from Francis
Darwin, ed., *The Life and Letters of
Charles Darwin* (1887).
1. For this and other localities mentioned in Darwin's writing, see map,
p. *xiv* above [Editor].

you may nearly guess at our disappointment, when a small pale man informed us we must perform a strict quarantine of twelve days. There was a death-like stillness in the ship till the Captain cried "up jib," and we left this longwished for place.

We were becalmed for a day between Teneriffe and the Grand Canary, and here I first experienced any enjoyment. The view was glorious. The Peak of Teneriffe was seen amongst the clouds like another world. Our only drawback was the extreme wish of visiting this glorious island *Tell Eyton never to forget either the Canary Islands or South America;* that I am sure it will well repay the necessary trouble, but that he must make up his mind to find a good deal of the latter. I feel certain he will regret it if he does not make the attempt. From Teneriffe to St. Jago the voyage was extremely pleasant. I had a net astern the vessel which caught great numbers of curious animals, and fully occupied my time in my cabin, and on deck the weather was so delightful and clear, that the sky and water together made a picture. On the 16th we arrived at Port Praya, the capital of the Cape de Verds, and there we remained twenty-three days, viz., till yesterday, the 7th of February. The time has flown away most delightfully, indeed nothing can be pleasanter; exceedingly busy, and that business both a duty and a great delight. I do not believe I have spent one half-hour idly since leaving Teneriffe. St. Jago has afforded me an exceedingly rich harvest in several branches of Natural History. I find the descriptions scarcely worth anything of many of the commoner animals that inhabit the Tropics. I allude, of course, to those of the lower classes.

Geologising in a volcanic country is most delightful; besides the interest attached to itself, it leads you into most beautiful and retired spots. Nobody but a person fond of Natural History can imagine the pleasure of strolling under cocoa-nuts in a thicket of bananas and coffee-plants, and an endless number of wild flowers. And this island, that has given me so much instruction and delight, is reckoned the most uninteresting place that we perhaps shall touch at during our voyage. It certainly is generally very barren, but the valleys are more exquisitely beautiful, from the very contrast. It is utterly useless to say anything about the scenery; it would be as profitable to explain to a blind man colours, as to a person who has not been out of Europe, the total dissimilarity of a tropical view. Whenever I enjoy anything, I always either look forward to writing it down, either in my log-book (which increases in bulk), or in a letter; so you must excuse raptures, and those raptures badly expressed. I find my collections are increasing wonderfully, and from Rio I think I shall be obliged to send a cargo home.

All the endless delays which we experienced at Plymouth have been most fortunate, as I verily believe no person ever went out better provided for collecting and observing in the different branches of Natural History. In a multitude of counsellors I certainly found good. I find to my great surprise that a ship is singularly comfortable for all sorts of work. Everything is so close at hand, and being cramped makes one so methodical, that in the end I have been a gainer. I already have got to look at going to sea as a regular quiet place, like going back to home after staying away from it. In short, I find a ship a very comfortable house, with everything you want, and if it was not for sea-sickness the whole world would be sailors. I do not think there is much danger of Erasmus setting the example, but in case there should be, he may rely upon it he does not know one-tenth of the sufferings of sea-sickness.

I like the officers much more than I did at first, especially Wickham, and young King and Stokes, and indeed all of them. The Captain continues steadily very kind, and does everything in his power to assist me. We see very little of each other when in harbour, our pursuits lead us in such different tracks. I never in my life met with a man who could endure nearly so great a share of fatigue. He works incessantly, and when apparently not employed, he is thinking. If he does not kill himself, he will during this voyage do a wonderful quantity of work. I find I am very well, and stand the little heat we have had as yet as well as anybody. We shall soon have it in real earnest. We are now sailing for Fernando Noronha, off the coast of Brazil, where we shall not stay very long, and then examine the shoals between there and Rio, touching perhaps at Bahia. I will finish this letter when an opportunity of sending it occurs.

February 26th.—About 280 miles from Bahia. On the 10th we spoke the packet *Lyra*, on her voyage to Rio. I sent a short letter by her, to be sent to England on [the] first opportunity. We have been singularly unlucky in not meeting with any homeward-bound vessels, but I suppose [at] Bahia we certainly shall be able to write to England. Since writing the first part of [this] letter nothing has occurred except crossing the Equator, and being shaved. This most disagreeable operation consists in having your face rubbed with paint and tar, which forms a lather for a saw which represents the razor, and then being half drowned in a sail filled with salt water. About 50 miles north of the line we touched at the rocks of St. Paul; this little speck (about ¼ of a mile across) in the Atlantic has seldom been visited. It is totally barren, but is covered by hosts of birds; they were so unused to men that we found we could kill plenty with stones and sticks. After remaining some hours on the island, we returned on board with the boat loaded with our prey. From this we went to Fernando Noronha, a small island where the

[Brazilians] send their exiles. The landing there was attended with so much difficulty owing [to] a heavy surf that the Captain determined to sail the next day after arriving. My one day on shore was exceedingly interesting, the whole island is one single wood so matted together by creepers that it is very difficult to move out of the beaten path. I find the Natural History of all these unfrequented spots most exceedingly interesting, especially the geology. I have written this much in order to save time at Bahia.

Decidedly the most strking thing in the Tropics is the novelty of the vegetable forms. Cocoa-nuts could well be imagined from drawings, if you add to them a graceful lightness which no European tree partakes of. Bananas and plantains are exactly the same as those in hothouses, the acacias or tamarinds are striking from the blueness of their foliage; but of the glorious orange trees, no description, no drawings, will give any just idea; instead of the sickly green of our oranges, the native ones exceed the Portugal laurel in the darkness of their tint, and infinitely exceed it in beauty of form. Cocoa-nuts, papaws, the light green bananas, and oranges, loaded with fruit, generally surround the more luxuriant villages. Whilst viewing such scenes, one feels the impossibility that any description should come near the mark, much less be overdrawn. * * *

The conviction that I am walking in the New World is even yet marvellous in my own eyes, and I dare say it is little less so to you, the receiving a letter from a son of yours in such a quarter.

> Believe me my dear Father,
> Your most affectionate son,
> Charles Darwin.

To J. S. Henslow

Rio de Janeiro, May 18, 1832.

My Dear Henslow,
* * *

Till arriving at Teneriffe (we did not touch at Madeira) I was scarcely out of my hammock, and really suffered more than you can well imagine from such a cause. At Santa Cruz, whilst looking amongst the clouds for the Peak, and repeating to myself Humboldt's sublime descriptions, it was announced we must perform twelve days' strict quarantine. We had made a short passage, so "Up jib," and away for St. Jago. You will say all this sounds very bad, and so it was; but from that to the present time it has been nearly one scene of continual enjoyment. A net over the stern kept me at full work till we arrived at St. Jago. Here we spent three most delightful weeks. The geology was pre-eminently interesting, and

I believe quite new; there are some facts on a large scale of upraised coast (which is an excellent epoch for all the volcanic rocks to date from), that would interest Mr. Lyell.

One great source of perlexity to me is an utter ignorance whether I note the right facts, and whether they are of sufficient importance to interest others. In the one thing collecting I cannot go wrong. St. Jago is singularly barren, and produces few plants or insects, so that my hammer was my usual companion, and in its company most delightful hours I spent. On the coast I collected many marine animals, chiefly gasteropodous (I think some new). I examined pretty accurately a *Caryopyllia*, and, if my eyes are not bewitched, former descriptions have not the slightest resemblance to the animal. I took several specimens of an Octopus which possessed a most marvellous power of changing its colours, equalling any chameleon, and evidently accommodating the changes to the colour of the ground which it passed over. Yellowish green, dark brown, and red, were the prevailing colours; this fact appears to be new, as far as I can find out. Geology and the invertebrate animals will be my chief object of pursuit through the whole voyage.

We then sailed for Bahia, and touched at the rock of St. Paul. This is a serpentine formation. Is it not the only island in the Atlantic which is not volcanic? We likewise stayed a few hours at Fernando Noronha; a tremendous surf was running so that a boat was swamped, and the Captain would not wait. I find my life on board when we are on blue water most delightful, so very comfortable and quiet—it is almost impossible to be idle, and that for me is saying a good deal. Nobody could possibly be better fitted in every respect for collecting than I am; many cooks have not spoiled the broth this time. Mr. Brown's little hints about microscopes, &c., have been invaluable. I am well off in books, the 'Dictionnaire Classique' *is most useful.* * * *

> Ever yours,
> Charles Darwin.

To J. S. Henslow

April 11, 1833.

My dear Henslow,

We are now running up from the Falkland Islands to the Rio Negro (or Colorado). The *Beagle* will proceed to Monte Video; but if it can be managed I intend staying at the former place. It is now some months since we have been at a civilised port; nearly all this time has been spent in the most southern part of Tierra del Fuego. It is a detestable place; gales succeed gales with such short intervals that it is difficult to do anything. We were twenty-three days off Cape Horn, and could by no means get to the westward. The last and final gale before we gave up the attempt was unusually severe. A sea stove one of the boats, and there was so much water on the decks that every place was afloat; nearly all the paper for drying plants is spoiled, and half of this curious collection.

We at last ran into harbour, and in the boats got to the west by the inland channels. As I was one of this party I was very glad of it. With two boats we went about 300 miles, and thus I had an excellent opportunity of geologising and seeing much of the savages. The Fuegians are in a more miserable state of barbarism than I had expected ever to have seen a human being. In this inclement country they are absolutely naked, and their temporary houses are like what children make in summer with boughs of trees. I do not think any spectacle can be more interesting than the first sight of man in his primitive wildness. It is an interest which cannot well be imagined until it is experienced. I shall never forget this when entering Good Success Bay—the yell with which a party received us. They were seated on a rocky point, surrounded by the dark forest of beech; as they threw their arms wildly round their heads, and their long hair streaming, they seemed the troubled spirits of another world. * * *

To Miss S. Darwin

Valparaiso, April 23, 1835.

My dear Susan,

I received, a few days since, your letter of November; the three letters which I before mentioned are yet missing, but I do not doubt they will come to life. I returned a week ago from my excursion across the Andes to Mendoza. Since leaving England I have never made so successful a journey; it has, however, been very expensive. I am sure my father would not regret it, if he could know how deeply I have enjoyed it: it was something more than enjoyment; I cannot express the delight which I felt at such a famous winding-up of all my geology in South America. I literally could hardly sleep at nights for thinking over my day's work. The scenery was so new, and so majestic; everything at an elevation of 12,000 feet bears so different an aspect from that in a lower country. I have seen many views more beautiful, but none with so strongly marked a character. To a geologist, also, there are such manifest proofs of excessive violence; the strata of the highest pinnacles are tossed about like the crust of a broken pie.

I crossed by the Portillo Pass, which at this time of the year is apt to be dangerous, so could not afford to delay there. After staying a day in the stupid town of Mendoza, I began my return by Uspallate, which I did very leisurely. My whole trip only took up twenty-two days. I travelled with, for me, uncommon comfort, as I carried a *bed*! My party consisted of two Peons and ten mules, two of which were with baggage, or rather food, in case of being snowed up. Everything, however, favoured me; not even a speck of this year's snow had fallen on the road. I do not suppose any of you can be much interested in geological details, but I will just mention my principal results:—Besides understanding to a certain extent the description and manner of the force which has elevated this great line of mountains, I can clearly demonstrate that one part of the double line is of an age long posterior to the other. In the more ancient line, which is the true chain of the Andes, I can describe the sort and order of the rocks which compose it. These are chiefly remarkable by containing a bed of gypsum nearly 2000 feet thick— a quantity of this substance I should think unparalleled in the world. What is of much greater consequence, I have procured fossil shells (from an elevation of 12,000 feet). I think an examination of these will give an approximate age to these mountains, as compared to the strata of Europe. In the other line of the Cordilleras there is a strong presumption (in my own mind, conviction) that the enormous mass of mountains, the peaks of which rise to 13,000 and 14,000 feet, are so very modern as to be contemporaneous with the plains of Patagonia (or about with the *upper* strata of the Isle of Wight). If this result shall be considered as proved,[2] it is a very important fact in the theory of the formation of the world; because, if such wonderful changes have taken place so recently in the crust of the globe, there can be no reason for supposing former epochs of excessive violence. These modern strata are very remarkable by being threaded with metallic veins of silver, gold, copper, &c.; hitherto these have been considered as appertaining to older formations. In these same beds, and close to a goldmine, I found a clump of petrified trees, standing upright, with layers of fine sandstone deposited round them, bearing the impression of their bark. These trees are covered by other sandstones and streams of lava to the thickness of several thousand feet. These rocks have been deposited beneath the water; yet it is clear the spot where the trees grew must once have been above the level of the sea, so that it is certain the land must have been depressed by at least as many thousand feet as the superincumbent subaqueous deposits are thick. But I am afraid you will tell me I am prosy with my geological descriptions and theories. . . .[3]

Your account of Erasmus' visit to Cambridge has made me long

2. The importance of these results has been fully recognized by geologists [Francis Darwin's note].

3. (. . .) indicates deletions made by Francis Darwin [Editor].

to be back there. I cannot fancy anything more delightful than his Sunday round of King's, Trinity, and those talking giants, Whewell and Sedgwick; I hope your musical tastes continue in due force. I shall be ravenous for the pianoforte. . . .

I have not quite determined whether I will sleep at the 'Lion' the first night when I arrive per 'Wonder,' or disturb you all in the dead of the night; everything short of that is absolutely planned. Everything about Shrewsbury is growing in my mind bigger and more beautiful, I am certain the acacia and copper beech are two superb trees; I shall know every bush, and I will trouble you young ladies, when each of you cut down your tree, to spare a few. As for the view behind the house, I have seen nothing like it. It is the same with North Wales; Snowdon, to my mind, looks much higher and much more beautiful than any peak in the Cordilleras. So you will say, with my benighted faculties, it is time to return, and so it is, and I long to be with you. Whatever the trees are, I know what I shall find all you. I am writing nonsense, so farewell. My most affectionate love to all, and I pray forgiveness from my father.

Yours most affectionately,
Charles Darwin.

To L. Jenyns (Blomefield)

Down, Oct. 12th. [1845].

My dear Jenyns,—Thanks for your note. I am sorry to say I have not even the tail-end of a fact in English Zoology to communicate. I have found that even trifling observations require, in my case, some leisure and energy, both of which ingredients I have had none to spare, as writing my Geology thoroughly expends both. I had always thought that I would keep a journal and record everything, but in the way I now live I find I observe nothing to record. Looking after my garden and trees, and occasionally a very little walk in an idle frame of mind, fills up every afternoon in the same manner. I am surprised that with all your parish affairs, you have had time to do all that which you have done. I shall be very glad to see your little work [4] (and proud should I have been if I could have added a single fact to it). My work on the species question has impressed me very forcibly with the importance of all such works as your intended one, containing what people are pleased generally to call trifling facts. These are the facts which make one understand the

4. Mr. Jenyns' 'Observations in Natural History.' It is prefaced by an Introduction on "Habits of observing as connected with the study of Natural History," and followed by a "Calendar of Periodic Phenomena in Natural History," with "Remarks on the importance of such Registers." My father seems to be alluding to this Register in the P.S. to the letter dated Oct. 17, 1846 [F. Darwin's note].

working or economy of nature. There is one subject, on which I am very curious, and which perhaps you may throw some light on, if you have ever thought on it; namely, what are the checks and what the periods of life,—by which the increase of any given species is limited. Just calculate the increase of any bird, if you assume that only half the young are reared, and these breed: within the *natural* (*i.e.*, if free from accidents) life of the parents the number of individuals will become enormous, and I have been much surprised to think how great destruction *must* annually or occasionally be falling on every species, yet the means and period of such destruction is scarcely perceived by us.

I have continued steadily reading and collecting facts on variation of domestic animals and plants, and on the question of what are species. I have a grand body of facts, and I think I can draw some conclusions. The general conclusions at which I have slowly been driven from a directly opposite conviction, is that species are mutable, and that allied species are co-descendants from common stocks. I know how much I open myself to reproach for such a conclusion, but I have at least honestly and deliberately come to it. I shall not publish on this subject for several years. At present I am on the Geology of South America. I hope to pick up from your book some facts on slight variations in structure or instincts in the animals of your acquaintance.

Believe me, ever yours,
C. Darwin.

To L. Jenyns [5]

Down, [1845?].

My dear Jenyns,—I am very much obliged to you for the trouble you have taken in having written me so long a note. The question of where, when, and how the check to the increase of a given species falls appears to me particularly interesting, and our difficulty in answering it shows how really ignorant we are of the lives and habits of our most familiar species. I was aware of the bare fact of old birds driving away their young, but had never thought of the effect you so clearly point out, of local gaps in number being thus immediately filled up. But the original difficulty remains; for if your farmers had not killed your sparrows and rooks, what would have become of those which now immigrate into your parish? in the middle of England one is too far distant from the natural limits of the rook and sparrow to suppose that the young are thus far expelled from Cambridgeshire. The check must fall heavily at some

5. Rev. L. Blomefield [F. Darwin's note].

time of each species' life; for, if one calculates that only half the progeny are reared and bred, how enormous is the increase! One has, however, no business to feel so much surprise at one's ignorance, when one knows how impossible it is without statistics to conjecture the duration of life and percentage of deaths to births in mankind. If it could be shown that apparently the birds of passage *which breed here* and increase, return in the succeeding years in about the same number, whereas those that come here for their winter and non-breeding season annually, come here with the same numbers, but return with greatly decreased numbers, one would know (as indeed seems probable) that the check fell chiefly on full-grown birds in the winter season, and not on the eggs and very young birds, which has appeared to me often the most probable period. If at any time any remarks on this subject should occur to you, I should be most grateful for the benefit of them.

With respect to my far distant work on species, I must have expressed myself with singular inaccuracy if I led you to suppose that I meant to say that my conclusions were inevitable. They have become so, after years of weighing puzzles, to myself *alone*; but in my wildest day-dream, I never expect more than to be able to show that there are two sides to the question of the immutability of species, *i. e.* whether species are *directly* created or by intermediate laws (as with the life and death of individuals). I did not approach the subject on the side of the difficulty in determining what are species and what are varieties, but (though, why I should give you such a history of my doings it would be hard to say) from such facts as the relationship between the living and extinct mammifers in South America, and between those living on the Continent and on adjoining islands, such as the Galapagos. It occurred to me that a collection of all such analogous facts would throw light either for or against the view of related species being co-descendants from a common stock. A long searching amongst agricultural and horticultural books and people makes me believe (I well know how absurdly presumptuous this must appear) that I see the way in which new varieties become exquisitely adapted to the external conditions of life and to other surrounding beings. I am a bold man to lay myself open to being thought a complete fool, and a most deliberate one. From the nature of the grounds which make me believe that species are mutable in form, these grounds cannot be restricted to the closest-allied species; but how far they extend I cannot tell, as my reasons fall away by degrees, when applied to species more and more remote from each other. Pray do not think that I am so blind as not to see that there are numerous immense difficulties in my notions, but they appear to me less than on the common view. I have drawn up a sketch and had it copied (in 200 pages) of my conclusions; and if I thought at some future time that you would think it worth reading, I should, of course, be most thankful to have the criticism of so competent a critic. Excuse this very long and egotistical and ill-written letter, which by your re- marks you had led me into, and believe me,

Yours very truly,
C. Darwin.

To C. Lyell

May 3 [1856].

. . . With respect to your suggestion of a sketch of my views, I hardly know what to think, but will reflect on it, but it goes against my prejudices. To give a fair sketch would be absolutely impossible, for every proposition requires such an array of facts. If I were to do anything, it could only refer to the main agency of change— selection—and perhaps point out a very few of the leading fea- tures, which countenance such a view, and some few of the main difficulties. But I do not know what to think; I rather hate the idea of writing for priority, yet I certainly should be vexed if any one were to publish my doctrines before me. Anyhow, I thank you heartily for your sympathy. I shall be in London next week, and I will call on you on Thursday morning for one hour precisely, so as not to lose much of your time and my own; but will you let me this time come as early as 9 o'clock, for I have much which I must do in the morning in my strongest time? Farewell, my dear old patron.

Yours,
C. Darwin.

To J. D. Hooker

May 9th, [1856].

. . . I very much want advice and *truthful* consolation if you can give it. I had a good talk with Lyell about my species work, and he urges me strongly to publish something. I am fixed against any periodical or Journal, as I positively will *not* expose myself to an Editor or a Council, allowing a publication for which they might be abused. If I publish anything it must be a *very thin* and little vol- ume, giving a sketch of my views and difficulties; but it is really dreadfully unphilosophical to give a *resumé*, without exact refer- ences, of an unpublished work. But Lyell seemed to think I might do this, at the suggestion of friends, and on the ground, which I might state, that I had been at work for eighteen [6] years, and yet could not publish for several years, and especially as I could point out difficulties which seemed to me to require especial investigation. Now what think you? I should be really grateful for advice. I thought of giving up a couple of months and writing such a sketch, and trying to keep my judgment open whether or no to publish it when completed. It will be simply impossible for me to give exact references; anything important I should state on the authority of the author generally; and instead of giving all the facts on which I ground my opinion, I could give by memory only one or two. In the Preface I would state that the work could not be considered strictly scientific, but a mere sketch or outline of a future work in which full references, &c., should be given. Eheu, eheu, I believe I should sneer at any one else doing this, and my only comfort is, that I *truly* never dreamed of it, till Lyell suggested it, and seems deliberately to think it advisable.

I am in a peck of troubles and do pray forgive me for troubling you.

Yours affectionately,
C. Darwin.

To Asa Gray

Down, July 20th [1856].

. . . It is not a little egotistical, but I should like to tell you (and I do not *think* I have) how I view my work. Nineteen years (!) ago it occurred to me that whilst otherwise employed on Nat. Hist., I might perhaps do good if I noted any sort of facts bearing on the question of the origin of species, and this I have since been doing. Either species have been independently created, or they have descended from other species, like varieties from one species. I think it can be shown to be probable that man gets his most distinct varieties by preserving such as arise best worth keeping and destroying the others, but I should fill a quire if I were to go on. To be brief, I *assume* that species arise like our domestic varieties with *much* extinction; and then test this hypothesis by comparison with as many general and pretty well-established propositions as I can find made out,—in geographical distribution, geological history, affinities, &c., &c. And it seems to me that, *supposing* that such hypothesis were to explain such general propositions, we ought, in accordance with the common way of following all sciences, to admit

6. The interval of eighteen years, from 1837 when he began to collect facts, would bring the date of this letter to 1855, not 1856, nevertheless the latter seems the more probable date [F. Darwin's note].

it till some better hypothesis be found out. For to my mind to say that species were created so and so is no scientific explanation, only a reverent way of saying it is so and so. But it is nonsensical trying to show how I try to proceed in the compass of a note. But as an honest man, I must tell you that I have come to the heterodox conclusion that there are no such things as independently created species—that species are only strongly defined varieties. I know that this will make you despise me. I do not much underrate the many *huge* difficulties on this view, but yet it seems to me to explain too much, otherwise inexplicable, to be false. Just to allude to one point in your last note, viz., about species of the same genus *generally* having a common or continuous area; if they are actual lineal descendants of one species, this of course would be the case; and the sadly too many exceptions (for me) have to be explained by climatal and geological changes. A *fortiori* on this view (but on exactly same grounds), all the individuals of the same species should have a continous distribution. On this latter branch of the subject I have put a chapter together, and Hooker kindly read it over. I thought the exceptions and difficulties were so great that on the whole the balance weighed against my notions, but I was much pleased to find that it seemed to have considerable weight with Hooker, who said he had never been so much staggered about the permanence of species. * * *

To A. R. Wallace

Moor Park, May 1st, 1857.

My dear Sir,—I am much obliged for your letter of October 10th, from Celebes, received a few days ago; in a laborious undertaking, sympathy is a valuable and real encouragement. By your letter and even still more by your paper [7] in the Annals, a year or more ago, I can plainly see that we have thought much alike and to a certain extent have come to similar conclusions. In regard to the Paper in the Annals, I agree to the truth of almost every word of your paper; and I dare say that you will agree with me that it is very rare to find oneself agreeing pretty closely with any theoretical paper; for it is lamentable how each man draws his own different conclusions from the very same facts. This summer will make the 20th year (!) since I opened my first note-book, on the question how and in what way do species and varieties differ from each other. I am now preparing my work for publication, but I find the subject so very large, that though I have written many chapters, I do not

7. 'On the law that has regulated the   Nat. Hist., 1855 [F. Darwin's note]. introduction of new species.'—Ann.

suppose I shall go to press for two years. I have never heard how long you intend staying in the Malay Archipelago; I wish I might profit by the publication of your Travels there before my work appears, for no doubt you will reap a large harvest of facts. * * *

To A. R. Wallace

Down, Dec. 22nd, 1857.

My dear Sir,—I thank you for your letter of Sept. 27th. I am extremely glad to hear that you are attending to distribution in accordance with theoretical ideas. I am a firm believer that without speculation there is no good and original observation. Few travellers have attended to such points as you are now at work on; and, indeed, the whole subject of distribution of animals is dreadfully behind that of plants. . . .

You ask whether I shall discuss "man." I think I shall avoid the whole subject, as so surrounded with prejudices; though I fully admit that it is the highest and most interesting problem for the naturalist. My work, on which I have now been at work more or less for twenty years, will not fix or settle anything; but I hope it will aid by giving a large collection of facts, with one definite end. I get on very slowly, partly from ill-health, partly from being a very slow worker. I have got about half written; but I do not suppose I shall published under a couple of years. I have now been three whole months on one chapter on Hybridism!

I am astonished to see that you expect to remain out three or four years more. What a wonderful deal you will have seen, and what interesting areas—the grand Malay Archipelago and the richest parts of South America! I infinitely admire and honour your zeal and courage in the good cause of Natural Science; and you have my very sincere and cordial good wishes for success of all kinds, and may all your theories succeed, except that on Oceanic Islands, on which subject I will do battle to the death.

Pray believe me, my dear sir, yours very sincerely,

C. Darwin.

To Mrs. Darwin

Moor Park, Wednesday, April [1858].

The weather is quite delicious. Yesterday, after writing to you, I strolled a little beyond the glade for an hour and a half, and enjoyed myself—the fresh yet dark-green of the grand Scotch firs, the brown of the catkins of the old birches, with their white stems, and a fringe of distant green from the larches made an excessively pretty view. At last I fell fast asleep on the grass, and awoke with a chorus of birds singing around me, and squirrels running up the trees, and some woodpeckers laughing, and it was as pleasant and rural a scene as ever I saw, and I did not care one penny how any of the beasts or birds had been formed. * * *

To C. Lyell

Down, 18th [June 1858].

My dear Lyell,—Some year or so ago you recommended me to read a paper by Wallace in the 'Annals,' [8] which had interested you, and, as I was writing to him, I knew this would please him much, so I told him. He has to-day sent me the enclosed, and asked me to forward it to you. It seems to me well worth reading. Your words have come true with a vengeance—that I should be forestalled. You said this, when I explained to you here very briefly my views of 'Natural Selection' depending on the struggle for existence. I never saw a more striking coincidence; if Wallace had my MS. sketch written out in 1842, he could not have made a better short abstract! Even his terms now stand as heads of my chapters. Please return me the MS., which he does not say he wishes me to publish, but I shall of course, at once write and offer to send to any journal. So all my originality, whatever it may amount to, will be smashed, though my book, if it will ever have any value, will not be deteriorated; as all the labour consists in the application of the theory.

I hope you will approve of Wallace's sketch, that I may tell him what you say.

My dear Lyell, yours most truly,
C. Darwin.

To C. Lyell

Down, Friday [June 25, 1858].

My dear Lyell,—I am very sorry to trouble you, busy as you are, in so merely a personal an affair; but if you will give me your deliberate opinion, you will do me as great a service as ever man did, for I have entire confidence in your judgment and honour. . . .

There is nothing in Wallace's sketch which is not written out much fuller in my sketch, copied out in 1844, and read by Hooker some dozen years ago. About a year ago I sent a short sketch, of which I have a copy, of my views (owing to correspondence on several points) to Asa Gray, so that I could most truly say and prove

8. Annals and Mag. of Nat. Hist., 1855 [F. Darwin's note].

that I take nothing from Wallace. I should be extremely glad now to publish a sketch of my general views in about a dozen pages or so; but I cannot persuade myself that I can do so honourably. Wallace says nothing about publication, and I enclose his letter. But as I had not intended to publish any sketch, can I do so honourably, because Wallace has sent me an outline of his doctrine? I would far rather burn my whole book, than that he or any other man should think that I had behaved in a paltry spirit. Do you not think his having sent me this sketch ties my hands? . . . If I could honourably publish, I would state that I was induced now to publish a sketch (and I should be very glad to be permitted to say, to follow your advice long ago given) from Wallace having sent me an outline of my general conclusions. We differ only, [in] that I was led to my views from what artificial selection has done for domestic animals. I would send Wallace a copy of my letter to Asa Gray, to show him that I had not stolen his doctrine. But I cannot tell whether to publish now would not be base and paltry. This was my first impression, and I should have certainly acted on it had it not been for your letter.

This is a trumpery affair to trouble you with, but you cannot tell how much obliged I should be for your advice.

By the way, would you object to send this and your answer to Hooker to be forwarded to me, for then I shall have the opinion of my two best and kindest friends. This letter is miserably written, and I write it now, that I may for a time banish the whole subject; and I am worn out with musing. . . .

My good dear friend forgive me. This is a trumpery letter, influenced by trumpery feelings.

Yours most truly,
C. Darwin.

I will never trouble you or Hooker on the subject again.

To J. D. Hooker

Tuesday night [June 29, 1858].

My dear Hooker,—I have just read your letter, and see you want the papers at once. I am quite prostrated, and can do nothing, but I send Wallace, and the abstract [9] of my letter to Asa Gray, which gives most imperfectly only the means of change, and does not touch on reasons for believing that species do change. I dare say all is too late. I hardly care about it. But you are too generous to sacrifice so much time and kindness. It is most generous, most kind. I

9. "Abstract" is here used in the sense of "extract;" in this sense also it occurs in the 'Linnean Journal,' where the sources of my father's paper are described [F. Darwin's note].

send my sketch of 1844 solely that you may see by your own hand-writing that you did read it. I really cannot bear to look at it. Do not waste much time. It is miserable in me to care at all about priority.

The table of contents will show what it is.

I would make a similar, but shorter and more accurate sketch for the 'Linnean Journal.'

I will do anything. God bless you, my dear kind friend.

I can write no more. I send this by my servant to Kew.

Yours,
C. Darwin.

To A. R. *Wallace*

Down, Jan. 25th [1859].

My dear Sir,—I was extremely much pleased at receiving three days ago your letter to me and that to Dr. Hooker. Permit me to say how heartily I admire the spirit in which they are written. Though I had absolutely nothing whatever to do in leading Lyell and Hooker to what they thought a fair course of action, yet I naturally could not but feel anxious to hear what your impression would be. I owe indirectly much to you and them; for I almost think that Lyell would have proved right, and I should never have completed my larger work, for I have found my Abstract hard enough with my poor health, but now, thank God, I am in my last chapter but one. My Abstract will make a small volume of 400 or 500 pages. Whenever published, I will, of course, send you a copy, and then you will see what I mean about the part which I believe selection has played with domestic productions. It is a very different part, as you suppose, from that played by "Natural Selection." I sent off, by the same address as this note, a copy of the 'Journal of the Linnean Society,' and subsequently I have sent some half-dozen copies of the paper. I have many other copies at your disposal. . . .

* * *

You ask about Lyell's frame of mind. I think he is somewhat staggered, but does not give in, and speaks with horror, often to me, of what a thing it would be, and what a job it would be for the next edition of 'The Principles,' if he were "*perverted.*" But he is most candid and honest, and I think will end by being *perverted.* Dr. Hooker had become almost as heterodox as you or I, and I look at Hooker as *by far* the most capable judge in Europe.

Most cordially do I wish you health and entire success in all your pursuits, and, God knows, if admirable zeal and energy deserve success, most amply do you deserve it. I look at my own career as nearly run out. If I can publish my Abstract and perhaps my greater work on the same subject, I shall look at my course as done.

Believe me, my dear sir, yours very sincerely,

C. Darwin.

Darwin's Notebooks on Transmutation of Species (1837–1839) †

Introduction to the British Museum Edition,
by Sir Gavin de Beer

In Darwin's *Journal* [1] the year 1837 contains an entry which runs, "In July opened first notebook on 'Transmutation of Species'—Had been greatly struck from about month of previous March on character of S. American fossils—& species on Galapagos Archipelago. These facts origin (especially latter) of all my views." This notebook is transcribed and printed below and forms the subject of the present study.

The four Notebooks on Transmutation of Species are the first implementation of the suggestion put forward by Darwin in his Ornithological Notebook [2] referring to his visit to the Galapagos Islands in September and October 1835. There he wrote:—"When I recollect the fact, that from the form of body, shape of scale and general size, the Spaniards can at once pronounce from which Isd. any tortoise may have been brought:—When I see these Islands in sight of each other and possessed of but a scanty stock of animals, tenanted by these birds but slightly different in structure and filling the same place in Nature, I must suspect they are only varieties. The only fact of a similar kind of which I am aware is the constant asserted difference between the Wolf-like Fox of East and West Falkland Islands.—If there is the slightest foundation for these remarks, the Zoology of Archipelagoes will be well worth examining; for such facts would undermine the stability of species."

The First Notebook, begun in July 1837, represents the state of Darwin's opinion as it developed six months after his return to England, the results of his consulting the literature on the subject, and the first formulation of his conviction that the stability of spe-

† The present text is excerpted from Sir Gavin de Beer, ed., *Darwin's Notebooks on Transmutation of Species* (Bulletin of the British Museum, Natural History, Historical Series, II, 2–5; London, 1960). The footnotes and emendations are de Beer's; the index numbers in the left margin are the page numbers in Darwin's notebooks. De Beer's later (1961) corrigenda have been incorporated into the text.

1. "Darwin's Journal", edited by Sir Gavin de Beer, *Bull. Brit. Mus. (Nat. Hist.)* Historical Series, vol. 2, p. 1, 1959.
2. *Charles Darwin and the Voyage of the Beagle*, edited by Nora Barlow, London 1945, p. 246. It is not known at what exact date these words were written.

cies had been "undermined."

It will be noticed that the passage from the *Journal* quoted above must have been a retrospective entry written at a later date, for if he only began his Notebook in July 1837 he could not then have known what "all his views" were. In this First Notebook itself Darwin stated that he finished it "probably" in February 1838, and this was nine months before he read Malthus's *Essay on Population*, which, as he said [3] (and Wallace also admitted [4] in his own case) supplied him with the remaining piece that he required to complete the construction of his argument. What that argument was is known from Darwin's *Sketch* of 1842 and *Essay* of 1844,[5] from which the *Origin of Species* was elaborated without much novelty of principle.

The First Notebook is therefore of great importance in tracing the course of his thoughts and the extent of his knowledge before his cognisance of Malthus's work, and will throw light on what it was in the latter which gave Darwin that extra idea which acted as a spark and launched him on his course.

At the outset, however, it must be made clear that the Notebooks all suffer from a grave defect. In the First Notebook Darwin himself wrote on the first page [6]: "All useful pages cut out. December 7, 1856. (and again looked through April 29, 1873)." In spite of all attempts to trace the missing fifty pages, in the Cambridge University Library where Mr. P. J. Gautrey searched for them, at Down House and the Royal College of Surgeons where Miss J. Dobson looked for them, and in the British Museum (Natural History) where Miss M. Skramovsky hunted for them among the letters addressed to Darwin deposited by Mr. Robin Darwin, they could not be found. The nature of their contents can only be surmised after a close study of the two hundred and thirty pages that remain, and an estimate can be made of what is missing from the information and the argument.

Another reason why the Notebooks are important is because Darwin has from time to time been reproached for having obtained information from the writings of other men without acknowledging the source. The *Origin of Species*, as is well known, contains the

3. *The Autobiography of Charles Darwin*, edited by Nora Barlow, London 1958, p. 120.
4. Alfred Russel Wallace, "Note on the passages of Malthus's 'Principles of Population' which suggested the idea of natural selection to Darwin and myself." *The Darwin and Wallace Celebration held on Thursday, 1 July 1908 by the Linnean Society of London*, London 1908, pp. 111–118; especially p. 117.

5. Darwin's *Sketch* of 1842, and *Essay* of 1844 are reprinted in Charles Darwin and Alfred Russel Wallace: *Evolution by Natural Selection* with a Foreword by Sir Gavin de Beer, Cambridge, 1958.
6. All page references to Darwin's Notebooks on transmutation of species are to the pagination of the original manuscripts indicated in the margin of the transcription printed below.

names of Darwin's authorities for the facts stated, but not their bibliographical references, for Darwin regarded his book as only an abstract from the much larger work on which he was then engaged but never finished. The *Sketch* of 1842 and the *Essay* of 1844, likewise, contain names without bibliographical references, but they were written only as an exercise in reviewing the state of his own argument and not intended for publication. The Notebooks, as will be seen, contain names and references.

Before any conclusion can be drawn on Darwin's indebtedness to his predecessors three considerations must be borne in mind. The first is the precise identification of what the original contribution to science was which Darwin himself claimed to have made. This is known from a letter [7] which he sent on 18th January 1860 to Baden Powell. "No educated person", he wrote, "not even the most ignorant, could suppose that I meant to arrogate to myself the origination of the doctrine that species had not been independently created. The only novelty in my work is the attempt to explain *how* species became modified, & to a certain extent how the theory of descent explains certain large classes of facts; & in these respects I received no assistance from my predecessors."

In arriving at a just appraisal of Darwin's character, this quoted passage is very important, and his contention is correct. Some of his predecessors, as will be seen, acknowledged evolution but had no notion of any mechanism adequate to explain its cause, let alone any idea of natural selection; two contemporaries [8] recognized natural selection but used it to prove that evolution could not occur. Unknown to Darwin, two other men [9] had, before him, grasped the solution of the problem and stated that natural selection could cause modification of species; but they were very far from being able to appreciate the significance of what they had done, provide evidence to support it, or work out its consequences.

The second consideration to bear in mind is that while Darwin was always on the look-out for facts, what he most hoped for in the works of his predecessors and contemporaries was ideas.

The third consideration is the necessity of appreciating what information and opinions, correct and false, were available in 1837 when Darwin "opened" his Notebook. Chief among these was the folk-belief in the inheritance of acquired characters. As Conway Zirkle has shown,[1] this is based on an uncritical combination of two propositions each of which by itself is approximately correct.

7. "Some Unpublished Letters of Charles Darwin," edited by Sir Gavin de Beer, *Notes and Records of the Royal Society of London*, vol. 14, 1959, p. 52.
8. Charles Lyell and Edward Blyth.
9. William Charles Wells and Patrick Matthew.
1. Conway Zirkle. "The early history of the idea of the inheritance of acquired characters and pangenesis", *Trans. Amer. Phil. Soc.*, vol. 35, 1946, p. 91.

The first is that organisms can be changed, often in an adaptive manner, by the conditions of the environment. The blacksmith's muscles are enlarged as a result of wielding his hammer. The second proposition is that organisms tend to produce offspring like themselves not only in physical features but in functional characters like gait and voice. Hence the conclusion is drawn that parents modified by the environment will produce offspring showing the same modifications.

This syllogism is invalidated because its middle term (resemblance between parent and offspring) is not only undistributed, but, as modern genetics has proved, fallacious. Offspring are not the product of their parents, but of germ-cells of which the parents are only the life-custodians. The old block produces no chip but is the elder brother, and the chip resembles him, if he does, because both are the product of the same line of germ-plasm. * * *

First Notebook (July 1837–February 1838)

* * * Aegyptian cats and dogs, ibis—same as formerly, but separate a pair and place them on fresh island, it is very doubtful whether they would remain constant; is it not said that marrying-in *deteriorates* a race, that is alters it from some end which is good for man.

Let a pair be introduced and increase slowly, from many enemies, so as often to intermarry—who will dare say what result.

According to this view animals on separate islands, ought to become different if kept long enough apart, with slightly differ[ent] circumstances. Now Galapagos [1] tortoises, mocking birds, Falkland fox, Chiloe fox. English and Irish Hare.

As we thus believe species vary, in changing climate we ought to find representative species; this we do in South America closely approaching. But as they inosculate, we must suppose the change is effected at once,—something like a variety produced—every grade in that case surely is not produced?

Species according to Lamarck [2] disappear as collection made perfect. Truer even than in Lamarck's time. Gray's [3] remark, best known species (as some common land shells) most difficult to separate. [Difference in] Every character continues to vanish,—bones, instinct, etc. etc. etc.

Non-fertility of hybridity etc. etc.

1. For this and other localities mentioned in Darwin's writing, see map, p. xiv above [Editor].
2. Jean-Baptiste de Lamarck. *Philosophie Zoologique*, Paris 1809, vol. 1, p. 75: "à mesure que nos collections s'enrichissent, nous voyons presque tous les vides se remplir et nos lignes de séparation s'effacer . . . plus nous rencontrons de preuves que tout est nuancé, que les différences remarquables s'évanouissent."
3. John Edward Gray. Probably personal communication.

If species (1) may be derived from form (2) etc., then (remembering Lyell's [4] arguments of transportal) island near continents might have some species same as nearest land, which were late arrivals, others old ones (of which none of same kind had in interval arrived) might have grown altered. Hence the type would be of the continent, though species all different. * * *

* * * Countries longest separated—greatest differences, if separated from immense ages possibly two distinct type[s], but each having its representatives—as in Australia.

This presupposes time when no mammalia existed; Australia; Mamm[alia] were produced from propagation from different set as the rest of the world.

This view supposes that in course of ages, and therefore changes, every animal has tendency to change.

This difficult to prove cats etc. from Egypt no answer, because time short and no great change has happened.

I look at two Ostriches as strong argument of possibility of such change; as we see them in space, so might they in time.

As I have before said, *isolate* species, especially with some change, probably vary quicker.

Unknown causes of change. Volcanic island. Electricity. Each species changes. Does it progress. * * *

* * * Changes not result of will of animal, but law of adaptation as much as acid and alkali. * * *

* * * With respect to extinction we can easy see that variety of ostrich Petise may not be well adapted, and thus perish out, or on other hand like Orpheus being favourable, many might be produced. This requires principle that the permanent varieties, produced by confined breeding and changing circumstances are continued and produce according to the adaptation of such circumstances, and therefore that death of species is a consequence (contrary to what would appear from America) of non-adaptation of circumstances. * * *

The largeness of present genera renders it probable that many contemporary [genera] would have left scarcely any type of their existence in the present world. Or we may suppose only each species in each generation only breeds, *like* individuals in a country not rapidly increasing.

If we thus go very far back to look to the source of the Mammalian type of organization, it is extremely inprobable that any of the successors of his relations shall now exist.

In same manner, if we take a man from any large family of 12 brothers and sisters in a state which does not increase, it will be chances against any one of them having progeny living ten thousand years hence; because at present day many are relatives, so that by

4. Charles Lyell. *Principles of Geology*, vol. 2, London 1832, pp. 96–104.

tracing back the fathers would be reduced to small percentage: therefore the chances are excessively great against any two of the 12 having progeny after that distant period.

Hence if this is true that the *greater the groups* the *greater the gaps* (or *solutions* of *continuous structure*) between them.— for instance, there would be great gap between birds and mammalia, still greater between vertebrate and articulate, still greater between animals and plants.

But yet besides affinities from three elements, from the infinite variations, and all coming from one stock and obeying one law, they may approach—some birds may approach animals and some of the vertebrate invertebrate. just a few on each side will yet present some anomaly and bearing stamp of some great main type, and the gradation will be sudden.

Heaven know whether this agrees with Nature: *Cuidado!* * * *

It is a wonderful fact—Horse, Elephant and Mastodon dying out about same time in such different quarters. Will Mr. Lyell[5] say that some circumstance killed it [them] over a tract from Spain to S. America? (*Never*). They die, without they change, like golden Pippins; it is a *generation* of *species* like generation of *individuals*.

Why does individual die? To perpetuate certain peculiarities (therefore adaption), and to obliterate accidental varieties, and to accommodate itself to change (for, of course change even in varieties is accomodation). Now this argument applies to species. If individual cannot procreate he has no issue; so with species.

I should expect that Bears & Foxes &c. are same in N. America and Asia; but many species closely allied, but different, because country separated since time of extinct quadrupeds;—same argument applies to England. Mem. Sh[r]ew mice.

Animals common to South and North America ? *Are there any?*

Rhinoceros peculiar to Java and another to Sumatra. Mem. Parrots peculiar, according to Swainson,[6] to certain islets in East India archipelago.

Dr. Smith[7] considers probable true northern species *replace* southern kinds.

Gnu reaches Orange river and says: so far will I go and no further.

Prof. Henslow[8] says that when race once established, so difficult

5. Charles Lyell. *Principles of Geology,* 5th edition, London 1837, vol. 3, p. 142: "Successive extinction of species consistent with their limited geographical distribution" (cross-heading) . . . "They must die out", to borrow an emphatical expression from Buffon; "because Time fights against them." 6. William Swainson. *A treatise on the geography and classification of animals,* Lardner's Cabinet Cyclopaedia, London 1835, p. 52: "The suctorial cockatoos of Malacca, the elegant ring-necked parrakeets of the continent, and the crimson-coloured lories of the islands, are appropriated solely to these regions." 7. Andrew Smith. Probably personal communication. 8. John Stevens Henslow. Probably personal communication.

to root out. For instance ever so many seeds of white flower all would come up white, though planted in same soil with blue. Now this is same bearing with Dr. Smith's fact of races of men * * *

The question if creative power acted at Galapagos, it so acted that birds with plumage and tone of voice purely American, North and South,—so permanent a breath cannot reside in space before island existed. Such an influence must exist in such spots. We know birds do arrive and seeds. (And geographical division are arbitrary and not permanent. This might be made very strong if we believe the Creator creates by any laws, which I think is shown by the very facts of the geological character of these islands.)

The same remarks applicable to fossil animals same type,—armadillos like every created [edentate]. Passage for vertebrae in neck—same cause; such beautiful adaptation, yet other animals live so well. This kind of propagation gives hiding-place for many unintelligible structures—it might have been of use in progenitor, or it may be of use,—like mammae on men's breast.

How does it come wandering birds such [as] sandpipers not new at Galapagos. Did the creative force know these species could arrive —did it only create those kinds not so likely to wander—did it create two species closely allied to Mus[cicapa] coronata, but not coronata. We know that domestic animals vary in countries without any assignable reason.

Astronomers might formerly have said that God ordered each planet to move in its particular destiny. In same manner God orders each animal created with certain form in certain country, but how much more simple and sublime power let attraction act according to law, such are inevitable consequences—let animal be created, then by the fixed laws of generation, such will be their successors. Let the powers of transportal be such, and so will be the forms of one country to another. Let geological changes go at such a rate, so will be the number and distribution of the species!! * * *

Definition of species: one that remains at large with constant characters, together with other beings of very near structure. Hence species may be good ones and differ scarcely in any external character. For instance, two wrens, found to haunt two islands—one with one kind of herbage and one with other—might change organization of stomach and hence remain distinct.

When country changes rapidly, we should expect most species.

The difference [between] intellect of man and animals not so great as between living thing without thought (plants) and living thing with thought (animal).

∴ My theory very distinct from Lamarck's.[9]

9. Darwin's point appears to be that Lamarck placed a great distinction between the higher animals which possessed a "sentiment intérieur", and the lower animals which do not. (*Philosophie Zoologique*, Paris 1809, vol. 2, p. 256).

Without *two* species will generate common kind, which is not probable, then monkeys will never produce man, but both monkeys and man may produce other species. Man already has produced marked varieties and may someday produce something else, but not probable owing to mixture of races. When all mixed physical changes (? intellectual [faculty] being acquired alters case) other species or angels produced.

Has the Creator since the Cambrian formation gone on creating animals with same general structure. Miserable limited view.

With respect to how species are [formed], Lamarck's [1] "willing" doctrine absurd (as equally are arguments against it [2]—namely how did otter live before being made otter—why to be sure there were a thousand intermediate forms. Opponent will say: show them me. I will answer yes, if you will show me every step between bull Dog and greyhound). I should say the changes were effects of external causes, of which we are as ignorant, as why millet seed turns a Bullfinch black, or iodine on glands of throat, or colour of plumage altered during passage of birds (where is this statement? I remember L. Jenyns [3] talking of it), or how to make Indian cow with hump or pig's foot with cloven hoof. * * *

If my theory true, we get 1st a *horizontal* history of earth within recent times, and many curious points of speculation; for having ascertained means of transport, we should then know whether former lands intervened. 2ᵈ) By character of any two ancient fauna, we may form some idea of connection of those two countries. Hence India, Mexico and Europe—one great sea. (Coral reefs ∴ shallow water at Melville island). 3ᵈ) We know that structure of every organ in A.B.C., three species of one genus can pass into each other by steps we see; but this cannot be predicated of structures in two genera. Although D.E.F. follow close to A.B.C., we cannot be sure that structure (C) could pass into (D). We may foretell species, limits of good species being known. It explains the blending of two genera. It explains typical structure. Every species is due to adaptation hereditary structure; Latter far chief element. ∴ Little service habits in classification or rather for the fact that they are *not* far the most serviceable. We may speculate of durability of succession from what we have seen in old world and on amount changes which may happen.

It leads you to believe the world older than *geologists* think; it agrees with excessive inequality of numbers of species in divisions, —look at articulata!!? It leads to [knowledge of] nature of physical

---

1. Jean Baptiste de Lamarck. *See* Introduction.
2. Darwin means that arguments against the formation of species are absurd. The argument about the evolution of the otter through intermediate forms is developed in the *Essay* of 1844, p. 152.
3. Leonard Jenyns, afterwards Blomefield. Probably personal communication.

change between one group of animals and a successive one. It leads to knowledge what kinds of structure may pass into each other; now on this view no one need look for intermediate structure, say in brain, between lowest mammal and reptile (or between extremities of any great divisions); thus a knowledge of possible changes is discovered, for speculating on future.

∴. Fish never become a man. Does not require fresh creation. If continent had sprung up round Galapagos on Pacific side, the Oolite order of things might have easily been formed.

With belief of transmutation and geographical grouping we are led to endeavour to discover *causes* of changes,—the manner of adaptation (wish of parents??), instinct and structure becomes full of speculation and line of observation. View of generation being condensation, test of highest organization intelligible. May look to first germ, led to comprehend true affinities. My theory would give zest to recent and fossil Comparative Anatomy; it would lead to study of instincts, heredity and mind heredity, whole [of] metaphysics. It would lead to closest examination of hybridity,—to what circumstances favour crossing and what prevent it; and generation, causes of change in order to know what we have come from and to what we tend, this and direct examination of direct passages of structure in species might lead to laws of change, which would then be [the] main object of study, to guide our speculations with respect to past and future.

The grand question which every naturalist ought to have before him when dissecting a whale, or classifying a mite, a fungus or an infusorian is What are the Laws of Life? * * *

The soul by consent of all is superadded, animals not got it, not look forward. If we choose to let conjecture run wild, then animals —our fellow brethren in pain, disease, death, suffering and famine, our slaves in the most laborious works, our companions in our amusements,—they may partake from our origin in one common ancestor, we may be all netted [4] together. * * *

Second Notebook (February–July 1838)

Once grant that species and genus may pass into each other,— grant that one instinct to be acquired (if the medullary point in ovum has such organization as to force in one man the development

4. Darwin's handwriting in the Notebooks is notoriously hard reading. Francis Darwin, in the *Life and Letters of Charles Darwin* (1887), transcribed this word as "melted," which is metaphorically attractive. But Sir Gavin de Beer, editor of the notebooks; P. J. Gautrey, who is in charge of the Darwin manuscripts at the University Library, Cambridge; and Lady Nora Barlow, Darwin's granddaughter, editor of his autobiography, and expert in his handwriting, all testify to "netted" as Darwin's intention [Editor].

of a brain capable of producing more glowing imagining or more profound reasoning than other, if this be granted!!) & whole fabric totters & falls. Look abroad, study gradation, study unity of type, study geographical distribution, study relation of fossil with recent. The fabric falls! But man—wonderful man "divino ore versum coelum attentior" is an exception. He is mammalian, his origin has not been indefinite. he is not a deity, his end under present form will come, (or how dreadfully we are deceived) then he is no exception. He possesses some of the same general instincts all & feelings as animals. They on other hand can reason—but man has reasoning powers in excess, instead of definite instincts—that is a replacement in mental machinery so analogous to what we see in bodily, that it does not stagger me. What circumstances may have been necessary to have made man! Seclusion want &c & perhaps a train of animals of hundred generations of species to produce contingents proper.—Present monkeys might not,—but probably would,—the world now being fit, for such an animal—man, (rude uncivilized man) might not have lived when certain other animals were alive, which have perished. Let man visit Ourang-outang in domestication, hear expressive whine, see its intelligence when spoken [to], as if it understood every word said—see its affection to those it knows,—see its passion & rage, sulkiness & very extreme of despair; let him look at savage, roasting his parent, naked, artless, not improving, yet improvable and then let him dare to boast of his proud preeminence. * * *

* * * Mention persecution of early Astronomers, then add chief good of individual scientific men is to push their science a few years in advance only of their age, (differently from literary men,) must remember that if they *believe* & do not openly avow their belief they do as much to retard as those whose opinion they believe have endeavoured to advance cause of truth. * * *

Third Notebook (July 15, 1838–October 2, 1838)

16th Aug. What a magnificent view one can take of the world Astronomical causes modified by unknown ones, cause changes in geography & changes of climate suspended to change of climate from physical causes,—then suspended changes of form in the organic world, as adaptation, & these changing affect each other, & their bodies by certain laws of harmony keep perfect in these themselves. instincts alter, reason is formed & the world peopled with myriads of distinct forms from a period short of eternity to the present time, to the future. How far grander than idea from cramped imagination that God created (warring against those very laws he established in all organic nature) the Rhinoceros of Java &

Sumatra,[5] that since the time of the Silurian he has made a long succession of vile molluscous animals. How beneath the dignity of him, who is supposed to have said let there be light & there was light. * * * bad taste. * * *

The line of argument often pursued throughout my theory is to establish a point as a probability by induction, & to apply it as hypotheses to other points, & see whether it will solve them. * * *

* * * It is absolutely necessary that some but not great difference (for every brother & sister are somewhat different) should be added to each individual before he can procreate. then change may be effect of differences of parents, or external circumstances during life. if the circumstances which must be external which induce change are always of one nature species is formed, if not—the changes oscillate backwards & forwards & are individual differences. (hence every individual is different). (All this agrees well with my view of those forms slightly favoured getting the upper hand & forming species.) * * *

Fourth Notebook (October, 1838–July 10, 1839)

* * * The dog being so much more intellectual than fox, wolf &c &c—is precisely analogous case to man exceeding monkeys.

Having proved mens & brutes bodies on one type: almost superfluous to consider minds. as difference between mind of a dog & a porpoise was not thought overwhelming—yet I will not shirk difficulty—I have felt some difficulty in conceiving how inhabitant of Tierra del Fuego is to be connected with civilized man. ask the Missionaries about Australian yet slow progress has done so. Show a savage dog, & ask him how wolf was so changed. * * *

* * * I [6] utterly deny the right to argue against my theory because it makes the world far *older* than what geologists think: it would be doing what others but fifty years since [did] to geologists,—& what is older—what relation in duration of planet to our lives. Being myself a geologist, I have thus argued to myself, till I can honestly reject such false reasoning.

Bell [7] Bridgewater Treatise on the Hand. p. 94. "The resemblance of the foot of the Ostrich to that of the camel has not escaped naturalists". Before he alludes to the resemblance of the snout of the mole & Pig in having two additional bones to give strength to it. p. 139. Doubts altogether the law of balancing of

5. Cf. Darwin's *Sketch* of 1842 and his *Essay* of 1844; in *Evolution by Natural Selection* with a Foreword by Sir Gavin de Beer, Cambridge 1958, pp. 83 and 249.
6. From here to the end of page 156 the Text is written in pencil.
7. Sir Charles Bell. *The Bridgewater Treatises. The Hand, its mechanism and vital endowments as evincing design*, London 1833, p. 94.

organs.[8] In the Batrac[h]ian Order the 32 ribs are wanting. p. 144 in the Ichthyosaurus 60 or 70 bones in the paddle, yet all in the arm are perfect. p. 144. Alludes to two theories;—the species are the result of circumstances; [9]—or the will of the animal. p. 145. Seems to argue, that as the transformation from the egg, a larva, or foetus to perfect animal are adapted by foreknowledge,[1] so must the mutations of species!! * * *

CHARLES DARWIN AND
ALFRED RUSSEL WALLACE

The Linnean Society Papers (1858) †

ON THE TENDENCY OF SPECIES TO FORM VARIETIES;
AND ON THE PERPETUATION OF VARIETIES AND SPECIES
BY NATURAL MEANS OF SELECTION.

BY CHARLES DARWIN, ESQ., F.R.S., F.L.S., & F.G.S.,

AND ALFRED WALLACE, ESQ.

COMMUNICATED BY SIR CHARLES LYELL, F.R.S., F.L.S.,

AND J. D. HOOKER, ESQ., M.D., V.P.R.S., F.L.S., &C.

(READ JULY 1ST, 1858.)

London, June 30th, 1858.

My dear Sir,—The accompanying papers, which we have the honour of communicating to the Linnean Society, and which all relate to the same subject, viz. the Laws which affect the Production of Varieties, Races, and Species, contain the results of the investiga-

8. Sir Charles Bell. *Ibid.* p. 139: "Shall we follow a system which informs us that when a bone is wanting in the cavity of the ear we are to seek for it in the jaw?" With a rare degree of irony, this is exactly what Reichert's established theory of homologies of the mammalian ear-ossicles requires in demonstrating that the malleus and incus of the mammal are the articular and quadrate of the reptile.
9. Sir Charles Bell. *Ibid.* p. 144: "It is, above all, surprising with what perverse ingenuity men seek to obscure the conception of a Divine Author, an intelligent, designing and benevolent Being—rather clinging to the greatest absurdities, or interposing the cold and inanimate influence of the mere "elements", in a manner to extinguish all feelings of dependence in our minds, and all feelings of gratitude."
1. Sir Charles Bell. *Ibid.* p. 145: "We

do perceive surprising charges in the conformity of animals. Some of them are very familiar to us; but all show a foreknowledge and a prospective plan."
† *Journal of the Linnean Society,* Zoology (1858), III, 45–62. (The Linnean Society was founded in 1788 for the immediate purpose of preserving the scientific collections of the great taxonomist Linnaeus (1707–1778), but it later developed broader bases of interest in natural history.) Alfred Russel Wallace (1823–1913) independently arrived at the theory of natural selection in 1858, two decades after Darwin opened his first notebooks on the subject. His discovery prompted Darwin to allow a brief account of his ideas to be given before the Linnean Society (along with Wallace's) and, the next year, to publish the *Origin* itself, which Darwin then thought of as a relatively short "abstract" of his ideas.

tions of two indefatigable naturalists, Mr. Charles Darwin and Mr. Alfred Wallace.

These gentlemen having, independently and unknown to one another, conceived the same very ingenious theory to account for the appearance and perpetuation of varieties and of specific forms on our planet, may both fairly claim the merit of being original thinkers in this important line of inquiry; but neither of them having published his views, though Mr. Darwin has for many years past been repeatedly urged by us to do so, and both authors having now unreservedly placed their papers in our hands, we think it would best promote the interests of science that a selection from them should be laid before the Linnean Society.

Taken in the order of their dates, they consist of:—

1. Extracts from a MS. work on Species,[1] by Mr. Darwin, which was sketched in 1839, and copied in 1844, when the copy was read by Dr. Hooker, and its contents afterwards communicated to Sir Charles Lyell. The first Part is devoted to "The Variation of Organic Beings under Domestication and in their Natural State;" and the second chapter of that Part, from which we propose to read to the Society the extracts referred to, is headed, "On the Variation of Organic Beings in a state of Nature; on the Natural Means of Selection; on the Comparison of Domestic Races and true Species."

2. An abstract of a private letter addressed to Professor Asa Gray, of Boston, U.S., in October 1857, by Mr. Darwin, in which he repeats his views, and which shows that these remained unaltered from 1839 to 1857.

3. An Essay by Mr. Wallace, entitled "On the Tendency of Varieties to depart indefinitely from the Original Type." This was written at Ternate in February 1858, for the perusal of his friend and correspondent Mr. Darwin, and sent to him with the expressed wish that it should be forwarded to Sir Charles Lyell, if Mr. Darwin thought it sufficiently novel and interesting. So highly did Mr. Darwin appreciate the value of the views therein set forth, that he proposed, in a letter to Sir Charles Lyell, to obtain Mr. Wallace's consent to allow the Essay to be published as soon as possible. Of this step we highly approved, provided Mr. Darwin did not withhold from the public, as he was strongly inclined to do (in favour of Mr. Wallace), the memoir which he had himself written on the same subject, and which, as before stated, one of us had perused in 1844, and the contents of which we had both of us been privy to for many years. On representing this to Mr. Darwin, he gave us permission to make what use we thought proper of his memoir, &c.; and in adopting our present course, of presenting it to the Linnean

1. This MS. work was never intended for publication, and therefore was not written with care.—C.D. 1858.

Society, we have explained to him that we are not solely considering the relative claims to priority of himself and his friend, but the interests of science generally; for we feel it to be desirable that views founded on a wide deduction from facts, and matured by years of reflection, should constitute at once a goal from which others may start, and that, while the scientific world is waiting for the appearance of Mr. Darwin's complete work, some of the leading results of his labours, as well as those of his able correspondent, should together be laid before the public.

We have the honour to be yours very obediently,

Charles Lyell
Jos. D. Hooker

J. J. Bennett, Esq.,
Secretary of the Linnean Society.

EXTRACT FROM AN UNPUBLISHED WORK ON SPECIES, BY C. DARWIN, ESQ., CONSISTING OF A PORTION OF A CHAPTER ENTITLED, "ON THE VARIATION OF ORGANIC BEINGS IN A STATE OF NATURE; ON THE NATURAL MEANS OF SELECTION; ON THE COMPARISON OF DOMESTIC RACES AND TRUE SPECIES."

De Candolle, in an eloquent passage, has declared that all nature is at war, one organism with another, or with external nature. Seeing the contented face of nature, this may at first well be doubted; but reflection will inevitably prove it to be true. The war, however, is not constant, but recurrent in a slight degree at short periods, and more severely at occasional more distant periods; and hence its effects are easily overlooked. It is the doctrine of Malthus applied in in most cases with tenfold force. As in every climate there are reasons, for each of its inhabitants, of greater and less abundance, so all annually breed; and the moral restraint which in some small degree checks the increase of mankind is entirely lost. Even slow-breeding mankind has doubled in twenty-five years; and if he could increase his food with greater ease, he would double in less time. But for animals without artificial means, the amount of food for each species must, *on an average*, be constant, whereas the increase of all organisms tends to be geometrical, and in a vast majority of cases at an enormous ratio. Suppose in a certain spot there are eight pairs of birds, and that *only* four pairs of them annually (including double hatches) rear only four young, and that these go on rearing their young at the same rate, then at the end of seven years (a short life, excluding violent deaths, for any bird) there will be 2048 birds, instead of the original sixteen. As this increase is quite impossible, we must conclude either that birds do not rear nearly half

their young, or that the average life of a bird is, from accident, not
nearly seven years. Both checks probably concur. The same kind of
calculation applied to all plants and animals affords results more or
less striking, but in very few instances more striking than in man.

Many practical illustrations of this rapid tendency to increase are
on record, among which, during peculiar seasons, are the extraordinary numbers of certain animals; for instance, during the years
1826 to 1828, in La Plata, when from drought some millions of
cattle perished, the whole country actually *swarmed* with mice. Now
I think it cannot be doubted that during the breeding-season all
the mice (with the exception of a few males or females in excess)
ordinarily pair, and therefore that this astounding increase during
three years must be attributed to a greater number than usual surviving the first year, and then breeding, and so on till the third
year, when their numbers were brought down to their usual limits
on the return of wet weather. Where man has introduced plants and
animals into a new and favourable country, there are many accounts
in how surprisingly few years the whole country has become stocked
with them. This increase would necessarily stop as soon as the
country was fully stocked; and yet we have every reason to believe,
from what is known of wild animals, that *all* would pair in the
spring. In the majority of cases it is most difficult to imagine
where the checks fall—though generally, no doubt, on the seeds,
eggs, and young; but when we remember how impossible, even in
mankind (so much better known than any other animal), it is to
infer from repeated casual observations what the average duration
of life is, or to discover the different percentage of deaths to births
in different countries, we ought to feel no surprise at our being
unable to discover where the check falls in any animal or plant. It
should always be remembered, that in most cases the checks are
recurrent yearly in a small, regular degree, and in an extreme degree during unusually cold, hot, dry, or wet years, according to the
constitution of the being in question. Lighten any check in the least
degree, and the geometrical powers of increase in every organism
will almost instantly increase the average number of the favoured
species. Nature may be compared to a surface on which rest ten
thousand sharp wedges touching each other and driven inwards by
incessant blows. Fully to realize these views much reflection is
requisite. Malthus on man should be studied; and all such cases as
those of the mice in La Plata, of the cattle and horses when first
turned out in South America, of the birds by our calculations,
&c., should be well considered. Reflect on the enormous multiplying
power *inherent and annually in action* in all animals; reflect on
the countless seeds scattered by a hundred ingenious contrivances,
year after year, over the whole face of the land; and yet we have

every reason to suppose that the average percentage of each of the inhabitants of a country usually remains constant. Finally, let it be borne in mind that this average number of individuals (the external conditions remaining the same) in each country is kept up by recurrent struggles against other species or against external nature (as on the borders of the Arctic regions, where the cold checks life), and that ordinarily each individual of every species holds its place, either by its own struggle and capacity of acquiring nourishment in some period of its life, from the egg upwards; or by the struggle of its parents (in short-lived organisms, when the main check occurs at longer intervals) with other individuals of the *same* or *different* species.

But let the external conditions of a country alter. If in a small degree, the relative proportions of the inhabitants will in most cases simply be slightly changed; but let the number of inhabitants be small, as on an island, and free access to it from other countries be circumscribed, and let the change of conditions continue progressing (forming new stations), in such a case the original inhabitants must ccase to be as perfectly adapted to the changed conditions as they were originally. It has been shown in a former part of this work, that such changes of external conditions would, from their acting on the reproductive system, probably cause the organization of those beings which were most affected to become, as under domestication, plastic. Now, can it be doubted, from the struggle each individual has to obtain subsistence, that any minute variation in structure, habits, or instincts, adapting that individual better to the new conditions, would tell upon its vigour and health? In the struggle it would have a better *chance* of surviving; and those of its offspring which inherited the variation, be it ever so slight, would also have a better *chance*. Yearly more are bred than can survive; the smallest grain in the balance, in the long run, must tell on which death shall fall, and which shall survive. Let this work of selection on the one hand, and death on the other, go on for a thousand generations, who will pretend to affirm that it would produce no effect, when we remember what, in a few years, Bakewell effected in cattle, and Western in sheep, by this identical principle of selection?

To give an imaginary example from changes in progress on an island:—let the organization of a canine animal which preyed chiefly on rabbits, but sometimes on hares, become slightly plastic; let these same changes cause the number of rabbits very slowly to decrease, and the number of hares to increase; the effect of this would be that the fox or dog would be driven to try to catch more hares: his organization, however, being slightly plastic, those individuals with the lightest forms, longest limbs, and best eyesight, let the difference be ever so small, would be slightly favoured, and would tend to live longer, and to survive during that time of the year when food was scarcest; they would also rear more young, which would tend to inherit these slight peculiarities. The less fleet ones would be rigidly destroyed. I can see no more reason to doubt that these causes in a thousand generations would produce a marked effect, and adapt the form of the fox or dog to the catching of hares instead of rabbits, than that greyhounds can be improved by selection and careful breeding. So would it be with plants under similar circumstances. If the number of individuals of a species with plumed seeds could be increased by greater powers of dissemination within its own area (that is, if the check to increase fell chiefly on the seeds), those seeds which were provided with ever so little more down, would in the long run be most disseminated; hence a greater number of seeds thus formed would germinate, and would tend to produce plants inheriting the slightly better-adapted down.[2]

Besides this natural means of selection, by which those individuals are preserved, whether in their egg, or larval, or mature state, which are best adapted to the place they fill in nature, there is a second agency at work in most unisexual animals, tending to produce the same effect, namely, the struggle of the males for the females. These struggles are generally decided by the law of battle, but in the case of birds, apparently, by the charms of their song, by their beauty or their power of courtship, as in the dancing rock-thrush of Guiana. The most vigorous and healthy males, implying perfect adaptation, must generally gain the victory in their contests. This kind of selection, however, is less rigorous than the other; it does not require the death of the less successful, but gives to them fewer descendants. The struggle falls, moreover, at a time of year when food is generally abundant, and perhaps the effect chiefly produced would be the modification of the secondary sexual characters, which are not related to the power of obtaining food, or to defence from enemies, but to fighting with or rivalling other males. The result of this struggle amongst the males may be compared in some respects to that produced by those agriculturists who pay less attention to the careful selection of all their young animals, and more to the occasional use of a choice mate.

ABSTRACT OF A LETTER FROM C. DARWIN, ESQ., TO PROF. ASA GRAY, BOSTON, U.S., DATED DOWN, SEPTEMBER 5TH, 1857.

1. It is wonderful what the principle of selection by man, that is the picking out of individuals with any desired quality, and breed-

2. I can see no more difficulty in this, than in the planter improving his varie-   ties of the cotton plant.—C.D. 1858.

ing from them, and again picking out, can do. Even breeders have been astounded at their own results. They can act on differences inappreciable to an uneducated eye. Selection has been *methodically* followed in *Europe* for only the last half century; but it was occasionally, and even in some degree methodically, followed in the most ancient times. There must have been also a kind of unconscious selection from a remote period, namely in the preservation of the individual animals (without any thought of their offspring) most useful to each race of man in his particular circumstances. The "roguing," as nurserymen call the destroying of varieties which depart from their type, is a kind of selection. I am convinced that intentional and occasional selection has been the main agent in the production of our domestic races; but however this may be, its great power of modification has been indisputably shown in later times. Selection acts only by the accumulation of slight or greater variations, caused by external conditions, or by the mere fact that in generation the child is not absolutely similar to its parent. Man, by this power of accumulating variations, adapts living beings to his wants—may be said to make the wool of one sheep good for carpets, of another for cloth, &c.

2. Now suppose there were a being who did not judge by mere external appearances, but who could study the whole internal organization, who was never capricious, and should go on selecting for one object during millions of generations; who will say what he might not effect? In nature we have some *slight* variation occasionally in all parts; and I think it can be shown that changed conditions of existence is the main cause of the child not exactly resembling its parents; and in nature geology shows us what changes have taken place, and are taking place. We have almost unlimited time; no one but a practical geologist can fully appreciate this. Think of the Glacial period, during the whole of which the same species at least of shells have existed; there must have been during this period millions on millions of generations.

3. I think it can be shown that there is such an unerring power at work in *Natural Selection* (the title of my book), which selects exclusively for the good of each organic being. The elder De Candolle, W. Herbert, and Lyell have written excellently on the struggle for life; but even they have not written strongly enough. Reflect that every being (even the elephant) breeds at such a rate, that in a few years, or at most a few centuries, the surface of the carth would not hold the progeny of one pair. I have found it hard constantly to bear in mind that the increase of every single species is checked during some part of its life, or during some shortly recurrent generation. Only a few of those annually born can live to propagate their kind. What a trifling difference must often determine which shall survive, and which perish!

4. Now take the case of a country undergoing some change. This will tend to cause some of its inhabitants to vary slightly—not but that I believe most beings vary at all times enough for selection to act on them. Some of its inhabitants will be exterminated; and the remainder will be exposed to the mutual action of a different set of inhabitants, which I believe to be far more important to the life of each being than mere climate. Considering the infinitely various methods which living beings follow to obtain food by struggling with other organisms, to escape danger at various times of life, to have their eggs or seeds disseminated, &c. &c., I cannot doubt that during millions of generations individuals of a species will be occasionally born with some slight variation, profitable to some part of their economy. Such individuals will have a better chance of surviving, and of propagating their new and slightly different structure; and the modification may be slowly increased by the accumulative action of natural selection to any profitable extent. The variety thus formed will either coexist with, or, more commonly, will exterminate its parent form. An organic being, like the woodpecker or misseltoe, may thus come to be adapted to a score of contingencies—natural selection accumulating those slight variations in all parts of its structure, which are in any way useful to it during any part of its life.

5. Multiform difficulties will occur to every one, with respect to this theory. Many can, I think, be satisfactorily answered. *Natura non facit saltum* answers some of the most obvious. The slowness of the change, and only a very few individuals undergoing change at any one time, answers others. The extreme imperfection of our geological records answers others.

6. Another principle, which may be called the principle of divergence, plays, I believe, an important part in the origin of species. The same spot will support more life if occupied by very diverse forms. We see this in the many generic forms in a square yard of turf, and in the plants or insects on any little uniform islet, belonging almost invariably to as many genera and families as species. We can understand the meaning of this fact amongst the higher animals, whose habits we understand. We know that it has been experimentally shown that a plot of land will yield a greater weight if sown with several species and genera of grasses, than if sown with only two or three species. Now, every organic being, by propagating so rapidly, may be said to be striving its utmost to increase in numbers. So it will be with the offspring of any species after it has become diversified into varieties, or subspecies, or true species. And it follows, I think, from the foregoing facts, that the varying offspring of each species will try (only few will succeed) to seize on as many and as diverse places in the economy of nature as possible.

Each new variety or species, when formed, will generally take the place of, and thus exterminate its less well-fitted parent. This I believe to be the origin of the classification and affinities of organic beings at all times; for organic beings always *seem* to branch and sub-branch like the limbs of a tree from a common trunk, the flourishing and diverging twigs destroying the less vigorous—the dead and lost branches rudely representing extinct genera and families.

This sketch is *most* imperfect; but in so short a space I cannot make it better. Your imagination must fill up very wide blanks.

C. Darwin

ON THE TENDENCY OF VARIETIES TO DEPART INDEFINITELY FROM THE ORIGINAL TYPE. BY ALFRED RUSSEL WALLACE.

One of the strongest arguments which have been adduced to prove the original and permanent distinctness of species is, that *varieties* produced in a state of domesticity are more or less unstable, and often have a tendency, if left to themselves, to return to the normal form of the parent species; and this instability is considered to be a distinctive peculiarity of all varieties, even of those occurring among wild animals in a state of nature, and to constitute a provision for preserving unchanged the originally created distinct species.

In the absence of scarcity of facts and observations as to *varieties* occurring among wild animals, this argument has had great weight with naturalists, and has led to a very general and somewhat prejudiced belief in the stability of species. Equally general, however, is the belief in what are called "permanent or true varieties,"—races of animals which continually propagate their like, but which differ so slightly (although constantly) from some other race, that the one is considered to be a *variety* of the other. Which is the *variety* and which the original *species*, there is generally no means of determining, except in those rare cases in which the one race has been known to produce an offspring unlike itself and resembling the other. This, however, would seem quite incompatible with the "permanent invariability of species," but the difficulty is overcome by assuming that such varieties have strict limits, and can never again vary further from the original type, although they may return to it, which, from the analogy of the domesticated animals, is considered to be highly probable, if not certainly proved.

It will be observed that this argument rests entirely on the assumption, that *varieties* occurring in a state of nature are in all respects analogous to or even identical with those of domestic animals, and are governed by the same laws as regards their permanence or further variation. But it is the object of the present paper to show that this assumption is altogether false, that there is a general principle in nature which will cause many *varieties* to survive the parent species, and to give rise to successive variations departing further and further from the original type, and which also produces, in domesticated animals, the tendency of varieties to return to the parent form.

The life of wild animals is a struggle for existence. The full exertion of all their faculties and all their energies is required to preserve their own existence and provide for that of their infant offspring. The possibility of procuring food during the least favourable seasons, and of escaping the attacks of their most dangerous enemies, are the primary conditions which determine the existence both of individuals and of entire species. These conditions will also determine the population of a species; and by a careful consideration of all the circumstances we may be enabled to comprehend, and in some degree to explain, what at first sight appears so inexplicable—the excessive abundance of some species, while others closely allied to them are very rare.

The general proportion that must obtain between certain groups of animals is readily seen. Large animals cannot be so abundant as small ones; the carnivora must be less numerous than the herbivora; eagles and lions can never be so plentiful as pigeons and antelopes; the wild asses of the Tartarian deserts cannot equal in numbers the horses of the more luxuriant prairies and pampas of America. The greater or less fecundity of an animal is often considered to be one of the chief causes of its abundance or scarcity; but a consideration of the facts will show us that it really has little or nothing to do with the matter. Even the least prolific of animals would increase rapidly if unchecked, whereas it is evident that the animal population of the globe must be stationary, or perhaps, through the influence of man, decreasing. Fluctuations there may be; but permanent increase, except in restricted localities, is almost impossible. For example, our own observation must convince us that birds do not go on increasing every year in a geometrical ratio, as they would do, were there not some powerful check to their natural increase. Very few birds produce less than two young ones each year, while many have six, eight, or ten; four will certainly be below the average; and if we suppose that each pair produce young only four times in their life, that will also be below the average, supposing them not to die either by violence or want of food. Yet at this rate how tremendous would be the increase in a few years from a single pair! A simple calculation will show that in fifteen years each pair of birds would have increased to nearly ten millions! whereas we have no reason to believe that the number of the birds of any country increases at all in fifteen or in one hundred and fifty years. With such powers of increase the population must have reached its limits, and have become stationary, in a very few years after the origin of each species. It is evident, therefore, that each year an immense number of birds must perish—as many in fact as are born; and as on the lowest calculation the progeny are each year twice as numerous as their parents, it follows that, whatever be the average number of individuals existing in any given country, *twice that number must perish annually,*—a striking result, but one which seems at least highly probable, and is perhaps under rather than over the truth. It would therefore appear that, as far as the continuance of the species and the keeping up the average number of individuals are concerned, large broods are superfluous. On the average all above *one* become food for hawks and kites, wild cats and weasels, or perish of cold and hunger as winter comes on. This is strikingly proved by the case of particular species; for we find that their abundance in individuals bears no relation whatever to their fertility in producing offspring. Perhaps the most remarkable instance of an immense bird population is that of the passenger pigeon of the United States, which lays only one, or at most two eggs, and is said to rear generally but one young one. Why is this bird so extraordinarily abundant, while others producing two or three times as many young are much less plentiful? The explanation is not difficult. The food most congenial to this species, and on which it thrives best, is abundantly distributed over a very extensive region, offering such difference of soil and climate, that in one part or another of the area the supply never fails. The bird is capable of a very rapid and long-continued flight, so that it can pass without fatigue over the whole of the district it inhabits, and as soon as the supply of food begins to fail in one place is able to discover a fresh feeding-ground. This example strikingly shows us that the procuring a constant supply of wholesome food is almost the sole condition requisite for ensuring the rapid increase of a given species, since neither the limited fecundity, nor the unrestrained attacks of birds of prey and of man are here sufficient to check it. In no other birds are these peculiar circumstances so strikingly combined. Either their food is more liable to failure, or they have not sufficient power of wing to search for it over an extensive area, or during some season of the year it becomes very scarce, and less wholesome substitutes have to be found; and thus, though more fertile in offspring, they can never increase beyond the supply of food in the least favourable seasons. Many birds can only exist by migrating, when their food becomes scarce, to regions possessing a milder, or at least a different climate, though, as these migrating birds are seldom excessively abaundant, it is evident that the countries they visit are still deficient in a constant and abundant supply of wholesome food. Those whose organization does not permit them to migrate when their food becomes periodically scarce, can never attain a large population. This is probably the reason why woodpeckers are scarce with us, while in the tropics they are among the most abundant of solitary birds. Thus the house sparrow is more abundant than the redbreast, because its food is more constant and plentiful,—seeds of grasses being preserved during the winter, and our farm-yards and stubble-fields furnishing an almost inexhaustible supply. Why, as a general rule, are aquatic, and especially sea birds, very numerous in individuals? Not because they are more prolific than others, generally the contrary; but because their food never fails, the sea-shores and river-banks daily swarming with a fresh supply of small mollusca and crustacea. Exactly the same laws will apply to mammals. Wild cats are prolific and have few enemies; why then are they never as abundant as rabbits? The only intelligible answer is, that their supply of food is more precarious. It appears evident, therefore, that so long as a country remains physically unchanged, the numbers of its animal population cannot materially increase. If one species does so, some others requiring the same kind of food must diminish in proportion. The numbers that die annually must be immense; and as the individual existence of each animal depends upon itself, those that die must be the weakest—the very young, the aged, and the diseased,—while those that prolong their existence can only be the most perfect in health and vigour—those who are best able to obtain food regularly, and avoid their numerous enemies. It is, as we commenced by remarking, "a struggle for existence," in which the weakest and least perfectly organized must always succumb.

Now it is clear that what takes place among the individuals of a species must also occur among the several allied species of a group, —viz. that those which are best adapted to obtain a regular supply of food, and to defend themselves against the attacks of their enemies and the vicissitudes of the seasons, must necessarily obtain and preserve a superiority in population; while those species which from some defect of power or organization are the least capable of counteracting the vicissitudes of food, supply, &c., must diminish in numbers, and, in extreme cases, become altogether extinct. Between these extremes the species will present various degrees of capacity for ensuring the means of preserving life; and it is thus we account for the abundance or rarity of species. Our ignorance will generally prevent us from accurately tracing the effects to their causes; but could we become perfectly acquainted with the organization and habits of the various species of animals, and could we measure the capacity of each for performing the different acts necessary to its safety and existence under all the varying circumstances by which it is surrounded, we might be able even to calculate the proportionate abundance of individuals which is the necessary result.

If now we have succeeded in establishing these two points—1st, *that the animal population of a country is generally stationary, being kept down by a periodical deficiency of food, and other checks;* and, 2nd, *that the comparative abundance or scarcity of the individuals of the several species is entirely due to their organization and resulting habits, which, rendering it more difficult to procure a regular supply of food and to provide for their personal safety in some cases than in others, can only be balanced by a difference in the population which have to exist in a given area*—we shall be in a condition to proceed to the consideration of *varieties,* to which the preceding remarks have a direct and very important application.

Most or perhaps all the variations from the typical form of a species must have some definite effect, however slight, on the habits or capacities of the individuals. Even a change of colour might, by rendering them more or less distinguishable, affect their safety; a greater or less development of hair might modify their habits. More important changes, such as an increase in the power or dimensions of the limbs or any of the external organs, would more or less affect their mode of procuring food or the range of country which they inhabit. It is also evident that most changes would affect, either favourably or adversely, the powers of prolonging existence. An antelope with shorter or weaker legs must necessarily suffer more from the attacks of the feline carnivora; the passenger pigeon with less powerful wings would sooner or later be affected in its powers of procuring a regular supply of food; and in both cases the result must necessarily be a diminution of the population of the modified species. If, on the other hand, any species should produce a variety having slightly increased powers of preserving existence, that variety must inevitably in time acquire a superiority in numbers. These results must follow as surely as old age, intemperance, or scarcity of food produce an increased mortality. In both cases there may be many individual exceptions; but on the average the rule will invariably be found to hold good. All varieties will therefore fall into two classes—those which under the same conditions would never reach the population of the parent species, and those which would in time obtain and keep a numerical superiority. Now, let some alteration of physical conditions occur in the district—a long period of drought, a destruction of vegetation by locusts, the irruption of some new carnivorous animal seeking "pastures new" —any change in fact tending to render existence more difficult to the species in question, and tasking its utmost powers to avoid complete extermination; it is evident that, of all the individuals composing the species, those forming the least numerous and most feebly organized variety would suffer first, and, were the pressure severe, must soon become extinct. The same causes continuing in action, the parent species would next suffer, would gradually diminish in numbers, and with a recurrence of similar unfavourable conditions might also become extinct. The superior variety would then alone remain, and on a return to favourable circumstances would rapidly increase in numbers and occupy the place of the extinct species and variety.

The *variety* would now have replaced the *species*, of which it would be a more perfectly developed and more highly organized form. It would be in all respects better adapted to secure its safety, and to prolong its individual existence and that of the race. Such a variety *could not* return to the original form; for that form is an inferior one, and could never compete with it for existence. Granted, therefore, a "tendency" to reproduce the original type of the species, still the variety must ever remain preponderant in numbers, and under adverse physical conditions *again alone survive*. But this new, improved, and populous race might itself, in course of time, give rise to new varieties, exhibiting several diverging modifications of form, any of which, tending to increase the facilities for preserving existence, must by the same general law, in their turn become predominant. Here, then, we have *progression and continued divergence* deduced from the general laws which regulate the existence of animals in a state of nature, and from the undisputed fact that varieties do frequently occur. It is not, however, contended that this result would be invariable; a change of physical conditions in the district might at times materially modify it, rendering the race which had been the most capable of supporting existence under the former conditions now the least so, and even causing the extinction of the newer and, for a time, superior race, while the old or parent species and its first inferior varieties continued to flourish. Variations in unimportant parts might also occur, having no perceptible effect on the life-preserving powers; and the varieties so furnished might run a course parallel with the parent species, either giving rise to further variations or returning to the former type. All we argue for is, that certain varieties have a tendency to maintain their existence longer than the original species, and this tendency must make itself felt; for though the doctrine of chances or averages can never be trusted to on a limited scale, yet, if applied to high numbers, the results come nearer to what theory demands, and, as we approach to an infinity of examples, become strictly accurate. Now the scale on which nature works is so vast—the numbers of individuals and periods of time with which she deals approach so near to infinity, that any cause, however slight, and however liable to be veiled and counteracted by accidental circumstances, must in the end produce its full legitimate results.

Let us now turn to domesticated animals, and inquire how varieties produced among them are affected by the principles here enunciated. The essential difference in the condition of wild and domestic animals is this,—that among the former, their well-being and very existence depend upon the full exercise and healthy condition of all their senses and physical powers, whereas, among the latter, these are only partially exercised, and in some cases are absolutely unused. A wild animal has to search, and often to labour, for every mouthful of food—to exercise sight, hearing, and smell in seeking it, and in avoiding dangers, in procuring shelter from the inclemency of the seasons, and in providing for the subsistence and safety of its offspring. There is no muscle of its body that is not called into daily and hourly activity; there is no sense or faculty that is not strengthened by continual exercise. The domestic animal, on the other hand, has food provided for it, is sheltered, and often confined, to guard it against the vicissitudes of the seasons, is carefully secured from the attacks of its natural enemies, and seldom even rears its young without human assistance. Half of its senses and faculties are quite useless; and the other half are but occasionally called into feeble exercise, while even its muscular system is only irregularly called into action.

Now when a variety of such an animal occurs, having increased power or capacity in any organ or sense, such increase is totally useless, is never called into action, and may even exist without the animal ever becoming aware of it. In the wild animal, on the contrary, all its faculties and powers being brought into full action for the necessities of existence, any increase becomes immediately available, is strengthened by exercise, and must even slightly modify the food, the habits, and the whole economy of the race. It creates as it were a new animal, one of superior powers, and which will necessarily increase in numbers and outlive those inferior to it.

Again, in the domesticated animal all variations have an equal chance of continuance; and those which would decidedly render a wild animal unable to compete with its fellows and continue its existence are no disadvantage whatever in a state of domesticity. Our quickly fattening pigs, short-legged sheep, pouter pigeons, and poodle dogs could never have come into existence in a state of nature, because the very first step towards such inferior forms would have led to the rapid extinction of the race; still less could they now exist in competition with their wild allies. The great speed but slight endurance of the race horse, the unwieldly strength of the ploughman's team, would both be useless in a state of nature. If turned wild on the pampas, such animals would probably soon become extinct, or under favorable circumstances might each lose those extreme qualities which would never be called into action, and in a few generations would revert to a common type, which must be that in which the various powers and faculties are so proportioned to each other as to be best adapted to procure food and secure safety,—that in which by the full exercise of every part of his organization the animal can alone continue to live. Domestic varieties, when turned wild, *must* return to something near the type of the original wild stock, *or become altogether extinct.*

We see, then, that no inferences as to varieties in a state of nature can be deduced from the observation of those occurring among domestic animals. The two are so much opposed to each other in every circumstance of their existence, that what applies to the one is almost sure not to apply to the other. Domestic animals are abnormal, irregular, artificial; they are subject to varieties which never occur and never can occur in a state of nature; their very existence depends altogether on human care: so far are many of them removed from that just proportion of faculties, that true balance of organization, by means of which alone an animal left to its own resources can preserve its existence and continue its race.

The hypothesis of Lamarck—that progressive changes in species have been produced by the attempts of animals to increase the development of their own organs, and thus modify their structure and habits—has been repeatedly and easily refuted by all writers on the subject of varieties and species, and it seems to have been considered that when this was done the whole question has been finally settled; but the view here developed renders such an hypothesis quite unnecessary, by showing that similar results must be produced by the action of principles constantly at work in nature. The powerful retractile talons of the falcon- and the cat-tribes have not been produced or increased by the volition of those animals; but among the different varieties which occurred in the earlier and less highly organized forms of these groups, *those always survived longest which had the greatest facilities for seizing their prey.* Neither did the giraffe acquire its long neck by desiring to reach the foliage of the more lofty shrubs, and constantly stretching its neck for the purpose, but because any varieties which occurred among its antitypes with a longer neck than usual *at once secured a fresh range of pasture over the same ground as their shorter-necked companions, and on the first scarcity of food were thereby enabled to outlive them.* Even the peculiar colours of many animals, especially insects, so closely resembling the soil or the leaves or the trunks on which they habitually reside, are explained on the same principle; for though in the course of ages varieties of many tints may have occurred, *yet those races having colours best adapted to conceal-ment from their enemies would inevitably survive the longest.* We have also here an acting cause to account for that balance so often observed in nature,—a deficiency in one set of organs always being compensated by an increased development of some others—power-ful wings accompanying weak feet, or great velocity making up for the absence of defensive weapons; for it has been shown that all varieties in which an unbalanced deficiency occurred could not long continue their existence. The action of this principle is exactly like that of the centrifugal governor of the stream engine, which checks and corrects any irregularities almost before they become evident; and in like manner no unbalanced deficiency in the animal kingdom can ever reach any conspicuous magnitude, because it would make itself felt at the very first step, by rendering existence difficult and extinction almost sure to follow. An origin such as is here advocated will also agree with the peculiar character of the modifications of form and structure which obtain in organized beings—the many lines of divergence from a central type, the increasing efficiency and power of a particular organ through a succession of allied species, and the remarkable persistence of un-important parts such as colour, texture of plumage and hair, form of horns or crests, through a series of species differing considerably in more essential characters. It also furnishes us with a reason for that "more specialized structure" which Professor Owen states to be a characteristic of recent compared with extinct forms, and which would evidently be the result of the progressive modification of any organ applied to a special purpose in the animal economy.

We believe we have now shown that there is a tendency in na-ture to the continued progression of certain classes of *varieties* further and further from the original type—a progression to which there appears no reason to assign any definite limits—and that the same principle which produces this result in a state of nature will also explain why domestic varieties have a tendency to revert to the original type. This progression, by minute steps, in various directions, but always checked and balanced by the necessary condi-tions, subject to which alone existence can be preserved, may, it is believed, be followed out so as to agree with all the phenomena presented by organized beings, their extinction and succession in past ages, and all the extraordinary modifications of form, instinct, and habits which they exhibit.

Ternate, February, 1858.

CHARLES DARWIN

The Origin of Species (1859) †

Introduction to the variorum edition, by Morse Peckham

"Much the greatest event that ever happened and much the best," Charles James Fox said of the French Revolution—to me, a remark even more pertinent to the publication of *On the Origin of Species*. Its greatness would justify the preparation of a variorum text, but there are sounder reasons. The scale on which Darwin carried out five revisions makes it impossible, without such a text, to comprehend the development of his book. Of the 3,878 sentences in the first edition, nearly 3,000, about 75 per cent, were rewritten from one to five times each. Over 1,500 sentences were added, and of the original sentences plus these, nearly 325 were dropped. Of the original and added sentences there are nearly 7,500 variants of all kinds.[1] In terms of net added sentences, the sixth edition is nearly a third as long again as the first.

But I have not undertaken this task because of the greatness of the book or even the scale of the revisions; I hope, rather, that the text will be a contribution to the history of biology, of ideas, and of modern culture. As a student of Victorian literature and its background, I became increasingly tantalized some years ago by the unsatisfactory discussion of the reception of the book, by confusing interpretations, by inadequate sketches of the development of Darwinism and the very different matter of evolutionary thought and its relation to the *Origin*. The larger outlines were fuzzily visible, but the illuminating detail was absent. Turning to the work itself, I quickly found part of the answer. Darwin complained often enough that few really understood the theory of Natural Selection, and were he to examine various cultural histories and even certain respected histories of science published since his death, he would still complain, perhaps quite bitterly. Yet the real reason for the fuzziness was not apparent. Modern editions, since 1898, have not included his tables of corrections, first introduced in the third edition, nor have any American editions I have examined, including

† The present text is excerpted from the sixth edition of the *Origin* (1872), the last edition during Darwin's lifetime. The textual history of the first six editions of the *Origin* is a complex one, but it has been clarified by Morse Peckham's valuable variorum edition of the *Origin* (Philadelphia, 1959). Morse Peckham (b. 1914) is professor of English at the University of South Carolina.

1. By "variant" is here meant "variant sentence." It may have one change in punctuation or a half-dozen verbal changes, or be a canceled sentence or a new one. I have not calculated the number of variants within sentences. There must be somewhere between 15,000 and 20,000.

the authorized Appleton edition of 1872.[2] By accident I came upon a passage taken from the 1859 edition. I was familiar with the passage, the heavily revised opening of the last chapter. At once I began to seek out, to examine, and to collect the earlier editions. The tables of changes surprised me. I was amazed at the extent and variety of the variations. Nothing I had read prepared me for such a situation, not even the *Life and Letters*. Nor did the lists of changes prepare me for what I was to discover when I did a little collation. * * *

The new [second] edition had the type, paper, and binding of the original. For textual purposes the fact that the same type was used is most important. In revising the work Darwin's determination to make only a few changes was carried out, at least in terms of the number of changes he made in later editions, particularly in the fourth, fifth, and sixth. Still, the total number in this edition is impressive enough: 9 sentences dropped; 483 rewritten or re-punctuated; 30 added. No chapter was untouched. * * *

The third edition contained two important new features: a table of "Additions and Corrections, to the Second and Third Editions," by which is meant only the thirty-five passages he considered important enough to record, and "An Historical Sketch of the Recent Progress of Opinion on the Origin of Species." Altogether he dropped 33 sentences, altered 617, and added 266, together 14 per cent of the total number of variations, while the second edition had only 7 per cent. The text was 35 pages longer than in the two previous editions, and the "Historical Sketch" added six and a half pages in smaller type. * * *

The fourth edition was the most extensively revised yet, containing 21 per cent of the total number of variants. Darwin dropped 36 sentences, rewrote 1,073, and added 435, although in his new table of differences between the third and fourth editions he listed only 34 passages. He added two pages to the "Historical Sketch" and fifty-two pages to the text. An important structural change involved the addition of a number of new sub-headings within the chapters, and the change from the former place at the beginning of paragraphs to a position centered above paragraphs. * * *

The fifth edition was to be the most important yet published. We first hear of it on December 5, 1868, when Murray still had a large enough stock of the fourth to make it worth his while to advertise. * * *

It was notable on several counts. For the first time Darwin used the famous phrase, taken from Spencer, "Survival of the Fittest," and it was the most extensively revised edition yet—indeed, if we

2. An American will rarely happen on one of the original editions, or any English edition, so widely was the book published in the United States. Several university libraries I have examined have nothing but American editions; of these, few are early.

except the bulk of the extra chapter added in the sixth edition, the most extensively revised of all. It contains 29 per cent of the total number of variants: 178 sentences dropped, 1,770 altered, and 227 added. Hence only two pages were added to the total length of the text. * * * But the sixth was to be an entirely new kind of edition, a popular edition to retail at 7/6.[3]

According to Francis Darwin, the new edition was begun in June, 1871, and finished January 10, 1872. By the middle of July, Darwin was struggling with his refutation of Mivart, the Roman Catholic biologist, about whom he had harsh and "mortified" things to say in his letters and whom Huxley was to trounce so thoroughly and deservedly the following November in the *Contemporary Review*. In August he expected to start correcting the sheets in a few weeks, and by late September he was satisfied with what he proposed to do to Mivart and had decided to devote a new chapter mainly to the cleverest enemy who had yet appeared, as well as the least fair. By late December he could write of being almost finished. * * *

The edition contained several important changes. The first word, "On," was dropped from the title. The considerations of objections were taken from Chapter IV and placed with new material, chiefly rebutting Mivart's attacks, in a new Chapter VII. Thus the old Chapters VII through XIV were renumbered VIII through XV. At the end was added a "Glossary of the Principal Scientific Terms used in the Present Volume," prepared by W. S. Dallas. This very useful addition was probably part of the plan to appeal to a popular market. Such a scheme was very likely Murray's, and my guess is that he suggested the glossary; it is more a publisher's idea than a scientist's. Including the new material on Mivart, the new edition had more variants than any of the previous five. Excluding that, it had fewer than the fifth but considerably more than the fourth. Darwin dropped 63 sentences, rewrote 1,669, and added 571. As in the fifth, hundreds of sentences were completely recast with only slight changes in meaning, the cumulative effect of which, however, was of great importance, as detailed studies of the text, if they are forthcoming, will show. * * *

Darwin's Introduction

When on board H.M.S. 'Beagle,' as naturalist, I was much struck with certain facts in the distribution of the organic beings inhabit-

3. The fifth edition is the cause of complete mystery. Of all the editions, I have found the fifth the hardest to find. One I found in Boston, another was found for me in London, and a third in Dublin. Both the first and fourth are easier, the first for obvious reasons. But why should the fourth, in an edition of 1,500, be easier to come by than the fifth, with its 2,000 copies?

ing South America, and in the geological relations of the present to the past inhabitants of that continent. These facts, as will be seen in the latter chapters of this volume, seemed to throw some light on the origin of species—that mystery of mysteries, as it has been called by one of our greatest philosophers. On my return home, it occurred to me, in 1837, that something might perhaps be made out on this question by patiently accumulating and reflecting on all sorts of facts which could possibly have any bearing on it. After five years' work I allowed myself to speculate on the subject, and drew up some short notes; these I enlarged in 1844 into a sketch of the conclusions, which then seemed to me probable: from that period to the present day I have steadily pursued the same object. I hope that I may be excused for entering on these personal details, as I give them to show that I have not been hasty in coming to a decision.

My work is now (1859) nearly finished; but as it will take me many more years to complete it, and as my health is far from strong, I have been urged to publish this Abstract. I have more especially been induced to do this, as Mr. Wallace, who is now studying the natural history of the Malay archipelago, has arrived at almost exactly the same general conclusions that I have on the origin of species. In 1858 he sent me a memoir on this subject, with a request that I would forward it to Sir Charles Lyell, who sent it to the Linnean Society, and it is published in the third volume of the Journal of that society. Sir C. Lyell and Dr. Hooker, who both knew of my work—the latter having read my sketch of 1844—honoured me by thinking it advisable to publish, with Mr. Wallace's excellent memoir, some brief extracts from my manuscripts.

This Abstract, which I now publish, must necessarily be imperfect. I cannot here give references and authorities for my several statements; and I must trust to the reader reposing some confidence in my accuracy. No doubt errors will have crept in, though I hope I have always been cautious in trusting to good authorities alone. I can here give only the general conclusions at which I have arrived, with a few facts in illustration, but which, I hope, in most cases will suffice. No one can feel more sensible than I do of the necessity of hereafter publishing in detail all the facts, with references, on which my conclusions have been grounded; and I hope in a future work to do this. For I am well aware that scarcely a single point is discussed in this volume on which facts cannot be adduced, often apparently leading to conclusions directly opposite to those at which I have arrived. A fair result can be obtained only by fully stating and balancing the facts and arguments on both sides of each question; and this is here impossible.

I much regret that want of space prevents my having the satisfaction of acknowledging the generous assistance which I have received from very many naturalists, some of them personally unknown to me. I cannot, however, let this opportunity pass without expressing my deep obligations to Dr. Hooker, who, for the last fifteen years, has aided me in every possible way by his large stores of knowledge and his excellent judgment.

In considering the Origin of Species, it is quite conceivable that a naturalist, reflecting on the mutual affinities of organic beings, on their embryological relations, their geographical distribution, geological succession, and other such facts, might come to the conclusion that species had not been independently created, but had descended, like varieties, from other species. Nevertheless, such a conclusion, even if well founded, would be unsatisfactory, until it could be shown how the innumerable species inhabiting this world have been modified, so as to acquire that perfection of structure and coadaptation which justly excites our admiration. Naturalists continually refer to external conditions, such as climate, food, &c., as the only possible source of variation. In one limited sense, as we shall hereafter see, this may be true; but it is preposterous to attribute to mere external conditions, the structure, for instance, of the woodpecker, with its feet, tail, beak, and tongue, so admirably adapted to catch insects under the bark of trees. In the case of the mistletoe, which draws its nourishment from certain trees, which has seeds that must be transported by certain birds, and which has flowers with separate sexes absolutely requiring the agency of certain insects to bring pollen from one flower to the other, it is equally preposterous to account for the structure of this parasite, with its relations to several distinct organic beings, by the effects of external conditions, or of habit, or of the volition of the plant itself.

It is, therefore, of the highest importance to gain a clear insight into the means of modification and coadaptation. At the commencement of my observations it seemed to me probable that a careful study of domesticated animals and of cultivated plants would offer the best chance of making out this obscure problem. Nor have I been disappointed; in this and in all other perplexing cases I have invariably found that our knowledge, imperfect though it be, of variation under domestication, afforded the best and safest clue. I may venture to express my conviction of the high value of such studies, although they have been very commonly neglected by naturalists.

From these considerations, I shall devote the first chapter of this Abstract to Variation under Domestication. We shall thus see that a large amount of hereditary modification is at least possible; and, what is equally or more important, we shall see how great is the power of man in accumulating by his Selection successive slight variations. I will then pass on to the variability of species in a state of nature; but I shall, unfortunately, be compelled to treat this subject far too briefly, as it can be treated properly only by giving long catalogues of facts. We shall, however, be enabled to discuss what circumstances are most favourable to variation. In the next chapter the Struggle for Existence amongst all organic beings throughout the world, which inevitably follows from the high geometrical ratio of their increase, will be considered. This is the doctrine of Malthus, applied to the whole animal and vegetable kingdoms. As many more individuals of each species are born than can possibly survive; and as, consequently, there is a frequently recurring struggle for existence, it follows that any being, if it vary however slightly in any manner profitable to itself, under the complex and sometimes varying conditions of life, will have a better chance of surviving, and thus be *naturally selected*. From the strong principle of inheritance, any selected variety will tend to propagate its new and modified form.

This fundamental subject of Natural Selection will be treated at some length in the fourth chapter; and we shall then see how Natural Selection almost inevitably causes much Extinction of the less improved forms of life, and leads to what I have called Divergence of Character. In the next chapter I shall discuss the complex and little known laws of variation. In the five succeeding chapters, the most apparent and gravest difficulties in accepting the theory will be given: namely, first, the difficulties of transitions, or how a simple being or a simple organ can be changed and perfected into a highly developed being or into an elaborately constructed organ; secondly, the subject of Instinct, or the mental powers of animals; thirdly, Hybridism, or the infertility of species and the fertility of varieties when intercrossed; and fourthly, the imperfection of the Geological Record. In the next chapter I shall consider the geological succession of organic beings throughout time; in the twelfth and thirteenth, their geographical distribution throughout space; in the fourteenth, their classification or mutual affinities, both when mature and in an embryonic condition. In the last chapter I shall give a brief recapitulation of the whole work, and a few concluding remarks.

No one ought to feel surprise at much remaining as yet unexplained in regard to the origin of species and varieties, if he make due allowance for our profound ignorance in regard to the mutual relations of the many beings which live around us. Who can explain why one species ranges widely and is very numerous, and why another allied species has a narrow range and is rare? Yet these relations are of the highest importance, for they determine the present welfare and, as I believe, the future success and modification of every inhabitant of this world. Still less do we know of the mutual relations of the innumerable inhabitants of the world during the many past geological epochs in its history. Although much remains obscure, and will long remain obscure, I can entertain no doubt, after the most deliberate study and dispassionate judgment of which I am capable, that the view which most naturalists until recently entertained, and which I formerly entertained—namely, that each species has been independently created—is erroneous. I am fully convinced that species are not immutable; but that those belonging to what are called the same genera are lineal descendants of some other and generally extinct species, in the same manner as the acknowledged varieties of any one species are the descendants of that species. Furthermore, I am convinced that Natural Selection has been the most important, but not the exclusive, means of modification.

Chapter I

VARIATION UNDER DOMESTICATION

Causes of variability —Effects of habit and the use or disuse of parts—Correlated variation—Inheritance—Character of domestic varieties—Difficulty of distinguishing between varieties and species —Origin of domestic varieties from one or more species—Domestic pigeons, their differences and origin—Principles of selection, anciently followed, their effects—Methodical and unconscious selection—Unknown origin of our domestic productions—Circumstances favourable to man's power of selection.

CAUSES OF VARIABILITY

When we compare the individuals of the same variety or subvariety of our older cultivated plants and animals, one of the first points which strikes us is, that they generally differ more from each other than do the individuals of any one species or variety in a state of nature. And if we reflect on the vast diversity of the plants and animals which have been cultivated, and which have varied during all ages under the most different climates and treatment, we are driven to conclude that this great variability is due to our domestic productions having been raised under conditions of life not so uniform as, and somewhat different from, those to which the parent species had been exposed under nature. There is, also, some probability in the view propounded by Andrew Knight, that this variability may be partly connected with excess of food. It seems clear that organic beings must be exposed during several generations to new conditions to cause any great amount of variation; and that, when the organisation has once begun to vary, it generally continues varying for many generations. No case is on record of a variable organism ceasing to vary under cultivation. Our oldest cultivated plants, such as wheat, still yield new varieties: our oldest domesticated animals are still capable of rapid improvement or modification.

As far as I am able to judge, after long attending to the subject, the conditions of life appear to act in two ways,—directly on the whole organisation or on certain parts alone, and indirectly by affecting the reproductive system. With respect to the direct action, we must bear in mind that in every case, as Professor Weismann has lately insisted, and as I have incidentally shown in my work on 'Variation under Domestication,' there are two factors: namely, the nature of the organism, and the nature of the conditions. The former seems to be much the more important; for nearly similar variations sometimes arise under, as far as we can judge, dissimilar conditions; and, on the other hand, dissimilar variations arise under conditions which appear to be nearly uniform. The effects on the offspring are either definite or indefinite. They may be considered as definite when all or nearly all the offspring of individuals exposed to certain conditions during several generations are modified in the same manner. It is extremely difficult to come to any conclusion in regard to the extent of the changes which have been thus definitely induced. There can, however, be little doubt about many slight changes,—such as size from the amount of food, colour from the nature of the food, thickness of the skin and hair from climate, &c. Each of the endless variations which we see in the plumage of our fowls must have had some efficient cause; and if the same cause were to act uniformly during a long series of generations on many individuals, all probably would be modified in the same manner. * * *

EFFECTS OF HABIT AND OF THE USE OR DISUSE OF PARTS; CORRELATED
VARIATION; INHERITANCE

* * * The laws governing inheritance are for the most part unknown. No one can say why the same peculiarity in different individuals of the same species, or in different species, is sometimes inherited and sometimes not so; why the child often reverts in certain characters to its grandfather or grandmother or more remote ancestor; why a peculiarity is often transmitted from one sex to both sexes, or to one sex alone, more commonly but not exclusively to the like sex. It is a fact of some importance to us, that peculiarities appearing in the males of our domestic breeds are often transmitted, either exclusively or in a much greater degree, to the males

alone. A much more important rule, which I think may be trusted, is that, at whatever period of life a peculiarity first appears, it tends to reappear in the offspring at a corresponding age, though sometimes earlier. In many cases this could not be otherwise; thus the inherited peculiarities in the horns of cattle could appear only in the offspring when nearly mature; peculiarities in the silkworm are known to appear at the corresponding caterpillar or cocoon stage. But hereditary diseases and some other facts make me believe that the rule has a wider extension, and that, when there is no apparent reason why a peculiarity should appear at any particular age, yet that it does tend to appear in the offspring at the same period at which it first appeared in the parent. I believe this rule to be of the highest importance in explaining the laws of embryology. * * *

CHARACTER OF DOMESTIC VARIETIES; DIFFICULTY OF DISTINGUISHING
BETWEEN VARIETIES AND SPECIES; ORIGIN OF DOMESTIC VARIETIES
FROM ONE OR MORE SPECIES

When we look to the hereditary varieties or races of our domestic animals and plants, and compare them with closely allied species, we generally perceive in each domestic race, as already remarked, less uniformity of character than in true species. Domestic races often have a somewhat monstrous character; by which I mean, that, although differing from each other, and from other species of the same genus, in several trifling respects, they often differ in an extreme degree in some one part, both when compared one with another, and more especially when compared with the species under nature to which they are nearest allied. With these exceptions (and with that of the perfect fertility of varieties when crossed,—a subject hereafter to be discussed), domestic races of the same species differ from each other in the same manner as do the closely-allied species of the same genus in a state of nature, but the differences in most cases are less in degree. This must be admitted as true, for the domestic races of many animals and plants have been ranked by some competent judges as the descendants of aboriginally distinct species, and by other competent judges as mere varieties. If any well marked distinction existed between a domestic race and a species, this source of doubt would not so perpetually recur. It has often been stated that domestic races do not differ from each other in character of generic value. It can be shown that this statement is not correct; but naturalists differ much in determining what characters are of generic value; all such valuations being at present empirical. When it is explained how genera originate under nature, it will be seen that we have no right to expect often to find a generic amount of difference in our domesticated races.

In attempting to estimate the amount of structural difference between allied domestic races, we are soon involved in doubt, from not knowing whether they are descended from one or several parent species. This point, if it could be cleared up, would be interesting; if, for instance, it could be shown that the greyhound, bloodhound, terrier, spaniel, and bull-dog, which we all know propagate their kind truly, were the offspring of any single species, then such facts would have great weight in making us doubt about the immutability of the many closely allied natural species—for instance, of the many foxes—inhabiting different quarters of the world. I do not believe, as we shall presently see, that the whole amount of difference between the several breeds of the dog has been produced under domestication, I believe that a small part of the difference is due to their being descended from distinct species. In the case of strongly marked races of some other domesticated species, there is presumptive or even strong evidence, that all are descended from a single wild stock. * * *

BREEDS OF THE DOMESTIC PIGEON, THEIR DIFFERENCES AND ORIGIN

Believing that it is always best to study some special group, I have, after deliberation, taken up domestic pigeons. I have kept every breed which I could purchase or obtain, and have been most kindly favoured with skins from several quarters of the world, more especially by the Hon. W. Elliot from India, and by the Hon. C. Murray from Persia. Many treatises in different languages have been published on pigeons, and some of them are very important, as being of considerable antiquity. I have associated with several eminent fanciers, and have been permitted to join two of the London Pigeon Clubs. The diversity of the breeds is something astonishing. Compare the English carrier and the short-faced tumbler, and see the wonderful difference in their beaks, entailing corresponding differences in their skulls. The carrier, more especially the male bird, is also remarkable from the wonderful development of the carunculated skin about the head; and this is accompanied by greatly elongated eyelids, very large external orifices to the nostrils, and a wide gape of mouth. The short-faced tumbler has a beak in outline almost like that of a finch; and the common tumbler has the singular inherited habit of flying at a great height in a compact flock, and tumbling in the air head over heels. The runt is a bird of great size, with long massive beak and large feet; some of the sub-breeds of runts have very long necks, others very long wings and tails, others singularly short tails. The barb is allied to the carrier, but, instead of a long beak has a very short and broad one. The pouter has a much elongated body, wings, and legs; and its enormously developed crop, which it glories in inflating, may well excite astonishment and even laughter. The turbit has a short and conical beak, with a line of reversed feathers down the breast; and it has the habit of continually expanding slightly, the upper part of the œsophagus. The Jacobin has the feathers so much reversed along the back of the neck that they form a hood; and it has, proportionately to its size, elongated wing and tail feathers. The trumpeter and laugher, as their names express, utter a very different coo from the other breeds. The fantail has thirty or even forty tail-feathers, instead of twelve or fourteen—the normal number in all the members of the great pigeon family: these feathers are kept expanded, and are carried so erect, that in good birds the head and tail touch: the oil-gland is quite aborted. Several other less distinct breeds might be specified.

In the skeletons of the several breeds, the development of the bones of the face in length and breadth and curvature differs enormously. The shape, as well as the breadth and length of the ramus of the lower jaw, varies in a highly remarkable manner. The caudal and sacral vertebræ vary in number; as does the number of the ribs, together with their relative breadth and the presence of processes. The size and shape of the apertures in the sternum are highly variable; so is the degree of divergence and relative size of the two arms of the furcula. The proportional width of the gape of mouth, the proportional length of the eyelids, of the orifice of the nostrils, of the tongue (not always in strict correlation with the length of beak), the size of the crop and of the upper part of the œsophagus; the development and abortion of the oil-gland; the number of the primary wing and caudal feathers; the relative length of the wing and tail to each other and to the body; the relative length of the leg and foot; the number of scutellæ on the toes, the development of skin between the toes, are all points of structure which are variable. The period at which the perfect plumage is acquired varies, as does the state of the down with which the nestling birds are clothed when hatched. The shape and size of the eggs vary. The manner of flight, and in some breeds the voice and disposition, differ remarkably. Lastly, in certain breeds, the males and females have come to differ in a slight degree from each other.

Altogether at least a score of pigeons might be chosen, which, if shown to an ornithologist, and he were told that they were wild birds, would certainly be ranked by him as well-defined species. Moreover, I do not believe that any ornithologist would in this case place the English carrier, the short-faced tumbler, the runt, the barb, pouter, and fantail in the same genus; more especially as in each of these breeds several truly-inherited sub-breeds, or species, as he would call them, could be shown him.

Great as are the differences between the breeds of the pigeon, I am fully convinced that the common opinion of naturalists is correct, namely, that all are descended from the rock-pigeon (Columba livia), including under this term several geographic races or sub-species, which differ from each other in the most trifling respects. * * *

From these several reasons, namely,—the improbability of man having formerly made seven or eight supposed species of pigeons to breed freely under domestication;—these supposed species being quite unknown in a wild state, and their not having become anywhere feral;—these species presenting certain very abnormal characters, as compared with all other Columbidæ, though so like the rock-pigeon in most respects;—the occasional re-appearance of the blue colour and various black marks in all the breeds, both when kept pure and when crossed;—and lastly, the mongrel offspring being perfectly fertile;—from these several reasons taken together, we may safely conclude that all our domestic breeds are descended from the rock-pigeon or Columba livia with its geographical sub-species.

In favour of this view, I may add, firstly, that the wild C. livia has been found capable of domestication in Europe and in India; and that it agrees in habits and in a great number of points of structure with all the domestic breeds. Secondly, that, although an English carrier or a short-faced tumbler differs immensely in certain characters from the rock-pigeon, yet that, by comparing the several sub-breeds of these two races, more especially those brought from distant countries, we can make, between them and the rock-pigeon, an almost perfect series; so we can in some other cases, but not with all the breeds. Thirdly, those characters which are mainly distinctive of each breed are in each eminently variable, for instance the wattle and length of beak of the carrier, the shortness of that of the tumbler, and the number of tail-feathers in the fantail; and the explanation of this fact will be obvious when we treat of Selection. Fourthly, pigeons have been watched and tended with the utmost care, and loved by many people. They have been domesticated for thousands of years in several quarters of the world * * * The paramount importance of these considerations in explaining the immense amount of variation which pigeons have undergone, will likewise be obvious when we treat of Selection. We shall then, also, see how it is that the several breeds so often have a somewhat monstrous character. It is also a most favourable circumstance for the production of distinct breeds, that male and female pigeons can be easily mated for life; and thus different breeds can be kept together in the same aviary.

I have discussed the probable origin of domestic pigeons at

some, yet quite insufficient, length; because when I first kept pigeons and watched the several kinds, well knowing how truly they breed, I felt fully as much difficulty in believing that since they had been domesticated they had all proceeded from a common parent, as any naturalist could in coming to a similar conclusion in regard to the many species of finches, or other groups of birds, in nature. One circumstance has struck me much; namely, that nearly all the breeders of the various domestic animals and the cultivators of plants, with whom I have conversed, or whose treatises I have read, are firmly convinced that the several breeds to which each has attended, are descended from so many aboriginally distinct species. Ask, as I have asked, a celebrated raiser of Hereford cattle, whether his cattle might not have descended from Long-horns, or both from a common parent-stock, and he will laugh you to scorn. I have never met a pigeon, or poultry, or duck, or rabbit fancier, who was not fully convinced that each main breed was descended from a distinct species. Van Mons, in his treatise on pears and apples, shows how utterly he disbelieves that the several sorts, for instance a Ribston-pippin or Codlin-apple, could ever have proceeded from the seeds of the same tree. Innumerable other examples could be given. The explanation, I think, is simple: from long-continued study they are strongly impressed with the differences between the several races; and though they well know that each race varies slightly, for they win their prizes by selecting such slight differences, yet they ignore all general arguments, and refuse to sum up in their minds slight differences accumulated during many successive generations. May not those naturalists who, knowing far less of the laws of inheritance than does the breeder, and knowing no more than he does of the intermediate links in the long lines of descent, yet admit that many of our domestic races are descended from the same parents—may they not learn a lesson of caution, when they deride the idea of species in a state of nature being lineal descendants of other species?

PRINCIPLES OF SELECTION ANCIENTLY FOLLOWED, AND THEIR EFFECTS

Let us now briefly consider the steps by which domestic races have been produced, either from one or from several allied species. Some effect may be attributed to the direct and definite action of the external conditions of life, and some to habit; but he would be a bold man who would account by such agencies for the differences between a dray- and race-horse, a greyhound and bloodhound, a carrier and tumbler pigeon. One of the most remarkable features in our domesticated races is that we see in them adaptation, not indeed to the animal's or plant's own good, but to man's use or fancy. Some variations useful to him have probably arisen suddenly, or by one step; many botanists, for instance, believe that the fuller's teasel, with its hooks, which cannot be rivalled by any mechanical contrivance, is only a variety of the wild Dipsacus; and this amount of change may have suddenly arisen in a seedling. So it has probably been with the turnspit dog; and this is known to have been the case with the ancon sheep. But when we compare the dray-horse and race-horse, the dromedary and camel, the various breeds of sheep fitted either for cultivated land or mountain pasture, with the wool of one breed good for one purpose, and that of another breed for another purpose; when we compare the many breeds of dogs, each good for man in different ways; when we compare the game-cock, so pertinacious in battle, with other breeds so little quarrelsome, with "everlasting layers" which never desire to sit, and with the bantam so small and elegant; when we compare the host of agricultural, culinary, orchard, and flower-garden races of plants, most useful to man at different seasons and for different purposes, or so beautiful in his eyes, we must, I think, look further than to mere variability. We cannot suppose that all the breeds were suddenly produced as perfect and as useful as we now see them; indeed, in many cases, we know that this has not been their history. The key is man's power of accumulative selection: nature gives successive variations; man adds them up in certain directions useful to him. In this sense he may be said to have made for himself useful breeds. * * *

At the present time, eminent breeders try by methodical selection, with a distinct object in view, to make a new strain or sub-breed, superior to anything of the kind in the country. But, for our purpose, a form of Selection, which may be called Unconscious, and which results from every one trying to possess and breed from the best individual animals, is more important. Thus, a man who intends keeping pointers naturally tries to get as good dogs as he can, and afterwards breeds from his own best dogs, but he has no wish or expectation of permanently altering the breed. Nevertheless we may infer that this process, continued during centuries, would improve and modify any breed, in the same way as Bakewell, Collins, &c., by this very same process, only carried on more methodically, did greatly modify, even during their lifetimes, the forms and qualities of their cattle. Slow and insensible changes of this kind can never be recognised unless actual measurements or careful drawings of the breeds in question have been made long ago, which may serve for comparison. In some cases, however, unchanged, or but little changed individuals of the same breed exist in less civilised districts, where the breed has been less improved. There is reason to believe that King Charles's spaniel has been unconsciously modified to a large extent since the time of that monarch. Some highly competent authorities are convinced that the setter is directly derived from the spaniel, and has probably been slowly altered from it. It is known that the English pointer has been greatly changed within the last century, and in this case the change has, it is believed, been chiefly effected by crosses with the foxhound; but what concerns us is, that the change has been effected unconsciously and gradually, and yet so effectually, that, though the old Spanish pointer certainly came from Spain, Mr. Borrow has not seen, as I am informed by him, any native dog in Spain like our pointer.

By a similar process of selection, and by careful training, English racehorses have come to surpass in fleetness and size the parent Arabs, so that the latter, by the regulations for the Goodwood Races, are favoured in the weights which they carry. Lord Spencer and others have shown how the cattle of England have increased in weight and in early maturity, compared with the stock formerly kept in this country. By comparing the accounts given in various old treatises of the former and present state of carrier and tumbler pigeons in Britain, India, and Persia, we can trace the stages through which they have insensibly passed, and come to differ so greatly from the rock-pigeon. * * *

CIRCUMSTANCES FAVOURABLE TO MAN'S POWER OF SELECTION

* * * To sum up on the origin of our domestic races of animals and plants, Changed conditions of life are of the highest importance in causing variability, both by acting directly on the organisation, and indirectly by affecting the reproductive system. It is not probable that variability is in inherent and necessary contingent, under all circumstances. The greater or less force of inheritance and reversion, determine whether variations shall endure. Variability is governed by many unknown laws, of which correlated growth is probably the most important. Something, but how much we do not know, may be attributed to the definite action of the conditions of life. Some, perhaps a great, effect may be attributed to the increased use or disuse of parts. The final result is thus rendered infinitely complex. In some cases the intercrossing of aboriginally distinct species appears to have played an important part in the origin of our breeds. When several breeds have once been formed in any country, their occasional intercrossing, with the aid of selection, has, no doubt, largely aided in the formation of new sub-breeds; but the importance of crossing has been much exaggerated, both in regard to animals and to those plants which are propagated by seed. With plants which are temporarily propagated by cuttings, buds, &c., the importance of crossing is immense; for the cultivator may here disregard the extreme variability both of hybrids and of mongrels, and the sterility of hybrids; but plants not propagated by

sccd are of little importance to us, for their endurance is only temporary. Over all these causes of Change, the accumulative action of Selection, whether applied methodically and quickly, or unconsciously and slowly but more efficiently seems to have been the predominant Power.

Chapter II

VARIATION UNDER NATURE

Variability — Individual differences — Doubtful species — Wide-ranging, much diffused, and common species vary most—Species of the larger genera in each country vary more frequently than the species of the smaller genera—Many of the species of the larger genera resemble varieties in being very closely, but unequally, related to each other, and in having restricted ranges.

Before applying the principles arrived at in the last chapter to organic beings in a state of nature, we must briefly discuss whether these latter are subject to any variation. To treat this subject properly, a long catalogue of dry facts ought to be given; but these I shall reserve for a future work. Nor shall I here discuss the various definitions which have been given of the term species. No one definition has satisfied all naturalists; yet every naturalist knows vaguely what he means when he speaks of a species. Generally the term includes the unknown element of a distant act of creation. The term "variety" is almost equally difficult to define; but here community of descent is almost universally implied, though it can rarely be proved. * * *

WIDE-RANGING, MUCH DIFFUSED, AND COMMON SPECIES VARY MOST

* * * Alphonse de Candolle and others have shown that plants which have very wide ranges generally present varieties; and this might have been expected, as they are exposed to diverse physical conditions, and as they come into competition (which, as we shall hereafter see, is an equally or more important circumstance) with different sets of organic beings. But my tables further show that, in any limited country, the species which are the most common, that is abound most in individuals, and the species which are most widely diffused within their own country (and this is a different consideration from wide range, and to a certain extent from commonness), oftenest give rise to varieties sufficiently well marked to have been recorded in botanical works. Hence it is the most flourishing, or, as they may be called, the dominant species,—those which range widely, are the most diffused in their own country, and are the most numerous in individuals,—which oftenest produce well-

marked varieties, or, as I consider them, incipient species. And
this, perhaps, might have been anticipated; for, as varieties, in
order to become in any degree permanent, necessarily have to
struggle with the other inhabitants of the country, the species
which are already dominant will be the most likely to yield offspring, which, though in some slight degree modified, still inherit
those advantages that enabled their parents to become dominant
over their compatriots. * * *

SUMMARY

Finally, varieties cannot be distinguished from species,—except,
first, by the discovery of intermediate linking forms; and, secondly,
by a certain indefinite amount of difference between them; for two
forms, if differing very little, are generally ranked as varieties, notwithstanding that they cannot be closely connected; but the
amount of difference considered necessary to give to any two forms
the rank of species cannot be defined. In genera having more than
the average number of species in any country, the species of these
genera have more than the average number of varieties. In large
genera the species are apt to be closely, but unequally, allied together, forming little clusters round other species. Species very
closely allied to other species apparently have restricted ranges. In
all these respects the species of large genera present a strong
analogy with varieties. And we can clearly understand these analogies, if species once existed as varieties, and thus originated;
whereas, these analogies are utterly inexplicable if species are independent creations.

We have, also, seen that it is the most flourishing or dominant
species of the larger genera within each class which on an average
yield the greatest number of varieties; and varieties, as we shall
hereafter see, tend to become converted into new and distinct species. Thus the larger genera tend to become larger; and throughout
nature the forms of life which are now dominant tend to become
still more dominant by leaving many modified and dominant descendants. But by steps hereafter to be explained, the larger genera
also tend to break up into smaller genera. And thus, the forms of
life throughout the universe become divided into groups subordinate to groups.

Chapter III

STRUGGLE FOR EXISTENCE

*Its bearing on natural selection—The term used in a wide sense—
Geometrical ratio of increase—Rapid increase of naturalised ani-*

mals and plants—Nature of the checks in increase—Competition universal—Effects of climate—Protection from the number of individuals—Complex relations of all animals and plants throughout nature—Struggle for life most severe between individuals and varieties of the same species: often severe between species of the same genus—The relation of organism to organism the most important of all relations.

Before entering on the subject of this chapter, I must make a few preliminary remarks, to show how the struggle for existence bears on Natural Selection. It has been seen in the last chapter that amongst organic beings in a state of nature there is some individual variability: indeed I am not aware that this has ever been disputed. It is immaterial for us whether a multitude of doubtful forms be called species or sub-species or varieties; what rank, for instance, the two or three hundred doubtful forms of British plants are entitled to hold, if the existence of any well-marked varieties be admitted. But the mere existence of individual variability and of some few well-marked varieties, though necessary as the foundation for the work, helps us but little in understanding how species arise in nature. How have all those exquisite adaptations of one part of the organisation to another part, and to the conditions of life, and of one organic being to another being, been perfected? We see these beautiful co-adaptations most plainly in the woodpecker and the mistletoe; and only a little less plainly in the humblest parasite which clings to the hairs of a quadruped or feathers of a bird; in the structure of the beetle which dives through the water; in the plumed seed which is wafted by the gentlest breeze; in short, we see beautiful adaptations everywhere and in every part of the organic world.

Again, it may be asked, how is it that varieties, which I have called incipient species, become ultimately converted into good and distinct species which in most cases obviously differ from each other far more than do the varieties of the same species? How do those groups of species, which constitute what are called distinct genera, and which differ from each other more than do the species of the same genus, arise? All these results, as we shall more fully see in the next chapter, follow from the struggle for life. Owing to this struggle, variations, however slight and from whatever cause proceeding, if they be in any degree profitable to the individuals of a species, in their infinitely complex relations to other organic beings and to their physical conditions of life, will tend to the preservation of such individuals, and will generally be inherited by the offspring. The offspring, also, will thus have a better chance of surviving, for, of the many individuals of any species which are periodically born, but a small number can survive. I have called this principle, by which each slight variation, if useful, is preserved, by the term Natural Selection, in order to mark its relation to man's power of selection. But the expression often used by Mr. Herbert Spencer of the Survival of the Fittest is more accurate, and is sometimes equally convenient. We have seen that man by selection can certainly produce great results, and can adapt organic beings to his own uses, through the accumulation of slight but useful variations, given to him by the hand of Nature. But Natural Selection, as we shall hereafter see, is a power incessantly ready for action, and is as immeasurably superior to man's feeble efforts, as the works of Nature are to those of Art.

We will now discuss in a little more detail the struggle for existence. In my future work this subject will be treated, as it well deserves, at greater length. The elder De Candolle and Lyell have largely and philosophically shown that all organic beings are exposed to severe competition. In regard to plants, no one has treated this subject with more spirit and ability than W. Herbert, Dean of Manchester, evidently the result of his great horticultural knowledge. Nothing is easier than to admit in words the truth of the universal struggle for life, or more difficult—at least I have found it so—than constantly to bear this conclusion in mind. Yet unless it be thoroughly engrained in the mind, the whole economy of nature, with every fact on distribution, rarity, abundance, extinction, and variation, will be dimly seen or quite misunderstood. We behold the face of nature bright with gladness, we often see superabundance of food; we do not see or we forget, that the birds which are idly singing round us mostly live on insects or seeds, and are thus constantly destroying life; or we forget how largely these songsters, or their eggs, or their nestlings, are destroyed by birds and beasts of prey; we do not always bear in mind, that, though food may be now superabundant, it is not so at all seasons of each recurring year.

THE TERM, STRUGGLE FOR EXISTENCE, USED IN A LARGE SENSE

I should premise that I use this term in a large and metaphorical sense including dependence of one being on another, and including (which is more important) not only the life of the individual, but success in leaving progeny. Two canine animals, in a time of dearth, may be truly said to struggle with each other which shall get food and live. But a plant on the edge of a desert is said to struggle for life against the drought, though more properly it should be said to be dependent on the moisture. A plant which annually produces a thousand seeds, of which only one of an average comes to maturity, may be more truly said to struggle with the plants of the same and other kinds which already clothe the ground. The mistletoe is dependent on the apple and a few other trees, but can only in a far-fetched sense be said to struggle with these trees, for, if too many of these parasites grow on the same tree, it languishes and dies. But several seedling mistletoes, growing close together on the same branch, may more truly be said to struggle with each other. As the mistletoe is disseminated by birds, its existence depends on them; and it may methodically be said to struggle with other fruit-bearing plants, in tempting the birds to devour and thus disseminate its seeds. In these several senses, which pass into each other, I use for convenience' sake the general term of Struggle for Existence.

GEOMETRICAL RATIO OF INCREASE

A struggle for existence inevitably follows from the high rate at which all organic beings tend to increase. Every being, which during its natural lifetime produces several eggs or seeds, must suffer destruction during some period of its life, and during some season or occasional year, otherwise, on the principle of geometrical increase, its numbers would quickly become so inordinately great that no country could support the product. Hence, as more individuals are produced than can possibly survive, there must in every case be a struggle for existence, either one individual with another of the same species, or with the individuals of distinct species, or with the physical conditions of life. It is the doctrine of Malthus applied with manifold force to the whole animal and vegetable kingdoms; for in this case there can be no artificial increase of food, and no prudential restraint from marriage. Although some species may be now increasing, more or less rapidly, in numbers, all cannot do so, for the world would not hold them.

There is no exception to the rule that every organic being naturally increases at so high a rate, that, if not destroyed, the earth would soon be covered by the progeny of a single pair. Even slow-breeding man has doubled in twenty-five years, and at this rate, in less than a thousand years, there would literally not be standing-room for his progeny. Linnæus has calculated that if an annual plant produced only two seeds—and there is no plant so unproductive as this—and their seedlings next year produced two, and so on, then in twenty years there should be a million plants. The elephant is reckoned the slowest breeder of all known animals, and I have taken some pains to estimate its probable minimum rate of natural increase; it will be safest to assume that it begins breeding when thirty years old, and goes on breeding till ninety years old, bringing forth six young in the interval, and surviving till one hundred years old; if this be so, after a period of from 740 to 750 years there would be nearly nineteen million elephants alive, descended from the first pair.

But we have better evidence on this subject than mere theoretical calculations, namely, the numerous recorded cases of the astonishingly rapid increase of various animals in a state of nature, when circumstances have been favourable to them during two or three following seasons. Still more striking is the evidence from our domestic animals of many kinds which have run wild in several parts of the world; if the statements of the rate of increase of slow-breeding cattle and horses in South America, and latterly in Australia, had not been well authenticated, they would have been incredible. So it is with plants; cases could be given of introduced plants which have become common throughout whole islands in a period of less than ten years. Several of the plants, such as the cardoon and a tall thistle, which are now the commonest over the whole plains of La Plata, clothing square leagues of surface almost to the exclusion of every other plant, have been introduced from Europe; and there are plants which now range in India, as I hear from Dr. Falconer, from Cape Comorin to the Himalaya, which have been imported from America since its discovery. In such cases, and endless others could be given, no one supposes, that the fertility of the animals or plants has been suddenly and temporarily increased in any sensible degree. The obvious explanation is that the conditions of life have been highly favourable, and that there has consequently been less destruction of the old and young, and that nearly all the young have been enabled to breed. Their geometrical ratio of increase, the result of which never fails to be surprising, simply explains their extraordinarily rapid increase and wide diffusion in their new homes.

In a state of nature almost every full-grown plant annually produces seed, and amongst animals there are very few which do not annually pair. Hence we may confidently assert, that all plants and animals are tending to increase at a geometrical ratio,—that all would rapidly stock every station in which they could anyhow exist, —and that this geometrical tendency to increase must be checked by destruction at some period of life. Our familiarity with the larger domestic animals tends, I think, to mislead us: we see no great destruction falling on them, but we do not keep in mind that thousands are annually slaughtered for food, and that in a state of nature an equal number would have somehow to be disposed of.

The only difference between organisms which annually produce eggs or seeds by the thousand, and those which produce extremely few, is, that the slow-breeders would require a few more years to people, under favourable conditions, a whole district, let it be ever so large. The condor lays a couple of eggs and the ostrich a score, and yet in the same country the condor may be the more numerous of the two; the Fulmar petrel lays but one egg, yet it is believed to be the most numerous bird in the world. One fly deposits hundreds of eggs, and another, like the hippobosca, a single one; but this difference does not determine how many individuals of the two species can be supported in a district. A large number of eggs is of some importance to those species which depend on a fluctuating amount of food, for it allows them rapidly to increase in number. But the real importance of a large number of eggs or seeds is to make up for much destruction at some period of life; and this period in the great majority of cases is an early one. If an animal can in any way protect its own eggs or young, a small number may be produced, and yet the average stock be fully kept up; but if many eggs or young are destroyed, many must be produced, or the species will become extinct. It would suffice to keep up the full number of a tree, which lived on an average for a thousand years, if a single seed were produced once in a thousand years, supposing that this seed were never destroyed, and could be ensured to germinate in a fitting place. So that, in all cases, the average number of any animal or plant depends only indirectly on the number of its eggs or seeds.

In looking at Nature, it is most necessary to keep the foregoing considerations always in mind—never to forget that every single organic being may be said to be striving to the utmost to increase in numbers; that each lives by a struggle at some period of its life; that heavy destruction inevitably falls either on the young or old, during each generation or at recurrent intervals. Lighten any check, mitigate the destruction ever so little, and the number of the species will almost instantaneously increase to any amount. * * *

Chapter IV

NATURAL SELECTION; OR THE SURVIVAL OF THE FITTEST

Natural Selection—its power compared with man's selection—its power on characters of trifling importance—its power at all ages and on both sexes—Sexual selection—On the generality of intercrosses between individuals of the same species—Circumstances favourable and unfavourable to the results of natural selection, namely, intercrossing, isolation, number of individuals—Slow action—Extinction caused by natural selection—Divergence of character, related to the diversity of inhabitants of any small area, and to naturalisation—Action of natural selection, through divergence of character and extinction, on the descendants from a common parent—Explains the grouping of all organic beings—Advance in

organisation—Low forms preserved—Convergence of character—
Indefinite multiplication of species—Summary.

How will the struggle for existence, briefly discussed in the last chapter, act in regard to variation? Can the principle of selection, which we have seen is so potent in the hands of man, apply under nature? I think we shall see that it can act most efficiently. Let the endless number of slight variations and individual differences occurring in our domestic productions, and, in a lesser degree, in those under nature, be borne in mind; as well as the strength of the hereditary tendency. Under domestication, it may be truly said that the whole organisation becomes in some degree plastic. But the variability, which we almost universally meet with in our domestic productions, is not directly produced, as Hooker and Asa Gray have well remarked, by man; he can neither originate varieties, nor prevent their occurrence; he can preserve and accumulate such as do occur. Unintentionally he exposes organic beings to new and changing conditions of life, and variability ensues; but similar changes of conditions might and do occur under nature. Let it also be borne in mind how infinitely complex and close-fitting are the mutual relations of all organic beings to each other and to their physical conditions of life; and consequently what infinitely varied diversities of structure might be of use to each being under changing conditions of life. Can it, then, be thought improbable, seeing that variations useful to man have undoubtedly occurred, that other variations useful in some way to each being in the great and complex battle of life, should occur in the course of many successive generations. If such do occur, can we doubt (remembering that many more individuals are born than can possibly survive) that individuals having any advantage, however slight, over others, would have the best chance of surviving and of procreating their kind? On the other hand, we may feel sure that any variation in the least degree injurious would be rigidly destroyed. This preservation of favourable individual differences and variations, and the destruction of those which are injurious, I have called Natural Selection, or the Survival of the Fittest. Variations neither useful nor injurious would not be affected by natural selection, and would be left either a fluctuating element, as perhaps we see in certain polymorphic species, or would ultimately become fixed, owing to the nature of the organism and the nature of the conditions.

Several writers have misapprehended or objected to the term Natural Selection. Some have even imagined that natural selection induces variability, whereas it implies only the preservation of such variations as arise and are beneficial to the being under its conditions of life. No one objects to agriculturists speaking of the potent effects of man's selection; and in this case the individual differences given by nature, which man for some object selects, must of necessity first occur. Others have objected that the term selection implies conscious choice in the animals which become modified; and it had even been urged that, as plants have no volition, natural selection is not applicable to them! In the literal sense of the word, no doubt, natural selection is a false term; but who ever objected to chemists speaking of the elective affinities of the various elements?—and yet an acid cannot strictly be said to elect the base which which it in preference combines. It has been said that I speak of natural selection as an active power or Deity; but who objects to an author speaking of the attraction of gravity as ruling the movements of the planets? Every one knows what is meant and is implied by such metaphorical expressions; and they are almost necessary for brevity. So again it is difficult to avoid personifying the word Nature; but I mean by Nature, only the aggregate action and product of many natural laws, and by laws the sequence of events as ascertained by us. With a little familiarity such superficial objections will be forgotten.

We shall best understand the probable course of natural selection by taking the case of a country undergoing some slight physical change, for instance, of climate. The proportional numbers of its inhabitants will almost immediately undergo a change, and some species will probably become extinct. We may conclude, from what we have seen of the intimate and complex manner in which the inhabitants of each country are bound together, that any change in the numerical proportions of the inhabitants, independently of the change of climate itself, would seriously affect the others. If the country were open on its borders, new forms would certainly immigrate, and this would likewise seriously disturb the relations of some of the former inhabitants. Let it be remembered how powerful the influence of a single introduced tree or mammal has been shown to be. But in the case of an island, or of a country partly surrounded by barriers, into which new and better adapted forms could not freely enter, we should then have places in the economy of nature which would assuredly be better filled up, if some of the original inhabitants were in some manner modified; for, had the area been open to immigration, these same places would have been seized on by intruders. In such cases, slight modifications, which in any way favoured the individuals of any species, by better adapting them to their altered conditions, would tend to be preserved; and natural selection would have free scope for the work of improvement.

We have good reason to believe, as shown in the first chapter, that changes in the conditions of life give a tendency to increased variability; and in the foregoing cases the conditions have changed, and this would manifestly be favourable to natural selection, by affording a better chance of the occurrence of profitable variations. Unless such occur, natural selection can do nothing. Under the term of "variations," it must never be forgotten that mere individual differences are included. As man can produce a great result with his domestic animals and plants by adding up in any given direction individual differences, so could natural selection, but far more easily from having incomparably longer time for action. Nor do I believe that any great physical change, as of climate, or any unusual degree of isolation to check immigration, is necessary in order that new and unoccupied places should be left, for natural selection to fill up by improving some of the varying inhabitants. For as all the inhabitants of each country are struggling together with nicely balanced forces, extremely slight modifications in the structure or habits of one species would often give it an advantage over others; and still further modifications of the same kind would often still further increase the advantage, as long as the species continued under the same conditions of life and profited by similar means of subsistence and defence. No country can be named in which all the native inhabitants are now so perfectly adapted to each other and to the physical conditions under which they live, that none of them could be still better adapted or improved; for in all countries, the natives have been so far conquered by naturalised productions, that they have allowed some foreigners to take firm possession of the land. And as foreigners have thus in every country beaten some of the natives, we may safely conclude that the natives might have been modified with advantage, so as to have better resisted the intruders.

As man can produce, and certainly has produced, a great result by his methodical and unconscious means of selection, what may not natural selection effect? Man can act only on external and visible characters: Nature, if I may be allowed to personify the natural preservation or survival of the fittest, cares nothing for appearances, except in so far as they are useful to any being. She can act on every internal organ, on every shade of constitutional difference, on the whole machinery of life. Man selects only for his own good: Nature only for that of the being which she tends. Every selected character is fully exercised by her, as is implied by the fact of their selection. Man keeps the natives of many climates in the same country; he seldom exercises each selected character in some peculiar and fitting manner; he feeds a long and a short beaked pigeon on the same food; he does not exercise a long-backed or long-legged quadruped in any peculiar manner; he exposes sheep with long and short wool to the same climate. He does not allow the most vigorous males to struggle for the females. He does not rigidly destroy all inferior animals, but protects during each varying season, as far as lies in his power, all his productions. He often begins his selection by some half-monstrous form; or at least by some modification prominent enough to catch the eye or to be plainly useful to him. Under Nature, the slightest differences of structure or constitution may well turn the nicely balanced scale in the struggle for life, and so be preserved. How fleeting are the wishes and efforts of man! how short his time! and consequently how poor will be his results, compared with those accumulated by Nature during whole geological periods! Can we wonder, then, that Nature's productions should be far "truer" in character than man's productions that they should be infinitely better adapted to the most complex conditions of life and should plainly bear the stamp of far higher workmanship?

It may metaphorically be said that natural selection is daily and hourly scrutinising, throughout the world, the slightest variations; rejecting those that are bad, preserving and adding up all that are good; silently and insensibly working, *whenever and wherever opportunity offers*, at the improvement of each organic being in relation to its organic and inorganic conditions of life. We see nothing of these slow changes in progress, until the hand of time has marked the lapse of ages, and then so imperfect is our view into long-past geological ages, that we see only that the forms of life are now different from what they formerly were.

In order that any great amount of modification should be effected in a species, a variety when once formed must again, perhaps after a long interval of time, vary or present individual differences of the same favourable nature as before; and these must be again preserved, and so onwards step by step. Seeing that individual differences of the same kind perpetually recur, this can hardly be considered as an unwarrantable assumption. But whether it is true, we can judge only by seeing how far the hypothesis accords with and explains the general phenomena of nature. On the other hand, the ordinary belief that the amount of possible variation is a strictly limited quantity is likewise a simple assumption.

Although natural selection can act only through and for the good of each being, yet characters and structures, which we are apt to consider as of very trifling importance, may thus be acted on. When we see leaf-eating insects green, and bark-feeders mottled-grey; the alpine ptarmigan white in winter, the red-grouse the colour of heather, we must believe that these tints are of service to these birds and insects in preserving them from danger. Grouse, if not destroyed at some period of their lives would increase in countless numbers; they are known to suffer largely from birds of prey; and hawks are guided by eyesight to their prey—so much so, that on parts of the Continent persons are warned not to keep white pigeons, as being the most liable to destruction. Hence natural selection might be effective in giving the proper colour to each kind of grouse, and in keeping that colour, when once acquired, true and constant. Nor ought we to think that the occasional destruction of an animal of any particular colour would produce little effect: we should remember how essential it is in a flock of white sheep to destroy a lamb with the faintest trace of black. We have seen how the colour of the hogs, which feed on the "paint-root" in Virginia, determines whether they shall live or die. In plants, the down on the fruit and the colour of the flesh are considered by botanists as characters of the most trifling importance: yet we hear from an excellent horticulturist, Downing, that in the United States, smooth-skinned fruits suffer far more from a beetle, a Curculio, than those with down; that purple plums suffer far more from a certain disease than yellow plums; whereas another disease attacks yellow-fleshed peaches far more than those with other coloured flesh. If, with all the aids of art, these slight differences make a great difference in cultivating the several varieties, assuredly, in a state of nature, where the trees would have to struggle with other trees, and with a host of enemies, such differences would effectually settle which variety, whether a smooth or downy, a yellow or purple fleshed fruit, should succeed.

In looking at many small points of difference between species, which, as far as our ignorance permits us to judge, seem quite unimportant, we must not forget that climate, food, &c., have no doubt produced some direct effect. It is also necessary to bear in mind that, owing to the law of correlation, when one part varies, and the variations are accumulated through natural selection, other modifications, often of the most unexpected nature, will ensue.

As we see that those variations which, under domestication, appear at any particular period of life, tend to reappear in the offspring at the same period;—for instance, in the shape, size, and flavour of the seeds of the many varieties of our culinary and agricultural plants; in the caterpillar and cocoon stages of the varieties of the silk-worm; in the eggs of poultry, and in the colour of the down of their chickens; in the horns of our sheep and cattle when nearly adult;—so in a state of nature natural selection will be enabled to act on and modify organic beings at any age, by the accumulation of variations profitable at that age, and by their inheritance at a corresponding age. If it profit a plant to have its seeds more and more widely disseminated by the wind, I can see no greater difficulty in this being effected through natural selection, than in the cotton-planter increasing and improving by selection the down in the pods on his cotton-trees. Natural selection may modify and adapt the larva of an insect to a score of contingencies, wholly different from those which concern the mature insect; and these modifications may effect, through correlation, the structure of the adult. So, conversely, modifications in the adult may affect the structure of the larva; but in all cases natural selection will ensure that they shall not be injurious: for if they were so, the species would become extinct.

Natural selection will modify the structure of the young in relation to the parent, and of the parent in relation to the young. In social animals it will adapt the structure of each individual for the benefit of the whole community; if the community profits by the selected change. What natural selection cannot do, is to modify the structure of one species, without giving it any advantage, for the good of another species; and though statements to this effect may be found in works of natural history, I cannot find one case which will bear investigation. A structure used only once in an animal's life, if of high importance to it, might be modified to any extent by natural selection; for instance, the great jaws possessed by certain insects, used exclusively for opening the cocoon—or the hard tip to the beak of unhatched birds, used for breaking the egg. It has been asserted, that of the best short-beaked tumbler-pigeons a greater number perish in the egg than are able to get out of it; so that fanciers assist in the act of hatching. Now if nature had to make the beak of a full-grown pigeon very short for the bird's own advantage, the process of modification would be very slow, and there would be simultaneously the most rigorous selection of all the young birds within the egg, which had the most powerful and hardest beaks, for all with weak beaks would inevitably perish; or, more delicate and more easily broken shells might be selected, the thickness of the shell being known to vary like every other structure.

It may be well here to remark that with all beings there must be much fortuitous destruction, which can have little or no influence on the course of natural selection. For instance a vast number of eggs or seeds are annually devoured, and these could be modified through natural selection only if they varied in some manner which protected them from their enemies. Yet many of these eggs or seeds would perhaps, if not destroyed, have yielded individuals better adapted to their conditions of life than any of those which happened to survive. So again a vast number of mature animals and plants, whether or not they be the best adapted to their conditions, must be annually destroyed by accidental causes, which would not be in the least degree mitigated by certain changes of structure or constitution which would in other ways be beneficial to the species. But let the destruction of the adults be ever so heavy, if the number which can exist in any district be not wholly kept down by such causes,—or again let the destruction of eggs or seeds be so great that only a hundredth or a thousandth part are developed,—yet of those which do survive, the best adapted individuals, supposing that there is any variability in a favourable direction, will tend to propagate their kind in larger numbers than the less well adapted. If the numbers be wholly kept down by the causes just indicated, as will often have been the case, natural selection will be powerless in certain beneficial directions; but this is no valid objection to its efficiency at other times and in other ways; for we are far from having any reason to suppose that many species ever undergo modification and improvement at the same time in the same area.

SEXUAL SELECTION

Inasmuch as peculiarities often appear under domestication in one sex and become hereditarily attached to that sex, so no doubt it will be under nature. Thus it is rendered possible for the two sexes to be modified through natural selection in relation to different habits of life, as is sometimes the case; or for one sex to be modified in relation to the other sex, as commonly occurs. This leads me to say a few words on what I have called Sexual Selection. This form of selection depends, not on a struggle for existence in relation to other organic beings or to external conditions, but on a struggle between the individuals of one sex, generally the males, for the possession of the other sex. The result is not death to the unsuccessful competitor, but few or no offspring. Sexual selection is, therefore, less rigorous than natural selection. Generally, the most vigorous males, those which are best fitted for their places in nature, will leave most progeny. But in many cases, victory depends not so much on general vigor, as on having special weapons, confined to the male sex. A hornless stag or spurless cock would have poor chance of leaving numerous offspring. Sexual selection, by always allowing the victor to breed, might surely give indomitable courage, length to the spur, and strength to the wing to strike in the spurred leg, in nearly the same manner as does the brutal cock-fighter by the careful selection of his best cocks. How low in the scale of nature the law of battle descends, I know not; male alligators have been described as fighting, bellowing, and whirling round, like Indians in a war-dance, for the possession of the females; male salmons have been observed fighting all day long; male stag-beetles sometimes bear wounds from the huge mandibles of other males; the males of certain hymenopterous insects have been frequently seen by that inimitable observer M. Fabre, fighting for a particular female who sits by, an apparently unconcerned beholder of the struggle, and then retires with the conqueror. The war is, perhaps, severest between the males of polygamous animals, and these seem oftenest provided with special weapons. The males of carnivorous animals are already well armed; though to them and to others, special means of defence may be given through means of sexual selection, as the mane of the lion, and the hooked jaw to the male salmon; for the shield may be as important for victory, as the sword or spear.

Amongst birds, the contest is often of a more peaceful character. All those who have attended to the subject, believe that there is the severest rivalry between the males of many species to attract, by singing, the females. The rock-thrush of Guiana, birds of paradise, and some others, congregate; and successive males display with the most elaborate care, and show off in the best manner, their gorgeous plumage; they likewise perform strange antics before the females, which, standing by as spectators, at last choose the most attractive partner. Those who have closely attended to birds in confinement well know that they often take individual preferences and dislikes: thus Sir R. Heron has described how a pied peacock was eminently attractive to all his hen birds. I cannot here enter on the necessary details; but if man can in a short time give beauty and an elegant carriage to his bantams, according to the standard of beauty, I can see no good reason to doubt that female birds, by selecting, during thousands of generations, the most melodious or beautiful males according to their standard of beauty, might produce a marked effect. Some well-known laws, with respect to the plumage of male and female birds, in comparison with the plumage of the young, can partly be explained through the action of sexual selection on variations occurring at different ages, and transmitted to the males alone or to both sexes at corresponding ages; but I have not space here to enter on this subject.

Thus it is, as I believe, that when the males and females of any animal have the same general habits of life, but differ in structure, colour, or ornament, such differences have been mainly caused by sexual selection: that is, by individual males having had, in successive generations, some slight advantage over other males, in their weapons, means of defence, or charms, which they have transmitted to their male offspring alone. Yet, I would not wish to attribute all sexual differences to this agency: for we see in our domestic animals peculiarities arising and becoming attached to the male sex, which apparently have not been augmented through selection by man. The tuft of hair on the breast of the wild turkey-cock cannot be of any use, and it is doubtful whether it can be ornamental in the eyes of the female bird;—indeed, had the tuft appeared under domestication, it would have been called a monstrosity.

ILLUSTRATIONS OF THE ACTION OF NATURAL SELECTION, OR THE SURVIVAL OF THE FITTEST

In order to make it clear how, as I believe, natural selection acts, I must beg permission to give one or two imaginary illustrations. Let us take the case of a wolf, which preys on various animals, securing some by craft, some by strength and some by fleetness; and let us suppose that the fleetest prey, a deer for instance, had from any change in the country increased in numbers or that other prey had decreased in numbers, during that season of the year when the wolf was hardest pressed for food. Under such circumstances the swiftest and slimmest wolves would have the best chance of surviving and so be preserved or selected,—provided always that they retained strength to master their prey at this or some other period of the year, when they were compelled to prey on other animals. I can see no more reason to doubt that this would be the result, than that man should be able to improve the fleetness of his greyhounds by careful and methodical selection, or by that kind of unconscious selection which follows from each man trying to keep the best dogs without any thought of modifying the breed. I may add, that, according to Mr. Pierce, there are two varieties of the wolf inhabiting the Catskill Mountains, in the United States, one with a light greyhound-like form, which pursues deer, and the other more bulky, with shorter legs, which more frequently attacks the shepherd's flocks.

It should be observed that, in the above illustration, I speak of the slimmest individual wolves, and not of any single strongly-marked variation having been preserved. In former editions of this work I sometimes spoke as if this latter alternative had frequently occurred. I saw the great importance of individual differences, and this led me fully to discuss the results of unconscious selection by man, which depends on the preservation of all the more or less valuable individuals, and on the destruction of the worst. I saw, also, that the preservation in a state of nature of any occasional deviation of structure, such as a monstrosity, would be a rare event; and that, if at first preserved, it would generally be lost by subsequent intercrossing with ordinary individuals. Nevertheless, until reading an able and valuable article in the 'North British Review' (1867), I did not appreciate how rarely single variations, whether slight or strongly marked, could be perpetuated. The author takes the case of a pair of animals, producing during their lifetime two hundred offspring, of which, from various causes of destruction, only two on an average survive to procreate their kind. This is rather an extreme estimate for most of the higher animals, but by no means so for many of the lower organisms. He then shows that if a single individual were born, which varied in some manner, giving it twice as good a chance of life as that of the other individuals, yet the chances would be strongly against its survival. Supposing it to survive and to breed, and that half its young inherited the favourable variation; still, as the Reviewer goes on to show, the young would have only a slightly better chance of surviving and breeding; and this chance would go on decreasing in the succeeding generations. The justice of these remarks cannot, I think, be disputed. If, for instance, a bird of some kind could procure its food more easily by having its beak curved, and if one were born with its beak strongly curved, and which consequently flourished, nevertheless there would be a very poor chance of this one individual perpetuating its kind to the exclusion of the common form; but there can hardly be a doubt, judging by what we see taking place under domestication, that this result would follow from the preservation during many generations of a large number of individuals with more or less strongly curved beaks, and from the destruction of a still larger number with the straightest beaks.

It should not, however, be overlooked that certain rather strongly marked variations, which no one would rank as mere individual differences, frequently recur owing to a similar organisation being similarly acted on—of which fact numerous instances could be given with our domestic productions. In such cases, if the varying individual did not actually transmit to its offspring its newly-acquired character, it would undoubtedly transmit to them, as long as the existing conditions remained the same, a still stronger tendency to vary in the same manner. There can also be little doubt that the tendency to vary in the same manner has often been so strong that all the individuals of the same species have been similarly modified without the aid of any form of selection. Or only a third, fifth, or tenth part of the individuals may have been thus affected, of which fact several instances could be given. Thus Graba estimates that about one-fifth of the guillemots in the Faroe Islands consist of a variety so well marked, that it was formerly ranked as a distinct species under the name of Uria lacrymans. In cases of this kind, if the variation were of a beneficial nature, the original form would soon be supplanted by the modified form, through the survival of the fittest.

To the effects of intercrossing in eliminating variations of all kinds, I shall have to recur; but it may be here remarked that most animals and plants keep to their proper homes, and do not needlessly wander about; we see this even with migratory birds, which almost always return to the same spot. Consequently each newly-formed variety would generally be at first local, as seems to be the common rule with varieties in a state of nature; so that similarly modified individuals would soon exist in a small body together, and would often breed together. If the new variety were successful in its battle for life, it would slowly spread from a central district, competing with and conquering the unchanged individuals on the margins of an ever-increasing circle.

It may be worth while to give another and more complex illustration of the action of natural selection. Certain plants excrete sweet juice, apparently for the sake of eliminating something injurious from the sap: this is effected, for instance, by glands at the base of the stipules in some Leguminosæ, and at the backs of the leaves of the common laurel. This juice, though small in quantity, is greedily sought by insects; but their visits do not in any way benefit the plant. Now, let us suppose that the juice or nectar was excreted from the inside of the flowers of a certain number of plants of any species. Insects in seeking the nectar would get dusted with pollen, and would often transport it from one flower to another. The flowers of two distinct individuals of the same species would thus get crossed; and the act of crossing, as can be fully proved, gives rise to vigorous seedlings which consequently would have the best chance of flourishing and surviving. The plants which produced flowers with the largest glands or nectaries, excreting most nectar, would oftenest be visited by insects, and would oftenest be crossed; and so in the long-run would gain the upper hand and form a local variety. The flowers, also, which had their stamens and pistils placed, in relation to the size and habits of the particular insects which visited them, so as to favour in any degree the transportal of the pollen, would likewise be favoured. We might have taken the case of insects visiting flowers for the sake of collecting pollen instead of nectar; and as pollen is formed for the sole purpose of fertilisation, its destruction appears to be a simple loss to the plant; yet if a little pollen were carried, at first occasionally and then habitually, by the pollen-devouring insects from flower to flower, and a cross thus effected, although nine-tenths of the pollen were destroyed it might still be a great gain to the plant to be thus robbed; and the individuals which produced more and more pollen, and had larger anthers, would be selected.

When our plant, by the above process long continued, had been rendered highly attractive to insects, they would, unintentionally on their part, regularly carry pollen from flower to flower; and that they do this effectually, I could easily show by many striking facts. I will give only one, as likewise illustrating one step in the separation of the sexes of plants. Some holly-trees bear only male flowers, which have four stamens producing a rather small quantity of pollen, and a rudimentary pistil: other holly-trees bear only female flowers; these have a full-sized pistil, and four stamens with shrivelled anthers, in which not a grain of pollen can be detected. Having found a female tree exactly sixty yards from a male tree, I put the stigmas of twenty flowers, taken from different branches, under the microscope, and on all, without exception, there were a few pollen-grains, and on some a profusion. As the wind had set for several days from the female to the male tree, the pollen could not thus have been carried. The weather had been cold and boisterous, and therefore not favourable to bees, nevertheless every female flower which I examined had been effectually fertilised by the bees, which had flown from tree to tree in search of nectar. But to return to our imaginary case: as soon as the plant had been rendered so highly attractive to insects that pollen was regularly carried from flower to flower, another process might commence. No naturalist doubts the advantage of what has been called the "physiological division of labour"; hence we may believe that it would be advantageous to a plant to produce stamens alone in one flower or on one whole plant, and pistils alone in another flower or on another plant. In plants under culture and placed under new conditions of life, sometimes the male organs and sometimes the female organs become more or less impotent; now if we suppose this to occur in ever so slight a degree under nature, then, as pollen is already carried regularly from flower to flower, and as a more complete separation of the sexes of our plant would be advantageous on the principle of the division of labour, individuals with this tendency more and more increased would be continually favoured or selected, until at last a complete separation of the sexes might be effected. It would take up too much space to show the various steps, through dimorphism and other means, by which the separation of the sexes in plants of various kinds is apparently now in progress; but I may add that some of the species of holly in North America, are, according to Asa Gray, in an exactly intermediate condition, or, as he expresses it, are more or less diœciously polygamous.

Let us now turn to the nectar-feeding insects; we may suppose the plant, of which we have been slowly increasing the nectar by continued selection, to be a common plant; and that certain insects depended in main part on its nectar for food. I could give many facts showing how anxious bees are to save time: for instance, their habit of cutting holes and sucking the nectar at the bases of certain flowers, which, with a very little more trouble, they can enter by the mouth. Bearing such facts in mind, it may be believed that under certain circumstances individual differences in the curvature or length of the proboscis, &c., too slight to be appreciated by us, might profit a bee or other insect, so that certain individuals would be able to obtain their food more quickly than others; and thus the communities to which they belonged would flourish and throw off many swarms inheriting the same peculiarities. The tubes of the corolla of the common red and incarnate clovers (Trifolium pratense and incarnatum) do not on a hasty glance appear to differ in length; yet the hive-bee can easily suck the nectar out of the incarnate clover, but not out of the common red clover, which is visited by humble-bees alone; so that whole fields of red clover offer in vain an abundant supply of precious nectar to the hive-bee. That this nectar is much liked by the hive-bee is certain; for I have repeatedly seen, but only in the autumn, many hive-bees sucking the flowers through holes bitten in the base of the tube by bumble-bees. The difference in the length of the corolla in the two kinds of clover, which determines the visits of the hive-bee, must be very trifling; for I have been assured that when red clover has been mown, the flowers of the second crop are somewhat smaller, and that these are visited by many hive-bees. I do not know whether this statement is accurate; nor whether another published statement can be trusted, namely, that the Ligurian bee which is generally considered a mere variety of the common hive-bee, and which freely crosses with it, is able to reach and suck the nectar of the red clover. Thus, in a country where this kind of clover abounded, it might be a great advantage to the hive-bee to have a slightly longer or differently constructed proboscis. On the other hand, as the fertility of this clover absolutely depends on bees visiting the flowers, if humble-bees were to become rare in any country, it might be a great advantage to the plant to have a shorter or more deeply divided corolla, so that the hive-bees should be enabled to suck its flowers. Thus I can understand how a flower and a bee might slowly become, either simultaneously or one after the other, modified and adapted to each other in the most perfect manner, by the continued preservation of all the individuals which presented slight deviations of structure mutually favourable to each other.

I am well aware that this doctrine of natural selection, exemplified in the above imaginary instances, is open to the same objections which were first urged against Sir Charles Lyell's noble views on "the modern changes of the earth, as illustrative of geology"; but we now seldom hear the agencies which we see still at work, spoken of as trifling or insignificant, when used in explaining the excavation of the deepest valleys of the formation of long lines of inland cliffs. Natural selection acts only by the preservation and accumulation of small inherited modifications, each profitable to the preserved being; and as modern geology has almost banished such views as the excavation of a great valley by a single diluvial wave, so will natural selection banish the belief of the continued creation of new organic beings, or of any great and sudden modification in their structure. * * *

CIRCUMSTANCES FAVOURABLE FOR THE PRODUCTION OF NEW FORMS THROUGH NATURAL SELECTION

This is an extremely intricate subject. A great amount of variability, under which term individual differences are always included, will evidently be favourable. A large number of individuals, by giving a better chance within any given period for the appearance of profitable variations, will conpensate for a lesser amount of variability in each individual, and is, I believe, a highly important element of success. Though Nature grants long periods of time for the work of natural selection, she does not grant an indefinite period; for as all organic beings are striving to seize on each place in the economy of nature, if any one species does not become modified and improved in a corresponding degree with its competitors, it will be exterminated. Unless favourable variations be inherited by some at least of the offspring, nothing can be effected by natural selection. The tendency to reversion may often check or prevent the work; but as this tendency has not prevented man from forming by selection numerous domestic races, why should it prevail against natural selection?

In the case of methodical selection, a breeder selects for some definite object, and if the individuals be allowed freely to intercross, his work will completely fail. But when many men, without intending to alter the breed, have a nearly common standard of perfection, and all try to procure and breed from the best animals, improvement surely but slowly follows from this unconscious process of selection, notwithstanding that there is no separation of selected individuals. Thus it will be under nature; for within a confined area, with some place in the natural polity not perfectly occupied, all the individuals varying in the right direction, though in different degrees, will tend to be preserved. But if the area be large, its several districts will almost certainly present different conditions of life; and then, if the same species undergoes modification in different districts, the newly-formed varieties will intercross on the confines of each. But we shall see in the sixth chapter that intermediate varieties, inhabiting intermediate districts, will in the long run generally be supplanted by one of the adjoining varieties. Intercrossing will chiefly affect those animals which unite for each birth and wander much, and which do not breed at a very quick rate. Hence with animals of this nature, for instance, birds, varieties will generally be confined to separated countries; and this I find to be the case. With hermaphrodite organisms which cross only occasionally, and likewise with animals which unite for each birth, but which wander little and can increase at a rapid rate, a new and improved variety might be quickly formed on any one spot, and might there maintain itself in a body and afterwards spread, so that the individuals of the new variety would chiefly cross together. On this principle, nurserymen always prefer saving seed from a large body of plants, as the chance of intercrossing is thus lessened.

Even with animals which unite for each birth, and which do not propagate rapidly, we must not assume that free intercrossing would always eliminate the effects of natural selection; for I can bring forward a considerable body of facts showing that within the same area, two varieties of the same animal may long remain distinct, from haunting different stations, from breeding at slightly different seasons, or from the individuals of each variety preferring to pair together.

Intercrossing plays a very important part in nature by keeping the individuals of the same species, or of the same variety, true and uniform in character. It will obviously thus act far more efficiently with those animals which unite for each birth; but, as already stated, we have reason to believe that occasional intercrosses take place with all animals and plants. Even if these take place only at long intervals of time, the young thus produced will gain so much in vigour and fertility over the offspring from long-continued self-fertilisation, that they will have a better chance of surviving and propagating their kind; and thus in the long run the influence of crosses, even at rare intervals, will be great. With respect to organic beings extremely low in the scale, which do not propagate sexually, nor conjugate, and which cannot possibly intercross, uniformity of character can be retained by them under the same conditions of life, only through the principle of inheritance, and through natural selection which will destroy any individuals departing from the proper type. If the conditions of life change and the form undergoes modification, uniformity of character can be given to the modified offspring, solely by natural selection preserving similar favourable variations.

Isolation, also, is an important element in the modification of species through natural selection. In a confined or isolated area, if not very large, the organic and inorganic conditions of life will generally be almost uniform; so that natural selection will tend to modify all the varying individuals of the same species in the same manner. Intercrossing with the inhabitants of the surrounding districts will, also, be thus prevented. Moritz Wagner has published an interesting essay on this subject, and has shown that the service rendered by isolation in preventing crosses between newly-formed varieties is probably greater even than I supposed. But from reasons already assigned I can by no means agree with this naturalist, that migration and isolation are necessary elements for the formation of new species. The importance of isolation is likewise great in preventing, after any physical change in the conditions, such as of climate, elevation of the land, &c., the immigration of better adapted organisms; and thus new places in the natural economy of the district will be left open to be filled up by the modification of the old inhabitants. Lastly, isolation will give time for a new variety to be improved at a slow rate; and this may sometimes be of much importance. If, however, an isolated area be very small, either from being surrounded by barriers, or from having very peculiar physical conditions, the total number of the inhabitants will be small; and this will retard the production of new species, through natural selection by decreasing the chances of favourable variations arising.

The mere lapse of time by itself does nothing, either for or against natural selection. I state this because it has been erroneously asserted that the element of time has been assumed by me to play an all-important part in modifying species, as if all the forms of life were necessarily undergoing change through some innate law. Lapse of time is only so far important, and its importance in this respect is great, that it gives a better chance of beneficial variations arising and of their being selected, accumulated, and fixed. It likewise tends to increase the direct action of the physical conditions of life, in relation to the constitution of each organism.

If we turn to nature to test the truth of these remarks, and look at any small isolated area, such as an oceanic island, although the number of species inhabiting it is small, as we shall see in our chapter on Geographical Distribution; yet of these species a very large proportion are endemic,—that is, have been produced there and nowhere else in the world. Hence an oceanic island at first sight seems to have been highly favourable for the production of new species. But we may thus deceive ourselves, for to ascertain whether a small isolated area, or a large open area like a continent, has been most favourable for the production of new organic forms, we ought to make the comparison within equal times; and this we are incapable of doing.

Although isolation is of great importance in the production of new species, on the whole I am inclined to believe that largeness of area is still more important, especially for the production of species which shall prove capable of enduring for a long period, and of spreading widely. Throughout a great and open area, not only will there be a better chance of favourable variations, arising from the large number of individuals of the same species there supported, but the conditions of life are much more complex from the large number of already existing species; and if some of these many species become modified and improved, others will have to be improved in a corresponding degree, or they will be exterminated. Each new form, also, as soon as it has been much improved, will be able to spread over the open and continuous area, and will thus come into competition with many other forms. Moreover, great areas, though now continuous, will often, owing to former oscillations of level, have existed in a broken condition; so that the good effects of isolation will generally, to a certain extent, have concurred. Finally, I conclude that, although small isolated areas

have been in some respects highly favourable for the production of
new species, yet that the course of modification will generally have
been more rapid on large areas; and what is more important, that
the new forms produced on large areas, which already have been
victorious over many competitors, will be those that will spread
most widely, and will give rise to the greatest number of new varieties and species. They will thus play a more important part in the
changing history of the organic world.

In accordance with this view, we can, perhaps, understand some
facts which will be again alluded to in our chapter on Geographical Distribution; for instance, the fact of the productions of the
smaller continent of Australia now yielding before those of the
larger Europæo-Asiatic area. Thus, also, it is that continental productions have everywhere become so largely naturalised on islands.
On a small island, the race for life will have been less severe, and
there will have been less modification and less extermination.
Hence, we can understand how it is that the flora of Madeira, according to Oswald Heer, resembles to a certain extent the extinct
tertiary flora of Europe. All fresh-water basins, taken together, make
a small area compared with that of the sea or of the land. Consequently, the competition between fresh-water productions will
have been less severe than elsewhere; new forms will have been then
more slowly produced, and old forms more slowly exterminated.
And it is in fresh-water basins that we find seven genera of Ganoid
fishes, remnants of a once preponderant order: and in fresh water
we find some of the most anomalous forms now known in the world
as the Ornithorhynchus and Lepidosiren which, like fossils, connect
to a certain extent orders at present widely sundered in the natural
scale. These anomalous forms may be called living fossils; they
have endured to the present day, from having inhabited a confined
area, and from having been exposed to less varied, and therefore
less severe, competition.

To sum up, as far as the extreme intricacy of the subject permits,
the circumstances favourable and unfavourable for the production
of new species through natural selection. I conclude that for
terrestrial productions a large continental area, which has undergone
many oscillations of level, will have been the most favourable for the
production of many new forms of life, fitted to endure for a long time
and to spread widely. Whilst the area existed as a continent, the inhabitants will have been numerous in individuals and kinds, and will
have been subjected to severe competition. When converted by
subsidence into large separate islands, there will still have existed
many individuals of the same species on each island: intercrossing
on the confines of the range of each new species will have been
checked: after physical changes of any kind, immigration will have

been prevented, so that new places in the polity of each island will have had to be filled up by the modification of the old inhabitants; and time will have been allowed for the varieties in each to become well modified and perfected. When, by renewed elevation, the islands were reconverted into a continental area, there will again have been very severe competition: the most favoured or improved varieties will have been enabled to spread: there will have been much extinction of the less improved forms, and the relative proportional numbers of the various inhabitants of the reunited continent will again have been changed; and again there will have been a fair field for natural selection to improve still further the inhabitants, and thus to produce new species.

That natural selection generally acts with extreme slowness I fully admit. It can act only when there are places in the natural polity of a district which can be better occupied by the modification of some of its existing inhabitants. The occurrence of such places will often depend on physical changes, which generally take place very slowly, and on the immigration of better adapted forms being prevented. As some few of the old inhabitants become modified, the mutual relations of others will often be disturbed; and this will create new places, ready to be filled up by better adapted forms, but all this will take place very slowly. Although all the individuals of the same species differ in some slight degree from each other, it would often be long before differences of the right nature in various parts of the organisation might occur. The result would often be greatly retarded by free intercrossing. Many will exclaim that these several causes are amply sufficient to neutralise the power of natural selection. I do not believe so. But I do believe that natural selection will generally act very slowly, only at long intervals of time, and only on a few of the inhabitants of the same region. I further believe that these slow, intermittent results accord well with what geology tells us of the rate and manner at which the inhabitants of the world have changed.

Slow though the process of selection may be, if feeble man can do much by artificial selection, I can see no limit to the amount of change, to the beauty and complexity of the coadaptations between all organic beings, one with another and with their physical conditions of life, which may have been effected in the long course of time through nature's power of selection, that is by the survival of the fittest. * * *

DIVERGENCE OF CHARACTER

The principle, which I have designated by this term, is of high importance, and explains, as I believe, several important facts. In the first place, varieties, even strongly-marked ones, though having somewhat of the character of species—as is shown by the hopeless doubts in many cases how to rank them—yet certainly differ far less from each other than do good and distinct species. Nevertheless, according to my view, varieties are species in the process of formation, or are, as I have called them, incipient species. How, then, does the lesser difference between varieties become augmented into the greater difference between species? That this does habitually happen, we must infer from most of the innumerable species throughout nature presenting well-marked differences; whereas varieties, the supposed prototypes and parents of future well-marked species, present slight and ill-defined differences. Mere chance, as we may call it, might cause one variety to differ in some character from its parents, and the offspring of this variety again to differ from its parent in the very same character and in a greater degree; but this alone would never account for so habitual and large a degree of difference as that between the species of the same genus.

As has always been my practice, I have sought light on this head from our domestic productions. We shall here find something analogous. It will be admitted that the production of races so different as short-horn and Hereford cattle, race and cart horses, the several breeds of pigeons, &c., could never have been effected by the mere chance accumulation of similar variations during many successive generations. In practice, a fancier is, for instance, struck by a pigeon having a slightly shorter beak; another fancier is struck by a pigeon having a rather longer beak; and on the acknowledged principle that "fanciers do not and will not admire a medium standard, but like extremes," they both go on (as has actually occurred with the sub-breeds of the tumbler-pigeon) choosing and breeding from birds with longer and longer beaks, or with shorter and shorter beaks. Again, we may suppose that at an early period of history, the men of one nation or district required swifter horses, whilst those of another required stronger and bulkier horses. The early differences would be very slight; but, in the course of time, from the continued selection of swifter horses in the one case, and of stronger ones in the other, the differences would become greater, and would be noted as forming two sub-breeds. Ultimately, after the lapse of centuries, these sub-breeds would become converted into two well-established and distinct breeds. As the differences became greater, the inferior animals with intermediate characters, being neither swift nor very strong, would not have been used for breeding, and will thus have tended to disappear. Here, then, we see in man's productions the action of what may be called the principle of divergence, causing differences, at first barely appreciable, steadily to increase, and the breeds to diverge in character, both from each other and from their common parent.

But how, it may be asked, can any analogous principle apply in nature? I believe it can and does apply most efficiently (though it was a long time before I saw how), from the simple circumstance that the more diversified the descendants from any one species become in structure, constitution, and habits, by so much will they be better enabled to seize on many and widely diversified places in the polity of nature, and so be enabled to increase in numbers.

We can clearly discern this in the case of animals with simple habits. Take the case of a carnivorous quadruped, of which the number that can be supported in any country has long ago arrived at its full average. If its natural power of increase be allowed to act, it can succeed in increasing (the country not undergoing any change in conditions) only by its varying descendants seizing on places at present occupied by other animals: some of them, for instance, being enabled to feed on new kinds of prey, either dead or alive; some inhabiting new stations, climbing trees, frequenting water, and some perhaps becoming less carnivorous. The more diversified in habits and structure the descendants of our carnivorous animals become, the more places they will be enabled to occupy. What applies to one animal will apply throughout all time to all animals—that is, if they vary—for otherwise natural selection can effect nothing. So it will be with plants. It has been experimentally proved, that if a plot of ground be sown with one species of grass, and a similar plot be sown with several distinct genera of grasses, a greater number of plants and a greater weight of dry herbage can be raised in the latter than in the former case. The same has been found to hold good when one variety and several mixed varieties of wheat have been sown on equal spaces of ground. Hence, if any one species of grass were to go on varying, and the varieties were continually selected which differed from each other in the same manner, though in a very slight degree, as do the distinct species and genera of grasses, a greater number of individual plants of this species, including its modified descendants, would succeed in living on the same piece of ground. And we know that each species and each variety of grass is annually sowing almost countless seeds; and is thus striving, as it may be said, to the utmost to increase in number. Consequently, in the course of many thousand generations, the most distinct varieties of any one species of grass would have the best chance of succeeding and of increasing in numbers, and thus of supplanting the less distinct varieties; and varieties, when rendered very distinct from each other, take the rank of species.

The truth of the principle that the greatest amount of life can be supported by great diversification of structure, is seen under many natural circumstances. In an extremely small area, especially if

freely open to immigration, and where the contest between individual and individual must be very severe, we always find great diversity in its inhabitants. For instance, I found that a piece of turf,
three feet by four in size, which had been exposed for many years
to exactly the same conditions, supported twenty species of plants,
and these belonged to eighteen genera and to eight orders, which
shows how much these plants differed from each other. So it is with
the plants and insects on small and uniform islets: also in small
ponds of fresh water. Farmers find that they can raise most food
by a rotation of plants belonging to the most different orders:
nature follows what may be called a simultaneous rotation. Most of
the animals and plants which live close round any small piece of
ground, could live on it (supposing its nature not to be in any way
peculiar), and may be said to be striving to the utmost to live there;
but, it is seen, that where they come into the closest competition,
the advantages of diversification of structure, with the accompanying differences of habit and constitution, determine that the inhabitants, which thus jostle each other most closely, shall, as a general
rule, belong to what we call different genera and orders.

The same principle is seen in the naturalisation of plants through
man's agency in foreign lands. It might have been expected that the
plants which would succeed in becoming naturalised in any land
would generally have been closely allied to the indigenes; for these
are commonly looked at as specially created and adapted for their
own country. It might also, perhaps, have been expected that naturalised plants would have belonged to a few groups more especially adapted to certain stations in their new homes. But the case
is very different; and Alph. de Candolle has well remarked, in his
great and admirable work, that floras gain by naturalisation, propor-
tionally with the number of the native genera and species far more
in new genera than in new species. To give a single instance: in the
last edition of Dr. Asa Gray's 'Manual of the Flora of the Northern
United States,' 260 naturalised plants are enumerated, and these
belong to 162 genera. We thus see that these naturalised plants are
of a highly diversified nature. They differ, moreover, to a large extent, from the indigenes, for out of the 162 naturalised genera, no
less than 100 genera are not there indigenous, and thus a large proportional addition is made to the genera now living in the United
States.

By considering the nature of the plants or animals which have in
any country struggled successfully with the indigenes and have
there become naturalised, we may gain some crude idea in what
manner some of the natives would have to be modified, in order to
gain an advantage over their compatriots; and we may at least infer
that diversification of structure, amounting to new generic differ-

ences, would be profitable to them.

The advantage of diversification of structure in the inhabitants of the same region is, in fact, the same as that of the physiological division of labour in the organs of the same individual body—a subject so well elucidated by Milne Edwards. No physiologist doubts that a stomach adapted to digest vegetable matter alone, or flesh alone, draws most nutriment from these substances. So in the general economy of any land, the more widely and perfectly the animals and plants are diversified for different habits of life, so will a greater number of individuals be capable of there supporting themselves. A set of animals, with their organisation but little diversified, could hardly compete with a set more perfectly diversified in structure. It may be doubted, for instance, whether the Australian marsupials, which are divided into groups differing but little from each other, and feebly representing, as Mr. Waterhouse and others have remarked, our carnivorous, ruminant, and rodent mammals, could successfully compete with these well-developed orders. In the Australian mammals, we see the process of diversification in an early and incomplete stage of development.

THE PROBABLE EFFECTS OF THE ACTION OF NATURAL SELECTION
THROUGH DIVERGENCE OF CHARACTER AND EXTINCTION, ON THE
DESCENDANTS OF A COMMON ANCESTOR

After the foregoing discussion, which has been much compressed, we may assume that the modified descendants of any one species will succeed so much the better as they become more diversified in structure, and are thus enabled to encroach on places occupied by other beings. Now let us see how this principle of benefit being derived from divergence of character, combined with the principles of natural selection and of extinction, tends to act.

The accompanying diagram will aid us in understanding this rather perplexing subject. Let A to L represent the species of a genus large in its own country; these species are supposed to resemble each other in unequal degrees, as is so generally the case in nature, and as is represented in the diagram by the letters standing at unequal distances. I have said a large genus, because as we saw in the second chapter, on an average more species vary in large genera than in small genera; and the varying species of the large genera present a greater number of varieties. We have, also, seen that the species, which are the commonest and the most widely diffused, vary more than do the rare and restricted species. Let (A) be a common, widely-diffused, and varying species, belonging to a genus large in its own country. The branching and diverging dotted lines of unequal lengths proceeding from (A), may represent its varying offspring. The variations are supposed to be extremely slight, but

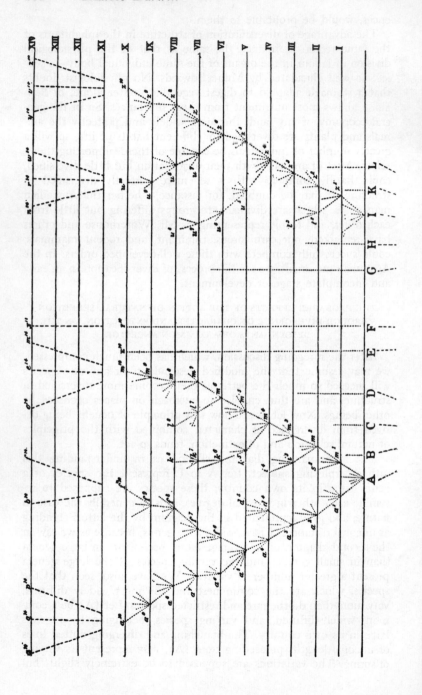

of the most diversified nature; they are not supposed all to appear simultaneously, but often after long intervals of time; nor are they all supposed to endure for equal periods. Only those variations which are in some way profitable will be preserved or naturally selected. And here the importance of the principle of benefit derived from divergence of character comes in; for this will generally lead to the most different or divergent variations (represented by the outer dotted lines) being preserved and accumulated by natural selection. When a dotted line reaches one of the horizontal lines, and is there marked by a small numbered letter, a sufficient amount of variation is supposed to have been accumulated to form it into a fairly well-marked variety, such as would be thought worthy of record in a systematic work.

The intervals between the horizontal lines in the diagram, may represent each a thousand or more generations. After a thousand generations, species (A) is supposed to have produced two fairly well-marked varieties, namely a^1 and m^1. These two varieties will generally still be exposed to the same conditions which made their parents variable, and the tendency to variability is in itself hereditary; consequently they will likewise tend to vary, and commonly in nearly the same manner as did their parents. Moreover, these two varieties, being only slightly modified forms, will tend to inherit those advantages which made their parent (A) more numerous than most of the other inhabitants of the same country; they will also partake of those more general advantages which made the genus to which the parent-species belonged, a large genus in its own country. And all these circumstances are favourable to the production of new varieties.

If, then, these two varieties be variable, the most divergent of their variations will generally be preserved during the next thousand generations. And after this interval, variety a^1 is supposed in the diagram to have produced variety a^2, which will, owing to the principle of divergence, differ more from (A) than did variety a^1. Variety m^1 is supposed to have produced two varieties, namely m^2 and s^2, differing from each other, and more considerably from their common parent (A). We may continue the process by similar steps for any length of time; some of the varieties, after each thousand generations, producing only a single variety, but in a more and more modified condition, some producing two or three varieties, and some failing to produce any. Thus the varieties or modified descendants of the common parent (A), will generally go on increasing in number and diverging in character. In the diagram the process is represented up to the ten-thousandth generation, and under a condensed and simplified form up to the fourteen-thousandth generation.

But I must here remark that I do not suppose that the process ever goes on so regularly as is represented in the diagram, though in itself made somewhat irregular, nor that it goes on continuously; it is far more probable that each form remains for long periods unaltered, and then again undergoes modification. Nor do I suppose that the most divergent varieties are invariably preserved: a medium form may often long endure, and may or may not produce more than one modified descendant; for natural selection will always act according to the nature of the places which are either un-occupied or not perfectly occupied by other beings; and this will depend on infinitely complex relations. But as a general rule, the more diversified in structure the descendants from any one species can be rendered, the more places they will be enabled to seize on, and the more their modified progeny will increase. In our diagram the line of succession is broken at regular intervals by small num-bered letters marking the successive forms which have become suf-ficiently distinct to be recorded as varieties. But these breaks are imaginary, and might have been inserted anywhere, after intervals long enough to allow the accumulation of a considerable amount of divergent variation.

As all the modified descendants from a common and widely-diffused species, belonging to a large genus, will tend to partake of the same advantages which made their parent successful in life, they will generally go on multiplying in number as well as diverg-ing in character: this is represented in the diagram by the several divergent branches proceeding from (A). The modified offspring from the later and more highly improved branches in the lines of descent, will, it is probable, often take the place of, and so de-stroy, the earlier and less improved branches: this is represented in the diagram by some of the lower branches not reaching to the upper horizontal lines. In some cases no doubt the process of modi-fication will be confined to a single line of descent and the number of modified descendants will not be increased; although the amount of divergent modification may have been augmented. This case would be represented in the diagram, if all the lines proceeding from (A) were removed, excepting that from a^1 to a^{10}. In the same way the English racehorse and English pointer have apparently both gone on slowly diverging in character from their original stocks, without either having given off any fresh branches or races.

After ten thousand generations, species (A) is supposed to have produced three forms, a^{10}, f^{10}, and m^{10}, which, from having diverged in character during the successive generations, will have come to differ largely, but perhaps unequally, from each other and from their common parent. If we suppose the amount of change between each horizontal line in our diagram to be excessively small, these three forms may still be only well-marked varieties; but we have only to suppose the steps in the process of modification to be more numerous or greater in amount, to convert these three forms into doubtful or at least into well-defined species. Thus the diagram illustrates the steps by which the small differences distinguishing varieties are increased into the larger differences distinguishing species. By continuing the same process for a greater number of generations (as shown in the diagram in a condensed and simplified manner), we get eight species, marked by the letters between a^{14} and m^{14}, all descended from (A). Thus, as I believe, species are multiplied and genera are formed.

In a large genus it is probable that more than one species would vary. In the diagram I have assumed that a second species (I) has produced, by analogous steps, after ten thousand generations, either two well-marked varieties (w^{10} and z^{10}) or two species, according to the amount of change supposed to be represented between the horizontal lines. After fourteen thousand generations, six new species marked by the letters n^{14} to z^{14}, are supposed to have been produced. In any genus, the species which are already very different in character from each other, will generally tend to produce the greatest number of modified descendants; for these will have the best chance of seizing on new and widely different places in the polity of nature: hence in the diagram I have chosen the extreme species (A), and the nearly extreme species (I), as those which have largely varied, and have given rise to new varieties and species. The other nine species (marked by capital letters) of our original genus, may for long but unequal periods continue to transmit unaltered descendants; and this is shown in the diagram by the dotted lines unequally prolonged upwards.

But during the process of modification, represented in the diagram, another of our principles, namely that of extinction, will have played an important part. As in each fully stocked country natural selection necessarily acts by the selected form having some advantage in the struggle for life over other forms, there will be a constant tendency in the improved descendants of any one species to supplant and exterminate in each stage of descent their predecessors and their original progenitor. For it should be remembered that the competition will generally be most severe between those forms which are most nearly related to each other in habits, constitution, and structure. Hence all the intermediate forms between the earlier and later states, that is between the less and more improved states of the same species, as well as the original parent-species itself, will generally tend to become extinct. So it probably will be with many whole collateral lines of descent, which will be conquered by later and improved lines. If, however, the modified offspring of a species get into some distinct country, or become quickly adapted to some quite new station, in which offspring and progenitor do not come into competition, both may continue to exist.

If, then, our diagram be assumed to represent a considerable amount of modification, species (A) and all the earlier varieties will have become extinct, being replaced by eight new species (a^{14} to m^{14}); and species (I) will be replaced by six (n^{14} to z^{14}) new species.

But we may go further than this. The original species of our genus were supposed to resemble each other in unequal degrees, as is so generally the case in nature; species (A) being more nearly related to B, C, and D, than to the other species; and species (I) more to G, H, K, L, than to the others. These two species (A) and (I) were also supposed to be very common and widely diffused species, so that they must originally have had some advantage over most of the other species of the genus. Their modified descendants, fourteen in number at the fourteen-thousandth generation, will probably have inherited some of the same advantages: they have also been modified and improved in a diversified manner at each stage of descent, so as to have become adapted to many related places in the natural economy of their country. It seems, therefore, extremely probable that they will have taken the places of, and thus exterminated not only their parents (A) and (I), but likewise some of the original species which were most nearly related to their parents. Hence very few of the original species will have transmitted offspring to the fourteen-thousandth generation. We may suppose that only one, (F), of the two species (E and F) which were least closely related to the other nine original species, has transmitted descendants to this late stage of descent.

The new species in our diagram descended from the original eleven species, will now be fifteen in number. Owing to the divergent tendency of natural selection, the extreme amount of difference in character between species a^{14} and z^{14} will be much greater than that between the most distinct of the original eleven species. The new species, moreover, will be allied to each other in a widely different manner. Of the eight descendants from (A) the three marked a^{14}, q^{14}, p^{14}, will be nearly related from having recently branched off from a^{10}, b^{14}, and f^{14}, from having diverged at an earlier period from a^5, will be in some degree distinct from the three first-named species; and lastly, o^{14}, e^{14}, and m^{14}, will be nearly related one to the other, but, from having diverged at the first commencement of the process of modification, will be widely different from the other five species, and may constitute a subgenus or a distinct genus.

The six descendants from (I) will form two sub-genera or genera. But as the original species (I) differed largely from (A), standing nearly at the extreme end of the original genus, the six descendants from (I) will, owing to inheritance alone, differ considerably from the eight descendants from (A); the two groups, moreover, are supposed to have gone on diverging in different directions. The intermediate species, also (and this is a very important consideration), which connected the original species (A) and (I), have become, expecting (F), extinct, and have left no descendants. Hence the six new species descended from (I), and the eight descendants from (A), will have to be ranked as very distinct genera, or even as distinct sub-families.

Thus it is, as I believe, that two or more genera are produced by descent with modification, from two or more species of the same genus. And the two or more parent-species are supposed to be descended from some one species of an earlier genus. In our diagram, this is indicated by the broken lines, beneath the capital letters, converging in sub-branches downwards towards a single point; this point represents a species, the supposed progenitor of our several new sub-genera and genera.

It is worth while to reflect for a moment on the character of the new species F^{14}, which is supposed not to have diverged much in character, but to have retained the form of (F), either unaltered or altered only in a slight degree. In this case, its affinities to the other fourteen new species will be of a curious and circuitous nature. Being descended from a form which stood between the parent-species (A) and (I), now supposed to be extinct and unknown, it will be in some degree intermediate in character between the two groups descended from these two species. But as these two groups have gone on diverging in character from the type of their parents, the new species (F^{14}) will not be directly intermediate between them, but rather between types of the two groups; and every naturalist will be able to call such cases before his mind.

In the diagram, each horizontal line has hitherto been supposed to represent a thousand generations, but each may represent a million or more generations; it may also represent a section of the successive strata of the earth's crust including extinct remains. We shall, when we come to our chapter on Geology, have to refer again to this subject, and I think we shall then see that the diagram throws light on the affinities of extinct beings, which, though generally belonging to the same orders, families, or genera, with those now living, yet are often, in some degree, intermediate in character between existing groups; and we can understand this fact, for the extinct species lived at various remote epochs when the branching lines of descent had diverged less.

I see no reason to limit the process of modification, as now explained, to the formation of genera alone. If, in the diagram, we suppose the amount of change, represented by each successive group of diverging dotted lines to be great, the forms marked a^{14} to p^{14}, those marked b^{14} and f^{14}, and those marked o^{14} to m^{14}, will form three very distinct genera. We shall also have two very distinct genera descended from(I), differing widely from the descendants of (A). These two groups of genera will thus form two distinct families, or orders, according to the amount of divergent modification supposed to be represented in the diagram. And the two new families, or orders, are descended from two species of the original genus, and these are supposed to be descended from some still more ancient and unknown form.

We have seen that in each country it is the species belonging to the larger genera which oftenest present varieties or incipient species. This, indeed, might have been expected; for, as natural selection acts through one form having some advantage over other forms in the struggle for existence, it will chiefly act on those which already have some advantage; and the largeness of any group shows that its species have inherited from a common ancestor some advantage in common. Hence, the struggle for the production of new and modified descendants will mainly lie between the larger groups which are all trying to increase in number. One large group will slowly conquer another large group, reduce its numbers, and thus lessen its chance of further variation and improvement. Within the same large group, the later and more highly perfected sub-groups, from branching out and seizing on many new places in the polity of Nature, will constantly tend to supplant and destroy the earlier and less improved sub-groups. Small and broken groups and sub-groups will finally disappear. Looking to the future, we can predict that the groups of organic beings which are now large and triumphant, and which are least broken up, that is, which have as yet suffered least extinction, will, for a long period, continue to increase. But which groups will ultimately prevail, no man can predict; for we know that many groups formerly most extensively developed, have now become extinct. Looking still more remotely to the future, we may predict that, owing to the continued and steady increase of the larger groups, a multitude of smaller groups will become utterly extinct, and leave no modified descendants; and consequently that, of the species living at any one period, extremely few will transmit descendants to a remote futurity. I shall have to return to this subject in the chapter on Classification, but I may add that as, according to this view, extremely few of the more ancient species have transmitted descendants to the present day, and, as all the descendants of the same species form a class, we can understand how it is that there exist so few classes in each main division of the animal and vegetable kingdoms. Although few of the most ancient species have left modified descendants, yet, at remote geological periods, the earth may have been almost as well peopled with species of many genera, families, orders, and classes, as at the present time.

ON THE DEGREE TO WHICH ORGANISATION TENDS TO ADVANCE

Natural Selection acts exclusively by the preservation and accumulation of variations, which are beneficial under the organic and inorganic conditions to which each creature is exposed at all periods of life. The ultimate result is that each creature tends to become more and more improved in relation to its conditions. This improvement inevitably leads to the gradual advancement of the organisation of the greater number of living beings throughout the world. But here we enter on a very intricate subject, for naturalists have not defined to each other's satisfaction what is meant by an advance in organisation. Amongst the vertebrata the degree of intellect and an approach in structure to man clearly come into play. It might be thought that the amount of change which the various parts and organs pass through in their development from the embryo to maturity would suffice as a standard of comparison; but there are cases, as with certain parasitic crustaceans, in which several parts of the structure become less perfect, so that the mature animal cannot be called higher than its larva. Von Baer's standard seems the most widely applicable and the best, namely, the amount of differentiation of the parts of the same organic being, in the adult state as I should be inclined to add, and their specialisation for different functions; or, as Milne Edwards would express it, the completeness of the division is physiological labour. But we shall see how obscure this subject is if we look, for instance, to fishes, amongst which some naturalists rank those as highest which, like the sharks, approach nearest to amphibians; whilst other naturalists rank the common bony or teleostean fishes as the highest, inasmuch as they are most strictly fish-like and differ most from the other vertebrate classes. We see still more plainly the obscurity of the subject by turning to plants, amongst which the standard of intellect is of course quite excluded; and here some botanists rank those plants as highest which have every organ, as sepals, petals, stamens, and pistils, fully developed in each flower; whereas other botanists, probably with more truth, look at the plants which have their several organs much modified and reduced in number as the highest.

If we take as the standard of high organisation, the amount of differentiation and specialisation of the several organs in each being when adult (and this will include the advancement of the brain for intellectual purposes), natural selection clearly leads towards this standard: for all physiologists admit that the specialisation of organs, inasmuch as in this state they perform their functions better, is an advantage to each being; and hence the accumulation of variations tending towards specialisation is within the scope of natural selection. On the other hand, we can see, bearing in mind that all organic beings are striving to increase at a high ratio and to seize on every unoccupied or less well occupied place in the economy of nature, that it is quite possible for natural selection gradually to fit a being to a situation in which several organs would be superfluous or useless: in such cases there would be retrogression in the scale of organisation. Whether organisation on the whole has actually advanced from the remotest geological periods to the present day will be more conveniently discussed in our chapter on Geological Succession.

But it may be objected that if all organic beings thus tend to rise in the scale, how is it that throughout the world a multitude of the lowest forms still exist; and how is it that in each great class some forms are far more highly developed than others? Why have not the more highly developed forms everywhere supplanted and exterminated the lower? Lamarck, who believed in an innate and inevitable tendency towards perfection in all organic beings, seems to have felt this difficulty so strongly, that he was led to suppose that new and simple forms are continually being produced by spontaneous generation. Science has not as yet proved the truth of this belief, whatever the future may reveal. On our theory the continued existence of lowly organisms offers no difficulty; for natural selection, or the survival of the fittest, does not necessarily include progressive development—it only takes advantage of such variations as arise and are beneficial to each creature under its complex relations of life. And it may be asked what advantage, as far as we can see, would it be to an infusorian animalcule—to an intestinal worm—or even to an earthworm, to be highly organised. If it were no advantage, these forms would be left, by natural selection, unimproved or but little improved, and might remain for indefinite ages in their present lowly condition. And geology tells us that some of the lowest forms, as the infusoria and rhizopods, have remained for an enormous period in nearly their present state. But to suppose that most of the many now existing low forms have not in the least advanced since the first dawn of life would be extremely rash; for every naturalist who has dissected some of the beings now ranked as very low in the scale, must have been struck with their really wondrous and beautiful organisation.

Nearly the same remarks are applicable if we look to the different grades of organisation within the same great group; for instance, in the vertebrata, to the co-existence of mammals and fish —amongst mammalia, to the co-existence of man and the ornithorhynchus—amongst fishes, to the co-existence of the shark and the lancelet (Amphioxus), which latter fish in the extreme simplicity of its structure approaches the invertebrate classes. But mammals and fish hardly come into competition with each other; the advancement of the whole class of mammals, or of certain members in this class, to the highest grade would not lead to their taking the place of fishes. Physiologists believe that the brain must be bathed by warm blood to be highly active, and this requires aërial respiration; so that warm-blooded mammals when inhabiting the water lie under a disadvantage in having to come continually to the surface to breathe. With fishes, members of the shark family would not tend to supplant the lancelet; for the lancelet, as I hear from Fritz Müller, has as sole companion and competitor on the barren sandy shore of South Brazil, an anomalous annelid. The three lowest orders of mammals, namely, marsupials, edentata, and rodents, co-exist in South America in the same region with numerous monkeys, and probably interfere little with each other. Although organisation, on the whole, may have advanced and be still advancing throughout the world, yet the scale will always present many degrees of perfection; for the high advancement of certain whole classes, or of certain members of each class, does not at all necessarily lead to the extinction of those groups with which they do not enter into close competition. In some cases, as we shall hereafter see, lowly organised forms appear to have been preserved to the present day, from inhabiting confined or peculiar stations, where they have been subjected to less severe competition, and where their scanty numbers have retarded the chance of favourable variations arising.

Finally, I believe that many lowly organised forms now exist throughout the world, from various causes. In some cases variations or individual differences of a favourable nature may never have arisen for natural selection to act on and accumulate. In no case, probably, has time sufficed for the utmost possible amount of development. In some few cases there has been what we must call retrogression of organisation. But the main cause lies in the fact that under very simple conditions of life a high organisation would be of no service,—possibly would be of actual disservice, as being of a more delicate nature, and more liable to be put out of order and injured.

Looking to the first dawn of life, when all organic beings, as we may believe, presented the simplest structure, how, it has been asked, could the first steps in the advancement or differentiation of parts have arisen? Mr. Herbert Spencer would probably answer that, as soon as simple unicellular organism came by growth or division to be compounded of several cells, or became attached to any supporting surface, his law "that homologous units of any order become differentiated in proportion as their relations to incident forces become different" would come into action. But as we have no facts to guide us, speculation on the subject is almost useless. It is, however, an error to suppose that there would be no struggle for existence, and, consequently, no natural selection, until many forms had been produced: variations in a single species inhabiting an isolated station might be beneficial, and thus the whole mass of individuals might be modified, or two distinct forms might arise. But, as I remarked towards the close of the Introduction, no one ought to feel surprise at much remaining as yet unexplained on the origin of species, if we make due allowance for our profound ignorance on the mutual relations of the inhabitants of the world at the present time, and still more so during past ages. * * *

SUMMARY OF CHAPTER

If under changing conditions of life organic beings present individual differences in almost every part of their structure, and this cannot be disputed; if there be, owing to their geometrical rate of increase, a severe struggle for life at some age, season, or year, and this certainly cannot be disputed; then, considering the infinite complexity of the relations of all organic beings to each other and to their conditions of life, causing an infinite diversity in structure, constitution, and habits, to be advantageous to them, it would be a most extraordinary fact if no variations had ever occurred useful to each being's own welfare, in the same manner as so many variations have occurred useful to man. But if variations useful to any organic being ever do occur, assuredly individuals thus characterised will have the best chance of being preserved in the struggle for life; and from the strong principle of inheritance, these will tend to produce offspring similarly characterised. This principle of preservation, or the survival of the fittest, I have called Natural Selection. It leads to the improvement of each creature in relation to its organic and inorganic conditions of life; and consequently, in most cases, to what must be regarded as an advance in organisation. Nevertheless, low and simple forms will long endure if well fitted for their simple conditions of life.

Natural selection, on the principle of qualities being inherited at corresponding ages, can modify the egg, seed, or young, as easily as the adult. Amongst many animals, sexual selection will have given its aid to ordinary selection, by assuring to the most vigorous and best adapted males the greatest number of offspring. Sexual selection will also give characters useful to the males alone, in their struggles or rivalry with other males; and these characters will be transmitted to one sex or to both sexes, according to the form of inheritance which prevails.

Whether natural selection has really thus acted in adapting the various forms of life to their several conditions and stations, must be judged by the general tenor and balance of evidence given in the following chapters. But we have already seen how it entails extinction; and how largely extinction has acted in the world's history, geology plainly declares. Natural selection, also leads to divergence of character; for the more organic beings diverge in structure, habits, and constitution, by so much the more can a large number be supported on the area,—of which we see proof by looking to the inhabitants of any small spot, and to the productions naturalised in foreign lands. Therefore, during the modification of the descendants of any one species, and during the incessant struggle of all species to increase in numbers, the more diversified the descendants become, the better will be their chance of success in the battle for life. Thus the small differences distinguishing varieties of the same species, steadily tend to increase, till they equal the greater differences between species of the same genus, or even of distinct genera.

We have seen that it is the common, the widely-diffused and widely-ranging species, belonging to the larger genera within each class, which vary most; and these tend to transmit to their modified offspring that superiority which now makes them dominant in their own countries. Natural selection, as has just been remarked, leads to divergence of character and to much extinction of the less improved and intermediate forms of life. On these principles, the nature of the affinities, and the generally well-defined distinctions between the innumerable organic beings in each class throughout the world, may be explained. It is a truly wonderful fact—the wonder of which we are apt to overlook from familiarity—that all animals and all plants throughout all time and space should be related to each other in groups, subordinate to groups, in the manner which we everywhere behold—namely, varieties of the same species most closely related, species of the same genus less closely and unequally related, forming sections and sub-genera, species of distinct genera much less closely related, and genera related in different degrees, forming sub-families, families, orders, sub-classes and classes. The several subordinate groups in any class cannot be ranked in a single file, but seem clustered round points, and these round other points, and so on in almost endless cycles. If species had been independently created, no explanation would have been possible of this kind of classification; but it is explained through inheritance and the complex action of natural selection, entailing extinction and divergence of character, as we have seen illustrated in the diagram.

The affinities of all the beings of the same class have sometimes been represented by a great tree. I believe this simile largely speaks the truth. The green and budding twigs may represent existing species; and those produced during former years may represent the long succession of extinct species. At each period of growth all the growing twigs have tried to branch out on all sides, and to overtop and kill the surrounding twigs and branches, in the same manner as species and groups of species have at all times overmastered other species in the great battle for life. The limbs divided into great branches, and these into lesser and lesser branches, were themselves once, when the tree was young, budding twigs, and this connection of the former and present buds by ramifying branches may well represent the classification of all extinct and living species in groups subordinate to groups. Of the many twigs which flourished when the tree was a mere bush, only two or three, now grown into great branches, yet survive and bear the other branches; so with the species which lived during long-past geological periods, very few have left living and modified descendants. From the first growth of the tree, many a limb and branch has decayed and dropped off; and these fallen branches of various sizes may represent those whole orders, families, and genera which have now no living representatives, and which are known to us only in a fossil state. As we here and there see a thin straggling branch springing from a fork low down in a tree, and which by some chance has been favoured and is still alive on its summit, so we occasionally see an animal like the Ornithorhynchus or Lepidosiren, which in some small degree connects by its affinities two large branches of life, and which has apparently been saved from fatal competition by having inhabited a protected station. As buds give rise by growth to fresh buds, and these, if vigorous, branch out and overtop on all sides many a feebler branch, so by generation I believe it has been with the great Tree of Life, which fills with its dead and broken branches the crust of the earth, and covers the surface with its ever-branching and beautiful ramifications.

Chapter VI

DIFFICULTIES OF THE THEORY

Difficulties of the theory of descent with modification—Absence or rarity of transitional varieties—Transitions in habits of life—Diversified habits in the same species—Species with habits widely differ-

*ent from those of their allies—Organs of extreme perfection—
Modes of transition—Cases of difficulty—Natura non facit saltum
—Organs of small importance—Organs not in all cases absolutely
perfect—The law of unity of type and of the conditions of existence
embraced by the theory of natural selection.*

Long before the reader has arrived at this part of my work, a
crowd of difficulties will have occurred to him. Some of them are
so serious that to this day I can hardly reflect on them without
being in some degree staggered; but, to the best of my judgment,
the greater number are only apparent, and those that are real are
not, I think, fatal to the theory.

These difficulties and objections may be classed under the following heads:—First, why, if species have descended from other
species by fine gradations, do we not everywhere see innumerable
transitional forms? Why is not all nature in confusion instead of
the species being, as we see them, well defined?

Secondly, is it possible that an animal having, for instance, the
structure and habits of a bat, could have been formed by the modification of some other animal with widely different habits and
structure? Can we believe that natural selection could produce, on
the one hand, an organ of trifling importance, such as the tail of a
giraffe, which serves as a fly-flapper, and, on the other hand, an
organ so wonderful as the eye?

Thirdly, can instincts be acquired and modified through natural
selection? What shall we say to the instinct which leads the bee to
make cells, and which has practically anticipated the discoveries of
profound mathematicians?

Fourthly, how can we account for species, when crossed, being
sterile and producing sterile offspring, whereas, when varieties are
crossed, their fertility is unimpaired?

The two first heads will here be discussed; some miscellaneous
objections in the following chapter; Instinct and Hybridism in the
two succeeding chapters.

ON THE ABSENCE OR RARITY OF TRANSITIONAL VARIETIES

As natural selection acts solely by the preservation of profitable
modifications, each new form will tend in a fully-stocked country to
take the place of, and finally to exterminate, its own less improved
parent-form and other less favoured forms with which it comes into
competition. Thus extinction and natural selection go hand in
hand. Hence, if we look at each species as descended from some
unknown form, both the parent and all the transitional varieties
will generally have been exterminated by the very process of the
formation and perfection of the new form.

But, as by this theory innumerable transitional forms must have existed, why do we not find them embedded in countless numbers in the crust of the earth? It will be more convenient to discuss this question in the chapter on the Imperfection of the Geological Record; and I will here only state that I believe the answer mainly lies in the record being incomparably less perfect than is generally supposed. The crust of the earth is a vast museum; but the natural collections have been imperfectly made, and only at long intervals of time.

But it may be urged that when several closely-allied species inhabit the same territory, we surely ought to find at the present time many transitional forms. Let us take a simple case: in travelling from north to south over a continent, we generally meet at successive intervals with closely allied or representative species, evidently filling nearly the same place in the natural economy of the land. These representative species often meet and interlock; and as the one becomes rarer and rarer, the other becomes more and more frequent, till the one replaces the other. But if we compare these species where they intermingle, they are generally as absolutely distinct from each other in every detail of structure as are specimens taken from the metropolis inhabited by each. By my theory these allied species are descended from a common parent; and during the process of modification, each has become adapted to the conditions of life of its own region, and has supplanted and exterminated its original parent-form and all the transitional varieties between its past and present states. Hence we ought not to expect at the present time to meet with numerous transitional varieties in each region, though they must have existed there, and may be embedded there in a fossil condition. But in the intermediate region, having intermediate conditions of life, why do we not now find closely-linking intermediate varieties? This difficulty for a long time quite confounded me. But I think it can be in large part explained.

In the first place we should be extremely cautious in inferring, because an area is now continuous, that it has been continuous during a long period. Geology would lead us to believe that most continents have been broken up into islands even during the later tertiary periods; and in such islands distinct species might have been separately formed without the possibility of intermediate varieties existing in the intermediate zones. By changes in the form of the land and of climate, marine areas now continuous must often have existed within recent times in a far less continuous and uniform condition than at present. But I will pass over this way of escaping from the difficulty; for I believe that many perfectly defined species have been formed on strictly continuous areas; though I do not doubt that the formerly broken condition of areas now continuous, has played an important part in the formation of new species, more especially with freely-crossing and wandering animals.

In looking at species as they are now distributed over a wide area, we generally find them tolerably numerous over a large territory, then becoming somewhat abruptly rarer and rarer on the confines, and finally disappearing. Hence the neutral territory, between two representative species is generally narrow in comparison with the territory proper to each. We see the same fact in ascending mountains, and sometimes it is quite remarkable how abruptly, as Alph. de Candolle has observed, a common alpine species disappears. The same fact has been noticed by E. Forbes in sounding the depths of the sea with the dredge. To those who look at climate and the physical conditions of life as the all-important elements of distribution, these facts ought to cause surprise, as climate and height or depth graduate away insensibly. But when we bear in mind that almost every species, even in its metropolis, would increase immensely in numbers, were it not for other competing species; that nearly all either prey on or serve as prey for others; in short, that each organic being is either directly or indirectly related in the most important manner to other organic beings,—we see that the range of the inhabitants of any country by no means exclusively depends on insensibly changing physical conditions, but in a large part on the presence of other species, on which it lives, or by which it is destroyed, or with which it comes into competition; and as these species are already defined objects, not blending one into another by insensible gradations, the range of any one species, depending as it does on the range of others, will tend to be sharply defined. Moreover, each species on the confines of its range, where it exists in lessened numbers, will, during fluctuations in the number of its enemies or of its prey, or in the nature of the seasons, be extremely liable to utter extermination; and thus its geographical range will come to be still more sharply defined.

As allied or representative species, when inhabiting a continuous area, are generally distributed in such a manner that each has a wide range, with a comparatively narrow neutral territory between them, in which they become rather suddenly rarer and rarer; then, as varieties do not essentially differ from species, the same rule will probably apply to both; and if we take a varying species inhabiting a very large area, we shall have to adapt two varieties to two large areas, and a third variety to a narrow intermediate zone. The intermediate variety, consequently, will exist in lesser numbers from inhabiting a narrow and lesser area; and practically, as far as I can make out, this rule holds good with varieties in a state of nature. I have met with striking instances of the rule in the case of varieties intermediate between well-marked varieties in the genus Balanus. And it would appear from information given me by Mr. Watson, Dr. Asa Gray, and Mr. Wollaston, that generally, when varieties intermediate between two other forms occur, they are much rarer numerically than the forms which they connect. Now, if we may trust these facts and inferences, and conclude that varieties linking two other varieties together generally have existed in lesser numbers than the forms which they connect, then we can understand why intermediate varieties should not endure for very long periods: —why, as a general rule, they should be exterminated and disappear, sooner than the forms which they originally linked together.

For any form existing in lesser numbers would, as already remarked, run a greater chance of being exterminated than one existing in large numbers; and in this particular case the intermediate form would be eminently liable to the inroads of closely-allied forms existing on both sides of it. But it is a far more important consideration, that during the process of further modification, by which two varieties are supposed to be converted and perfected into two distinct species, the two which exist in larger numbers, from inhabiting larger areas, will have a great advantage over the intermediate variety, which exists in smaller numbers in a narrow and intermediate zone. For forms existing in larger numbers will have a better chance, within any given period, of presenting further favourable variations for natural selection to seize on, than will the rarer forms which exist in lesser numbers. Hence, the more common forms, in the race for life, will tend to beat and supplant the less common forms, for these will be more slowly modified and improved. It is the same principle which, as I believe, accounts for the common species in each country, as shown in the second chapter, presenting on an average a greater number of well-marked varieties than do the rarer species. I may illustrate what I mean by supposing three varieties of sheep to be kept, one adapted to an extensive mountainous region; a second to a comparatively narrow, hilly tract; and a third to the wide plains at the base; and that the inhabitants are all trying with equal steadiness and skill to improve their stocks by selection; the chances in this case will be strongly in favour of the great holders on the mountains or on the plains, improving their breeds more quickly than the small holders on the intermediate narrow, hilly tract; and consequently the improved mountain or plain breed will soon take the place of the less improved hill breed; and thus the two breeds, which originally existed in greater numbers, will come into close contact with each other, without the interposition of the supplanted, intermediate hill variety.

To sum up, I believe that species come to be tolerably well-defined objects, and do not at any one period present an inextricable chaos of varying and intermediate links; first, because new varieties are very slowly formed, for variation is a slow process, and natural selection can do nothing until favourable individual differences or variations occur, and until a place in the natural polity of the country can be better filled by some modification of some one or more of its inhabitants. And such new places will depend on slow changes of climate, or on the occasional immigration of new inhabitants, and, probably, in a still more important degree, on some of the old inhabitants becoming slowly modified, with the new forms thus produced, and the old ones acting and reacting on each other. So that, in any one region and at any one time, we ought to see only a few species presenting slight modifications of structure in some degree permanent; and this assuredly we do see.

Secondly, areas now continuous must often have existed within the recent period as isolated portions, in which many forms, more especially amongst the classes which unite for each birth and wander much, may have separately been rendered sufficiently distinct to rank as representative species. In this case, intermediate varieties between the several representative species and their common parent, must formerly have existed within each isolated portion of the land, but these links during the process of natural selection will have been supplanted and exterminated, so that they will no longer be found in a living state.

Thirdly, when two or more varieties have been formed in different portions of a strictly continuous area, intermediate varieties will, it is probable, at first have been formed in the intermediate zones, but they will generally have had a short duration. For these intermediate varieties will, from reasons already assigned (namely from what we know of the actual distribution of closely allied or representative species, and likewise of acknowledged varieties), exist in the intermediate zones in lesser numbers than the varieties which they tend to connect. From this cause alone the intermediate varieties will be liable to accidental extermination; and during the process of further modification through natural selection, they will almost certainly be beaten and supplanted by the forms which they connect; for these from existing in greater numbers will, in the aggregate, present more varieties, and thus be further improved through natural selection and gain further advantages.

Lastly, looking not to any one time, but to all time, if my theory be true, numberless intermediate varieties, linking closely together all the species of the same group, must assuredly have existed; but the very process of natural selection constantly tends, as has been so often remarked, to exterminate the parent-forms and the intermediate links. Consequently evidence of their former existence could be found only amongst fossil remains, which are preserved, as we shall attempt to show in a future chapter, in an extremely imperfect and intermittent record.

ON THE ORIGIN AND TRANSITIONS OF ORGANIC BEINGS WITH PECULIAR HABITS AND STRUCTURE

It has been asked by the opponents of such views as I hold, how, for instance, could a land carnivorous animal have been converted into one with aquatic habits; for how could the animal in its transitional state have subsisted? It would be easy to show that there now exist carnivorous animals presenting close intermediate grades from strictly terrestrial to aquatic habits; and as each exists by a struggle for life, it is clear that each must be well adapted to its place in nature. Look at the Mustela vison of North America, which has webbed feet, and which resembles an otter in its fur, short legs, and form of tail. During the summer this animal dives for and preys on fish, but during the long winter it leaves the frozen waters, and preys, like other pole-cats, on mice and land animals. If a different case had been taken, and it had been asked how an insectivorous quadruped could possibly have been converted into a flying bat, the question would have been far more difficult to answer. Yet I think such difficulties have little weight.

Here, as on other occasions, I lie under a heavy disadvantage, for, out of the many striking cases which I have collected, I can only give one or two instances of transitional habits and structures in allied species; and of diversified habits, either constant or occasional, in the same species. And it seems to me that nothing less than a long list of such cases is sufficient to lessen the difficulty in any particular case like that of the bat.

Look at the family of squirrels; here we have the finest gradation from animals with their tails only slightly flattened, and from others, as Sir J. Richardson has remarked, with the posterior part of their bodies rather wide and with the skin on their flanks rather full, to the so-called flying squirrels; and flying squirrels have their limbs and even the base of the tail united by a broad expanse of skin, which serves as a parachute and allows them to glide through the air to an astonishing distance from tree to tree. We cannot doubt that each structure is of use to each kind of squirrel in its own country, by enabling it to escape birds or beasts of prey, to collect food more quickly, or, as there is reason to believe, to lessen the danger from occasional falls. But it does not follow from this fact that the structure of each squirrel is the best that it is possible to conceive under all possible conditions. Let the climate and vegetation change, let other competing rodents or new beasts of prey immigrate, or old ones become modified, and all analogy would lead us to believe that some at least of the squirrels would decrease in numbers or become exterminated, unless they also become modified and improved in structure in a corresponding manner. Therefore, I can see no difficulty, more especially under changing conditions of life, in the continued preservation of individuals with fuller and fuller flank-membranes, each modification being useful, each being propagated, until by the accumulated effects of this process of natural selection, a perfect so-called flying squirrel was produced.

Now look at the Galeopithecus or so-called flying lemur, which formerly was ranked amongst bats, but is now believed to belong to the Insectivora. An extremely wide flank-membrane stretches from the corners of the jaw to the tail, and includes the limbs with the elongated fingers. This flank-membrane is furnished with an extensor muscle. Although no graduated links of structure, fitted for gliding through the air, now connect the Galeopithecus with the other Insectivora, yet there is no difficulty in supposing that such links formerly existed, and that each was developed in the same manner as with the less perfectly gliding squirrels; each grade of structure having been useful to its possessor. Nor can I see any insuperable difficulty in further believing that the membrane connected fingers and fore-arm of the Galeopithecus might have been greatly lengthened by natural selection; and this, as far as the organs of flight are concerned, would have converted the animal into a bat. In certain bats in which the wing-membrane extends from the top of the shoulder to the tail and includes the hind-legs, we perhaps see traces of an apparatus originally fitted for gliding through the air rather than for flight.

If about a dozen genera of birds were to become extinct, who would have ventured to surmise that birds might have existed which used their wings solely as flappers, like the logger-headed duck (Micropterus of Eyton); as fins in the water and as front-legs on the land, like the penguin; as sails, like the ostrich; and functionally for no purpose, like the Apteryx? Yet the structure of each of these birds is good for it, under the conditions of life to which it is exposed, for each has to live by a struggle; but it is not necessarily the best possible under all possible conditions. It must not be inferred from these remarks that any of the grades of wing-structure here alluded to, which perhaps may all be the result of disuse, indicate the steps by which birds actually acquired their perfect power of flight; but they serve to show what diversified means of transition are at least possible.

Seeing that a few members of such water-breathing classes as the Crustacea and Mollusca are adapted to live on the land; and seeing that we have flying birds and mammals, flying insects of the most diversified types, and formerly had flying reptiles, it is conceivable that flying-fish, which now glide far through the air, slightly rising and turning by the aid of their fluttering fins, might have been modified into perfectly winged animals. If this had been effected, who would have ever imagined that in an early transitional state they had been the inhabitants of the open ocean, and had used their incipient organs of flight exclusively, as far as we know, to escape being devoured by other fish?

When we see any structure highly perfected for any particular habit, as the wings of a bird for flight, we should bear in mind that animals displaying early transitional grades of the structure will seldom have survived to the present day, for they will have been supplanted by their successors, which were gradually rendered more perfect through natural selection. Furthermore, we may conclude that transitional states between structures fitted for very different habits of life will rarely have been developed at an early period in great numbers and under many subordinate forms. Thus, to return to our imaginary illustration of the flying-fish, it does not seem probable that fishes capable of true flight would have been developed under many subordinate forms, for taking prey of many kinds in many ways, on the land and in the water, until their organs of flight had come to a high stage of perfection, so as to have given them a decided advantage over other animals in the battle for life. Hence the chance of discovering species with transitional grades of structure in a fossil condition will always be less, from their having existed in lesser numbers, than in the case of species with fully developed structures.

I will now give two or three instances both of diversified and of changed habits in the individuals of the same species. In either case it would be easy for natural selection to adapt the structure of the animal to its changed habits, or exclusively to one of its several habits. It is, however, difficult to decide, and immaterial for us, whether habits generally change first and structure afterwards; or whether slight modifications of structure lead to changed habits; both probably often occurring almost simultaneously. Of cases of changed habits it will suffice merely to allude to that of the many British insects which now feed on exotic plants, or exclusively on artificial substances. Of diversified habits innumerable instances could be given: I have often watched a tyrant flycatcher (Saurophagus sulphuratus) in South America, hovering over one spot and then proceeding to another, like a kestrel, and at other times standing stationary on the margin of water, and then dashing into it like a king-fisher at a fish. In our own country the larger titmouse (Parus major) may be seen climbing branches, almost like a creeper; it sometimes, like a shrike, kills small birds by blows on the head; and I have many times seen and heard it hammering the seeds of the yew on a branch, and thus breaking them like a nuthatch. In North America the black bear was seen by Hearne swimming for hours with widely open mouth, thus catching, almost like a whale, insects in the water.

As we sometimes see individuals following habits different from those proper to their species and to the other species of the same genus, we might expect that such individuals would occasionally give rise to new species, having anomalous habits, and with their structure either slightly or considerably modified from that of their type. And such instances occur in nature. Can a more striking instance of adaptation be given than that of a woodpecker for climbing trees and seizing insects in the chinks of the bark? Yet in North America there are woodpeckers which feed largely on fruit, and others with elongated wings which chase insects on the wing. On the plains of La Plata, where hardly a tree grows, there is a woodpecker (Colaptes campestris) which has two toes before and two behind, a long pointed tongue, pointed tail-feathers, sufficiently stiff to support the bird in a vertical position on a post, but not so stiff as in the typical woodpeckers, and a straight strong beak. The beak, however, is not so straight or so strong as in the typical woodpeckers, but it is strong enough to bore into wood. Hence this Colaptes in all the essential parts of its structure is a woodpecker. Even in such trifling characters as the colouring, the harsh tone of the voice, and undulatory flight, its close blood-relationship to our common woodpecker is plainly declared; yet, as I can assert, not only from my own observation, but from those of the accurate Azara, in certain large districts it does not climb trees, and it makes its nest in holes in banks! In certain other districts, however, this same woodpecker, as Mr. Hudson states, frequents trees, and bores holes in the trunk for its nest. I may mention as another illustration of the varied habits of this genus, that a Mexican Colaptes has been described by De Saussure as boring holes into hard wood in order to lay up a store of acorns.

Petrels are the most aërial and oceanic of birds, but in the quiet sounds of Tierra del Fuego, the Puffinuria berardi, in its general habits, in its astonishing power of diving, in its manner of swimming and of flying when made to take flight, would be mistaken by any one for an auk or a grebe; nevertheless it is essentially a petrel, but with many parts of its organisation profoundly modified in relation to its new habits of life; whereas the woodpecker of La Plata has had its structure only slightly modified. In the case of the water-ouzel, the acutest observer by examining its dead body would never have suspected its sub-aquatic habits; yet this bird, which is allied to the thrush family, subsists by diving—using its wings under water, and grasping stones with its feet. All the members of the great order of Hymenopterous insects are terrestrial, excepting the genus Proctotrupes, which Sir John Lubbock has discovered to be aquatic in its habits; it often enters the water and dives about by the use not of its legs but of its wings, and remains as long as four hours beneath the surface; yet it exhibits no modification in structure in accordance with its abnormal habits.

He who believes that each being has been created as we now see it, must occasionally have felt surprise when he has met with an animal having habits and structure not in agreement. What can be plainer than that the webbed feet of ducks and geese are formed for swimming? Yet there are upland geese with webbed feet which rarely go near the water; and no one except Audubon has seen the frigate-bird, which has all its four toes webbed, alight on the surface of the ocean. On the other hand, grebes and coots are eminently aquatic, although their toes are only bordered by membrane. What seems plainer than that the long toes, not furnished with membrane of the Grallatores are formed for walking over swamps and floating plants?—the waterhen and landrail are members of this order, yet the first is nearly as aquatic as the coot, and the second nearly as terrestrial as the quail or partridge. In such cases, and many others could be given, habits have changed without a corresponding change of structure. The webbed feet of the upland goose may be said to have become almost rudimentary in function, though not in structure. In the frigate-bird, the deeply scooped membrane between the toes shows that structure has begun to change.

He who believes in separate and innumerable acts of creation may say, that in these cases it has pleased the Creator to cause a being of one type to take the place of one belonging to another type; but this seems to me only re-stating the fact in dignified language. He who believes in the struggle for existence and in the principle of natural selection, will acknowledge that every organic being is constantly endeavouring to increase in numbers; and that if any one being varies ever so little, either in habits or structure, and thus gains an advantage over some other inhabitant of the same country, it will seize on the place of that inhabitant, however different that may be from its own place. Hence it will cause him no surprise that there should be geese and frigate-birds with webbed feet, living on the dry land and rarely alighting on the water, that there should be long-toed corncrakes, living in meadows instead of in swamps; that there should be woodpeckers where hardly a tree grows; that there should be diving thrushes and diving Hymenoptera, and petrels with the habits of auks.

ORGANS OF EXTREME PERFECTION AND COMPLICATION

To suppose that the eye with all its inimitable contrivances for adjusting the focus to different distances, for admitting different amounts of light, and for the correction of spherical and chromatic aberration, could have been formed by natural selection, seems, I freely confess, absurd in the highest degree. When it was first said that the sun stood still and the world turned round, the common sense of mankind declared the doctrine false; but the old saying of *Vox populi, vox Dei,* as every philosopher knows, cannot be trusted in science. Reason tells me, that if numerous gradations from a simple and imperfect eye to one complex and perfect can be shown to exist, each grade being useful to its possessor, as is certainly the case; if further, the eye ever varies and the variations be inherited, as is likewise certainly the case; and if such variations should be useful to any animal under changing conditions of life, then the difficulty of believing that a perfect and complex eye could be formed by natural selection, though insuperable by our imagination, should not be considered as subversive of the theory. How a nerve comes to be sensitive to light, hardly concerns us more than how life itself originated; but I may remark that, as some of the lowest organisms, in which nerves cannot be detected, are capable of perceiving light, it does not seem impossible that certain elements in their sarcode should become aggregated and developed into nerves, endowed with this special sensibility.

In searching for the gradations through which an organ in any species has been perfected, we ought to look exclusively to its lineal progenitors; but this is scarcely ever possible, and we are forced to look to other species and genera of the same group, that is to the collateral descendants from the same parent-form, in order to see what gradations are possible, and for the chance of some gradations having been transmitted in an unaltered or little altered condition. But the state of the same organ in distinct classes may incidentally throw light on the steps by which it has been perfected.

The simplest organ which can be called an eye consists of an optic nerve, surrounded by pigment-cells and covered by translucent skin, but without any lens or other refractive body. We may, however, according to M. Jourdain, descend even a step lower and find aggregates of pigment-cells, apparently serving as organs of vision, without any nerves, and resting merely on sarcodic tissue. Eyes of the above simple nature are not capable of distinct vision, and serve only to distinguish light from darkness. In certain starfishes, small depressions in the layer of pigment which surrounds the nerve are filled, as described by the author just quoted, with transparent gelatinous matter, projecting with a convex surface, like the cornea in the higher animals. He suggests that this serves not to form an image, but only to concentrate the luminous rays and render their perception more easy. In this concentration of the rays we gain the first and by far the most important step towards the formation of a true, picture-forming eye; for we have only to place the naked extremity of the optic nerve, which in some of the lower animals lies deeply buried in the body, and in some near the surface, at the right distance from the concentrating apparatus, and an image will be formed on it.

In the great class of the Articulata, we may start from an optic nerve simply coated with pigment, the latter sometimes forming a sort of pupil, but destitute of a lens or other optical contrivance. With insects it is now known that the numerous facets on the cornea of their great compound eyes form true lenses, and that the cones include curiously modified nervous filaments. But these organs in the Articulata are so much diversified that Müller formerly made three main classes with seven subdivisions, besides a fourth main class of aggregated simple eyes.

When we reflect on these facts, here given much too briefly, with respect to the wide, diversified, and graduated range of structure in the eyes of the lower animals; and when we bear in mind how small the number of all living forms must be in comparison with those which have become extinct, the difficulty ceases to be very great in believing that natural selection may have converted the simple apparatus of an optic nerve, coated with pigment and invested by transparent membrane, into an optical instrument as perfect as is possessed by any member of the Articulate Class.

He who will go thus far, ought not to hesitate to go one step further, if he finds on finishing this volume that large bodies of facts, otherwise inexplicable, can be explained by the theory of modification through natural selection; he ought to admit that with a structure even as perfect as an eagle's eye might thus be formed, although in this case he does not know the transitional states. It has been objected that in order to modify the eye and still preserve it as a perfect instrument, many changes would have to be effected simultaneously, which, it is assumed, could not be done through natural selection; but as I have attempted to show in my work on the variation of domestic animals, it is not necessary to suppose that the modifications were all simultaneous, if they were extremely slight and gradual. Different kinds of modification would, also, serve for the same general purpose: as Mr. Wallace has remarked, "if a lens has too short or too long a focus, it may be amended either by an alteration of curvature, or an alteration of density; if the curvature be irregular, and the rays do not converge to a point, then any increased regularity of curvature will be an improvement. So the contraction of the iris and the muscular movements of the eye are neither of them essential to vision, but only improvements which might have been added and perfected at any stage of the construction of the instrument." Within the highest division of the animal kingdom, namely, the Vertebrata, we can start from an eye so simple, that it consists, as in the lancelet, of a little sack of transparent skin, furnished with a nerve and lined with pigment, but destitute of any other apparatus. In fishes and reptiles, as Owen has remarked, "the range of gradations of dioptric structures is very great." It is a significant fact that even in man, according to the high authority of Virchow, the beautiful crystalline lens is formed in the embryo by an accumulation of epidermic cells, lying in a sack-like fold of the skin; and the vitreous body is formed from embryonic subcutaneous tissue. To arrive, however, at a just conclusion regarding the formation of the eye, with all its marvellous yet not absolutely perfect characters, it is indispensable that the reason should conquer the imagination; but I have felt the difficulty far too keenly to be surprised at others hesitating to extend the principle of natural selection to so startling a length.

It is scarcely possible to avoid comparing the eye with a telescope. We know that this instrument has been perfected by the long-continued efforts of the highest human intellects; and we naturally infer that the eye has been formed by a somewhat analogous process. But may not this inference be presumptuous? Have we any right to assume that the Creator works by intellectual powers like those of man? If we must compare the eye to an optical instrument, we ought in imagination to take a thick layer of transparent tissue, with spaces filled with fluid, and with a nerve sensitive to light beneath, and then suppose every part of this layer to be continually changing slowly in density, so as to separate into layers of different densities and thicknesses, placed at different distances from each other, and with the surfaces of each layer slowly changing in form. Further we must suppose that there is a power, represented by natural selection or the survival of the fittest, always intently watching each slight alteration in the transparent layers; and carefully preserving each which, under varied circumstances, in any way or in any degree, tends to produce a distincter image. We must suppose each new state of the instrument to be multiplied by the million; each to be preserved until a better one is produced, and then the old ones to be all destroyed. In living bodies, variation will cause the slight alterations, generation will multiply them almost infinitely, and natural selection will pick out with unerring skill each improvement. Let this process go on for millions of years; and during each year on millions of individuals of many kinds; and may we not believe that a living optical instrument might thus be formed as superior to one of glass, as the works of the Creator are to those of man? * * *

SUMMARY: THE LAW OF UNITY OF TYPE AND OF THE CONDITIONS OF EXISTENCE EMBRACED BY THE THEORY OF NATURAL SELECTION

We have in this chapter discussed some of the difficulties and objections which may be urged against the theory. Many of them are serious; but I think that in the discussion light has been thrown on several facts, which on the belief of independent acts of creation are utterly obscure. We have seen that species at any one period are not indefinitely variable, and are not linked together by a multitude of intermediate gradations, partly because the process of natural selection is always very slow, and at any one time acts only on a few forms; and partly because the very process of natural selection implies the continual supplanting and extinction of preceding and intermediate gradations. Closely allied species, now living on a continuous area, must often have been formed when the area was not continuous, and when the conditions of life did not insensibly graduate away from one part to another. When two varieties are formed in two districts of a continuous area, an intermediate variety will often be formed, fitted for an intermediate zone; but from reasons assigned, the intermediate variety will usually exist in lesser numbers than the two forms which it connects; consequently the two latter, during the course of further modification, from existing in greater numbers, will have a great advantage over the less numerous intermediate variety, and will thus generally succeed in supplanting and exterminating it.

We have seen in this chapter how cautious we should be in concluding that the most different habits of life could not graduate into each other; that a bat, for instance, could not have been formed by natural selection from an animal which at first only glided through the air.

We have seen that a species under new conditions of life may change its habits; or it may have diversified habits, with some very unlike those of its nearest congeners. Hence we can understand, bearing in mind that each organic being is trying to live wherever it can live, how it has arisen that there are upland geese with webbed feet, ground woodpeckers, diving thrushes, and petrels with the habits of auks.

Although the belief that an organ so perfect as the eye could have been formed by natural selection, is enough to stagger any one; yet in the case of any organ, if we know of a long series of gradations in complexity, each good for its possessor, then, under changing conditions of life, there is no logical impossibility in the acquirement of any conceivable degree of perfection through natural selection. In the cases in which we know of no intermediate or transitional states, we should be extremely cautious in concluding that none can have existed, for the metamorphoses of many organs show what wonderful changes in function are at least possible. For instance, a swimbladder has apparently been converted into an air-breathing lung. The same organ having performed simultaneously very different functions, and then having been in part or in whole specialised for one function; and two distinct organs having performed at the same time the same function, the one having been perfected whilst aided by the other, must often have largely facilitated transitions.

We have seen that in two beings widely remote from each other in the natural scale, organs serving for the same purpose and in external appearance closely similar may have been separately and independently formed; but when such organs are closely examined, essential differences in their structure can almost always be detected; and this naturally follows from the principle of natural selection. On the other hand, the common rule throughout nature is infinite diversity of structure for gaining the same end; and this again naturally follows from the same great principle.

In many cases we are far too ignorant to be enabled to assert that a part or organ is so unimportant for the welfare of a species, that modifications in its structure could not have been slowly accumulated by means of natural selection. In many other cases, modifications are probably the direct result of the laws of variation or of growth, independently of any good having been thus gained. But even such structures have often, as we may feel assured, been subsequently taken advantage of, and still further modified, for the good of species under new conditions of life. We may, also, believe that a part formerly of high importance has frequently been retained (as the tail of an aquatic animal by its terrestrial descendants), though it has become of such small importance that it could not, in its present state, have been acquired by means of natural selection.

Natural selection can produce nothing in one species for the exclusive good or injury of another; though it may well produce parts, organs, and excretions highly useful or even indispensable, or again highly injurious to another species, but in all cases at the same time useful to the possessor. In each well-stocked country natural selection acts through the competition of the inhabitants, and consequently leads to success in the battle for life, only in accordance with the standard of that particular country. Hence the inhabitants of one country, generally the smaller one, often yield to the inhabitants of another and generally the larger country. For in the larger country there will have existed more individuals and more diversified forms, and the competition will have been severer, and thus the standard of perfection will have been rendered higher. Natural selection will not necessarily lead to absolute perfection; nor, as far as we can judge by our limited faculties, can absolute perfection be everywhere predicated.

On the theory of natural selection we can clearly understand the full meaning of that old canon in natural history, "Natura non facit saltum." This canon, if we look to the present inhabitants alone of the world, is not strictly correct; but if we include all those of past times, whether known or unknown, it must on this theory be strictly true.

It is generally acknowledged that all organic beings have been formed on two great laws—Unity of Type, and the Conditions of Existence. By unity of type is meant that fundamental agreement in structure which we see in organic beings of the same class, and which is quite independent of their habits of life. On my theory, unity of type is explained by unity of descent. The expression of conditions is fully embraced by the principle of natural selection. For natural selection acts by either now adapting the varying parts of each being to its organic and inorganic conditions of life; or by having adapted them during past periods of time: the adaptations being aided in many cases by the increased use or disuse of parts, being affected by the direct action of the external conditions of life, and subjected in all cases to the several laws of growth and variation. Hence, in fact, the law of the Conditions of Existence is the higher law; as it includes, through the inheritance of former variations and adaptations, that of Unity of Type.

Chapter X

ON THE IMPERFECTION OF THE GEOLOGICAL RECORD

On the absence of intermediate varieties at the present day—On the nature of extinct intermediate varieties; on their number—On the lapse of time, as inferred from the rate of denudation and of deposition—On the lapse of time as estimated by years—On the poorness of our palæontological collections—On the intermittence of geological formations—On the denudation of granitic areas—On the absence of intermediate varieties in any one formation—On the sudden appearance of groups of species—On their sudden appearance in the lowest known fossiliferous strata—Antiquity of the habitable earth.

In the sixth chapter I enumerated the chief objections which might be justly urged against the views maintained in this volume. Most of them have now been discussed. One, namely the distinctness of specific forms, and their not being blended together by innumerable transitional links, is a very obvious difficulty. I assigned reasons why such links do not commonly occur at the present day under the circumstances apparently most favourable for their presence, namely, on an extensive and continuous area with graduated physical conditions. I endeavoured to show, that the life of each species depends in a more important manner on the presence of other already defined organic forms, than on climate, and, therefore, that the really governing conditions of life do not graduate away quite insensibly like heat or moisture. I endeavoured, also, to show that intermediate varieties, from existing in lesser numbers than the forms which they connect, will generally be beaten out and exterminated during the course of further modification and improvement. The main cause, however, of innumerable intermediate links not now occurring everywhere throughout nature, depends on the very process of natural selection, through which new varieties continually take the places of and supplant their parent-forms. But just in proportion as this process of extermination has acted on an enormous scale, so must the number of intermediate varieties, which have formerly existed, be truly enormous. Why then is not every geological formation and every stratum full of such intermediate links? Geology assuredly does not reveal any such finely-graduated organic chain; and this, perhaps, is the most obvious and serious objection which can be urged against the theory. The explanation lies, as I believe, in the extreme imperfection of the geological record.

In the first place, it should always be borne in mind what sort of intermediate forms must, on the theory, have formerly existed. I have found it difficult, when looking at any two species, to avoid picturing to myself forms *directly* intermediate between them. But this is a wholly false view; we should always look for forms intermediate between each species and a common but unknown progenitor; and the progenitor will generally have differed in some respects from all its modified descendants. To give a simple illustration: the fantail and pouter pigeons are both descended from the rock-pigeon; if we possessed all the intermediate varieties which have ever existed, we should have an extremely close series between both and the rock-pigeon; but we should have no varieties directly intermediate between the fantail and pouter; none, for instance, combining a tail somewhat expanded with a crop somewhat enlarged, the characteristic features of these two breeds. These two breeds, moreover, have become so much modified, that, if we had no historical or indirect evidence regarding their origin, it would not have been possible to have determined, from a mere comparison of their structure with that of the rock-pigeon, C. livia, whether they had descended from this species or from some allied form, such as C. œnas.

So, with natural species, if we look to forms very distinct, for instance to the horse and tapir, we have no reason to suppose that links directly intermediate between them ever existed, but between each and an unknown common parent. The common parent will have had in its whole organisation much general resemblance to the tapir and to the horse; but in some points of structure may have differed considerably from both, even perhaps more than they differ from each other. Hence, in all such cases, we should be unable to recognise the parent-form of any two or more species, even if we closely compared the structure of the parent with that of its modified descendants, unless at the same time we had a nearly perfect chain of the intermediate links.

It is just possible by the theory, that one of two living forms might have descended from the other; for instance, a horse from a tapir; and in this case *direct* intermediate links will have existed between them. But such a case would imply that one form had remained for a very long period unaltered, whilst its descendants had undergone a vast amount of change; and the principle of competition between organism and organism, between child and parent, will render this a very rare event; for in all cases the new and improved forms of life tend to supplant the old and unimproved forms.

By the theory of natural selection all living species have been connected with the parent-species of each genus, by differences not greater than we see between the natural and domestic varieties of the same species at the present day; and these parent-species, now generally extinct, have in their turn been similarly connected with more ancient forms; and so on backwards, always converging to the common anestor of each great class. So that the number of intermediate and transitional links, between all living and extinct species, must have been inconceivably great. But assuredly, if this theory be true, such have lived upon the earth.

ON THE LAPSE OF TIME, AS INFERRED FROM THE RATE OF DEPOSITION AND EXTENT OF DENUDATION

Independently of our not finding fossil remains of such infinitely numerous connecting links, it may be objected that time cannot have sufficed for so great an amount of organic change, all changes having been effected slowly. It is hardly possible for me to recall to the reader who is not a practical geologist, the facts leading the mind feebly to comprehend the lapse of time. He who can read Sir Charles Lyell's grand work on the Principles of Geology, which the future historian will recognise as having produced a revolution in natural science, and yet does not admit how vast have been the past periods of time, may at once close this volume. Not that it suffices to study the Principles of Geology, or to read special treatises by different observers on separate formations, and to mark how each author attempts to give an inadequate idea of the duration of each formation, or even of each stratum. We can best gain some idea of past time by knowing the agencies at work, and learning how deeply the surface of the land has been denuded, and how much sediment has been deposited. As Lyell has well remarked, the extent and thickness of our sedimentary formations are the result and the measure of the denudation which the earth's crust has elsewhere undergone. Therefore a man should examine for himself the great piles of superimposed strata, and watch the rivulets bringing down mud, and the waves wearing away the sea-cliffs, in order to comprehend something about the duration of past time, the monuments of which we see all around us. * * *

ON THE POORNESS OF PALAEONTOLOGICAL COLLECTIONS

Now let us turn to our richest geological museums, and what a paltry display we behold! That our collections are imperfect is admitted by every one. The remark of that admirable palæontologist, Edward Forbes, should never be forgotten, namely, that very many fossil species are known and named from single and often broken specimens, or from a few specimens collected on some one spot. Only a small portion of the surface of the earth has been geologically explored, and no part with sufficient care, as the important discoveries made every year in Europe prove. No organism wholly soft can be preserved. Shells and bones decay and disappear when left on the bottom of the sea, where sediment is not accumulating. We probably take a quite erroneous view, when we assume that sediment is being deposited over nearly the whole bed of the sea, at a rate sufficiently quick to embed and preserve fossil remains. Throughout an enormously large proportion of the ocean, the bright blue tint of the water bespeaks its purity. The many cases on record of a formation conformably covered, after an immense interval of time, by another and later formation, without the underlying bed having suffered in the interval any wear and tear, seem explicable only on the view of the bottom of the sea not rarely lying for ages in an unaltered condition. The remains which do become embedded, if in sand or gravel, will, when the beds are upraised generally be dissolved by the percolation of rain-water charged with carbonic acid. Some of the many kinds of animals which live on the beach between high and low water mark seem to be rarely preserved. For instance, the several species of the Chthamalinæ (a subfamily of sessile cirripedes) coat the rocks all over the world in infinite numbers: they are all strictly littoral, with the exception of a single Mediterranean species, which inhabits deep water, and this has been found fossil in Sicily, whereas not one other species has hitherto been found in any tertiary formation: yet it is known that the genus Chthamalus existed during the Chalk period. Lastly, many great deposits requiring a vast length of time for their accumulation, are entirely destitute of organic remains, without our being able to assign any reason: one of the most striking instances is that of the Flysch formation, which consists of shale and sandstone, several thousand, occasionally even six thousand feet in thickness, and extending for at least 300 miles from Vienna to Switzerland; and although this great mass has been most carefully searched, no fossils, except a few vegetable remains, have been found.

With respect to the terrestrial productions which lived during the Secondary and Palæozoic periods, it is superfluous to state that our evidence is fragmentary in an extreme degree. For instance, until recently not a land-shell was known belonging to either of these vast periods, with the exception of one species discovered by Sir C. Lyell and Dr. Dawson in the carboniferous strata of North America; but now land-shells have been found in the lias. In regard to mammiferous remains, a glance at the historical table published in Lyell's Manual will bring home the truth, how accidental and rare is their preservation, far better than pages of detail. Nor is their rarity surprising, when we remember how large a proportion of the bones of tertiary mammals have been discovered either in caves or in lacustrine deposits; and that not a cave or true lacustrine bed is known belonging to the age of our secondary or palæozoic formations.

But the imperfection in the geological record largely results from another and more important cause than any of the foregoing; namely, from the several formations being separated from each other by wide intervals of time. This doctrine has been emphatically admitted by many geologists and palæontologists, who, like E. Forbes, entirely disbelieve in the change of species. When we see the formations tabulated in written works, or when we follow them in nature, it is difficult to avoid believing that they are closely consecutive. But we know, for instance, from Sir R. Murchison's great work on Russia, what wide gaps there are in that country between the superimposed formations; so it is in North America, and in many other parts of the world. The most skilful geologist, if his attention had been confined exclusively to these large territories, would never have suspected that, during the periods which were blank and barren in his own country, great piles of sediment, charged with new and peculiar forms of life, had elsewhere been accumulated. And if, in each separate territory, hardly any idea can be formed of the length of time which has elapsed between the consecutive formations, we may infer that this could nowhere be ascertained. The frequent and great changes in the mineralogical composition of consecutive formations, generally implying great changes in the geography of the surrounding lands, whence the sediment was derived, accord with the belief of vast intervals of time having elapsed between each formation. * * *

ON THE SUDDEN APPEARANCE OF GROUPS OF ALLIED SPECIES IN THE
LOWEST KNOWN FOSSILIFEROUS STRATA

* * * Those who believe that the geological record is in any degree perfect, will undoubtedly at once reject the theory. For my part, following out Lyell's metaphor, I look at the geological record as a history of the world imperfectly kept, and written in a changing dialect; of this history we possess the last volume alone, relating only to two or three countries. Of this volume, only here and there a short chapter has been preserved; and of each page, only here and there a few lines. Each word of the slowly-changing language, more or less different in the successive chapters, may represent the forms of life, which are entombed in our consecutive formations, and which falsely appear to have been abruptly introduced. On this view, the difficulties above discussed are greatly diminished, or even disappear.

Chapter XV

RECAPITULATION AND CONCLUSION

Recapitulation of the objections to the theory of natural selection —Recapitulation of the general and special circumstances in its favour—Causes of the general belief in the immutability of species —How far the theory of natural selection may be extended—Effects of its adoption on the study of natural history—Concluding remarks.

As this whole volume is one long argument, it may be convenient to the reader to have the leading facts and inferences briefly recapitulated.

That many and serious objections may be advanced against the theory of descent with modification through variation and natural selection, I do not deny. I have endeavored to give to them their full force. Nothing at first can appear more difficult to believe than that the more complex organs and instincts have been perfected, not by means superior to, though analogous with, human reason, but by the accumulation of innumerable slight variations, each good for the individual possessor. Nevertheless, this difficulty, though appearing to our imagination insuperably great, cannot be considered real if we admit the following propositions, namely, that all parts of the organisation and instincts offer, at least, individual differences—that there is a struggle for existence leading to the preservation of profitable deviations of structure or instinct—and, lastly, that gradations in the state of perfection of each organ may have existed, each good of its kind. The truth of these propositions cannot, I think, be disputed.

It is, no doubt, extremely difficult even to conjecture by what gradations many structures have been perfected, more especially amongst broken and failing groups of organic beings, which have suffered much extinction, but we see so many strange gradations in nature, that we ought to be extremely cautious in saying that any organ or instinct, or any whole structure, could not have arrived at its present state by many graduated steps. There are, it must be admitted, cases of special difficulty opposed to the theory of natural selection; and one of the most curious of these is the existence in the same community of two or three defined castes of workers or sterile female ants; but I have attempted to show how these difficulties can be mastered.

With respect to the almost universal sterility of species when first crossed, which forms so remarkable a contrast with the almost universal fertility of varieties when crossed, I must refer the reader to the recapitulation of the facts given at the end of the ninth chapter, which seem to me conclusively to show that this sterility is no more a special endowment than is the incapacity of two distinct kinds of trees to be grafted together; but that it is incidental on differences confined to the reproductive systems of the intercrossed species. We see the truth of this conclusion in the vast difference in the results of crossing the same two species reciprocally,—that is, when one species is first used as the father and then as the mother. Analogy from the consideration of dimorphic and trimorphic plants clearly leads to the same conclusion, for when the forms are illegitimately united, they yield few or no seed, and their offspring are more or less sterile; and these forms belong to the same undoubted species, and differ from each other in no respect except in their reproductive organs and functions.

Although the fertility of varieties when intercrossed and of their mongrel offspring has been asserted by so many authors to be universal, this cannot be considered as quite correct after the facts given on the high authority of Gärtner and Kölreuter. Most of the varieties which have been experimented on have been produced under domestication; and as domestication (I do not mean mere confinement) almost certainly tends to eliminate that sterility which, judging from analogy, would have affected the parent-species if intercrossed, we ought not to expect that domestication would likewise induce sterility in their modified descendants when crossed. This elimination of sterility apparently follows from the same cause which allows our domestic animals to breed freely under diversified circumstances; and this again apparently follows from their having been gradually accustomed to frequent changes in their conditions of life.

A double and parallel series of facts seems to throw much light on the sterility of species, when first crossed, and of their hybrid offspring. On the one side, there is good reason to believe that slight changes in the conditions of life give vigour and fertility to all organic beings. We know also that a cross between the distinct individuals of the same variety, and between distinct varieties, increases the number of their offspring, and certainly gives to them increased size and vigour. This is chiefly owing to the forms which are crossed having been exposed to somewhat different conditions of life; for I have ascertained by a laborious series of experiments that if all the individuals of the same variety be subjected during several generations to the same conditions, the good derived from crossing is often much diminished or wholly disappears. This is one side of the case. On the other side, we know that species which have long been exposed to nearly uniform conditions, when they are subjected under confinement to new and greatly changed conditions, either perish, or if they survive, are rendered sterile, though retaining perfect health. This does not occur, or only in a very slight degree, with our domesticated productions, which have long been exposed to fluctuating conditions. Hence when we find that hybrids produced by a cross between two distinct species are few in number, owing to their perishing soon after conception or at a very early age, or if surviving that they are rendered more or less sterile, it seems highly probable that this result is due to their having been in fact subjected to a great change in their conditions of life, from being compounded of two distinct organisations. He who will explain in a definite manner why, for instance, an elephant or a fox will not breed under confinement in its native country, whilst the domestic pig or dog will breed freely under the most diversified conditions, will at the same time be able to give a definite answer to the question why two distinct species, when crossed, as well as their hybrid offspring, are generally rendered more or less sterile, whilst two domesticated varieties when crossed and their mongrel offspring are perfectly fertile.

Turning to geographical distribution, the difficulties encountered on the theory of descent with modification are serious enough. All the individuals of the same species, and all the species of the same genus, or even higher group, are descended from common parents; and therefore, in however distant and isolated parts of the world they may now be found, they must in the course of successive generations have travelled from some one point to all the others. We are often wholly unable even to conjecture how this could have been effected. Yet, as we have reason to believe that some species have retained the same specific form for very long periods of time, immensely long as measured by years, too much stress ought not to be laid on the occasional wide diffusion of the same species; for during very long periods there will always have been a good chance for wide migration by many means. A broken or interrupted range may often be accounted for by the extinction of the species in the intermediate regions. It cannot be denied that we are as yet very ignorant as to the full extent of the various climatal and geographical changes which have affected the earth during modern periods; and such changes will often have facilitated migration. As an example, I have attempted to show how potent has been the influence of the Glacial period on the distribution of the same and of allied species throughout the world. We are as yet profoundly ignorant of the many occasional means of transport. With respect to distinct species of the same genus inhabiting distant and isolated regions, as the process of modification has necessarily been slow, all the means of migration will have been possible during a very long period; and consequently the difficulty of the wide diffusion of the species of the same genus is in some degree lessened.

As according to the theory of natural selection an interminable number of intermediate forms must have existed, linking together all the species in each group by gradations as fine are our existing varieties, it may be asked: Why do we not see these linking forms all around us? Why are not all organic beings blended together in an inextricable chaos? With respect to existing forms, we should remember that we have no right to expect (excepting in rare cases) to discover *directly* connecting links between them, but only between each and some extinct and supplanted form. Even on a wide area, which has during a long period remained continuous, and of which the climatic and other conditions of life change insensibly in proceeding from a district occupied by one species into another district occupied by a closely allied species, we have no just right to expect often to find intermediate varieties in the intermediate zones. For we have reason to believe that only a few species of a genus ever undergo change; the other species becoming utterly extinct and leaving no modified progeny. Of the species which do change, only a few within the same country change at the same time; and all modifications are slowly effected. I have also shown that the intermediate varieties which probably at first existed in the intermediate zones, would be liable to be supplanted by the allied forms on either hand; for the latter, from existing in greater numbers, would generally be modified and improved at a quicker rate than the intermediate varieties, which existed in lesser numbers; so that the intermediate varieties would, in the long run, be supplanted and exterminated.

On this doctrine of the extermination of an infinitude of connecting links, between the living and extinct inhabitants of the world, and at each successive period between the extinct and still older species, why is not every geological formation charged with such links? Why does not every collection of fossil remains afford plain evidence of the gradation and mutation of the forms of life? Although geological research has undoubtedly revealed the former existence of many links, bringing numerous forms of life much closer together, it does not yield the infinitely many fine gradations between past and present species required on the theory; and this is the most obvious of the many objections which may be urged against it. Why, again, do whole groups of allied species appear, though this appearance is often false, to have come in suddenly on the successive geological stages? Although we now know that organic beings appeared on this globe, at a period incalculably remote, long before the lowest bed of the Cambrian system was deposited, why do we not find beneath this system great piles of strata stored with the remains of the progenitors of the Cambrian fossils? For on the theory, such strata must somewhere have been deposited at these ancient and utterly unknown epochs of the world's history.

I can answer these questions and objections only on the supposition that the geological record is far more imperfect than most geologists believe. The number of specimens in all our museums is absolutely as nothing compared with the countless generations of countless species which have certainly existed. The parent-form of any two or more species would not be in all its characters directly intermediate between its modified offspring, any more than the rock-pigeon is directly intermediate in crop and tail between its descendants, the pouter and fantail pigeons. We should not be able to recognise a species as the parent of another and modified species, if we were to examine the two ever so closely, unless we possessed most of the intermediate links; and owing to the imperfection of the geological record, we have no just right to expect to find so many links. If two or three, or even more linking forms were discovered, they would simply be ranked by many naturalists as so many new species, more especially if found in different geological sub-stages, let their differences be ever so slight. Numerous existing doubtful forms could be named which are probably varieties; but who will pretend that in future ages so many fossil links will be discovered, that naturalists will be able to decide whether or not these doubtful forms ought to be called varieties? Only a small portion of the world has been geologically explored. Only organic beings of certain classes can be preserved in a fossil condition, at least in any great number. Many species when once formed never undergo any further change but become extinct without leaving modified descendants; and the periods, during which species have undergone modification, though long as measured by years, have probably been short in comparison with the periods during which they retain the same form. It is the dominant and widely ranging species which vary most frequently and vary most, and varieties are often at first local—both causes rendering the discovery of intermediate links in any one formation less likely. Local varieties will not spread into other and distant regions until they are considerably modified and improved; and when they have spread, and are discovered in a geological formation, they appear as if suddenly created there, and will be simply classed as new species. Most formations have been intermittent in their accumulation; and their duration has probably been shorter than the average duration of specific forms. Successive formations are in most cases separated from each other by blank intervals of time of great length; for fossiliferous formations thick enough to resist future degradations can as a general rule be accumulated only where much sediment is deposited on the subsiding bed of the sea. During the alternate periods of elevation and of stationary level the record will generally be blank. During these latter periods there will probably be more variability in the forms of life; during periods of subsidence, more extinction.

With respect to the absence of strata rich in fossils beneath the Cambrian formation, I can recur only to the hypothesis given in the tenth chapter; namely, that though our continents and oceans have endured for an enormous period in nearly their present relative positions, we have no reason to assume that this has always been the case; consequently formations much older than any now known may lie buried beneath the great oceans. With respect to the lapse of time not having been sufficient since our planet was consolidated for the assumed amount of organic change, and this objection, as urged by Sir William Thompson, is probably one of the gravest as yet advanced, I can only say, firstly, that we do not know at what rate species change as measured by years, and secondly, that many philosophers are not as yet willing to admit that we know enough of the constitution of the universe and of the interior of our globe to speculate with safety on its past duration.

That the geological record is imperfect all will admit; but that it is imperfect to the degree required by our theory, few will be inclined to admit. If we look to long enough intervals of time, geology plainly declares that species have all changed; and they have changed in the manner required by the theory, for they have changed slowly and in a graduated manner. We clearly see this in the fossil remains from consecutive formations invariably being much more closely related to each other, than are the fossils from widely separated formations.

Such is the sum of the several chief objections and difficulties which may be justly urged against the theory; and I have now briefly recapitulated the answers and explanations which, as far as I can see, may be given. I have felt these difficulties far too heavily during many years to doubt their weight. But it deserves especial notice that the more important objections relate to questions on which we are confessedly ignorant; nor do we know how ignorant we are. We do not know all the possible transitional gradations between the simplest and the most perfect organs; it cannot be pretended that we know all the varied means of distribution during the long lapse of years, or that we know how imperfect is the Geological Record. Serious as these several objections are, in my judgment they are by no means sufficient to overthrow the theory of descent with subsequent modification.

Now let us turn to the other side of the argument. Under domestication we see much variability, caused, or at least excited, by changed conditions of life; but often in so obscure a manner, that we are tempted to consider the variations as spontaneous. Variability is governed by many complex laws,—by correlated growth, compensation, the increased use and disuse of parts, and the definite action of the surrounding conditions. There is much difficulty in ascertaining how largely our domestic productions have been modified; but we may safely infer that the amount has been large, and that modifications can be inherited for long periods. As long as the conditions of life remain the same, we have reason to believe that a modification, which has already been inherited for many generations, may continue to be inherited for an almost infinite number of generations. On the other hand, we have evidence that variability when it has once come into play, does not cease under domestication for a very long period; nor do we know that it ever ceases, for new varieties are still occasionally produced by our oldest domesticated productions.

Variability is not actually caused by man; he only unintentionally exposes organic beings to new conditions of life, and then nature acts on the organisation and causes it to vary. But man can and does select the variations given to him by nature, and thus accumulates them in any desired manner. He thus adapts animals and plants for his own benefit or pleasure. He may do this methodically, or he may do it unconsciously by preserving the individuals most useful or pleasing to him without any intention of altering the breed. It is certain that he can largely influence the character of a breed by selecting, in each successive generation, individual differences so slight as to be inappreciable except by an educated eye. This unconscious process of selection has been the great agency in the formation of the most distinct and useful domestic breeds. That many breeds produced by man have to a large extent the character of natural species, is shown by the inextricable doubts whether many of them are varieties or aboriginally distinct species.

There is no reason why the principles which have acted so efficiently under domestication should not have acted under nature. In the survival of favoured individuals and races, during the constantly-recurrent Struggle for Existence, we see a powerful and ever-acting form of Selection. The struggle for existence inevitably follows from the high geometrical ratio of increase which is common to all organic beings. This high rate of increase is proved by calculation,—by the rapid increase of many animals and plants during a succession of peculiar seasons, and when naturalised in new countries. More individuals are born than can possibly survive. A grain in the balance may determine which individuals shall live and which shall die,—which variety or species shall increase in number, and which shall decrease, or finally become extinct. As the individuals of the same species come in all respects into the closest competition with each other, the struggle will generally be most severe between them; it will be almost equally severe between the varieties of the same species, and next in severity between the species of the same genus. On the other hand the struggle will often be severe between beings remote in the scale of nature. The slightest advantage in certain individuals, at any age or during any season, over those with which they come into competition, or better adaptation in however slight a degree to the surrounding physical conditions, will, in the long run, turn the balance.

With animals having separated sexes, there will be in most cases a struggle between the males for the possession of the females. The most vigorous males, or those which have most successfully struggled with their conditions of life, will generally leave most progeny. But success will often depend on the males having special weapons, or means of defense, or charms; and a slight advantage will lead to victory.

As geology plainly proclaims that each land has undergone

great physical changes, we might have expected to find that organic beings have varied under nature, in the same way as they have varied under domestication. And if there has been any variability under nature, it would be an unaccountable fact if natural selection had not come into play. It has often been asserted, but the assertion is incapable of proof, that the amount of variation under nature is a strictly limited quantity. Man, though acting on external characters alone and often capriciously, can produce within a short period a great result by adding up mere individual differences in his domestic productions; and every one admits that species present individual differences. But, besides such differences, all naturalists admit that natural varieties exist, which are considered sufficiently distinct to be worthy of record in systematic works. No one has drawn any clear distinction between individual differences and slight varieties; or between more plainly marked varieties and sub-species, and species. On separate continents, and on different parts of the same continent when divided by barriers of any kind, and on outlying islands, what a multitude of forms exist, which some experienced naturalists rank as varieties, others as geographical races or sub-species, and others as distinct, though closely allied species!

If then, animals and plants do vary, let it be ever so slightly or slowly, why should not variations or individual differences, which are in any way beneficial, be preserved and accumulated through natural selection, or the survival of the fittest? If man can by patience select variations useful to him, why, under changing and complex conditions of life, should not variations useful to nature's living products often arise, and be preserved or selected? What limit can be put to this power, acting during long ages and rigidly scrutinising the whole constitution, structure, and habits of each creature,—favouring the good and rejecting the bad? I can see no limit to this power, in slowly and beautifully adapting each form to the most complex relations of life. The theory of natural selection, even if we look no farther than this, seems to be in the highest degree probable. I have already recapitulated, as fairly as I could, the opposed difficulties and objections: now let us turn to the special facts and arguments in favour of the theory.

On the view that species are only strongly marked and permanent varieties, and that each species first existed as a variety, we can see why it is that no line of demarcation can be drawn between species, commonly supposed to have been produced by special acts of creation, and varities which are acknowledged to have been produced by secondary laws. On this same view we can understand how it is that in a region where many species of a genus have been produced, and where they now flourish, these same species should present many varieties; for where the manufactory of species has been active, we might expect, as a general rule, to find it still in action; and this is the case if varieties be incipient species. Moreover, the species of the larger genera, which afford the greater number of varieties or incipient species, retain to a certain degree the character of varieties; for they differ from each other by a less amount of difference than do the species of smaller genera. The closely allied species also of the larger genera apparently have restricted ranges, and in their affinities they are clustered in little groups round other species—in both respects resembling varieties. These are strange relations on the view that each species was independently created, but are intelligible if each existed first as a variety.

As each species tends by its geometrical rate of reproduction to increase inordinately in number; and as the modified descendants of each species will be enabled to increase by as much as they become more diversified in habits and structure, so as to be able to seize on many and widely different places in the economy of nature, there will be a constant tendency in natural selection to preserve the most divergent offspring of any one species. Hence, during a long-continued course of modification, the slight differences characteristic of varieties of the same species, tend to be augmented into the greater differences characteristic of the species of the same genus. New and improved varieties will inevitably supplant and exterminate the older, less improved, and intermediate varieties; and thus species are rendered to a large extent defined and distinct objects. Dominant species belonging to the larger groups within each class tend to give birth to new and dominant forms; so that each large group tends to become still larger, and at the same time more divergent in character. But as all groups cannot thus go on increasing in size, for the world would not hold them, the more dominant groups beat the less dominant. This tendency in the large groups to go on increasing in size and diverging in character, together with the inevitable contingency of much extinction, explains the arrangement of all the forms of life in groups subordinate to groups, all within a few great classes, which has prevailed throughout all time. This grand fact of the grouping of all organic beings under what is called the Natural System, is utterly inexplicable on the theory of creation.

As natural selection acts solely by accumulating slight, successive, favourable variations, it can produce no great or sudden modifications; it can act only by short and slow steps. Hence, the canon of "Natura non facit saltum," which every fresh addition to our knowledge tends to confirm, is on this theory intelligible. We can see why throughout nature the same general end is gained by an almost infinite diversity of means, for every peculiarity when once acquired is long inherited, and structures already modified in many different ways have to be adapted for the same general purpose. We can, in short, see why nature is prodigal in variety, though niggard in innovation. But why this should be a law of nature if each species has been independently created no man can explain.

Many other facts are, as it seems to me, explicable on this theory. How strange it is that a bird, under the form of a woodpecker, should prey on insects on the ground; that upland geese which rarely or never swim, should possess webbed feet; that a thrush-like bird should dive and feed on sub-aquatic insects; and that a petrel should have the habits and structure fitting it for the life of an auk! and so in endless other cases. But on the view of each species constantly trying to increase in number, with natural selection always ready to adapt the slowly varying descendants of each to any unoccupied or ill-occupied place in nature, these facts cease to be strange, or might even have been anticipated.

We can to a certain extent understand how it is that there is so much beauty throughout nature; for this may be largely attributed to the agency of selection. That beauty, according to our sense of it, is not universal, must be admitted by every one who will look at some venomous snakes, at some fishes, and at certain hideous bats with a distorted resemblance to the human face. Sexual selection has given the most brilliant colours, elegant patterns, and other ornaments to the males, and sometimes to both sexes of many birds, butterflies, and other animals. With birds it has often rendered the voice of the male musical to the female, as well as to our ears. Flowers and fruit have been rendered conspicuous by brilliant colours in contrast with the green foliage, in order that the flowers may be readily seen, visited and fertilised by insects, and the seeds disseminated by birds. How it comes that certain colours, sounds, and forms should give pleasure to man and the lower animals,—that is, how the sense of beauty in its simplest form was first acquired,—we do not know any more than how certain odours and flavours were first rendered agreeable.

As natural selection acts by competition, it adapts and improves the inhabitants of each country only in relation to their co-inhabitants; so that we need feel no surprise at the species of any one country, although on the ordinary view supposed to have been created and specially adapted for that country, being beaten and supplanted by the naturalised productions from another land. Nor ought we to marvel if all the contrivances in nature be not, as far as we can judge, absolutely perfect, as in the case even of the human eye; or if some of them be abhorrent to our ideas of fitness. We need not marvel at the sting of the bee, when used against an enemy, causing the bee's own death; at drones being produced in such great numbers for one single act, and being then slaughtered by their sterile sisters; at the astonishing waste of pollen by our fir-trees; at the instinctive hatred of the queenbee for her own fertile daughters; at the ichneumonidæ feeding within the living bodies of caterpillars; or at other such cases. The wonder indeed is, on the theory of natural selection, that more cases of the want of absolute perfection have not been detected.

The complex and little known laws governing the production of varieties are the same, as far as we can judge, with the laws which have governed the production of distinct species. In both cases physical conditions seem to have produced some direct and definite effect, but how much we cannot say. Thus, when varieties enter any new station, they occasionally assume some of the characters proper to the species of that station. With both varieties and species, use and disuse seem to have produced a considerable effect; for it is impossible to resist this conclusion when we look, for instance, at the logger-headed duck, which has wings incapable of flight, in nearly the same condition as in the domestic duck; or when we look at the burrowing tucu-tucu, which is occasionally blind, and then at certain moles, which are habitually blind and have their eyes covered with skin; or when we look at the blind animals inhabiting the dark caves of America and Europe. With varieties and species, correlated variation seems to have played an important part, so that when one part has been modified other parts have been necessarily modified. With both varieties and species, reversions to long-lost characters occasionally occur. How inexplicable on the theory of creation is the occasional appearance of stripes on the shoulders and legs of the several species of the horse-genus and of their hybrids! How simply is this fact explained if we believe that these species are all descended from a striped progenitor, in the same manner as the several domestic breeds of the pigeon are descended from the blue and barred rock-pigeon!

On the ordinary view of each species having been independently created, why should specific characters, or those by which the species of the same genus differ from each other, be more variable than generic characters in which they all agree? Why, for instance, should the colour of a flower be more likely to vary in any one species of a genus, if the other species possess differently coloured flowers, than if all possessed the same coloured flowers? If species are only well-marked varieties, of which the characters have become in a high degree permanent, we can understand this fact; for they have already varied since they branched off from a common progenitor in certain characters, by which they have come to be specifically distinct from each other; therefore these same characters would be more likely again to vary than the generic characters which have been inherited without change for an immense period. It is inexplicable on the theory of creation why a part developed in a very unusual manner in one species alone of a genus, and therefore, as we may naturally infer, of great importance to that species, should be eminently liable to variation; but, on our view, this part has undergone, since the several species branched off from a common progenitor, an unusual amount of variability and modification, and therefore we might expect the part generally to be still variable. But a part may be developed in the most unusual manner, like the wing of a bat, and yet not be more variable than any other structure, if the part be common to many subordinate forms, that is, if it has been inherited for a very long period; for in this case, it will have been rendered constant by long-continued natural selection.

Glancing at instincts, marvellous as some are, they offer no greater difficulty than do corporeal structures on the theory of the natural selection of successive slight, but profitable modifications. We can thus understand why nature moves by graduated steps in endowing different animals of the same class with their several instincts. I have attempted to show how much light the principle of gradation throws on the admirable architectural powers of the hive-bee. Habit no doubt often comes into play in modifying instincts; but it certainly is not indispensable, as we see in the case of neuter insects, which leave no progeny to inherit the effects of long-continued habit. On the view of all the species of the same genus having descended from a common parent, and having inherited much in common, we can understand how it is that allied species, when placed under widely different conditions of life, yet follow nearly the same instincts; why the thrushes of tropical and temperate South America, for instance, line their nests with mud like our British species. On the view of instincts having been slowly acquired through natural selection, we need not marvel at some instincts being not perfect and liable to mistakes, and at many instincts causing other animals to suffer.

If species be only well-marked and permanent varieties, we can at once see why their crossed offspring should follow the same complex laws in their degrees and kinds of resemblance to their parents,—in being absorbed into each other by successive crosses, and in other such points,—as do the crossed offspring of acknowledged varieties. This similarity would be a strange fact, if species had been independently created and varieties had been produced through secondary laws.

If we admit that the geological record is imperfect to an extreme degree, then the facts, which the record does give, strongly support the theory of descent with modifications. New species have come on the stage slowly and at successive intervals; and the amount of change, after equal intervals of time, is widely different in different groups. The extinction of species and of whole groups of species which has played so conspicuous a part in the history of the organic world, almost inevitably follows from the principle of natural selection; for old forms are supplanted by new and improved forms. Neither single species nor groups of species reappear when the chain of ordinary generation is once broken. The gradual diffusion of dominant forms, with the slow modification of their descendants, causes the forms of life, after long intervals of time, to appear as if they had changed simultaneously throughout the world. The fact of the fossil remains of each formation being in some degree intermediate in character between the fossils in the formations above and below, is simply explained by their intermediate position in the chain of descent. The grand fact that all extinct beings can be classed with all recent beings, naturally follows from the living and the extinct being the offspring of common parents. As species have generally diverged in character during their long course of descent and modification, we can understand why it is that the more ancient forms, or early progenitors of each group, so often occupy a position in some degree intermediate between existing groups. Recent forms are generally looked upon as being, on the whole, higher in the scale of organisation than ancient forms; and they must be higher, in so far as the later and more improved forms have conquered the older and less improved forms in the struggle for life; they have also generally had their organs more specialised for different functions. This fact is perfectly compatible with numerous beings still retaining simple and but little improved structures, fitted for simple conditions of life; it is likewise compatible with some forms having retrograded in organisation, by having become at each stage of descent better fitted for new and degraded habits of life. Lastly, the wonderful law of the long endurance of allied forms on the same continent,—of marsupials in Australia, of edentata in America, and other such cases,—is intelligible, for within the same country the existing and the extinct will be closely allied by descent.

Looking to geographical distribution, if we admit that there has been during the long course of ages much migration from one part of the world to another, owing to former climatal and geographical changes and to the many occasional and unknown means of dispersal, then we can understand, on the theory of descent with modification, most of the great leading facts in Distribution. We can see why there should be so striking a parallelism in the distribution of organic beings throughout space, and in their geological succession throughout time; for in both cases the beings have been connected by the bond of ordinary generation, and the means of modification have been the same. We see the full meaning of the wonderful fact, which has struck every traveller, namely, that on the same continent, under the most diverse conditions, under heat and cold, on mountain and lowland, on deserts and marshes, most of the inhabitants within each great class are plainly related; for they are the descendants of the same progenitors and early colonists. On this same principle of former migration, combined in most cases with modification, we can understand, by the aid of the Glacial period, the identity of some few plants, and the close alliance of many others, on the most distant mountains, and in the northern and southern temperate zones; and likewise the close alliance of some of the inhabitants of the sea in the northern and southern temperate latitudes, though separated by the whole intertropical ocean. Although two countries may present physical conditions as closely similar as the same species ever require, we need feel no surprise at their inhabitants being widely different, if they have been for a long period completely sundered from each other; for as the relation of organism to organism is the most important of all relations, and as the two countries will have received colonists at various periods and in different proportions, from some other country or from each other, the course of modification in the two areas will inevitably have been different.

On this view of migration, with subsequent modification, we see why oceanic islands are inhabited by only few species, but of these, why many are peculiar or endemic forms. We clearly see why species belonging to those groups of animals which cannot cross wide spaces of the ocean, as frogs and terrestrial mammals, do not inhabit oceanic islands; and why, on the other hand, new and peculiar species of bats, animals which can traverse the ocean, are found on islands far distant from any continent. Such cases as the presence of peculiar species of bats on oceanic islands and the absence of all other terrestrial mammals, are facts utterly inexplicable on the theory of independent acts of creation.

The existence of closely allied or representative species in any two areas, implies, on the theory of descent with modification, that the same parent-forms formerly inhabited both areas; and we almost invariably find that wherever many closely allied species inhabit two areas, some identical species are still common to both. Wherever many closely allied yet distinct species occur, doubtful forms and varieties belonging to the same groups likewise occur. It is a rule of high generality that the inhabitants of each area are related to the inhabitants of the nearest source whence immigrants might have been derived. We see this in the striking relation of nearly all plants and animals of the Galapagos archipelago, of Juan

Fernandez, and of the other American islands, to the plants and animals of the neighbouring American mainland; and of those of the Cape de Verde Archipelago, and of the other African islands to the African mainland. It must be admitted that these facts receive no explanation on the theory of creation.

The fact, as we have seen, that all past and present organic beings can be arranged within a few great classes, in groups subordinate to groups, and with the extinct groups often falling in between the recent groups, is intelligible on the theory of natural selection with its contingencies of extinction and divergence of character. On these same principles we see how it is, that the mutual affinities of the forms within each class are so complex and circuitous. We see why certain characters are far more serviceable than others for classification;—why adaptive characters, though of paramount importance to the beings, are of hardly any importance in classification; why characters derived from rudimentary parts, though of no service to the beings, are often of high classificatory value; and why embryological characters are often the most valuable of all. The real affinities of all organic beings, in contradistinction to their adaptive resemblances, are due to inheritance or community of descent. The Natural System is a genealogical arrangement, with the acquired grades of difference, marked by the terms, varieties, species, genera, families, &c.; and we have to discover the lines of descent by the most permanent characters whatever they may be and of however slight vital importance.

The similar framework of bones in the hand of a man, wing of a bat, fin of the porpoise, and leg of the horse,—the same number of vertebræ forming the neck of the giraffe and of the elephant,—and innumerable other such facts, at once explain themselves on the theory of descent with slow and slight successive modifications. The similarity of pattern in the wing and in the leg of a bat, though used for such different purpose,—in the jaws and legs of a crab,—in the petals, stamens, and pistils of a flower, is likewise, to a large extent, intelligible on the view of the gradual modification of parts or organs, which were aboriginally alike in an early progenitor in each of these classes. On the principle of successive variations not always supervening at an early age, and being inherited at a corresponding not early period of life, we clearly see why the embryos of mammals, birds, reptiles, and fishes should be so closely similar, and so unlike the adult forms. We may cease marvelling at the embryo of an airbreathing mammal or bird having branchial slits and arteries running in loops, like those of a fish which has to breathe the air dissolved in water by the aid of well-developed branchiæ.

Disuse, aided sometimes by natural selection, will often have reduced organs when rendered useless under changed habits or conditions of life; and we can understand on this view the meaning of rudimentary organs. But disuse and selection will generally act on each creature, when it has come to maturity and has to play its full part in the struggle for existence, and will thus have little power on an organ during early life; hence the organ will not be reduced or rendered rudimentary at this early age. The calf, for instance, has inherited teeth, which never cut through the gums of the upper jaw, from an early progenitor having well-developed teeth; and we may believe, that the teeth in the mature animal were formerly reduced by disuse, owing to the tongue and palate, or lips, having become excellently fitted through natural selection to browse without their aid; whereas in the calf, the teeth have been left unaffected, and on the principle of inheritance at corresponding ages have been inherited from a remote period to the present day. On the view of each organism with all its separate parts having been specially created, how utterly inexplicable is it that organs bearing the plain stamp of inutility, such as the teeth in the embryonic calf or the shrivelled wings under the soldered wing-covers of many beetles, should so frequently occur. Nature may be said to have taken pains to reveal her scheme of modification, by means of rudimentary organs, of embryological and homologous structures, but we are too blind to understand her meaning.

I have now recapitulated the facts and considerations which have thoroughly convinced me that species have been modified, during a long course of descent. This has been effected chiefly through the natural selection of numerous successive, slight, favourable variations; aided in an important manner by the inherited effects of the use and disuse of parts; and in an unimportant manner, that is in relation to adaptive structures, whether past or present, by the direct action of external conditions, and by variations which seem to us in our ignorance to arise spontaneously. It appears that I formerly underrated the frequency and value of these latter forms of variation, as leading to permanent modifications of structure independently of natural selection. But as my conclusions have lately been much misrepresented, and it has been stated that I attribute the modification of species exclusively to natural selection, I may be permitted to remark that in the first edition of this work, and subsequently, I placed in a most conspicuous position—namely, at the close of the Introduction—the following words: "I am convinced that natural selection has been the main but not the exclusive means of modification." This has been of no avail. Great is the power of steady misrepresentation; but the history of science shows that fortunately this power does not long endure.

It can hardly be supposed that a false theory would explain, in so satisfactory a manner as does the theory of natural selection, the several large classes of facts above specified. It has recently been objected that this is an unsafe method of arguing; but it is a method used in judging of the common events of life, and has often been used by the greatest natural philosophers. The undulatory theory of light has thus been arrived at; and the belief in the revolution of the earth on its own axis was until lately supported by hardly any direct evidence. It is no valid objection that science as yet throws no light on the far higher problem of the essence or origin of life. Who can explain what is the essence of the attraction of gravity? No one now objects to following out the results consequent on this unknown element of attraction; notwithstanding that Leibnitz formerly accused Newton of introducing "occult qualities and miracles into philosophy."

I see no good reason why the views given in this volume should shock the religious feelings of any one. It is satisfactory, as showing how transient such impressions are, to remember that the greatest discovery ever made by man, namely, the law of the attraction of gravity, was also attacked by Leibnitz, "as subversive of natural, and inferentially of revealed, religion." A celebrated author and divine has written to me that "he has gradually learnt to see that it is just as noble a conception of the Deity to believe that He created a few original forms capable of self-development into other and needful forms, as to believe that He required a fresh act of creation to supply the voids caused by the action of His laws."

Why, it may be asked, until recently did nearly all the most eminent living naturalists and geologists disbelieve in the mutability of species? It cannot be asserted that organic beings in a state of nature are subject to no variation; it cannot be proved that the amount of variation in the course of long ages is a limited quality; no clear distinction has been, or can be, drawn between species and well-marked varieties. It cannot be maintained that species when intercrossed are invariably sterile, and varieties invariably fertile; or that sterility is a special endowment and sign of creation. The belief that species were immutable productions was almost unavoidable as long as the history of the world was thought to be of short duration; and now that we have acquired some idea of the lapse of time, we are too apt to assume, without proof, that the geological record is so perfect that it would have afforded us plain evidence of the mutation of species, if they had undergone mutation.

But the chief cause of our natural unwillingness to admit that one species has given birth to clear and distinct species, is that we are always slow in admitting great changes of which we do not see the steps. The difficulty is the same as that felt by so many geologists, when Lyell first insisted that long lines of inland cliffs had been formed, the great valleys excavated, by the agencies which we see still at work. The mind cannot possibly grasp the full meaning of the term of even a million years; it cannot add up and perceive the full effects of many slight variations, accumulated during an almost infinite number of generations.

Although I am fully convinced of the truth of the views given in this volume under the form of an abstract, I by no means expect to convince experienced naturalists whose minds are stocked with a multitude of facts all viewed, during a long course of years, from a point of view directly opposite to mine. It is so easy to hide our ignorance under such expressions as the "plan of creation," "unity of design," &c., and to think that we give an explanation when we only re-state a fact. Any one whose disposition leads him to attach more weight to unexplained difficulties than to the explanation of a certain number of facts will certainly reject the theory. A few naturalists, endowed with much flexibility of mind, and who have already begun to doubt the immutability of species, may be influenced by this volume; but I look with confidence to the future,— to young and rising naturalists, who will be able to view both sides of the question with impartiality. Whoever is led to believe that species are mutable will do good service by conscientiously expressing his conviction; for thus only can the load of prejudice by which this subject is overwhelmed be removed.

Several eminent naturalists have of late published their belief that a multitude of reputed species in each genus are not real species; but that other species are real, that is, have been independently created. This seems to me a strange conclusion to arrive at. They admit that a multitude of forms, which till lately they themselves thought were special creations, and which are still thus looked at by the majority of naturalists, and which consequently have all the external characteristic features of true species,—they admit that these have been produced by variation, but they refuse to extend the same view to other and slightly different forms. Nevertheless they do not pretend that they can define, or even conjecture, which are the created forms of life, and which are those produced by secondary laws. They admit variation as a *vera causa* in one case, they arbitrarily reject it in another, without assigning any distinction in the two cases. The day will come when this will be given as a curious illustration of the blindness of preconceived opinion. These authors seem no more startled at a miraculous act of creation than at an ordinary birth. But do they really believe that at innumerable periods in the earth's history certain elemental atoms have been commanded suddenly to flash into living tissues? Do they believe that at each supposed act of creation one individual or many were produced? Were all the infinitely numerous kinds of animals and plants created as eggs or seed, or as full grown? and in the case of mammals, were they created bearing the false marks of nourishment from the mother's womb? Undoubtedly some of these same questions cannot be answered by those who believe in the appearance or creation of only a few forms of life, or of some one form alone. It has been maintained by several authors that it is as easy to believe in the creation of a million beings as of one; but Maupertuis' philosophical axiom "of least action" leads the mind more willingly to admit the smaller number; and certainly we ought not to believe that innumerable beings within each great class have been created with plain, but deceptive, marks of descent from a single parent.

As a record of a former state of things, I have retained in the foregoing paragraphs, and elsewhere, several sentences which imply that naturalists believe in the separate creation of each species; and I have been much censured for having thus expressed myself. But undoubtedly this was the general belief when the first edition of the present work appeared. I formerly spoke to very many naturalists on the subject of evolution, and never once met with any sympathetic agreement. It is probable that some did then believe in evolution, but they were either silent, or expressed themselves so ambiguously that it was not easy to understand their meaning. Now things are wholly changed, and almost every naturalist admits the great principle of evolution. There are, however, some who still think that species have suddenly given birth, through quite unexplained means, to new and totally different forms: but, as I have attempted to show, weighty evidence can be opposed to the admission of great and abrupt modifications. Under a scientific point of view, and as leading to further investigation, but little advantage is gained by believing that new forms are suddenly developed in an inexplicable manner from old and widely different forms, over the old belief in the creation of species from the dust of the earth.

It may be asked how far I extend the doctrine of the modification of species. The question is difficult to answer, because the more distinct the forms are which we consider, by so much the arguments in favour of community of descent become fewer in number and less in force. But some arguments of the greatest weight extend very far. All the members of whole classes are connected together by a chain of affinities, and all can be classed on the same principle, in groups subordinate to groups. Fossil remains sometimes tend to fill up very wide intervals between existing orders.

Organs in a rudimentary condition plainly show that an early progenitor had the organ in a fully developed condition; and this in some cases implies an enormous amount of modification in the descendants. Throughout whole classes various structures are formed on the same pattern, and at a very early age the embryos closely resemble each other. Therefore I cannot doubt that the theory of descent with modification embraces all the members of the same great class or kingdom. I believe that animals are descended from at most only four or five progenitors, and plants from an equal or lesser number.

Analogy would lead me one step farther, namely, to the belief that all animals and plants are descended from some one prototype. But analogy may be a deceitful guide. Nevertheless all living things have much in common, in their chemical composition, their cellular structure, their laws of growth, and their liability to injurious influences. We see this even in so trifling a fact as that the same poison often similarly affects plants and animals; or that the poison secreted by the gall-fly produces monstrous growths on the wild rose or oak-tree. With all organic beings excepting perhaps some of the very lowest, sexual production seems to be essentially similar. With all, as far as is at present known the germinal vesicle is the same; so that all organisms start from a common origin. If we look even to the two main divisions—namely, to the animal and vegetable kingdoms—certain low forms are so far intermediate in character that naturalists have disputed to which kingdom they should be referred. As Professor Asa Gray has remarked, "the spores and other reproductive bodies of many of the lower algæ may claim to have first a characteristically animal, and then an unequivocally vegetable existence." Therefore, on the principle of natural selection with divergence of character, it does not seem incredible that, from such low and intermediate form, both animals and plants may have been developed; and, if we admit this, we must likewise admit that all the organic beings which have ever lived on this earth may be descended from some one primordial form. But this inference is chiefly grounded on analogy and it is immaterial whether or not it be accepted. No doubt it is possible, as Mr. G. H. Lewes has urged, that at the first commencement of life many different forms were evolved; but if so we may conclude that only a very few have left modified descendants. For, as I have recently remarked in regard to the members of each great kingdom, such as the Vertebrata, Articulata &c., we have distinct evidence in their embryological homologous and rudimentary structures that within each kingdom all the members are descended from a single progenitor.

When the views advanced by me in this volume, and by Mr. Wallace, or when analogous views on the origin of species are generally admitted, we can dimly foresee that there will be a considerable revolution in natural history. Systematists will be able to pursue their labours as at present; but they will not be incessantly haunted by the shadowy doubt whether this or that form be a true species. This, I feel sure and I speak after experience, will be no slight relief. The endless disputes whether or not some fifty species of British brambles are good species will cease. Systematists will have only to decide (not that this will be easy) whether any form be sufficiently constant and distinct from other forms, to be capable of definition; and if definable, whether the differences be sufficiently important to deserve a specific name. This latter point will become a far more essential consideration than it is at present; for differences, however slight, between any two forms if not blended by intermediate gradations, are looked at by most naturalists as sufficient to raise both forms to the rank of species.

Hereafter we shall be compelled to acknowledge that the only distinction between species and well-marked varieties is, that the latter are known, or believed, to be connected at the present day by intermediate gradations, whereas species were formerly thus connected. Hence, without rejecting the consideration of the present existence of intermediate gradations between any two forms we shall be led to weigh more carefully and to value higher the actual amount of difference between them. It is quite possible that forms now generally acknowledged to be merely varieties may hereafter be thought worthy of specific names; and in this case scientific and common language will come into accordance. In short, we shall have to treat species in the same manner as those naturalists treat genera, who admit that genera are merely artificial combinations made for convenience. This may not be a cheering prospect; but we shall at least be free from the vain search for the undiscovered and undiscoverable essence of the term species.

The other and more general departments of natural history will rise greatly in interest. The terms used by naturalists, of affinity, relationship, community of type, paternity, morphology, adaptive characters, rudimentary and aborted organs, &c., will cease to be metaphorical, and will have a plain signification. When we no longer look at an organic being as a savage looks at a ship, as something wholly beyond his comprehension; when we regard every production of nature as one which has had a long history; when we contemplate every complex structure and instinct as the summing up of many contrivances, each useful to the possessor, in the same way as any great mechanical invention is the summing up of the labour, the experience, the reason, and even the blunders of numerous workmen; when we thus view each organic being, how far more interesting—I speak from experience—does the study of natural history become!

A grand and almost untrodden field of inquiry will be opened, on the causes and laws of variation, on correlation, on the effects of use and disuse, on the direct action of external conditions, and so forth. The study of domestic productions will rise immensely in value. A new variety raised by man will be a more important and interesting subject for study than one more species added to the infinitude of already recorded species. Our classifications will come to be, as far as they can be so made, genealogies; and will then truly give what may be called the plan of creation. The rules for classifying will no doubt become simpler when we have a definite object in view. We possess no pedigrees or armorial bearings; and we have to discover and trace the many diverging lines of descent in our natural genealogies, by characters of any kind which have long been inherited. Rudimentary organs will speak infallibly with respect to the nature of long-lost structures. Species and groups of species which are called aberrant, and which may fancifully be called living fossils, will aid us in forming a picture of the ancient forms of life. Embryology will often reveal to us the structure, in some degree obscured, of the prototype of each great class.

When we feel assured that all the individuals of the same species, and all the closely allied species of most genera, have within a not very remote period descended from one parent, and have migrated from some one birth-place; and when we better know the many means of migration, then, by the light which geology now throws, and will continue to throw, on former changes of climate and of the level of the land, we shall surely be enabled to trace in an admirable manner the former migrations of the inhabitants of the whole world. Even at present, by comparing the differences between the inhabitants of the sea on the opposite sides of a continent, and the nature of the various inhabitants on that continent, in relation to their apparent means of immigration, some light can be thrown on ancient geography.

The noble science of Geology loses glory from the extreme imperfection of the record. The crust of the earth with its imbedded remains must not be looked at as a well-filled museum, but as a poor collection made at hazard and at rare intervals. The accumulation of each great fossiliferous formation will be recognised as having depended on an unusual concurrence of favourable circumstances, and the blank intervals between the successive stages as having been of vast duration. But we shall be able to gauge with some security the duration of these intervals by a comparison of the preceding and succeeding organic forms. We must be cautious in attempting to correlate as strictly contemporaneous two formations, which do not include many identical species, by the general succession of the forms of life. As species are produced and exterminated by slowly acting and still existing causes, and not by miraculous acts of creation; and as the most important of all causes of organic change is one which is almost independent of altered and perhaps suddenly altered physical conditions, namely, the mutual relation of organism to organism,—the improvement of one organism entailing the improvement or the extermination of others; it follows, that the amount of organic change in the fossils of consecutive formations probably serves as a fair measure of the relative though not actual lapse of time. A number of species, however, keeping in a body might remain for a long period unchanged, whilst within the same period several of these species by migrating into new countries and coming into competition with foreign associates, might become modified; so that we must not overrate the accuracy of organic change as a measure of time.

In the future I see open fields for far more important researches. Psychology will be securely based on the foundation already well laid by Mr. Herbert Spencer, that of the necessary acquirement of each mental power and capacity by gradation. Much light will be thrown on the origin of man and his history.

Authors of the highest eminence seem to be fully satisfied with the view that each species has been independently created. To my mind it accords better with what we know of the laws impressed on matter by the Creator, that the production and extinction of the past and present inhabitants of the world should have been due to secondary causes, like those determining the birth and death of the individual. When I view all beings not as special creations, but as the lineal descendants of some few beings which lived long before the first bed of the Cambrian system was deposited, they seem to me to become ennobled. Judging from the past, we may safely infer that not one living species will transmit its unaltered likeness to a distant futurity. And of the species now living very few will transmit progeny of any kind to a far distant futurity; for the manner in which all organic beings are grouped, shows that the greater number of species in each genus, and all the species in many genera, have left no descendants, but have become utterly extinct. We can so far take a prophetic glance into futurity as to foretell that it will be the common and widely-spread species, belonging to the larger and dominant groups within each class, which will ultimately prevail and procreate new and dominant species. As all the living forms of life are the lineal descendants of those which lived long before the Cambrian epoch, we may feel certain that the ordinary succession by generation has never once been broken, and that no cataclysm has desolated the whole world. Hence we may look with some confidence to a secure future of great length. And as natural selection works solely by and for the good of each being, all corporeal and mental endowments will tend to progress towards perfection.

It is interesting to contemplate a tangled bank, clothed with many plants of many kinds, with birds singing on the bushes, with various insects flitting about, and with worms crawling through the damp earth, and to reflect that these elaborately constructed forms, so different from each other, and dependent upon each other in so complex a manner, have all been produced by laws acting around us. These laws, taken in the largest sense, being Growth with Reproduction; Inheritance which is almost implied by reproduction; Variability from the indirect and direct action of the conditions of life, and from use and disuse: a Ratio of Increase so high as to lead to a Struggle for Life, and as a consequence to Natural Selection, entailing Divergence of Character and the Extinction of less-improved forms. Thus, from the war of nature, from famine and death, the most exalted object which we are capable of conceiving, namely, the production of the higher animals, directly follows. There is grandeur in this view of life, with its several powers, having been originally breathed by the Creator into a few forms or into one; and that, whilst this planet has gone cycling on according to the fixed law of gravity, from so simple a beginning endless forms most beautiful and most wonderful have been, and are being evolved.

CHARLES DARWIN

The Descent of Man (1871) †

Introduction

The nature of the following work will be best understood by a brief account of how it came to be written. During many years I collected notes on the origin or descent of man, without any intention of publishing on the subject, but rather with the determination not to publish, as I thought that I should thus only add to the prejudices against my views. It seemed to me sufficient to indicate, in the first edition of my 'Origin of Species,' that by this work "light would be thrown on the origin of man and his history;" and this implies that man must be included with other organic beings in any general conclusion respecting his manner of appearance on this earth. Now the case wears a wholly different aspect. When a naturalist like Carl Vogt ventures to say in his address as President of the National Institution of Geneva (1869), "personne, en Eu-

---

† The present text is excerpted from the second edition (1874), an extensive revision which contains a note by T. H. Huxley on the brains of humans and apes.

rope au moins, n'ose plus soutenir la création indépendante et de toutes pièces, des espèces," it is manifest that at least a large number of naturalists must admit that species are the modified descendants of other species; and this especially holds good with the younger and rising naturalists. The greater number accept the agency of natural selection; though some urge, whether with justice the future must decide, that I have greatly overrated its importance. Of the older and honoured chiefs in natural science, many unfortunately are still opposed to evolution in every form

In consequence of the views now adopted by most naturalists, and which will ultimately, as in every other case, be followed by others who are not scientific, I have been led to put together my notes, so as to see how far the general conclusions arrived at in my former works were applicable to man. This seemed all the more desirable, as I had never deliberately applied these views to a species taken singly. When we confine our attention to any one form, we are deprived of the weighty arguments derived from the nature of the affinities which connect together whole groups of organisms —their geographical distribution in past and present times, and their geological succession. The homological structure, embryological development, and rudimentary organs of a species remain to be considered, whether it be man or any other animal, to which our attention may be directed; but these great classes of facts afford, as it appears to me, ample and conclusive evidence in favour of the principle of gradual evolution. The strong support derived from the other arguments should, however, always be kept before the mind.

The sole object of this work is to consider, firstly, whether man, like every other species, is descended from some pre-existing form; secondly, the manner of his development; and thirdly, the value of the differences between the so-called races of man. As I shall confine myself to these points, it will not be necessary to describe in detail the differences between the several races—an enormous subject which has been fully discussed in many valuable works. The high antiquity of man has recently been demonstrated by the labours of a host of eminent men, beginning with M. Boucher de Perthes; and this is the indispensable basis for understanding his origin. I shall, therefore, take this conclusion for granted, and may refer my readers to the admirable treatises of Sir Charles Lyell, Sir John Lubbock, and others. Nor shall I have occasion to do more than to allude to the amount of difference between man and the anthropomorphous apes; for Prof. Huxley, in the opinion of most competent judges, has conclusively shewn that in every visible character man differs less from the higher apes, than these do from the lower members of the same order of Primates.

This work contains hardly any original facts in regard to man; but as the conclusions at which I arrived, after drawing up a rough draft, appeared to me interesting, I thought that they might interest others. It has often and confidently been asserted, that man's origin can never be known: but ignorance more frequently begets confidence than does knowledge: it is those who know little, and not those who know much, who so positively assert that this or that problem will never be solved by science. The conclusion that man is the co-descendant with other species of some ancient, lower, and extinct form, is not in any degree new. Lamarck long ago came to this conclusion, which has lately been maintained by several eminent naturalists and philosophers; for instance, by Wallace, Huxley, Lyell, Vogt, Lubbock, Büchner, Rolle, &c.,[1] and especially by Häckel. This last naturalist, besides his great work, 'Generelle Morphologie' (1866), has recently (1868, with a second edit. in 1870), published his 'Natürliche Schöpfungsgeschichte,' in which he fully discusses the genealogy of man. If this work had appeared before my essay had been written, I should probably never have completed it. Almost all the conclusions at which I have arrived I find confirmed by this naturalist, whose knowledge on many points is much fuller than mine. Wherever I have added any fact or view from Prof. Häckel's writings, I give his authority in the text; other statements I leave as they originally stood in my manuscript, occasionally giving in the foot-notes references to his works, as a confirmation of the more doubtful or interesting points.

During many years it has seemed to me highly probable that sexual selection has played an important part in differentiating the races of man; but in my 'Origin of Species' (first edition, p. 199) I contented myself by merely alluding to this belief. When I came to apply this view to man, I found it indispensable to treat the whole subject in full detail.[2] Consequently the second part of the present work, treating of sexual selection, has extended to an inordinate length, compared with the first part; but this could not be avoided.

I had intended adding to the present volumes an essay on the expression of the various emotions by man and the lower animals. My attention was called to this subject many years ago by Sir

1. As the works of the first-named authors are so well known, I need not give the titles; but as those of the latter are less well known in England, I will give them:—'Sechs Vorlesungen über die Darwin'sche Theorie:' zweite Auflage, 1868, von Dr. L. Büchner; translated into French under the title 'Conférences sur la Théorie Darwinienne,' 1869. 'Der Mensch, im Lichte der Darwin'sche Lehre,' 1865, von Dr. F. Rolle. I will not attempt to give references to all the authors who have taken the same side of the question. Thus G. Canestrini has published ('Annuario della Soc. d. Nat.,' Mo-

dena, 1867, p. 81) a very curious paper on rudimentary characters, as bearing on the origin of man. Another work has (1869) been published by Dr. Francesco Barrago, bearing in Italian the title of "Man, made in the image of God, was also made in the image of the ape."
2. Prof. Häckel was the only author who, at the time when this work first appeared, had discussed the subject of sexual selection, and had seen its full importance, since the publication of the 'Origin'; and this he did in a very able manner in his various works.

Charles Bell's admirable work. This illustrious anatomist maintains that man is endowed with certain muscles solely for the sake of expressing his emotions. As this view is obviously opposed to the belief that man is descended from some other and lower form, it was necessary for me to consider it. I likewise wished to ascertain how far the emotions are expressed in the same manner by the different races of man. But owing to the length of the present work, I have thought it better to reserve my essay for separate publication.

Chapter I

THE EVIDENCE OF THE DESCENT OF MAN FROM SOME LOWER FORM

Nature of the evidence bearing on the origin of man—Homologous structures in man and the lower animals—Miscellaneous points of correspondence—Development—Rudimentary structures, muscles, sense-organs, hair, bones, reproductive organs, &c.—The bearing of these three great classes of facts on the origin of man.

He who wishes to decide whether man is the modified descendant of some pre-existing form, would probably first enquire whether man varies, however slightly, in bodily structure and in mental faculties; and if so, whether the variations are transmitted to his offspring in accordance with the laws which prevail with the lower animals. Again, are the variations the result, as far as our ignorance permits us to judge, of the same general causes, and are they governed by the same general laws, as in the case of other organisms; for instance, by correlation, the inherited effects of use and disuse, &c.? Is man subject to similar malconformations, the result of arrested development, of reduplication of parts, &c., and does he display in any of his anomalies reversion to some former and ancient type of structure? It might also naturally be enquired whether man, like so many other animals, has given rise to varieties and sub-races, differing but slightly from each other, or to races differing so much that they must be classed as doubtful species? How are such races distributed over the world; and how, when crossed, do they react on each other in the first and succeeding generations? And so with many other points.

The enquirer would next come to the important point, whether man tends to increase at so rapid a rate, as to lead to occasional severe struggles for existence; and consequently to beneficial variations, whether in body or mind, being preserved, and injurious ones eliminated. Do the races or species of men, whichever term may be applied, encroach on and replace one another, so that some finally become extinct? We shall see that all these questions, as indeed is obvious in respect to most of them, must be answered in the affirmative, in the same manner as with the lower animals. But the several considerations just referred to may be conveniently deferred for a time: and we will first see how far the bodily structure of man shows traces, more or less plain, of his descent from some lower form. In succeeding chapters the mental powers of man, in comparison with those of the lower animals, will be considered.

THE BODILY STRUCTURE OF MAN

It is notorious that man is constructed on the same general type or model as other mammals. All the bones in his skeleton can be compared with corresponding bones in a monkey, bat, or seal. So it is with his muscles, nerves, blood-vessels and internal viscera. The brain, the most important of all the organs, follows the same law, as shewn by Huxley and other anatomists. Bischoff,[1] who is a hostile witness, admits that every chief fissure and fold in the brain of man has its analogy in that of the orang; but he adds that at no period of development do their brains perfectly agree; nor could perfect agreement by expected, for otherwise their mental powers would have been the same. Vulpian [2] remarks: "Les différences réelles qui existent entre l'encéphale de l'homme et celui des singes supérieurs, sont bien minimes. Il ne faut pas se faire d'illusions à cet égard. L'homme est bien plus près des singes anthropomorphes par les caractères anatomiques de son cerveau que ceux-ci ne le sont non seulement des autres mammifères, mais même de certains quadrumanes, des guenons et des macaques." But it would be superfluous here to give further details on the correspondence between man and the higher mammals in the structure of the brain and all other parts of the body.

It may, however, be worth while to specify a few points, not directly or obviously connected with structure, by which this correspondence or relationship is well shewn.

Man is liable to receive from the lower animals, and to communicate to them, certain diseases, as hydrophobia, variola, the glanders, syphilis, cholera, herpes, &c.; [3] and this fact proves the close similarity [4] of their tissues and blood, both in minute structure and

1. 'Grosshirnwindungen des Menschen,' 1868, s. 96. The conclusions of this author, as well as those of Gratiolet and Aeby, concerning the brain, will be discussed by Prof. Huxley in the Appendix alluded to in the Preface to this edition.
2. 'Leç. sur la Phys.' 1866, p. 890, as quoted by M. Dally, 'L'Ordre des Primates et le Transformisme,' 1868, p. 29.
3. Dr. W. Lauder Lindsay has treated this subject at some length in the 'Journal of Mental Science,' July 1871;

and in the 'Edinburgh Veterinary Review,' July 1858.
4. A Reviewer has criticised ('British Quarterly Review,' Oct. 1st, 1871, p. 472) what I have here said with much severity and contempt; but as I do not use the term identity, I cannot see that I am greatly in error. There appears to me a strong analogy between the same infection or contagion producing the same result, or one closely similar, in two distinct animals, and the testing of two distinct fluids by the same chemical reagent.

composition, far more plainly than does their comparison under the best microscope, or by the aid of the best chemical analysis. Monkeys are liable to many of the same non-contagious diseases as we are; thus Rengger,[5] who carefully observed for a long time the *Cebus Azaræ* in its native land, found it liable to catarrh, with the usual symptoms, and which, when often recurrent, led to consumption. These monkeys suffered also from apoplexy, inflammation of the bowels, and cataract in the eye. The younger ones when shedding their milk-teeth often died from fever. Medicines produced the same effect on them as on us. Many kinds of monkeys have a strong taste for tea, coffee, and spirituous liquors: they will also, as I have myself seen, smoke tobacco with pleasure.[6] Brehm asserts that the natives of north-eastern Africa catch the wild baboons by exposing vessels with strong beer, by which they are made drunk. He has seen some of these animals, which he kept in confinement, in this state; and he gives a laughable account of their behaviour and strange grimaces. On the following morning they were very cross and dismal; they held their aching heads with both hands, and wore a most pitiable expression: when beer or wine was offered them, they turned away with disgust, but relished the juices of lemons.[7] An American monkey, an Ateles, after getting drunk on brandy, would never touch it again, and thus was wiser than many men. These trifling facts prove how similar the nerves of taste must be in monkeys and man, and how similarly their whole nervous system is affected.

Man is infested with internal parasites, sometimes causing fatal effects; and is plagued by external parasites, all of which belong to the same genera or families as those infesting other mammals, and in the case of scabies to the same species.[8] Man is subject, like other mammals, birds, and even insects,[9] to that mysterious law, which causes certain normal processes, such as gestation, as well as the maturation and duration of various diseases, to follow lunar periods. His wounds are repaired by the same process of healing; and the stumps left after the amputation of his limbs, especially during an embryonic period, occasionally possess some power of regeneration, as in the lowest animals.[1]

5. 'Naturgeschichte der Säugethiere von Paraguay,' 1830, s. 50.
6. The same tastes are common to some animals much lower in the scale. Mr. A. Nicols informs me that he kept in Queensland, in Australia, three individuals of the *Phaseolarctus cinereus;* and that, without having been taught in any way, they acquired a strong taste for rum, and for smoking tobacco.
7. Brehm, 'Thierleben,' B. i. 1864, s. 75, 86. On the Ateles, s. 105. For other analogous statements, see s. 25, 107.
8. Dr. W. Lauder Lindsay, 'Edinburgh

Vet. Review,' July 1858, p. 13.
9. With respect to insects see Dr. Laycock, "On a General Law of Vital Periodicity," 'British Association,' 1842. Dr. Macculloch, 'Silliman's North American Journal of Science,' vol. xvii. p. 305, has seen a dog suffering from tertian ague. Hereafter I shall return to this subject.
1. I have given the evidence on this head in my 'Variation of Animals and Plants under Domestication,' vol. ii. p. 15, and more could be added.

The whole process of that most important function, the reproduction of the species, is strikingly the same in all mammals, from the first act of courtship by the male,[2] to the birth and nurturing of the young. Monkeys are born in almost as helpless a condition as our own infants; and in certain genera the young differ fully as much in appearance from the adults, as do our children from their full-grown parents.[3] It has been urged by some writers, as an important distinction, that with man the young arrive at maturity at a much later age than with any other animal: but if we look to the races of mankind which inhabit tropical countries the difference is not great, for the orang is believed not to be adult till the age of from ten to fifteen years.[4] Man differs from woman in size, bodily strength, hairiness, &c., as well as in mind, in the same manner as do the two sexes of many mammals. So that the correspondence in general structure, in the minute structure of the tissues, in chemical composition and in constitution, between man and the higher animals, especially the anthropomorphous apes, is extremely close.

EMBRYONIC DEVELOPMENT

Man is developed from an ovule, about the 125th of an inch in diameter, which differs in no respect from the ovules of other animals. The embryo itself at a very early period can hardly be distinguished from that of other members of the vertebrate kingdom. At this period the arteries run in arch-like branches, as if to carry the blood to branchiæ which are not present in the higher vertebrate, though the slits on the sides of the neck still remain (f, g, fig. 1), marking their former position. At a somewhat later period, when the extremities are developed, "the feet of lizards and mammals," as the illustrious Von Baer remarks, "the wings and feet of birds, no less than the hands and feet of man, all arise from the same fundamental form." It is, says Prof. Huxley,[5] quite in the later stages of development that the young human being presents marked differences from the young ape, while the latter departs as much from the dog in its developments, as the man does. Startling as this last assertion may appear to be, it is demonstrably true."

2. Mares e diversis generibus Quadrumanorum sine dubio dignoscunt feminas humanas a maribus. Primum, credo, odoratu, postea aspectu. Mr. Youatt, qui diu in Hortis Zoologicis (Bestiariis) medicus animalium erat, vir in rebus observandis cautus et sagax, hoc mihi certissime probavit, et curatores ejusdem loci et alii e ministris confirmaverunt. Sir Andrew Smith et Brehm notabant idem in Cynocephalo. Illustrissimus Cuvier etiam narrat multa de hâc re, quâ ut opinor, nihil turpius potest indicari inter omnia hominibus et Quadrumanis communia.

Narrat enim Cynocephalum quendam in furorem incidere aspectu feminarum aliquarem, sed nequaquam accendi tanto furore ab omnibus. Semper eligebat juniores, et dignoscebat in turbâ, et advocabat voce gestûque.
3. This remark is made with respect to Cynocephalus and the anthropomorphous apes by Geoffroy Saint-Hilaire and F. Cuvier, 'Hist. Nat. des Mammifères,' tom. i. 1824.
4. Huxley, 'Man's Place in Nature,' 1863, p. 34.
5. 'Man's Place in Nature,' 1863, p. 67.

As some of my readers may never have seen a drawing of an embryo, I have given one of man and another of a dog, at about the same early stage of development, carefully copied from two works of undoubted accuracy.[6]

After the foregoing statements made by such high authorities, it would be superfluous on my part to give a number of borrowed details, shewing that the embryo of man closely resembles that of other mammals. It may, however, be added, that the human embryo likewise resembles certain low forms when adult in various points of structure. For instance, the heart at first exists as a simple pulsating vessel; the excreta are voided through a cloacal passage; and the os coccyx projects like a true tail, "extending considerably beyond the rudimentary legs." [7] In the embryos of all air-breathing vertebrates, certain glands, called the corpora Wolffiana, correspond with, and act like the kidneys of mature fishes.[8] Even at a later embryonic period, some striking resemblances between man and the lower animals may be observed. Bischoff says "that the convolutions of the brain in a human fœtus at the end of the seventh month reach about the same stage of development as in a baboon when adult." [9] The great toe, as Professor Owen remarks,[1] "which forms the fulcrum when standing or walking, is perhaps the most characteristic peculiarity in the human structure;" but in an embryo, about an inch in length, Prof. Wyman [2] found "that the great toe was shorter than the others; and, instead of being parallel to them, projected at an angle from the side of the foot, thus corresponding with the permanent condition of this part in the quadrumana." I will conclude with a quotation from Huxley,[3] who after asking, does man originate in a different way from a dog, bird, frog or fish? says, "the reply is not doubtful for a moment; without question, the mode of origin, and the early stages of the development of man, are identical with those of the animals immediately below him in the scale: without a doubt in these respects, he is far nearer to apes than the apes are to the dog."

6. The human embryo (upper fig.) is from Ecker, 'Icones Phys.,' 1851–1859, tab. xxx. fig. 2. This embryo was ten lines in length, so that the drawing is much magnified. The embryo of the dog is from Bischoff, 'Entwicklungsgeschichte des Hunde-Eies,' 1845, tab. xi. fig. 42 B. This drawing is five times magnified, the embryo being twenty-five days old. The internal viscera have been omitted, and the uterine appendages in both drawings removed. I was directed to these figures by Prof. Huxley, from whose work, 'Man's Place in Nature,' the idea of giving them was taken. Häckel has also given analogous drawings in his 'Schöpfungsgeschichte.'

7. Prof. Wyman in 'Proc. of American Acad. of Sciences,' vol. iv. 1860, p. 17.

8. Owen, 'Anatomy of Vertebrates,' vol. i. p. 533.

9. 'Die Grosshirnwindungen des Menschen,' 1868, s. 95.

1. 'Anatomy of Vertebrates,' vol. ii. p. 553.

2. 'Proc. Soc. Nat. Hist.' Boston, 1863, vol. ix. p. 185.

3. 'Man's Place in Nature,' p. 65.

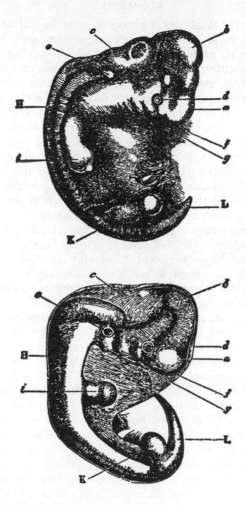

FIG. 1.—Upper figure human embryo, from Ecker. Lower figure that of a dog, from Bischoff.

a. Fore-brain, cerebral hemispheres, &c.
b. Mid-brain, corpora, quadrigemina.
c. Hind-brain, cerebellum, medulla oblongata.
d. Eye. e. Ear. f. First visceral arch. g. Second visceral arch.
H. Vertebral columns and muscles in process of development.
i. Anterior ⎱ extremities.
K. Posterior ⎰
L. Tail or os coccyx.

RUDIMENTS

This subject, though not intrinsically more important than the two last, will for several reasons be treated here more fully.[4] Not one of the higher animals can be named which does not bear some part in a rudimentary condition; and man forms no exception to the rule. Rudimentary organs must be distinguished from those that are nascent; though in some cases the distinction is not easy. The former are either absolutely useless, such as the mammæ of male quadrupeds, or the incisor teeth of ruminants which never cut through the gums; or they are of such slight service to their present possessors, that we can hardly suppose that they were developed under the conditions which now exist. Organs in this latter state are not strictly rudimentary, but they are tending in this direction. Nascent organs, on the other hand, though not fully developed, are of high service to their possessors, and are capable of further development. Rudimentary organs are eminently variable; and this is partly intelligible, as they are useless, or nearly useless, and consequently are no longer subjected to natural selection. They often become wholly suppressed. When this occurs, they are nevertheless liable to occasional reappearance through reversion—a circumstance well worthy of attention.

The chief agents in causing organs to become rudimentary seem to have been disuse at that period of life when the organ is chiefly used (and this is generally during maturity), and also inheritance at a corresponding period of life. The term "disuse" does not relate merely to the lessened action of muscles, but includes a diminished flow of blood to a part or organ, from being subjected to fewer alterations of pressure, or from becoming in any way less habitually active. Rudiments, however, may occur in one sex of those parts which are normally present in the other sex; and such rudiments, as we shall hereafter see, have often originated in a way distinct from those here referred to. In some cases, organs have been reduced by means of natural selection, from having become injurious to the species under changed habits of life. The process of reduction is probably often aided through the two principles of compensation and economy of growth; but the later stages of reduction, after disuse has done all that can fairly be attributed to it, and when the saving to be effected by the economy of growth would be

4. I had written a rough copy of this chapter before reading a valuable paper, "Caratteri rudimentali in ordine all' origine dell' uomo" ('Annuario della Soc. d. Nat.,' Modena, 1867, p. 81), by G. Canestrini, to which paper I am considerably indebted. Häckel has given admirable discussions on this whole subject, under the title of Dysteleology, in his 'Generelle Morphologie' and 'Schöpfungsgeschichte.'

very small,[5] are difficult to understand. The final and complete suppression of a part, already useless and much reduced in size, in which case neither compensation nor economy can come into play, is perhaps intelligible by the aid of the hypothesis of pangenesis. But as the whole subject of rudimentary organs has been discussed and illustrated in my former works,[6] I need here say no more on this head.

Rudiments of various muscles have been observed in many parts of the human body;[7] and not a few muscles, which are regularly present in some of the lower animals can occasionally be detected in man in a greatly reduced condition. Every one must have noticed the power which many animals, especially horses, possess of moving or twitching their skin; and this is effected by the *panniculus carnosus*. Remnants of this muscle in an efficient state are found in various parts of our bodies; for instance, the muscle on the forehead, by which the eyebrows are raised. The *platysma myoides*, which is well developed on the neck, belongs to this system. Prof. Turner, of Edinburgh, has occasionally detected, as he informs me, muscular fasciculi in five different situations, namely in the axillæ, near the scapulæ, &c., all of which must be referred to the system of the *panniculus*. He has also shewn [8] that the *musculus sternalis* or *sternalis brutorum*, which is not an extension of the *rectus abdominalis*, but is closely allied to the *panniculus*, occurred in the proportion of about three percent. in upward of 600 bodies: he adds, that this muscle affords "an excellent illustration of the statement that occasional and rudimentary structures are especially liable to variation in arrangement."

Some few persons have the power of contracting the superficial muscles on their scalps; and these muscles are in a variable and partially rudimentary condition. M. A. de Candolle has communicated to me a curious instance of the long-continued persistence or inheritance of this power, as well as of its unusual development. He knows a family, in which one member, the present head of the family, could, when a youth, pitch several heavy books from his head by the movement of the scalp alone; and he won wagers by

---

5. Some good criticisms on this subject have been given by Messrs. Murie and Mivart, in 'Transact. Zoolog. Soc.' 1869, vol. vii p. 92.
6. 'Variation of Animals and Plants under Domestication,' vol. ii. pp. 317 and 397. See also 'Origin of Species,' fifth edition, p. 535.
7. For instance, M. Richard ('Annales des Sciences Nat.,' 3d series, Zoolog.

1852, tom. xviii. p. 13) describes and figures rudiments of what he calls the "muscle pédieux de la main," which he says is sometimes "infiniment petit." Another muscle, called "le tibial postérieur," is generally quite absent in the hand, but appears from time to time in a more or less rudimentary condition.
8. Prof. W. Turner, 'Proc. Royal Soc. Edinburgh,' 1866–67, p. 65.

performing this feat. His father, uncle, grandfather, and his three children possess the same power to the same unusual degree. This family became divided eight generations ago into two branches; so that the head of the above-mentioned branch is cousin in the seventh degree to the head of the other branch. This distant cousin resides in another part of France; and on being asked whether he possessed the same faculty, immediately exhibited his power. This case offers a good illustration how persistent may be the transmission of an absolutely useless faculty, probably derived from our remote semi-human progenitors; since many monkeys have, and frequently use the power, of largely moving their scalps up and down.[9]

The extrinsic muscles which serve to move the external ear, and the intrinsic muscles which move the different parts, are in a rudimentary condition in man, and they all belong to the system of the *panniculus;* they are also variable in development, or at least in function. I have seen one man who could draw the whole ear forwards; other men can draw it upwards; another who could draw it backwards;[1] and from what one of these persons told me, it is probable that most of us, by often touching our ears, and thus directing our attention towards them, could recover some power of movement by repeated trials. The power of erecting and directing the shell of the ears to the various points of the compass, is no doubt of the highest service to many animals, as they thus perceive the direction of danger; but I have never heard, on sufficient evidence, of a man who possessed this power, the one which might be of use to him. The whole external shell may be considered a rudiment, together with the various folds and prominences (helix and anti-helix, tragus and anti-tragus, &c.) which in the lower animals strengthen and support the ear when erect, without adding much to its weight. Some authors, however, suppose that the cartilage of the shell serves to transmit vibrations to the acoustic nerve; but Mr. Toynbee,[2] after collecting all the known evidence on this head, concludes that the external shell is of no distinct use. The ears of the chimpanzee and orang are curiously like those of man, and the proper muscles are likewise but very slightly developed.[3] I am also assured by the keepers in the Zoological Gardens that these

9. See my 'Expression of the Emotions in Man and Animals,' 1872, p. 144.
1. Canestrini quotes Hyrtl. ('Annuario della Soc. dei Naturalisti,' Modena, 1897, p. 97) to the same effect.
2. 'The Diseases of the Ear,' by J. Toynbee, F. R. S., 1860, p. 12. A distinguished physiologist, Prof. Preyer,

informs me that he had lately been experimenting on the function of the shell of the ear, and has come to nearly the same conclusion as that given here.
3. Prof. A. Macalister, 'Annals and Mag. of Nat. History,' vol. vii., 1871, p. 342.

animals never move or erect their ears; so that they are in an equally rudimentary condition with those of man, as far as function is concerned. Why these animals, as well as the progenitors of man, should have lost the power of erecting their ears, we can not say. It may be, though I am not satisfied with this view, that owing to their arboreal habits and great strength they were but little exposed to danger, and so during a lengthened period moved their ears but little, and thus gradually lost the power of moving them. This would be a parallel case with that of those large and heavy birds, which, from inhabiting oceanic islands, have not been exposed to the attacks of beasts of prey, and have consequently lost the power of using their wings for flight. The inability to move the ears in man and several apes is, however, partly compensated by the freedom with which they can move the head in a horizontal plane, so as to catch sounds from all directions. It has been asserted that the ear of man alone possesses a lobule; but "a rudiment of it is found in the gorilla;" [4] and, as I hear from Prof. Preyer, it is not rarely absent in the negro.

The celebrated sculptor, Mr. Woolner, informs me of one little peculiarity in the external ear, which he has often observed both in men and women, and of which he perceived the full significance. His attention was first called to the subject whilst at work on his figure of Puck, to which he had given pointed ears. He was thus led to examine the ears of various monkeys, and subsequently more carefully those of man. The peculiarity consists in a little blunt point, projecting from the inwardly folded margin, or helix. When present, it is developed at birth, and according to Prof. Ludwig Meyer, more frequently in man than in woman. Mr. Woolner made an exact model of one such case, and sent me the accompanying drawing. (Fig. 2.) These points not only project inwards towards the centre of the ear, but often a little outwards from its plane, so as to be visible when the head is viewed from directly in front or behind. They are variable in size, and somewhat in position, standing either a little higher or lower; and they sometimes occur on one ear and not on the other. They are not confined to mankind, for I observed a case in one of the spider-monkeys (*Ateles beelzebuth*) in our Zoological Gardens; and Mr. E. Ray Lankester informs me of another case in a chimpanzee in the gardens at Hamburg. The helix obviously consists of the extreme margin of the ear folded inwards; and this folding appears to be in some manner connected with the whole external ear being permanently pressed

4. Mr. St. George Mivart, 'Elementary Anatomy,' 1873, p. 396.

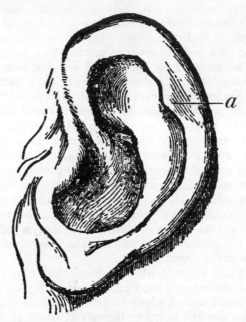

FIG. 2.—Human Ear, modelled and drawn by Mr. Woolner.
   a. The projecting point.

backwards. In many monkeys, which do not stand high in the order, as baboons and some species of macacus,[5] the upper portion of the ear is slightly pointed, and the margin is not at all folded inwards; but if the margin were to be thus folded, a slight point would necessarily project inwards towards the centre, and probably a little outwards from the plane of the ear; and this I believe to be their origin in many cases. On the other hand, Prof. L. Meyer, in an able paper recently published,[6] maintains that the whole case is one of mere variability; and that the projections are not real ones, but are due to the internal cartilage on each side of the points not having been fully developed. I am quite ready to admit that this is the correct explanation in many instances, as in those figured by Prof. Meyer, in which there are several minute points, or the whole margin is sinuous. I have myself seen, through the kindness

5. See also some remarks, and the drawings of the ears of the Lemuroidea, in Messrs. Murie and Mivart's excellent paper in 'Transact. Zoolog. Soc.' vol. vii. 1869, pp. 6 and 90.

6. Ueber das Darwin'sche Spitzohr, Archiv für Path. Anat. und Phys. 1871, p. 485.

of Dr. L. Down, the ear of a microcephalous idiot, on which there
is a projection on the outside of the helix, and not on the inward
folded edge, so that this point can have no relation to a former apex
of the ear. Nevertheless in some cases, my original view, that the
points are vestiges of the tips of formerly erect and pointed ears,
still seems to me probable. I think so from the frequency of their
occurrence, and from the general correspondence in position with
that of the tip of a pointed ear. In one case, of which a photograph
has been sent me, the projection is so large, that supposing, in
accordance with Prof. Meyer's view, the ear to be made perfect by
the equal development of the cartilage throughout the whole extent
of the margin, it would have covered fully one-third of the whole
ear. Two cases have been communicated to me, one in North America, and the other in England, in which the upper margin is not at
all folded inwards, but is pointed, so that it closely resembles the
pointed ear of an ordinary quadruped in outline. In one of these
cases, which was that of a young child, the father compared the ear
with the drawing which I have given [7] of the ear of a monkey, the
Cynopithecus niger, and says that their outlines are closely similar.
If, in these two cases, the margin had been folded inwards in the
normal manner, an inward projection must have been formed. I
may add that in two other cases the outline still remains somewhat
pointed, although the margin of the upper part of the ear is normally folded inwards—in one of them, however, very narrowly. The
following woodcut (No. 3) is an accurate copy of a photograph of
the fœtus of an orang (kindly sent me by Dr. Nitsche), in which it
may be seen how different the pointed outline of the ear is at this
period from its adult condition, when it bears a close general resemblance to that of man. It is evident that the folding over of the
tip of such an ear, unless it changed greatly during its further
development, would give rise to a point projecting inwards. On the
whole, it still seems to me probable that the points in question are
in some cases, both in man and apes, vestiges of a former condition.

The nictitating membrane, or third eyelid, with its accessory
muscles and other structures, is especially well developed in birds,
and is of much functional importance to them, as it can be rapidly
drawn across the whole eye-ball. It is found in some reptiles and
amphibians, and in certain fishes, as in sharks. It is fairly well
developed in the two lower divisions of the mammalian series,
namely, in the monotremata and marsupials, and in some few of
the higher mammals, as in the walrus. But in man, the quadrumana, and most other mammals, it exists, as is admitted by all

7. 'The Expression of the Emotions,' p. 136.

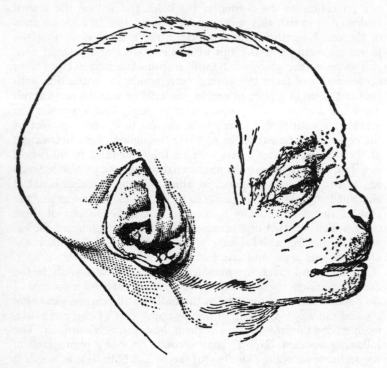

FIG. 3.—Fœtus of an Orang. Exact copy of a photograph, showing the form of the ear at this early age.

anatomists, as a mere rudiment, called the semilunar fold.[8]

The sense of smell is of the highest importance to the greater number of mammals—to some, as the ruminants, in warning them of danger; to others, as the carnivora, in finding their prey; to others, again, as the wild boar, for both purposes combined. But the sense of smell is of extremely slight service, if any, even to the dark coloured races of men, in whom it is much more highly developed than in the white and civilised races.[9] Nevertheless it

8. Müller's 'Elements of Physiology,' Eng. translat., 1842, vol. ii. p. 1117. Owen, 'Anatomy of Vertebrates,' vol. iii. p. 260; ibid. on the Walrus, 'Proc. Zoolog. Soc.' November 8th, 1854. See also R. Knox, 'Great Artists and Anatomists,' p. 106. This rudiment apparently is somewhat larger in Negroes and Australians than in Europeans, see Carl Vogt, 'Lectures on Man,' Eng. translat. p. 129.

9. The account given by Humboldt of the power of smell possessed by the natives of South America is well known, and has been confirmed by others. M. Houzeau ('Études sur les Facultés Mentales,' &c., tom. i. 1872, p. 91) asserts that he repeatedly made experiments, and proved that Negroes and Indians could recognise persons in the dark by their odour. Dr. W. Ogle has made some curious observations on the connection

does not warn them of danger, nor guide them to their food; nor does it prevent the Esquimaux from sleeping in the most fetid atmosphere, nor many savages from eating half-putrid meat. In Europeans the power differs greatly in different individuals, as I am assured by an eminent naturalist who possesses this sense highly developed, and who has attended to the subject. Those who believe in the principle of gradual evolution, will not readily admit that the sense of smell in its present state was originally acquired by man, as he now exists. He inherits the power in an enfeebled and so far rudimentary condition, from some early progenitor, to whom it was highly serviceable, and by whom it was continually used. In those animals which have this sense highly developed, such as dogs and horses, the recollection of persons and of places is strongly associated with their odour; and we can thus perhaps understand how it is, as Dr. Maudsley has truly remarked,[1] that the sense of smell in man "is singularly effective in recalling vividly the ideas and images of forgotten scenes and places."

Man differs conspicuously from all the other Primates in being almost naked. But a few short straggling hairs are found over the greater part of the body in the man, and fine down on that of a woman. The different races differ much in hairiness; and in the individuals of the same race the hairs are highly variable, not only in abundance, but likewise in position: thus in some Europeans the shoulders are quite naked, whilst in others they bear thick tufts of hair.[2] There can be little doubt that the hairs thus scattered over the body are the rudiments of the uniform hairy coat of the lower animals. This view is rendered all the more probable, as it is known that fine, short, and pale-coloured hairs on the limbs and other parts of the body, occasionally become developed into "thickset, long, and rather coarse dark hairs," when abnormally nourished near old-standing inflamed surfaces.[3]

I am informed by Sir James Paget that often several members of a family have a few hairs in their eyebrows much longer than the others; so that even this slight peculiarity seems to be inherited. These hairs, too, seem to have their representatives; for in the chimpanzee, and in certain species of Macacus, there are scattered hairs of considerable length rising from the naked skin above the eyes, and corresponding to our eyebrows; similar long hairs project

between the power of smell and the colouring matter of the membrane of the olfactory region as well as of the skin of the body. I have, therefore, spoken in the text of the dark-coloured races having a finer sense of smell than the white races. See his paper, 'Medico-Chirurgical Transactions,' London, vol. liii., 1870, p. 276.

1. 'The Physiology and Pathology of Mind,' 2nd edit. 1868, p. 134.
2. Eschricht, Ueber die Richtung der Haare am menschlichen Körper, 'Müller's Archiv für Anat. und Phys. 1837, s. 47. I shall often have to refer to this very curious paper.
3. Paget, 'Lectures on Surgical Pathology,' 1853, vol. i. p. 71.

from the hairy covering of the superciliary ridges in some baboons.

The fine wool-like hair, or so-called lanugo, with which the human fœtus during the sixth month is thickly covered, offers a more curious case. It is first developed, during the fifth month, on the eyebrows and face, and especially round the mouth, where it is much longer than that on the head. A moustache of this kind was observed by Eschricht [4] on a female fœtus; but this is not so surprising a circumstance as it may at first appear, for the two sexes generally resemble each other in all external characters during an early period of growth. The direction and arrangement of the hairs on all parts of the fœtal body are the same as in the adult, but are subject to much variability. The whole surface, including even the forehead and ears, is thus thickly clothed; but it is a significant fact that the palms of the hands and the soles of the feet are quite naked, like the inferior surfaces of all four extremities in most of the lower animals. As this can hardly be an accidental coincidence, the woolly covering of the fœtus probably represents the first permanent coat of hair in those mammals which are born hairy. Three or four cases have been recorded of persons born with their whole bodies and faces thickly covered with fine long hairs; and this strange condition is strongly inherited, and is correlated with an abnormal condition of the teeth.[5] Prof. Alex. Brandt informs me that he has compared the hair from the face of a man thus characterised, aged thirty-five, with the lanugo of a fœtus, and finds it quite similar in texture; therefore, as he remarks, the case may be attributed to an arrest of development in the hair, together with its continued growth. Many delicate children, as I have been assured by a surgeon to a hospital for children, have their backs covered by rather long silky hairs; and such cases probably come under the same head.

It appears as if the posterior molar or wisdom-teeth were tending to become rudimentary in the more civilised races of man. These teeth are rather smaller than the other molars, as is likewise the case with the corresponding teeth in the chimpanzee and orang; and they have only two separate fangs. They do not cut through the gums till about the seventeenth year, and I have been assured that they are much more liable to decay, and are earlier lost than the other teeth; but this is denied by some eminent dentists. They are also much more liable to vary, both in structure and in the period of their development, than the other teeth.[6] In the Melanian races, on the other hand, the wisdom-teeth are usually furnished with

4. Eschricht, ibid. s. 40, 47.
5. See my 'Variation of Animals and Plants under Domestication,' vol. ii. p. 327. Prof. Alex Brandt has recently sent me an additional case of a father and son, born in Russia, with these peculiarities. I have received drawings of both from Paris.
6. Dr. Webb, 'Teeth in Man and the Anthropoid Apes,' as quoted by Dr. C. Carter Blake in 'Anthropological Review,' July 1867, p. 299.

three separate fangs, and are generally sound; they also differ from the other molars in size, less than in the Caucasian races.[7] Prof. Schaaffhausen accounts for this difference between the races by "the posterior dental portion of the jaw being always shortened" in those that are civilised,[8] and this shortening may, I presume, be attributed to civilised men habitually feeding on soft, cooked food, and thus using their jaws less. I am informed by Mr. Brace that it is becoming quite a common practice in the United States to remove some of the molar teeth of children, as the jaw does not grow large enough for the perfect development of the normal number.[9]

With respect to the alimentary canal, I have met with an account of only a single rudiment, namely the vermiform appendage of the cæcum. The cæcum is a branch or diverticulum of the intestine, ending in a cul-de-sac, and is extremely long in many of the lower vegetable-feeding mammals. In the marsupial koala it is actually more than thrice as long as the whole body.[1] It is sometimes produced into a long gradually-tapering point, and is sometimes constricted in parts. It appears as if, in consequence of changed diet or habits, the cæcum had become much shortened in various animals, the vermiform appendage being left as a rudiment of the shortened part. That this appendage is a rudiment, we may infer from its small size, and from the evidence which Prof. Canestrini [2] has collected of its variability in man. It is occasionally quite absent, or again is largely developed. The passage is sometimes completely closed for half or two-thirds of its length, with the terminal part consisting of a flattened solid expansion. In the orang this appendage is long and convoluted: in man it arises from the end of the short cæcum, and is commonly from four to five inches in length, being only about the third of an inch in diameter. Not only is it useless, but it is sometimes the cause of death, of which fact I have lately heard two instances: this is due to small hard bodies, such as seeds, entering the passage, and causing inflammation.[3]

In some of the lower Quadrumana, in the Lemuridæ and Carnivora, as well as in many marsupials, there is a passage near the lower end of the humerus, called the supra-condyloid foramen, through which the great nerve of the fore limb and often the great

7. Owen, 'Anatomy of Vertebrates,' vol. iii. pp. 320, 321, and 325.
8. 'On the Primitive Form of the Skull,' Eng. translat. in 'Anthropological Review,' Oct. 1868, p. 426.
9. Prof. Montegazza writes to me from Florence, that he has lately been studying the last molar teeth in the different races of man, and has come to the same conclusion as that given in my text, viz., that in the higher or civilized races they are on the road towards atrophy or elimination.

1. Owen, 'Anatomy of Vertebrates,' vol. iii. pp. 416, 434, 441.
2. 'Annuario della Soc. d. Nat.' Modena, 1867, p. 94.
3. M. C. Martins ("De l'Unité Organique," in 'Revue des Deux Mondes,' June 15, 1862, p. 16), and Häckel ("Generelle Morphologie,' B. ii. s. 278), have both remarked on the singular fact of this rudiment sometimes causing death.

artery pass. Now in the humerus of man, there is generally a trace of this passage, which is sometimes fairly well developed, being formed by a depending hook-like process of bone, completed by a band of ligament. Dr. Struthers,[4] who has closely attended to the subject, has now shewn that this peculiarity is sometimes inherited, as it has occurred in a father, and in no less than four out of his seven children. When present, the great nerve invariably passes through it; and this clearly indicates that it is the homologue and rudiment of the supra-condyloid foramen of the lower animals. Prof. Turner estimates, as he informs me, that it occurs in about one per cent. of recent skeletons. But if the occasional development of this structure in man is, as seems probable, due to reversion, it is a return to a very ancient state of things, because in the higher Quadrumana it is absent.

There is another foramen or perforation in the humerus, occasionally present in man, which may be called the inter-condyloid. This occurs, but not constantly, in various anthropoid and other apes,[5] and likewise in many of the lower animals. It is remarkable that this perforation seems to have been present in man much more frequently during ancient times than recently. Mr. Busk [6] has collected the following evidence on this head: Prof. Broca "noticed the perforation in four and a half per cent. of the arm-bones collected in the 'Cimetière du Sud,' at Paris; and in the Grotto of Orrony, the contents of which are referred to the Bronze period, as many as eight humeri out of thirty-two were perforated; but this extraordinary proportion, he thinks, might be due to the cavern having been a sort of 'family vault.' Again, M. Dupont found thirty per cent. of perforated bones in the caves of the Valley of the Lesse, belonging to the Reindeer period; whilst M. Leguay, in a sort of *dolmen* at Argenteuil, observed twenty-five per cent. to be perforated; and M. Pruner-Bey found twenty-six per cent. in the same condition in bones from Vauréal. Nor should it be left unnoticed that M. Pruner-Bey states that this condition is common in Guanche skeletons." It is an interesting fact that ancient races, in this and several other cases, more frequently present structures which resemble those of the lower animals than do the modern. One chief cause seems to be that the ancient races stand somewhat

4. With respect to inheritance, see Dr. Struthers in the 'Lancet,' Feb. 15, 1873, and another important paper, ibid., Jan. 24, 1863, p. 83. Dr. Knox, as I am informed, was the first anatomist who drew attention to this peculiar structure in man; see his 'Great Artists and Anatomists,' p. 63. See also an important memoir on this process by Dr. Gruber, in the 'Bulletin de l'Acad. Imp. de St. Pétersbourg,' tom xii. 1867, p. 448.
5. Mr. St. George Mivart, 'Transact.

Phil. Soc.' 1867, p. 310.
6. "On the Caves of Gibraltar," 'Transact. Internat. Congress of Prehist. Arch.' Third Session, 1869, p. 159. Prof. Wyman has lately shown (Fourth Annual Report, Peabody Museum, 1871, p. 20), that this perforation is present in thirty-one per cent. of some human remains from ancient mounds in the Western United States, and in Florida. It frequently occurs in the negro.

nearer in the long line of descent to their remote animal-like progenitors.

In man, the os coccyx, together with certain other vertebræ hereafter to be described, though functionless as a tail, plainly represent this part in other vertebrate animals. At an early embryonic period it is free, and projects beyond the lower extremities; as may be seen in the drawing (Fig. i.) of a human embryo. Even after birth it has been known, in certain rare and anomalous cases,[7] to form a small external rudiment of a tail. The os coccyx is short, usually including only four vertebræ, all anchylosed together: and these are in a rudimentary condition, for they consist, with the exception of the basal one, of the centrum alone.[8] They are furnished with some small muscles; one of which, as I am informed by Prof. Turner, has been expressly described by Theile as a rudimentary repetition of the extensor of the tail, a muscle which is so largely developed in many mammals.

The spinal cord in man extends only as far downwards as the last dorsal or first lumbar vertebra; but a thread-like structure (the *filum terminale*) runs down the axis of the sacral part of the spinal canal, and even along the back of the coccygeal bones. The upper part of this filament, as Prof. Turner informs me, is undoubtedly homologous with the spinal cord; but the lower part apparently consists merely of the *pia mater*, or vascular investing membrane. Even in this case the os coccyx may be said to possess a vestige of so important a structure as the spinal cord, though no longer enclosed within a bony canal. The following fact, for which I am also indebted to Prof. Turner, shews how closely the os coccyx corresponds with the true tail in the lower animals: Luschka has recently discovered at the extremity of the coccygeal bones a very peculiar convoluted body, which is continuous with the middle sacral artery; and this discovery led Krause and Meyer to examine the tail of a monkey (Macacus), and of a cat, in both of which they found a similarly convoluted body, though not at the extremity.

The reproductive system offers various rudimentary structures; but these differ in one important respect from the foregoing cases. Here we are not concerned with the vestige of a part which does not belong to the species in an efficient state, but with a part efficient in the one sex, and represented in the other by a mere rudiment. Nevertheless, the occurrence of such rudiments is as difficult to explain, on the belief of the separate creation of each

7. Quatrefages has lately collected the evidence on this subject. 'Revue des Cours Scientifiques,' 1867–1868, p. 625. In 1840 Fleischmann exhibited a human fœtus bearing a free tail, which, as is not always the case, included vertebral bodies; and this tail was critically examined by the many anatomists present at the meeting of naturalists at Erlangen (see Marshall in Niederländischen Archiv Für Zoologie, December 1871).
8. Owen, 'On the Nature of Limbs,' 1849, p. 114.

species, as in the foregoing cases. Hereafter I shall have to recur to these rudiments, and shall shew that their presence generally depends merely on inheritance, that is, on parts acquired by one sex having been partially transmitted to the other. I will in this place only give some instances of such rudiments. It is well known that in the males of all mammals, including man, rudimentary mammæ exist. These in several instances have become well developed, and have yielded a copious supply of milk. Their essential identity in the two sexes is likewise shewn by their occasional sympathetic enlargement in both during an attack of the measles. The *vesicula prostatica*, which has been observed in many male mammals, is now universally acknowledged to be the homologue of the female uterus, together with the connected passage. It is impossible to read Leuckart's able description of this organ, and his reasoning, without admitting the justness of his conclusion. This is especially clear in the case of those mammals in which the true female uterus bifurcates, for in the males of these the vesicula likewise bifurcates.[9] Some other rudimentary structures belonging to the reproductive system might have been here adduced.[1]

The bearing of the three great classes of facts now given is unmistakable. But it would be superfluous fully to recapitulate the line of argument given in detail in my 'Origin of Species.' The homological construction of the whole frame in the members of the same class is intelligible, if we admit their descent from a common progenitor, together with their subsequent adaptation to diversified conditions. On any other view, the similarity of pattern between the hand of a man or monkey, the foot of a horse, the flipper of a seal, the wing of a bat, &c., is utterly inexplicable.[2] It is no scientific explanation to assert that they have all been formed

9. Leuckart, in Todd's 'Cyclop. of Anat.' 1849–52, vol. iv. p. 1415. In man this organ is only from three to six lines in length, but, like so many other rudimentary parts, it is variable in development as well as in other characters.
1. See, on this subject, Owen, 'Anatomy of Vertebrates,' vol. iii. pp. 675, 676, 706.
2. Prof. Bianconi, in a recently published work, illustrated by admirable engravings ('La Théorie Darwinienne et la création dite indépendante,' 1874), endeavours to show that homological structures, in the above and other cases, can be fully explained on mechanical principles, in accordance with their uses. No one has shewn so well, how admirably such structures are adapted for their final purpose; and this adaptation can, as I believe, be explained through natural selection. In considering the wing of a bat, he brings forward (p. 218) what appears to me (to use Auguste Comte's words) a mere metaphysical principle, namely, the preservation "in its integrity of the mammalian nature of the animal." In only a few cases does he discuss rudiments, and then only those parts which are partially rudimentary, such as the little hoofs of the pig and ox, which do not touch the ground; these he shows clearly to be of service to the animal. It is unfortunate that he did not consider such cases as the minute teeth, which never cut through the jaw in the ox, or the mammæ of male quadrupeds, or the wings of certain beetles, existing under the soldered wing-covers, or the vestiges of the pistil and stamens in various flowers, and many other such cases. Although I greatly admire Prof. Bianconi's work, yet the belief now held by most naturalists seems to me left unshaken, that homological structures are inexplicable on the principle of mere adaptation.

on the same ideal plan. With respect to development, we can clearly understand, on the principle of variation supervening at a rather late embryonic period, and being inherited at a corresponding period, how it is that the embryos of wonderfully different forms should still retain, more or less perfectly, the structure of their common progenitor. No other explanation has ever been given of the marvellous fact that the embryos of a man, dog, seal, bat, reptile, &c., can at first hardly be distinguished from each other. In order to understand the existence of rudimentary organs, we have only to suppose that a former progenitor possessed the parts in question in a perfect state, and that under changed habits of life they became greatly reduced, either from simple disuse, or through the natural selection of those individuals which were least encumbered with a superfluous part, aided by the other means previously indicated.

Thus we can understand how it has come to pass that man and all other vertebrate animals have been constructed on the same general model, why they pass through the same early stages of development, and why they retain certain rudiments in common. Consequently we ought frankly to admit their community of descent; to take any other view, is to admit that our own structure, and that of all the animals around us, is a mere snare laid to entrap our judgment. This conclusion is greatly strengthened, if we look to the members of the whole animal series, and consider the evidence derived from their affinities or classification, their geographical distribution and geological succession. It is only our natural prejudice, and that arrogance which made our forefathers declare that they were descended from demi-gods, which leads us to demur to this conclusion. But the time will before long come, when it will be thought wonderful that naturalists, who were well acquainted with the comparative structure and development of man, and other mammals, should have believed that each was the work of a separate act of creation.

Chapter II

ON THE MANNER OF DEVELOPMENT OF MAN FROM SOME LOWER FORM

Variability of body and mind in man—Inheritance—Causes of variability—Laws of variation the same in man as in the lower animals—Direct action of the conditions of life—Effects of the increased use and disuse of parts—Arrested development—Reversion—Correlated variation—Rate of increase—Checks to increase —Natural selection—Man the most dominant animal in the world

—Importance of his corporeal structure—The causes which have led to his becoming erect—Consequent changes of structure—Decrease in size of the canine teeth—Increased size and altered shape of the skull—Nakedness—Absence of a tail—Defenceless condition of man.

It is manifest that man is now subject to much variability. No two individuals of the same race are quite alike. We may compare millions of faces, and each will be distinct. There is an equally great amount of diversity in the proportions and dimensions of the various parts of the body; the length of the legs being one of the most variable points.[1] Although in some quarters of the world an elongated skull, and in other quarters a short skull prevails, yet there is great diversity of shape even within the limits of the same race, as with the aborigines of America and South Australia—the latter a race "probably as pure and homogeneous in blood, customs, and language as any in existence"—and even with the inhabitants of so confined an area as the Sandwich Islands.[2] An eminent dentist assures me that there is nearly as much diversity in the teeth as in the features. The chief arteries so frequently run in abnormal courses, that it has been useful for surgical purposes to calculate from 1040 corpses how often each course prevails.[3] The muscles are eminently variable: thus those of the foot were found by Prof. Turner [4] not to be strictly alike in any two out of fifty bodies; and in some the deviations were considerable. He adds, that the power of performing the appropriate movements must have been modified in accordance with the several deviations. Mr. J. Wood has recorded [5] the occurrence of 295 muscular variations in thirty-six subjects, and in another set of the same number no less than 558 variations, those occurring on both sides of the body being only reckoned as one. In the last set, not one body out of the thirty-six was "found totally wanting in departures from the standard descriptions of the muscular system given in anatomical text books." A single body presented the extraordinary number of twenty-five distinct abnormalities. The same muscle sometimes varies in many ways: thus Prof. Macalister describes [6] no less than twenty distinct variations in the *palmaris accessorius.*

1. Investigations in Military and Anthropolog. Statistics of American Soldiers,' by B. A. Gould, 1869, p. 256.
2. With respect to the "Cranial forms of the American aborigines," see Dr. Aitken Meigs in 'Proc. Acad. Nat. Sci.' Philadelphia, May, 1868. On the Australians, see Huxley, in Lyell's 'Antiquity of Man,' 1863, p. 87. On the Sandwich Islanders, Prof. J. Wyman, 'Observations on Crania,' Boston, 1868, p. 18.
3. 'Anatomy of the Arteries,' by R. Quain. Preface, vol. i. 1844.
4. 'Transact. Royal Soc. Edinburgh,' vol. xxiv. pp. 175, 189.
5. 'Proc. Royal Soc.' 1867, p. 544; also 1868, pp. 483, 524. There is a previous paper, 1866, p. 229.
6. 'Proc. R. Irish Academy,' vol. x. 1868, p. 141.

The famous old anatomist, Wolff,[7] insists that the internal viscera are more variable than the external parts: *Nulla particula est quæ non aliter et aliter in aliis se habeat hominibus.* He has even written a treatise on the choice of typical examples of the viscera for representation. A discussion on the beau-ideal of the liver, lungs, kidneys, &c., as of the human face divine, sounds strange in our ears.

The variability or diversity of the mental faculties in men of the same race, not to mention the greater differences between the men of distinct races, is so notorious that not a word need here be said. So it is with the lower animals. All who have had charge of menageries admit this fact, and we see it plainly in our dogs and other domestic animals. Brehm especially insists that each individual monkey of those which he kept tame in Africa had its own peculiar disposition and temper: he mentions one baboon remarkable for its high intelligence; and the keepers in the Zoological Gardens pointed out to me a monkey, belonging to the New World division, equally remarkable for intelligence. Rengger, also, insists on the diversity in the various mental characters of the monkeys of the same species which he kept in Paraguay; and this diversity, as he adds, is partly innate, and partly the result of the manner in which they have been treated or educated.[8]

I have elsewhere [9] so fully discussed the subject of Inheritance, that I need here add hardly anything. A greater number of facts have been collected with respect to the transmission of the most trifling, as well as of the most important characters in man, than in any of the lower animals; though the facts are copious enough with respect to the latter. So in regard to mental qualities, their transmission is manifest in our dogs, horses, and other domestic animals. Besides special tastes and habits, general intelligence, courage, bad and good temper, &c., are certainly transmitted. With man we see similar facts in almost every family; and we now know, through the admirable labours of Mr. Galton,[1] that genius which implies a wonderfully complex combination of high faculties, tends to be inherited; and, on the other hand, it is too certain that insanity and deteriorated mental powers likewise run in families.

With respect to the causes of variability, we are in all cases very ignorant; but we can see that in man as in the lower animals, they stand in some relation to the conditions to which each species has been exposed, during several generations. Domesticated animals vary more than those in a state of nature; and this is apparently

7. 'Act. Acad. St. Petersburg,' 1778, part ii. p. 217.
8. Brehm, 'Thierleben,' B. i. s. 58, 87. Rengger, 'Säugethiere von Paraguay,' s. 57.
9. Variation of Animals and Plants under Domestication,' vol. ii. chap. xii.
1. 'Hereditary Genius: an Inquiry into its Laws and Consequences, 1869.

due to the diversified and changing nature of the conditions to which they have been subjected. In this respect the different races of man resemble domesticated animals, and so do the individuals of the same race, when inhabiting a very wide area, like that of America. We see the influence of diversified conditions in the more civilised nations; for the members belonging to different grades of rank, and following different occupations, present a greater range of character than do the members of barbarous nations. But the uniformity of savages has often been exaggerated, and in some cases can hardly be said to exist.[2] It is, nevertheless, an error to speak of man, even if we look only to the conditions to which he has been exposed, as "far more domesticated" [3] than any other animal. Some savage races, such as the Australians, are not exposed to more diversified conditions than are many species which have a wide range. In another and much more important respect, man differs widely from any strictly domesticated animal; for his breeding has never long been controlled, either by methodical or unconscious selection. No race or body of men has been so completely subjugated by other men, as that certain individuals should be preserved, and thus unconsciously selected, from somehow excelling in utility to their masters. Nor have certain male and female individuals been intentionally picked out and matched, except in the well-known case of the Prussian grenadiers; and in this case man obeyed, as might have been expected, the law of methodical selection; for it is asserted that many tall men were reared in the villages inhabited by the grenadiers and their tall wives. In Sparta, also, a form of selection was followed, for it was enacted that all children should be examined shortly after birth; the well-formed and vigorous being preserved, the others left to perish.[4]

If we consider all the races of man as forming a single species, his range is enormous; but some separate races, as the Americans and Polynesians, have very wide ranges. It is a well-known law that

2. Mr. Bates remarks ('The Naturalist on the Amazons,' 1863, vol. ii. p. 159), with respect to the Indians of the same South American tribe, "no two of them were at all similar in the shape of the head; one man had an oval visage with fine features, and another was quite Mongolian in breadth and prominence of cheek, spread of nostrils, and obliquity of eyes."
3. Blumenbach, 'Treatises on Anthropolog.' Eng. translat., 1865, p. 205.
4. Mitford's 'History of Greece,' vol. i. p. 282. It appears also from a passage in Xenophon's 'Memorabilia,' B. ii. 4 (to which my attention has been called by the Rev. J. N. Hoare), that it was a well recognised principle with the Greeks, that men ought to select their

wives with a view to the health and vigour of their children. The Grecian poet, Theognis, who lived 550 B. C., clearly saw how important selection, if carefully applied, would be for the improvement of mankind. He saw, likewise, that wealth often checks the proper action of sexual selection. He thus writes:

"With kine and horses, Kurnus! we proceed
By reasonable rules, and choose a breed
For profit and increase, at any price:
Of a sound stock, without defect or vice.

widely-ranging species are much more variable than species with restricted ranges; and the variability of man may with more truth be compared with that of widely-ranging species, than with that of domesticated animals.

Not only does variability appear to be induced in man and the lower animals by the same general causes, but in both the same parts of the body are effected in a closely analogous manner. This has been proved in such full detail by Godron and Quatrefages, that I need here only refer to their works.[5] Monstrosities, which graduate into slight variations, are likewise so similar in man and the lower animals, that the same classification and the same terms can be used for both, as has been shewn by Isidore Geoffroy St.-Hilaire.[6] In my work on the variation of domestic animals, I have attempted to arrange in a rude fashion the laws of variation under the following heads:—The direct and definite action of changed conditions, as exhibited by all or nearly all the individuals of the same species, varying in the same manner under the same circumstances. The effects of the long-continued use or disuse of parts. The cohesion of homologous parts. The variability of multiple parts. Compensation of growth; but of this law I have found no good instance in the case of man. The effects of the mechanical pressure of one part on another; as of the pelvis on the cranium of the infant in the womb. Arrests of development, leading to the diminution or suppression of parts. The reappearance of long-lost characters through reversion. And lastly, correlated variation. All these so-called laws apply equally to man and the lower animals; and most of them even to plants. It would be superfluous here to discuss all of them;[7] but several are so important, that they must be treated at considerable length. * * *

RATE OF INCREASE

Civilised populations have been known under favourable conditions, as in the United States, to double their numbers in twenty-five years; and, according to a calculation, by Euler, this might occur in a little over twelve years.[8] At the former rate, the present population of the United States (thirty millions), would in 657 years cover the whole terraqueous globe so thickly, that four men would have to stand on each square yard of surface. The primary or

5. Godron, 'De l'Espèce,' 1859, tom. ii. livre 3. Quatrefages, 'Unité de l'Espèce Humaine,' 1861. Also Lectures on Anthropology, given in the 'Revue des Cours Scientifiques,' 1866–1868.
6. 'Hist. Gén. et Part. des Anomalies de l'Organisation,' in three volumes, tom. i. 1832.
7. I have fully discussed these laws in my 'Variation of Animals and Plants under Domestication,' vol. ii. chap. xxii. and xxiii. M. J. P. Durand has lately (1868) published a valuable essay 'De l'Influence des Milieux,' &c. He lays much stress, in the case of plants, on the nature of the soil.
8. See the ever memorable 'Essay on the Principle of Population,' by the Rev. T. Malthus, vol. i. 1826, pp. 6, 517.

fundamental check to the continued increase of man is the difficulty of gaining subsistence, and of living in comfort. We may infer that this is the case from what we see, for instance, in the United States, where subsistence is easy, and there is plenty of room. If such means were suddenly doubled in Great Britain, our number would be quickly doubled. With civilised nations, this primary check acts chiefly by restraining marriages. The greater death-rate of infants in the poorest classes is also very important; as well as the greater mortality, from various diseases, of the inhabitants of crowded and miserable houses, at all ages. The effects of severe epidemics and wars are soon counterbalanced, and more than counterbalanced, in nations placed under favourable conditions. Emigration also comes in aid as a temporary check, but, with the extremely poor classes, not to any great extent.

There is great reason to suspect, as Malthus has remarked, that the reproductive power is actually less in barbarous, than in civilised races. We know nothing positively on this head, for with savages no census has been taken; but from the concurrent testimony of missionaries, and of others who have long resided with such people, it appears that their families are usually small, and large ones rare. This may be partly accounted for, as it is believed, by the women suckling their infants during a long time; but it is highly probable that savages, who often suffer much hardships, and who do not obtain so much nutritious food as civilised men, would be actually less prolific. I have shewn in a former work,[9] that all our domesticated quadrupeds and birds, and all our cultivated plants, are more fertile than the corresponding species in a state of nature. It is no valid objection to this conclusion that animals suddenly supplied with an excess of food, or when grown very fat; and that most plants on sudden removal from very poor to very rich soil, are rendered more or less sterile. We might, therefore, expect that civilised men, who in one sense are highly domesticated, would be more prolific than wild men. It is also probable that the increased fertility of civilised nations would become, as with our domestic animals, an inherited character: it is at least known that with mankind a tendency to produce twins runs in families.[1]

Notwithstanding that savages appear to be less prolific than civilised people, they would no doubt rapidly increase if their numbers were not by some means rigidly kept down. The Santali, or hill-tribes of India, have recently afforded a good illustration of this fact; for, as shewn by Mr. Hunter,[2] they have increased at an

9. 'Variation of Animals and Plants under Domestication,' vol. ii. pp. 111–113, 163.
1. Mr. Sedgwick, 'British and Foreign Medico-Chirurg. Review,' July, 1863, p. 170.
2. 'The Animals of Rural Bengal,' by W. W. Hunter, 1868, p. 259.

extraordinary rate since vaccination has been introduced, other pestilences mitigated, and war sternly repressed. This increase, however, would not have been possible had not these rude people spread into the adjoining districts, and worked for hire. Savages almost always marry; yet there is some prudential restraint, for they do not commonly marry at the earliest possible age. The young men are often required to shew that they can support a wife; and they generally have first to earn the price with which to purchase her from her parents. With savages the difficulty of obtaining subsistence occasionally limits their number in a much more direct manner than with civilised people, for all tribes periodically suffer from severe famines. At such times savages are forced to devour much bad food, and their health can hardly fail to be injured. Many accounts have been published of their protruding stomachs and emaciated limbs after and during famines. They are then, also, compelled to wander much, and, as I was assured in Australia, their infants perish in large numbers. As famines are periodical, depending chiefly on extreme seasons, all tribes must fluctuate in number. They cannot steadily and regularly increase, as there is no artificial increase in the supply of food. Savages, when hard pressed, encroach on each other's territories, and war is the result; but they are indeed almost always at war with their neighbours. They are liable to many accidents on land and water in their search for food; and in some countries they suffer much from the larger beasts of prey. Even in India, districts have been depopulated by the ravages of tigers.

Malthus has discussed these several checks, but he does not lay stress enough on what is probably the most important of all, namely infanticide, especially of female infants and the habit of procuring abortion. These practices now prevail in many quarters of the world; and infanticide seems formerly to have prevailed, as Mr. M'Lennan [3] has shewn on a still more extensive scale. These practices appear to have originated in savages recognising the difficulty, or rather the impossibility of supporting all the infants that are born. Licentiousness may also be added to the foregoing checks; but this does not follow from failing means of subsistence; though there is reason to believe that in some cases (as in Japan) it has been intentionally encouraged as a means of keeping down the population.

If we look back to an extremely remote epoch, before man had arrived at the dignity of manhood, he would have been guided more by instinct and less by reason than are the lowest savages at the present time. Our early semi-human progenitors would not

3. 'Primitive Marriage,' 1865.

have practised infanticide or polyandry; for the instincts of the lower animals are never so perverted [4] as to lead them regularly to destroy their own offspring, or to be quite devoid of jealousy. There would have been no prudential restraint from marriage, and the sexes would have freely united at an early age. Hence the progenitors of man would have tended to increase rapidly; but checks of some kind, either periodical or constant, must have kept down their numbers, even more severely than with existing savages. What the precise nature of these checks were, we cannot say, any more than with most other animals. We know that horses and cattle, which are not extremely prolific animals, when first turned loose in South America, increased at an enormous rate. The elephant, the slowest breeder of all known animals, would in a few thousand years stock the whole world. The increase of every species of monkey must be checked by some means; but not, as Brehm remarks, by the attacks of beasts of prey. No one will assume that the actual power of reproduction in the wild horses and cattle of America, was at first in any sensible degree increased; or that, as each district became fully stocked, this same power was diminished. No doubt in this case, and in all others, many checks concur, and different checks under different circumstances; periodical dearths, depending on unfavourable seasons, being probably the most important of all. So it will have been with the early progenitors of man.

NATURAL SELECTION

We have now seen that man is variable in body and mind; and that the variations are induced, either directly or indirectly, by the same general causes, and obey the same general laws, as with the lower animals. Man has spread widely over the face of the earth, and must have been exposed, during his incessant migration,[5] to the most diversified conditions. The inhabitants of Tierra del Fuego, the Cape of Good Hope, and Tasmania in the one hemisphere, and of the Arctic regions in the other, must have passed through many climates, and changed their habits many times, before they reached their present homes.[6] The early progenitors of

4. A writer in the 'Spectator' (March 12th, 1871, p. 320) comments as follows on this passage:—"Mr. Darwin finds himself compelled to reintroduce a new doctrine of the fall of man. He shews that the instincts of the higher animals are far nobler than the habits of savage races of men, and he finds himself, therefore, compelled to re-introduce,—in a form of the substantial orthodoxy of which he appears to be quite unconscious,—and to introduce as a scientific hypothesis the doctrine that man's gain of *knowledge* was the cause of a temporary but long-enduring moral deterioration as indicated by the many foul customs, especially as to marriage, of savage tribes. What does the Jewish tradition of the moral degeneration of man through his snatching at a knowledge forbidden him by his highest instinct assert beyond this?"

5. See some good remarks to this effect by W. Stanley Jevons, "A Deduction from Darwin's Theory," 'Nature,' 1869, p. 231.

6. Latham, 'Man and his Migrations,' 1851, p. 135.

man must also have tended, like all other animals, to have increased beyond their means of subsistence; they must, therefore, occasionally have been exposed to a struggle for existence, and consequently to the rigid law of natural selection. Beneficial variations of all kinds will thus, either occasionally or habitually, have been preserved and injurious ones eliminated. I do not refer to strongly-marked deviations of structure, which occur only at long intervals of time, but to mere individual differences. We know, for instance, that the muscles of our hands and feet, which determine our powers of movement, are liable, like those of the lower animals,[7] to incessant variability. If then the progenitors of man inhabiting any district, especially one undergoing some change in its conditions, were divided into two equal bodies, the one half which included all the individuals best adapted by their powers of movement for gaining subsistence, or for defending themselves, would on an average survive in greater numbers, and procreate more offspring than the other and less well endowed half.

Man in the rudest state in which he now exists is the most dominant animal that has ever appeared on this earth. He has spread more widely than any other highly organised form: and all others have yielded before him. He manifestly owes this immense superiority to his intellectual faculties, to his social habits, which lead him to aid and defend his fellows, and to his corporeal structure. The supreme importance of these characters has been proved by the final arbitrament of the battle for life. Through his powers of intellect, articulate language has been evolved; and on this his wonderful advancement has mainly depended. As Mr. Chauncey Wright remarks: [8] "a psychological analysis of the faculty of language shews, that even the smallest proficiency in it might require more brain power than the greatest proficiency in any other direction." He has invented and is able to use various weapons, tools, traps, &c. with which he defends himself, kills or catches prey, and otherwise obtains food. He has made rafts or canoes for fishing or crossing over to neighbouring fertile islands. He has discovered the art of making fire, by which hard and stringy roots can be rendered digestible, and poisonous roots or herbs innocuous. This discovery of fire, probably the greatest ever made by man, excepting language, dates from before the dawn of history. These several inventions, by which man in the rudest state has become so pre-eminent, are the direct results of the development of his powers of observation, memory, curiosity, imagination, and reason. I cannot, there-

7. Messrs. Murie and Mivart in their 'Anatomy of the Lemuroidea' ('Transact. Zoolog. Soc.' vol. vii. 1869, pp. 96–98) say, "some muscles are so irregular in their distribution that they cannot be well classed in any of the above groups." These muscles differ even on the opposite sides of the same individual.
8. Limits of Natural Selection, 'North American Review,' Oct. 1870, p. 295.

fore, understand how it is that Mr. Wallace [9] maintains, that "natural selection could only have endowed the savage with a brain a little superior to that of an ape."

Although the intellectual powers and social habits of man are of paramount importance to him, we must not underrate the importance of his bodily structure, to which subject the remainder of this chapter will be devoted; the development of the intellectual and social or moral faculties being discussed in a later chapter.

Even to hammer with precision is no easy matter, as every one who has tried to learn carpentry will admit. To throw a stone with as true an aim as a Fuegian in defending himself, or in killing birds, requires the most consummate perfection in the correlated action of the muscles of the hand, arm, and shoulder, and, further, a fine sense of touch. In throwing a stone or spear, and in many other actions, a man must stand firmly on his feet; and this again demands the perfect co-adaptation of numerous muscles. To chip a flint into the rudest tool, or to form a barbed spear or hook from a bone, demands the use of a perfect hand; for, as a most capable judge, Mr. Schoolcraft,[1] remarks, the shaping fragments of stone into knives, lances, or arrow-heads, shews "extraordinary ability and long practice." This is to a great extent proved by the fact that primeval men practised a division of labour; each man did not manufacture his own flint tools or rude pottery, but certain individuals appear to have devoted themselves to such work, no doubt receiving in exchange the produce of the chase. Archæologists are convinced that an enormous interval of time elapsed before our ancestors thought of grinding chipped flints into smooth tools. One can hardly doubt, that a man-like animal who possessed a hand and arm sufficiently perfect to throw a stone with precision, or to form a flint into a rude tool, could, with sufficient practice, as far as mechanical skill alone is concerned, make almost anything which a civilised man can make. The structure of the hand in this respect may be compared with that of the vocal organs, which in

9. 'Quarterly Review,' April 1869, p. 392. This subject is more fully discussed in Mr. Wallace's 'Contributions to the Theory of Natural Selection,' 1870, in which all the essays referred to in this work are republished. The 'Essay on Man,' has been ably criticised by Prof. Claparède, one of the most distinguished zoologists in Europe, in an article published in the 'Bibliothèque Universelle,' June 1870. The remark quoted in my text will surprise every one who has read Mr. Wallace's celebrated paper on 'The origin of Human Races deduced from the Theory of Natural Selection,' originally published in the 'Anthropological Review,' May 1864, p. clviii. I cannot here resist quoting a most just remark by Sir J. Lubbock ('Prehistoric Times,' 1865, p. 479) in reference to this paper, namely, that Mr. Wallace, "with characteristic unselfishness, ascribes it (i. e. the idea of natural selection) unreservedly to Mr. Darwin, although, as is well known, he struck out the idea independently, and published it, though not with the same elaboration, at the same time."

1. Quoted by Mr. Lawson Tait in his 'Law of Natural Selection,'—'Dublin Quarterly Journal of Medical Science,' Feb. 1869. Dr. Keller is likewise quoted to the same effect.

the apes are used for uttering various signal-cries, as in one genus, musical cadences; but in man the closely similar vocal organs have become adapted through the inherited effects of use for the utterance of articulate language.

Turning now to the nearest allies of man, and therefore to the best representatives of our early progenitors, we find that the hands of the Quadrumana are constructed on the same general pattern as our own, but are far less perfectly adapted for diversified uses. Their hands do not serve for locomotion so well as the feet of a dog; as may be seen in such monkeys as the chimpanzee and orang, which walk on the outer margins of the palms, or on the knuckles.[2] Their hands, however, are admirably adapted for climbing trees. Monkeys seize thin branches or ropes, with the thumb on one side and the fingers and palm on the other, in the same manner as we do. They can thus also lift rather large objects, such as the neck of a bottle, to their mouths. Baboons turn over stones, and scratch up roots with their hands. They seize nuts, insects, or other small objects with the thumb in opposition to the fingers, and no doubt they thus extract eggs and young from the nests of birds. American monkeys beat the wild oranges on the branches until the rind is cracked, and then tear it off with the fingers of the two hands. In a wild state they break open hard fruits with stones. Other monkeys open mussel-shells with the two thumbs. With their fingers they pull out thorns and burs, and hunt for each other's parasites. They roll down stones, or throw them at their enemies: nevertheless, they are clumsy in these various actions, and, as I have myself seen, are quite unable to throw a stone with precision.

It seems to me far from true that because "objects are grasped clumsily" by monkeys, "a much less specialised organ of prehension" would have served them [3] equally well with their present hands. On the contrary, I see no reason to doubt that more perfectly constructed hands would have been an advantage to them, provided that they were not thus rendered less fitted for climbing trees. We may suspect that a hand as perfect as that of man would have been disadvantageous for climbing; for the most arboreal monkeys in the world, namely, Ateles in America, Colobus in Africa, and Hylobates in Asia, are either thumbless, or their toes partially cohere, so that their limbs are converted into mere grasping hooks.[4]

2. Owen, 'Anatomy of Vertebrates,' vol. iii. p. 71.
3. 'Quarterly Review,' April 1869, p. 392.
4. In *Hylobates syndactylus*, as the name expresses, two of the toes regularly cohere; and this, as Mr. Blyth informs me, is occasionally the case with the toes of *H. agilis, lar*, and *leuciscus*. Colobus is strictly arboreal and extraordinarily active (Brehm, 'Thierleben,' B. i. s. 50), but whether a better climber than the species of the allied genera, I do not know. It deserves notice that the feet of the sloths, the most arboreal animals in the world, are wonderfully hook-like.

As soon as some ancient member in the great series of the Primates came to be less aboreal, owing to a change in its manner of procuring subsistence, or to some change in the surrounding conditions, its habitual manner of progression would have been modified: and thus it would have been rendered more strictly quadrupedal or bipedal. Baboons frequent hilly and rocky districts, and only from necessity climb high trees; [5] and they have acquired almost the gait of a dog. Man alone has become a biped; and we can, I think, partly see how he has come to assume his erect attitude, which forms one of his most conspicuous characters. Man could not have attained his present dominant position in the world without the use of his hands, which are so admirably adapted to act in obedience to his will. Sir C. Bell [6] insists that "the hand supplies all instruments, and by its correspondence with the intellect gives him universal dominion." But the hands and arms could hardly have become perfect enough to have manufactured weapons, or to have hurled stones and spears with a true aim, as long as they were habitually used for locomotion and for supporting the whole weight of the body, or, as before remarked, so long as they were especially fitted for climbing trees. Such rough treatment would also have blunted the sense of touch, on which their delicate use largely depends. From these causes alone it would have been an advantage to man to become a biped; but for many actions it is indispensable that the arms and whole upper part of the body should be free; and he must for this end stand firmly on his feet. To gain this great advantage, the feet have been rendered flat; and the great toe has been peculiarly modified, though this has entailed the almost complete loss of its power of prehension. It accords with the principle of the division of physiological labour, prevailing throughout the animal kingdom, that as the hands became perfected for prehension, the feet should have become perfected for support and locomotion. With some savages, however, the foot has not altogether lost its prehensile power, as shewn by their manner of climbing trees, and of using them in other ways. [7]

If it be an advantage to man to stand firmly on his feet and to have his hands and arms free, of which, from his pre-eminent success in the battle of life, there can be no doubt, then I can see no reason why it should not have been advantageous to the progenitors of man to have become more and more erect or bipedal. They

5. Brehm, 'Thierleben,' B. i. s. 80.
6. "The Hand," &c. 'Bridgewater Treatise,' 1833, p. 38.
7. Häckel has an excellent discussion on the steps by which man became a biped: 'Natürliche Schöpfungsgeschichte,' 1868, s. 507. Dr. Büchner ('Conférences sur la Théorie Darwinienne,' 1869, p. 135) has given good cases of the use of the foot as a prehensile organ by man; and has also written on the manner of progression of the higher apes, to which I allude in the following paragraph: see also Owen ('Anatomy of Vertebrates,' vol. iii. p. 71) on this latter subject.

would thus have been better able to defend themselves with stones or clubs, to attack their prey, or otherwise to obtain food. The best built individuals would in the long run have succeeded best, and have survived in large numbers. If the gorilla and a few allied forms had become extinct, it might have been argued, with great force and apparent truth, that an animal could not have been gradually converted from a quadruped into a biped, as all the individuals in an intermediate condition would have been miserably ill-fitted for progression. But we know (and this is well worthy of reflection) that the anthropomorphous apes are now actually in an intermediate condition; and no one doubts that they are on the whole well adapted for their conditions of life. Thus the gorilla runs with a sidelong shambling gait, but more commonly progresses by resting on its bent hands. The long-armed apes occasionally use their arms like crutches, swinging their bodies forward between them, and some kinds of Hylobates, without having been taught, can walk or run upright with tolerable quickness; yet they move awkwardly, and much less securely than man. We see, in short, in existing monkeys a manner of progression intermediate between that of a quadruped and a biped; but, as an unprejudiced judge [8] insists, the anthropomorphous apes approach in structure more nearly to the bipedal than to the quadrupedal type.

As the progenitors of man became more and more erect, with their hands and arms more and more modified for prehension and other purposes, with their feet and legs at the same time transformed for firm support and progression, endless other changes of structure would have become necessary. The pelvis would have to be broadened, the spine peculiarly curved, and the head fixed in an altered position, all which changes have been attained by man. Prof. Schaaffhausen [9] maintains that "the powerful mastoid processes of the human skull are the result of his erect position;" and these processes are absent in the orang, chimpanzee, &c., and are smaller in the gorilla than in man. Various other structures, which appear connected with man's erect position, might here have been added. It is very difficult to decide how far these correlated modifications are the result of natural selection, and how far of the inherited effects of the increased use of certain parts, or of the action of one part on another. No doubt these means of change often co-operate: thus when certain muscles, and the crests of bone to which they are attached, become enlarged by habitual use, this shews that certain actions are habitually performed and must be

---

8. Prof. Broca, La Constitution des Vertèbres caudales; 'La Revue d'Anthropologie,' 1872, p. 26, (separate copy).
9. 'On the Primitive Form of the Skull,' translated in 'Anthropological Review,' Oct. 1868, p. 428. Owen ('Anatomy of Vertebrates,' vol. ii. 1866, p. 551) on the mastoid processes in the higher apes.

serviceable. Hence the individuals which performed them best, would tend to survive in greater numbers.

The free use of the arms and hands, partly the cause and partly the result of man's erect position, appears to have led to an indirect manner to other modifications of structure. The early male forefathers of man were, as previously stated, probably furnished with great canine teeth; but as they gradually acquired the habit of using stones, clubs, or other weapons, for fighting with their enemies or rivals, they would use their jaws and teeth less and less. In this case, the jaws, together with the teeth, would become reduced in size, as we may feel almost sure from innumerable analogous cases. In a future chapter we shall meet with a closely parallel case, in the reduction or complete disappearance of the canine teeth in male ruminants, apparently in relation with the development of their horns; and in horses, in relation to their habit of fighting with their incisor teeth and hoofs.

In the adult male anthropomorphous apes, as Rütimeyer,[1] and others, have insisted, it is the effect on the skull of the great development of the jaw-muscles that causes it to differ so greatly in many respects from that of man, and has given to these animals "a truly frightful physiognomy." Therefore, as the jaws and teeth in man's progenitors gradually become reduced in size, the adult skull would have come to resemble more and more that of existing man. As we shall hereafter see, a great reduction of the canine teeth in the males would almost certainly affect the teeth of the females through inheritance.

As the various mental faculties gradually developed themselves the brain would almost certainly become larger. No one, I presume, doubts that the large proportion which the size of man's brain bears to his body, compared to the same proportion in the gorilla or orang, is closely connected with his higher mental powers. We meet with closely analogous facts with insects, for in ants the cerebral ganglia are of extraordinary dimensions, and in all the Hymenoptera these ganglia are many times larger than in the less intelligent orders, such as beetles.[2] On the other hand, no one supposes that the intellect of any two animals or of any two men can be accurately gauged by the cubic contents of their skulls. It is certain that there may be extraordinary mental activity with an extremely small absolute mass of nervous matter: thus the wonderfully diversified instincts, mental powers, and affections of ants are notorious, yet their cerebral ganglia are not so large as the quarter

1. 'Die Grenzen der Thierwelt, eine Betrachtung zu Darwin's Lehre,' 1868, s. 51.
2. Dujardin, 'Annales des Sc. Nat.' 3rd series Zoolog. tom. xiv. 1850. p. 203. See also Mr. Lowne, 'Anatomy and Phys. of the *Musca vomitoria*,' 1870, p. 14. My son, Mr. F. Darwin, dissected for me the cerebral ganglia of the *Formica rufa*.

of a small pin's head. Under this point of view, the brain of an ant is one of the most marvellous atoms of matter in the world, perhaps more so than the brain of a man.

The belief that there exists in man some close relation between the size of the brain and the development of the intellectual faculties is supported by the comparison of the skulls of savage and civilised races, of ancient and modern people, and by the analogy of the whole vertebrate series. Dr. J. Bernard Davis has proved,[3] by many careful measurements, that the mean internal capacity of the skull in Europeans is 92.3 cubic inches; in Americans 87.5; in Asiatics 87.1; and in Australians only 81.9 cubic inches. Professor Broca [4] found that the nineteenth century skulls from graves in Paris were larger than those from vaults of the twelfth century, in the proportion of 1484 to 1426; and that the increased size, as ascertained by measurements, was exclusively in the frontal part of the skull—the seat of the intellectual faculties. Prichard is persuaded that the present inhabitants of Britain have "much more capacious braincases" than the ancient inhabitants. Nevertheless, it must be admitted that some skulls of very high antiquity, such as the famous one of Neanderthal, are well developed and capacious.[5] With respect to the lower animals, M. E. Lartet,[6] by comparing the crania of tertiary and recent mammals belonging to the same groups, has come to the remarkable conclusion that the brain is generally larger and the convolutions are more complex in the more recent forms. On the other hand, I have shewn [7] that the brains of domestic rabbits are considerably reduced in bulk, in comparison with those of the wild rabbit or hare; and this may be attributed to their having been closely confined during many generations, so that they have exerted their intellect, instincts, senses, and voluntary movements but little.

The gradually increasing weight of the brain and skull in man must have influenced the development of the supporting spinal column, more especially whilst he was becoming erect. As this change of position was being brought about, the internal pressure

3. 'Philosophical Transactions,' 1869, p. 513.
4. 'Les Sélections,' M. P. Broca, 'Revue d'Anthropologies,' 1873; see also, as quoted in C. Vogt's 'Lectures on Man,' Eng. Translat. 1864, pp. 88, 90. Prichard, 'Phys. Hist. of Mankind,' vol. i. 1838, p. 305.
5. In the interesting article just referred to, Prof. Broca has well remarked, that in civilised nations, the average capacity of the skull must be lowered by the preservation of a considerable number of individuals, weak in mind and body, who would have been promptly eliminated in the savage state. On the other hand, with savages, the average includes only the more capable individuals, who have been able to survive under extremely hard conditions of life. Broca thus explains the otherwise inexplicable fact, that the mean capacity of the skull of the ancient Troglodytes of Lozère is greater than that of modern Frenchmen.
6. 'Comptes-rendus des Sciences,' &c., June 1, 1868.
7. 'The Variation of Animals and Plants under Domestication,' vol. i. pp. 124–129.

of the brain will also have influenced the form of the skull; for many facts shew how easily the skull is thus affected. Ethnologists believe that it is modified by the kind of cradle in which infants sleep. Habitual spasms of the muscles, and a cicatrix from a severe burn, have permanently modified the facial bones. In young persons whose heads have become fixed either sideways or backwards, owing to disease, one of the two eyes has changed its position, and the shape of the skull has been altered apparently by the pressure of the brain in a new direction.[8] I have shewn that with long-eared rabbits even so trifling a cause as the lopping forward of one ear drags forward almost every bone of the skull on that side; so that the bones on the opposite side no longer strictly correspond. Lastly, if any animal were to increase or diminish much in general size, without any change in its mental powers, or if the mental powers were to be much increased or diminished, without any great change in the size of the body, the shape of the skull would almost certainly be altered. I infer this from my observations on domestic rabbits, some kinds of which have become very much larger than the wild animal, whilst others have retained nearly the same size, but in both cases the brain has been much reduced relatively to the size of the body. Now I was at first much surprised on finding that in all these rabbits the skull had become elongated or dolichocephalic; for instance, of two skulls of nearly equal breadth, the one from a wild rabbit and the other from a large domestic kind, the former was 3.15 and the latter 4.3 inches in length.[9] One of the most marked distinctions in different races of men is that the skull in some is elongated, and in others rounded; and here the explanation suggested by the case of the rabbits may hold good; for Welcker finds that short "men incline more to brachycephaly, and tall men to dolichocephaly;" [1] and tall men may be compared with the larger and longer-bodied rabbits, all of which have elongated skulls, or are dolichocephalic.

From these several facts we can understand, to a certain extent, the means by which the great size and more or less rounded form of the skull have been acquired by man; and these are characters eminently distinctive of him in comparison with the lower animals.

Another most conspicuous difference between man and the lower animals is the nakedness of his skin. Whales and porpoises

8. Schaaffhausen gives from Blumenbach and Busch, the cases of the spasms and cicatrix, in 'Anthropolog. Review,' Oct. 1868, p. 420. Dr. Jarrold ('Anthropologia,' 1808, pp. 115, 116) adduces from Camper and from his own observations, cases of the modification of the skull from the head being fixed in an unnatural position. He believes that in certain trades, such as that of a shoemaker, where the head is habitually held forward, the forehead becomes more rounded and prominent.

9. 'Variation of Animals', &c., vol. i. p. 117, on the elongation of the skull; p. 119, on the effect of the lopping of one ear.

1. Quoted by Schaaffhausen, in 'Anthropolog. Review,' Oct. 1868, p. 419.

(Cetacea), dugongs (Sirenia) and the hippopotamus are naked; and this may be advantageous to them for gliding through the water; nor would it be injurious to them from the loss of warmth, as the species, which inhabit the colder regions, are protected by a thick layer of blubber, serving the same purpose as the fur of seals and others. Elephants and rhinoceroses are almost hairless; and as certain extinct species, which formerly lived under an Arctic climate, were covered with long wool or hair, it would almost appear as if the existing species of both genera had lost their hairy covering from exposure to heat. This appears the most probable, as the elephants in India which live on elevated and cool districts are more hairy [2] than those on the lowlands. May we then infer that man became divested of hair from having aboriginally inhabited some tropical land? That the hair is chiefly retained in the male sex on the chest and face, and in both sexes at the junction of all four limbs with the trunk, favours this inference—on the assumption that the hair was lost before man became erect; for the parts which now retain most hair would then have been most protected from the heat of the sun. The crown of the head, however, offers a curious exception, for at all times it must have been one of the most exposed parts, yet it is thickly clothed with hair. The fact, however, that the other members of the order of Primates, to which man belongs, although inhabiting various hot regions, are well clothed with hair, generally thickest on the upper surface,[3] is opposed to the supposition that man became naked through the action of the sun. Mr. Belt believes [4] that within the tropics it is an advantage to man to be destitute of hair, as he is thus enabled to free himself of the multitude of ticks (acari) and other parasites, with which he is often infested, and which sometimes cause ulceration. But whether this evil is of sufficient magnitude to have led to the denudation of his body through natural selection, may be doubted, since none of the many quadrupeds inhabiting the tropics have, as far as I know, acquired any specialised means of relief. The view which seems to me the most probable is that man, or rather primarily woman, became divested of hair for ornamental purposes, as we shall see under Sexual Selection; and, according to this belief, it is not surprising that man should differ so greatly in hairiness from all other Primates, for

2. Owen, 'Anatomy of Vertebrates,' vol. iii. p. 619.
3. Isidore Geoffroy St.-Hilaire remarks ('Hist. Nat. Générale,' tom. ii. 1859, pp. 215–217) on the head of man being covered with long hair; also on the upper surfaces of monkeys and of other mammals being more thickly clothed than the lower surfaces. This has likewise been observed by various authors. Prof. P. Gervais ('Hist. Nat. des Mammifères,' tom. i. 1854, p. 28), however, states that in the Gorilla the hair is thinner on the back, where it is partly rubbed off, than on the lower surface.
4. The 'Naturalist in Nicaragua,' 1874, p. 209. As some confirmation of Mr. Belt's view, I may quote the following passage from Sir W. Denison ('Varieties of Vice-Regal Life,' vol. i. 1870, p. 440): "It is said to be a practice with the Australians, when the vermin get troublesome, to singe themselves."

characters, gained through sexual selection, often differ to an extraordinary degree in closely related forms.

According to a popular impression, the absence of a tail is eminently distinctive of man; but as those apes which come nearest to him are destitute of this organ, its disappearance does not relate exclusively to man. The tail often differs remarkably in length within the same genus: thus in some species of Macacus it is longer than the whole body, and is formed of twenty-four vertebræ; in others it consists of a scarcely visible stump, containing only three or four vertebræ. In some kinds of baboons there are twenty-five, whilst in the mandrill there are ten very small stunted caudal vertebræ, or, according to Cuvier,[5] sometimes only five. The tail, whether it be long or short, almost always tapers toward the end; and this, I presume, results from the atrophy of the terminal muscles, together with their arteries and nerves, through disuse, leading to the atrophy of the terminal bones. But no explanation can at present be given of the great diversity which often occurs in its length. Here, however, we are more specially concerned with the complete external disappearance of the tail. Professor Broca has recently shewn [6] that the tail in all quadrupeds consists of two portions, generally separated abruptly from each other; the basal portion consists of vertebræ, more or less perfectly channelled and furnished with apophyses like ordinary vertebræ; whereas those of the terminal portion are not channelled, are almost smooth, and scarcely resemble true vertebræ. A tail, though not externally visible, is really present in man and the anthropomorphous apes, and is constructed on exactly the same pattern in both. In the terminal portion the vertebræ, constituting the *os coccyx*, are quite rudimentary, being much reduced in size and number. In the basal portion, the vertebræ are likewise few, are united firmly together, and are arrested in development; but they have been rendered much broader and flatter than the corresponding vertebræ in the tails of other animals: they constitute what Broca calls the accessory sacral vertebræ. These are of functional importance by supporting certain internal parts and in other ways; and their modification is directly connected with the erect or semi-erect attitude of man and the anthropomorphous apes. This conclusion is the more trustworthy, as Broca formerly held a different view, which he has now abandoned. The modification, therefore, of the basal caudal vertebræ in man and the higher apes may have been effected, directly or indirectly, through natural selection.

But what are we to say about the rudimentary and variable

5. Mr. St. George Mivart, 'Proc. Zoolog. Soc.' 1865, pp. 562, 583. Dr. J. E. Gray, 'Cat. Brit. Mus.: Skeletons.' Owen, 'Anatomy of Vertebrates,' vol. ii. p. 517. Isidore Geoffroy, 'Hist. Nat. Gén.' tom. ii. p. 244.
6. 'Revue d'Anthropologie,' 1872; 'La Constitution des Vertèbres caudales.'

vertebræ of the terminal portion of the tail, forming the *os coccyx*? A notion which has often been, and will no doubt again be ridiculed, namely, that friction has had something to do with the disappearance of the external portion of the tail, is not so ridiculous as it at first appears. Dr. Anderson [7] states that the extremely short tail of *Macacus brunneus* is formed of eleven vertebræ, including the imbedded basal ones. The extremity is tendonous and contains no vertebræ; this is succeeded by five rudimentary ones, so minute that together they are only one line and a half in length, and these are permanently bent to one side in the shape of a hook. The free part of the tail, only a little above an inch in length, includes only four more small vertebræ. This short tail is carried erect; but about a quarter of its total length is doubled on to itself to the left; and this terminal part, which includes the hook-like portion, serves "to fill up the interspace between the upper divergent portion of the callosities;" so that the animal sits on it, and thus renders it rough and callous. Dr. Anderson thus sums up his observations: "These facts seem to me to have only one explanation; this tail, from its short size, is in the monkey's way when it sits down, and frequently becomes placed under the animal while it is in this attitude; and from the circumstance that it does not extend beyond the extremity of the ischial tuberosities, it seems as if the tail originally had been bent round by the will of the animal, into the interspace between the callosities, to escape being pressed between them and the ground, and that in time the curvature became permanent, fitting in of itself when the organ happens to be sat upon." Under these circumstances it is not surprising that the surface of the tail should have been roughened and rendered callous, and Dr. Murie,[8] who carefully observed this species in the Zoological Gardens, as well as three other closely allied forms with slightly longer tails, says that when the animal sits down, the tail "is necessarily thrust to one side of the buttocks; and whether long or short its root is consequently liable to be rubbed or chafed." As we now have evidence that mutilations occasionally produce an inherited effect,[9] it is not very improbable that in short-tailed monkeys, the projecting part of the tail, being functionally useless, should after many generations have become rudimentary and distorted, from being continually rubbed and chafed. We see the projecting part in this condition in the *Macacus brunneus*, and

7. 'Proc. Zoolog. Soc.,' 1872, p. 210.
8. 'Proc. Zoolog. Soc.,' 1872, p. 786.
9. I allude to Dr. Brown-Séquard's observations on the transmitted effect of an operation causing epilepsy in guinea-pigs, and likewise more recently on the analogous effects of cutting the sympathetic nerve in the neck. I shall hereafter have occasion to refer to Mr. Salvin's interesting case of the apparently inherited effects of motmots biting off the barbs of their own tail-feathers. See also on the general subject 'Variation of Animals and Plants under Domestication,' vol. ii. pp. 22–24.

absolutely aborted in the M. *ecaudatus* and in several of the higher apes. Finally, then, as far as we can judge, the tail has disappeared in man and the anthropomorphous apes, owing to the terminal portion having been injured by friction during a long lapse of time; the basal and embedded portion having been reduced and modified, so as to become suitable to the erect or semi-erect position.

I have now endeavoured to shew that some of the most distinctive characters of man have in all probability been acquired, either directly, or more commonly indirectly, through natural selection. We should bear in mind that modifications in structure or constitution which do not serve to adapt an organism to its habits of life, to the food which it consumes, or passively to the surrounding conditions, cannot have been thus acquired. We must not, however, be too confident in deciding what modifications are of service to each being: we should remember how little we know about the use of many parts, or what changes in the blood tissues may serve to fit an organism for a new climate or new kinds of food. Nor must we forget the principle of correlation, by which, as Isidore Geoffroy has shewn in the case of man, many strange deviations of structure are tied together. Independently of correlation, a change in one part often leads, through the increased or decreased use of other parts, to other changes of a quite unexpected nature. It is also well to reflect on such facts, as the wonderful growth of galls on plants caused by the poison of an insect, and on the remarkable changes of colour in the plumage of parrots when fed on certain fishes, or inoculated with the poison of toads; [1] for we can thus see that the fluids of the system, if altered for some special purpose, might induce other changes. We should especially bear in mind that modifications acquired and continually used during past ages for some useful purpose, would probably become firmly fixed, and might be long inherited.

Thus a large yet undefined extension may safely be given to the direct and indirect results of natural selection; but I now admit, after reading the essay by Nägeli on plants, and the remarks by various authors with respect to animals, more especially those recently made by Professor Broca, that in the earlier editions of my 'Origins of Species' I perhaps attributed too much to the action of natural selection or the survival of the fittest. I have altered the fifth edition of the 'Origin' so as to confine my remarks to adaptive changes of structure; but I am convinced, from the light gained during even the last few years, that very many structures which now appear to us useless, will hereafter be proved to be useful, and

1. "The Variation of Animals and Plants under Domestication,' vol. ii. pp. 280, 282.

will therefore come within the range of natural selection. Nevertheless, I did not formerly consider sufficiently the existence of structures, which, as far as we can at present judge, are neither beneficial nor injurious; and this I believe to be one of the greatest oversights as yet detected in my work. I may be permitted to say, as some excuse, that I had two distinct objects in view; firstly, to shew that species had not been separately created, and secondly, that natural selection had been the chief agent of change, though largely aided by the inherited effects of habit, and slightly by the direct action of the surrounding conditions. I was not, however, able to annul the influence of my former belief, then almost universal, that each species had been purposely created; and this led to my tacit assumption that every detail of structure, excepting rudiments, was of some special, though unrecognised, service. Any one with this assumption in his mind would naturally extend too far the action of natural selection, either during past or present times. Some of those who admit the principle of evolution, but reject natural selection, seem to forget, when criticising my book, that I had the above two objects in view; hence if I have erred in giving to natural selection great power, which I am very far from admitting, or in having exaggerated its power, which is in itself probable, I have at least, as I hope, done good service in aiding to overthrow the dogma of separate creations.

It is, as I can now see, probable that all organic beings, including man, possess peculiarities of structure, which neither are now, nor were formerly of any service to them, and which, therefore, are of no physiological importance. We know not what produces the numberless slight differences between the individuals of each species, for reversion only carries the problem a few steps backwards, but each peculiarity must have had its efficient cause. If these causes, whatever they may be, were to act more uniformly and energetically during a lengthened period (and against this no reason can be assigned), the result would probably be not a mere slight individual difference, but a well-marked and constant modification, though one of no physiological importance. Changed structures, which are in no way beneficial, cannot be kept uniform through natural selection, though the injurious will be thus eliminated. Uniformity of character would, however, naturally follow from the assumed uniformity of the exciting causes, and likewise from the free intercrossing of many individuals. During successive periods, the same organism might in this manner acquire successive modifications, which would be transmitted in a nearly uniform state as long as the exciting causes remained the same and there was free intercrossing. With respect to the exciting causes we can only say, as when speaking of so-called spontaneous variations, that they relate much more closely to the constitution of the varying organism, than to the nature of the conditions to which it has been subjected.

In this chapter we have seen that as man at the present day is liable, like every other animal, to multiform individual differences or slight variations, so no doubt were the early progenitors of man; the variations being formerly induced by the same general causes, and governed by the same general and complex laws as at present. As all animals tend to multiply beyond their means of subsistence, so it must have been with the progenitors of man; and this would inevitably lead to a struggle for existence and to natural selection. The latter process would be greatly aided by the inherited effects of the increased use of parts, and these two processes would incessantly react on each other. It appears, also, as we shall hereafter see, that various unimportant characters have been acquired by man through sexual selection. An unexplained residuum of change must be left to the assumed uniform action of those unknown agencies, which occasionally induce strongly marked and abrupt deviations of structure in our domestic productions.

Judging from the habits of savages and of the greater number of the Quadrumana, primeval men, and even their ape-like progenitors, probably lived in society. With strictly social animals, natural selection sometimes acts on the individual, through the preservation of variations which are beneficial to the community. A community which includes a large number of well-endowed individuals increases in number, and is victorious over other less favoured ones; even although each separate member gains no advantage over the others of the same community. Associated insects have thus acquired many remarkable structures, which are of little or no service to the individual, such as the pollen-collecting apparatus, or the sting of the worker-bee, or the great jaws of soldier-ants. With the higher social animals, I am not aware that any structure has been modified solely for the good of the community, though some are of secondary service to it. For instance, the horns of ruminants and the great canine teeth of baboons appear to have been acquired by the males as weapons for sexual strife, but they are used in defence of the herd or troop. In regard to certain mental powers the case, as we shall see in the fifth chapter, is wholly different; for these faculties have been chiefly, or even exclusively, gained for the benefit of the community, and the individuals thereof have at the same time gained an advantage indirectly.

It has often been objected to such views as the foregoing, that man is one of the most helpless and defenceless creatures in the world; and that during his early and less well-developed condition, he would have been still more helpless. The Duke of Argyll, for instance, insists [2] that "the human frame has diverged from the structure of brutes, in the direction of greater physical helplessness and weakness. That is to say, it is a divergence which of all others it is most impossible to ascribe to mere natural selection." He adduces the naked and unprotected state of the body, the absence of great teeth or claws for defence, the small strength and speed of man, and his slight power of discovering food or of avoiding danger by smell. To these deficiencies there might be added one still more serious, namely, that he cannot climb quickly, and so escape from enemies. The loss of hair would not have been a great injury to the inhabitants of a warm country. For we know that the unclothed Fuegians can exist under a wretched climate. When we compare the defenceless state of man with that of apes, we must remember that the great canine teeth with which the latter are provided, are possessed in their full development by the males alone, and are chiefly used by them for fighting with their rivals; yet the females, which are not thus provided, manage to survive.

In regard to bodily size or strength, we do not know whether man is descended from some small species, like the chimpanzee, or from one as powerful as the gorilla; and, therefore, we cannot say whether man has become larger and stronger, or smaller and weaker, than his ancestors. We should, however, bear in mind that an animal possessing great size, strength, and ferocity, and which, like the gorilla, could defend itself from all enemies, would not perhaps have become social: and this would most effectually have checked the acquirement of the higher mental qualities, such as sympathy and the love of his fellows. Hence it might have been an immense advantage to man to have sprung from some comparatively weak creature.

The small strength and speed of man, his want of natural weapons, &c., are more than counterbalanced, firstly, by his intellectual powers, through which he has formed for himself weapons, tools, &c., though still remaining in a barbarous state, and secondly, by his social qualities which lead him to give and receive aid from his fellow-men. No country in the world abounds in a greater degree with dangerous beasts than Southern Africa; no country presents more fearful physical hardships than the Arctic regions; yet one of the puniest of races, that of the Bushmen, maintains itself in Southern Africa, as do the dwarfed Esquimaux in the Arctic regions. The ancestors of man were, no doubt, inferior in intellect, and probably in social disposition, to the lowest existing savages;

2. 'Primeval Man,' 1869, p. 66.

but it is quite conceivable that they might have existed, or even flourished, if they had advanced in intellect, whilst gradually losing their brute-like powers, such as that of climbing trees, &c. But these ancestors would not have been exposed to any special danger, even if far more helpless and defenceless than any existing savages, had they inhabited some warm continent or large island, such as Australia, New Guinea, or Borneo, which is now the home of the orang. And natural selection arising from the competition of tribe with tribe, in some large area as one of these, together with the inherited effects of habit, would, under favourable conditions, have sufficed to raise man to his present high position in the organic scale.

Chapter III

COMPARISON OF THE MENTAL POWERS OF MAN AND THE LOWER ANIMALS

The difference in mental power between the highest ape and the lowest savage, immense—Certain instincts in common—The emotions—Curiosity—Imitation—Attention—Memory—Imagination—Reason—Progressive improvement—Tools and weapons used by animals—Abstraction, self-consciousness—Language—Sense of Beauty—Belief in God, spiritual agencies, superstitions.

We have seen in the last two chapters that man bears in his bodily structure clear traces of his descent from some lower form; but it may be urged that, as man differs so greatly in his mental power from all other animals, there must be some error in this conclusion. No doubt the difference in this respect is enormous, even if we compare the mind of one of the lowest savages, who has no words to express any number higher than four, and who uses hardly any abstract terms for common objects or for the affections,[1] with that of the most highly organised ape. The difference would, no doubt, still remain immense, even if one of the higher apes had been improved or civilised as much as a dog has been in comparison with its parent-form, the wolf or jackal. The Fuegians rank amongst the lowest barbarians; but I was continually struck with surprise how closely the three natives on board H. M. S. "Beagle," who had lived some years in England, and could talk a little English, resembled us in disposition and in most of our mental faculties. If no organic being excepting man had possessed any mental power, or if his powers had been of a wholly different nature from those of the lower animals, then we should never have

1. See the evidence on those points, as given by Lubbock, 'Prehistoric Times,' p. 354, &c.

been able to convince ourselves that our high faculties had been gradually developed. But it can be shewn that there is no fundamental difference of this kind. We must also admit that there is a much wider interval in mental power between one of the lowest fishes, as a lamprey or lancelet, and one of the higher apes, than between an ape and man; yet this interval is filled up by numberless gradations.

Nor is the difference slight in moral disposition between a barbarian, such as the man described by the old navigator Byron, who dashed his child on the rocks for dropping a basket of sea-urchins, and a Howard or Clarkson; and in intellect, between a savage who uses hardly any abstract terms, and a Newton or Shakespeare. Differences of this kind between the highest men of the highest races and the lowest savages, are connected by the finest gradations. Therefore it is possible that they might pass and be developed into each other.

My object in this chapter is to shew that there is no fundamental difference between man and the higher mammals in their mental faculties. Each division of the subject might have been extended into a separate essay, but must here be treated briefly. As no classification of the mental powers has been universally accepted, I shall arrange my remarks in the order most convenient for my purpose; and will select those facts which have struck me most, with the hope that they may produce some effect on the reader.

* * * The lower animals, like man, manifestly feel pleasure and pain, happiness and misery. Happiness is never better exhibited than by young animals, such as puppies, kittens, lambs, &c., when playing together, like our own children. Even insects play together, as has been described by that excellent observer, P. Huber,[2] who saw ants chasing and pretending to bite each other, like so many puppies.

The fact that the lower animals are excited by the same emotions as ourselves is so well established, that it will not be necessary to weary the reader by many details. Terror acts in the same manner on them as on us, causing the muscles to tremble, the heart to palpitate, the sphincters to be relaxed, and the hair to stand on end. Suspicion, the offspring of fear, is eminently characteristic of most wild animals. It is, I think, impossible to read the account given by Sir E. Tennent, of the behaviour of the female elephants, used as decoys, without admitting that they intentionally practise deceit, and well know what they are about. Courage and timidity are extremely variable qualities in the individuals of the same species, as is plainly seen in our dogs. Some dogs and horses are ill-

2. 'Recherches sur les Mœurs des Fourmis,' 1810, p. 173.

tempered, and easily turn sulky; others are good-tempered; and these qualities are certainly inherited. Every one knows how liable animals are to furious rage, and how plainly they shew it. Many, and probably true, anecdotes have been published on the long-delayed and artful revenge of various animals. The accurate Rengger, and Brehm[3] state that the American and African monkeys which they kept tame, certainly revenged themselves. Sir Andrew Smith, a zoologist whose scrupulous accuracy was known to many persons, told me the following story of which he was himself an eye-witness; at the Cape of Good Hope an officer had often plagued a certain baboon, and the animal, seeing him approaching one Sunday for parade, poured water into a hole and hastily made some thick mud, which he skilfully dashed over the officer as he passed by, to the amusement of many bystanders. For long afterwards the baboon rejoiced and triumphed whenever he saw his victim.

The love of a dog for his master is notorious; as an old writer quaintly says,[4] "A dog is the only thing on this earth that luvs you more than he luvs himself."

In the agony of death a dog has been known to caress his master, and every one has heard of the dog suffering under vivisection, who licked the hand of the operator; this man, unless the operation was fully justified by an increase of our knowledge, or unless he had a heart of stone, must have felt remorse to the last hour of his life.

As Whewell[5] has well asked, "who that reads the touching instances of maternal affection, related so often of the women of all nations, and of the females of all animals, can doubt that the principle of action is the same in the two cases?" We see maternal affection exhibited in the most trifling details; thus Rengger observed an American monkey (a Cebus) carefully driving away the flies which plagued her infant; and Duvaucel saw a Hylobates washing the faces of her young ones in a stream. So intense is the grief of female monkeys for the loss of their young, that it invariably caused the death of certain kinds kept under confinement by Brehm in N. Africa. Orphan monkeys were always adopted and carefully guarded by the other monkeys, both males and females. One female baboon had so capacious a heart that she not only adopted young monkeys of other species, but stole young dogs and cats, which she continually carried about. Her kindness, however, did not go so far as to share her food with her adopted offspring, at

3. All the following statements, given on the authority of these two naturalists, are taken from Rengger's 'Naturgesch. der Säugethiere von Paraguay,' 1830, s. 41–57, and from Brehm's 'Thierleben,' B. i. s. 10–87.

4. Quoted by Dr. Lauder Lindsay, in his 'Physiology of Mind in the Lower Animals;' 'Journal of Mental Science,' April 1871, p. 38.
5. 'Bridgewater Treatise,' p. 263.

which Brehm was surprised, as his monkeys always divided everything quite fairly with their own young ones. An adopted kitten scratched this affectionate baboon, who certainly had a fine intellect, for she was much astonished at being scratched, and immediately examined the kitten's feet, and without more ado bit off the claws.[6] In the Zoological Gardens, I heard from the keeper that an old baboon (*C. chacma*) had adopted a Rhesus monkey; but when a young drill and mandrill were placed in the cage, she seemed to perceive that these monkeys, though distinct species, were her nearer relatives, for she at once rejected the Rhesus and adopted both of them. The young Rhesus, as I saw, was greatly discontented at being thus rejected, and it would, like a naughty child, annoy and attack the young drill and mandrill whenever it could do so with safety; this conduct exciting great indignation in the old baboon. Monkeys will also, according to Brehm, defend their master when attacked by any one, as well as dogs to whom they are attached, from the attacks of other dogs. But we here trench on the subjects of sympathy and fidelity, to which I shall recur. Some of Brehm's monkeys took much delight in teasing a certain old dog whom they disliked, as well as other animals, in various ingenious ways.

Most of the more complex emotions are common to the higher animals and ourselves. Every one has seen how jealous a dog is of his master's affection, if lavished on any other creature; and I have observed the same fact with monkeys. This shews that animals not only love, but have desire to be loved. Animals manifestly feel emulation. They love approbation or praise; and a dog carrying a basket for his master exhibits in a high degree self-complacency or pride. There can, I think, be no doubt that a dog feels shame, as distinct from fear, and something very like modesty when begging too often for food. A great dog scorns the snarling of a little dog, and this may be called magnanimity. Several observers have stated that monkeys certainly dislike being laughed at; and they sometimes invent imaginary offences. In the Zoological Gardens I saw a baboon who always got into a furious rage when his keeper took out a letter or book and read it aloud to him; and his rage was so violent that, as I witnessed on one occasion, he bit his own leg till the blood flowed. Dogs shew what may be fairly called a sense of humour, as distinct from mere play; if a bit of stick or other such object be thrown to one, he will often carry it away for a short distance; and then squatting down with it on the ground close before him, will wait until his master comes quite close to take it away.

6. A critic, without any grounds ('Quarterly Review,' July, 1871, p. 72), disputes the possibility of this act as described by Brehm, for the sake of discrediting my work. Therefore I tried, and found that I could readily seize with my own teeth the sharp little claws of a kitten nearly five weeks old.

The dog will then seize it and rush away in triumph, repeating the same manœuvre, and evidently enjoying the practical joke.

We will now turn to the more intellectual emotions and faculties, which are very important, as forming the basis for the development of the higher mental powers. Animals manifestly enjoy excitement, and suffer from ennui, as may be seen with dogs, and, according to Rengger, with monkeys. All animals feel Wonder, and many exhibit Curiosity. They sometimes suffer from this latter quality, as when the hunter plays antics and thus attracts them; I have witnessed this with deer, and so it is with the wary chamois, and with some kinds of wild-ducks. Brehm gives a curious account of the instinctive dread, which his monkeys exhibited, for snakes; but their curiosity was so great that they could not desist from occasionally satiating their horror in a most human fashion, by lifting up the lid of the box in which the snakes were kept. I was so much surprised at this account, that I took a stuffed and coiled-up snake into the monkey-house at the Zoological Gardens, and the excitement thus caused was one of the most curious spectacles which I ever beheld. Three species of Cercopithecus were the most alarmed; they dashed about their cages, and uttered sharp signal cries of danger, which were understood by the other monkeys. A few young monkeys and one old Anubis baboon alone took no notice of the snake. I then placed the stuffed specimen on the ground in one of the larger compartments. After a time all the monkeys collected round it in a large circle, and staring intently, presented a most ludicrous appearance. They became extremely nervous; so that when a wooden ball, with which they were familiar as a plaything, was accidentally moved in the straw, under which it was partly hidden, they all instantly started away. These monkeys behaved very differently when a dead fish, a mouse,[7] a living turtle, and other new objects were placed in their cages; for though at first frightened, they soon approached, handled and examined them. I then placed a live snake in a paper bag, with the mouth loosely closed, in one of the larger compartments. One of the monkeys immediately approached, cautiously opened the bag a little, peeped in, and instantly dashed away. Then I witnessed what Brehm has described, for monkey after monkey, with head raised high and turned on one side, could not resist taking a momentary peep into the upright bag, at the dreadful object lying quietly at the bottom. It would almost appear as if monkeys had some notion of zoological affinities, for those kept by Brehm exhibited a strange, though mistaken, instinctive dread of innocent lizards and frogs. An orang, also, has been known to be much alarmed at the first

7. I have given a short account of their behaviour on this occasion in my "Expression of the Emotions,' p. 43.

sight of a turtle.[8]

The principle of Imitation is strong in man, and especially, as I have myself observed, with savages. In certain morbid states of the brain this tendency is exaggerated to an extraordinary degree: some hemiplegic patients and others, at the commencement of inflammatory softening of the brain, unconsciously imitate every word which is uttered, whether in their own or in a foreign language, and every gesture or action which is performed near them.[9] Desor[1] has remarked that no animal voluntarily imitates an action performed by man, until in the ascending scale we come to monkeys, which are well known to be ridiculous mockers. Animals, however, sometimes imitate each other's actions: thus two species of wolves, which had been reared by dogs, learned to bark, as does sometimes the jackal,[2] but whether this can be called voluntary imitation is another question. Birds imitate the songs of their parents, and sometimes of other birds; and parrots are notorious imitators of any sound which they often hear. Dureau de la Malle gives an account[3] of a dog reared by a cat, who learnt to imitate the well-known action of a cat licking her paws, and thus washing her ears and face; this was also witnessed by the celebrated naturalist Audouin. I have received several confirmatory accounts; in one of these, a dog had not been suckled by a cat, but had been brought up with one, together with kittens, and had thus acquired the above habit, which he ever afterwards practised during his life of thirteen years. Dureau de la Malle's dog likewise learnt from the kittens to play with a ball by rolling it about with his fore paws, and springing on it. A correspondent assures me that a cat in his house used to put her paws into jugs of milk having too narrow a mouth for her head. A kitten of this cat soon learned the same trick, and practised it ever afterwards, whenever there was an opportunity.

The parents of many animals, trusting to the principle of imitation in their young, and more especially to their instinctive or inherited tendencies, may be said to educate them. We see this when a cat brings a live mouse to her kittens; and Dureau de la Malle has given a curious account (in the paper above quoted) of his observations on hawks which taught their young dexterity, as well as judgment of distances, by first dropping through the air dead mice and sparrows, which the young generally failed to catch, and then bringing them live birds and letting them loose.

Hardly any faculty is more important for the intellectual progress of man than Attention. Animals clearly manifest this power,

8. W. C. L. Martin, 'Nat. Hist. of Mammalia,' 1841, p. 405.
9. Dr. Bateman 'On Aphasia,' 1870, p. 110.
1. Quoted by Vogt, 'Mémoire sur les Microcéphales,' 1867, p. 168.
2. 'The Variation of Animals and Plants under Domestication,' vol. i. p. 27.
3. 'Annales des Sc. Nat.' (1st Series), tom. xxii. p. 397.

as when a cat watches by a hole and prepares to spring on its prey. Wild animals sometimes become so absorbed when thus engaged, that they may be easily approached. Mr. Bartlett has given me a curious proof how variable this faculty is in monkeys. A man who trains monkeys to act in plays, used to purchase common kinds from the Zoological Society at the price of five pounds for each; but he offered to give double the price, if he might keep three or four of them for a few days, in order to select one. When asked how he could possibly learn so soon, whether a particular monkey would turn out a good actor, he answered that it all depended on their power of attention. If when he was talking and explaining anything to a monkey, its attention was easily distracted, as by a fly on the wall or other trifling object, the case was hopeless. If he tried by punishment to make an inattentive monkey act, it turned sulky. On the other hand, a monkey which carefully attended to him could always be trained.

It is almost superfluous to state that animals have excellent Memories for persons and places. A baboon at the Cape of Good Hope, as I have been informed by Sir Andrew Smith, recognised him with joy after an absence of nine months. I had a dog who was savage and averse to all strangers, and I purposely tried his memory after an absence of five years and two days. I went near the stable where he lived, and shouted to him in my old manner; he shewed no joy, but instantly followed me out walking, and obeyed me, exactly as if I had parted with him only half an hour before. A train of old associations, dormant during five years, had thus been instantaneously awakened in his mind. Even ants, as P. Huber[4] has clearly shewn, recognised their fellow-ants belonging to the same community after a separation of four months. Animals can certainly by some means judge of the intervals of time between recurrent events.

The Imagination is one of the highest prerogatives of man. By this faculty he unites former images and ideas, independently of the will, and thus creates brilliant and novel results. A poet, as Jean Paul Richter remarks,[5] "who must reflect whether he shall make a character say yes or no—to the devil with him; he is only a stupid corpse." Dreaming gives us the best notion of this power; as Jean Paul again says, "The dream is an involuntary art of poetry." The value of the products of our imagination depends of course on the number, accuracy, and clearness of our impressions, on our judgment and taste in selecting or rejecting the involuntary combinations, and to a certain extent on our power of vol-

4. 'Les Mœurs des Fourmis,' 1810, p. 150.
5. Quoted in Dr. Maudsley's 'Physiol- ogy and Pathology of Mind,' 1868, pp. 19, 220.

untarily combining them. As dogs, cats, horses, and probably all the higher animals, even birds [6] have vivid dreams, and this is shewn by their movements and the sounds uttered, we must admit that they possess some power of imagination. There must be something special, which causes dogs to howl in the night, and especially during moonlight, in that remarkable and melancholy manner called baying. All dogs do not do so; and, according to Houzeau,[7] they do not then look at the moon, but at some fixed point near the horizon. Houzeau thinks that their imaginations are disturbed by the vague outlines of the surrounding objects, and conjure up before them fantastic images: if this be so, their feelings may almost be called superstitious.

Of all the faculties of the human mind, it will, I presume, be admitted that Reason stands at the summit. Only a few persons now dispute that animals possess some power of reasoning. Animals may constantly be seen to pause, deliberate, and resolve. It is a significant fact, that the more the habits of any particular animal are studied by a naturalist, the more he attributes to reason and the less to unlearnt instincts.[8] In future chapters we shall see that some animals extremely low in the scale apparently display a certain amount of reason. No doubt it is often difficult to distinguish between the power of reason and that of instinct. For instance, Dr. Hayes, in his work on 'The Open Polar Sea,' repeatedly remarks that his dogs, instead of continuing to draw the sledges in a compact body, diverged and separated when they came to thin ice, so that their weight might be more evenly distributed. This was often the first warning which the travellers received that the ice was becoming thin and dangerous. Now, did the dogs act thus from the experience of each individual, or from the example of the older and wiser dogs, or from an inherited habit, that is from instinct? This instinct, may possibly have arisen since the time, long ago, when dogs were first employed by the natives in drawing their sledges; or the Arctic wolves, the parent-stock of the Esquimaux dog, may have acquired an instinct impelling them not to attack their prey in a close pack, when on thin ice.

We can only judge by the circumstances under which actions are performed, whether they are due to instinct, or to reason, or to the mere association of ideas: this latter principle, however, is intimately connected with reason. A curious case has been given by Prof. Möbius,[9] of a pike, separated by a plate of glass from an ad-

6. Dr. Jerdon, 'Birds of India,' vol. i. 1862, p. xxi. Houzeau says that his parokeets and canary-birds dreamt: 'Facultés Mentales,' tom. ii. p. 136.
7. 'Facultés Mentales des Animaux,' 1872, tom. ii. p. 181.
8. Mr. L. H. Morgan's work on 'The American Beaver,' 1868, offers a good illustration of this remark. I cannot help thinking, however, that he goes too far in underrating the power of instinct.
9. 'Die Bewegungen der Thiere,' &c., 1873, p. 11.

joining aquarium stocked with fish, and who often dashed himself with such violence against the glass in trying to catch the other fishes, that he was sometimes completely stunned. The pike went on thus for three months, but at last learnt caution, and ceased to do so. The plate of glass was then removed, but the pike would not attack these particular fishes, though he would devour others which were afterwards introduced; so strongly was the idea of a violent shock associated in his feeble mind with the attempt on his former neighbours. If a savage, who had never seen a large plate-glass window, were to dash himself even once against it, he would for a long time afterwards associate a shock with a window-frame; but very differently from the pike, he would probably reflect on the nature of the impediment, and be cautious under analogous circumstances. Now with monkeys, as we shall presently see, a painful or merely a disagreeable impression, from an action once performed, is sometimes sufficient to prevent the animal from repeating it. If we attribute this difference between the monkey and the pike solely to the association of ideas being so much stronger and more persistent in the one than the other, though the pike often received much the more severe injury, can we maintain in the case of man that a similar difference implies the possession of a fundamentally different mind?

Houzeau relates [1] that, whilst crossing a wide and arid plain in Texas, his two dogs suffered greatly from thirst, and that between thirty and forty times they rushed down the hollows to search for water. These hollows were not valleys, and there were no trees in them, or any other difference in the vegetation, and as they were absolutely dry there could have been no smell of damp earth. The dogs behaved as if they knew that a dip in the ground offered them the best chance of finding water, and Houzeau has often witnessed the same behaviour in other animals.

I have seen, as I daresay have others, that when a small object is thrown on the ground beyond the reach of one of the elephants in the Zoological Gardens, he blows through his trunk on the ground beyond the object, so that the current reflected on all sides may drive the object within his reach. Again a well-known ethnologist, Mr. Westropp, informs me that he observed in Vienna a bear deliberately making with his paw a current in some water, which was close to the bars of his cage, so as to draw a piece of floating bread within his reach. These actions of the elephant and bear can hardly be attributed to instinct or inherited habit, as they would be of little use to an animal in a state of nature. Now, what is the difference between such actions, when performed by an uncultivated man, and by one of the higher animals?

The savage and the dog have often found water at a low level,

1. 'Facultés Mentales des Animaux,' 1872, tom. ii. p. 265.

and the coincidence under such circumstances has become associated in their minds. A cultivated man would perhaps make some
general proposition on the subject; but from all that we know of
savages it is extremely doubtful whether they would do so, and a
dog certainly would not. But a savage, as well as a dog, would
search in the same way, though frequently disappointed; and in
both it seems to be equally an act of reason, whether or not any
general proposition on the subject is consciously placed before the
mind.[2] The same would apply to the elephant and the bear making currents in the air or water. The savage would certainly neither
know nor care by what law the desired movements were effected;
yet his act would be guided by a rude process of reasoning, as
surely as would a philosopher in his longest chain of deductions.
There would no doubt be this difference between him and one of
the higher animals, that he would take notice of much slighter circumstances and conditions, and would observe any connection
between them after much less experience and this would be of
paramount importance. I kept a daily record of the actions of one
of my infants, and when he was about eleven months old, and
before he could speak a single word, I was continually struck with
the greater quickness, with which all sorts of objects and sounds
were associated together in his mind, compared with that of the
most intelligent dogs I ever knew. But the higher animals differ in
exactly the same way in this power of association from those low
in the scale, such as the pike, as well as in that of drawing inferences and of observation.

The promptings of reason, after very short experience, are well
shewn by the following actions of American monkeys, which stand
low in their order. Rengger, a most careful observer, states that
when he first gave eggs to his monkeys in Paraguay, they smashed
them, and thus lost much of their contents; afterwards they gently
hit one end against some hard body, and picked off the bits of shell
with their fingers. After cutting themselves only *once* with any
sharp tool, they would not touch it again, or would handle it with
the greatest caution. Lumps of sugar were often given them
wrapped up in paper; and Rengger sometimes put a live wasp in the
paper, so that in hastily unfolding it they got stung; after this had
once happened, they always first held the packet to their ears to
detect any movement within.[3]

The following cases relate to dogs. Mr. Colquhoun [4] winged two

2. Prof. Huxley has analysed with admirable clearness the mental steps by
which a man, as well as a dog, arrives
at a conclusion in a case analogous to
that given in my text. See his article,
'Mr. Darwin's Critics,' in the 'Contemporary Review,' Nov. 1871, p. 462, and
in his 'Critques and Essays,' 1873, p.
279.

3. Mr. Belt, in his most interesting
work, 'The Naturalist in Nicaragua,'
1874 (p. 119), likewise describes various actions of a tamed Cebus, which, I
think, clearly shew that this animal
possessed some reasoning power.
4. 'The Moor and the Loch,' p. 45. Col.
Hutchinson on 'Dog Breaking,' 1850, p.
46.

wild-ducks, which fell on the further side of a stream; his retriever tried to bring over both at once, but could not succeed; she then, though never before known to ruffle a feather, deliberately killed one, brought over the other, and returned for the dead bird. Col. Hutchinson relates that two partridges were shot at once, one being killed, the other wounded; the latter ran away, and was caught by the retriever, who on her return came across the dead bird; "she stopped, evidently greatly puzzled, and after one or two trials, finding she could not take it up without permitting the escape of the winged bird, she considered a moment, then deliberately murdered it by giving it a severe crunch, and afterwards brought away both together. This was the only known instance of her ever having wilfully injured any game." Here we have reason though not quite perfect, for the retriever might have brought the wounded bird first and then returned for the dead one, as in the case of the two wild-ducks. I give the above cases, as resting on the evidence of two independent witnesses, and because in both instances the retrievers, after deliberation, broke through a habit which is inherited by them (that of not killing the game retrieved), and because they shew how strong their reasoning faculty must have been to overcome a fixed habit.

I will conclude by quoting a remark by the illustrious Humboldt.[5] "The muleteers in S. America say, 'I will not give you the mule whose step is easiest, but la mas racional,—the one that reasons best;'" and as he adds, "this popular expression, dictated by long experience, combats the system of animated machines, better perhaps than all the arguments of speculative philosophy." Nevertheless some writers even yet deny that the higher animals possess a trace of reason; and they endeavor to explain away, by what appears to be mere verbiage,[6] all such facts as those above given.

It has, I think, now been shewn that man and the higher animals, especially the Primates, have some few instincts in common. * * *

Chapter VI

ON THE AFFINITIES AND GENEALOGY OF MAN

Position of man in the animal series—The natural system genealogical—Adaptive characters of slight value—Various small points

5. 'Personal Narrative,' Eng. translat., vol. iii. p. 106.

6. I am glad to find that so acute a reasoner as Mr. Leslie Stephen ('Darwinism and Divinity, Essays on Freethinking,' 1873, p. 80), in speaking of the supposed impassable barrier between the minds of man and the lower animals, says, "The distinctions, indeed, which have been drawn, seem to us to rest upon no better foundation than a great many other metaphysical distinctions; that is, the assumption that because you can give two things different names, they must therefore have different natures. It is difficult to understand how anybody who has ever kept a dog, or seen an elephant, can have any doubt as to an animal's power of performing the essential processes of reasoning."

of resemblance between man and the Quadrumana—Rank of man in the natural system—Birthplace and antiquity of man—Absence of fossil connecting links—Lower stages in the genealogy of man, as inferred, firstly from his affinities and secondly from his structure— Early androgynous condition of the Vertebrata—Conclusion.

Even if it be granted that the difference between man and his nearest allies is as great in corporeal structure as some naturalists maintain, and although we must grant that the difference between them is immense in mental power, yet the facts given in the earlier chapters appear to declare, in the plainest manner, that man is descended from some lower form, notwithstanding that connecting-links have not hitherto been discovered.

Man is liable to numerous, slight, and diversified variations, which are induced by the same general causes, are governed and transmitted in accordance with the same general laws, as in the lower animals. Man has multiplied so rapidly, that he has necessarily been exposed to struggle for existence, and consequently to natural selection. He has given rise to many races, some of which differ so much from each other, that they have often been ranked by naturalists as distinct species. His body is constructed on the same homological plan as that of other mammals. He passes through the same phases of embryological development. He retains many rudimentary and useless structures, which no doubt were once serviceable. Characters occasionally make their re-appearance in him, which we have reason to believe were possessed by his early progenitors. If the origin of man had been wholly different from that of all other animals, these various appearances would be mere empty deceptions; but such an admission is incredible. These appearances, on the other hand, are intelligible, at least to a large extent, if man is the co-descendant with other mammals of some unknown and lower form.

Some naturalists, from being deeply impressed with the mental and spiritual powers of man, have divided the whole organic world into three kingdoms, the Human, the Animal, and the Vegetable, thus giving to man a separate kingdom.[1] Spiritual powers cannot be compared or classed by the naturalist: but he may endeavour to shew, as I have done, that the mental faculties of man and the lower animals do not differ in kind, although immensely in degree. A difference in degree, however great, does not justify us in placing man in a distinct kingdom, as will perhaps be best illustrated by comparing the mental powers of two insects, namely, a coccus or scale-insect and an ant, which undoubtedly belong to the same

---

1. Isidore Geoffroy St.-Hilaire gives a detailed account of the position assigned to man by various naturalists in their classifications: 'Hist. Nat. Gén.' tom. ii. 1859, pp. 170–189.

class. The difference is here greater than, though of a somewhat different kind from, that between man and the highest mammal. The female coccus, whilst young, attaches itself by its proboscis to a plant; sucks the sap, but never moves again; is fertilised and lays eggs; and this is its whole history. On the other hand, to describe the habits and mental powers of worker-ants, would require, as Pierre Huber has shewn, a large volume; I may, however, briefly specify a few points. Ants certainly communicate information to each other, and several unite for the same work, or for games of play. They recognise their fellow-ants after months of absence, and feel sympathy for each other. They build great edifices, keep them clean, close the doors in the evening, and post sentries. They make roads as well as tunnels under rivers, and temporary bridges over them, by clinging together. They collect food for the community, and when an object, too large for entrance, is brought to the nest, they enlarge the door, and afterwards build it up again. They store up seeds, of which they prevent the germination, and which, if damp, are brought up to the surface to dry. They keep aphides and other insects as milch-cows. They go out to battle in regular bands, and freely sacrifice their lives for the common weal. They emigrate according to a preconcerted plan. They capture slaves. They move the eggs of their aphides, as well as their own eggs and cocoons, into warm parts of the nest, in order that they may be quickly hatched; and endless similar facts could be given.[2] On the whole, the difference in mental power between an ant and a coccus is immense; yet no one has ever dreamed of placing these insects in distinct classes, much less in distinct kingdoms. No doubt the difference is bridged over by other insects; and this is not the case with man and the higher apes. But we have every reason to believe that the breaks in the series are simply the results of many forms having become extinct.

Professor Owen, relying chiefly on the structure of the brain, has divided the mammalian series into four sub-classes. One of these he devotes to man; in another he places both the Marsupials and the Monotremata; so that he makes man as distinct from all other mammals as are these two latter groups conjoined. This view has not been accepted, as far as I am aware, by any naturalist capable of forming an independent judgment and therefore need not here be further considered.

We can understand why a classification founded on any single character or organ—even an organ so wonderfully complex and im-

2. Some of the most interesting facts ever published on the habits of ants are given by Mr. Belt, in his 'Naturalist in Nicaragua,' 1874. See also Mr. Moggridge's admirable work, 'Harvesting Ants,' &c., 1873, also L'Instinct chez les Insectes,' by M. George Pouchet, 'Revue des Deux Mondes,' Feb. 1870, p. 682.

portant as the brain—or on the high development of the mental faculties, is almost sure to prove unsatisfactory. This principle has indeed been tried with hymenopterous insects; but when thus classed by their habits or instincts, the arrangement proved thoroughly artificial.[3] Classifications may, of course, be based on any character whatever, as on size, colour, or the element inhabited; but naturalists have long felt a profound conviction that there is a natural system. This system, it is now generally admitted, must be, as far as possible, genealogical in arrangement,—that is the co-descendants of the same form must be kept together in one group, apart from the co-descendants of any other form; but if the parent-forms are related, so will be their descendants, and the two groups together will form a larger group. The amount of difference between the several groups—that is the amount of modification which each has undergone—is expressed by such terms as genera, families, orders, and classes. As we have no record of the lines of descent, the pedigree can be discovered only by observing the degrees of resemblance between the beings which are to be classed. For this object numerous points of resemblance are of much more importance than the amount of similarity or dissimilarity in a few points. If two languages were found to resemble each other in a multitude of words and points of construction, they would be universally recognised as having sprung from a common source, notwithstanding that they differed greatly in some few words or points of construction. But with organic beings the points of resemblance must not consist of adaptations to similar habits of life: two animals may, for instance, have had their whole frames modified for living in the water, and yet they will not be brought any nearer to each other in the natural system. Hence we can see how it is that resemblances in several unimportant structures, in useless and rudimentary organs, or not now functionally active, or in an embryological condition, are by far the most serviceable for classification; for they can hardly be due to adaptations within a late period; and thus they reveal the old lines of descent or of true affinity.

We can further see why a great amount of modification in some one character ought not to lead us to separate widely any two organisms. A part which already differs much from the same part in other allied forms has already, according to the theory of evolution, varied much; consequently it would (as long as the organism remained exposed to the same exciting conditions) be liable to further variations of the same kind; and these, if beneficial, would be preserved, and thus be continually augmented. In many cases the continued development of a part, for instance, of the beak of a bird, or of the teeth of a mammal, would not aid the species in gaining its

3. Westwood, 'Modern Class of Insects,' vol. ii. 1840, p. 87.

food, or for any other object; but with man we can see no definite limit to the continued development of the brain and mental faculties, as far as advantage is concerned. Therefore in determining the position of man in the natural or genealogical system, the extreme development of his brain ought not to outweigh a multitude of resemblances in other less important or quite unimportant points.

The greater number of naturalists who have taken into consideration the whole structure of man, including his mental faculties, have followed Blumenbach and Cuvier, and have placed man in a separate Order, under the title of the Bimana, and therefore on an equality with the orders of the Quadrumana, Carnivora, &c. Recently many of our best naturalists have recurred to the view first propounded by Linnæus, so remarkable for his sagacity, and have placed man in the same Order with the Quadrumana, under the title of the Primates. The justice of this conclusion will be admitted: for in the first place, we must bear in mind the comparative insignificance for classification of the great development of the brain in man, and that the strongly-marked differences between the skulls of man and the Quadrumana (lately insisted upon by Bischoff, Aeby, and others) apparently follow from their differently developed brains. In the second place, we must remember that nearly all the other and more important differences between man and the quadrumana are manifestly adaptive in their nature, and relate chiefly to the erect position of man; such as the structure of his hand, foot, and pelvis, the curvature of his spine, and the position of his head. The family of Seals offers a good illustration of the small importance of adaptive characters for classification. These animals differ from all other Carnivora in the form of their bodies and in the structure of their limbs, far more than does man from the higher apes; yet in most systems, from that of Cuvier to the most recent one by Mr. Flower,[4] seals are ranked as a mere family in the Order of the Carnivora. If man had not been his own classifier, he would never have thought of founding a separate order for his own reception.

It would be beyond my limits, and quite beyond my knowledge, even to name the innumerable points of structure in which man agrees with the other Primates. Our great anatomist and philosopher, Prof. Huxley, has fully discussed this subject,[5] and concludes that man in all parts of his organization differs less from the higher apes, than these do from the lower members of the same group. Consequently there "is no justification for placing man in a distinct order." * * *

4. 'Proc. Zoolog. Soc.' 1863, p. 4.

5. 'Evidence as to Man's Place in Nature,' 1863, p. 70, *et passim*.

LOWER STAGES IN THE GENEALOGY OF MAN

* * * We have thus far endeavoured rudely to trace the genealogy of the Vertebrata by the aid of their mutual affinities. We will
now look to man as he exists; and we shall, I think, be able partially
to restore the structure of our early progenitors, during successive
periods, but not in due order of time. This can be effected by
means of the rudiments which man still retains, by the characters
which occasionally make their appearance in him through reversion,
and by the aid of the principles of morphology and embryology. The
various facts, to which I shall here allude, have been given in the
previous chapters.

The early progenitors of man must have been once covered with
hair, both sexes having beards; their ears were probably pointed,
and capable of movement; and their bodies were provided with a
tail, having the proper muscles. Their limbs and bodies were also
acted on by many muscles which now only occasionally reappear,
but are normally present in the Quadrumana. At this or some
earlier period, the great artery and nerve of the humerus ran through
a supra-condyloid foramen. The intestine gave forth a much larger
diverticulum or cæcum than that now existing. The foot was then
prehensile, judging from the condition of the great toe in the
fœtus; and our progenitors, no doubt, were arboreal in their habits,
and frequented some warm, forest-clad land. The males had great
canine teeth, which served them as formidable weapons. At a much
earlier period the uterus was double; the excreta were voided
through a cloaca; and the eye was protected by a third eyelid or nictitating membrane. At a still earlier period the progenitors of man must have been aquatic in their habits; for morphology
plainly tells us that our lungs consist of a modified swim-bladder,
which once served as a float. The clefts on the neck in the embryo
of man show where the branchiæ once existed. In the lunar or
weekly recurrent periods of some of our functions we apparently
still retain traces of our primordial birthplace, a shore washed by
the tides. At about this same early period the true kidneys were
replaced by the corpora wolffiana. The heart existed as a simple
pulsating vessel; and the chorda dorsalis took the place of a vertebral
column. These early ancestors of man, thus seen in the dim recesses
of time, must have been as simply, or even still more simply organised than the lancelet or amphioxus.

There is one other point deserving a fuller notice. It has long
been known that in the vertebrate kingdom one sex bears rudiments
of various accessory parts, appertaining to the reproductive system,
which properly belongs to the opposite sex; and it has now been

ascertained that at a very early embryonic period both sexes possess true male and female glands. Hence some remote progenitor of the whole vertebrate kingdom appears to have been hermaphrodite or androgynous.[6] But here we encounter a singular difficulty. In the mammalian class the males possess rudiments of a uterus with the adjacent passage, in their vesiculæ prostaticæ; they bear also rudiments of mammæ, and some male Marsupials have traces of a marsupial sack.[7] Other analogous facts could be added. Are we, then, to suppose that some extremely ancient mammal continued androgynous, after it had acquired the chief distinctions of its class, and therefore after it had diverged from the lower classes of the vertebrate kingdom? This seems very improbable, for we have to look to fishes, the lowest of all the classes, to find any still existent androgynous forms.[8] That various accessory parts, proper to each sex, are found in a rudimentary condition in the opposite sex, may be explained by such organs having been gradually acquired by the one sex, and then transmitted in a more or less imperfect state to the other. When we treat of sexual selection, we shall meet with innumerable instances of this form of transmission,—as in the case of the spurs, plumes, and brilliant colours, acquired for battle or ornament by male birds, and inherited by the females in an imperfect or rudimentary condition.

The possession by male mammals of functionally imperfect mammary organs is, in some respects, especially curious. The Monotremata have the proper milk-secreting glands with orifices, but no nipples; and as these animals stand at the very base of the mammalian series, it is probable that the progenitors of the class also had milk-secreting glands, but no nipples. This conclusion is supported by what is known of their manner of development; for Professor Turner informs me, on the authority of Kölliker and Langer, that in the embryo the mammary glands can be distinctly traced before the nipples are in the least visible; and the development of successive parts in the individual generally represents and accords

6. This is the conclusion of Prof. Gegenbaur, one of the highest authorities in comparative anatomy: see 'Grundzüge der vergleich. Anat.' 1870, s. 876. The result has been arrived at chiefly from the study of the Amphibia; but it appears from the researches of Waldeyer (as quoted in 'Journal of Anat. and Phys.' 1869, p. 161), that the sexual organs of even "the higher vertebrata are, in their early condition, hermaphrodite." Similar views have long been held by some authors, though until recently without a firm basis.
7. The male Thylacinus offers the best instance. Owen, 'Anatomy of Vertebrates,' vol. iii. p. 771.

8. Hermaphroditism has been observed in several species of Serranus, as well as in some other fishes, where it is either normal and symmetrical, or abnormal and unilateral. Dr. Zouteveen has given me references on this subject, more especially to a paper by Prof. Halbertsma, in the 'Transact. of the Dutch Acad. of Sciences,' vol. xvi. Dr. Günther doubts the fact, but it has now been recorded by too many good observers to be any longer disputed. Dr. M. Lessona writes to me, that he has verified the observations made by Cavolini on Serranus. Prof. Ercolani has recently shewn ('Acad. delle Scienze,' Bologna, Dec. 28, 1871) that eels are androgynous.

with the development of successive beings in the same line of descent. The Marsupials differ from the Monotremata by possessing nipples; so that probably these organs were first acquired by the Marsupials, after they had diverged from, and risen above, the Monotremata, and were then transmitted to the placental mammals.[9] No one will suppose that the Marsupials still remained androgynous, after they had approximately acquired their present structure. How then are we to account for male mammals possessing mammæ? It is possible that they were first developed in the females and then transferred to the males, but from what follows this is hardly probable.

It may be suggested, as another view, that long after the progenitors of the whole mammalian class had ceased to be androgynous, both sexes yielded milk, and thus nourished their young; and in the case of the Marsupials, that both sexes carried their young in marsupial sacks. This will not appear altogether improbable, if we reflect that the males of existing syngnathous fishes receive the eggs of the females in their abdominal pouches, hatch them, and afterwards, as some believe, nourish the young;[1]—that certain other male fishes hatch the eggs within their mouths or branchial cavities;—that certain male toads take the chaplets of eggs from the females, and wind them round their own thighs, keeping them there until the tadpoles are born;—that certain male birds undertake the whole duty of incubation, and that male pigeons, as well as the females, feed their nestlings with a secretion from their crops. But the above suggestion first occurred to me from mammary glands of male mammals being so much more perfectly developed than the rudiments of the other accessory reproductive parts, which are found in the one sex though proper to the other. The mammary glands and nipples, as they exist in male mammals, can indeed hardly be called rudimentary; they are merely not fully developed, and not functionally active. They are sympathetically affected under the influence of certain diseases, like the same organs in the female. They often secrete a few drops of milk at birth and at puberty: this latter fact occurred in the curious case before referred to, where a young man possessed two pairs of mammæ. In man and some other male

9. Prof. Gegenbaur has shewn ('Jenaische Zeitschrift,' Bd. vii. p. 212) that two distinct types of nipples prevail throughout the several mammalian orders, but that it is quite intelligible how both could have been derived from the nipples of the Marsupials, and the latter from those of the Monotremata. See, also, a memoir by Dr. Max Huss, on the mammary glands, ibid. B. viii. p. 176.

1. Mr. Lockwood believes (as quoted in 'Quart. Journal of Science,' April, 1868, p. 269), from what he has observed of the development of Hippocampus, that the walls of the abdominal pouch of the male in some way afford nourishment. On male fishes hatching the ova in their mouths, see a very interesting paper by Prof. Wyman, in 'Proc. Boston Soc. of Nat. Hist.' Sept. 15, 1857; also Prof. Turner, in 'Journal of Anat. and Phys.' Nov. 1, 1866, p. 78. Dr. Günther has likewise described similar cases.

mammals these organs have been known occasionally to become so well developed during maturity as to yield a fair supply of milk. Now if we suppose that during a former prolonged period male mammals aided the females in nursing their offspring,[2] and that afterwards from some cause (as from the production of a smaller number of young) the males ceased to give this aid, disuse of the organs during maturity would lead to their becoming inactive; and from two well-known principles of inheritance, this state of inactivity would probably be transmitted to the males at the corresponding age of maturity. But at an earlier age these organs would be left unaffected, so that they would be almost equally well developed in the young of both sexes.

CONCLUSION

Von Baer has defined advancement or progress in the organic scale better than any one else, as resting on the amount of differentiation and specialisation of the several parts of a being,—when arrived at maturity, as I should be inclined to add. Now as organisms have become slowly adapted to diversified lines of life by means of natural selection, their parts will have become more and more differentiated and specialised for various functions from the advantage gained by the division of physiological labour. The same part appears often to have been modified first for one purpose, and then long afterwards for some other and quite distinct purpose; and thus all the parts are rendered more and more complex. But each organism still retains the general type of structure of the progenitor from which it was aboriginally derived. In accordance with this view it seems, if we turn to geological evidence, that organisation on the whole has advanced throughout the world by slow and interrupted steps. In the great kingdom of the Vertebrata it has culminated in man. It must not, however, be supposed that groups of organic beings are always supplanted, and disappear as soon as they have given birth to other and more perfect groups. The latter, though victorious over their predecessors, may not have become better adapted for all places in the economy of nature. Some old forms appear to have survived from inhabiting protected sites, where they have not been exposed to very severe competition; and these often aid us in constructing our genealogies, by giving us a fair idea of former and lost populations. But we must not fall into the error of looking at the existing members of any lowly-organised group as perfect representatives of their ancient predecessors.

The most ancient progenitors in the kingdom of the Vetebrata, at which we are able to obtain an obscure glance, apparently con-

2. Maddle. C. Royer has suggested a similar view in her 'Origine de l'Homme,' &c., 1870.

sisted of a group of marine animals,[3] resembling the larvæ of existing Ascidians. These animals probably gave rise to a group of fishes, as lowly organised as the lancelet; and from these the Ganoids, and other fishes like the Lepidosiren, must have been developed. From such fish a very small advance would carry us on to the Amphibians. We have seen that birds and reptiles were once intimately connected together; and the Monotremata now connect mammals with reptiles in a slight degree. But no one can at present say by what line of descent the three higher and related classes, namely, mammals, birds, and reptiles, were derived from the two lower vertebrate classes, namely, amphibians and fishes. In the class of mammals the steps are not difficult to conceive which led from the ancient Monotremata to the ancient Marsupials; and from these to the early progenitors of the placental mammals. We may thus ascend to the Lemuridæ; and the interval is not very wide from these to the Simiadæ. The Simiadæ then branched off into two great stems, the New World and Old World monkeys; and from the latter, at a remote period, Man, the wonder and glory of the Universe, proceeded.

Thus we have given to man a pedigree of prodigious length, but not, it may be said, of noble quality. The world, it has often been remarked, appears as if it had long been preparing for the advent of man: and this, in one sense is strictly true, for he owes his birth to a long line of progenitors. If any single link in this chain had never existed, man would not have been exactly what he now is. Unless we wilfully close our eyes, we may, with our present knowledge, approximately recognise our parentage; nor need we feel ashamed of it. The most humble organism is something much higher than the inorganic dust under our feet; and no one with an un-

3. The inhabitants of the seashore mus* be greatly affected by the tides; animais living either about the *mean* high-water mark, or about the *mean* low-water mark, pass through a complete cycle of tidal changes in a fortnight. Consequently, their food supply will undergo marked changes week by week. The vital functions of such animals, living under these conditions for many generations, can hardly fail to run their course in regular weekly periods. Now it is a mysterious fact that in the highest and now terrestrial Vertebrata, as well as in other classes, many normal and abnormal processes have one or more whole weeks as their periods; this would be rendered intelligible if the Vetebrata are descended from an animal allied to the existing tidal Ascidians. Many instances of such periodic processes might be given, as the gestation of mammals, the duration of fevers, &c. The hatching of eggs affords also a good example, for, according to Mr. Bartlett ('Land and Water,' Jan. 7, 1871), the eggs of the pigeon are hatched in two weeks; those of the fowl in three; those of the duck in four; those of the goose in five; and those of the ostrich in seven weeks. As far as we can judge, a recurrent period, if approximately of the right duration for any process or function, would not, when once gained, be liable to change; consequently it might be thus transmitted through almost any number of generations. But if the function changed, the period would have to change, and would be apt to change almost abruptly by a whole week. This conclusion, if sound, is highly remarkable; for the period of gestation in each mammal, and the hatching of each bird's eggs, and many other vital processes, thus betray to us the primordial birthplace of these animals.

biased mind can study any living creature, however humble, without being struck with enthusiasm at its marvellous structure and properties.

Chapter XXI

GENERAL SUMMARY AND CONCLUSION

Main conclusion that man is descended from some lower form— Manner of development—Genealogy of man—Intellectual and moral faculties—Sexual Selection—Concluding remarks.

A brief summary will be sufficient to recall to the reader's mind the more salient points in this work. Many of the views which have been advanced are highly speculative, and some no doubt will prove erroneous; but I have in every case given the reasons which have led me to one view rather than to another. It seemed worth while to try how far the principle of evolution would throw light on some of the more complex problems in the natural history of man. False facts are highly injurious to the progress of science, for they often endure long; but false views, if supported by some evidence, do little harm, for every one takes a salutary pleasure in proving their falseness and when this is done, one path towards error is closed and the road to truth is often at the same time opened.

The main conclusion here arrived at, and now held by many naturalists who are well competent to form a sound judgment, is that man is descended from some less highly organised form. The grounds upon which this conclusion rests will never be shaken, for the close similarity between man and the lower animals in embryonic development, as well as in innumerable points of structure and constitution, both of high and of the most trifling importance,—the rudiments which he retains, and the abnormal reversions to which he is occasionally liable,—are facts which cannot be disputed. They have long been known, but until recently they told us nothing with respect to the origin of man. Now when viewed by the light of our knowledge of the whole organic world, their meaning is unmistakable. The great principle of evolution stands up clear and firm, when these groups or facts are considered in connection with others, such as the mutual affinities of the members of the same group, their geographical distribution in past and present times, and their geological succession. It is incredible that all these facts should speak falsely. He who is not content to look, like a savage, at the phenomena of nature as disconnected, cannot any longer believe that man is the work of a separate act of creation. He will be forced to admit that the close resemblance of the embryo of man to that, for instance, of a dog—the construction of his skull, limbs and whole frame on the same plan with that of other mammals, independently of the uses to which the parts may be put—the occasional re-appearance of various structures, for instance of several muscles, which man does not normally possess, but which are common to the Quadrumana—and a crowd of analogous facts—all point in the plainest manner to the conclusion that man is the co-descendant with other mammals of a common progenitor.

We have seen that man incessantly presents individual differences in all parts of his body and in his mental faculties. These differences or variations seem to be induced by the same general causes, and to obey the same laws as with the lower animals. In both cases similar laws of inheritance prevail. Man tends to increase at a greater rate than his means of subsistence; consequently he is occasionally subjected to a severe struggle for existence, and natural selection will have effected whatever lies within its scope. A succession of strongly-marked variations of a similar nature is by no means requisite; slight fluctuating differences in the individual suffice for the work of natural selection; not that we have any reason to suppose that in the same species, all parts of the organisation tend to vary to the same degree. We may feel assured that the inherited effects of the long-continued use or disuse of parts will have done much in the same direction with natural selection. Modifications formerly of importance, though no longer of any special use, are long-inherited. When one part is modified, other parts change through the principle of correlation, of which we have instances in many curious cases of correlated monstrosities. Something may be attributed to the direct and definite action of the surrounding conditions of life, such as abundant food, heat or moisture; and lastly, many characters of slight physiological importance, some indeed of considerable importance, have been gained through sexual selection.

No doubt man, as well as every other animal, presents structures, which seem to our limited knowledge, not to be now of any service to him, nor to have been so formerly, either for the general conditions of life, or in the relations of one sex to the other. Such structures cannot be accounted for by any form of selection, or by the inherited effects of the use and disuse of parts. We know, however, that many strange and strongly-marked peculiarities of structure occasionally appear in our domesticated productions, and if their unknown causes were to act more uniformly, they would probably become common to all the individuals of the species. We may hope hereafter to understand something about the causes of such occasional modifications, especially through the study of monstrosities: hence the labours of experimentalists such as those of M. Camille Dareste, are full of promise for the future. In general we can only say that the cause of each slight variation and of each monstrosity lies much more in the constitution of the organism, than in the nature of the surrounding conditions; though new and changed conditions certainly play an important part in exciting organic changes of many kinds.

Through the means just specified, aided perhaps by others as yet undiscovered, man has been raised to his resent state. But since he attained to the rank of manhood, he has diverged into distinct races, or as they may be more fitly called, sub-species. Some of these, such as the Negro and European, are so distinct that, if specimens had been brought to a naturalist without any further information, they would undoubtedly have been considered by him as good and true species. Nevertheless all the races agree in so many unimportant details of structure and in so many mental peculiarities that these can be accounted for only by inheritance from a common progenitor; and a progenitor thus characterised would probably deserve to rank as man.

It must not be supposed that the divergence of each race from the other races, and of all from a common stock, can be traced back to any one pair of progenitors. On the contrary, at every stage in the process of modification, all the individuals which were in any way better fitted for their conditions of life, though in different degrees, would have survived in greater numbers than the less well-fitted. The process would have been like that followed by man, when he does not intentionally select particular individuals, but breeds from all the superior individuals, and neglects the inferior. He thus slowly but surely modifies his stock, and unconciously forms a new strain. So with respect to modifications acquired independently of selection, and due to variations arising from the nature of the organism and the action of the surrounding conditions, or from changed habits of life, no single pair will have been modified much more than the other pairs inhabiting the same country, for all will have been continually blended through free intercrossing.

By considering the embryological structure of man,—the homologies which he presents with the lower animals,—the rudiments which he retains,—and the reversions to which he is liable, we can partly recall in imagination the former condition of our early progenitors; and can approximately place them in their proper place in the zoological series. We thus learn that man is descended from a hairy, tailed quadruped, probably arboreal in its habits, and an inhabitant of the Old World. This creature, if its whole structure had been examined by a naturalist, would have been classed amongst the Quadrumana, as surely as the still more ancient progenitor of the Old and New World monkeys. The Quadrumana and all the higher mammals are probably derived from an ancient marsupial animal, and this through a long series of diversified forms, from some amphibian-like creature, and this again from some fish-like animal. In the dim obscurity of the past we can see that the early progenitor of all the Vertebrata must have been an aquatic animal provided with branchiæ, with the two sexes united in the same individual, and with the most important organs of the body (such as the brain and heart) imperfectly or not at all developed. This animal seems to have been more like the larvæ of the existing marine Ascidians than any other known form.

The high standard of our intellectual powers and moral disposition is the greatest difficulty which presents itself, after we have been driven to this conclusion on the origin of man. But every one who admits the principle of evolution, must see that the mental powers of the higher animals, which are the same in kind with those of man, though so different in degree, are capable of advancement. Thus the interval between the mental powers of one of the higher apes and of a fish, or between those of an ant and scale-insect, is immense; yet their development does not offer any special difficulty; for with our domesticated animals, the mental faculties are certainly variable, and the variations are inherited. No one doubts that they are of the utmost importance to animals in a state of nature. Therefore the conditions are favourable for their development through natural selection. The same conclusion may be extended to man; the intellect must have been all-important to him, even at a very remote period, as enabling him to invent and use language, to make weapons, tools, traps, &c., whereby with the aid of his social habits, he long ago became the most dominant of all living creatures.

A great stride in the development of the intellect will have followed, as soon as the half-art and half-instinct of language came into use; for the continued use of language will have reacted on the brain and produced an inherited effect; and this again will have reacted on the improvement of language. As Mr. Chauncey Wright [1] has well remarked, the largeness of the brain in man relatively to his body, compared with the lower animals, may be attributed in chief part to the early use of some simple form of language,—that wonderful engine which affixes signs to all sorts of objects and qualities, and excites trains of thought which would never arise from the mere impression of the senses, or if they did arise could not be followed out. The higher intellectual powers of man, such as those of ratiocination, abstraction, self-consciousness, &c., probably follow from the continued improvement and exercise of the other mental

1. 'On the Limits of Natural Selection,' in the 'North American Review,' Oct. 1870, p. 295.

faculties.

The development of the moral qualities is a more interesting problem. The foundation lies in the social instincts, including under this term the family ties. These instincts are highly complex, and in the case of the lower animals give special tendencies towards certain definite actions; but the more important elements are love, and the distinct emotion of sympathy. Animals endowed with the social instincts take pleasure in one another's company, warn one another of danger, defend and aid one another in many ways. These instincts do not extend to all the individuals of the species, but only to those of the same community. As they are highly beneficial to the species, they have in all probability been acquired through natural selection.

A moral being is one who is capable of reflecting on his past actions and their motives—of approving of some and disapproving of others; and the fact that man is the one being who certainly deserves this designation, is the greatest of all distinctions between him and the lower animals. But in the fourth chapter I have endeavoured to shew that the moral sense follows, firstly, from the enduring and ever-present nature of the social instincts; secondly, from man's appreciation of the approbation and disapprobation of his fellows; and thirdly, from the high activity of his mental faculties, with past impressions extremely vivid; and in these latter respects he differs from the lower animals. Owing to this condition of mind, man cannot avoid looking both backwards and forwards, and comparing past impressions. Hence after some temporary desire or passion has mastered his social instincts, he reflects and compares the now weakened impression of such past impulses with the ever-present social instincts; and he then feels that sense of dissatisfaction which all unsatisfied instincts leave behind them, he therefore resolves to act differently for the future,—and this is conscience. Any instinct, permanently stronger or more enduring than another, gives rise to a feeling which we express by saying that it ought to be obeyed. A pointer dog, if able to reflect on his past conduct, would say to himself, I ought (as indeed we say of him) to have pointed at that hare and not have yielded to the passing temptation of hunting it.

Social animals are impelled partly by a wish to aid the members of their community in a general manner, but more commonly to perform certain definite actions. Man is impelled by the same general wish to aid his fellows; but has few or no special instincts. He differs also from the lower animals in the power of expressing his desires by words, which thus become a guide to the aid required and bestowed. The motive to give aid is likewise much modified in man; it no longer consists solely of a blind instinctive impulse, but is much influenced by the praise or blame of his fellows. The appreciation and the bestowal of praise and blame both rest on sympathy; and this emotion, as we have seen, is one of the most important elements of the social instincts. Sympathy, though gained as an instinct, is also much strengthened by exercise or habit. As all men desire their own happiness, praise or blame is bestowed on actions and motives, according as they lead to this end; and as happiness is an essential part of the general good, the greatest-happiness principle indirectly serves as a nearly safe standard of right and wrong. As the reasoning powers advance and experience is gained, the remoter effects of certain lines of conduct on the character of the individual, and on the general good, are perceived; and then the self-regarding virtues come within the scope of public opinion, and receive praise, and their opposites blame. But with the less civilised nations reason often errs, and many bad customs and base superstitions come within the same scope, and are then esteemed as high virtues, and their breach as heavy crimes.

The moral faculties are generally and justly esteemed as of higher value than the intellectual powers. But we should bear in mind that the activity of the mind in vividly recalling past impressions is one of the fundamental though secondary bases of conscience. This affords the strongest argument for educating and stimulating in all possible ways the intellectual faculties of every human being. No doubt a man with a torpid mind, if his social affections and sympathies are well developed, will be led to good actions, and may have a fairly sensitive conscience. But whatever renders the imagination more vivid and strengthens the habit of recalling and comparing past impressions, will make the conscience more sensitive, and may even somewhat compensate for weak social affections and sympathies.

The moral nature of man has reached its present standard, partly through the advancement of his reasoning powers and consequently of a just public opinion, but especially from his sympathies having been rendered more tender and widely diffused through the effects of habit, example, instruction, and reflection. It is not improbable that after long practice virtuous tendencies may be inherited. With the more civilised races, the conviction of the existence of an all-seeing Deity has had a potent influence on the advance of morality. Ultimately man does not accept the praise or blame of his fellows as his sole guide, though few escape this influence, but his habitual convictions, controlled by reason, afford him the safest rule. His conscience then becomes the supreme judge and monitor. Nevertheless the first foundation or origin of the moral sense lies in the social instincts, including sympathy; and these instincts no doubt were primarily gained, as in the case of the lower animals, through natural selection.

The belief in God has often been advanced as not only the greatest, but the most complete of all the distinctions between man and the lower animals. It is however impossible, as we have seen, to maintain that this belief is innate or instinctive in man. On the other hand a belief in all-pervading spiritual agencies seems to be universal; and apparently follows from a considerable advance in man's reason, and from a still greater advance in his faculties of imagination, curiosity and wonder. I am aware that the assumed instinctive belief in God has been used by many persons as an argument for His existence. But this is a rash argument, as we should thus be compelled to believe in the existence of many cruel and malignant spirits, only a little more powerful than man; for the belief in them is far more general than in a beneficent Deity. The idea of a universal and beneficent Creator does not seem to arise in the mind of man, until he has been elevated by long-continued culture.

He who believes in the advancement of man from some low organised form, will naturally ask how does this bear on the belief in the immortality of the soul. The barbarous races of man, as Sir J. Lubbock has shewn, possess no clear belief of this kind; but arguments derived from the primeval beliefs of savages are, as we have just seen, of little or no avail. Few persons feel any anxiety from the impossibility of determining at what precise period in the development of the individual, from the first trace of a minute germinal vesicle, man becomes an immortal being; and there is no greater cause for anxiety because the period cannot possibly be determined in the gradually ascending organic scale.[2]

I am aware that the conclusions arrived at in this work will be denounced by some as highly irreligious; but he who denounces them is bound to shew why it is more irreligious to explain the origin of man as a distinct species by descent from some lower form, through the laws of variation and natural selection, than to explain the birth of the individual through the laws of ordinary reproduction. The birth both of the species and of the individual are equally parts of that grand sequence of events, which our minds refuse to accept as the result of blind chance. The understanding revolts at such a conclusion, whether or not we are able to believe that every slight variation of structure,—the union of each pair in marriage,— the dissemination of each seed,—and other such events, have all been ordained for some special purpose.

2. The Rev. J. A. Picton gives a discussion to this effect in his 'New Theories and the Old Faith,' 1870.

Sexual selection has been treated at great length in this work; for, as I have attempted to shew, it has played an important part in the history of the organic world. I am aware that much remains doubtful, but I have endeavoured to give a fair view of the whole case. In the lower divisions of the animal kingdom, sexual selection seems to have done nothing: such animals are often affixed for life to the same spot, or have the sexes combined in the same individual, or what is still more important, their perceptive and intellectual faculties are not sufficiently advanced to allow of the feelings of love and jealousy, or of the exertion of choice. When, however, we come to the Arthropoda and Vertebrata, even to the lowest classes in these two great Sub-Kingdoms, sexual selection has effected much.

In the several great classes of the animal kingdom,—in mammals, birds, reptiles, fishes, insects, and even crustaceans,—the differences between the sexes follow nearly the same rules. The males are almost always the wooers; and they alone are armed with special weapons for fighting with their rivals. They are generally stronger and larger than the females, and are endowed with the requisite qualities of courage and pugnacity. They are provided, either exclusively or in a much higher degree than the females, with organs for vocal or instrumental music, and with odoriferous glands. They are ornamental with infinitely diversified appendages, and with the most brilliant or conspicuous colours, often arranged in elegant patterns, whilst the females are unadorned. When the sexes differ in more important structures, it is the male which is provided with special sense-organs for discovering the female, with locomotive organs for reaching her, and often with prehensile organs for holding her. These various structures for charming or securing the female are often developed in the male during only part of the year, namely the breeding-season. They have in many cases been more or less transferred to the females; and in the latter case they often appear in her as mere rudiments. They are lost or never gained by the males after emasculation. Generally they are not developed in the male during early youth, but appear a short time before the age for reproduction. Hence in most cases the young of both sexes resemble each other; and the female somewhat resembles her young offspring throughout life. In almost every great class a few anomalous cases occur, where there has been an almost complete transposition of the characters proper to the two sexes; the females assuming characters which properly belong to the males. This surprising uniformity in the laws regulating the differences between the sexes in so many and such widely separated classes, is intelligible if we admit the action of one common cause, namely sexual selection.

Sexual selection depends on the success of certain individuals over others of the same sex, in relation to the propagation of the species; whilst natural selection depends on the success of both sexes, at all ages, in relation to the general conditions of life. The sexual struggle is of two kinds; in the one it is between individuals of the same sex, generally the males, in order to drive away or kill their rivals, the females remaining passive; whilst in the other, the struggle is likewise between the individuals of the same sex, in order to excite or charm those of the opposite sex, generally the females, which no longer remain passive, but select the more agreeable partners. This latter kind of selection is closely analogous to that which man unintentionally, yet effectually, brings to bear on his domesticated productions, when he preserves during a long period the most pleasing or useful individuals, without any wish to modify the breed.

The laws of inheritance determine whether characters gained through sexual selection by either sex shall be transmitted to the same sex, or to both; as well as the age at which they shall be developed. It appears that variations arising late in life are commonly transmitted to one and the same sex. Variability is the necessary basis for the action of selection, and is wholly independent of it. It follows from this, that variations of the same general nature have often been taken advantage of and accumulated through sexual selection in relation to the propagation of the species, as well as through natural selection in relation to the general purposes of life. Hence secondary sexual characters, when equally transmitted to both sexes can be distinguished from ordinary specific characters only by the light of analogy. The modifications acquired through sexual selection are often so strongly pronounced that the two sexes have frequently been ranked as distinct species, or even as distinct genera. Such strongly-marked differences must be in some manner highly important; and we know that they have been acquired in some instances at the cost not only of inconvenience, but of exposure to actual danger.

The belief in the power of sexual selection rests chiefly on the following considerations. Certain characters are confined to one sex; and this alone renders it probable that in most cases they are connected with the act of reproduction. In innumerable instances these characters are fully developed only at maturity, and often during only a part of the year, which is always the breeding-season. The males (passing over a few exceptional cases) are the more active in courtship; they are the better armed, and are rendered the more attractive in various ways. It is to be especially observed that the males display their attractions with elaborate care in the presence of the females; and that they rarely or never display them excepting during the season of love. It is incredible that all this should be purposeless. Lastly we have distinct evidence with some quadrupeds and birds, that the individuals of one sex are capable of feeling a strong antipathy or preference for certain individuals of the other sex.

Bearing in mind these facts, and the marked results of man's unconscious selection, when applied to domesticated animals and cultivated plants, it seems to me almost certain that if the individuals of one sex were during a long series of generations to prefer pairing with certain individuals of the other sex, characterised in some peculiar manner, the offspring would slowly but surely become modified in this same manner. I have not attempted to conceal that, excepting when the males are more numerous than the females, or when polygamy prevails, it is doubtful how the more attractive males succeed in leaving a large number of offspring to inherit their superiority in ornaments or other charms than the less attractive males; but I have shewn that this would probably follow from the females,—especially the more vigorous ones, which would be the first to breed,—preferring not only the more attractive but at the same time the more vigorous and victorious males.

Although we have some positive evidence that birds appreciate bright and beautiful objects, as with the bower-birds of Australia, and although they certainly appreciate the power of song, yet I fully admit that it is astonishing that the females of many birds and some mammals should be endowed with sufficient taste to appreciate ornaments, which we have reason to attribute to sexual selection; and this is even more astonishing in the case of reptiles, fish, and insects. But we really know little about the minds of the lower animals. It cannot be supposed, for instance, that male birds of paradise or peacocks should take such pains in erecting, spreading, and vibrating their beautiful plumes before the females for no purpose. We should remember the fact given on excellent authority in a former chapter, that several peahens, when debarred from an admired male, remained widows during a whole season rather than pair with another bird.

Nevertheless I know of no fact in natural history more wonderful than that of the female Argus pheasant should appreciate the exquisite shading of the ball-and-socket ornaments and the elegant patterns on the wing-feathers of the male. He who thinks that the male was created as he now exists must admit that the great plumes, which prevent the wings from being used for flight, and which are displayed during courtship and at no other time in a manner quite peculiar to this one species, were given to him as an ornament. If so, he must likewise admit that the female was cre-

ated and endowed with the capacity of appreciating such ornaments. I differ only in the conviction that the male Argus pheasant
acquired his beauty gradually, through the preference of the females
during many generations for the more highly ornamented males;
the æsthetic capacity of the females having been advanced through
exercise or habit, just as our own taste is gradually improved. In the
male through the fortunate chance of a few feathers being left unchanged, we can distinctly trace how simple spots with a little
fulvous shading on one side may have been developed by small
steps into the wonderful ball-and-socket ornaments; and it is probable that they were actually thus developed.

Everyone who admits the principle of evolution, and yet feels
great difficulty in admitting that female mammals, birds, reptiles,
and fish, could have acquired the high taste implied by the beauty
of the males, and which generally coincides with our own standard,
should reflect that the nerve-cells of the brain in the highest as well
as in the lowest members of the Vertebrate series, are derived from
those of the common progenitor of this great Kingdom. For we can
thus see how it has come to pass that certain mental faculties, in
various and widely distinct groups of animals, have been developed
in nearly the same manner and to nearly the same degree.

The reader who has taken the trouble to go through the several
chapters devoted to sexual selection, will be able to judge how far
the conclusions at which I have arrived are supported by sufficient
evidence. If he accepts these conclusions he may, I think, safely
extend them to mankind; but it would be superfluous here to repeat what I have so lately said on the manner in which sexual
selection apparently has acted on man, both on the male and female side, causing the two sexes to differ in body and mind, and
the several races to differ from each other in various characters, as
well as from their ancient and lowly-organised progenitors.

He who admits the principle of sexual selection will be led to the
remarkable conclusion that the nervous system not only regulates
most of the existing functions of the body, but has indirectly influenced the progressive development of various bodily structures
and of certain mental qualities. Courage, pugnacity, perseverance,
strength and size of body, weapons of all kinds, musical organs,
both vocal and instrumental, bright colours and ornamental appendages, have all been indirectly gained by the one sex or the
other, through the exertion of choice, the influence of love and
jealousy, and the appreciation of the beautiful in sound, colour or
form; and these powers of the mind manifestly depend on the development of the brain.

Man scans with scrupulous care the character and pedigree of his
horses, cattle, and dogs before he matches them; but when he

comes to his own marriage he rarely, or never, takes any such care. He is impelled by nearly the same motives as the lower animals, when they are left to their own free choice, though he is in so far superior to them that he highly values mental charms and virtues. On the other hand he is strongly attracted by mere wealth or rank. Yet he might by selection do something not only for the bodily constitution and frame of his offspring, but for their intellectual and moral qualities. Both sexes ought to refrain from marriage if they are in any marked degree inferior in body or mind; but such hopes are Utopian and will never be even partially realised until the laws of inheritance are thoroughly known. Everyone does good service, who aids toward this end. When the principles of breeding and inheritance are better understood, we shall not hear ignorant members of our legislature rejecting with scorn a plan for ascertaining whether or not consanguineous marriages are injurious to man.

The advancement of the welfare of mankind is a most intricate problem: all ought to refrain from marriage who cannot avoid abject poverty for their children; for poverty is not only a great evil, but tends to its own increase by leading to recklessness in marriage. On the other hand, as Mr. Galton has remarked, if the prudent avoid marriage, whilst the reckless marry, the inferior members tend to supplant the better members of society. Man, like every other animal, has no doubt advanced to his present high condition through a struggle for existence consequent on his rapid multiplication; and if he is to advance still higher, it is to be feared that he must remain subject to a severe struggle. Otherwise he would sink into indolence, and the more gifted men would not be more successful in the battle of life than the less gifted. Hence our natural rate of increase, though leading to many and obvious evils, must not be greatly diminished by any means. There should be open competition for all men; and the most able should not be prevented by laws or customs from succeeding best and rearing the largest number of offspring. Important as the struggle for existence has been and even still is, yet as far as the highest part of man's nature is concerned there are other agencies more important. For the moral qualities are advanced, either directly or indirectly, much more through the effects of habit, the reasoning powers, instruction, religion, &c., than through natural selection; though to this latter agency may be safely attributed the social instincts, which afforded the basis for the development of the moral sense.

The main conclusion arrived at in this work, namely, that man is descended from some lowly organised form, will, I regret to think, be highly distasteful to many. But there can hardly be a doubt that we are descended from barbarians. The astonishment which I felt on first seeing a party of Fuegians on a wild and broken shore will never be forgotten by me, for the reflection at once rushed into my mind—such were our ancestors. These men were absolutely naked and bedaubed with paint, their long hair was tangled, their mouths, frothed with excitement, and their expression was wild, startled, and distrustful. They possessed hardly any arts, and like wild animals lived on what they could catch; they had no government, and were merciless to every one not of their own small tribe. He who has seen a savage in his native land will not feel much shame, if forced to acknowledge that the blood of some more humble creature flows in his veins. For my own part I would as soon be descended from that heroic little monkey, who braved his dreaded enemy in order to save the life of his keeper, or from that old baboon, who descending from the mountains, carried away in triumph his young comrade from a crowd of astonished dogs—as from a savage who delights to torture his enemies, offers up bloody sacrifices, practises infanticide without remorse, treats his wives like slaves, knows no decency, and is haunted by the grossest superstitutions.

Man may be excused for feeling some pride at having risen, though not through his own exertions, to the very summit of the organic scale; and the fact of his having thus risen, instead of having been aboriginally placed there, may give him hope for a still higher destiny in the distant future. But we are not here concerned with hopes or fears, only with the truth as far as our reason permits us to discover it; and I have given the evidence to the best of my ability. We must, however, acknowledge, as it seems to me, that man with all his noble qualities, with sympathy which feels for the most debased, with benevolence which extends not only to other men but to the humblest living creature, with his god-like intellect which has penetrated into the movements and constitution of the solar system—with all these exalted powers—Man still bears in his bodily frame the indelible stamp of his lowly origin.

PART III

Darwin's Influence on Science

I do not expect my ideas to be adopted all at once. The human mind gets creased into a way of seeing things. Those who have envisaged nature according to a certain point of view during much of their career, rise only with difficulty to new ideas.

—Lavoisier, 1785

It is manifest that at least a large number of naturalists must admit that species are the modified descendants of other species; and this especially holds good with the younger and rising naturalists. * * * Of the older and honoured chiefs in natural science, many unfortunately are still opposed to evolution in every form.

—Darwin, 1871

Neo-Darwinism, as we may call the modern theory of gradual transformation operated by natural selection upon a Mendelian genetic outfit of self-reproducing and self-varying genes, is fully accepted by the great majority of students of evolution.

—Sir Julian Huxley, 1958

Introduction

BERT JAMES LOEWENBERG

The Mosaic of Darwinian Thought (1959) †

The Darwinian revolution established the hypothesis of trans-mutation; the establishment of the hypothesis of transmutation of species widened the scope of scientific method and absorbed biology within the realm of objective science. Darwin, in Kant's prophetic phrase, was "the Newton of the grass blades," for Darwin accomplished for biology what Galileo and Newton had already accomplished for mechanics and physics. The revolution in biology, spurred by Darwinism, was premised on a new way of looking at nature and a new way of looking at life. It was likewise premised on newer concepts of man which remolded the profile of humanity and therefore the cast of society. New views of life, of nature, and of society reshaped the metaphysics of the ultimate and reformed the philosophy of the temporal. The mosaic of Darwinian thought transcends Charles Darwin. The implications of Darwinian thought are wedged into a pattern which goes back to the Greeks and stretches into the future. * * *

Darwin's data was actually overwhelming. The *Origin of Species* was crammed with data and the evidence was expanded, refined, and elaborated in later editions of the *Origin* and in Darwin's subsequent works. The facts, often new and rare, were garnered from innumerable sources and covered virtually the entire range of natural history. Old and familiar facts were placed in startlingly novel perspective.

But the genius of the *Origin of Species* and the *Descent of Man* resides in its conceptual organization, the hypotheses of descent, natural selection, struggle, isolation, sexual selection, heredity, and kindred theories. The genius of Darwin lies in the capacity for marshalling the data, new and old, in a framework of theoretical analysis. Darwin ferreted data out of horticultural journals and breeders' records. He observed seedlings, insects, and birds with unbelievable patience. Monographs of research gave him what he

† *Victorian Studies*, III (1959), 3–18. Bert James Loewenberg (b. 1905) is professor of history at Sarah Lawrence College.

called a harvest of facts and he extracted additional facts and additional ideas from his friends and coworkers. He discovered data as the result of his experiments with animals, with orchids, and with climbing plants; with volcanoes, coral reefs, and barnacles. Darwin's data were varied and magnificent, but the validity of the evidence for the Darwinian doctrine of descent by modification rested on the validity of the Darwinian hypothesis of development. And the validity of the hypothesis of evolution depended on the validity of the special hypotheses that explained its operation. Both depended on concepts of scientific method which were in turn rooted in a logic justifying its principles and its philosophy. Darwin's greatest contribution was to weld these elements together. He merged the evidence, the hypotheses, and the method in a grand analytical synthesis. As a consequence he legitimized the methodology by which the evidence was clarified and by which the hypotheses were validated.

While the evidence, to use a favorite Darwinian word, was truly "staggering," the hypothesis of natural selection was more important than the data. The hypothesis of natural selection, crucial to the establishment of the concept of evolution, is historically less vital than the mode of its establishment. It is the method which constitutes Darwin's claim to enduring greatness. Darwin's greatness rests on his total contribution, but the refinement of the evidence of transmutation taken alone is no more than a detail in the history of science. The expansion of the method of science exemplified by Darwin in establishing the doctrine of evolution constitutes an epoch in the history of science and a landmark in the history of thought.

Whether old or new, Darwin's evidence concentrated on difficulties, difficulties hard to explain on any current biological theory. How could conventional arguments receive so wide an acceptance when they failed to eliminate stark exceptions or to explain away incongruities with other bodies of fact? Genetic derivation, he repeatedly urged, at least offered a plausible explanation. Evolution by descent, moreover, provided an hypothesis which explained many apparently diverse facts and offered a unifying interpretation of the variety and alternations of living forms. Darwin did not generally encounter opposition to his specific data; it was his interpretation of the data which was suspect. The facts of geology were as rarely in dispute as the facts of embryology. No one doubted the existence of rudimentary organs, but Darwin's explanation of them was frequently spurned. That different plants and animals were distributed over the earth was an elementary principle; but Darwin's theories of geographical distribution were hardly elementary and were not universally accepted as principles. Darwin's hypotheses were criticized because Darwin's method and its logic defied regnant philosophical views.

Darwin's exposition of classification as of embryology and taxonomy was a calculated refutation of contemporary postulates.[1] He not only set forth the evidence in evolutionary categories but he also challenged accepted maxims of interpretation and method. When discussing the natural system he remarked that "scarcely two naturalists will give the same answer" when seeking to define it. Charles Darwin was invariably temperate and polite, but his queries and comments were not on that account less devastating: "How it comes, that certain facts of the structure, by which the habits and functions of the species are settled, are of no use in classification, whilst, other parts, formed at the same time, are of the greatest, it would be difficult to say, on the theory of separate creations" (*Foundations* [1844], p. 199).

To a Richard Owen or a Louis Agassiz it must have seemed that Darwin was deliberately irritating. He was forever accenting the negative, probing into difficulties that had long agonized his adversaries. He was purposely exposing the weaknesses of the opposition case. That there was no other way of making his own was beside the point. And Darwin was bent on making it. Certain naturalists, he commented, "believe that the degree of affinity on the natural system depends on the degrees of resemblance in organs more or less physiologically important for the preservation of life" (*Foundations* [1844], p. 200). To discover a scale of importance was unquestionably difficult. Nevertheless, the general proposition, said Darwin, "must be rejected as false; though it may be partially true." The reasons for so blunt a statement were not abstruse. Classification as interpreted by Owen or Agassiz did not work in Darwinian terms. Such systems of classification failed to work because they bore little resemblance to the conditions of life in which the organs actually functioned. Darwin was not seeking a universal plan of nature; he was seeking specific causal explanations, explanations of functioning organs in organic life and in a series of changing environments. Regardless of the particular Darwinian argument, the contention was always the same: what was the explanation of specific change? Regardless of the particular Darwinian contention, men were asked to see familiar data in new relations and the new relations were conceptual, constructs based upon methodological principles which many felt were invalid and inappropriate.

Darwin's search took him to the most unexpected places and in-

1. Charles Darwin, *The Foundations of the Origin of Species, Two Essays Written in 1842 and 1844*, Francis Darwin, ed. (1909), pp. 198, 199; George John Romanes, *Darwin, and After Darwin* 3 vols. (1892, 1895, 1897), I, 24 ff.

duced him to ask all manner of unorthodox questions. "If you knew," he wrote Hooker, "some of the experiments (if they may be so called) which I am trying, you would have a good right to sneer, for they are so *absurd* even in *my* opinion that I dare not tell you." [2] Darwin's efforts to extract fresh meanings from established convictions taught him to suspect definitive solutions and to abjure the ideal of finality. He urged Hooker, who slashed at difficulties with a candor only friendship permitted, to do his worst, but he admonished him to remember that "you cannot have thought so freely on the subject as I have." [3] In making this point Darwin made an essential point about himself and about scientific method. Darwin's free-ranging explorations disposed him to regard all questions as open, to accept no conclusions drained from observed facts as beyond further extension by hypothesis. But it was just this tendency which invited dissent, for such queries as Darwin asked were exactly the queries which had been definitely settled. Yet Darwin was simply exemplifying another facet of scholarship: the determination to reject provisionally all prescribed formulations while examining competing formulations. The principle of exclusion possesses the advantage of apparent finality but it is bought at the price of ruling out probabilities. "This is experiment after my own heart," Darwin once wrote illustrating the principle, "with chances 1000 to 1 against its success." [4]

Darwin was rarely inhibited by epistemological reservations. Darwin accepted the facts of nature as provisionally given; he did not begin his inquiry with the problems of knowledge. He was in no sense an aggressive empiricist; he simply was not concerned with metaphysics.[5] If variations were accepted as given for purposes of further analysis, then subsequent changes or further variations occurred as the result of natural causes, the interactivities of the total environments. The word "origin" was never used in its sense of "beginning"; it always implied changes in the development of life-forms already in existence.

Criticisms levelled at Darwin's theory of variation have confounded his own conception of it. Whatever inferences are latent in the text of the *Origin* and other Darwin writings, Darwin's own thinking was unambiguous. "I imagine," he once wrote to Hooker, successfully restraining his irritation, "that you look at variability as some necessary contingency" within the organism, "that there is some necessary tendency in the variability to go on diverging in

2. Darwin to Hooker, 14 Apr., 1855, in Francis Darwin, ed., *The Life and Letters of Charles Darwin*, 3 vols. (1887), II, 55 (italics in original).
3. Darwin to Hooker, 12 Oct., 1858, *Life*, II, 138, and Oct., 1856, p. 85.
4. Darwin to Hooker [1855], *Life*, II, 57.
5. *Life*, I, 69. But see Robert E. Fitch, "Charles Darwin: Science and the Saintly Sentiments," *Columbia University Forum*, II (1959), 7–12.

character or degree." "I do not agree," he said simply.[6] "The formation of a strong variety or species I look at as almost wholly due to the selection of what may be incorrectly called *chance* variations or variability." "No doubt . . . variability is governed by laws, some of which I am endeavouring very obscurely to trace." [7] They were incorrectly called chance variations because factors as yet unknown doubtless explained them, but they were none the less random in the sense that they were unwilled and unplanned. Wallace, as so often happened, was even clearer. Variation, after all, was no more than *"the absence of identity,"* [8] and required no additional elaboration. To Darwin he wrote: "variations of every kind are always occurring in every part of every species, and . . . favourable variations are always ready when wanted." [9]

Darwin was employing the objective method of science. He was seeking to define "natural laws," by which he meant the identification of sequences occurring in nature. These sequences expressed relations among phenomena and offered explanations of their behavior without reference to ultimate causes exterior to the phenomena under review. Darwin did not seek to explain the quality or essence of a prehistoric barnacle or to assign a primary cause for the existence of the varieties of Alpine flora. He observed, compared, and measured varieties in historical and contemporary contexts, and sought to discover connections within the economy of the individual organism as well as within the economy of nature. Darwin did not seek for final causes of gill, fin, wing, or bone. He always asked what these organs did, how they changed, what purposes they served under one set of conditions or under another.

Darwin held universal theories in abeyance. "I find," he wrote the cosmic philosopher, John Fiske, "that my mind is so fixed by the inductive method, that I cannot appreciate deductive reasoning." He did not deny Fiske's right to construct a cosmic philosophy, he simply explained why he was unable to do so. "I must begin with a good body of facts, and not from principle (in which I always suspect some fallacy), and then as much deduction as you please." [1] Darwin understood by deduction not only reasoning from the general to the particular, from a principle or law to a particular fact, but deducing facts from principles which were fixed beyond investigation. "I have no faith in anything," he once remarked, "short of actual measurement and the Rule of Three." [2]

6. Darwin to Hooker, 11 May [1859], *Life*, II, 158; Darwin to Lyell, 25 Oct. [1859], pp. 176–177.
7. Darwin to Hooker, 23 Nov. [1856], *Life*, II, 87.
8. Alfred Russel Wallace, "The Origin of Species and Genera," *Studies Scientific and Social* (1900), I, 302 (italics in original).

9. Wallace to Darwin, 2 July [1866], in Francis Darwin and A. C. Seward, eds., *More Letters of Charles Darwin*, 2 vols. (1903), I, 270; Darwin, *Foundations* [1842], pp. 1–2.
1. Darwin to Fiske, 8 Dec. [1874], *Life*, III, 193–194.
2. *Life*, II, 51 [1855].

Darwin stuck to his scientific guns and often fired broadsides at his detractors. "It is mere rubbish," he exploded in a letter to Hooker, "thinking at present of the origin of life; one might as well think of the origin of matter." [3] "What," he asked in the 1842 Sketch, "would the Astronomer say to the doctrine that the planets moved [not] according to the laws of gravitation, but from the Creator having willed each separate planet to move in its particular orbit?" (*Foundations*, p. 22). Darwin was unequivocal. In an early criticism of the manuscript that was to become the *Origin*, Lyell unravelled his reservations. Darwin gratefully acknowledged them, but he had already outdistanced his master in refining a philosophy of science. Lyell propounded what for him was a fundamental question: *"must you not assume a primordial creative power which does not act with uniformity, or how else could man supervene?"* [4] To this question Darwin replied: "under present knowledge [we must assume] the creation of one or a few new forms in the same manner as philosophers assume a power of attraction without any explanation." The remainder of Darwin's answer is an excellent statement of his own position and one of the best statements of the philosophy of scientific method.

> I entirely reject, as in my judgment quite unnecessary, any subsequent addition of "new powers and attributes and forces": or of any "principle of improvement", except in so far as every character which is naturally selected or preserved is in some way an advantage or improvement, otherwise it would not have been selected. If I were convinced that I required such additions to the theory of natural selection, I would reject it as rubbish, but I have firm faith in it, as I cannot believe, that if false, it would explain so many whole classes of facts, which, if I am in my senses, it seems to explain. . . . I would give absolutely nothing for the theory of Natural Selection, if it requires miraculous additions at any one stage or descent. I think Embryology, Homology, Classification, &c., &c., show us that all vertebrata have descended from one parent; how that parent appeared we know not. If you admit in ever so little a degree . . . you will find it difficult to say: thus far the explanation holds good, but no further; here we must call in "the addition of new creative forces." I think you will be driven to reject all or admit all: I fear by your letter it will be the former alternative; and in that case I shall feel sure it is my fault, and not the theory's fault, and this will certainly comfort me. [5]

The Darwinian theory of evolution itself was Darwin's most impressive witness. Darwinian evolution was an hypothesis. As such

3. Darwin to Hooker [29 Mar. 1863], *Life*, III, 18.
4. Darwin to Lyell, 11 Oct. [1859],
Life, II, 210 (italics in original).
5. *Life*, II, 210–211.

it was a theoretical instrument devised to organize and test the data. There were no incontrovertible facts attesting that one variety had been transmuted into another. There was no concrete evidence to establish that random variations, basic to the operation of natural selection, existed in nature and had always so existed. Darwin could not even demonstrate concretely the process by which altered physical characters in a given organism were transmitted to succeeding generations. General critics flayed the theory as "mere hypothesis," hypothesis in the sense of unsubstantial speculation. That Darwin's theory was "vain" was underscored by the popular notion of the role of the scientist as a collector of facts. When the facts were collected and organized, they then spoke for themselves. Scholars—philosophers, scientists, and theologians—rejected Darwin's theory on more sophisticated grounds. For them the hypothesis violated the logic of hypothesis. It constituted a perversion of the canons of induction, for assumptions, not facts, were offered as the ground of its credibility. The learned William Whewell's critique of Hume applied with equal force to Darwin: "Our inference from Hume's observations is, not the truth of his conclusions, but the falsehood of his premises: not that, therefore, we can know nothing of natural connexion, but that, therefore, we have some other source of knowledge than experience." The philosophy of induction derived from the philosophy of causation. "Cause is to be conceived as some abstract quality, power, or efficacy, by which change is produced; a quality not identical with the events, but disclosed by means of them." [6]

With Lyell, constantly concerned about the ultimate, Darwin conducted a running debate, a debate Darwin called "our quasi-theological controversy about natural selection." "Do you consider," he asked Lyell, "the successive variations in the size of the crop of a Pouter Pigeon, which man has accumulated to please his caprice, . . . due to the creative and sustaining powers of Brahma?" [7] Darwin could not accept this inference. Since he could not imagine that Lyell would think otherwise, he wondered how any logical difference could be established between selection produced by the breeder under domestication and the result of selection in a state of nature.

If Darwin's debate with Lyell was quasi-theological, his debate with Asa Gray was frankly theological. He was, he confessed, "in an

6. William Whewell, *The Philosophy of the Inductive Sciences* (1840), I, 72; Alvar Ellegård, "Darwin's Theory and Nineteenth Century Philosophy of Science," in *Roots of Scientific Thought*, pp. 537–568; C. J. Ducasse, "Whewell's Philosophy of Scientific Discovery," *Philosophical Review*, LX (1951), 56–69, 213–234; E. W. Strong, "William Whewell and John Stuart Mill: Their Controversy About Scientific Knowledge," *Journal of the History of Ideas*, XVI (1955), 209–231.
7. Darwin to Lyell, Apr. [1860], *Life*, II, 303–304.

utterly hopeless muddle." Yet he could not endorse Gray's resolute faith in design: "I cannot look at each separate thing as the result of Design." [8] However, he was not sufficiently muddled to be without a point of view. Questions of ultimate purpose, he told Lyell, are "beyond the human intellect, like 'predestination' and 'free will,' or the 'origin of evil'." [9] Darwin entertained wistful thoughts about ultimate meanings, but he never permitted such thoughts to interfere with his operations. He did not know, to be sure, where he was coming out, but he struggled conscientiously to suspend judgment about the purpose of the universe while he was engaged in the scientific examination of its terrestrial parts. "I am inclined," he admitted to Gray, certain his admission would not please him, "to look at everything as resulting from designed laws, with the details, whether good or bad, left to the working out of what we call chance. Not that this notion *at all* satisfies me. I feel most deeply that the whole subject is too profound for the human intellect. A dog might as well speculate on the mind of a Newton. Let each man hope and believe what he can." [1]

Darwin's attitude toward cosmic purpose resembles the attitude of Chauncey Wright. "When it was objected to him," William James recalled, "that there must be some principle of oneness in the diversity of phenomena—some *glue* to hold them together . . . he would reply that there is no need of a glue to join things unless we apprehend some reason why they should fall asunder. Phenomena *are* grouped—more we cannot say of them." [2]

Darwin and Chauncey Wright were in general accord. Both were advocates of the neutrality of science. "True science," wrote the American logician, "should approach . . . questions, avoiding . . . the terms which have attached to them *good* and *bad* meanings in place of scientific distinctness,—terms which have a moral connotation as well as a scientific one . . .Words have 'reputations' as well as other authorities, and there is a tyranny in their reputations even more fatal to freedom of thought. True science deals with nothing but questions of facts—and in terms, if possible, which shall not determine beforehand how we ought to feel about the facts; for this is one of the most certain and fatal means of corrupting evidence." [3]

Darwin granted special weight to no category of probable meanings. Neither Cause, Being, Life, or Design was accorded any special prior significance. Darwin accounted life a given of nature. If

8. Darwin to Gray, 26 Nov. 1860, *Life,* II, 353.
9. Darwin to Lyell, 25 Apr. [1860], *Life,* II, 304.
1. Darwin to Gray, 22 May [1860], *Life,* II, 310–311, 312.

2. William James, "Chauncey Wright," *Nation,* XXI (1875), 194.
3. Cited from the Wright papers by Philip P. Wiener, *Evolution and the Founders of Pragmatism* (Cambridge, Mass., 1949), pp. 44–45.

it had larger meanings, those meanings were yet to be determined. Ultimate meanings were not within the scope of science. Wright, following Kant, distinguished between science and ethics, and Darwin in practice agreed with both. "If the facts are determined, and, as far as may be, free from moral biases, then practical science comes in to determine what, in view of the facts, our feelings and rules of conduct ought to be; but practical science has no inherent postulates any more than speculative science. Its ultimate grounds are the particular goods or ends of human life." [4]

A vital aspect of the Darwinian revolution consists in Darwin's contribution to the method and philosophy of science. The nature of the Darwinian revolution is the revolution in man's conception of nature. Copernicus brought astronomy within the domain of science. Darwin brought zoology within the domain of science. Darwin made the biological sciences objective, experimental, phenomenal, and empirical. As Darwin viewed the world of Reality, Being possessed no antecedent priority. Being, if Being there was, was to be found in the process of natural exploration. Darwin contributed to reverse the order of Being and process. Being and permanence were conceived, not as ultimate coordinates of temporal change within an antecedent transcendental system. They were conceived as logical coordinates emergent in the study of natural parts. Historically, the question is not whether Parmenides was wrong and Darwin and his successors right. Significant is the fact that Darwin separated the study of process from the concept of Being. The impact of Darwin is the impact of scientific method on the life sciences and on the sciences of human life. The laws of moral "harmony," Chauncey Wright is reported to have said, "are of a wholly different order, *different in meaning* . . . neither contradictory to nor in conformity with those of the scientific cosmos." [5]

4. Wiener, pp. 44–45; A. D. Lindsay, *Kant* (London, 1934), pp. 163–164.
5. Wiener, p. 36 (italics in original);

Charles C. Gillispie, "Lamarck and Darwin in the History of Science," in *Forerunners of Darwin*, pp. 265–291.

The Victorian Opposition
to Darwin

BERNARD BARBER

Resistance by Scientists to Scientific Discovery (1961) †

In the study of the history and sociology of science, there has been a relative lack of attention to one of the interesting aspects of the social process of discovery—the resistance on the part of scientists themselves to scientific discovery. * * *

Substantive Concepts

Several different kinds of cultural resistance to discovery may be distinguished. We may turn first to the way in which the substantive concepts and theories held by scientists at any given time become a source of resistance to new ideas. And our illustrations begin with the very origins of modern science. In his magisterial discussion of the Copernican revolution, Kuhn [1] tells us not only about the nonscientific opposition to the heliocentric theory but also about the resistance from the astronomer-scientists of the time. Even after the publication of De Revolutionibus, the belief of most astronomers in the stability of the earth was unshaken. The idea of the earth's motion was either ignored or dismissed as absurd. Even the great astronomer-observer Brahe remained a life-long opponent of Copernicanism; he was unable to break with the traditional patterns of thought about the earth's lack of motion. And his immense prestige helped to postpone the conversion of other astronomers to the new theory. * * *

Methodological Conceptions

The methodological conceptions scientists entertain at any given time constitute a second cultural source of resistance to scientific

† Science, CXXXIV (1961), 596–602. Bernard Barber (b. 1918) is professor of sociology at Barnard College, Columbia University.

1. T. S. Kuhn, The Copernican Revolution (Cambridge, Mass.: Harvard University Press, 1957).

discovery and are as important as substantive ideas in determining response to innovations. Some scientists, for example, tend to be antitheoretical, resisting, on that methodological ground, certain discoveries. "In Baconian science," says Gillispie, "the bird-watcher comes into his own while genius, ever theorizing in far places, is suspect. And this is why Bacon would have none of Kepler or Copernicus or Gilbert or anyone who would extend a few ideas of calculations into a system of the world." [2]

Religious Ideas

Although we have heard more of the way in which religious forces outside science have hindered its progress, the religious ideas of scientists themselves constitute, after substantive and methodological conceptions, a third cultural source of resistance to scientific innovation. Such internal resistance goes back to the beginning of modern science. We have seen that the astronomer colleagues of Copernicus resisted his ideas in part because of their religious beliefs, and we know that Leibniz, for example, criticized Newton "for failing to make providential destiny part of physics." [3] Scientists themselves felt that science should justify God and His world. Gradually, of course, physics and religion were accommodated one to the other, certainly among scientists themselves. But all during the first half of the 19th century resistance to discovery in geology persisted among scientists for religious reasons. The difficulty, as Gillispie has put it on the basis of his classic analysis of geology during this period, "appears to be one of religion (in a crude sense) *in* science rather than one of religion *versus* scientists." The most embarrassing obstacles faced by the new sciences were cast up by the curious providential materialism of the scientists themselves.[4] When, in the 1840's, Robert Chambers published his *Vestiges of Creation*, declaring a developmental view of the universe, the theory of development was so at variance with the religous views which all scientists accepted that "they all spoke out: Herschel, Whewell, Forbes, Owen, Prichard, Huxley, Lyell, Sedgwick, Murchison, Buckland, Agassiz, Miller, and others." [5]

Religious resistance continued and was manifested against Darwin, of course, although many of the scientists who had resisted earlier versions of developmentalism accepted Darwin's evolutionary theory, Huxley being not the least among them. In England,

2. C. C. Gillispie, *The Edge of Objectivity* (Princeton: Princeton University Press, 1960).
3. *Ibid.*
4. C. C. Gillispie, *Genesis and Geology* (Cambridge, Mass.: Harvard University Press, 1951).
5. *Ibid.*, p. 133. That scientists were religious also, and in the same way, in America, can be seen in A. H. Dupree, *Asa Gray* (Cambridge, Mass.; Harvard University Press, 1959).

Richard Owen offered the greatest resistance on scientific grounds, while in America and, in fact, internationally, Louis Agassiz was the leading critic of Darwinism on religious grounds.[6] * * *

In addition to shared idea-systems, the patterns of social interaction among scientists also become sources of resistance to discovery. Here again we are dealing with elements that, on the whole, probably serve to advance science but that occasionally produce negative, or dysfunctional, effects.

Professional Standing

The first of these social sources of resistance is the relative professional standing of the discoverer. In general, higher professional standing in science is achieved by the more competent, those who have demonstrated their capacity for being creative in their own right and for judging the discoveries of others. But sometimes, when discoveries are made by scientists of lower standing, they are resisted by scientists of higher standing partly because of the authority the higher position provides. Huxley commented on this social source of resistance in a letter he wrote in 1852: "For instance, I know that the paper I have just sent in is very original and of some importance, and I am equally sure that if it is referred to the judgment of my 'particular' friend, that it will not be published. He won't be able to say a word against it, but he will pooh-pooh it to a dead certainty. You will ask with wonderment, Why? Because for the last twenty years [. . . .] has been regarded as the great authority in these matters, and has had no one tread on his heels, until, at last, I think, he has come to look upon the Natural World as his special preserve, and 'no poachers allowed.' So I must manoeuvre a little to get my poor memoir kept out of his hands."[7] * * *

Professional Specialization

Another social source of resistance is the pattern of specialization that prevails in science at any given time. On the whole, of course, as with any social or other type of system, such specialization is efficient for internal and environmental purposes. Specialization concentrates and focuses the requisite knowledge and skill where they are needed. But occasionally the negative aspect of specialization shows itself, and innovative "outsiders" to a field of specialization are resisted by the "insiders." Thus, when Helmholtz announced his theory of the conservation of energy, it met with

o. Gillispie, *Genesis and Geology;* Dupree; E. Lurie, *Louis Agazziz: A Life in Science* (Chicago: University of Chicago Press, 1960).

7. R. H. Murray, *Science and Scientists in the Nineteenth Century* (London: Sheldon, 1925), p. 367.

resistance partly because he was not a specialist in what we now think of as physics. * * *

Societies, "Schools," and Seniority

Scientific organizations, as we may safely infer from their large number and their historical persistence, serve a variety of useful purposes for their members. And of course scientific publications are indispensable for communication in science. But occasionally, when organizations or publications are incompetently staffed and run, they may serve as another social source of resistance to innovation in science.

The rivalries of what are called "schools" are frequently alleged to be another social source of resistance in science. Huxley, for example, is reported to have said, two years before his death, " 'Authorities,' 'disciples,' and 'schools' are the curse of science; and do more to interfere with the work of the scientific spirit than all its enemies." 8 * * *

That the older resist the younger in science is another pattern that has often been noted by scientists themselves and by those who study science as a social phenomenon. "I do not," said Lavoisier in the closing sentences of his memoir *Reflections on Phlogiston* (read before the Academy of Sciences in 1785), "expect my ideas to be adopted all at once. The human mind gets creased into a way of seeing things. Those who have envisaged nature according to a certain point of view during much of their career, rise only with difficulty to new ideas. It is the passage of time, therefore, which must confirm or destroy the opinions I have presented. Meanwhile, I observe with great satisfaction that the young people are beginning to study the science without prejudice. . . ." 9 * * *

After this long recital of the cultural and social sources of resistance, by scientists, to scientific discovery, I need to emphasize a point I have already made. That some resistance occurs, that it has specifiable sources in culture and social interaction, that it may be in some measure inevitable, is not proof either that there is more resistance than acceptance in science or that scientists are no more open-minded than other men. On the contrary, the powerful norm of open-mindedness in science, the objective tests by which concepts and theories often can be validated, and the social mechanisms for ensuring competition among ideas new and old—all these make up a social system in which objectivity is greater than it is in other social areas, resistance less. The development of modern science demonstrates this ever so clearly. Nevertheless, some re-

8. C. Bibby, *T. H. Huxley: Scientist, Humanist, and Educator* (New York: Horizon, 1959), p. 18.
9. Gillispie, *The Edge of Objectivity.*

sistance remains, and it is this we seek to understand and thus perhaps to reduce. If "the edge of objectivity" in science, as Charles Gillispie has recently pointed out, requires us to take physical and biological nature as it is, without projecting our wishes upon it, so also we have to take man's social nature, or his behavior in society, as it is. As men in society, scientists are sometimes the agents, sometimes the objects, of resistance to their own discoveries.

ADAM SEDGWICK

Objections to Mr. Darwin's Theory of the Origin of Species (1860) †

[The Archbishop of Dublin has received the following remarks, in answer to an inquiry he had made of a friend (eminent in the world of science) on the subject of Darwin's theory of the origin of species.]

* * * I must in the first place observe that Darwin's theory is not *inductive,*—not based on a series of acknowledged facts pointing to a *general* conclusion,—not a proposition evolved out of the facts, logically, and of course including them. To use an old figure, I look on the theory as a vast pyramid resting on its apex, and that apex a mathematical point. The only facts he pretends to adduce, as true elements of proof, are the *varieties* produced by domestication, or the *human artifice* of cross-breeding. We all admit the varieties, and the very wide limits of variation, among domestic animals. How very unlike are poodles and greyhounds. Yet they are of one species. And how nearly alike are many animals,—allowed to be of distinct species, on any acknowledged views of species. Hence there may have been very many blunders among naturalists, in the discrimination and enumeration of species. But this does not undermine the grand truth of nature, and the continuity of species. Again, the varieties, built upon by Mr. Darwin, are varieties of domestication and human *design*. Such varieties could have no existence in the old world. Something may be done by cross-breeding; but mules are generally sterile, or the progeny (in some rare instances) passes into one of the original crossed forms. The Author of Nature will not permit His work to be spoiled by the wanton curiosity of Man. And in a state of nature (such as that of the old

† Adam Sedgwick (1785–1873) was Woodwardian Professor of Geology at Cambridge and president of the Geological Society and of the British Associa-tion. His review appeared anonymously in *The Spectator*, XXXIII (March 24, 1860), 285–286.

world before Man came upon it) wild animals of different species do not desire to cross and unite.

Species have been constant for thousands of years; and time (so far as I see my way) though multiplied by millions and billions would never change them, so long as the conditions remained constant. Change the conditions, and old species would disappear; and new species *might* have room to come in and flourish. But how, and by what causation? I say by *creation*. But, what do I mean by creation? I reply, the operation of a power quite beyond the powers of a pigeon-fancier, a cross-breeder, or hybridizer; a power I cannot imitate or comprehend; but in which I can believe, by a legitimate conclusion of sound reason drawn from the laws and harmonies of Nature,—proving in all around me, a design and purpose, and a mutual adaptation of parts, which I *can* comprehend,— and which prove that there is exterior to, and above, the mere phenomena of Nature a great prescient and designing cause. Believing this, I have no difficulty in the repetition of new species.

But Darwin would say that I am introducing a *miracle* by the supposition. In one sense I am; in another I am not. The hypothesis does not suspend or interrupt an established law of Nature. It does suppose the introduction of a new phenomenon unaccounted for by the operation of any *known* law of Nature; and it appeals to a power above established laws, and yet acting in conformity with them. * * *

I place the theory against facts viewed collectively. 1st. I see no proofs of enormous *gaps* of geological time, (I say nothing of years or centuries,) in those cases where there is a sudden change in the ancient fauna and flora. I am willing, out of the stock of past time, to lavish millions or billions upon each epoch, if thereby we can gain rational results from the operation of *true causes*. But time and "natural selection" can do nothing if there be not a vera causa working in them. [Note—see remark on *Time*, in the *Annotations on Bacon's Essays*.] I must confine myself to a few of the collective instances.

2d. Towards the end of the carboniferous period, there was a vast extinction of animal and vegetable life. We can, I think, account for this extinction mechanically. The old crust was broken up. The sea bottom underwent a great change. The old flora and fauna went out; a new flora and fauna appeared, in the ground now called Permian, at the base of the new red sandstone, which overlie the carboniferous. I take the fact as it *is*, and I have no difficulty. The time in which all this was brought *may* have been very long, even upon a geological scale of time. But where do the *intervening* and connecting types exist, which are to mark the *work of natural selection?* We do not find them. Therefore the step onwards gives no true resting-place to a baseless theory; and is, in fact, a stumbling-block in its way.

3d. Before we rise through the new red sandstone, we find the muschel-kalk (wanting in England, though its place on the scale is well-known) with *an entirely new* fauna: where have we a proof of any enormous lapse of geological time to account for the change? We have no proof in the deposits themselves: the presumption they offer to our senses is of a contrary kind.

4th. If we rise from the muschel-kalk to the Lias, we find again a new fauna. All the anterior species are gone. Yet the passage through the upper members of the new red sandstone to the Lias is by insensible gradation, and it is no easy matter to fix the physical line of their demarcation. I think it would be a very rash assertion to affirm that a great interval took place between the formation of the upper part of the new red sandstone and the Lias. Physical evidence is against it. To support a baseless theory, Darwin would require a countless lapse of ages of which we have *no* commensurate physical monuments; and he is unable to supply any of the connecting organic links that ought to bind together the older fauna with that of the Lias.

I need hardly go on any further with these objections. But I cannot conclude without expressing my detestation of the theory, because of its unflinching materialism;—because it has deserted the inductive track, the only track that leads to physical truth;—because it utterly repudiates final causes, and thereby indicates a demoralized understanding on the part of its advocates. In some rare instances it shows a wonderful credulity. Darwin seems to believe that a white bear, by being confined to the slops floating in the Polar basin, might be turned into a whale; that a Lemur might easily be turned into a bat; that a three-toed Tapir might be the great grandfather of a horse! or the progeny of a horse may (in America) have gone back to the tapir.

But any startling and (supposed) novel paradox, maintained very boldly and with something of imposing plausibility, produces, in some minds, a kind of pleasing excitement, which predisposes them in its favour; and if they are unused to careful reflection, and averse to the labour of accurate investigation, they will be likely to conclude that what is (apparently) *original*, must be a production of original *genius*, and that anything very much opposed to prevailing notions must be a grand *discovery*,—in short, that whatever comes from "the bottom of a well" must be the "truth" supposed to be hidden there.

SIR RICHARD OWEN

Darwin on the Origin of Species (1860) †

* * * Mr. Darwin refers to the multitude of the individuals of every species, which, from one cause or another, perish either before, or soon after attaining maturity.

'Owing to this struggle for life, any variation, however slight and from whatever cause proceeding, if it be in any degree profitable to an individual of any species, in its infinitely complex relations to other organic beings and to external nature, will tend to the preservation of that individual, and will generally be inherited by its offspring. The offspring, also, will thus have a better chance of surviving, for, of the many individuals of any species which are periodically born, but a small number can survive. I have called this principle, by which each slight variation, if useful, is preserved, by the term of Natural Selection, in order to mark its relation to man's power of selection. We have seen that man by selection can certainly produce great results, and can adapt organic beings to his own uses, through the accumulation of slight but useful variations, given to him by the hand of Nature. But Natural Selection, as we shall hereafter see, is a power incessantly ready for action, and is as immeasurably superior to man's feeble efforts, as the works of Nature are to those of Art.' (P. 61.)

The scientific world has looked forward with great interest to the facts which Mr. Darwin might finally deem adequate to the support of his theory on this supreme question in biology, and to the course of inductive original research which might issue in throwing light on 'that mystery of mysteries.' But having now cited the chief, if not the whole, of the original observations adduced by its author in the volume now before us, our disappointment may be conceived. Failing the adequacy of such observations, not merely to carry conviction, but to give a colour to the hypothesis, we were then left to confide in the superior grasp of mind, strength of intellect, clearness and precision of thought and expression, which might raise one man so far above his contemporaries, as to enable him to discern in the common stock of facts, of coincidences, correlations and analogies in Natural History, deeper and truer conclusions than his fellow-labourers had been able to reach.

† Sir Richard Owen (1804–1892), superintendent of the Natural History Department of the British Museum, was a distinguished comparative anatomist and a pioneer in vertebrate paleontology. His review of the *Origin of Species* appeared anonymously in the *Edinburgh Review*, CXI (1860), 251–275.

These expectations, we must confess, received a check on perusing the first sentence in the book.

'When on board H.M.S "Beagle," as naturalist, I was much struck with certain facts in the distribution of the inhabitants of South America, and in the geological relations of the present to the past inhabitants of that continent. These facts seemed to me to throw some light on the origin of species—that mystery of mysteries, as it has been called by some of our greatest philosophers.' (P. 1.)

What is there, we asked ourselves, as we closed the volume to ponder on this paragraph,—what can there possibly be in the inhabitants, we suppose he means aboriginal inhabitants, of South America, or in their distribution on that continent, to have suggested to any mind that man might be a transmuted ape, or to throw any light on the origin of the human or other species? Mr. Darwin must be aware of what is commonly understood by an 'uninhabited island;' he may, however, mean by the inhabitants of South America, not the human kind only, whether aboriginal or otherwise, but all the lower animals. Yet again, why are the freshwater polypes or sponges to be called 'inhabitants' more than the plants? Perhaps what was meant might be, that the distribution and geological relations of the organised beings generally in South America, had suggested transmutational views. They have commonly suggested ideas as to the independent origin of such localized kinds of plants and animals. But what the 'certain facts' were, and what may be the nature of the light which they threw upon the mysterious beginning of species, is not mentioned or further alluded to in the present work. * * *

'Isolation also,' says Mr. Darwin, 'is an important element in the process of natural selection.' But how can one select if a thing be 'isolated'? Even using the word in the sense of a confined area, Mr. Darwin admits that the conditions of life 'throughout such area, will tend to modify all the individuals of a species in the same manner, in relation to the same conditions.' (P. 104.) No evidence, however, is given of a species having ever been created in that way; but granting the hypothetical influence and transmutation, there is no selection here. The author adds, 'Although I do not doubt that isolation is of considerable importance in the production of new species, on the whole, I am inclined to believe, that largeness of area is of more importance in the production of species capable of spreading widely.' (P. 105.)

Now, on such a question as the origin of species, and in an express, formal, scientific treatise on the subject, the expression of a belief, where one looks for a demonstration, is simply provoking.

We are not concerned in the author's beliefs or inclinations to believe. Belief is a state of mind short of actual knowledge. It is a state which may govern action, when based upon a tacit admission of the mind's incompetency to prove a proposition, coupled with submissive acceptance of an authoritative dogma, or worship of a favourite idol of the mind. We readily concede, and it needs, indeed, no ghost to reveal the fact, that the wider the area in which a species may be produced, the more widely it will spread. But we fail to discern its import in respect of the great question at issue.

We have read and studied with care most of the monographs conveying the results of close investigations of particular groups of animals, but have not found, what Darwin asserts to be the fact, at least as regards all those investigators of particular groups of animals and plants whose treatises he has read, viz., that their authors 'are one and all firmly convinced that each of the well-marked forms or species was at the first independently created.' Our experience has been that the monographers referred to have rarely committed themselves to any conjectural hypothesis whatever, upon the origin of the species which they have closely studied.

Darwin appeals from the 'experienced naturalists whose minds are stocked with a multitude of facts' which he assumes to have been 'viewed from a point of view opposite to his own,' to the 'few naturalists endowed with much flexibility of mind,' for a favourable reception of his hypothesis. We must confess that the minds to whose conclusions we incline to bow belong to that truth-loving, truth-seeking, truth-imparting class, which Robert Brown [1], Bojanus [2], Rudolphi, Cuvier [3], Ehrenberg [4], Herold [4], Kölliker [5], and Siebold,[6] worthily exemplify. The rightly and sagaciously generalising intellect is associated with the power of endurance of continuous and laborious research, exemplarily manifested in such monographs as we have quoted below. Their authors are the men who trouble the intellectual world little with their beliefs, but enrich it greatly with their proofs. If close and long-continued research, sustained by the determination to get accurate results, blunted, as Mr. Darwin seems to imply, the far-seeing discovering faculty, then are we driven to this paradox, viz., that the elucidation of the higher problems, nay the highest, in Biology, is to be sought for or expected in the lucubrations of those naturalists whose minds are not weighed or troubled with more than a discursive and superficial knowledge of nature.

Lasting and fruitful conclusions have, indeed, hitherto been based

1. Prodromus Floræ Novæ Hollandiæ.
2. Anatome Testudinis Europæ.
3. Mémoires pour servir à l'Anatomie des Mollusques.
4. Die Infusionsthierchen, als vollkommene Organismen.
5. Disquisitiones de Animalium vertebris carentium, &c.
6. Entwickelungsgeschichte des Cephalopoden.

only on the possession of knowledge; now we are called upon to accept an hypothesis on the plea of want of knowledge. The geological record, it is averred, is so imperfect! But what human record is not? Especially must the record of past organisms be must less perfect than of present ones. We freely admit it. But when Mr. Darwin, in reference to the absence of the intermediate fossil forms required by his hypothesis—and only the zootomical zoologist can approximatively appreciate their immense numbers—the countless hosts of transitional links which, on 'natural selection,' must certainly have existed at one period or another of the world's history —when Mr. Darwin exclaims what may be, or what may not be, the forms yet forthcoming out of the graveyards of strata, we would reply, that our only ground for prophesying of what may come, is by the analogy of what has come to light. We may expect, e.g., a chambered-shell from a secondary rock; but not the evidence of a creature linking on the cuttle-fish to the lump-fish.

Mr. Darwin asks, 'How is it that varieties, which I have called incipient species, become ultimately good and distinct species?' To which we rejoin with the question:—Do they become good and distinct species? Is there any one instance proved by observed facts of such transmutation? We have searched the volume in vain for such. When we see the intervals that divide most species from their nearest congeners, in the recent and especially the fossil series, we either doubt the fact of progressive conversion, or, as Mr. Darwin remarks in his letter to Dr. Asa Gray [7], one's 'imagination must fill up very wide blanks.' * * *

The essential element in the complex idea of species, as it has been variously framed and defined by naturalists, viz., the blood-relationship between all the individuals of such species, is annihilated on the hypothesis of 'natural selection.' According to this view a genus, a family, an order, a class, a sub-kingdom,—the individuals severally representing these grades of difference or relationship,— now differ from individuals of the same species only in degree: the species, like every other group, is a mere creature of the brain; it is no longer from nature. With the present evidence from form, structure, and procreative phenomena, of the truth of the opposite proposition, that 'classification is the task of science, but species the work of nature,' we believe that this aphorism will endure; we are certain that it has not yet been refuted; and we repeat in the words of Linnæus, 'Classis et Ordo est sapientiæ, Species naturæ opus.'

7. Proceedings of the Linnæan Society, 1858, p. 61.

ERNST MAYR

Agassiz, Darwin, and Evolution (1959) †

* * *

The Publication of On the Origin of Species

Darwin's publication must have been a staggering blow to Agassiz. Not because it was another publication upholding the detestable theory of transmutation but because it was so obviously immune to the majority of the arguments against the evolutionary theory elaborated by Agassiz just two years before. Cuvier's opponents—and they were mostly the same as those against whom Agassiz had been arguing—had based their theories essentially on a priori considerations of various sorts. It was easy to counter them with other a priori considerations. As naturalists they were dilettantes and no match for zoologists as erudite as Cuvier and Agassiz. That Darwin's was a totally new approach to the subject of evolution was well appreciated by Agassiz:

> Darwin has placed the subject on a different basis from that of all his predecessors, and has brought to the discussion a vast amount of well-arranged information, a convincing cogency of argument, and a captivating charm of presentation. His doctrine appealed the more powerfully to the scientific world because he maintained it at first not upon metaphysical ground but upon observation. Indeed it might be said that he treated his subject according to the best scientific methods, had he not frequently overstepped the boundaries of actual knowledge and allowed his imagination to supply the links which science does not furnish.[1]

Darwin's strictly empirical approach of patiently piling fact upon fact in an almost pedestrian manner until the sheer weight of the evidence made a conclusion inevitable was received by his contemporaries with mixed feelings. The non-biologists, in particular, felt excluded by an approach not based on 'pure reason' and relieved their frustration by ridiculing Darwin's 'clumsiness' as compared, for instance, with the grandiose sweep of Lamarck's *Philosophie zoologique*. It is, to put it mildly, amusing to read how Agassiz re-

† *Harvard Library Bulletin*, XIII (1959), 165–194. Ernst Mayr (b. 1904) is Alexander Agassiz Professor of Zoology and Director of the Museum of Comparative Zoology at Harvard University.

1. Louis Agassiz, "Evolution and Permanence of Type," *Atlantic Monthly*, XXXIII (January 1874), 94.

fers to Darwin's inductive method as 'speculation.' There is no doubt that the year 1859 ushered in a new era in the history of evolutionary biology, the era of the scientific method. It is indeed fully justifiable to refer to the entire preceding period, dominated by speculation and intuition, as the prehistory of evolutionary science. Evolutionary biology as a science started in 1859.

Agassiz was fifty-two years old when Darwin's work was published. He was in the midst of building his great new natural history museum, he was the most popular lecturer in America, and he had his teaching and enormous social obligations. All in all, he was unable to find the intellectual peace to undertake a critical evaluation of the foundation of his concepts and beliefs. So different was Darwin's approach that Agassiz was unable not only to understand it fully, but, where he attempted to rephrase Darwin's arguments in his own words, to do so correctly. Yet he tried manfully to refute Darwin's evolutionary proofs, particularly in two publications, one issued in 1860 and the other prepared in 1873 shortly before his death and published posthumously in 1874.

Agassiz' Refutation of the Evolutionary Evidence

Among Darwin's many arguments in favor of common descent by modification Agassiz singled out for criticism primarily two series, those dealing with the geological record, and those dealing with the mechanisms responsible for evolutionary change. As palaeontologist and embryologist Agassiz felt best qualified to deal with these two sectors.[2]

The Geological Record

The first point he takes up is the diversity of different faunas. 'Before it could be granted that the great variety of types which occur at any later periods has arisen from a successive differentiation of a few still earlier types, it should be shown that in reality in former periods the types are fewer and less diversified.'[3] This, however, says Agassiz, is not the case. There are 1,200 species of fossil sea shells known from the Eocene beds of the Paris Basin, and only 600 living species in the Mediterranean, 'affording, at once, a very striking evidence of the greater diversity and greater number of species of that geological period [the Eocene of more than sixty million years ago] when compared even with those of a wider geographical

---

2. Quotations in the following summary are sometimes taken from earlier works of Agassiz, as affording more complete statements.

3. Agassiz, "The Primitive Diversity and Number of Animals in Geological Times," *American Journal of Science and Arts*, 2nd. ser., XVII (1854), 318.

area at the present day.' [4] Even admitting that the Paris fauna was so rich because it was a tropical fauna, yet its richness, says Agassiz, 'is much greater than that of any local fauna of the present period, even within the tropics.' Subsequent researches have not substantiated Agassiz' claims. Some recent local lists of sea shells record the following number of species: Port Alfred, South Africa (non-tropical) 721, west coast of America from California to Panama 1,600, east coast of America from Greenland to Texas 2,632, and Philippines 4,152. Indeed, the recent fauna of marine mollusks of the Indo-Malayan area is estimated to be 6,000 to 8,000 species, far in excess of the 1,200 species from the Eocene of Paris.[5]

If all types of organisms have existed from the beginning, it follows that all major types must be present in the oldest fossil-bearing rocks, while the still earlier rocks must be void of any evidence of organic life. This, claims Agassiz, is indeed the case. Every piece of inconvenient evidence is eliminated by a special *ad hoc* explanation: the absence of coelenterates ('Acalephs') in the older strata is due to the absence of hard parts in their bodies; the absence of vertebrates in these formations is due, he says, to the incompleteness of the fossil record, for vertebrates should be present upon 'physiological grounds.' [6] His major thesis, that there were as many species of animals at the very beginning of the world as there are now, is the same that Bonnet defended so vigorously, the same that, as Lovejoy has shown, goes back explicitly or implicitly all the way to Plato and his principle of plenitude.

Agassiz' second argument is based on the apparent fixity of species. Whenever animals and plants of two successive geological periods are compared, he says, they are either completely identical or quite different. 'None of those primordial forms of life, which naturalists call species, are known to have changed during any of these periods. It cannot be denied, that the species of different successive periods are supposed by some naturalists to derive their distinguishing features from changes which have taken place in those of preceding ages; but this is a mere supposition.' [7] As the strongest argument in favor of the fixity of species he considers the demonstration that the animals and plants discovered in the Egyptian tombs during Napoleon's expedition were indistinguishable from living species, as pointed out by Cuvier and other naturalists. It was not realized by Agassiz that the approximately five thousand years elapsed since the entombments compare to the total length of duration of a species as do about eighty days to the life expectancy

4. *Ibid.*, 310.
5. According to information kindly supplied by Dr. W. J. Clench, Museum of Comparative Zoology, Harvard University.

6. *Agassiz, Contributions to the Natural History of the United States of America,* V (Boston, 1857), 24.
7. *Ibid.*, 51.

of a man. It would be highly improbable that one could demonstrate an evolutionary change in such an exceedingly short fraction of the total life span of a species. Agassiz concludes the argument with the statement that he will not accept the transmutation theory 'as long as no fact is adduced to show that any one well known species among the many thousands that are buried in the whole series of fossiliferous rocks, is actually the parent of any one of the species now living.' [8] He nowhere states, however, what kind of evidence he would accept as proof. If one wishes to be obstinate, it is possible to claim to this very day that even the most perfect vertical series of intergrading species of fossil is nothing but proof for the 'unfolding' (*evolutio*) of preformed germs in the sense of Bonnet.

Agassiz' next anti-evolutionary argument is best stated in his own words. 'The supporters of the transmutation theory . . . never can make it appear that the definiteness of the characters of the class of Birds is the result of a common descent of all Birds, for the first Bird must have been brother or cousin to some other animal that was not a Bird, since there are other animals besides Birds in this world, to no one of which any bird bears as close a relation as it bears to its own class.' [9] By a curious coincidence this statement was published exactly one year before the description of *Archaeopteryx*, a virtually perfect intermediate between birds and reptiles. Although numerous additional 'missing links' have been discovered since that day, hardly any other of them connects two major types of animals in quite so ideal a manner as does *Archaeopteryx*. It is, of course, virtually impossible to comprehend gradual evolution if one places the diversity of the organic world in the rigid pigeonholes of 'types.' No doubt Agassiz would have reacted to *Archaeopteryx* as did the few remaining anti-evolutionists of a later period, who placed it as a separate type of its own that had nothing to do with the evolution of birds from reptilian ancestors.

One of Agassiz' chief arguments is based on Cuvier's demonstration of the sharp distinction between consecutive faunas as well as the absence of any missing links between the major types. He was, therefore, particularly upset by Kowalevsky's discovery of a chorda in the ascidians, which would indicate that they are a link between the mollusks (with which the ascidians had been classified by Cuvier and Agassiz) and the vertebrates (which are characterized by the chorda). It would have pleased Agassiz to learn that this discovery does not make the ascidians a missing link. It is now known that they are not to be connected with the mollusks but form the

8. Agassiz, "Prof. Agassiz on the Origin of Species," *American Journal of Science* *and Arts,* 2nd. ser., XXX (July 1860), 144.
9. *Ibid.,* 154.

phylum chordates together with the vertebrates. The great phyla of the animal kingdom are as far apart now as they were in Agassiz' time. All the evidence indicates that they diverged from each other but that this happened in the Pre-Cambrian days (more than five hundred million years ago). There is no fossil record available to indicate the steps by which this divergence took place. Our ignorance concerning the origin of the major types is as great today as it was in Agassiz' time.

Finally, Agassiz raises one point concerning the fossil record by which he thinks he can inflict a mortal wound on the transmutation theory. If this theory were right, says Agassiz, the 'lowest' representative of a type should be found in the lowest strata and the 'highest' in the most recent strata. But this is not what one finds!

> What then are the earliest known Vertebrates? They are Selachians (sharks and their allies) and Ganoids (garpikes and the like), the highest of all living fishes, structurally speaking. . . . In all their features the Selachians, more than any other fishes, resemble the higher animals. They lay few eggs, the higher kinds giving birth only to three, four, or five at a brood, whereas the common fishes lay myriads of eggs, hundreds of thousands in some instances, and these are for the greater part cast into the water to be developed at random.[1]

In this argument Agassiz is quite oblivious to the fact that he speaks like a true Aristotelian, selecting his criteria of 'high' and 'low' on the basis of a priori considerations:

> The limitation of the young is unquestionably a mark of superiority. The higher we rise in the scale of animal life the more restricted is the number of offspring. In proportion to this reduction in number, the connection of the offspring with the parent is drawn closer, organically and morally, till this relation becomes finally the foundation of all social organization, of all human civilization.

The facts of internal fertilization and placenta formation among the sharks are quoted as additional evidence of their 'superiority,' and yet, Agassiz continues, these are the first vertebrates to be found in the fossil record, while *Amphioxus* and the lampreys (primitive chordates) are not found as fossils at all, but only in the present period, to which we ourselves belong. 'This certainly does not look like a connected series beginning with the lowest and ending with the highest, for the highest fishes come first and the lowest come last.' Discoveries in the fossil history of the fishes, made since Agassiz, have completely demolished his argument. Preceding the selachians, groups of primitive fishes have been found

---

1. Agassiz, "Evolution and Permanence of Type," 100.

that appear to be directly ancestral to the lampreys and to the more advanced fishes. The bony fishes, in spite of the myriads of eggs they lay, are a comparatively recent development, derived from ganoid-like ancestors. More importantly, these finds show the complete invalidity of Agassiz' a priori criteria of what is 'low' and what is 'high.' Many of the earliest fishes were as elaborate in their structure as any of their descendants. No wonder Agassiz finally came to the conclusion: 'The whole history of geological succession shows us that the lowest in structure is by no means necessarily the earliest in time, either in the vertebrate type or any other.' [2] It all depends on how we define 'lowest in structure.'

The Mechanisms of Evolution

Agassiz throughout his life was scornful of any of the theories that attempted to elaborate on the causes and mechanisms that might be responsible for evolutionary changes. We have already discussed how he considered 'physical causes' as a brute sledge hammer that could not improve a delicate watch. Furthermore, wherever environment does have a slight effect, as in raising the milk production of a well-fed cow, it has no lasting influence, for this improvement will not be transmitted to her offspring. Agassiz was entirely right in his refutation of the inheritance of acquired characters. Indeed, most of his arguments against the environmentalists of the schools of Lamarck and Geoffroy St Hilaire are well taken, and supported by any modern evolutionist. But where Agassiz uses strictly genetic arguments, he is a child of his times: the century of genetics had not yet arrived. Yet, on the whole, Agassiz' discussion of heredity is not much worse than Darwin's excursions in this field. Fortunately Darwin was satisfied, particularly in the *Origin*, to take for granted the existence of genetic variability and the replenishment of genetic variability as the source material for natural selection. Indeed, as Huxley [3] has correctly pointed out, if Darwin had been familiar with Mendel's work he might well have been misled into some sort of saltational mutationism like De Vries, Bateson, and other early Mendelians.

In this centenary year of the *Origin of Species* it is no longer doubted by thinking biologists that natural selection is the key mechanism of evolution. Hundreds if not thousands of objections against the universal power of natural selection have been raised during the past hundred years but have uniformly been shown to be

2. *Ibid.*, 101.
3. Julian Huxley, "The Emergence of Darwinism," *Journal of the Linnean So-* *ciety of London, Zoology*, XLV (1958), 1–14, *Botany*, LVI (1958), 1–14.

ill considered. It is interesting to look into Agassiz' stand on this problem. Let me say beforehand that no typologist has ever understood natural selection, because he can not possibly understand it. Natural selection is a population phenomenon, a shifting of statistical averages owing to differential reproduction. This is a mode of thinking so different from that of a typologist that it is bound to be incomprehensible to him.[4] Agassiz was no exception. For him, 'the organized beings which live now, and have lived in former geological periods, constitute an organic whole, intelligibly and methodically combined in all of its parts.'[5] This, he says, cannot have possibly resulted from the play of blind physical forces. To apply the term 'natural selection' to such accidental causes is a mistake, because 'selection implies design; the powers to which Darwin refers the order of species, can design nothing.' Here he is merely arguing against the term 'selection,' which Darwin had chosen in deliberate analogy with the artificial selection of the animal and plant breeders. This, as we now see it, was an entirely legitimate terminology since, in either case, the survival into the next generation is determined by 'superiority.' In one case it is superiority in the eyes of the breeder, in the other case superiority of reproductive success. What Agassiz plainly missed was that no two individuals are genetically identical and, as Darwin emphasized, not all individuals that are born reach reproductive age and reproduce with equal success. One has a choice of only two possibilities. Either one ascribes the differences in survival and reproductive success entirely to chance or one admits that the genetic endowment of an individual may contribute to this success. If one admits the second alternative, one automatically admits natural selection. And, to express this once more in terms of 'information,' one can say that, owing to the genetic phenomena of mutation and recombination, every individual has a slightly different code of information controlling its development and response to the total environment. Some of these codes are more "successful" than others and therefore will contribute more than their share to the genetic reservoir of the next generation. Unsuitable codes, on the other hand, will produce less successful phenotypes and will have a smaller chance to be returned to the gene reservoir of the population. It has taken us a hundred years to reach such a sophisticated way of expressing natural selection. It is therefore understandable that Agassiz, rooted in an alien conceptual world, never really came to grips with the problem at all.

4. Ernst Mayr, "Darwin and the Evolutionary Theory in Biology," *Evolution and Anthropology: A Centennial Appraisal* (Anthropological Society of Washington, 1959).

5. Agassiz, "Prof. Agassiz on the Origin of Species," 147.

The Passing of the Years

Agassiz' first great outburst against the Darwinian theory came in a series of open discussions at the American Academy of Arts and Sciences, culminating in a detailed rebuttal published in the introduction to Volume III of his *Natural History of the United States* (1861) and preprinted verbatim in the *American Journal of Science and Arts*.[6] This was the end of the scientific debate. In the next dozen years Agassiz took his case to the public. In lectures, popular articles, and books he pleaded the cause of creationism, reiterating his previous arguments in a form intelligible to the layman. However, shortly before his death, he turned once again to a more serious and systematic consideration of the question of evolution. The results of these studies he presented, in the fall of 1873, in a series of lectures, of which only the first was completed for the press, to be published posthumously in 1874. The situation with respect to Darwin had greatly changed since 1860. Darwin no longer was a maverick and rebel to whose theory Agassiz could refer as a 'scientific mistake, untrue in its facts, unscientific in its method, and mischievous in its tendency.' [7] The theory of evolution had by now been almost universally adopted and Darwin had become the grand old man of biology. As a consequence, Agassiz is far more gentle in his references to Darwin.

Indeed, he gives every impression of a sincere attempt to do justic to the new theory. Yet Louis Agassiz was unable to give up old loyalties. All his life he had felt himself the disciple of that great master, Cuvier, and in his old age he was not going to abandon him. As a consequence, he maintained what he had learned as a youth, even in the face of newly discovered zoological fact. When Leuckart proposed to divide Cuvier's radiates into coelenterates and echinoderms Agassiz protested strongly: 'The organs and the whole structural combination are the same in the two divisions.' [8] As Leuckart had shown and as is now known to every zoologist, this assertion is not correct: the two phyla are as different from each other in their basic structure as any phyla in the animal kingdom. In a similar spirit of loyalty Agassiz did not accept even the smallest part of the transmutation theory. One may question whether a compromise was possible. Both Darwin's theory of common descent by modification through natural selection and Agassiz' theory of successive special creations are so completely self-contained and mutually exclusive that their mingling is hardly conceivable. Once one

6. Agassiz, 'Prof. Agassiz on the Origin of Species.''
7. *Ibid.*, 154.
8. Agassiz, "Evolution and Permanence of Type," 93–94.

admits either a 'little bit' of special creation or a 'little bit' of gradual evolution, one has no reason for not accepting all of one or of the other.

Agassiz' attitude toward the theory of evolution is an extraordinarily interesting phenomenon in the history of the advance of scientific ideas. It is another illustration of the familiar concept that an age has to be ready for a new idea or a new discovery, with the corollary that contemporaries may live in different ages, some being directed more forward, others more backward. Darwin's great fortune was that he was just enough ahead of his time to be a leader and not enough ahead to be ignored. Agassiz' misfortune was to have absorbed in his youth a *Zeitgeist* that was unsuitable for mixing with the revolutionary new ideas. He was, one may say, a victim of the thoroughness of his education.

Victorian Supporters of Darwin

SIR JOSEPH DALTON HOOKER

Flora Tasmaniae (1859) †

* * * In the Introductory Essay to the New Zealand Flora, I advanced certain general propositions as to the origin of species, which I refrained from endorsing as articles of my own creed: amongst others was the still prevalent doctrine that these are, in the ordinary acceptation of the term, created as such, and are immutable. In the present Essay I shall advance the opposite hypothesis, that species are derivative and mutable; and this chiefly because, whatever opinions a naturalist may have adopted with regard to the origin and variation of species, every candid mind must admit that the facts and arguments upon which he has grounded his convictions require revision since the recent publication by the Linnean Society of the ingenious and original reasonings and theories of Mr. Darwin and Mr. Wallace. * * *

With regard to my own views on the subjects of the variability of existing species and the fallacy of supposing we can ascertain anything through these alone of their ancestry or of originally created types, they are, in so far as they are liable to influence my estimate of the value of the facts collected for the analysis of the Australian Flora, unaltered from those which I maintained in the 'Flora of New Zealand:' on such theoretical questions, however, as the origin and ultimate permanence of species, they have been greatly influenced by the views and arguments of Mr. Darwin and Mr. Wallace above alluded to, which incline me to regard more favourably the hypothesis that it is to variation that we must look as the means which Nature has adopted for peopling the globe with those diverse existing forms which, when they tend to transmit their characters

† Hooker and Thomas Henry Huxley were two of the earliest of Victorian scientists to rally to Darwin's support. This excerpt is from the "Introductory Essay" to the *Flora Tasmaniae*, Volume III of *The Botany of the Antarctic Voyage of H. M. Discovery Ships Erebus and Terror, in the Years 1839–* *1843* (London, 1859). It appeared in December, 1859, thus putting Hooker in public support of Darwin almost at the moment the *Origin* was published. Compare Hooker's earlier position in *Flora Nova-Zelandiae* (1853), pp. 19–23, above.

unchanged through many generations, are called species. * * *

In conformity with my plan of starting from the variable and not the fixed aspect of Nature, I have now set down the prominent features of the Vegetable Kingdom, as surveyed from this point of view. From the preceding paragraphs the evidence appears to be certainly in favour of proneness to change in individuals, and of the power to change ceasing only with the life of the individual; and we have still to account for the fact that there are limits to these mutations, and laws that control the changes both as to degree and kind; that species are neither visionary nor even arbitrary creations of the naturalist; that they are, in short, realities, whether only temporarily so or not.

13. Granting then that the tendency of Nature is first to multiply forms of existing plants by graduated changes, and next by destroying some to isolate the rest in area and in character, we are now in a condition to seek some theory of the *modus operandi* of Nature that will give temporary permanence of character to these changelings. And here we must appeal to theory or speculation; for our knowledge of the history of species in relation to one another, and to the incessant mutations of their environing physical conditions, is far too limited and incomplete to afford data for demonstrating the effects of these in the production of any one species in a native state.

Of these speculations by far the most important and philosophical is that of the delimitation of species by natural selection, for which we are indebted to two wholly independent and original thinkers, Mr. Darwin and Mr. Wallace.[1] These authors assume that all animal and vegetable forms are variable, that the average amount of space and annual supply of food for each species (or other group of individuals) is limited and constant, but that the increase of all organisms tends to proceed annually in a geometrical ratio; and that, as the sum of organic life on the surface of the globe does not increase, the individuals annually destroyed must be incalculably great; also that each species is ever warring against many enemies, and only holding its own by a slender tenure. In the ordinary course of nature this annual destruction falls upon the eggs or seeds and young of the organisms, and as it is effected by a multitude of antagonistic, ever-changing natural causes, each more destructive of one organism than of any other, it operates with different effect on each group of individuals, in every locality, and at every returning season. Here then we have an infinite number of varying conditions, and a superabundant supply of variable organisms, to accommodate themselves to these conditions. Now the organisms can have no power of surviving any change in these conditions, except they are endowed with the means of accommodating them-

1. Journal of the Linnean Society of London, Zoology, vol. iii. p. 45.

selves to it. The exercise of this power may be accompanied by a visible (morphological) change in the form or structure of the individual, or it may not, in which case there is still a change, but a physiological one, not outwardly manifested; but there is always a morphological change if the change of conditions be sudden, or when, through lapse of time, it becomes extreme. The new form is necessarily that best suited to the changed condition, and as its progeny are henceforth additional enemies to the old, they will eventually tend to replace their parent form in the same locality. Further, a greater proportion of the seeds and young of the old will annually be destroyed than of the new, and the survivors of the old, being less well adapted to the locality, will yield less seed, and hence have fewer descendants. * * *

35. From the sum then of our theories, as arranged in accordance with ascertained facts, we may make the following assumptions:— That the principal recognized families of plants which inhabited the globe at and since the Palæozoic period still exist, and therefore have as families survived all intervening geological changes. That of these types some have been transferred, or have migrated, from one hemisphere to another. That it is not unreasonable to suppose that further evidence may be forthcoming which will show that all existing species may have descended genealogically from fewer preexisting ones; that we owe their different forms to the variation of individuals, and the power of limiting them into genera and species to the destruction of some of these varieties, etc., and the increase in individuals of others. Lastly, that the fact of species being with so much uniformity the ultimate and most definable group (the leaves as it were of the family tree), may possibly be owing to the tendency to vary being checked, partly by the ample opportunities each brood of a variety possesses of being fertilized by the pollen of its nearest counterpart, partly by the temporary stability of its surrounding physical conditions, and partly by the superabundance of seeds shed by each individual, those only vegetating which are well suited to existing conditions: an appearance of stability is also, in the case of many perennials, due to the fact that the individuals normally attain a great age,[2] and thus survive many generations of other species, of which generations some present characters foreign

---

2. In considering the relative amount and rate at which different plants vary, it should be remembered that we habitually estimate them not only loosely but falsely. We assume annuals to be more variable than perennials, but we probably greatly overrate the amount to which they really are so, because a brief personal experience enables us to study many generations of an annual under many combinations of physical conditions; whereas the same experience embraces but a fractional period of the duration of (comparatively) very few perennials. It has also been well shown by Bentham (in his paper on the British Flora, read (1858) before the Linnæan Society) that an appearance of stability is given to many varieties of perennials, through their habitual increase by buds, offsets, etc., which propagate the individual; and in the case of *Rubi*, which comparatively seldom propagate by seed, a large tract of ground may be peopled by parts of a single individual.

to their parents. * * *

37. Again, it is argued by both Mr. Darwin and Mr. Wallace that the general effects of variation by selection must be to establish a general progressive development of the whole animal kingdom. But here again in botany we are checked by the question, What is the standard of progression? Is it physiological or morphological? Is it evidenced by the power of overcoming physical obstacles to dispersion or propagation, or by a nice adaptation of structure or constitution to very restricted or complex conditions? Are cosmopolites to be regarded as superior to plants of restricted range, hermaphrodite plants to unisexual, parasites to self-sustainers, albuminous-seeded to exalbuminous, gymnosperms to angiosperms, water plants to land, trees to herbs, perennials to annuals, insular plants to continental? and, in fine, what is the significance of the multitudinous differences in point of structure and complexity, and powers of endurance, presented by the members of the Vegetable Kingdom, and which have no recognized physiological end and interpretation, nor importance in a classificatory point of view? It is extremely easy to answer any of these questions, and to support the opinion by a host of arguments, morphological, physiological, and teleological; but any one gifted with a quick perception of relations, and whose mind is stored with a sufficiency of facts, will turn every argument to equal advantage for both sides of the question.

To my mind, however, the doctrine of progression, if considered in connection with the hypothesis of the origin of species being by variation, is by far the most profound of all that have ever agitated the schools of Natural History, and I do not think that it has yet been treated in the unprejudiced spirit it demands. The elements for its study are the vastest and most complicated which the naturalist can contemplate, and reside in the comprehension of the reciprocal action of the so-called inorganic on the organic world. Granting that multiplication and specialization of organs is the evidence and measure of progression, that variation explains the *rationale* of the operation which results in this progression, the question arises, What are the limits to the combinations of physical causes which determine this progreession, and how can the specializing power of Nature stop short of causing every race or family ultimately to represent a species? While the psychological philosophers persuade us that we see the tendency to specialize pervading every attribute of organic life, mental and physical; and the physicists teach that there are limits to the amount and duration of heat, light, and every other manifestation of physical force which our senses present or our intellects perceive, and which are all in process of consumption; the reflecting botanist, knowing that his ultimate results must accord with these facts, is perplexed at feeling that he has failed to establish on independent evidence the doctrines of variation and progressive specialization, or to co-ordinate his attempts to do so with the successive discoveries in physical science. * * *

The arguments deduced from genetic resemblance being (in the present state of science), as far as I can discover, exhausted, I have felt it my duty to re-examine the phenomena of variation in reference to the origin of existing species; these phenomena I have long studied independently of this question, and when treating either of whole Floras or of species, I have made it my constant aim to demonstrate how much more important and prevalent this element of variability is than is usually admitted, as also how deep it lies beneath the foundations of all our facts and reasonings concerning classification and distribution. I have hitherto endeavoured to keep my ideas upon variation in subjection to the hypothesis of species being immutable, both because a due regard to that theory checks any tendency to careless observation of minute facts, and because the opposite one is apt to lead to a precipitate conclusion that slight differences have no significance; whereas, though not of specific importance, they may be of high structural and physiological value, and hence reveal affinities that might otherwise escape us. I have already stated how greatly I am indebted to Mr. Darwin's [3] *rationale* of the phenomena of variation and natural selection in the production of species; and though it does not positively establish the doctrine of creation by variation, I expect that every additional fact and observation relating to species will gain great additional value from being viewed in reference to it, and that it will materially assist in developing the principles of classification and distribution.

THOMAS HENRY HUXLEY

On the Relations of Man to the Lower Animals (1863) †

* * * The question of questions for mankind—the problem which underlies all others, and is more deeply interesting than any

3. In this Essay I refer to the brief abstract only (Linn. Journ.) of my friend's views, not to his work now in the press, a deliberate study of which may modify my opinion on some points whereon we differ. Matured conclusions on these subjects are very slowly developed.

† Thomas Henry Huxley (1825–1895) studied medicine as a young man and matured as a naturalist during a voyage of discovery aboard H.M.S. *Rattlesnake*, at the end of which he was elected a Fellow of the Royal Society. His review of the *Origin* in the London *Times* was an important contribution to public understanding of the book, and for years Huxley was Darwin's ablest advocate, "Darwin's bulldog." The present excerpts are from Chapter 2 of *Man's Place in Nature* (London, 1863).

other—is the ascertainment of the place which Man occupies in nature and of his relations to the universe of things. Whence our race has come; what are the limits of our power over nature, and of nature's power over us; to what goal we are tending; are the problems which present themselves anew and with undiminished interest to every man born into the world. * * *

As if to demonstrate, by a striking example, the impossibility of erecting any cerebral barrier between man and the apes, Nature has provided us, in the latter animals, with an almost complete series of gradations from brains little higher than that of a Rodent, to brains little lower than that of Man. And it is a remarkable circumstance that though, so far as our present knowledge extends, there *is* one true structural break in the series of forms of Simian brains, this hiatus does not lie between Man and the man-like apes, but between the lower and the lowest Simians; or, in other words, between the old and new world apes and monkeys, and the Lemurs. Every Lemur which has yet been examined, in fact, has its cerebellum partially visible from above, and its posterior lobe, with the contained posterior cornu and hippocampus minor, more or less rudimentary. Every Marmoset, American monkey, old world monkey, Baboon, or Man-like ape, on the contrary, has its cerebellum entirely hidden, posteriorly, by the cerebral lobes, and possesses a large posterior cornu, with a well-developed hippocampus minor. * * *

As to the convolutions, the brains of the apes exhibit every stage of progress, from the almost smooth brain of the Marmoset, to the Orang and the Chimpanzee, which fall but little below Man. And it is most remarkable that, as soon as all the principal sulci appear, the pattern according to which they are arranged is identical with that of the corresponding sulci of man. The surface of the brain of a monkey exhibits a sort of skeleton map of man's, and in the man-like apes the details become more and more filled in, until it is only in minor characters, such as the greater excavation of the anterior lobes, the constant presence of fissures usually absent in man, and the different disposition and proportions of some convolutions, that the Chimpanzee's or the Orang's brain can be structurally distinguished from Man's.

So far as cerebral structure goes, therefore, it is clear that Man differs less from the Chimpanzee or the Orang, than these do even from the Monkeys, and that the difference between the brains of the Chimpanzee and of Man is almost insignificant, when compared with that between the Chimpanzee brain and that of a Lemur.

It must not be overlooked, however, that there is a very striking difference in the absolute mass and weight between the lowest human brain and that of the highest ape—a difference which is all

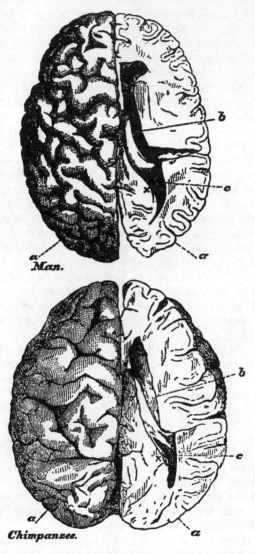

Drawings of the cerebral hemispheres of a Man and of a Chimpanzee of the same length, in order to show the relative proportions of the parts: the former taken from a specimen, which Mr. Flower, Conservator of the Museum of the Royal College of Surgeons, was good enough to dissect for me; the latter, from the photograph of a similarly dissected Chimpanzee's brain, given in Mr. Marshall's paper above referred to. *a*, posterior lobe; *b*, lateral ventricle; *c*, posterior cornu; *x*, the hippocampus minor.

the moie remarkable when we recollect that a full grown Gorilla is probably pretty nearly twice as heavy as a Bosjes man, or as many an European woman. It may be doubted whether a healthy human adult brain ever weighed less than thirty-one or two ounces, or that the heaviest Gorilla brain has exceeded twenty ounces.

This is a very noteworthy circumstance, and doubtless will one day help to furnish an explanation of the great gulf which intervenes between the lowest man and the highest ape in intellectual power; [1] but it has little systematic value, for the simple reason that, as may be concluded from what has been already said respecting cranial capacity, the difference in weight of brain between the highest and the lowest men is far greater, both relatively and absolutely, than that between the lowest man and the highest ape. The latter, as has been seen, is represented by, say twelve, ounces of cerebral substance absolutely, or by 32 : 20 relatively; but as the largest recorded human brain weighed between 65 and 66 ounces, the former difference is reprcsented by more than 33 ounces absolutely, or by 65 : 32 relatively. Regarded systematically the cerebral

1. I say *help* to furnish: for I by no means believe that it was any original difference of cerebral quality, or quantity, which caused that divergence between the human and the pithecoid stirpes, which has ended in the present enormous gulf between them. It is no doubt perfectly true, in a certain sense, that all difference of function is a result of difference of structure; or, in other words, of difference in the combination of the primary molecular forces of living substance; and, starting from this undeniable axiom, objectors occasionally, and with much seeming plausibility, argue that the vast intellectual chasm between the Ape and Man implies a corresponding structural chasm in the organs of the intellectual functions; so that, it is said, the non-discovery of such vast differences proves, not that they are absent, but that Science is incompetent to detect them. A very little consideration, however, will, I think, show the fallacy of this reasoning. Its validity hangs upon the assumption, that intellectual power depends altogether on the brain—whereas the brain is only one condition out of many on which intellectual manifestations depend; the others being, chiefly, the organs of the senses and the motor apparatuses, especially those which are concerned in prehension and in the production of articulate speech.

A man born dumb, notwithstanding his great cerebral mass and his inheritance of strong intellectual instincts, would be capable of few higher intellectual manifestations than an Orang or a Chimpanzee, if he were confined to the society of dumb associates. And yet there might not be the slightest discernible difference between brain and that of a highly intelligent and cultivated person. The dumbness might be the result of a defective structure of the mouth, or of the tongue, or a mere defective innervation of these parts; or it might result from congenital deafness, caused by some minute defect of the internal ear, which only a careful anatomist could discover.

The argument, that because there is an immense difference between a Man's intelligence and an Ape's, therefore, there must be an equally immense difference between their brains, appears to me to be about as well based as the reasoning by which one should endeavour to prove that, because there is a "great gulf" between a watch that keeps accurate time and another that will not go at all, there is therefore a great structural hiatus between the two watches. A hair in the balance-wheel, a little rust on a pinion, a bend in a tooth of the escapement, a something so slight that only the practised eye of the watchmaker can discover it, may be the source of all the difference.

And believing, as I do, with Cuvier, that the possession of articulate speech is the grand distinctive character of man (whether it bc absolutely peculiar to him or not), I find it very easy to comprehend, that some equally inconspicuous structural difference may have been the primary cause of the immeasurable and practically infinite divergence of the Human from the Simian Stirps.

differences, of man and apes, are not of more than generic value
—his Family distinction resting chiefly on his dentition, his pelvis,
and his lower limbs.

Thus, whatever system of organs be studied, the comparison of
their modifications in the ape series leads to one and the same result—that the structural differences which separate Man from the
Corilla and the Chimpanzee are not so great as those which separate the Gorilla from the lower apes.

But in enunciating this important truth 1 must guard myself
against a form of misunderstanding, which is very prevalent. I find,
in fact, that those who endeavour to teach what nature so clearly
shows us in this matter, are liable to have their opinions misrepresented and their phraseology garbled, until they seem to say that
the structural differences between man and even the highest apes
are small and insignificant. Let me take this opportunity then of
distinctly asserting, on the contrary, that they are great and significant; that every bone of a Gorilla bears marks by which it might
be distinguished from the corresponding bone of a Man; and that,
in the present creation, at any rate, no intermediate link bridges
over the gap between *Homo* and *Troglodytes*.

It would be no less wrong than absurd to deny the existence of
this chasm; but it is at least equally wrong and absurd to exaggerate
its magnitude, and, resting on the admitted fact of its existence, to
refuse to inquire whether it is wide or narrow. Remember, if you
will, that there is no existing link between Man and the Gorilla,
but do not forget that there is no less sharp line of demarcation, a
no less complete absence of any transitional form, between the
Gorilla and the Orang, or the Orang and the Gibbon. I say, not
less sharp, though it is somewhat narrower. The structural differences beween Man and the Man-like apes certainly justify our
regarding him as constituting a family apart from them; though,
inasmuch as he differs less from them than they do from other
families of the same order, there can be no justification for placing
him in a distinct order.

And thus the sagacious foresight of the great lawgiver of systematic zoology, Linnæus, becomes justified, and a century of anatomical research brings us back to his conclusion, that man is a
member of the same order (for which the Linnæan term PRIMATES
ought to be retained) as the Apes and Lemurs. This order is now
divisible into seven families, of about equal systematic value: the
first, the ANTHROPINI, contains Man alone; the second, the CATA-
RHINI, embraces the old world apes; the third, the PLATYRHINI,
all new world apes, except the Marmosets; the fourth, the ARC-
TOPITHECINI, contains the Marmosets; the fifth, the LEMURINI, the

Lemurs—from which *Cheiromys* should probably be excluded to form a sixth distinct family, the CHEIROMYINI; while the seventh, the GALEOPITHECINI, contains only the flying Lemur *Galeopithecus*, —a strange form which almost touches on the Bats, as the *Cheiromys* puts on a rodent clothing, and the Lemurs simulate Insectivora. Perhaps no order of mammals presents us with so extraordinary a series of gradations as this—leading us insensibly from the crown and summit of the animal creation down to creatures, from which there is but a step, as it seems, to the lowest, smallest, and least intelligent of the placental Mammalia. It is as if nature herself had foreseen the arrogance of man, and with Roman severity had provided that his intellect, by its very triumphs, should call into prominence the slaves, admonishing the conqueror that he is but dust.

These are the chief facts, this the immediate conclusion from them to which I adverted the commencement of this Essay. The facts, I believe, cannot be disputed; and if so, the conclusion appears to me to be inevitable.

But if Man be separated by no greater structural barrier, from the brutes than they are from one another—then it seems to follow that if any process of physical causation can be discovered by which the genera and families of ordinary animals have been produced, that process of causation is amply sufficient to account for the origin of Man. In other words, if it could be shown that the Marmosets, for example, have arisen by gradual modification of the ordinary Platyrhini, or that both Marmosets and Platyrhini are modified ramifications of a primitive stock—then, there would be no rational ground for doubting that man might have originated, in the one case, by the gradual modification of a man-like ape; or, in the other case, as a ramification of the same primitive stock as those apes.

At the present moment, but one such process of physical causation has any evidence in its favour; or, in other words, there is but one hypothesis regarding the origin of species of animals in general which has any scientific existence—that propounded by Mr. Darwin. For Lamarck, sagacious as many of his views were, mingled them with so much that was crude and even absurd, as to neutralize the benefit which his originality might have effected, had he been a more sober and cautious thinker; and though I have heard of the announcement of a formula touching "the ordained continuous becoming of organic forms," it is obvious that it is the first duty of a hypothesis to be intelligible, and that a qua-quâ-versal proposition of this kind, which may be read backwards, or forwards, or sideways, with exactly the same amount of signification, does not really exist, though it may seem to do so.

At the present moment, therefore, the question of the relation of man to the lower animals resolves itself, in the end, into the larger question of the tenability or untenability of Mr. Darwin's views. But here we enter upon difficult ground, and it behoves us to define our exact position with the greatest care.

It cannot be doubted, I think, that Mr. Darwin has satisfactorily proved that when he terms selection, or selective modification, must occur, and does occur, in nature; and he has also proved to superfluity that such selection is competent to product forms as distinct structurally, as some genera even are. If the animated world presented us with none but structural differences, I should have no hesitation in saying that Mr. Darwin had demonstrated the existence of a true physical cause, amply competent to account for the origin of living species, and of man among the rest.

But, in addition to their structural distinctions, the species of animals and plants, or at least a great number of them, exhibit physiological characters—what are known as distinct species, structurally, being for the most part either altogether incompetent to breed one with another; or if they breed, the resulting mule, or hybrid, is unable to perpetuate its race with another hybrid of the same kind.

A true physical cause is, however, admitted to be such only on one condition—that it shall account for all the phenomena which come within the range of its operation. If it is inconsistent with any one phenomenon, it must be rejected; if it fails to explain any one phenomenon, it is so far weak, so far to be suspected; though it may have a perfect right to claim provisional acceptance.

Now, Mr. Darwin's hypothesis is not, so far as I am aware, inconsistent with any known biological fact; on the contrary, if admitted, the facts of Development, of Comparative Anatomy, of Geographical Distribution, and of Palæontology, become connected together, and exhibit a meaning such as they never possessed before; and I, for one, am fully convinced, that if not precisely true, that hypothesis is as near an approximation to the truth as, for example, the Copernican hypothesis was to the true theory of the planetary motions.

But, for all this, our acceptance of the Darwinian hypothesis must be provisional so long as one link in the chain of evidence is wanting; and so long as all the animals and plants certainly produced by selective breeding from a common stock are fertile, and their progeny are fertile with one another, that link will be wanting. For, so long, selective breeding will not be proved to be competent to do all that is required of it to produce natural species.

I have put this conclusion as strongly as possible before the reader, because the last position in which I wish to find myself is that of an advocate for Mr. Darwin's, or any other views—if by an advocate is meant one whose business it is to smooth over real difficulties, and to persuade where he cannot convince.

In justice to Mr. Darwin, however, it must be admitted that the conditions of fertility and sterility are very ill understood, and that every day's advance in knowledge leads us to regard the hiatus in his evidence as of less and less importance, when set against the multitude of facts which harmonize with, or receive an explanation from, his doctrines.

I adopt Mr. Darwin's hypothesis, therefore, subject to the production of proof that physiological species may be produced by selective breeding; just as a physical philosopher may accept the undulatory theory of light, subject to the proof of the existence of the hypothetical ether; or as the chemist adopts the atomic theory, subject to the proof of the existence of atoms; and for exactly the same reasons, namely, that it has an immense amount of primâ facie probability; that it is the only means at present within reach of reducing the chaos of observed facts to order; and lastly, that it is the most powerful instrument of investigation which has been presented to naturalists since the invention of the natural system of classification, and the commencement of the systematic study of embryology.

But even leaving Mr. Darwin's views aside, the whole analogy of natural operations furnishes so complete and crushing an argument against the intervention of any but what are termed secondary causes, in the production of all the phenomena of the universe; that, in view of the intimate relations between Man and the rest of the living world; and between the forces exerted by the latter and all other forces, I can see no excuse for doubting that all are coordinated terms of Nature's great progression, from the formless to the formed—from the inorganic to the organic—from blind force to conscious intellect and will.

Science has fulfilled her function when she has ascertained and enunciated truth; and were these pages addressed to men of science only, I should now close this essay, knowing that my colleagues have learned to respect nothing but evidence, and to believe that their highest duty lies in submitting to it, however it may jar against their inclinations.

But desiring, as I do, to reach the wider circle of the intelligent public, it would be unworthy cowardice were I to ignore the repugnance with which the majority of my readers are likely to meet the conclusions to which the most careful and conscientious study I have been able to give to this matter, has led me.

On all sides I shall hear the cry—"We are men and women, not a mere better sort of apes, a little longer in the leg, more compact in the foot, and bigger in brain than your brutal Chimpanzees and Gorillas. The power of knowledge—the conscience of good and evil—the pitiful tenderness of human affections, raise us out of all real fellowship with the brutes, however closely they may seem to approximate us."

To this I can only reply that the exclamation would be most just and would have my own entire sympathy, if it were only relevant. But, it is not I who seek to base Man's dignity upon his great toe, or insinuate that we are lost if an Ape has a hippocampus minor. On the contrary, I have done my best to sweep away this vanity. I have endeavoured to show that no absolute structural line of demarcation, wider than that between the animals which immediately succeed us in the scale, can be drawn between the animal world and ourselves; and I may add the expression of my belief that the attempt to draw a psychical distinction is equally futile, and that even the highest faculties of feeling and of intellect begin to germinate in lower forms of life.[2] At the same time, no one is more strongly convinced than I am of the vastness of the gulf between civilized man and the brutes; or is more certain that whether *from* them or not, he is assuredly not *of* them. No one is less disposed to think lightly of the present dignity, or despairingly of the future hopes, of the only consciously intelligent denizen of this world.

We are indeed told by those who assume authority in these matters, that the two sets of opinions are incompatible, and that the belief in the unity of origin of man and brutes involves the brutalization and degradation of the former. But is this really so? Could not a sensible child confute, by obvious arguments, the shallow rhetoricians who would force this conclusion upon us? Is it, indeed, true, that the Poet, or the Philosopher, or the Artist whose genius is the glory of his age, is degraded from his high estate by

2. It is so rare a pleasure for me to find Professor Owen's opinions in entire accordance with my own, that I cannot forbear from quoting a paragraph which appeared in his Essay "On the Characters, &c., of the Class Mammalia," in the 'Journal of the Proceedings of the Linnean Society of London' for 1857, but is unaccountably omitted in the "Reade Lecture" delivered before the University of Cambridge two years later, which is otherwise nearly a reprint of the paper in question. Prof. Owen writes: "Not being able to appreciate or conceive of the distinction between the psychical phenomena of a Chimpanzee and of a Boschisman or of an Aztec, with arrested brain growth, as being of a nature so essential as to preclude a comparison between them, or as being other than a difference of degree, I cannot shut my eyes to the significance of that all-pervading similitude of structure—every tooth, every bone, strictly homologous—which makes the determination of the difference between *Homo* and *Pithecus* the anatomist's difficulty."

Surely it is a little singular that the 'anatomist,' who finds it 'difficult' to 'determine the difference' between *Homo* and *Pithecus*, should yet range them on anatomical grounds, in distinct sub-classes!

the undoubted historical probability, not to say certainty, that he is the direct descendant of some naked and bestial savage, whose intelligence was just sufficient to make him a little more cunning than the Fox, and by so much more dangerous than the Tiger? Or is he bound to howl and grovel on all fours because of the wholly unquestionable fact, that he was once an egg, which no ordinary power of discrimination could distinguish from that of a Dog? Or is the philanthropist or the saint to give up his endeavours to lead a noble life, because the simplest study of man's nature reveals, at its foundations, all the selfish passions and fierce appetites of the merest quadruped? Is mother-love vile because a hen shows it, or fidelity base because dogs possess it?

The common sense of the mass of mankind will answer these questions without a moment's hesitation. Healthy humanity, finding itself hard pressed to escape from real sin and degradation, will leave the brooding over speculative pollution to the cynics and the 'righteous overmuch' who, disagreeing in everything else, unite in blind insensibility to the nobleness of the visible world, and in inability to appreciate the grandeur of the place Man occupies therein.

Nay more, thoughtful men, once escaped from the blinding influences of traditional prejudice, will find in the lowly stock whence man has sprung, the best evidence of the splendour of his capacities; and will discern in his long progress through the Past, a reasonable ground of faith in his attainment of a nobler Future.

They will remember that in comparing civilized man with the animal world, one is as the Alpine traveller, who sees the mountains soaring into the sky and can hardly discern where the deep shadowed crags and roseate peaks end, and where the clouds of heaven begin. Surely the awe-struck voyager may be excused if, at first, he refuses to believe the geologist, who tells him that these glorious masses are, after all, the hardened mud of primeval seas, or the cooled slag of subterranean furnaces—of one substance with the dullest clay, but raised by inward forces to that place of proud and seemingly inaccessible glory.

But the geologist is right; and due reflection on his teachings, instead of diminishing our reverence and our wonder, adds all the force of intellectual sublimity to the mere esthetic intuition of the uninstructed beholder.

And after passion and prejudice have died away, the same result will attend the teachings of the naturalist respecting that great Alps and Andes of the living world—Man. Our reverence for the nobility of manhood will not be lessened by the knowledge, that Man is, in substance and in structure, one with the brutes; for, he alone possesses the marvellous endowment of intelligible and rational speech, whereby, in the secular period of his existence, he has slowly accumulated and organized the experience which is almost wholly lost with the cessation of every individual life in other animals; so that now he stands raised upon it as on a mountain top, far above the level of his humble fellows, and transfigured from his grosser nature by reflecting, here and there, a ray from the infinite source of truth.

SIR CHARLES LYELL

Principles of Geology (1867) †

* * * In former editions of this work from 1832 to 1853, I did not venture to differ from the opinion of Linnæus, that each species had remained from its origin such as we now see it, being variable, but only within certain fixed limits. The mystery in which the origin of each species was involved seemed to me no greater than that in which the beginning of all vital phenomena on the earth is shrouded. * * *

* * * Mr. Charles Darwin * * * had been for many years busily engaged in collecting materials for a great work on the origin of species; having made for that purpose a vast series of original observations and experiments on domesticated animals and cultivated plants, and having reflected profoundly on those problems in geology and biology which were calculated to throw most light on that question. For eighteen years these researches had all been pointing to the same conclusion, namely, that the species now living had been derived by variation and generation from those which had pre-existed, and these again from others of still older date. Several of his MS. volumes on this subject had been read by Dr. Hooker as long ago as 1844, and how long the ever-accumulating store of facts and reasonings might have remained unknown to the general public, had no one else attempted to work out the same problem, it is impossible to say. But at length Mr. Darwin received a communication, dated February 1858, from Mr. Wallace, then residing at Ternate in the Malay Archipelago, entitled 'On the Tendency of Varieties to depart indefinitely from the Original Type.'

The Author requested Mr. Darwin to show this essay to me

---

† Lyell was the most reluctant of Darwin's several confidants to come out publicly in support of evolution. His remarks on the subject in *The Antiquity of Man* (1863) were deeply disappointing to Darwin, and there was no new edition of the *Principles* until 1867, in which the present passage occurred. The text given here is from Chapter 35 of the eleventh edition (New York, 1883).

should he think it sufficiently novel and interesting. It was brought to me by Dr. Hooker, who remarked how complete was the coincidence of Mr. Wallace's new views and those contained in one of the chapters of Mr. Darwin's unpublished work. Accordingly, he suggested that it would be unfair to let Mr. Wallace's essay go to press unaccompanied by the older memoir on the same subject. Although, therefore, Mr. Darwin was willing to waive his claim to priority, the two papers were read on the same evening to the Linnæan Society and published in their Proceedings for 1858. The title of the chapter extracted from Mr. Darwin's MS. ran as follows: 'On the Tendency of Species to form Varieties, and on the Perpetuation of Species and Varieties by Natural Means of Selection.'

Already in the previous year, September 1857, Mr. Darwin had sent to Professor Asa Gray, the celebrated American botanist, a brief sketch of his forthcoming treatise on what he then termed 'Natural Selection.' This letter, also printed by the Linnæan Society together with the papers above alluded to, contained an outline of the leading features of his theory of selection as since explained, showing how new races were formed by the breeder, and how analogous results might or must occur in nature under changed conditions in the animate and inanimate world. Reference was made in the same letter to the law of human population first enunciated by Malthus, or the tendency in man to increase in a geometrical ratio, while the means of subsistence cannot be made to augment in the same ratio. We were reminded that in some countries the human population has doubled in twenty-five years, and would have multiplied faster if food could have been supplied. In like manner every animal and plant is capable of increasing so rapidly, that if it were unchecked by other species, it would soon occupy the greater part of the habitable globe; but in the general struggle for life few only of those which are born into the world can obtain subsistence and arrive at maturity. In any given species those alone survive which have some advantage over others, and this is often determined by a slight peculiarity capable in a severe competition of turning the scale in their favour. Notwithstanding the resemblance to each other and to their parents of all the individuals of the same family, no two of them are exactly alike. The breeder chooses out from among the varieties presented to him those best suited to his purpose, and the divergence from the original stock is more and more increased by breeding in each successive generation from individuals which possess the desired characters in the most marked degree. In this manner Mr. Darwin suggests that as the surrounding conditions in the organic and inorganic world slowly alter in the course of geological periods, new races which are more in harmony with the altered state of things must be formed in a state of nature, and must often supplant the parent type.

Although this law of natural selection constituted one only of the grounds on which Mr. Darwin relied for establishing his views as to the origin of species by variation, yet it formed so original and prominent a part of his theory that the fact of Mr. Wallace having independently thought out the same principle and illustrated it by singularly analogous examples, is remarkable. It raises at the same time a strong presumption in favour of the truth of the doctrine. * * *

After the publication of the detached chapter of his book in the Linnæan Proceedings, Mr. Darwin was persuaded by his friends that he ought no longer to withhold from the world the result of his investigations on the nature and origin of species, and his theory of Natural Selection. Great was the sensation produced in the scientific world by the appearance of the abridged and condensed statement of his views comprised in his work entitled 'On the Origin of Species by means of Natural Selection, or the Preservation of Favoured Races in the Struggle for Life.' From the hour of its appearance it gave, as Professor Huxley truly said, 'a new direction to biological speculation,' for even where it failed to make proselytes, it gave a shock to old and time-honoured opinions from which they have never since recovered. It effected this not merely by the manner in which it explained how new races and species might be formed by Natural Selection, but also by showing that, if we assume this principle, much light is thrown on many very distinct and otherwise unconnected classes of phenomena, both in the present condition and past history of the organic world. * * *

Darwin and Modern Science

SIR JULIAN HUXLEY

Evolution: The Modern Synthesis (1942, 1963) †

I. The Theory of Natural Selection

Evolution may lay claim to be considered the most central and the most important of the problems of biology. For an attack upon it we need facts and methods from every branch of the science—ecology, genetics, paleontology, geographical distribution, embryology, systematics, comparative anatomy—not to mention reinforcements from other disciplines such as geology, geography, and mathematics.

Biology at the present time is embarking upon a phase of synthesis after a period in which new disciplines were taken up in turn and worked out in comparative isolation. Nowhere is this movement towards unification more likely to be valuable than in this many-sided topic of evolution; and already we are seeing the first-fruits in the re-animation of Darwinism.

By Darwinism I imply that blend of induction and deduction which Darwin was the first to apply to the study of evolution. He was concerned both to establish the fact of evolution and to discover the mechanism by which it operated; and it was precisely because he attacked both aspects of the problem simultaneously, that he was so successful.[1] On the one hand he amassed enormous quantities of facts from which inductions concerning the evolutionary process could be drawn; and on the other, starting from a few general principles, he deduced the further principle of natural selection.

It is as well to remember the strong deductive element in Darwinism. Darwin based his theory of natural selection on three observable facts of nature and two deductions from them. The first fact is the tendency of all organisms to increase in a geometrical

† The following selections comprise Chapter 1 of the first edition (1942) and excerpts from the Introduction to the second edition (1963) of *Evolution: The Modern Synthesis*. Sir Julian Huxley (b. 1887), the grandson of Thomas Henry Huxley, is a distinguished zo-ologist and man of letters.

1. This method is not, as has sometimes been asserted, a circular argument. See discussion in J. S. Huxley, "Darwin's Theory of Sexual Selection . . . ," *American Naturalist*, LXXII (1938), 416.

ratio. The tendency of all organisms to increase is due to the fact that offspring, in the early stages of their existence, are always more numerous than their parents; this holds good whether reproduction is sexual or asexual, by fission or by budding, by means of seeds, spores, or eggs.[2] The second fact is that, in spite of this tendency to progressive increase, the numbers of a given species actually remain more or less constant.

The first deduction follows. From these two facts he deduced the struggle for existence. For since more young are produced than can survive, there must be competition for survival. In amplifying his theory, he extended the concept of the struggle for existence to cover reproduction. The struggle is in point of fact for survival of the stock; if its survival is aided by greater fertility, an earlier breeding season, or other reproductive function, these should be included under the same head.

Darwin's third fact of nature was variation: all organisms vary appreciably. And the second and final deduction, which he deduced from the first deduction and the third fact, was Natural Selection. Since there is a struggle for existence among individuals, and since these individuals are not all alike, some of the variations among them will be advantageous in the struggle for survival, others unfavourable. Consequently, a higher proportion of individuals with favourable variations will on the average survive, a higher proportion of those with unfavourable variations will die or fail to reproduce themselves. And since a great deal of variation is transmitted by heredity, these effects of differential survival will in large measure accumulate from generation to generation. Thus natural selection will act constantly to improve and to maintain the adjustment of animals and plants to their surroundings and their way of life.

A few comments on these points in the light of the historical development of biology since Darwin's day will clarify both his statement of the theory and the modern position in regard to it.

His first fact has remained unquestioned. All organisms possess the potentiality of geometric increase. We had better perhaps say *increase of geometric type*, since the ratio of offspring to parents may vary considerably from place to place, and from season to season. In all cases, however, the tendency or potentiality is not merely to a progressive increase, but to a multiplicative and not to an additive increase.

Equally unquestioned is his second fact, the general constancy of numbers of any species. As he himself was careful to point out, the constancy is only approximate. At any one time, there will

2. The only exception, so far as I am aware, is to be found in certain human populations which fall far short of replacing themselves.

always be some species that are increasing in their numbers, others that are decreasing. But even when a species is increasing, the actual increase is never as great as the potential: some young will fail to survive. Again, with our much greater knowledge of ecology, we know to-day that many species undergo cyclical and often remarkably regular fluctuations, frequently of very large extent, in their numbers.[3] But this fact, although it has certain interesting evolutionary consequences, does not invalidate the general principle.

The first two facts being accepted, the deduction from them also holds: a struggle for existence, or better, a struggle for survival, must occur.

The difficulties of the further bases of the theory are greater, and it is here that the major criticisms have fallen. In the first place, Darwin assumed that the bulk of variations were inheritable. He expressly stated that any which were not inheritable would be irrelevant to the discussion; but he continued in the assumption that those which are inheritable provide an adequate reservoir of potential improvement.[4]

As Haldane [5] has pointed out, the decreased interest in England in plant-breeding, caused by the repeal of the Corn Laws, led Darwin to take most of his evidence from animal-breeders. This was much more obscure than what the plant-breeders in France had obtained: in fact Vilmorin, before Darwin wrote, had fully established the roles of heritable and non-heritable variation in wheat.

Thus in Darwin's time, and still more in England than in France, the subject of inheritance was still very obscure. In any case the basic laws of heredity, or, as we should now say, the principles of genetics, had not yet emerged. In a full formulation of the theory of Natural Selection, we should have to add a further fact and a further deduction. We should begin, as he did, with the fact of variation, and deduce from it and our previous deduction of the struggle for existence that there must be a *differential survival* of different types of offspring in each generation. We should then proceed to the fact of inheritance. *Some* variation is inherited: and that fraction will be available for transmission to later generations. Thus our final deduction is that the result will be a differential transmission of inherited variation. The term Natural Selection is

3. See C. S. Elton, *Animal Ecology* (London, 1927), p. 110.
4. *The Origin of Species* (6th. ed., one vol. ed., p. 9): ". . . any variation which is not inherited is unimportant for us. But the number and diversity of inheritable deviations of structure, both those of slight and those of considerable physiological importance, are endless. No breeder doubts how strong is the tendency to inheritance: that like produces like is his fundamental belief." And so on.
5. J. B. S. Haldane, *The Marxist Philosophy and the Sciences* (London, 1938), p. 107.

thus seen to have two rather different meanings. In a broad sense it covers all cases of differential survival: but from the evolutionary point of view it covers only the differential transmission of inheritable variations.

Mendelian analysis has revealed the further fact, unsuspected by Darwin, that recombination of existing genetic units may both produce and modify new inheritable variations. And this, as we shall see later, has important evolutionary consequences.

Although both the principle of differential survival and that of its evolutionary accumulation by Natural Selection were for Darwin essentially deductions, it is important to realize that, if true, they are also facts of nature capable of verification by observation and experiment. And in point of fact differential mortality, differential survival, and differential multiplication among variants of the same species are now known in numerous cases.

The criticism, however, was early made that a great deal of the mortality found in nature appeared to be accidental and non-selective. This would hold for the destruction of the great majority of eggs and larvae of prolific marine animals, or the death of seeds which fell on stony ground or other unsuitable habitats. It remains true that we require many more quantitative experiments on the subject before we can know accurately the extent of non-selective elimination. Even a very large percentage of such elimination, however, in no way invalidates the selection principle from holding for the remaining fraction. The very fact that it is accidental and non-selective ensures that the residue shall be a random sample, and will therefore contain any variation of selective value in the same proportions as the whole population. It is, I think, fair to say that the fact of differential survival of different variations is generally accepted, although it still requires much clarification, especially on the quantitative side. In other words, natural selection within the bounds of the single generation is an active factor in biology.

2. The Nature of Variation

The really important criticisms have fallen upon Natural Selection as an evolutionary principle, and have centred round the nature of inheritable variation.

Darwin, though his views on the subject did not remain constant, was always inclined to allow some weight to Lamarckian principles, according to which the effects of use and disuse and of environmental influences were supposed to be in some degree inherited. However, later work has steadily reduced the scope that can be allowed to such agencies: Weismann drew a sharp distinction between soma and germplasm, between the individual body which was not concerned in reproduction, and the hereditary constitution contained in the germ-cells, which alone was transmitted in heredity. Purely somatic effects, according to him, could not be passed on: the sole inheritable variations were variations in the hereditary constitution.

Although the distinction between soma and germplasm is not always so sharp as Weismann supposed, and although the principle of Baldwin and Lloyd Morgan, usually called Organic Selection, shows how Lamarckism may be simulated by the later replacement of adaptive modifications by adaptive mutations, Weismann's conceptions resulted in a great clarification of the position. It is owing to him that we to-day classify variations into two fundamentally distinct cagetories—modifications and mutations (together with new arrangements of mutations, or recombinations; see below, p. 331). Modifications are produced by alterations in the environment (including modifications of the internal environment such as are brought about by use and disuse), mutations by alterations in the substance of the hereditary constitution. The distinction may be put in a rather different but perhaps more illuminating way. Variation is a study of the differences between organisms. On analysis, these differences may turn out to be due to differences in environment (as with an etiolated plant growing in a cellar as against a green one in light; or a sun-tanned sailor as against a pale slum-dweller); or they may turn out to be due to differences in hereditary constitution (as between an albino and a green seedling in the same plot, or a negro and a white man in the same city); or of course to a simultaneous difference both in environment and in constitution (as with the difference in stature between an undernourished pigmy and a well-nourished negro). Furthermore, only the second are inherited. We speak of them as genetic differences: at their first origin they appear to be due to mutations in the hereditary constitution. The former we call modifications, and are not inheritable.

The important fact is that only experiment can decide between the two. Both in nature and in the laboratory, one of two indistinguishable variants may turn out to be due to environment, the other to genetic peculiarity. A particular shade of human complexion may be due to genetic constitution making for fair complexion plus considerable exposure to the sun, or to a genetically dark complexion plus very little tanning: and similarly for stature, intelligence, and many other characters.

This leads to a further important conclusion: characters as such are not and cannot be inherited. For a character is always the joint product of a particular genetic composition and a particular set of environmental circumstances. Some characters are much more stable in regard to the normal range of environmental variation than are others—for instance, human eye-colour or hair-form as against skin-colour or weight. But these too are in principle similar. Alter the environment of the embryo sufficiently, and eyeless monsters with markedly changed brain-development are produced.

In the early days of Mendelian research, phrases such as "in fowls, the character rose-comb is inherited as a Mendelian dominant" were current. So long as such phrases are recognized as mere convenient shorthand, they are harmless; but when they are taken to imply the actual genetic transmission of the characters, they are wholly incorrect.

Even as shorthand, they may mislead. To say that rose-comb is inherited as a dominant, even if we know that we mean the genetic factor for rose-comb, is likely to lead to what I may call the one-to-one or billiard-ball view of genetics. There are assumed to be a large number of characters in the organism, each one represented in a more or less invariable way by a particular factor or gene, or a combination of a few factors. This crude particulate view is a mere restatement of the preformation theory of development: granted the rose-comb factor, the rose-comb character, nice and clear-cut, will always appear. The rose-comb factor, it is true, is not regarded as a sub-microscopic replica of the actual rose-comb, but is taken to represent it by some form of unanalysed but inevitable correspondence.

The fallacy in this view is again revealed by the use of the difference method. In asserting that rose-comb is a dominant character, we are merely stating in a too abbreviated form the results of experiments to determine what constitutes the difference between fowls with rose-combs and fowls with single combs. In reality, what is inherited as a Mendelian dominant is the gene in the rose-combed stock which differentiates it from the single-combed stock: we have no right to assert anything more as a result of our experiments than the existence of such a differential factor.

Actually, every character is dependent on a very large number (possibly all) of the genes in the hereditary constitution: but some of these genes exert marked differential effects upon the visible appearance. Both rose- and single-comb fowls contain all the genes needed to build up a full-sized comb: but "rose" genes build it up according to one growth-pattern, "single" genes according to another.

This principle is of great importance. For instance, up till very recently the chief data in human genetics have been pedigrees of abnormalities or diseases collected by medical men. And in collecting these data, medical men have usually been obsessed with the implications of the ideas of "character-inheritance". When the character has not appeared in orthodox and classical Mendelian fashion they have tended to dismiss it with some such phrase as "inheritance irregular", whereas further analysis might have shown a perfectly normal *inheritance* of the gene concerned, but an irregular *expression* of the character, dependent on the other genes with which it was associated and upon differences in environment.[6]

This leads on to a further and very vital fact, namely, the existence of a type of genetic process undreamt of until the Mendelian epoch. In Darwin's day biological inheritance meant the reappearance of similar characters in offspring and parent, and implied the physical transmission of some material basis for the characters. What would Darwin or any nineteenth-century biologist say to facts such as the following, which now form part of any elementary course in genetics? A black and an albino mouse are mated. All their offspring are grey, like wild mice: but in the second generation greys, blacks, and albinos appear in the ratio 9:3:4. Or again, fowls with rose-comb and pea-comb mated together produce nothing but so-called walnut combs: but in the next generation, in addition to walnut, rose, and pea, some single combs are produced.

To the biologist of the Darwinian period the production of the grey mice would have been not inheritance, but "reversion" to the wild type, and the reappearance of the blacks and whites in the next generation would have been "atavism" or "skipping a generation". Similarly the appearance of single combs in the fowl cross would have been described as reversion, while the production of walnut combs would have been regarded as some form of "sport."

In reality, the results are in both cases immediately explicable on the assumption of two pairs of genes, each transmitted from parent to offspring by the same fundamental genetic mechanism. The "reversions", "atavisms", and "sports" are all due to new combinations of old genes. Thus, although all the facts are in one sense phenomena of inheritance, it is legitimate and in some ways desirable to distinguish those in which the same characters reappear generation after generation from those in which new characters are generated. As Haldane has put it, modern genetics deals not only with inheritance, but with recombination.

Thus the raw material available for evolution by natural selection falls into two categories—mutation and recombination. Mutation is the only begetter of intrinsic change in the separate units of the hereditary constitution: it alters the nature of genes.[7]

Recombination, on the other hand, though it may produce quite

<hr/>

6. See discussion in L. T. Hogben, *Nature and Nurture* (London, 1933).
7. Strictly speaking, this applies only to gene-mutation. Chromosome-mutation, whether it adds or subtracts chromosome-sets, whole chromosomes, or parts of chromosomes, or inverts sections of chromosomes, merely provides new quantitative or positional combinations of old genes. However, chromosomes-mutation may alter the *effects* of genes. Thus we are covered if we say that mutation alters either the qualitative nature or the effective action (including the mode of transmission) of the hereditary constitution.

new combinations with quite new effects on characters, only juggles with existing genes. It is, however, almost as important for evolution. It cannot occur without sexual reproduction: and its importance in providing the possibility of speedily combining several favourable mutations doubtless accounts for the all-but-universal presence of the sexual process in the life-cycle of organisms. We shall in later chapters see its importance for adjusting mutations to the needs of the organism.

Darwinism to-day thus still contains an element of deduction, and is none the worse for that as a scientific theory. But the facts available in relation to it are both more precise and more numerous, with the result that we are able to check our deductions and to make quantitative prophecies with much greater fullness than was possible to Darwin. This has been especially notable as regards the mathematical treatment of the problem, which we owe to R. A. Fisher, J. B. S. Haldane, Sewall Wright, and others. We can now take mutation-rates and degrees of advantage of one mutation or combination over another, which are within the limits actually found in genetic experiments, and can calculate the rates of evolution which will then occur.

If mutation had a rate that was very high it would neutralize or over-ride selective effects: if one that was very low, it would not provide sufficient raw material for change; if it were not more or less at random in many directions, evolution would run in orthogenetic grooves. But mutation being in point of fact chiefly at random, and the mutation-rate being always moderately low, we can deduce that the struggle for existence will be effective in producing differential survival and evolutionary change.

3. The Eclipse of Darwinism

The death of Darwinism has been proclaimed not only from the pulpit, but from the biological laboratory; but, as in the case of Mark Twain, the reports seem to have been greatly exaggerated, since to-day Darwinism is very much alive.

The reaction against Darwinism set in during the nineties of last century. The younger zoologists of that time were discontented with the trends of their science. The major school still seemed to think that the sole aim of zoology was to elucidate the relationship of the larger groups. Had not Kovalevsky demonstrated the vertebrate affinities of the sea-squirts, and did not comparative embryology prove the common ancestry of groups so unlike as worms and molluscs? Intoxicated with such earlier successes of evolutionary phylogeny, they proceeded (like some Forestry Commission of science) to plant wildernesses of family trees over the beauty-spots of biology.

A related school, a little less prone to speculation, concentrated on the pursuit of comparative morphology within groups. This provides one of the most admirable of intellectual trainings for the student, and has yielded extremely important results for science. But if pursued too exclusively for its own sake, it leads, as Radl has pithily put it in his *History of Biological Theories*, to spending one's time comparing one thing with another without ever troubling about what either of them really is. In other words, zoology, becoming morphological, suffered divorce from physiology. And finally Darwinism itself grew more and more theoretical. The paper demonstration that such and such a character was or might be adaptive was regarded by many writers as sufficient proof that it must owe its origin to Natural Selection. Evolutionary studies became more and more merely case-books of real or supposed adaptations. Late nineteenth-century Darwinism came to resemble the early nineteenth-century school of Natural Theology. Paley *redivivus*, one might say, but philosophically upside down, with Natural Selection instead of a Divine Artificer as the *Deus ex machina*. There was little contact of evolutionary speculation with the concrete facts of cytology and heredity, or with actual experimentation.

A major symptom of revolt was the publication of William Bateson's *Materials for the Study of Variation* in 1894. Bateson had done valuable work on the embryology of *Balanoglossus*; but his sceptical and concrete mind found it distasteful to spend itself on speculations on the ancestry of the vertebrates, which was then regarded as the outstanding topic of evolution, and he turned to a task which, however different it might seem, he rightly regarded as piercing nearer to the heart of the evolutionary problems. Deliberately he gathered evidence of variation which was discontinuous, as opposed to the continuous variation postulated by Darwin and Weismann. The resultant volume of material, though its gathering might fairly be called biassed, was impressive in quantity and range, and deeply impressed the more active spirits in biology. It was the first symptom of what we may call the period of mutation theory, which postulated that large mutations, and not small "continuous variations", were the raw material of evolution, and actually determined most of its course, selection being relegated to a wholly subordinate position.

This was first formally promulgated by de Vries [8] as a result of his work with the evening primroses, *Oenothera*, and was later adopted by various other workers, notably T. H. Morgan, in his first genetical phase. The views of the early twentieth-century

8. II. de Vries, *Die Mutationstheorie* (Leipzig, 1901); *Species and Varieties; their Origin by Mutation* (Chicago, 1905).

geneticists, moreover, were coloured by the rediscovery of Mendel's laws by Correns, de Vries, and Tschermak in the spring of 1900, and the rapid generalization of them, notably by Bateson.

Naturally, the early Mendelians worked with clear-cut differences of large extent. As it became clearer that mendelian inheritance was universal, it was natural to suppose all mendelian factors produced large effects, that therefore mutation was sharp and discontinuous, and that the continuous variation which is obviously widespread in nature is not heritable.

Bateson did not hesitate to draw the most devastating conclusions from his reading of the mendelian facts. In his Presidential Address to the British Association in 1914, assuming first that change in the germplasm is always by large mutation and secondly that all mutation is loss, from a dominant something to a recessive nothing, he concluded that the whole of evolution is merely an unpacking. The hypothetical ancestral amoeba contained—actually and not just potentially—the entire complex of life's hereditary factors. The jettisoning of different portions of this complex released the potentialities of this, that, and the other group and form of life. Selection and adaptation were relegated to an unconsidered background.

Meanwhile the true-blue Darwinian stream, leaving Weismannism behind, had reached its biometric phase. Tracing its origin to Galton, biometry blossomed under the guidance of Karl Pearson and Weldon. Unfortunately this, the first thorough application of mathematics to evolution, though productive of many important results and leading to still more important advances in method, was for a considerable time rendered sterile by its refusal to acknowledge the genetic facts discovered by the Mendelians. Both sides, indeed, were to blame. The biometricians stuck to hypothetical modes of inheritance and genetic variation on which to exercise their mathematical skill; the Mendelians refused to acknowledge that continuous variation could be genetic, or at any rate dependent on genes, or that a mathematical theory of selection could be of any real service to the evolutionary biologist.

It was in this period, immediately prior to the war, that the legend of the death of Darwinism acquired currency. The facts of mendelism appeared to contradict the facts of paleontology, the theories of the mutationists would not square with the Weismannian views of adaptation, the discoveries of experimental embryology seemed to contradict the classical recapitulatory theories of development. Zoologists who clung to Darwinian views were looked down on by the devotees of the newer disciplines, whether cytology or genetics, *Entwicklungsmechanik* or comparative physiology, as old-fashioned theorizers; and the theological and philosophical antipathy to Darwin's great mechanistic generalization could once more raise its head without fearing too violent a knock.

But the old-fashioned selectionists were guided by a sound instinct. The opposing factions became reconciled as the younger branches of biology achieved a synthesis with each other and with the classical disciplines: and the reconciliation converged upon a Darwinian centre.

It speedily became apparent that mendelism applied to the heredity of all many-celled and many single-celled organisms, both animals and plants. The mendelian laws received a simple and general interpretation: they were due in the first place to inheritance being particulate, and in the second place to the particles being borne on the chromosomes, whose behaviour could be observed under the microscope. Many apparent exceptions to mendelian rules turned out to be due to aberrations of chromosome-behaviour. Segregation and recombination, the fundamental mendelian facts, are all but universal, being co-extensive with sexual reproduction; and mutation, the further corollary of the particulate theory of heredity, was found to occur even more widely, in somatic tissues and in parthenogenetic and sexually-reproducing strains as well as in the germtrack of bisexual species. Blending inheritance as originally conceived was shown not to occur, and cytoplasmic inheritance to play an extremely subsidiary role.

The Mendelians also found that mutations could be of any extent, and accordingly that apparently continuous as well as obviously discontinuous variation had to be taken into account in discussing heredity and evolution. The mathematicians found that biometric methods could be applied to neo-mendelian postulates, and then become doubly fruitful. Cytology became intimately linked with genetics. Experimental embryology and the study of growth illuminated heredity, recapitulation, and paleontology. Ecology and systematics provided new data and new methods of approach to the evolutionary problem. Selection, both in nature and in the laboratory, was studied quantitatively and experimentally. Mathematical analysis showed that only particulate inheritance would permit evolutionary change: blending inheritance, as postulated by Darwin, was shown by R. A. Fisher [9] to demand mutation-rates enormously higher than those actually found to occur. Thus, though it may still be true in a formal sense that, as such an eminent geneticist as Miss E. R. Saunders said at the British Association meeting in 1920, "Mendelism is a theory of heredity: it is not a theory of evolution", yet the assertion is purely formal. Mendelism is now seen as an essential part of the theory of evolution. Mendelian analysis does not merely explain the distribu-

9. R. A. Fisher, *The Genetical Theory of Natural Selection* (Oxford, 1930).

tive hereditary mechanism: it also, together with selection, explains the progressive mechanism of evolution.

Biology in the last twenty years, after a period in which new disciplines were taken up in turn and worked out in comparative isolation, has become a more unified science. It has embarked upon a period of synthesis, until to-day it no longer presents the spectacle of a number of semi-independent and largely contradictory sub sciences, but is coming to rival the unity of older sciences like physics, in which advance in any one branch leads almost at once to advance in all other fields, and theory and experiment march hand-in-hand. As one chief result, there has been a rebirth of Darwinism. The historical facts concerning this trend are summarized by Shull in a recent book.[1] It is noteworthy that T. H. Morgan, after having been one of the most extreme critics of selectionist doctrine, has recently, as a result of modern work in genetics (to which he has himself so largely contributed), again become an upholder of the Darwinian point of view;[2] while his younger colleagues, notably Muller and Sturtevant, are strongly selectionist in their evolutionary views.

The Darwinism thus reborn is a modified Darwinism, since it must operate with facts unknown to Darwin; but it is still Darwinism in the sense that it aims at giving a naturalistic interpretation of evolution, and that its upholders, while constantly striving for more facts and more experimental results, do not, like some cautious spirits, reject the method of deduction.

Hogben[3] disagrees with this conclusion. He accepts the findings of neo-Mendelism and the mathematical conclusions to be drawn from them; but, to use his own words, "the essential difference between the theory of natural selection expounded by such contemporary writers as J. B. S. Haldane, Sewall Wright, and R. A. Fisher, as contrasted with that of Darwin, resides in the fact that Darwin interpreted the process of artificial selection in terms of a theory of 'blending inheritance' universally accepted by his own generation, whereas the modern view is based on the Theory of Particulate Inheritance. The consequences of the two views are very different. According to the Darwinian doctrine, evolution is an essentially continuous process, and selection is essentially creative in the sense that no change would occur if selection were removed. According to the modern doctrine, evolution is discontinuous. The differentiation of varieties or species may suffer periods of stagnation. Selection is a destructive agency."

Accordingly, Hogben would entirely repudiate the title of Dar-

1. A. F. Shull, *Evolution* (New York and London, 1936).
2. T. H. Morgan, *Evolution and Genetics* (Princeton, 1925); and later writings.
3. L. T. Hogben, *Genetic Principles in Medicine and Social Science* (London, 1931), pp. 145 ff.

winism for the modern outlook, and would prefer to see the term Natural Selection replaced by another to mark the new connotations it has acquired, although on this latter point he is prepared to admit the convenience of retention.

These objections, coming from a biologist of Hogben's calibre, must carry weight. On the other hand we shall see reason in later chapters for finding them ungrounded. In the first place, evolution, as revealed in fossil trends, *is* "an essentially continuous process". The buildimg-blocks of evolution, in the shape of mutations, are, to be sure, discrete quanta of change. But firstly, the majority of them (and the very great majority of those which survive to become incorporated in the genetic constitution of living things) appear to be of small extent; secondly, the effect of a given mutation will be different according to the combinations of modifying genes present; and thirdly, its effect may be masked or modified by environmental modification. The net result will be that, for all practical purposes, most of the variability of a species at any given moment will be continuous, however accurate are the measurements made; and that most evolutionary change will be gradual, to be detected by a progressive shifting of a mean value from generation to generation.

In the second place, the statement that selection is a destructive agency is not true, if it is meant to imply that it is *merely* destructive. It is also directive, and because it is directive, it has a share in evolutionary creation. Neither mutation nor selection alone is creative of anything important in evolution; but the two in conjunction are creative.

Hogben is perfectly right in stressing the fact of the important differences in content and implication between the Darwinism of Darwin or Weismann and that of Fisher or Haldane. We may, however, reflect that the term *atom* is still in current use and the atomic theory not yet rejected by physicists, in spite of the supposedly indivisible units having been divided. This is because modern physicists still find that the particles called atoms by their predecessors do play an important role, even if they are compound and do occasionally lose or gain particles and even change their nature. If this is so, biologists may with a good heart continue to be Darwinians and to employ the term Natural Selection, even if Darwin knew nothing of mendelizing mutations, and if selection is by itself incapable of changing the constitution of a species or a line.[4]

4. It should be added that Hogben was in 1931 concerned to stress mutation-pressure as an agency of change—then a new and not generally accepted conception. Since then he has allowed much more weight to the joint role of selection and mutation in producing adaptive change. See Hogben, "Problems of the Origin of Species," in *The New Systematics*, J. S. Huxley, ed. (Oxford, 1940).

Introduction to the Second Edition

* * * In the twenty years since this book was first published, there has been an enormous volume of new work and new ideas on the subject of evolution. * * *

The main fact to note is that the neo-Darwinian, synthetic, or integrative theory of evolution that I maintained in 1942 has gained many new adherents and may now be regarded as the established view. It has been supported by Rensch in his *Evolution above the Species Level* (1959a); by G. G. Simpson in *Tempo and Mode in Evolution* (1944) and *Major Factors in Evolution* (1953), by Ernst Mayr in *Systematics and the Origin of Species* (1942), by Dobhansky in *Genetics and the Origin of Species* (1951) and in *Mankind Evolving* (1962), by Stebbins in *Variation and Evolution in Plants* (1954), by Carter in *A Hundred Years of Evolution* (1957): also by the mass of the contributors to *The Evolution of Life*, Vol. 1 of the University of Chicago centennial on *Evolution after Darwin* (1960), to the Society of Experimental Biology's Symposium on *Evolution* (1953), to *Hundert Jahre Evolutionsforschung*, edited by Heberer and Schwanitz (1960), to *Darwin's Biological Work*, edited by P. R. Bell (1959), and to *A Century of Darwin*, edited by S. A. Barnett (1958). See also Waddington's *The Nature of Life* (1961) and Moody's *Introduction to Evolution* (1953).

It underlies most recent works on genetics, like L. C. Dunn's symposium on *Genetics in the 20th Century* (1951) Srb and Owen's text-book of *General Genetics* (1952) or King's up-to-date *Genetics* (1962), and modern treatments of major animal groups such as J. Z. Young's remarkable *The Life of Vertebrates* (1950). Finally, it has been adopted or assumed by the great majority of the contributors to *Evolution*, the first scientific journal devoted to the subject, whose successful launching in 1947 marked a major step in the progress of evolutionary biology.

Darwin's original contention, that biological evolution is a natural process, effected primarily by natural selection, has thus become increasingly confirmed, and all other theories of evolution requiring a supernatural or vitalistic force or mechanism, such as Bergson's creative evolution, and all "autogenetic" theories (Dobzhansky) such as Berg's nomogenesis, Osborn's aristogenesis, and orthogenesis in the strict sense, together with all Lamarckian theories involving the inheritance of acquired characters, have become increasingly untenable.

Only in the U.S.S.R. has Lamarckism found favour. Here, under the influence of Lysenko, the peculiar brand of Lamarckism styled

Michurinism was given official sanction, and extravagant and ill-founded claims were made on its behalf, while neo-Mendelian genetics, which everywhere else was advancing in a spectacular way, was officially condemned as bourgeois or capitalist "Morganist-Mendelist," and Soviet geneticists were exiled or lost their jobs. See J. S. Huxley, *Soviet Genetics and World Science*, 1949; and C. Zirkle, *Evolution, Marxian Biology and the Social Scene*, 1959.

The Soviet opposition to genetical science was particularly strong in the field of human genetics, since the orthodox Marxists believed or wanted to believe that a few generations of socialism would improve the genetic quality of the population. Eventually Lysenko lost his dominant position. But though orthodox genetics is now once more permitted, some official encouragement is given to an uneasy mixture of Mendelism and Michurinism.

Meanwhile in Britain, Waddington [1] has made a notable contribution to evolutionary theory by his discovery that Lamarckian inheritance may be simulated by a purely neo-Darwinian mechanism. This he called *genetic assimilation*. It operates through the natural selection of genes which dispose the developing organism to become modified in reaction to some environmental stimulus. Waddington showed experimentally that after a number of generations of selection for individuals which showed the most pronounced reaction, a strain could be obtained which developed the modified character in the absence of the environmental stimulus. This applies to adaptive as well as to non-adaptive modifications, and, as Haldane [2] points out, could clearly be effective in regard to the origin of various types of instinctive behaviour, by the genetic assimilation of behavioural modifications.[3]

The upholders of orthogenetic evolution had claimed that good fossil series showed unvarying evolutionary trends in one definite direction, and that this could not be explained except by postulating some inherent directive force. Their standard example was the evolution of the horse. However, G. G. Simpson in his book *Horses* (1951) conclusively demonstrated that the facts are otherwise: not only are trends sometimes reversed in single branches of the group, but the main trend shows definite changes of direction during its course. This is consonant with the view that natural selection is "opportunistic" in its operations, a view especially championed by G. G. Simpson and accepted by most other modern authorities, such as Dobzhansky and Mayr.

---

1. C. H. Waddington, *The Strategy of the Genes* (London, 1957); "Evolutionary Adaptation," in *Evolution after Darwin*, I, Sol Tax, ed. (Chicago, 1960).
2. J.B.S. Haldane, "Natural Selection" in P. R. Bell, ed., *Darwin's Biological Work* (Cambridge, 1959), p. 146.
3. See also C. Stern, "Genetic Assimilation," Proceedings of the American Philosophical Society, CIII (1959), 183.

Sheppard in his book *Natural Selection and Heredity* (1958) has analysed the operation of natural selection in detail, especially in relation to population genetics, speciation, and adaptations such as mimicry.

The most comprehensive and up-to-date exposition of the synthetic theory of evolution has just been given by Ernst Mayr in his magistral book *Animal Species and Evolution* (1963). As he points out, a radical change in recent evolutionary theory has been "the replacement of typologic thinking by population thinking." However, the modern synthetic theory still retains the combination of induction and deduction that underlay Darwin's original theory of evolution by natural selection.

His main point is that the species is a highly organised unit of evolution, based on an integrated pattern of co-operative genes co-adapted to produce an optimal phenotype, highly homeostatic and resistant to major change. This results in what has been termed *genetic relativity*. No gene has a fixed selective value: one and the same gene may be highly advantageous on one genetic background, highly disadvantageous on another. A long-term consequence is that the range of mutations and recombinations available to any particular organism or taxon is a restricted one and its evolutionary possibilities are correpondingly limited. This presumably accounts for some so-called orthogenetic trends, and for various phenotypic tendencies of different families and orders of animals and plants.

As a further result, speciation, in the sense of the splitting of one species into two, appears to occur most frequent by divergence of isolated populations near the margins of a species' range. These, under the pressure of new selective forces and in the absence of gene-flow from the central gene-pool of the species, are able to escape from the old integration and undergo genetic reconstruction with formation of a new integrated genotypic pattern. * * *

As a result of the marked increase of interest in population genetics as against formal genetics, selection theory has undergone various changes. One striking and in my opinion undesirable innovation concerns the concept of *fitness*. It is now fashionable to define fitness solely in terms of differential reproductive advantage, without any reference to phenotypic fitness ensuring individual survival. Some authors, like Dobzhansky [4], go so far as to call differential reproductive advantage "Darwinian fitness," although Darwin never used fitness in this sense, and although it was Herbert Spencer who first introduced the term into evolutionary theory by his unfortunate phrase *The Survival of the Fittest*, which Darwin did not employ in the earlier editions of the *Origin of Species*.

4. T. Dobzhansky, "A Review of Some Fundamental Concepts and Problems of Population Genetics," *Cold Spring Harbor Symp. Quant. Biol.*, XX (1955), 1.

Dobzhansky writes that "Darwinian fitness is measurable only in terms of reproductive proficiency," and later (p.221) that "the only trend [or] direction . . . discernible in life and its evolution is the product of more life." Accordingly (p. 11) "natural selection *means* [5] *differential reproduction* of carriers of different genetic endowments . . ."

When we examine the problem more critically, we find that we must differentiate between two quite distinct modes of natural selection, leading to different types of evolutionary trend, which we may call *survival selection* and *reproductive selection*. Haldane [6] also distinguishes these two modes of natural selection, but calls them phenotypic and genotypic respectively. I prefer my terminology for natural selection, but suggest using *phenotypic* and *genotypic* for the corresponding types of social selection (see below).

In the actual processes of biological evolution, survival selection is much the more important: selection exerts its effects mainly on individual phenotypes, and operates primarily by means of their differential survival to maturity. This will produce evolutionary effects because, as Darwin saw, (a) the majority of individuals which survive to maturity will mate and leave offspring; (b) much of the phenotypic variance promoting survival has a genetic basis.

Natural selection clearly may also operate by means of the differential reproduction of mature individuals, but in point of fact this *reproductive selection* has only minor evolutionary effects. Its most general effect is to promote an optimum clutch-size, litter-size, or in general terms progeny-number. Its effect in organisms with separate sexes is to promote mechanisms for securing successful matings, from flower-colour in entomophilous plants to mating behaviour in birds.[7] Only when there is strong intra-sexual competition with a high premium on mating success, does reproductive selection promote special trends like those to striking display characters in polygamous-promiscuous birds like Birds of Paradise and Argus Pheasants; or those to large size, special weapons, and general combative character in mammals with a harem-system, like deer and Elephant Seals. Darwin recognized the basic difference between these two forms of selection when he coined the term *sexual selection* for reproductive selection operating by inter-male competition.[8]

Survival selection, on the other hand, as Darwin saw in 1859, inevitably promotes all kinds of trend leading to biological improve-

5. It would be more logical to say *operates by means of.*
6. Haldane, "Natural Selection."
7. See Maynard Smith, *The Theory of Evolution* (London, 1958), Chapters 8 and 11.

8. For important discussions of sexual selection, see Chapter 6 of R. A. Fisher, *Genetical Theory of Natural Selection*; Maynard Smith; and S. A. Barnett, ed., *A Century of Darwin* (London, 1958).

ment, whether improvement in close adaptation to environment, in specialisation, in functional efficiency of particular organ-systems, in self-regulation, or in general organisation.

As R. A. Fisher pointed out in chapters 8 to 11 of his great book *The Genetical Theory of Natural Selection*, man is reproductively unique among organisms in showing an enormous range of individual variation in fertility, instead of a single optimum value with low variance. Man is also unique in having markedly reduced the impact of natural selection on the survival of individuals by artificial means, such as medical care and sanitation. The relative importance of differential survival and differential reproduction has thus been completely reversed in most present-day communities.

The human situation is so different from the biological that it may prove best to abandon the attempt to apply concepts like natural selection to modern human affairs. All the evolutionary differentials now operating, whether in survival or in reproduction, have their roots in the special psychosocial character of human evolution. It would seem best to accept the fact that a novel form of selection, *psychosocial selection*, or more simply *social selection*, is now operating; to attempt to define and analyse it more closely; and to see how it could be applied to produce eugenic results. Both phenotypic (survival) social selection and genotypic (reproductive) social selection are now probably dysgenic in their effects.

Thus R. A. Fisher [9] says that evolution in certain early types of society proceeds by "the social promotion of fertility," whereas in most modern societies there is a "social selection of infertility." I have coined the word *euselection* to denote deliberate selection for what are deemed desirable genetic qualities. Herbert Brewer uses *eutelgenesis* to denote eugenic improvement by means of artificial insemination from selected donors; and H. J. Muller [1] and he have pointed out how it could be rendered much more effective by the use of the recent technique of preserving mammalian sperm (and eventually ova and immature germ-cells) in a deep-frozen state.

Eugenics and the general relation of human genetics to human evolution has been much discussed recently, notably by Dobzhansky [2] by Crow, Muller and others in the first part of the symposium on *Evolution and Man's Progress*,[3] by Medawar in his Reith Lectures (1960), and by myself in my Galton Lectures (1962). It is becoming clear that social euselection (eugenic selec-

9. Fisher, p. 245.
1. H. J. Müller, "The Guidance of Human Evolution," *Persp. Biol. Med.* III (1959), 1.; and "Should We Weaken or Strengthen our Genetic Heritage?" in H. Hoagland and R. W. Burhoe, *Evolution and Man's Progress* (New York and London, 1962).
2. Dobzhansky, *Mankind Evolving* (New Haven, 1962).
3. Hoagland and Burhoe, eds., *Evolution and Man's Progress* (London, 1962).

tion for the deliberate genetic improvement of man) will differ radically from artificial selection for the deliberate genetic improvement of domesticated plants and animals; and also from natural selection, which operates automatically to produce biological improvement in natural species of groups. It is also clear that, in so far as immediate threats to human progress are overcome, such as over-population, atomic war, and over-exploitation of natural resources, eugenic improvement will become an increasingly important goal of evolving man.

Much theoretical and experimental work has been done on selection in general. In addition to survival (phenotypic) and reproductive (genotypic), sexual, and social (psychosocial) selection (see above), the following main types of natural selection are now usually distinguished [4]:

(1) *Normalizing*, centripetal, or stabilizing selection: tending to reduce variance, to promote the continuance of the "normal" type, and to prevent change in a well-adapted organisation.

(2) *Directional*, directed, or dynamic selection: tending to produce change in an adaptive direction.

(3) *Diversifying*, disruptive, or centrifugal selection: tending to separate a single population into two genetically distinct populations.

(4) *Balancing* selection: tending to produce balanced polymorphisms and heteroses in populations.

(5) Selection for variability: leading to high variance in cryptic adaptation in certain conditions (see Sheppard, 1958). To which we may perhaps add

(6) *Post hoc* selection, as when a viable new species originates suddenly by allopolyploidy.

In recent years, much attention has been paid to the effects of population-density on survival, and a careful analysis has been made of the various density-dependent and density-independent factors involved and of their selective effects.[5]

In numerically very small populations, as Sewall Wright first pointed out, change in gene-frequency may occur by chance, through random survival without the intervention of selection. When this occurs through the loss of alleles which inevitably takes place in such populations, it is termed *genetic drift*, and may ac-

4. See Dobzhansky, *Mankind Evolving*, Haldane, "Natural Selection"; P. M. Sheppard, *Natural Selection and Heredity* (London, 1958); J. M. Thoday, "Natural Selection and Biological Progress," in S. A. Barnett, *A Century of Darwin* (London, 1958); etc. Haldane in particular has helped to quantify the subject.

5. W. C. Allee et al., *Principles of Animal Ecology* (Philadelphia and London, 1949); V. C. Wynne-Edwards, *Animal Dispersion in Relation to Social Behaviour* (Edinburgh and London, 1962); Ernst Mayr, *Animal Species and Evolution* (Cambridge, Mass., 1963).

tually override selection-pressure and even lead to reduction or extinction of the population. Further, as discussed in chaps. 2 and 5 of the present work it may also occur when an isolated habitat, such as an island or a lake, is colonized by a handful of invaders. These will almost certainly not have a full complement of the alleles in the gene-complex of the species, so that the local population will be genetically distinct from the outset, and will frequently show further divergence owing to genetic drift and to local selection (see below). This has been called the *founder principle* by Mayr, who gives numerous examples of its effects. * * *

Perhaps the most important fact to emerge from research in population genetics is that in most animal species, the majority of wild populations have a surprisingly high genetic variance, but that much of it is potential, and is not manifested phenotypically unless released under the influence of selection. This capacity of the integrated genotype for storing variance is highly adaptive in relation to the evolutionary survival of species. On the other hand, the species has to pay a considerable price for this capacity, in the shape of the genetic load of disadvantageous variations which may be released by recombination.

Most such populations are not even approximately homozygous, but are heterozygous for a large proportion, perhaps a majority, of their genes. There is considerable dispute as to how much of this heterozygosity is maintained through selectively balanced morphisms, through straight heterozygote advantage in single genes, through traditional heterosis due to the co-operation of complementary genes, through the establishment of complementary linked polygenic systems as described by Mather, or through that of complementary chromosomal types (chromosome morphisms) as found by Dobzhansky in wild Drosophila. In any case, the widespread existence of heterozygosity will lock up a great deal of the variance of a natural population in potential form. Linked polygenic systems are normally balanced so as to secure an optimum mean effect on a given character (or on a pair or set of balanced morphic characters; see below). Long-continued selection can change the manifestation of the character, by a slow but stepwise release of their latent (stored) variance, as shown for instance, by the work of Mather[6] and Thoday.[7]

In this and other ways high heterozygosity confers a marked degree of stability on a population, but it also ensures a large store of potential variance, which can be released by selection if circum-

6. K. Mather, "The Genetical Structure of Populations," in *Symp. Soc. Exp. Biol.* VII (Cambridge, England, 1953); and discussion of heterosis in *Proc. Roy. Soc.* (B) CXLIV (1956), 143.

7. J. M. Thoday, "Components of Fitness," *Symp. Soc. Exp. Biol.;* VII, Evolution, p. 96; and "Natural Selection and Biological Progress," in S. A. Barnett, *A Century of Darwin.*

stances demand it. Darwin's postulate that long-term and major evolution by natural selection is normally slow and manifested by gradual trends of change, largely in quantitative characters, has thus been confirmed, though modern population-genetics has shown that short-term minor changes may occur with surprising rapidity, under the influence of unexpectedly high selective pressures. * * *

I have left to the end the most important scientific event of our times—the discovery by Watson and Crick that the desoxyribonucleic acids—DNA for short—are the true physical basis of life, and provide the mechanism of heredity and evolution.[8] Their chemical structure, combining two elongated linear sequences in a linked double spiral or bihelix, makes them self-reproducing, and ensures that they can act as a code, providing an immense amount of genetical "information," together with occasional variations of information (mutations) which also reproduce themselves. Linear constructions of DNA are, of course, the primary structures in the genetic organelles we call chromosomes. In some primitive organisms there is only a single chromosome, including the species' entire apparatus of DNA.[9]

Specific DNA also plays the key role in determining the specific proteins, including enzymes, in living cells, through the intermediary of specific forms of RNA (ribose nucleic acid). The particular DNA code of each species thus provides epigenetic "instruction" as well as phylogenetic "information." Mayr[1] makes the same distinction in slightly different terms. In his formulation, the phenomena of ontogeny and physiology are manifestations of the decoding of the information provided by the genotypic DNA, while those of evolutionary change are the result of the provision of ever-new codes of genetic information.

It may well prove that DNA structure has the further intrinsic property of ensuring recombination of mutants by interchange between separate homologous sections of DNA (chromosomes). Even if this essentially sexual process were not intrinsic *ab origine*, it confers such a high degree of evolutionary advantage that it must have been incorporated into the stream of life very early in its evolution. * * *

The various properties of DNA which I have mentioned make evolution inevitable. The existence of an elaborate self-reproducing code of genetical information ensures continuity and specificity; the intrinsic capacity for mutation provides varability; the capacity for self-reproduction ensures potentially geometric increase and there-

8. For a brief account, see Davidson, 1960, and for a general discussion, see New Biology, No. 31, *Biological Replication*, 1960.

9. E. Chargaff and J. N. Davidson, eds., *The Nucleic Acids* (New York, 1955–1960).
1. *Animal Species and Evolution*.

fore a struggle for existence; the existence of genetic variability ensures differential survival of variants and therefore natural selection; and this results in evolutionary transformation.

Our detailed knowledge of the constitution and operation of DNA and RNA will help in the unravelling of many particular genetic-evolutionary problems. Among these may be mentioned the relation of genes to developmental processes, the interaction of different genes, and the relations of genes to immunology via antigens and antibodies. Light is already being shed on the fine structure of genes, which are proving to be far more complex than was originally supposed.[2]

It would also seem certain that more detailed knowledge about DNA will give us fuller understanding of mutation and the ways in which it depends on chemical structure, with the eventual possibility of influencing the type and direction of mutation by artificial means. In general, however, the discovery of DNA and its properties has not led to important new developments or significant modifications in evolutionary theory or in our understanding of the course of biological evolution. What it has done is to reveal the physical basis underlying the evolutionary mechanisms which Darwin's genius deduced must be operative in nature, and to open up new possibilities of detailed genetic analysis and of experimental control of the genetic-evolutionary process. The edifice of evolutionary theory is still essentially Darwinian after the incorporation of all our new knowledge of mendelian (particulate) genetics; it will remain so long after the incorporation of our knowledge of its detailed chemical basis.

THEODOSIUS DOBZHANSKY

The Nature of Heredity (1964) †

* * *

Chromosome Chemistry

The work of the Morgan school on Drosophila genetics and cytogenetics attained such a degree of refinement that after it the next development in the understanding of the physical basis of heredity could only come, and it did come, from the study of the

---

2. C. Pontecorvo, *Trends in Genetic Analysis* (New York and Oxford, 1959).
† From Chapter 1 of *Heredity and the Nature of Man* (New York, 1964).

Theodosius Dobzhansky (b. 1900) is professor of genetics at Rockefeller University.

chemistry of chromosomes. The two classes of chemical compounds that account for most of the material composing a chromosome are deoxyribonucleic acids (abbreviated as DNA) and proteins, loosely joined to form nucleoproteins. The question naturally arises, what makes one gene different from another? A human sex cell contains probably no fewer than 10,000 different genes, and there may be millions and millions of kinds of genes in different organisms in the living world.

Until fairly recently, say twenty years ago, most biologists were inclined to regard the proteins as probably responsible for the specific qualities of each gene. At present, it is considered extremely probable that heredity, genetic information, to use a now-fashionable phrase, is stored chiefly in the chromosomal DNA. Let us see what has led to this change of opinion. The nucleic acids are seemingly rather too simple and too uniform in chemical composition in most diverse organisms to produce a variety of structures at least equal to the variety of genes that exist in the living world. Proteins are, on the contrary, large, some of them being enormous, molecules; they exist in a great variety of forms, and they can be envisaged to produce almost infinite variety.

Facts began, however, to come to light that argued for the nucleic acids being the chief carriers of genetic information. A. E. Mirsky in the United States, R. Vendrely in France, and others found that the amount of DNA per cell doubles in the interval between successive cell divisions, and is reduced by half when the cell divides. However, this amount is remarkably constant in body cells of a given species of organism, except that the sex cells contain only half as much DNA and half as many chromosomes as do body cells. The chromosomal proteins are, on the contrary, quite variable, both in amount and in composition in different cells of the same body.

O. T. Avery, C. M. MacLeod, and M. McCarty discovered in 1944 that hereditary characteristics can be transferred from one strain of bacteria to other strains, causing pneumonia (*Pneumococcus*) by means of a transforming principle extracted from the donor strain. This "transforming principle" was identified as a nucleic acid. Such transformations of the hereditary endowment are now known in several species of bacteria; whether this is also possible in higher organisms remains to be seen. A. D. Hershey secured a very elegant demonstration of the importance of DNA in the transmission of heredity in his study of the bacteriophages (bacterial viruses). A bacteriophage is an organism too small to be seen in an ordinary light microscope but visible in electron microscopes; it enters living bacterial cells, multiplies therein, and causes the bacteria to disintegrate, releasing numerous new bacteriophages.

Now, the body of a bacteriophage consists of a DNA core and a protein envelope; Hershey showed that only the DNA enters the host bacterial cell, while the protein is left outside.

The amounts of the DNA involved in the transmission of heredity are actually remarkably small, even in higher organisms. For example, the nucleus of the spermatozoon of a fish (carp) contains about 1.6 billionths of a milligram (1.6×10^{-12} of a gram) of DNA, while the nuclei of the body cells (red blood cells) contain 3.0 to 3.3 billionths. (This variation is probably a matter of imprecision in measurement.) Another fish (trout) has 2.45 of the same units of DNA in a spermatozoon, and 4.9 in a bodycell nucleus. Spermatozoa of a bull have 3.3 units, body cells some 6.4 to 6.8. Human body cells contain 6.0 to 6.8 units; the amount in human sex cells does not seem to have been measured.

One can make an interesting calculation of the total amount of DNA that has contained and has transmitted the genetic endowment of mankind. Take three billion (3×10^9) as the number of human beings now living; each of them arose from a fertilized egg cell, the nucleus of which had between 6 and 7×10^{-12} gram of DNA; all these egg cells had, then, between 0.018 and 0.021 of a gram, roughly 20 milligrams of DNA. Truly, the powers concealed in this extraordinary substance exceed by far anything in the atomic and other bombs yet invented!

Lower organisms generally have less DNA than higher ones. Thus, a bacteriophage (bacterial virus) has only 0.0002×10^{-12} of a gram; a colon bacterium (*Escherichia coli*), 0.01; the nucleus of a cell of a sponge, 0.1; of a sea urchin, 1.97; of a mouse, 5; of a man, as stated above, between 6 and 7. Man is, however, far from the top of the series. More DNA than in human cells is contained in a cell nucleus of the amphibians, such as a toad (7.3), a frog (15.0), *Necturus* (48), and *Amphiuma* (168). The meaning of this is obscure—in our pride we would not like to entertain the notion that toads, frogs, and salamanders need either more numerous or more complicated genes than man does. One possible but unconfirmed explanation might be that in some organisms the chromosomes of the cell nuclei contain the set of genes each represented only once, while in other organisms each gene of the set is repeated several times.

The chemical structure of DNA is a fascinating story in its own right. Many outstanding investigators in different parts of the world have been working on it in recent years, and with outstanding success. The results obtained are of the greatest importance; so much so, that it seems in the highest degree likely that our time will stand, in the history of biology, as that of the discovery of the chemical basis of heredity. Furthermore, it is sometimes said that truly great discoveries in science are beautifully simple; I am not sure that this proposition can always be sustained, but it certainly applies to the DNA story. Its essentials can be stated briefly and simply, without going into chemical details. DNA (Figures 4 and 5) extracted from the chromosomes of cell nuclei can be broken down to a fairly small number of constituents. These are a kind of sugar called deoxyribose, a phosphoric acid, and four so-called nucleotide bases, namely adenine, guanine, cytosine, and thymine. We shall not discuss the chemical structure and chemical formulae

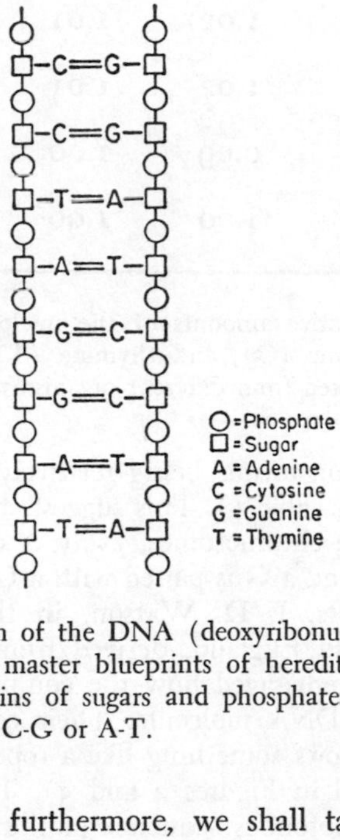

Figure 4. The comparison of the DNA (deoxyribonucleic acid), the substance which carries the master blueprints of heredity in the form of a genetic "code." Two chains of sugars and phosphates are cross-linked by pairs of nucleotide bases, C-G or A-T.

of these constituents; furthermore, we shall take the liberty of denoting the adenine, guanine, cytosine, and thymine nucleotide bases simply by their initial letters, A, G, C, and T. Only rarely, in some exceptional organisms, is one of the bases replaced by a closely related chemical compound. This uniformity is, of course, in itself a most remarkable fact, attesting the fundamental unity of all that lives.

The DNA obtained from a series of quite diverse organisms has been submitted to chemical analysis. A suggestive regularity has emerged: namely, the content of A always equals, within limits of analytical error, that of T, and the content of G is the same as C. By contrast, the amount of A + T in relation to that of G + C

ORGANISM	A : T	G : C	(A + T) : (G + C)
BACTERIOPHAGE	1.00	1.09	1.87
COLON BACTERIA	1.09	0.99	1.00
YEAST	0.96	1.08	1.80
SEA URCHIN	1.02	1.01	1.85
SALMON	1.02	1.01	1.43
CATTLE	0.99	1.00	1.37
MAN	1.00	1.00	1.54

TABLE 1. The relative amounts of the nucleotide bases adenine (A), cytosine (C), guanine (G), and thymine (T) in the deoxyribonucleic acids (DNA) extracted from different organisms.

is variable, some organisms being relatively richer in A + T and others in G + C (Table 1). This suggests that in the intact DNA, as it exists in the chromosomes, every A component is somehow paired with a T, and a G is paired with a C.

Two biochemists, J. D. Watson, in the United States, and F. H. C. Crick, in England, derived from these data a brilliant hypothesis. They envisaged how the component parts are put together to give a DNA molecule. Their celebrated model of the DNA structure shows something like a rope ladder wound up in a spiral (represented in Figures 4 and 5). The vertical part of the "ladder" is a monotonous sequence of the deoxyribose sugars and phosphates. The "rungs" of the "ladder" consist of the A, G, C, and T residues; there are two kinds of "rungs"—in one of them, A is coupled with T; in the other kind, G is coupled with C. Here, then, is an explanation of the fact that the DNA's obtained from most diverse organisms contain as many A's as T's and as many C's as G's, so that the ratios of their amount are always close to unity; the members of these pairs are the necessary complements of each other.

The Watson-Crick model provides a solution to the problem mentioned above, namely, how can there be so many kinds of genes if all of them have their distinctive properties specified by their DNA? This solution is best explained by means of an analogy. There are some 400,000 words in the English language, yet all these words can be spelled with only twenty-six letters of the alphabet. In fact, all of them can also be spelled with only three "letters" —in the Morse telegraphic code's dot, dash, and gap. A line in a printed page consists of words; words contain different letters, or the same letters differently arranged. The genetic "alphabet" consists of the four "letters" A, T, G, C; different combinations of them can give a virually infinite variety of genetic "words" or "messages." The matter may also be looked at in another light— in the light of evolution. The evolutionary development of the living world has evidently taken place on the levels of the genetic words and messages, while the genetic alphabet has remained virtually unaltered throughout. Man differs from a Drosophila fly, a corn plant, or a bacteriophage by virtue of the fact that his gene endowment contains different messages, but these messages are conveyed by means of the same alphabet.

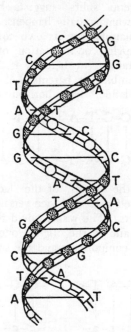

Figure 5. A representation of the Watson-Crick model of the structure of the DNA (deoxyribonucleic acid). The two cross-linked chains shown in Figure 4 are wound in a double helical spiral.

The genes are, then, sections of the DNA ladder-like molecules; different genes are different because they contain different sequences of the "letters" A, T, G, and C. It can be said that heredity is "coded" in the genes, or in the DNA of the chromosomes, in a manner similar to a message written in Morse code or in some secret code used by diplomats, generals, or spies. The day may not be far away when the sequences of the genetic "letters" in the various genes in man and in other organisms may become known. It is, however, a tremendous achievement to have understood the method of construction of the genetic messages, even if, for the time being, we cannot spell many of them out ourselves in the laboratory.

How Genes Make Their Own Copies

The Watson-Crick model has suggested a solution for another knotty biological problem. When a cell divides, its chromosomes split in equal halves, so that the daughter cells receive the same chromosomes, and presumably the same genes, the mother cell had. To say that a gene "splits" suggests, however, a crude and inaccurate picture of what actually happens. What a gene in fact appears to do is to manufacture its own copy, another gene just like itself. The self-copying, or replication, of the genes has to be very precise and accurate if the heredity is to be maintained and the progeny is to resemble the parents. Let us, then, represent a portion of the DNA "ladder" lying horizontally, like this:

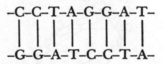

Now suppose that the "rungs" of the "ladder" break, and that each C attracts to itself a G and vice versa, and that each A attracts a T and vice versa. The result would then be two "ladders" similar to each other and to the original one. (The capital letters stand for the original components and the small ones for the new components.)

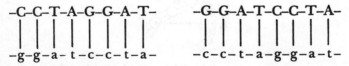

An individual receives, then, his heredity in the form of the two genetic "messages" encoded in the DNA of the two sex cells, the egg cell from the mother and the spermatozoon from the father.

These two cells unite at fertilization, and initiate the long and complex series of processes in the development of the individual. The fertilized egg is a single cell; it divides in two, four, eight, and finally billions of cells; the cells form an embryo, then a fetus, an infant, a child, an adolescent, an adult, an oldster. An individual develops as long as he lives. Growth and maturation, as well as senescence and old-age decrepitude, are parts of the sequence of the developmental process. Looked at from the standpoint of genetics, the development of an individual may be said to represent a translation, or a decoding, of the genetic messages this individual received from his parents. Little is known at present, and much is to be learned, about the precise ways in which this translation of the genetic messages really takes place in the growing and developing organism when its organs are formed and its cells differentiate. The physiology of the development is a field of study rapidly developing at present.

Genes and Proteins

Some of the most important constituents of all living bodies belong to the class of chemical compounds known as proteins. The hemoglobin of red blood cells, the myosin of the muscles, the pepsin and trypsin so essential for the digestion of food, and numerous enzymes indispensable to the life of body cells, all are proteins. The human body contains no fewer than 10,000 and possibly as many as 100,000 different kinds of proteins. Mention has already been made that proteins are large, some of them enormous, chemical molecules. Chemists discovered, however, that under the influence of acids or alkalis, proteins can be broken up into much smaller constituents. These constituents are amino acids. There is no need to describe here the chemical structure of the amino acids. What is important for us is that there are about twenty different kinds of amino acids which are the constituents of most known proteins. The proteins consist of long chains of amino-acid residues; these chains may be linked together by cross-connections, and may be coiled in various complicated but specific ways. Protein molecules may be long and slender fibers, or more or less spherical or globular in shape. Different proteins contain different sets and proportions of the twenty known amino acids. Moreover, the properties of a protein depend upon the exact alignment of the amino-acid residues in the chains.

One may say that the protein "alphabet" consists of about twenty "letters," the different amino acids. By analogy with the DNA nucleic acids, with their four genetic "letters," one may attempt to represent the structure of the proteins in terms of the twenty amino-acid "letters." The difficulty here is that, as indicated, a protein molecule may contain several different amino-acid chains with various cross-links and convolutions. In other words, the "letters" in a protein are not necessarily all disposed in a single line; they may form a complicated three-dimensional structure consisting of several amino-acid chains. The analogy with DNA is nevertheless a useful one, because the chief function the genes play in the development is to direct the synthesis of the proteins. Some authorities consider it probable that every gene specifies the sequence of the amino acids in just one chain composing a certain enzyme or some other protein the body must contain. To put it differently, the genetic message encoded in the DNA of the gene in the form of the sequence of the letters A, T, G, C is translated into the sequence of the amino-acid "letters" in a chain composing a certain protein.

In recent years, biochemists have obtained some very valuable information concerning the ways and means whereby this "translation" of the DNA four-letter code into the twenty-letter amino-acid code is actually accomplished (Figure 6). It appears that the "translators" are still-different substances, the ribonucleic acids, abbreviated RNA. RNA differs from DNA in several respects. It contains a different kind of sugar, a ribose instead of deoxyribose. It is at least usually single-stranded, instead of double-stranded with "rungs" like a ladder. It contains the base called uracil instead of thymine. The four-letter alphabet of RNA thus differs in one letter from DNA—it is A, U, G, C, instead of A, T, G, C.

The process of translation of the DNA message into the amino-acids sequence in the protein happens in the following way (Figure 6). First, a strand of RNA is formed, in which the sequence of the "letters" in a section of the DNA strand is impressed in a corresponding sequence of the RNA. The result is called the messenger RNA. It comes out from the cell nucleus into the cell cytoplasm, and attaches itself to the surface of very tiny bodies called ribosomes, visible only with the aid of electron microscopes. A series of amino acids then becomes arranged in a chain characteristic of a given protein and corresponding to the sequence of the "letters" in a given messenger RNA. Each amino acid in the protein is specified by a sequence of three "letters" in the RNA and the DNA. Successful attempts have been made in recent years to break this "triplet Code," that is, to determine just which groups of three "letters" in RNA and DNA correspond to each one of the twenty amino acids. So spectacularly rapid has been the progress in this line of endeavor that the code is now well on the way to being deciphered, although some problems still await solution. One, perhaps rather unexpected, feature is that the code proved to be a degenerate one. "Degeneracy" (the word here does not imply that the code was in the past somehow better or more efficient than it is now) means that instead of a strict one-to-one correspondence between an RNA triplet and an amino acid, some amino acids can be specified by two or more different triplets.

Origin of Life

The foregoing pages have attempted to outline, of necessity in a very condensed and even superficial manner, the remarkable progress the study of heredity has made since the pioneer microscopists first sighted the sex cells. The remainder of the present chapter will deal with a frankly speculative matter: the origin of life on earth. Man has discovered that he is a product of evolution of living matter, and he cannot refrain from asking whence he, together with everything that lives, ultimately came.

The development of ideas about the origin of life went through at least three phases. To those unfamiliar with biology, the problem appeared to be very simple, or, rather, the problem did not seem to exist at all. Primitive man was an animist, believing that all natural objects possess some sort of life or vitality. He was ready to assume that living beings arise from nonliving materials all the time. Countless legends and myths relate, often with great poetic elegance, how diverse animals and even men appeared out of stones, earth, or simply from the air. More prosaically, it was generally credited that fly maggots arise from putrid meat, lice from dirty clothing, and mice from old rags. As a cheeky youth, I remember having angered a dear old lady by refusing to believe that clothes moths will appear in the stored woolens if no moth comes in from the outside. She did not know, or care to know, that Francesco Redi and Spallanzani had already proved, in the seventeenth and eighteenth centuries, that spontaneous generation of life does not occur—an example, I suppose, of what is politely called the "academic lag."

After Louis Pasteur's classical work of 1862, the principle *omne vivum ex vivo* (all life arises from life) became the fundamental tenet of biology. Darwin's theory of evolution, of "descent with modification," was taken to explain the development of the living world, from the lowest to the highest forms, from "amoeba to man," as it used to be formulated. This theory did not, however, pretend to explain how the lowest organisms arose in the first place. Biological evolution was supposed to start with an "amoeba"; nowadays, we prefer to start with some primordial virus, since the amoeba is much too complicated an organism already. The Swedish astronomer S. A. Arrhenius in 1907 proposed an escape: Life is

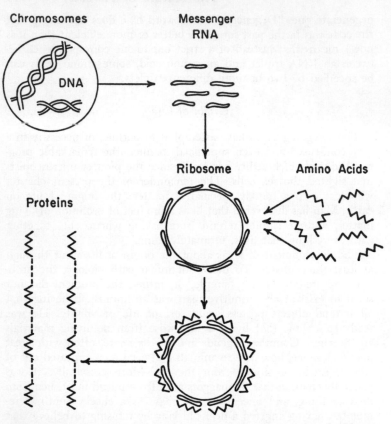

Figure 6. A schematic representation of how the genes act to build proteins, some of which act as enzymes. The DNA of the genes in the chromosomes impresses its specificity on another substance, the messenger RNA. This "messenger" passes from the cell nucleus to the cytoplasm, and settles on the surface of very minute bodies called ribosomes. Amino acids then become linked together in orders specified by the messenger RNA, to form different proteins.

present in many parts of the universe, and its seeds were introduced on our planet with some sort of cosmic dust. Nobody has ever found any such seeds coming in from cosmic space. This is not the only flaw in Arrhenius' hypothesis. The problem is merely pushed back in time, and the question immediately arises: How did life start in the cosmos?

The spectacular recent advances of biochemistry and genetics have imbued biologists with enough self-confidence to face again the problem that for so long seemed beyond reach, namely, creating life in the laboratory from nonliving constituents. Such a feat is yet to be achieved. It is, however, interesting to consider briefly some experiments that come nearest, to date, to this achievement. A. Kornberg (now at Stanford University) prepared a mixture of the component parts of DNA, that is, of the "letters" A, T, C, and G. His preparation actually contained them in the form of deoxynucleoside triphosphates of adenine, thymine, cytosine, and guanine. The problem was, of course, how to link these components together as they are linked in the DNA.

Kornberg extracted from the colon bacterium an enzyme that can mediate the reaction of linking. The addition of the enzyme to the mixture of the triphosphates of A, T, C, and G did not, however, suffice to accomplish the synthesis of DNA. What was missing was a "primer." Kornberg, in 1956, found that a small amount of DNA extracted from some living organism could serve as such a primer. The addition of a primer caused the appearance in the preparation of DNA molecules. Most important of all, the DNA synthesized was identical in the proportions of the different nucleotides (the "letters") not to the DNA of the organism furnishing the enzyme, in this case the colon bacterium, but to that furnishing the primer. Kornberg was able to induce the synthesis of the DNA characteristic of a bacteriophage, of at least two species of bacteria, and of cattle by using as primers DNA extracted from these organisms.

In Kornberg's experiments, the molecules of the primer DNA "reproduced" themselves. Or, to be more precise, they served as models, or templates, for the synthesis of their copies. The genes in the chromosomes of living cells reproduce themselves probably by means of a priming mechanism of the same kind that operated in Kornberg's experiments. One would, of course, like to see an experiment performed with a synthetic primer, instead of with a primer taken from a living cell. Is this a possible goal? In a recently published work, Kornberg and his colleagues L. L. Bertsch, J. F. Jackson, and H. G. Khorana seem to be well on the way to this achievement. When it is finally achieved, one will have to face a tough question: Does this mean that life has been created artificially? It must at the very least be admitted that this would give us a good model of life, even though it may not re-create a facsimile of any actually existing life.

At the base of it all there is, just the same, a real problem: What was the origin on earth, or anywhere in the universe, of the first "primer," which initiated the process of self-copying, the fundamental characteristic of life. For the time being this remains an unsolved riddle. But the problem is a meaningful one, and it is within this larger context that many biologists, chemists, astronomers, and geologists have been doing some interesting experiments, and a great deal of speculative writing. The results obtained by A. I. Oparin, in Russia, J. D. Bernal, in England, and Harold Urey, Stanley Miller, M. Calvin, S. W. Fox, and Harlow Shapley, in the United States, are in general agreement on one basic point: the primeval conditions on earth, which existed before there was any life, permitted the formation of certain chemical compounds that are now formed, exclusively or at least principally, in living bodies.

The atmosphere of the young planet Earth was very different from the one we breathe; it had little or no free oxygen, but it did contain, in addition to water vapor, the hydrocarbon methane (CH_4) and ammonia (NH_3). The chemical reactions that could take place in such an atmosphere have been explored by Stanley Miller and others. In Miller's classical experiment of 1953, at least two amino acids, alanine and glutamic acid, were obtained in a vessel containing water, hydrogen, methane, and ammonia under the influence of electric discharges. There is now good evidence that a number of organic compounds, formaldehyde, acetic and several other organic acids, as well as five amino acids, can be formed in a mixture of gases resembling the atmosphere of the primordial earth under the influence of high-energy ultraviolet radiations, electric discharges, and perhaps other agencies. The waters of the seas and oceans were probably a kind of thin "soup," a dilute solution of some of the substances now formed in living organisms. Larger and more complex organic molecules, particularly proteins and nucleic acids, could conceivably arise in such a "soup," although this has not yet been conclusively demonstrated experimentally under realistically contrived "primitive" conditions. Oparin believes that an important process was the formation of so-called coacervate droplets, simple colloidal suspensions; Bernal thinks that protein molecules may have been formed owing to absorption of amino acids on the surface of clay particles.

All this adds up to the surmise that the first life could have arisen under the conditions that once existed on earth. The critical step, the appearance of the first self-replicating molecule or a combination of molecules, still seems, however, to be an improbable event. As long as this step is not reproduced experimentally, there will exist a difference of opinion about how it occurred. Some scientists are so headstrong as to believe that the surmise is plausible enough to be accepted as a probable description of what happened in reality. Given eons of time—and our planet is known to be at least three billion years old—a highly improbable event can take place somewhere, or even in several places, in the universe. Perhaps the first spark that kindled the flame of life did occur on earth, this insignificant little speck in vast cosmic spaces. Shapley seems to be convinced that life *must* exist also on some other planets, in many solar systems, and in galaxies other than our own. On the other hand, some people continue to regard the origin of life not only as an unsolved but also as an unsolvable mystery. They are as firmly convinced as ever that an act of God must have been invoked to contribute that first spark. I strongly feel that this point of view must not be ignored but must be faced honestly in a book dealing with the humanistic aspects of biology, even though it is impossible to attempt here more than an indication of the broad lines of the relevant arguments.

That there occur in living bodies many chemical and physical processes similar in principle to those observable in inert bodies is not doubted by anyone. Thus, nutrition is analogous to stoking an engine with fuel, and respiration to the combustion of that fuel. The question is whether *in addition* to such processes there are also in life other processes, forces, or agents which are not composed of physicochemical ones. Mechanists hold that such additional, irreducible, specifically vital forces do not exist. Vitalists believe that they do, and call them by a variety of names—the vital force, entelechy, psyche. Vitalism is at present a minority opinion, but it is a minority not because the mechanists have actually "explained" every one and all biological phenomena by reducing them to physics and chemistry. It will be argued in the next chapter that reductionist explanations are not always the most meaningful ones. Mechanists have achieved something perhaps better than a simple reduction. The living world is, hopefully, understandable as the outcome of the formation of progressively more and more complex and perfect compounds or patterns of physico-chemical processes in the course of biological evolution.

Biologists have rejected vitalism not because it has been proved that in no biological phenomenon may there be lurking a vital force. One cannot prove a universal negative. It is, rather, that vitalism has been shown to be unnecessary. Actually, the best argument that a vitalist can offer is that a mechanistic universe is too dull, flat, and uninteresting. Most vitalists are also theists. They are looking for gaps left between scientifically understandable events, hoping to have these gaps filled with God's interventions. The origin of life is one such gap. There are certainly innumerable others. They become, however, inexorably fewer and fewer as science progresses. Therefore, a supernatural God becomes less and less necessary. I am convinced that religion in the Age of Science cannot be sustained by the assumption of miraculous events abrogating the order of Nature. It should, rather, see acts of God in events the natural causes of which it fully understands. Then and only then nature as a whole, organic and inorganic, human and prehuman,

macrocosmic and microcosmic, becomes a field for God's eternal
and continuing, immanent and transcendent, natural and providential activity.

To those who ascribe the origin of life to God's special intervention it can be pointed out that this makes God simply another
physico-chemical agent, but one perversely concealed from observation because it acts so very rarely. Suppose that it was God who
some two billion years ago compounded the four kinds of nucleotides into the first DNA strand capable of self-replication. Was God
then an enzyme of a peculiarly complex structure which no chemist
can synthesize? But what if some bright chemist in the future
synthesizes this enzyme, or at least figures out what chemical structure it must have had? And this predicament is not peculiar to the
problem of the origin of life—it occurs every time one chooses to
invoke God's intervention into natural processes. Does it make
sense, for example, to think that organic evolution is guided by
God's intervention? This would presumably mean that God induces from time to time some unusual mutations of a special kind,
or that He directs the chromosomes to form particular gene combinations. There is certainly no compelling reason to make such
assumptions. The origin of life and the emergence of human self-
awareness were the crucial events of the evolutionary deveyplopment
of the cosmos. They certainly did take place here, on earth; we do
not know whether similar events happened elsewhere in the universe. Be that as it may, creation is a process, not an act; it was
not completed some five thousand or any other number of years
ago; it continues now, before our eyes, and is accessible to scientific
study.

TRACY M. SONNEBORN

Implications of the New Genetics for Biology and Man (1963) †

During the last decade, genetics has been spectacularly fruitful,
developing with ever-increasing speed and ever more challenging
prospects. Each month, almost each day, advances are announced.
Questions are being posed—and answered—that seemed, until recently, beyond the scope of foreseeable experimental analysis. And
no end is in sight!

Intoxicated with their successes, many practitioners of the new

† *American Institute of Biological Sciences Bulletin*, XIII (April 1963),
pp. 22–26. Tracy M. Sonneborn (b. 1905) is Distinguished Professor of
Zoology at Indiana University.

revolutionary genetics exhibit unbounded assurance that no secret of living nature and no obstacle to controlling it are beyond their powers to expose or overcome. This leads some foremost biologists to startling views about the future of biology and of man. Biology, they contend, is undergoing a fundamental change which will soon make much of it—especially much of its methodology—obsolete. Further, they warn that the new genetics may provide the means of remaking man—and soon. They urge that no time be lost, for mankind may well be confronted with powers potentially greater than those of atomic energy; that they may be used for good or ill; that it behooves man to become aware of this new knowledge and its power and to hasten to acquire the wisdom needed to use it well, lest we are once again caught unprepared.

To close our eyes and ears to these visions and warnings might well be perilous. On the other hand, if there is another side to the story, we should hear it, too, before making judgments. For some time I have wanted to think through these problems. In arriving at my judgments which, I confess, turned out to be different from what I at first supposed they would be, I have had to take into account both the past and the present, both the classical and the new genetics: their essential natures, findings, implications, limitations, and prospects. I shall try to lead you over the path I have traversed.

Let us first look upon the past, upon classical genetics. Its great findings are now common knowledge. They include the concept of the gene as the indivisible unit, the atom, of heredity; the rules of genic transmission from parents to offspring; the organization of genes into linked groups; the linear architecture of each array of linked genes; the numerically assignable position or locus of each gene in the linear group; and the assignment of each linkage group to a chromosome.

These discoveries have two major implications for biology in general. First, by their complete generality—their universal applicability to all organisms from microbes to man—they conferred upon the whole of biology a magnificent unity matched by very few other generalizations. Second, and perhaps even more important for the issues that now divide biologists, they reveal the power and the fruitfulness of purely biological methods.* * *

* * * Simple, purely biological methods, without the essential aid of chemistry or physics, of biochemistry or biophysics, led to the exposure of some of the deepest secrets of living nature. Modern researchers and students often forget—or never knew—that they could not have guessed what questions to ask or what problems to attack at the biochemical and molecular levels, had not a sound and profound theoretical structure first been established by the elegant and powerful methods of pure biology. * * *

Nevertheless, knowledge of human genetics along classical lines does provide the means by which we could decisively affect the hereditary make-up of mankind many generations hence. * * *

The revolutionary and triumphant new genetics is often characterized as being distinctively biochemical and molecular and as differing thereby from classical genetics. In my opinion, this characterization is wrong for two reasons. First, this aspect of the new genetics is not in itself new. To some extent, genetics has been biochemical and molecular almost from the start. Nearly 60 years ago, Garrod pointed out the existence of gene-controlled biochemical traits in man. There has never been a time since then when comparable studies and theoretical constructs were not current. Second, some of the most spectacular triumphs of the new genetics —such as Benzer's revelations of the number and array of subunits in a gene—were achieved by classical genetic methodology.

The main point of difference is more fundamental. The essential nature of the new genetics is its deliberate refusal to concern itself with secondary complications and its hard concentration on a small number of the simplest possible systems, with the conscious objective of attacking the most basic problems and of putting everything else aside until they are solved. * * *

This remarkable concentration on one or a few relatively simple favorable materials constitutes the essential nature of the new genetics. It has paid off handsomely. Among its most important accomplishments are the discoveries of the chemical composition and structure of the genetic material of the chromosome and gene and the molecular events in genic replication, mutation, and action. * * *

The most basic questions of genetics and biology thus have been answered within a decade. In the process of doing so, there has been a marriage between biochemistry and genetics from which has issued a new generation of investigators well acquainted with both parental disciplines. They work in the faith that every problem of biology will sooner or later be solved in molecular terms by them or their descendants. They expect to proceed by the same concentrated and simplified mass effort that has already been shown to be so rewarding, going first to the next more complicated set of problems and then on and on to successively greater levels of complexity until they achieve complete molecularization of the whole of biology.

This is, I believe, what most of the brave, new molecular geneticists would tell you is the chief significance of the new genetics for the whole of biology. They say: "The old biology is sterile, dying, or dead. It is a waste of time. Only the molecular approach is fruitful. And the only sensible way is to proceed from the bottom up, tackling successively increasing orders of complexity as each underlying level has been reduced to molecular terms."

These molecular biologists have shown what they can do. Their views are not lightly to be dismissed. Yet, there are other biologists who take a diametrically opposed view. All molecular genetics and molecular biology is held by them to be a gross and fallacious oversimplification. They maintain that the essence of biology is complexity and that the simple schemes of molecular genetics are not biology at all but chemistry. Biologists of this sort maintain that *true* biology—like taxonomy, ecology, and evolution—will never be reduced to molecular terms. They point out that the idea of *Reductionism*—i.e., reduction of biology to physics and chemistry—is more than a century old and, in principle, no closer to achievement than it ever was.

What does our review imply about this conflict of views? The great success story of the new genetics in its approach from the bottom up, after a long prior history of failure by classical genetics to penetrate fully to the molecular level by starting at the other end, certainly forces us at least to say: "Well, let's see how much further this new approach can go." Twenty years ago, the enormous successes of today would have been judged impossible or tremendously remote; the problems of the gene, mutation, and gene action were then considered to be typically biological and complex. The successful solution of these problems in molecular terms came and came fast. Further progression upwards may also come.

Nevertheless, admitting all this is not the same as prophesying the sterility, doom, and demise of the old-fashioned, purely biological approach to biological problems. Our review of classical genetics showed how that biological approach yielded the knowledge without which the new molecular geneticists would have been unable to see the problems or to know how to start attacking them. In the light of these facts, there can be no doubt that *both* the biological and biochemical approaches have been indispensable.

The question before us is whether the same interrelation will repeat itself. I believe it will. The biological approach at each level will have the task of finding the most suitable materials, of discovering the phenomena to be attacked at the molecular level, and of inferring by indirection—in so far as it can—the nature of the mechanisms and the problems. Then, and only then, can the molecular biologists proceed to a deeper attack.

Actually, the biologist has already, to some extent, done this for the next domains to be attacked at the molecular level—the domains of the regulation of gene activity and of cellular differentiation. And much still remains to do in this domain. For example, in the past few years my coworkers and I have attempted to obtain a decisive answer, by purely biological methods, to a molecular question: whether certain hereditary, morphological differentiations of the cell are solely determined by properties of the products of gene action. These biological methods have permitted us to demonstrate that another factor is involved: namely, the *pre-existing* structure of the cell. Where the products of genic activity go and how they become integrated into the structural and functional features of the cell are decisively determined by the pre-existing structure and organization of the cell, particularly of its outer thin layer or cortex. These visible cortical differentiations and their experimentally produced variations are perpetuated in the absence of genic or nuclear differences in kind or in activity. To use the current cliché, a new dimension—pre-existing cell structure—has been added to the picture of cellular heredity and differentiation, one which would not be discovered by working exclusively with *in vitro* systems or with a molecular approach.

History thus appears to be repeating itself and probably will go on doing so. In the long run, it seems that the progress of biology would be cut off and the stream of advances of molecular biology would dry up unless we assure the lively continuation of both the biological and the biochemical approaches. * * *

So much for the implications of the new genetics for the future of biology. What are its implications for the future of man? As I hinted at the start, there is a division of judgment on this topic among biologists. Some believe that recent advances have brought us close to the day when man could use his knowledge of molecular genetics to remake man's hereditary constitution according to his wishes. Others do not agree that such knowledge is just around the corner or is likely to come as far ahead as we can now foresee. * * *

* * * Present knowledge of bacteria and viruses still gives no secure basis for concluding that directive control of their genetic constitutions is in prospect. And, if it were possible to conclude otherwise, we would still be left with the important fact that the sorts of controls now imaginable are inefficient. This means that of a large number of treated cells, few would respond to the control methods. This is no problem to viral and bacterial geneticists, who routinely use highly selective methods and ruthlessly throw away the million failures and keep the one success. But such wastage is out of the question with man. I, therefore, cannot yet visualize for the foreseeable future any important directive control of the hereditary constitution of man based upon carryover of our new knowledge of viruses and bacteria. * * *

What then about the second approach, that the new genetics of man himself poses the possibility of soon controlling his hereditary constitution? Let's see what we now know or are in process of discovering. As I mentioned at the start, the cells of man are now being handled and studied like bacteria, or more correctly, like Protozoa. Moreover, some of the main, new biochemical, genetic knowledge is on substances found in man, such as hemoglobin; and human chromosome study is proving highly feasible, popular, and fruitful. Human genetics is indeed at the focus of attention as never before.

Among the new discoveries are evidences that the DNA-RNA-protein story of microorganisms is essentially the same in man. This gives further foundation to the expectation of being able to extrapolate in principle from microbes to man. However, there are thus far, to my knowledge, no successes in extending transduction to mammals and very few claims for success in extending transformation. * * *

In fact, the genetic analysis of mammalian cell cultures has, as yet, hardly gotten off the ground. There are several reasons. First, unlike bacteria and viruses, human cells are diploid—they contain two genes of each kind. So, dominance and recessiveness complicate the picture. Consider just the first step: selecting mutations. If mutation occurs once in a hundred thousand genes—a reasonably high rate—then both genes of a pair would mutate in the same cell only once in 10 billion cells. And, since nearly all simple gene mutations from normal are recessive, usually both genes of the kind would have to mutate in order to detect the mutant cell. That would be pushing it a bit even for viruses or bacteria; for the enormously larger human cells, it is on the verge of impracticality. Although there have been a number of claims for finding and selecting genic mutations in human cell culture, alternative explanations of the observations are difficult to exclude at present. For, what seems to be a genic mutation may, in reality, be a very different phenomenon, discovered many years ago in our work on Protozoa and subsequently found by others in bacteria. A given set of genes may not always act the same. Certain external conditions activate or repress the functioning of certain genes, and, once done, cells with the active and inactive genes may reproduce side by side, true to their different phenotypes. In the absence of breeding analysis, such hereditary changes behave like gene mutations; but breeding analysis shows them to be merely persistent differences in gene *action*. Nearly all, if not all, of the persistent hereditary changes reported for human cell cultures could be of this kind. They cannot be accepted as gene mutations—especially if they occur with high frequencies—so long as this alternative is not excluded.

Finally, there is the associated fact that in cell culture most of the known genic actions that specifically characterized the phenotype in the intact body cease. These genes just don't act in the isolated cell cultures. Only a few, such as those determining galactosemia and acatalasia, have proved workable in cell culture.

There is, thus, nothing yet in our knowledge of the new human genetics that provides a basis for seeing an early control of human hereditary constitutions. Not only are the methods devised for bacteria and viruses and the results obtained with them far from providing such a basis, but we are almost completely ignorant of the genetics of human cell cultures, and we find in these cultures several nasty, special, and as yet unsolved difficulties. There is still a long way to go. Tomorrow or 10 or 20 years hence there may be breakthroughs, but they cannot at present be foreseen.

I, therefore, feel forced to conclude that there is no immediate prospect of radical new powers of controlling human heredity and evolution. This may well come eventually, but it does not seem to be just around the corner. There are still vast areas of ignorance to be converted into precise knowledge before such human engineering will be possible. For the present and for the foreseeable future, sound application of genetic knowledge to the improvement of man —if it is to be done at all—will necessarily have to be restricted to the slower and less spectacular, but sound, methods based upon classical genetics.

A. S. ROMER

Darwin and the Fossil Record (1958) †

* * *

Fossils and the "Origin"

Of exceeding interest to the palæontologist is Darwin's treatment of the fossil record in the *Origin*, and we shall discuss this at some length. Today, in an elementary book devoted to the topic of evolution, a substantial section is usually devoted to proofs of the reality of the evolutionary process—proofs derived from the consideration of the fossil record, particularly that of the vertebrates. Not so in Darwin's classic. The treatment of the subject is essentially a negative one. For the most part his argument is not that palæontology supports the evolutionary theory but, rather, that it need not be regarded as opposing it.

To understand this approach it is necessary to recall the history of palæontological work. Today, evolution and palæontology march

† From Chapter 6 of S. A. Barnett, ed., *A Century of Darwin* (Cambridge, Mass., 1958). A. S. Romer (b. 1894) is emeritus professor of zoology at Harvard University.

hand in hand. Palæontology supports evolution; the truth of evolution is a basic assumption underlying all palæontological work. This, however, was not the case in earlier days.

Little work of importance was done in palæontology until the late 1700's, at which time both vertebrate and invertebrate fields began to assume importance. Intensive work in the invertebrate area arose from recognition of the fact, first clearly seen by William Smith, an English civil engineer and amateur geologist of the period, that a given set of beds tended to contain the same species of shells over vast and widely separated areas. Accurate determination of fossils could thus be of great practical use to the stratigrapher; as a result, invertebrate palæontology tended to develop not as an independent science, but as a handmaiden to the geologist—a working tool for the stratigrapher looking for oil or ores or coal. The fossil shells were rarely thought of as the remains of once-living organisms, but merely as convenient markers for the identification of successive formations, and would have been as useful had they been identifiable mineral inclusions or distinctive assortments of nuts and bolts. This point of view, incidentally, is not confined to the early days, but has continued to a considerable degree to the present— much to the disadvantage of the science. Recent years, however, have seen a considerable increase of interest in the biological aspects of their subject among invertebrate palæontologists.

With this background the invertebrate workers of Darwin's day not merely lacked interest in evolutionary ideas, but were inclined to view them with suspicion as detrimental to their work. For clear-cut stratigraphic work the species in a given formation should be stable entities, clearly distinguishable from those in the strata above and below. The idea of gradual change and of transitional forms was abhorrent.

More striking is the fact that most vertebrate palæontologists, now ardent believers in evolution, were in early days to be found in the opposition camp. Cuvier, justly venerated as the true founder of the science of vertebrate palæontology as well as of comparative anatomy, first clearly pointed out that the true road to the proper interpretation of fossil forms is to consider them as once living organisms and to interpret them in the light of our knowledge of still existing forms. But Cuvier was flatly opposed to any evolutionary interpretations, as shown by his violent opposition to Lamarck and Geoffroy St. Hilaire. For him the fossil record was one of clearly distinct periods of life, separated from one another by major geological revolutions, with the creation of an entirely new fauna after each catastrophe. Man, for Cuvier, was a geologically recent form, not part of the true fossil record; mammals are not to be found earlier than the "Tertiary" beds; the older "Secondary" rocks contain a quite distinct type of life, in which mammals were absent and reptiles were prominent; still further back were "Primary" rocks in which land animals were absent and older creations of invertebrates and fishes constituted the faunas. This non-evolutionary attitude of Cuvier was maintained, despite increasing knowledge, by most of the more prominent palæontologists of Darwin's day, notably Richard Owen, greatest of nineteenth-century English workers in vertebrate palæontology and anatomy, and Louis Agassiz, the first major student of fossil fishes.

With this to contend with, it is apparent why Darwin was thrown on the defensive in his treatment of the fossil record. He could not call on the palæontologists for support; the most he could do was to attempt appeasement, to show that it was at least possible to interpret the geological story in evolutionary terms, and that there were no insuperable objections.

Palæontological data are cited in a variety of places in the *Origin*, as, for example, in the chapters on geographical distribution. His general argument on the fossil story is, however, concentrated in chapters X and XI, "On the interpretation of the geological record" and "On the geological succession of organic beings". Of these two chapters the first is by far the more important. In it he discusses some of the arguments which might be—and were— brought against an evolutionary interpretation of the geological record, and answers most of them in a convincing fashion. The major objections, certain of which continued (although with diminishing force) to be brought against evolutionary beliefs long after the time of the first publication of Darwin's work, may be stated as follows:

First, if the evolutionary theory were true, we should expect to find many fossil species or varieties of intermediate nature— "missing links", that is, in modern popular terminology. This, said the opponents, is not the case.

Second, the extent of geological time is too brief for major evolutionary changes to have occurred.

Third, known fossils from the various periods and formations do not show a well-arranged phyletic pattern, as would be expected on evolutionary grounds, but a scattered, seemingly random, distribution of forms.

Fourth, if the history of life has been a gradual evolutionary progression, we would expect to find gradual changes between forms in the lower and upper parts of geological formations. This is not the case.

Fifth, whole groups of species appear suddenly, in an abrupt manner, in certain formations, contrary to what one would expect if evolutionary development had occurred.

Sixth, a related and more serious problem is the sudden appearance, without known antecedents, in the lowest known fossiliferous strata—the Cambrian—of a whole series of members of a variety of major animal types.

Darwin discusses these objections *seriatim* and is able, for the most part, to give convincing answers.

First, there is the absence of intermediate varieties. In an earlier section of the *Origin* Darwin had given quite satisfactory reasons for the rarity, at the present day, of types intermediate between living forms, and the same situation should hold for any given geological formation. Further, if one is looking in the fossil record for "intermediates", what should they be intermediate between? For example, says Darwin, should we look—today or in any older formation—for an intermediate between a horse and a tapir—a form which "splits the difference" between the two? It is, he says, highly improbable that either one of these has descended from the other. Rather, the two have presumably descended from a remote common ancestor; and we would be unable to recognize this remote ancestor —the true "intermediate"—without a knowledge of the lines of descent of horse and tapir from it.

Darwin could not have hit upon a happier illustration. Already in Darwin's day his erstwhile friend and later opponent, Owen, had described the skull of a small browsing animal from the English Eocene which he named *Hyracotherium* because of the resemblance of its teeth to those of the living conies, or hyraxes, of Africa and Syria. Considerably later, with the discovery in the American West of linking types, it became apparent that *Hyracotherium* was an ancestral equid, and in recent decades it has been demonstrated that *Hyracotherium* and the widely-known *Eohippus*, the "dawn horse", are generically identical. But *Hyracotherium* is not merely a direct horse ancestor; it is at least very close to the ancestor of the tapirs and other odd-toed ungulates. It is thus one of the "intermediates", the supposed absence of which was argued as an objection to evolution; but just as Darwin pointed out would be the case, its nature was not recognized until further connecting links were discovered.

Second is the question whether geological time is insufficient. Our Christian ancestors were in general habituated to a chronology of the type promulgated by the learned Bishop Ussher, according to whose computations from the somewhat confused and conflicting data of the Old Testament the world is rather under 6,000 years of age. Even those of a more liberal cast of mind, who with that other, older, and more famous bishop, St. Augustine of Hippo, were willing to grant that the seven days of creation need not be taken literally, still tended to regard the lapse of time since the earth began as a relatively short period. Darwin presents the concept of the long span of geological time most persuasively. He had himself seen, in South America, geological processes proceeding in fast tempo. For his purposes here, however, he paints for his readers, instead, the picture of the English landscape and the immense amount of time necessary to effect the changes which have brought it from the conditions surely present in times past to those of the present. Strata are worn away but slowly. Even where the sea eats away a cliff on its shores, the degradation is generally slow; and, further, only a fraction of the shore-line is suffering in this fashion at any one time. But the action of the sea is only a minor process in the erosion of the land; much more important—and much slower, in general— are the breaking down of rocks by chemical and biological means and their transportation downhill and to the sea by rills and streams. Immense thicknesses of rock, it seems clear, have been completely worn away, over, surely, a vast period of time by this type of action. And equally impressive is a consideration of the sediments laid down in ancient seas and lowlands as a result of such degradation. Darwin cites an estimate of the thickness of sediments laid down since the beginning of the Palæozoic in one area or another of England as having a total thickness of over 72,000 feet—nearly fourteen miles of accumulation. A vast amount of time was surely needed to form these deposits; and since there are many gaps in the English sequence, further major additions must be added to give the total time since the fossil sequence became established in Cambrian days at the opening of the Palæozoic Era.

How long in terms of years have the various eras and periods covered? In his first edition Darwin estimates that the minimum time needed during the Tertiary to remove once overlying sediments —about 1,100 feet of them—from the Weald of Southern England must have been over 300,000,000 years, and that since the process of denudation was presumably intermittent, the actual elapsed time would have been far longer.

Darwin's figure here, it would seem, is very far above any acceptable to his contemporaries. In later editions of the book this calculation is omitted, and the only estimate of any sort for which figures in years are given is one cited from Croll to the effect that a thousand feet of sediments might be removed in about six million years. On this basis (although Darwin does not say this) the estimate for the Wealden degradation during the Tertiary might have been rather less than seven million years. This is on an order of magnitude which was more palatable, it would seem, to the geologists of the last century, and Darwin even offers a further sop to the hesitant conservative by saying of the Croll estimate that "some considerations lead to the suspicion that it may be too large", and that it might be halved or quartered.

Up to the early decades of the present century figures on the order of magnitude of the Croll calculations were those generally accepted; the time from the beginning of the Tertiary was frequently cited as about five million years, and from the beginning of the Palæozoic as about fifty millions. Such figures were based on estimates of the minimum time needed to lay down the known series of sediments, and it was agreed that in all probability some increase, although perhaps a modest one, might be needed to account for gaps in the sedimentary record. During the past quarter-century there has been a sharp upward revision of such figures due to a study of radioactive rocks present at a number of levels in the geological column and their degree of disintegration. The new figures have increased over the old by a factor of ten; the Tertiary is now commonly cited as having a duration of fifty to seventy million years, and the time elapsed since the beginning of the Palæozoic calculated to be five hundred million years or so. This is indeed a sharp jump, but even so falls far short of Darwin's original estimates. But whatever estimate one then accepted, or accepts now —the "short count", current figures, or Darwin's original long one —the span of geological time is certainly adequate for a very considerable amount of evolutionary change to have occurred.

Third, there is the assertion that known fossils do not form a phyletic pattern, as would be expected on an evolutionary hypothesis. At the time of the first publication of the *Origin* and, to a somewhat lesser degree, at the time of publication of later editions, this objection was one of seemingly great validity. The known record of past life was a very "spotty" one; to some extent the later formations in the sedimentary sequence showed the presence of "higher" forms of life, but this could just as well be explained on the basis of separate successive creations with "improved" forms being brought forth *de novo* in the later ones. Beyond this single general trend, there was no evidence of any phylogenetic "family tree". Even among the vertebrates, in which hard internal skeletal parts favour preservation as fossils, there was little indication at the time of any evolutionary arrangement of the animals then known. A fair assortment of fossil fishes had been described; but as Agassiz observed (even as late as in a posthumous paper in the '70s) forms of a presumed advanced type had been found in older strata than those containing any fishes of a supposedly more primitive nature—the reverse of an evolutionary sequence. Intermediates between fishes and land vertebrates were practically unknown. Plesiosaurs and ichthyosaurs, the only reptiles then adequately described, were isolated if spectacular types which shed no light on the possible evolution of reptiles. Nothing was known to connect either birds or mammals with lower groups.

Why this seeming contradiction between the known fossil record and that expected on the evolutionary hypothesis? Darwin attributes this to the poorness of palæontological collections in his day. Only a small portion of the earth had then been geologically explored, and no part explored thoroughly. Of the fossil species then described, very many were known and named from single and often broken or fragmentary specimens, rendering interpretation difficult. In addition to the inadequacies of our knowledge of fossils due to insufficient exploration, are those due to the imperfections of the geological record. Unless deposited in an area where sediments are being laid down, shells and bones decay quickly. It seems clear that at any past time, as is true today, sedimentation was taking place over only a very small portion of the earth's surface, leaving great gaps in the preserved record of life in any given area. Further, the fact that an animal was fossilized is no guarantee that it would be preserved down to modern times, for degradation of necessity goes hand in hand with sedimentation. Our knowledge of terrestrial formations in the earlier geological periods, Darwin points out, is hence extremely meagre. There are vast areas of the earth (the Canadian Shield, for example) in which no unaltered sediments at all are present today: "primordial" rocks form the surface; in consequence, we shall never obtain a record of any former inhabitant of the region. And—most discouraging fact of all—many of the connecting links between major animal phyla, according to the evolutionary hypothesis, would have been soft-bodied animals; and while Darwin's statement that "no organism wholly soft can be preserved as a fossil" is too extreme, identifiable remains of such forms are extremely rare.

Many of the reasons advanced by Darwin for the inadequacies of fossil remains—those concerned with the imperfections of the geological record—are as valid today as they were a century ago, and it is certain that we shall never be able to find and describe more than a very small fraction of the former inhabitants of the earth. But wider exploration and further exploitation of fossiliferous deposits already known have added vastly, over the intervening decades, to the number and variety of known forms. And it is of major importance that, although no "family tree", even that of the vertebrates, is fully documented, nearly every new discovery fits into once hypothetical phylogenies. There are still, among the vertebrates, areas in which there are major lacunæ—for example, the evolution of the earliest fishes, the origin of the modern amphibian orders and of certain reptile groups—but in many portions of the "tree" the phyletic pattern is becoming increasingly clear. Beyond the middle Devonian the general pattern of fish evolution is demonstrable. The gap between fishes and land vertebrates is gradually closing through such discoveries as that of the late Devonian amphibians of Greenland. Connections between early amphibians and the reptiles are so well documented that in the case of such an animal as *Seymouria* of the early Texas Permian, it is difficult to reach a decision concerning the class to which it should be assigned. A few years after the publication of Darwin's first edition came discovery of *Archæopteryx*, filling a half-way position on the branch of the vertebrate tree leading from reptiles to advanced birds. Discoveries, first in South Africa, later in other regions, have closed much of the gap between reptiles and mammals. (Much of the early material of mammal-like reptiles from South Africa was described by Owen. In a monograph on these forms published in the 1870s he discusses the morphological similarity of these reptiles to mammals without committing himself to biological evolution; this is a masterpiece of eloquent evasion.) It is still necessary today to call attention to the obvious imperfections of the palæontological record, but the need is much less than in the last century and the approach to the fossil story can be a positive rather than a negative one.

The fourth objection was the absence of intermediate varieties in any single formation. If, as assumed by Darwin, evolution had occurred in a slow but constant fashion, we should find, in any formation, a gradual transition between species present at the time of its commencement and the differing varieties or species presumably descended from them and present at its close. This did not appear in Darwin's day to be generally the case, although much invertebrate fossil material was known from a number of formations of marine origin. Darwin admitted the strength of this argument, but gave a number of suggestions which lessen its force. It is difficult to determine how long a term of years is necessary to effect an evolutionary change from one species to a derived one; possibly many formations did not persist for a sufficient length of time for noticeable evolutionary changes to have taken place in them. Again, to witness evolutionary progress within a formation, it is necessary that the populations present at its close be descended from those found there at its initiation; but it is not at all unlikely that there may have been considerable immigration from other areas, accompanied by extinction or emigration of old residents. Darwin believed (and many geneticists today are in agreement with this conclusion) that the development of a new variety or species which may eventually supplant the parent type generally takes place in a rather restricted area, and perhaps in a relatively short time; the chance of finding a formation in which the supplanting type developed is small.

The situation may be further obscured by a factor of quite another sort—a man-made one. There is no golden rule by which a palæontologist may distinguish varieties and species. Species are founded by some workers on the basis of excessively slight differences, by others only when obvious major differences are visible; whether or not specific changes are thought to have occurred within the limits of a formation may depend as much on the working methods of the palæontologist describing the material as on the nature of the fossils themselves.

Now, as in Darwin's day, there is still often no evidence of progressive evolutionary change within a formation. But over the course of the intervening century a number of detailed studies of formations have been made, ranging from the Devonian to the Tertiary, in which careful work has revealed series of finely graded changes in forms from successive levels. Some of this work was done during Darwin's lifetime. As a result, instead of being forced to state, as he did in 1859, that "geological research . . . has done scarcely anything in breaking down the distinction between species, by connecting them together by numerous, fine, intermediate varieties", he could in later editions say instead: "It has been asserted over and over again, by writers who believe in the immutability of species, that geology yields no linking forms. This assertion . . . is certainly erroneous."

The fifth difficulty is the sudden appearance of whole groups of allied species. "The abrupt manner in which whole groups of species suddenly appear in certain formations, has been urged by several palæontologists—for instance, by Aggassiz, Pictet, and Sedgwick—as a fatal objection to the belief in the transmutation of species." Were this phenomenon a reality, says Darwin, the objection would be a serious one. But the objection is based merely on negative evidence, which experience often shows to be worthless. He points out that, for example, Agassiz had maintained that teleost fishes first appeared—and appeared then in abundance—only in the Upper Cretaceous, but that he had later discovered teleosts, in lesser variety, in the earlier Jurassic and even Triassic. Since Darwin's day many further supposed examples of the sudden appearance, full-fledged, of animal and plant groups have been found to be equally illusory. The weakness of negative evidence can be further illustrated today by cases of supposed extinction. The most familiar example is the recent discovery in the sea off the Comoro Islands of a living cœlacanth fish, *Latimeria*, belonging to a group of which no fossils are known in beds later than the Cretaceous; this group had therefore been confidently stated to have been extinct for seventy million years. Still more striking is the very recent discovery by the *Galathea* expedition, off the west coast of Mexico, of an archaic segmented mollusc type long supposed (because of negative evidence) to have been extinct since the Ordovician—a period of perhaps 400 million years.

Finally, we have the sudden appearance of groups of allied species in the lowest known fossiliferous strata. This situation is a special case of the last, and one admitted by Darwin to be a serious difficulty for his theory. From the beginning of the Cambrian up through the rest of the geological sequence we have an abundant representation of animal life at every stage; even in Lower Cambrian formations marine invertebrates are numerous and varied. Below this, there are vast thicknesses of sediments in which the progenitors of the Cambrian forms would be expected. But we do not find them; these older beds are almost barren of evidence of life, and the general picture is reasonably consistent with the idea of a special creation at the beginning of Cambrian times.

"To the question why we do not find rich fossiliferous deposits belonging to these assumed earliest periods prior to the Cambrian system," says Darwin, "I can give no satisfactory answer." Nor can we give today any fully satisfactory answer, although some signs of pre-Cambrian life unknown to Darwin have been discovered, and although a number of palæontologists have devoted much thought to the question. Darwin advanced a hypothesis that in pre-Cambrian days the world "may have presented a different aspect, and that the older continents, formed of formations older than any known to us, exist now only as remnants in a metamorphosed condition, or lie still buried under the ocean". This hypothesis is none too convincing. Later workers have made various additional suggestions toward a solution of the problem. But even today we have not completely solved this greatest of remaining palæontological puzzles. * * *

WILFRID LE GROS CLARK

The Study of Man's Descent (1958) †

* * * In the introduction to the first edition of *The Descent of Man*, Darwin specifically stated that he had for many years been collecting notes on this subject, not with the intention of publishing them, "but rather with the determination not to publish", as he thought that by so doing he would only add to the prejudices against his general conclusions regarding the evolutionary process. It seems that he was led to change his mind as the result of several

† From Chapter 8 of S. A. Barnett, ed., *A Century of Darwin* (Cambridge, Mass., 1958). Wilfrid Le Gros Clark (b. 1895), distinguished anatomist and paleontologist, was formerly president of the British Association.

circumstances; these were: first, the publication of Haeckel's works on morphology and evolution; secondly, the comparative anatomical studies of T. H. Huxley; and thirdly, the evidence adduced by archæologists and geologists that man had a far greater antiquity than Archbishop Ussher's estimate of 4004 B.C. (his assumed date of the creation). Today we recognize in Haeckel's works many crudities and much far-reaching speculation, while Darwin's statement that Huxley "has conclusively shown that in every single visible character, man differs less from the higher apes than these do from the lower members of the same order of Primates" certainly requires some qualification. But the great quantity of anatomical data which these distinguished biologists had accumulated provided so much detailed evidence of man's relationship to the other Primates that Darwin felt he could rely on the strongest and most influential support when he came to focus attention on man as a product of evolution. * * *

Since Darwin's day, of course, the evidence relating to human evolution has grown to vast proportions. Comparative anatomical studies have multiplied almost indefinitely the structural details which ally man far more closely to the anthropoid ape family (Pongidæ) than to any other group of Primates, and the fossil evidence now carries back the zoological family to which man belongs (Hominidæ) not only a few thousands of years, but something near a million. No longer do we have to depend for conclusions regarding man's relationships on indirect comparisons of modern man with modern apes, for we now have available many fossil remains of their extinct precursors showing, in this or that feature, an intermediate character which appears to blur, or even to blot out completely, the contrasts seen in their successors today. We are not concerned in this essay with a detailed consideration of all the accumulated evidence. Rather shall we review briefly the nature of a few of the items of the purely morphological evidence adduced by Darwin for his thesis of man's descent, and discuss the validity of his arguments in the light of knowledge which has accrued over the last eighty years or more. * * *

Distinctive Characters of Man

The opposition to Darwin's thesis of the evolutionary origin of man naturally led his critics to search for anatomical characters in which the human body could be said to be "unique", thus providing arguments for removing man in any system of classification as far as possible from other mammals (especially the apes). In some cases, indeed, these arguments were pushed to an extreme of absurdity, which today we are apt to find rather astonishing. The celebrated wrangle over the comparatively unimportant feature of the brain called the "hippocampus minor" is a relevant example. This feature, present in the human brain, was said to be absent in the ape's brain, and its absence was assumed to be of great significance. Huxley's easy demonstration that, in fact, it is present also in the chimpanzee's brain was hailed as a great victory for the evolutionists—an interesting commentary on the emotional atmosphere of such discussions at the time, and amusingly satirized by Charles Kingsley in *The Water Babies*.

In the second edition of *The Descent of Man* there is included an appendix by Huxley on the comparative anatomy of the human and ape brain, in which he shows that the two are constructed on the same total morphological pattern and that the difference between the two groups is not greater than those which occur between the large anthropoid apes and the quadrupedal monkeys. These conclusions have certainly stood the test of time, for today it can be safely asserted that, in its gross and also its microscopical structure, the brain of a man has not been found to show any qualitative differences from that of a gorilla: the differences appear to be quantitative only. As we now know, even the quantitative difference is a good deal smaller than was commonly supposed. Thus in gorillas the largest cranial capacity so far recorded is 685 c.c., while the lowest capacity recorded for a human being of "normal" intelligence is less than 900 c.c. The difference between these extremes is therefore no more than about 200 c.c., and the difference in the volume of actual brain tissue is presumably even less, since the cranial capacity includes also the space occupied by the membranes of the brain, the cerebrospinal fluid and blood vessels. It is exceedingly difficult to suppose that such a small addition of brain substance in man could, by itself, account for his vastly superior mental powers, and it seems necessary to assume that the latter depend on some complexity of functional organization which is not reflected in structural organization so far as it has been possible to define this anatomically.

If this is so, obviously it is very hazardous to draw any inferences regarding the mental processes of extinct hominids simply by a consideration of their cranial capacity. Darwin remarks that "no one supposes that the intellect . . . of any two men can be accurately gauged by the cubic content of their skulls", and repeated statistical studies have since shown that this statement still holds true for *Homo sapiens*. * * *

Embryology

The great pioneer of comparative embryology, K. E. von Baer, had published his classic studies on the development of animals as early as 1828, and in *On the Origin of Species* Darwin referred to his observations on the astonishing similarity of the embryos of vertebrates which, when fully developed, are very different indeed. This is expressed in von Baer's formal proposition that during its development an animal departs more and more from the structural organization of other animals. In *The Descent of Man* Darwin referred to the observation that the proposition applies as much to the human embryo as it does to other mammals. Thus a human embryo of about three weeks is very similar to the embryo of a dog or monkey at a corresponding stage of development. The early development of the human embryo also involves a series of transformations during which one type of organization characteristic of lower vertebrates is exchanged for a more advanced type of organization. Such transformations appear sometimes to be almost dramatic, and they seem to have no rational explanation unless we suppose they have reference to evolutionary history. The suggestion that in a modified form ontogeny (embryonic development of the individual) repeats phylogeny (evolution of the type) has been termed "recapitulation". But it must be emphasized that this does not mean that the successive stages in the embryonic development of an individual in any way represent the *mature* forms of successive stages of its evolutionary history. It means only that, broadly speaking, in his ontogeny the developmental stages through which man passes reproduce the *embryonic* form of certain ancestral types. Thus, it is well known that in the early human embryo a foundation of gill arches is laid down in the neck region, similar to that which, in fishes, finally leads to the establishment of functional gills. But, as in other mammalian embryos, the elements of these gill arches become completely reorganized so as to form, not the gills for which it seems certain they were originally intended in past evolutionary history, but quite different structures such as the framework of the larynx and its muscles, the facial musculature, and so forth. This transformation of the gill arches involves a most remarkable rearrangement of skeletal elements, muscles, nerves and blood vessels, and it seems impossible to explain such a profound modification unless it is supposed that the embryonic basis of the gill arches has been inherited from a remote ancestor of fish-like form. Many other examples of similar kinds of change or replacement could be enumerated, such as the withdrawal of a projecting tail into the floor of the pelvis to form the coccyx, the sequence of events which leads to the partitioning of the heart, and the reorganization of certain groups of nerve cells in the brain. It may be argued that each stage in these transformations provides the essential preliminary for the next stage and that, such being the case, it is not logically necessary to postulate an evolutionary basis. It is true, for example, that certain elements of the gill arch system appear to function as "organizers" during development, determining and controlling the subsequent development of adjacent regions. But the most satisfying explanation of this phenomenon is still to be found in evolutionary terms, i.e. that, since during the course of phylogeny each stage in the sequence of evolutionary development is determined by the preceding stage and itself determines the subsequent stage, the same mechanism still persists as a requisite basis for the embryological development of the individual. Nor are the early stages in a sequence of transformations to be explained by reference to the immediate requirements of the embryo at that time. Darwin makes a point of this when he remarks (in the *Origin of Species*):

> We cannot, for instance, suppose that in the embryos of the vertebrates the peculiar loop-like course of the arteries near the branchial slits are related to similar conditions in the young mammal which is nourished in the womb of its mother, in the egg of the bird which is hatched in a nest, and in the spawn of a frog under water,

and again

> There is no obvious reason why, for instance, the wing of a bat, or the fin of a porpoise, should not have been sketched out with all the parts in proper proportion, as soon as any structure became visible in the embryo.

Perhaps a more striking example is provided by the development of the definitive arterial pattern of the limbs in the human embryo; in the latter the arteries are at first disposed in a pattern similar to that of lower vertebrates, but this subsequently becomes rearranged in a new pattern which is presumed to be functionally more suitable for limbs of human structure. But there is no evidence that the embryonic pattern is determined by the mechanical requirements of the circulation at that particular stage of development, and it happens from time to time that the pattern persists as an abnormality into adult life without any concomitant abnormality of muscles and other associated structures. The fact that in the development of the human embryo the various tissues and organs often do not proceed directly to the patterns of organization adapted to the functional requirements of the mature individual, but follow (as it were) a circuitous route which leads them through stages of development characteristic of lower forms of life, and which may involve the "scrapping" of temporary structures so that the latter can be replaced by structures of a very different pattern —all this provides formidable evidence for the thesis of the evolutionary origin of man. Much more evidence from the study of comparative embryology since Darwin's time has added support to his affirmation that "community in embryonic structure reveals community in descent". * * *

Rudiments

Darwin naturally laid great stress on the importance of vestigial structures as evidence for evolution, for, as he pointed out, the common explanations offered by the older naturalists that such vestiges had been created "for the sake of symmetry", or in order to "complete the scheme of nature," were really no explanations at all. In fact, such rudiments are entirely meaningless unless they are recognized to be relics of some organ or structure which was fully developed in a past ancestry. It may be (and has been) argued that, because it is not possible to ascribe a specific function to a rudimentary structure, it does not necessarily follow that it is completely functionless; indeed, the fact that a relic persists at all has been assumed to imply that it must have some selective value, however slight, or that its development must be in some way correlated with that of another feature which does have a selective advantage. But, in either case, the rudimentary or vestigial nature of a structure which no longer serves its original function is not in question.

Vestigial structures are so well known in the human body that there is no need to enumerate them here. Darwin himself drew attention to certain muscles (like those of the external ear) which are normally present in man and which clearly represent remnants

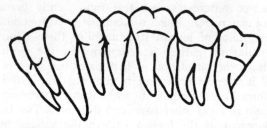

40.—A diagram illustrating the longer and more robust root of the canine tooth in our own species, compared with the roots of neighbouring teeth; this reflects the evolutionary history of the canine, since in our ancestors this was a much larger tooth.

of a more extensive and functional musculature in lower mammals, and also to such features as the nodular remnants of the tail in the coccyx, the lanugo covering of hair in the human fœtus, and so forth. These examples could be multiplied to make an impressive list. No one today doubts that they are properly regarded as evidence of a past ancestry: we can only be impressed with the remarkable conservatism of morphological elements whereby they persist in modified and apparently functionless form for, it may be, thousands or even millions of years after they have ceased to serve what was originally their main function. * * *

Postlude

We have seen that the morphological evidence advanced by Darwin in *The Descent of Man*, supported by the vast accumulation of knowledge since the publication of this book in 1871, provides a valid basis for the assumption of a natural relationship between man and other Primates, and that this relationship is particularly close with the anthropoid apes. It is also the case that predictions implied in the conclusions drawn from this evidence have been verified in a most remarkable way by the discovery of the actual remains of extinct hominids representing, or closely approximating to, some of the intermediate phases which had been postulated (particularly in the series *Australopithecus—Pithecanthropus—Homo*). In this essay, only the most cursory reference has been made to this palæontological evidence, though it is of quite crucial importance. But we have been concerned rather with the nature of the evidence on which Darwin himself relied, and he could only refer to "the absence of fossil remains seeming to connect man with his ape-like progenitors". Opinions today still vary on the *degree* of the relationship between the Hominidæ and the Pongidæ, and also on the approximate date in geological time when the two families became separated in the course of their evolutionary divergence. These differences of opinion are in some cases due to an evident misunderstanding of fundamental evolutionary principles, but they are partly due to the fact that the fossil record of hominid and pongid evolution, though year by year it becomes more ample, is still too incomplete. It is well to recognize this fact, for until the documentary evidence of the fossil record has been accumulated in greater quantity, it is not to be expected that there will be general agreement on the details of hominid evolution. Yet, even though there are still conspicuous gaps in the record, it is important, indeed essential, to offer the most probable interpretation of such evidence as is available. Such an interpretation may not be the only possible one, but only by the construction and deliberate formulation of hypotheses is the opportunity given of putting them to the test by further observation and discovery.

At the beginning of this essay we observed that Darwin must

have required considerable moral courage to publish *The Descent of Man* at the time he did. Almost ninety years afterwards, though from a somewhat different aspect, the study of human origins still requires a certain degree of moral courage—courage to advance interpretations some of which are quite likely to be proved erroneous by the accession of further evidence, and courage freely to acknowledge errors of interpretation when these come to be exposed

PART IV

Darwin's Influence on Theological and Philosophical Thought

And God said, Let us make man in our image, after our likeness: and let them have dominion over the fish of the sea, and
over the fowl of the air, and over the cattle, and over all the earth,
and over every creeping thing that creepeth upon the earth.

So God created man in his own image, in the image of God
created he him; male and female created he them.

—Genesis I, 26–27

Darwin threw down a challenge to the old rigidities, and his doctrine of evolution made everything a matter of degree, obliterating
the absoluteness of white-and-black, right-and-wrong. * * * It
seemed that everything, instead of being so or not so, as in the
logic books, was only more so or less so. And in this mush of
compromise all the old splendid certainties dissolved.

—Bertrand Russell, 1949

Intellectual progress usually occurs through sheer abandonment
of questions. * * * We do not solve them; we get over them.

—John Dewey, 1909

Today we know that we are not entirely the masters of our fate,
certainly not the captains of our souls, but neither are we innocent and passive bystanders. Many factors in nature interact to
cause and direct our evolution, but our understanding of evolution has itself become one of the factors.

—Conway Zirkle, 1958

Introduction

MORSE PECKHAM

Darwinism and Darwinisticism (1959) †

Everyone knows that the impact of the *Origin of Species* was immense and that it has had a profound influence upon the literature of England and of the West ever since that late November day in 1859. But when one tries to tally up the writers affected and to list the books and make an inventory of passages showing Darwinian influence and Darwinian assumptions in novels, poems, and essays, a fog seems to arise in one's mind, through which are discernible twinkles of what may or may not be bits of genuine Darwinism.

Indeed, here is the first problem. What is Darwinism? Or at least, what is the Darwinism found in the *Origin*, for that alone is the Darwinism with which I am here concerned. The name of Darwin has magnetized to itself a thousand bits and pieces of ideas which are certainly not to be found in the book itself, and some of which Darwin, had he been able to understand them, would certainly have repudiated. For example, it has been said a million times and will be said a million times more that for Darwin competition between species and members of species is the only mechanism of directive and progressive evolution. Thus he has been adulated for having revealed that in capitalism and its related and derived values was to be found the natural system of social and economic organization which assures the progress of man; and execrated for having led men to disbelieve the seemingly obvious truth that man's proper, natural, and normal mode of behavior is cooperation, harmony, and love. Again, it is always being rediscovered that in natural selection there are cooperative as well as competitive mechanisms at work. Alternatively, it is frequently stated that Darwin failed to perceive the element of cooperation because he was himself the product of a laissez-faire society: Marxists are particularly grand and imposing on the subject.

In this one example are to be found the typical confusions observable in many discussions of Darwinism carried on by non-scientists and even by scientists when they are not scientizing.

† *Victorian Studies*, III (1959), 3–40.

First, there is by the very use of the terms an introduction of values into a descriptive construct; or the misinterpretation of descriptive terms by ascribing to the words a moral significance and to the author a moral intention. The roots of this error are to be found in the ancient exhortation that Nature should be our basic model for Right Behavior. Not surprisingly it is constantly assumed that the *Origin* rests on moral assumptions: that a value statement may be verified in the same way that an empirical or predictive statement is verified is an attitude that only a small fraction of human beings have yet outgrown, and that in only a small part of their behavior. The difficulty arose because Darwin did not have the word "ecology." He was in fact an ecological thinker, and in ecology words like "competition" and "cooperation" are too inexact, too value-weighted, too metaphorical, and too anthropomorphic to be used at all.

Second, scientific statements are continuously subjected not only to moral interpretations but also, and more subtly, to metaphysical interpretations. Hence, the unconscious ascription to the *Origin* of a metaphysic. Darwin is said to have discovered the Law of Evolution, according to which the universe is characterized by a steady growth in richness and complexity and excellence. Now Spencer formulated a Law of Evolution, but there is no such law in the *Origin*. In fact, in the fourth edition there is a brief but profoundly important passage at the beginning of Chapter Four in which Darwin specifically disclaims any knowledge of and any statements about Laws of Nature, which he clearly labels mental conveniences, or constructs. He is a scientist, not a moralist and not a metaphysician, and he knows it. Unfortunately, most humanists then and now have little notion of what a scientist is and does. They are interested in metaphysics and morals, and when a science seems to have a metaphysical and moral implication, or when a scientist assumes another role and makes metaphysical and moral statements, then only do they evince an interest and subject themselves to what they think are scientific influences.

It will be apparent from what I have said so far that the problem of the impact of the *Origin* upon the culture of the last one hundred years is a complex one. It involves, above all, the question, what is the difference between "Darwinian" and "Darwinistic" (that is, between those propositions and implied assumptions which may be properly ascribed to a source in the *Origin,* and those propositions and derived assumptions which are not properly so ascribed). I shall attempt to clear the way for future studies of the *Origin* and literature, using "literature" generally and loosely.

The question to be answered, then, is, what was the Darwinian and Darwinistic impact of the *Origin* upon Western culture? But even this is much too vague. How is the culture of the past available and what do we mean by "culture"? It is said that historical investigation is concerned with the events of the past. But of course past events are not observable, and so we are left with the question as to what in fact the historian observes. The problem may be somewhat crudely, though I think not naïvely, tackled by observing what the historian actually does. He is engaged in the manipulation (with all that the word implies) of documents and artifacts. These are his data, not past events. The empirical referent of his "History," that is, his construct which purports to refer to the events of the past, or "history," is his own operations with those documents and artifacts which he assumes to have had an existence prior to the moment he began examining them. His History is a linguistic construct, characterized by what he hopes is at least an intuitive consistence, designed to justify his work. Since internal inconsistencies are always discoverable in his construct, and since his collection of documents and artifacts is never complete, nor its degree of completeness ever known, History, like any science, is characterized by instability. (Like physics, it is always being reconstructed.) Thus the process of historiography is the consequence of a continuous interaction, manipulated by historians, between construct and data.

One particular problem remains: what is the model of the historian's construct? Such models certainly are now, and perhaps always will be, intuitive. At least I know of no mathematical or logical model for a historical narrative. But though models for battles, parliamentary debates, and assassinations are probably pretty reliable, those for cultural history are probably not. In cultural history we are involved with matters of extraordinary difficulty and subtlety. Whereas the assassination of Lincoln was eminently observable at one time (there were witnesses; a reasonably consistent construct may be created of his murder and death), a priest may lose his religious belief and nobody be the wiser (Pater thought he could have a successful career as an Anglican clergyman with no religious belief whatsoever, and he was probably right). The difficulty lies in the fact that the locus of cultural history is covert behavior. When we realize that there is no such entity as "culture" but only human beings doing something, or behaving covertly, and that such behavior may or may not leave traces in documents and artifacts, the general problem of the inaccessibility of the past is twice compounded; for cultural behavior is not necessarily observable even when it is going on in a human being who is right before the observer's eyes or even at times, when it is going on inside the observer. When we talk about "culture" in the old-fashioned way, or "high-level culture" in the modern way, we are referring somewhat vaguely to two kinds of data, first, recorded verbal behavior, sufficiently complex and highly-valued to be called literature, philosophy, or science, and recorded sign-systems of a parallel complexity which we call the visual and auditory arts, and, second, unrecorded and covert linguistic and aesthetic semiotic behavior. On the model of our own behavior, insofar as we can and have trained ourselves to observe it, aided by various admittedly inadequate personality or psychological theories, we try to write cultural history. Now, we know very little about cultural transmission and cultural innovation at any level, let alone complex high-level transmission and innovation. It is not surprising that when we undertake to write cultural history we finish feeling a bit baffled and inadequate.

At least, however, we can now see our basic problem somewhat more precisely. On the one hand there are the Darwinian and Darwinistic documents, on the other, documents and artifacts which show Darwinian and Darwinistic influences, and in between, casually, we hope or assume for constructive purposes, connecting the two categories, a doubly inaccessible process of cultural history of which we wish to make a construct. But, alas! each part of the problem consists of a set of variables. For instance, a single Darwinistic sentence might have had a profoundly revolutionary impact upon the covert behavior of an individual, with the consequence that he wrote a single poem profoundly different from anything he had written before. (Did this happen in the case of Swinburne's "Hertha"?) Or a reading of the entire *Origin* might have had a slight impact which resulted, for the moment, at least, in a fairly brief document. (Was this the case of Kingsley's famous letter which Darwin was so happy to quote in later editions in order to avert the theological lightning?) Or a very thorough reading of Darwinian and Darwinistic material might so confirm the already existing attitudes of an individual that he perceived nothing innovative. (Was this the case with Browning, whose post-*Origin* work indicates that he not only read Darwin but read him with such extreme care that frequent re-reading is implied?) * * *

In 1859 a metaphysic of goal-directed organic growth was dominant in the higher levels of Western culture. Canon Raven has pointed out that the agitation produced by Darwin can not be understood without reference to the *Essays and Reviews,* which appeared only a few months after, or to Colenso's work, which appeared in 1862. The academic difficulties of Max Müller and of Benjamin Jowett are equally inseparable from the total situation. Today it is somewhat difficult to understand why all of these books and events should have been interconnected in the covert culture of the day. But a reading of *Essays and Reviews* shows the deep penetration of metaphysical evolutionism into the minds of its authors. That was their offense: they were addressing a world of a lower cultural level which still lived by a static metaphysic. I have referred to Newman's speculation about the possibility of applying his ideas of development to the biological world, and he has been praised for his profundity in thus anticipating and understanding Darwin. But the praise has come from individuals who did not themselves understand Darwin, for in fact the *Origin* was an embarrassment to the metaphysical evolutionists.

The evolutionists were already used to having their metaphysic apparently confirmed by scientific developments. Lyell and Herschel and Nichol seemed to support them, and they took the *Vestiges of Creation* to be a scientific work. Consequently, there is no indication that the *Origin* disturbed Tennyson, for example, or Newman, or George Eliot. "Hertha," again, is a good example. Written in the latter half of the 1860's, it appears to be a perfect instance of the impact of Darwin. Yet it can just as well be thought of as a humanistic and anti-religious interpretation of the concluding speech of *Paracelsus*. It could have been written had the *Origin* never been published. That it was written as a consequence of the *Origin* seems highly probable, but as a consequence of a misunderstanding of the *Origin*. For the biologic world that Darwin revealed, if you do not read him with the assumptions of metaphysical evolutionism as instruments for understanding the book, is a world totally lacking in the organized and teleological process characteristic of evolutionary metaphysics. New species come into existence by a process which can only be described as accidental. If a species has a range of variations among its individuals such that when the environment of the species changes, hitherto non-adaptive variations are selected as means of survival, a new species will in the course of time emerge, provided that the change in environment is not so great as to cause the total extinction of the species and provided that the population of the species is sufficient to maintain itself during the period of the development of the new species out of the old. No organism, Darwin said, is as perfectly adapted as it might be. That is, it includes within its population instincts and organs which are not instrumental to its environmental adaptation, although in its ancestry at some time or other such organs and instincts were adaptive. (To be sure, Darwin was not very certain about this and proposed other reasons, particularly morphology, for non-adaptive organs.) Further, there are numerous instances not only of extinction but of total or partial regression, or regression at some stage of an organism's life-cycle. Nor is there any reason to believe that natural selection operates in a morally or metaphysically progressive fashion. Indeed, from the *Origin* it is very easy to conclude that the more complex an organism the less its chances to survive. It is impossible to find in the *Origin* a basis in the biological world for any kind of orthogenesis or goal-directed process. Consequently it has been misread or simply not read at all, though discussed by all varieties of metaphysical evolutionists from Newman to Gerald Heard and current Catholic theologians.

Thus the grand thesis of metaphysical evolutionism—from simple to complex means from good to better, infinitely or finitely, as your metaphysical taste determines—not only received no support from the *Origin* but, if the book were properly understood and if the individual involved felt that a metaphysic should and could have scientific support, was positively demolished. Hence the curious spectacle, to be found so often, of orthodox fundamentalist Christians and anti-Christian or quasi-Christian metaphysical evolutionists ranged side by side in opposition to Darwin. And hence the equally curious spectacle of other metaphysical and Christian evolutionists swallowing the book without even a catch in the throat.

But the book presented an even deeper problem of which very few were apparently aware, although it was implied in the early editions and was clearly spelled out in the fourth. In the middle of the century most scientists characteristically conceived their task as discovering the laws of nature. Newton's Law of Gravity was held to be unrepealable, and for a hundred and fifty years Law had been gradually replacing Providence at the higher cultural levels. To be sure there were exceptions. Newman preferred to believe that the weather was controlled by angels, and he has several very pretty passages on the subject. But for the most part advanced thinkers felt like Nichol, who in 1839 hailed the advent of the comprehension of Nature through discoverable Laws and rejoiced at the disappearance of the capricious ways of Providence. He felt it added greatly to the dignity of God to think that He governed the world through Laws and not through unpredictable wilfullness. It is hard not to see the influence here of political liberalism. Or perhaps it is the other way around. Certainly the two seem to be connected, for the idea of the subjection of the Crown to the rational laws of elected representatives, the progress away from capricious tyranny, is remarkably like Nichol's conception. An Enlightenment idea, it was a basic ingredient of most Romantic metaphysics and fundamental to evolutionary metaphysics. The metaphor unconsciously used seems too transparent to be missed, and yet it was missed. The notion was that just as it is possible to study the political behavior of a people and hence deduce its laws, so it is possible to study the behavior of nature and arrive at the laws which govern it. It was a notion particularly appealing to Englishmen, who, because of the peculiar and highly admired nature of the English Constitution, were in part governed by written laws and in part by laws not spelled out in a written constitution in the style of the infidel Bentham and the misguided Americans but implicit in the political structure of the nation. In Nature the laws are there, they are immanent in the natural world, and it is the will of God that in our enlightened progress we should discover them. Constant reference to such economic ideas as the Law of Supply and Demand continually reinforced such concepts; and it is typical that Ruskin's aesthetic and socio-economic writings are filled with Laws of This and Laws of That.

The *Origin* did not fit into this conception at all. Not only was an apparently accidental world revealed, but even if one insisted upon discovering an order in the apparent chaos of the biological world, the incredible intricacy of ecological relations was such that Darwin himself felt that a full comprehension was beyond him or any human being. When biology can be studied mathematically —and biologists are making progress in that direction, particularly in genetics—perhaps a few people will comprehend the biologic world, but it is too much for mathematically unorganized descriptive language.

Thus at the time there were frequent complaints that Darwin did not really reveal the Laws of Nature. The culture was still penetrated by the Baconian notion that the Laws of Nature are not only immanent, because they had been put there by God, but also were few in number and essentially simple, because God had so designed them that the human mind might understand them. The culture accepted the Baconian notion that if one assembled all the data pertinent to a line of inquiry, the true relations between the separate bits of data and the laws that governed them would reveal themselves. Again we find, metaphysically, the desire to penetrate into a world of pure order.

But Darwin's notion of scientific law was empiricistic and extraordinarily modern. He implies it in his superb discussion of the term "species" and its related words. He demonstrates that to the term there is no corresponding reality or entity in the biological world. It is essential to his argument that species should not be regarded as fixed, and he disproves their fixity not so much by aligning data as by analyzing the term to demonstrate that the attempt to find distinct species in nature is necessarily fruitless, since the term is only of convenience in creating hypotheses, or, as we should say today, constructs. Further, he spelled his notion out in additions made to the opening of Chapter Four in the fourth edition. To him a scientific law was a mental convenience. The mind organized the data into meaningful structures; it did not discover the principles of organization immanent within the data. To a certain extent his public was at least intuitively aware of this position and responded to it negatively. Nevertheless for the most part the Legalists of Nature simply derived from the *Origin* further proof of their arguments. It is yet another example of how Darwinism was converted into Darwinisticism and is comparable and related to the similar absorption of the *Origin* and natural selection into metaphysical evolutionism.

There are further variables in this part of the basic question, such as adaptation, economy, and morality. Huxley, in his Romanes lecture, and Mill, earlier, in *Three Essays on Religion*, concluded that the ancient "Follow nature" as a basis for morality was in error, and that if a genuine morality were to be developed it must be on a purely human basis, indifferent to and even opposed to the workings of evolution. The economists, as we have seen, followed a different course, and with the aid of Spencer found in the *Origin* a basis for their own morality. And in the matter of adaptation, the final basis of British empirical theology, the notion of perfect adaptation of organism to environment was washed away by the *Origin*. Consequently, as might have been expected, Darwinisticism in the field of moralized psychology has used Darwin as a basis for attempting to make perfect adaptation of the individual personality to its social environment into the criterion of psychological health. There can be located still other variables, but I have attempted to go into at least two of the problems involved in the impact of the *Origin* in order to show the profound difference between Darwinism and Darwinisticism. Darwinism is a scientific theory about the origin of biological species from pre-existent species, the mechanism of that process being an extraordinarily complex ecology which can be observed only in fairly small and artificially isolated instances. It reveals a world not of accident precisely but rather one in which "accident" becomes a meaningless problem. Darwinisticism can be an evolutionary metaphysic about the nature of reality and the universe. It can be a metaphysical and simplistic notion of natural law. It can be an economic theory, or a moral theory, or an aesthetic theory, or a psychological theory. It can be anything which claims to have support from the *Origin*, or conversely anything which claims to have really understood what Darwin inadequately and partially presented. Once one is aware of the distinction, much which is ascribed to Darwin and much which appears to be Darwinian in the cultural documents of the past one hundred years turns out not to be Darwinian at all but Darwinistic. Is it true that what Darwin said had very little impact, but that what people thought he said, that is, what they already believed and believed to have been confirmed by Darwin, had an enormous impact? * * *

Philosophy

JOHN DEWEY

The Influence of Darwin on Philosophy (1909) †

I

That the publication of the "Origin of Species" marked an epoch in the development of the natural sciences is well known to the layman. That the combination of the very words origin and species embodied an intellectual revolt and introduced a new intellectual temper is easily overlooked by the expert. The conceptions that had reigned in the philosophy of nature and knowledge for two thousand years, the conceptions that had become the familiar furniture of the mind, rested on the assumption of the superiority of the fixed and final; they rested upon treating change and origin as signs of defect and unreality. In laying hands upon the sacred ark of absolute permanency, in treating the forms that had been regarded as types of fixity and perfection as originating and passing away, the "Origin of Species" introduced a mode of thinking that in the end was bound to transform the logic of knowledge, and hence the treatment of morals, politics, and religion.

No wonder, then, that the publication of Darwin's book, a half century ago, precipitated a crisis. The true nature of the controversy is easily concealed from us, however, by the theological clamor that attended it. The vivid and popular features of the anti-Darwinian row tended to leave the impression that the issue was between science on one side and theology on the other. Such was not the case—the issue lay primarily within science itself, as Darwin himself early recognized. The theological outcry he discounted from the start, hardly noticing it save as it bore upon the "feelings of his female relatives." But for two decades before final publication he contemplated the possibility of being put down by his scientific peers as a fool or as crazy; and he set, as the measure of

† Originally a lecture given at Columbia University in 1909 by the noted American philosopher John Dewey (1859–1952), this essay was subsequently included in Dewey's *The Influence of Darwin on Philosophy and Other Essays in Contemporary Thought* (New York, 1910).

his success, the degree in which he should affect three men of science: Lyell in geology, Hooker in botany, and Huxley in zoology.

Religious considerations lent fervor to the controversy, but they did not provoke it. Intellectually, religious emotions are not creative but conservative. They attach themselves readily to the current view of the world and consecrate it. They steep and dye intellectual fabrics in the seething vat of emotions; they do not form their warp and woof. There is not, I think, an instance of any large idea about the world being independently generated by religion. Although the ideas that rose up like armed men against Darwinism owed their intensity to religious associations, their origin and meaning are to be sought in science and philosophy, not in religion.

II

Few words in our language foreshorten intellectual history as much as does the word species. The Greeks, in initiating the intellectual life of Europe, were impressed by characteristic traits of the life of plants and animals; so impressed indeed that they made these traits the key to defining nature and to explaining mind and society. And truly, life is so wonderful that a seemingly successful reading of its mystery might well lead men to believe that the key to the secrets of heaven and earth was in their hands. The Greek rendering of this mystery, the Greek formulation of the aim and standard of knowledge, was in the course of time embodied in the word species, and it controlled philosophy for two thousand years. To understand the intellectual face-about expressed in the phrase "Origin of Species," we must, then, understand the long dominant idea against which it is a protest.

Consider how men were impressed by the facts of life. Their eyes fell upon certain things slight in bulk, and frail in structure. To every appearance, these perceived things were inert and passive. Suddenly, under certain circumstances, these things—henceforth known as seeds or eggs or germs—begin to change, to change rapidly in size, form, and qualities. Rapid and extensive changes occur, however, in many things—as when wood is touched by fire. But the changes in the living thing are orderly; they are cumulative; they tend constantly in one direction; they do not, like other changes, destroy or consume, or pass fruitless into wandering flux; they realize and fulfil. Each successive stage, no matter how unlike its predecessor, preserves its net effect and also prepares the way for a fuller activity on the part of its successor. In living beings, changes do not happen as they seem to happen elsewhere, any which way; the earlier changes are regulated in view of later results.

This progressive organization does not cease till there is achieved a true final term, a τελὸς, a completed, perfected end. This final form exercises in turn a plenitude of functions, not the least noteworthy of which is production of germs like those from which it took its own origin, germs capable of the same cycle of self-fulfilling activity.

But the whole miraculous tale is not yet told. The same drama is enacted to the same destiny in countless myriads of individuals so sundered in time, so severed in space, that they have no opportunity for mutual consultation and no means of interaction. As an old writer quaintly said, "things of the same kind go through the same formalities"—celebrate, as it were, the same ceremonial rites.

This formal activity which operates throughout a series of changes and holds them to a single course; which subordinates their aimless flux to its own perfect manifestation; which, leaping the boundaries of space and time, keeps individuals distant in space and remote in time to a uniform type of structure and function: this principle seemed to give insight into the very nature of reality itself. To it Aristotle gave the name, εἶδος. This term the scholastics translated as *species*.

The force of this term was deepened by its application to everything in the universe that observes order in flux and manifests constancy through change. From the casual drift of daily weather, through the uneven recurrence of seasons and unequal return of seed time and harvest, up to the majestic sweep of the heavens—the image of eternity in time—and from this to the unchanging pure and contemplative intelligence beyond nature lies one unbroken fulfillment of ends. Nature as a whole is a progressive realization of purpose strictly comparable to the realization of purpose in any single plant or animal.

The conception of εἶδος, species, a fixed form and final cause, was the central principle of knowledge as well as of nature. Upon it rested the logic of science. Change as change is mere flux and lapse; it insults intelligence. Genuinely to know is to grasp a permanent end that realizes itself through changes, holding them thereby within the metes and bounds of fixed truth. Completely to know is to relate all special forms to their one single end and good: pure contemplative intelligence. Since, however, the scene of nature which directly confronts us is in change, nature as directly and practically experienced does not satisfy the conditions of knowledge. Human experience is in flux, and hence the instrumentalities of sense-perception and of inference based upon observation are condemned in advance. Science is compelled to aim at realities lying behind and beyond the processes of nature, and to carry on its search for these realities by means of rational forms transcending ordinary modes of perception and inference.

There are, indeed, but two alternative courses. We must either find the appropriate objects and organs of knowledge in the mutual interactions of changing things; or else, to escape the infection of change, we *must* seek them in some transcendent and supernal region. The human mind, deliberately as it were, exhausted the logic of the changeless, the final, and the transcendent, before it essayed adventure on the pathless wastes of generation and transformation. We dispose all too easily of the efforts of the schoolmen to interpret nature and mind in terms of real essences, hidden forms, and occult faculties, forgetful of the seriousness and dignity of the ideas that lay behind. We dispose of them by laughing at the famous gentleman who accounted for the fact that opium put people to sleep on the ground it had a dormitive faculty. But the doctrine, held in our own day, that knowledge of the plant that yields the poppy consists in referring the peculiarities of an individual to a type, to a universal form, a doctrine so firmly established that any other method of knowing was conceived to be unphilosophical and unscientific, is a survival of precisely the same logic. This identity of conception in the scholastic and anti-Darwinian theory may well suggest greater sympathy for what has become unfamiliar as well as greater humility regarding the further unfamiliarities that history has in store.

Darwin was not, of course, the first to question the classic philosophy of nature and of knowledge. The beginnings of the revolution are in the physical science of the sixteenth and seventeenth centuries. When Galileo said: "It is my opinion that the earth is very noble and admirable by reason of so many and so different alterations and generations which are incessantly made therein," he expressed the changed temper that was coming over the world; the transfer of interest from the permanent to the changing. When Descartes said: "The nature of physical things is much more easily conceived when they are beheld coming gradually into existence, than when they are only considered as produced at once in a finished and perfect state," the modern world became self-conscious of the logic that was henceforth to control it, the logic of which Darwin's "Origin of Species" is the latest scientific achievement. Without the methods of Copernicus, Kepler, Galileo, and their successors in astronomy, physics, and chemistry, Darwin would have been helpless in the organic sciences. But prior to Darwin the impact of the new scientific method upon life, mind, and politics, had been arrested, because between these ideal or moral interests and the inorganic world intervened the kingdom of plants and animals. The gates of the garden of life were barred to the new ideas; and only through this garden was there access to mind and politics.

The influence of Darwin upon philosophy resides in his having conquered the phenomena of life for the principle of transition, and thereby freed the new logic for application to mind and morals and life. When he said of species what Galileo had said of the earth, *e pur se muove,* he emancipated, once for all, genetic and experimental ideas as an organon of asking questions and looking for explanations.

III

The exact bearings upon philosophy of the new logical outlook are, of course, as yet, uncertain and inchoate. We live in the twilight of intellectual transition. One must add the rashness of the prophet to the stubbornness of the partizan to venture a systematic exposition of the influence upon philosophy of the Darwinian method. At best, we can but inquire as to its general bearing—the effect upon mental temper and complexion, upon that body of half-conscious, half-instinctive intellectual aversions and preferences which determine, after all, our more deliberate intellectual enterprises. In this vague inquiry there happens to exist as a kind of touchstone a problem of long historic currency that has also been much discussed in Darwinian literature. I refer to the old problem of design *versus* chance, mind *versus* matter, as the causal explanation, first or final, of things.

As we have already seen, the classic notion of species carried with it the idea of purpose. In all living forms, a specific type is present directing the earlier stages of growth to the realization of its own perfection. Since this purposive regulative principle is not visible to the senses, it follows that it must be an ideal or rational force. Since, however, the perfect form is gradually approximated through the sensible changes, it also follows that in and through a sensible realm a rational ideal force is working out its own ultimate manifestation. These inferences were extended to nature: (*a*) She does nothing in vain; but all for an ulterior purpose. (*b*) Within natural sensible events there is therefore contained a spiritual causal force, which as spiritual escapes perception, but is apprehended by an enlightened reason. (*c*) The manifestation of this principle brings about a subordination of matter and sense to its own realization, and this ultimate fulfillment is the goal of nature and of man. The design argument thus operated in two directions. Purposefulness accounted for the intelligibility of nature and the possibility of science, while the absolute or cosmic character of this purposefulness gave sanction and worth to the moral and religious endeavors of man. Science was underpinned and morals authorized by one and the same principle, and their mutual agreement was eternally guaranteed.

This philosophy remained, in spite of sceptical and polemic out-bursts, the official and the regnant philosophy of Europe for over two thousand years. The expulsion of fixed first and final causes from astronomy, physics, and chemistry had indeed given the doc-trine something of a shock. But, on the other hand, increased acquaintance with the details of plant and animal life operated as a counterbalance and perhaps even strengthened the argument from design. The marvelous adaptations of organisms to their environment, of organs to the organism, of unlike parts of a com-plex organ—like the eye—to the organ itself; the foreshadowing by lower forms of the higher; the preparation in earlier stages of growth for organs that only later had their functioning—these things were increasingly recognized with the progress of botany, zoology, paleontology, and embryology. Together, they added such prestige to the design argument that by the late eighteenth cen-tury it was, as approved by the sciences of organic life, the central point of theistic and idealistic philosophy.

The Darwinian principle of natural selection cut straight under this philosophy. If all organic adaptations are due simply to con-stant variation and the elimination of those variations which are harmful in the struggle for existence that is brought about by excessive reproduction, there is no call for a prior intelligent causal force to plan and preordain them. Hostile critics charged Darwin with materialism and with making chance the cause of the universe.

Some naturalists, like Asa Gray, favored the Darwinian principle and attempted to reconcile it with design. Gray held to what may be called design on the installment plan. If we conceive the "stream of variations" to be itself intended, we may suppose that each successive variation was designed from the first to be selected. In that case, variation, struggle, and selection simply define the mechanism of "secondary causes" through which the "first cause" acts; and the doctrine of design is none the worse off because we know more of its *modus operandi*.

Darwin could not accept this mediating proposal. He admits or rather he asserts that it is "impossible to conceive this immense and wonderful universe including man with his capacity of looking far backwards and far into futurity as the result of blind chance or necessity." [1] But nevertheless he holds that since variations are in useless as well as useful directions, and since the latter are sifted out simply by the stress of the conditions of struggle for existence, the design argument as applied to living beings is unjustifiable; and its lack of support there deprives it of scientific value as ap-plied to nature in general. If the variations of the pigeon, which

1. "Life and Letters," Vol. I., p. 282; cf. 285.

under artificial selection give the pouter pigeon, are not preordained for the sake of the breeder, by what logic do we argue that variations resulting in natural species are pre-designed? [2]

IV

So much for some of the more obvious facts of the discussion of design *versus* chance, as causal principles of nature and of life as a whole. We brought up this discussion, you recall, as a crucial instance. What does our touchstone indicate as to the bearing of Darwinian ideas upon philosophy? In the first place, the new logic outlaws, flanks, dismisses—what you will—one type of problems and substitutes for it another type. Philosophy forswears inquiry after absolute origins and absolute finalities in order to explore specific values and the specific conditions that generate them.

Darwin concluded that the impossibility of assigning the world to chance as a whole and to design in its parts indicated the insolubility of the question. Two radically different reasons, however, may be given as to why a problem is insoluble. One reason is that the problem is too high for intelligence; the other is that the question in its very asking makes assumptions that render the question meaningless. The latter alternative is unerringly pointed to in the celebrated case of design *versus* chance. Once admit that the sole verifiable or fruitful object of knowledge is the particular set of changes that generate the object of study together with the consequences that then flow from it, and no intelligible question can be asked about what, by assumption, lies outside. To assert—as is often asserted—that specific values of particular truth, social bonds and forms of beauty, if they can be shown to be generated by concretely knowable conditions, are meaningless and in vain; to assert that they are justified only when they and their particular causes and effects have all at once been gathered up into some inclusive first cause and some exhaustive final goal, is intellectual atavism. Such argumentation is reversion to the logic that explained the extinction of fire by water through the formal essence of aqueousness and the quenching of thirst by water through the final cause of aqueousness. Whether used in the case of the special event or that of life as a whole, such logic only abstracts some aspect of the existing course of events in order to reduplicate it as a petrified eternal principle by which to explain the very changes of which it is the formalization.

When Henry Sidgwick casually remarked in a letter that as he

2. "Life and Letters," Vol. II, pp. 146, 170, 245; Vol. I., pp. 283–84. See also the closing portion of his "Variations of Animals and Plants under Domestication."

grew older his interest in what or who made the world was altered into interest in what kind of a world it is anyway, his voicing of a common experience of our own day illustrates also the nature of that intellectual transformation effected by the Darwinian logic. Interest shifts from the wholesale essence back of special changes to the question of how special changes serve and defeat concrete purposes; shifts from an intelligence that shaped things once for all to the particular intelligences which things are even now shaping; shifts from an ultimate goal of good to the direct increments of justice and happiness that intelligent administration of existent conditions may beget and that present carelessness or stupidity will destroy or forego.

In the second place, the classic type of logic inevitably set philosophy upon proving that life *must* have certain qualities and values—no matter how experience presents the matter—because of some remote cause and eventual goal. The duty of wholesale justification inevitably accompanies all thinking that makes the meaning of special occurrences depend upon something that once and for all lies behind them. The habit of derogating from present meanings and uses prevents our looking the facts of experience in the face; it prevents serious acknowledgment of the evils they present and serious concern with the goods they promise but do not as yet fulfil. It turns thought to the business of finding a wholesale transcendent remedy for the one and guarantee for the other. One is reminded of the way many moralists and theologians greeted Herbert Spencer's recognition of an unknowable energy from which welled up the phenomenal physical processes without and the conscious operations within. Merely because Spencer labeled his unknowable energy "God," this faded piece of metaphysical goods was greeted as an important and grateful concession to the reality of the spiritual realm. Were it not for the deep hold of the habit of seeking justification for ideal values in the remote and transcendent, surely this reference of them to an unknowable absolute would be despised in comparison with the demonstrations of experience that knowable energies are daily generating about us precious values.

The displacing of this wholesale type of philosophy will doubtless not arrive by sheer logical disproof, but rather by growing recognition of its futility. Were it a thousand times true that opium produces sleep because of its dormitive energy, yet the inducing of sleep in the tired, and the recovery to waking life of the poisoned, would not be thereby one least step forwarded. And were it a thousand times dialectically demonstrated that life as a whole is regulated by a transcendent principle to a final inclusive goal, none the less truth and error, health and disease, good and evil, hope and fear in the concrete, would remain just what and where they now are. To improve our education, to ameliorate our manners, to advance our politics, we must have recourse to specific conditions of generation.

Finally, the new logic introduces responsibility into the intellectual life. To idealize and rationalize the universe at large is after all a confession of inability to master the courses of things that specifically concern us. As long as mankind suffered from this impotency, it naturally shifted a burden of responsibility that it could not carry over to the more competent shoulders of the transcendent cause. But if insight into specific conditions of value and into specific consequences of ideas is possible, philosophy must in time become a method of locating and interpreting the more serious of the conflicts that occur in life, and a method of projecting ways for dealing with them: a method of moral and political diagnosis and prognosis.

The claim to formulate *a priori* the legislative constitution of the universe is by its nature a claim that may lead to elaborate dialectic developments. But it is also one that removes these very conclusions from subjection to experimental test, for, by definition, these results make no differences in the detailed course of events. But a philosophy that humbles its pretensions to the work of projecting hypotheses for the education and conduct of mind, individual and social, is thereby subjected to test by the way in which the ideas it propounds work out in practice. In having modesty forced upon it, philosophy also acquires responsibility.

Doubtless I seem to have violated the implied promise of my earlier remarks and to have turned both prophet and partizan. But in anticipating the direction of the transformations in philosophy to be wrought by the Darwinian genetic and experimental logic, I do not profess to speak for any save those who yield themselves consciously or unconsciously to this logic. No one can fairly deny that at present there are two effects of the Darwinian mode of thinking. On the one hand, there are making many sincere and vital efforts to revise our traditional philosophic conceptions in accordance with its demands. On the other hand, there is as definitely a recrudescence of absolutistic philosophies; an assertion of a type of philosophic knowing distinct from that of the sciences, one which opens to us another kind of reality from that to which the sciences give access; an appeal through experience to something that essentially goes beyond experience. This reaction affects popular creeds and religious movements as well as technical philosophies. The very conquest of the biological sciences by the new ideas has led many to proclaim an explicit and rigid separation of philosophy from science.

Old ideas give way slowly; for they are more than abstract logical forms and categories. They are habits, predispositions, deeply engrained attitudes of aversion and preference. Moreover, the conviction persists—though history shows it to be a hallucination—that all the questions that the human mind has asked are questions that can be answered in terms of the alternatives that the questions themselves present. But in fact intellectual progress usually occurs through sheer abandonment of questions together with both of the alternatives they assume—an abandonment that results from their decreasing vitality and a change of urgent interest. We do not solve them: we get over them. Old questions are solved by disappearing, evaporating, while new questions corresponding to the changed attitude of endeavor and preference take their place. Doubtless the greatest dissolvent in contemporary thought of old questions, the greatest precipitant of new methods, new intentions, new problems, is the one effected by the scientific revolution that found its climax in the "Origin of Species."

THOMAS HENRY HUXLEY

Evolution and Ethics (1893) †

* * *

The propounders of what are called the 'ethics of evolution', when the 'evolution of ethics' would usually better express the object of their speculations, adduce a number of more or less interesting facts and more or less sound arguments, in favour of the origin of the moral sentiments, in the same way as other natural phenomena, by a process of evolution. I have little doubt, for my own part, that they are on the right track; but as the immoral sentiments have no less been evolved, there is, so far, as much natural sanction for the one as the other. The thief and the murderer follow nature just as much as the philanthropist. Cosmic evolution may teach us how the good and the evil tendencies of man may have come about; but, in itself, it is incompetent to furnish any better reason why what we call good is preferable to what we call evil than we had before. Some day, I doubt not, we shall arrive at an understanding of the evolution of the æsthetic faculty; but all the understanding in the world will neither increase nor diminish the force of the intuition that this is beautiful

---

† Thomas Henry Huxley's essay was the Romanes lecture for 1893; it is reprinted in Thomas Henry Huxley and Julian Huxley, *Touchstone for Ethics* (New York and London, 1947), pp. 67–112.

and that is ugly.

There is another fallacy which appears to me to pervade the so-called 'ethics of evolution'. It is the notion that because, on the whole, animals and plants have advanced in perfection of organization by means of the struggle for existence and the consequent 'survival of the fittest'; therefore men in society, men as ethical beings, must look to the same process to help them towards perfection. I suspect that this fallacy has arisen out of the unfortunate ambiguity of the phrase 'survival of the fittest'. 'Fittest' has a connotation of 'best'; and about 'best' there hangs a moral flavour. In cosmic nature, however, what is 'fittest' depends upon the conditions. Long since,[1] I ventured to point out that if our hemisphere were to cool again, the survival of the fittest might bring about, in the vegetable kingdom, a population of more and more stunted and humbler and humbler organisms, until the 'fittest' that survived might be nothing but lichens, diatoms, and such microscopic organisms as those which give red snow its colour; while, if it became hotter, the pleasant valleys of the Thames and Isis might be uninhabitable by any animated beings save those that flourish in a tropical jungle. They, as the fittest, the best adapted to the changed conditions, would survive.

Men in society are undoubtedly subject to the cosmic process. As among other animals, multiplication goes on without cessation, and involves severe competition for the means of support. The struggle for existence tends to eliminate those less fitted to adapt themselves to the circumstances of their existence. The strongest, the most self-assertive, tend to tread down the weaker. But the influence of the cosmic process on the evolution of society is the greater the more rudimentary its civilization. Social progress means a checking of the cosmic process at every step and the substitution for it of another, which may be called the ethical process; the end of which is not the survival of those who may happen to be the fittest, in respect of the whole of the conditions which obtain, but of those who are ethically the best.[2]

1. 'Criticisms on the Origin of Species,' 1864. *Collected Essays,* vol. ii, p. 91. [1894].

2. Of course, strictly speaking, social life, and the ethical process in virtue of which it advances towards perfection, are part and parcel of the general process of evolution, just as the gregarious habit of innumerable plants and animals, which has been of immense advantage to them, is so. A hive of bees is an organic polity, a society in which the part played by each member is determined by organic necessities. Queens, workers, and drones are, so to speak, castes, divided from one another by marked physical barriers. Among birds and mammals, societies are formed, of which the bond in many cases seems to be purely psychological; that is to say, it appears to depend upon the liking of the individuals for one another's company. The tendency of individuals to over self-assertion is kept down by fighting. Even in these rudimentary forms of society, love and fear come into play, and enforce a greater or less renunciation of self-will. To this extent the general cosmic process begins to be checked by a rudimentary ethical process, which is, strictly speaking, part of the former, just as the 'governor' in a steam-engine is part of the mechanism of the engine.

As I have already urged, the practice of that which is ethically best—what we call goodness or virtue—involves a course of conduct which, in all respects, is opposed to that which leads to success in the cosmic struggle for existence. In place of ruthless self-assertion it demands self-restraint; in place of thrusting aside, or treading down, all competitors, it requires that the individual shall not merely respect, but shall help his fellows; its influence is directed, not so much to the survival of the fittest, as to the fitting of as many as possible to survive. It repudiates the gladiatorial theory of existence. It demands that each man who enters into the enjoyment of the advantages of a polity shall be mindful of his debt to those who have laboriously constructed it; and shall take heed that no act of his weakens the fabric in which he has been permitted to live. Laws and moral precepts are directed to the end of curbing the cosmic process and reminding the individual of his duty to the community, to the protection and influence of which he owes, if not existence itself, at least the life of something better than a brutal savage.

It is from neglect of these plain considerations that the fanatical individualism [3] of our time attempts to apply the analogy of cosmic nature to society. Once more we have a misapplication of the stoical injunction to follow nature; the duties of the individual to the State are forgotten, and his tendencies to self-assertion are dignified by the name of rights. It is seriously debated whether the members of a community are justified in using their combined strength to constrain one of their number to contribute his share to the maintenance of it; or even to prevent him from doing his best to destroy it. The struggle for existence, which has done such admirable work in cosmic nature, must, it appears, be equally beneficent in the ethical sphere. Yet if that which I have insisted upon is true; if the cosmic process has no sort of relation to moral ends; if the imitation of it by man is inconsistent with the first principles of ethics; what becomes of this surprising theory?

Let us understand, once for all, that the ethical progress of society depends, not on imitating the cosmic process, still less in running away from it, but in combating it. It may seem an audacious proposal thus to pit the microcosm against the macrocosm and to set man to subdue nature to his higher ends; but I venture to think that the great intellectual difference between the ancient times with which we have been occupied and our day, lies in the solid foundation we have acquired for the hope that such an enterprise may meet with a certain measure of success. * * *

---

3. See 'Government: Anarchy or Regimentation', *Collected Essays*, vol. i. pp. 413–418. It is this form of political philosophy to which I conceive the epithet of 'reasoned savagery' to be strictly applicable. [1894.]

SIR JULIAN HUXLEY

Evolutionary Ethics (1943) †

* * *

I. T. H. Huxley's Antithesis Between Ethics and Evolution

* * * For T. H. Huxley, fifty years ago, there was a fundamental contradiction between the ethical process and the cosmic process. By the former, he meant the universalist ethics of the Victorian enlightenment, bred by nineteenth-century humanitarianism out of traditional Christian ethics, and in him personally tinged by a noble but stern puritanism and an almost fanatical devotion to scientific truth and its pursuit. And the cosmic process he restricted almost entirely to biological evolution and to the selective struggle for existence on which it depends. 'The ethical progress of society'—this was the main conclusion of his Romanes lecture—'consists, not in imitating the cosmic process, still less in running away from it, but in combating it'.

To-day, that contradiction can, I believe, be resolved—on the one hand by extending the concept of evolution both backward into the inorganic and forward into the human domain, and on the other by considering ethics not as a body of fixed principles, but as a product of evolution, and itself evolving. In both cases, the intellectual tool which has given us new insight is that of developmental analysis—the scientific study of change, of becoming, of the production of novelty, whether of life from not-life, of a baby from an ovum and a man from a baby, of ants and swallows and tigers out of ancestral protozoa, of civilized societies out of barbarism and barbarism out of the dim beginnings of social life. * * *

V. Evolutionary Levels and Directions

During the thousand million years of organic evolution, the degree of organization attained by the highest forms of life increased enormously. And with this there increased also the possibilities of control, of independence, of inner harmony and self-regulation, of experience. Compared with what a protozoan or a polyp can show, the complexity of later forms of life, like bee or swallow or antelope, is stupendous, their capacity for self-regulation

† "Evolutionary Ethics" was the Romanes Lecture for 1943; it is reprinted in *Touchstone for Ethics*, pp. 113–166.

almost miraculous, their experience so much richer and more varied as to be different in kind.

And finally there is, in certain types of animals, an increase in consciousness or mind. Whether mind be a sudden emergent or, as biologists prefer to think, a gradual development of some universal property of the world-stuff, mind of the same general nature as ours is clearly present on the higher organizational levels of life, and at least in the birds and mammals we can trace its steady evolution towards greater capacities for feeling, knowing, willing, and understanding.

There is thus one direction within the multifariousness of evolution which we can legitimately call progress. It consists in the capacity to attain a higher degree of organization, but without closing the door to further advance. In the organic phase of evolution, this depends on all-round improvement as opposed to the limited improvement or one-sided specialiation which, it can be demonstrated, automatically leads sooner or later to a dead end, after which no true advance is possible, but only minor variations on an already existent theme. Insects appear to have reached an evolutionary dead end over 30 million years ago; birds a little later; and all the main lines of higher mammals except the primates— carnivores, ungulates, whales, bats, rodents, and so forth—at least no later than the early Pliocene. Most evolutionary lines or trends are specializations which either thus come to a stop or are extinguished; true progress or the unlimited capacity for advance is rare.

However, the details of biological evolution need not concern us overmuch, since during the last half-million years or so a new and more comprehensive type of order of organization has arisen; and on this new level, the world-stuff is once more introduced to altogether new possibilities, and has quite new methods of evolutionary operation at its disposal. Biological or organic evolution has at its upper end been merged into and largely succeeded by conscious or social evolution.

Just as biological evolution was rendered both possible and inevitable when material organization became self-reproducing, so conscious evolution was rendered both possible and inevitable when social organization became self-reproducing. This occurred when the evolving world-stuff, in the form of ancestral man, became capable of true speech and conceptual thought. For just as animal organization, however elaborate, had been transmissible across the generation by the vehicle of the chromosomes and genes, so from then on conscious experience could be transmitted down the stream of time on the vehicle of words and other symbols and representations. And somewhat as sexual fusion made possible the pooling of individual mutations, so reason made possible the pooling of individual experiences. For the first time in evolution, tradition and education became continuous and cumulative processes.

With this, a new type of organization came into being—that of self-reproducing society. So long as man survives as a species (and there is no reason for thinking he will not) there seems no possibility for any other form of life to push up to this new organizational level. Indeed there are grounds for suspecting that biological evolution has come to an end, so far as any sort of major advance is concerned. Thus further large-scale evolution has once again been immensely restricted in extent, being now it would seem confined to the single species man; but at the same time again immensely accelerated in its speed, through the operation of the new mechanisms now available.

In any case, it is only through social evolution that the world-stuff can now realize radically new possibilities. Mechanical interaction and natural selection still operate, but have become of secondary importance. For good or evil, the mechanism of evolution has in the main been transferred onto the social or conscious level. Part of the blind struggle for existence between separate individuals or groups is transposed into conflict in consciousness, either within the individual mind or within the tradition which is the vehicle of pooled social consciousness. The slow methods of variation and heredity are outstripped by the speedier processes of acquiring and transmitting experience. New tools of living originated *ex post facto* as biological adaptations or unconscious adjustments become increasingly unimportant compared with the tools deliberately produced by human design. Physical trial and error can be more and more transposed to the sphere of thought.

And in so far as the mechanism of evolution ceases to be blind and automatic and becomes conscious, ethics can be injected into the evolutionary process. Before man that process was merely amoral. After his emergence onto life's stage it became possible to introduce faith, courage, love of truth, goodness—in a word moral purpose—into evolution. It became possible, but the possibility has been and is too often unrealized. It is the business of an enlightened ethics to help in its realization.

The attainment of the social type of organization opens a new and apparently indefinite range of possibilities to the evolving world-stuff. It can now proceed to some understanding of the cosmos which gave it birth, and of the conflicts which it must endure; it can for the first time consciously both appreciate and create beauty, truth, and other values; it becomes aware of good and evil; it becomes capable of new emotional states like love, reverence, or mystical contemplation and peace; it can inject some of its own purpose into events; finally and most significantly, many of the new experiences that are being made available have inherent value.

Even in the brief space that man has been in existence, there has been considerable evolutionary advance in the degree of social organization, considerable realization of new possibilities previously unavailable to life. What is more, the general rate of advance, in spite of periodic setbacks, has been growing progressively quicker. There is every reason to believe that through the attainment of this new level of conscious and social organization, the evolutionary process has taken on a new and apparently indefinite lease of life.

VI.   *Evolution and general ethical standards*

What guidance does all this give us in our search for independent ethical standards? There are, it seems to me, three rather separate areas in which such guidance may be found—that of nature as a whole, that of human society, and that of the human individual. All three must be considered from the dynamic angle of evolution or development; and when thus considered, all three are interlocked.

In the broadest possible terms evolutionary ethics must be based on a combination of a few main principles: that it is right to realize ever new possibilities in evolution, notably those which are valued for their own sake; that it is right both to respect human individuality and to encourage its fullest development; that it is right to construct a mechanism for further social evolution which shall satisfy these prior conditions as fully, efficiently, and as rapidly as possible.

To translate these arid-sounding generalities into concrete terms and satisfying forms is beyond the scope of a lecture; it is a task for an entire generation. But I must attempt a certain expansion, and some development of their implications.

When we look at evolution as a whole, we find, among the many directions which it has taken, one which is characterized by introducing the evolving world-stuff to progressively higher levels of organization and so to new possibilities of being, action, and experience. This direction has culminated in the attainment of a state where the world-stuff (now moulded into human shape) finds that it experiences some of the new possibilities as having value in or for themselves; and further that among these it assigns higher and lower degrees of value, the higher values being those which are more intrinsically or more permanently satisfying, or involve a greater degree of perfection. * * *

If desirable direction of evolution provides the most comprehensive (though also the least specific) external standard for our ethics, then one very important corollary at once follows: namely that social organization should be planned, not to prevent change, nor merely to permit it, but to encourage it. Thus a static stability is undesirable, and a complete or static certitude of ethical belief itself becomes unethical. * * *

Furthermore, the rate as well as the direction of change is important. Theoretically, there must be an optimum rate of change, above which stability is endangered and the sacrifices of the present are excessive, below which advance is so slow that the welfare of future generations is needlessly impaired. Thus anything which retards advance below this optimum, even if it be moving in the same right direction, is wrong.

Next we have the guidance derived from an understanding of the workings of human societies. In the first place, it is clear on evlutionary grounds that the individual is in a real sense higher than the State or the social organism. The possibilities which are of value for their own sake, and whose realization must be one of our primary aims, are not experienced by society as a unit, but by some or all of the human beings which compose it.

All claims that the State has an intrinsically higher value than the individual are false. They turn out, on closer scrutiny, to be rationalizations or myths aimed at securing greater power or privilege for a limited group which controls the machinery of the State.

On the other hand the individual is meaningless in isolation, and the possibilities of development and self-realization open to him are conditioned and limited by the nature of the social organization. The individual thus has duties and responsibilities as well as rights and privileges, or if you prefer it, finds certain outlets and satisfactions (such as devotion to a cause, or participation in a joint enterprise) only in relation to the type of society in which he lives. * * *

With this we are brought into the area of the individual. The human individual is not merely inherently higher than the State, but the rightly-developed individual is, and will continue to be, the highest product of evolution, even though he needs the proper organization of society to achieve his welfare and realize his development.

The phrase *rightly-developed* begs a question. I would suggest that it includes not only the full, all-round development of potentialities, but also the one-sided development of particular possibilities or special talents, provided always that these restrict the development or interfere with the welfare of other individuals or groups as little as possible. * * *

If the right development of the individual is an evolutionary end in itself, then it is right that there should be universal equality of opportunity for development, and to the fullest degree. The reciprocal of this is the rightness of unselfishness and kindness, as the necessary means for realizing general well-being. Thus individual ethics will always in large measure be concerned with the conflict between the claims of self-expression and self-sacrifice, and their best reconciliation through love.

The Golden Rule, as various philosophers have pointed out, is an impossible ideal; it cannot ever be put into practice, not merely because of the imperfections of human nature, but also because it does not provide a real basis on which to make practical ethical decisions. However, it is the hyperbole beyond a perfectly practical ideal—the extension of more opportunity of fuller life to more human beings. Psychologically, this can be promoted by extending the child's love and sympathy to an ever-widening circle, and linking the idea of any and all avoidable suffering and stunting of development with his personal sense of wrong. And it can be promoted institutionally by the rational acceptance of certain moral principles, and then by laws and practical measures designed to give effect to those principles.

To accept this view is to give a new content to that sector of ethics concerned with justice. * * *

But in our grossly imperfect world the individual will continue to suffer painful conflict. He must reflect that this is one of the means by which we as a species have emerged into a new and more hopeful phase of evolution. It is part of the price we pay for being men.

And society will long be faced with the conflict between the general affirmation and the particular denial of principles that we know to be right. Our ethical principles assure us that war is a general wrong: yet to urge it may still be a particular right. Tolerance and kindness are general virtues: yet ruthless suppression of opponents may be a particular duty. It is the eternal conflict between means and ends. There is a slight comfort in the reflection that fuller understanding of general principles will give us more assurance of what ends are right.

Nor will clearer ethical vision prevent us from suffering what we feel as injustice at the hands of the cosmos—congenital deformity, unmerited suffering, physical disaster, the early death of loved ones. Such cosmic injustice represents the persistence of chance and its amorality into human life: we may gradually reduce its amount but we assuredly shall never abolish it. Man is the heir of evolution: but he is also its martyr. All living species provide their evolutionary sacrifice: only man knows that he is a victim.

But man is not only the heir of the past and the victim of the present: he is also the agent through whom evolution may unfold its further possibilities. Here, it seems, is the solution of our riddle of ethical relativity: the ultimate guarantees for the correctness of our labels of rightness and wrongness are to be sought for among the facts of evolutionary direction. Here, too, is to be found the reconciliation of T. H. Huxley's antithesis between the ethical and the cosmic process: for the cosmic process, we now perceive, is continued into human affairs. Thus man can impose moral principles upon ever-widening areas of the cosmic process, in whose further slow unfolding he is now the protagonist. He can inject his ethics into the heart of evolution.

JOHN HERMAN RANDALL, JR.

The Changing Impact of Darwin on Philosophy (1961) †

In the Darwin Centennial Number of the *Rice Institute Pamphlet*, Professor James Street Fulton writes:

> An essay on the philosophy of evolution in the century since the publication of Darwin's *Origin of Species* can be written in two sentences. By the end of the first fifty years, everybody in the educated world took evolution for granted, but the idea was still intellectually exciting and its philosophical exploitation was entering upon its period of full maturity. By the end of the next fifty years, evolution belongs to "common sense" almost as thoroughly as the Copernican hypothesis and other early landmarks of the scientific revolution; but the idea is no longer exciting, and evolutionary philosophy is out of fashion.[1]

Professor Fulton's closing comment is not quite exact. "Evolutionary philosophy" may be out of fashion today, in the sense he intends of the philosophies of "cosmic evolution" of half a century ago. But, after all, the philosophies of Herbert Spencer or Henri Bergson represent only an early stage of the impact of Darwin on philosophizing; and, it has now become clear, the least important stage.

† This article is based on two lectures on the theme, "Darwin and Philosophy," given on December 2 and 3, 1960, as part of the program of Darwin Centennial Lectures held at the University of California, Santa Barbara. It owes much to the suggestions offered in the panel discussion held on December 4 by the other participants, Mr. Aldous Huxley and Professors Harry Girvetz and Alexander Sesonske [Randall's note]. From the *Journal of the History of Ideas*, XXII (1961), 435–462. John Herman Randall, Jr. (b. 1899) is Woodbridge Professor of Philosophy at Columbia University.
1. Fulton, "Philosophical Adventures of the Idea of Evolution, 1859 1959," *Rice Institute Pamphlet*, Darwin Centennial Number, v. 46 (1959), 1.

For Charles Darwin is one of those significant thinkers who is not technically a "philosopher." He is at once something less, and something more. He is one of those men, like Copernicus, Galileo, Newton, Freud, Planck, Einstein, and Franz Boas, who succeed in formulating ideas that make philosophers necessary, and to whom philosophers should therefore look with a mixture of extreme annoyance and deep gratitude. It is safe to say, that had not Darwin —or someone else—published the *Origin of Species* in 1859, there is hardly a single subsequent thinker whose thought would not have been different.

As a matter of fact, someone else *did*, Alfred Russel Wallace. This makes clear, that in considering the idea of the evolution of biological species, we are not dealing with the brilliant hypothesis of a single man of genius, but rather with an idea for which men's intellectual experience was ready and prepared. But this serves only to make Darwin's own achievement the more significant. We are considering a fundamental intellectual revolution, like those associated with the other names mentioned, to which must be added that of the great intellectual revolutionary of the XIIIth century, a man who was a philosopher, Aristotle. For the coming of Aristotelian science, at the end of the XIIth and the beginning of the XIIIth centuries, set off the first of the great intellectual revolutions through which our Western culture has passed.

Now, all these successive intellectual revolutions in our cultural tradition illustrate a rather similar pattern of cultural change. The impact of a revolutionary idea again and again provokes typical reactions. First, there appears a group of partisans of the new idea, who see its promise, what illumination and suggestive further ideas it can afford. In reaction against their one-sided enthusiasm for the new idea, the partisans of the old, of tradition, consolidate their forces. This usually is accomplished too late for them to fight more than a rearguard action. By this time there has appeared a third group, the adjusters—the compromisers and mediators—who interrupt the new idea in the light of the traditional notions with which men are already familiar. They take it as really confirming in a new way the older and familiar ideas.

These three stages of cultural adjustment to a novel conception have normally in our tradition taken a generation or so to be worked out. Only then do men begin to suspect, and far-seeing thinkers to realize, that the new idea has been more disruptive and subversive than it at first seemed. For when taken seriously it has really been transforming the problems completely. And certain pioneer thinkers begin to perceive implications of that novel conception which the vast majority even of intelligent men were at first, and for about a generation, prevented from seeing by their inability to loosen the hold of older preconceptions upon their minds and imaginations. * * *

If "evolutionary philosophy" is now for us "out of fashion," the reference is to the third group, the adjusters. In my own lifetime, I have lived through the heyday of the evolutionary religious faiths, of the philosophies of cosmic evolution. I have seen them come, and I have seen them recede into the limbo of indifference. But we ourselves are in the midst of what I have distinguished as the work of the fourth stage, of the transformers. Even when, like so many philosophers today whose eyes are focused on new and quite different intellectual problems, we do not very clearly realize it, all our present-day philosophizing is still profoundly influenced by the intellectual consequences of accepting Darwinian evolution. * * *

In 1909, John Dewey gave a lecture in a course at Columbia University celebrating the fiftieth anniversary of the *Origin of Species*. He spoke on "The Influence of Darwinism on Philosophy." [2] * * *

* * * What Dewey pointed out was that while the "row" with the theologians had no philosophical significance, neither had the efforts at a "wholesale justification" of the meaning of life, of which he took Herbert Spencer's as the illustration. Evolution was not the answer to the old, traditional problems. Its significance for philosophy lay in its leading men to shift their attention to a wholly new set. For, said Dewey:

> In laying hands upon the sacred ark of absolute permanency, in treating the forms that had been treated as the types of fixity and perfection as originating and passing away, the "Origin of Species" introduced a *mode of thinking* that in the end was bound to transform the *logic of knowledge*, and hence the treatment of morals, politics, and religion.[3]

John Dewey has been proved right. The "new mode of thinking" is clearly the most important "influence" of Darwin on philosophy: the shifting of interest to a different set of problems. The realization of the further implications of the idea of evolution is not, of course, the only reason for this shift of interest. It has been helped also by the increasing impact of the experimental temper of mind: William James and John Dewey have been well called "the experimental method conscious of itself and its procedures." And it has been helped by the generalization of logical calculi into philosophies, in Bertrand Russell, the Logical Positivists, and the earlier Wittgenstein devoted to "logical atomism."

2. "The Influence of Darwinism on Philosophy," in *The Influence of Darwin on Philosophy and Other Essays in Contemporary Thought* (New York, 1910), 1–19.
3. John Dewey, *The Influence of Darwin on Philosophy*, 1.

Having pointed out this major shift, we must at the same time recognize the persistence of the Hegelian evolution of human history. This remains not only in the Marxian world, where the Marxists still feel the need of a cosmic sanction for their social philosophy: Diamat in its orthodox form is the outstanding survivor today of the cosmically rooted "evolutionary faiths" of the end of the XIXth century. The Marxists now claim, and rightly, that theirs is the only philosophy today that really believes in the inevitability of "progress," in the good old-fashioned XIXth-century religious sense. The doubts the rest of us have come to share only reflect the contradictions of capitalist society. Marxism thus betrays in this as in so many other ways its origin in the complacent and uncritical atmosphere of XIXth-century "idealism."

Marxism is the last of the great Romantic faiths, lingering on in a scientific world. But there remain other XXth-century versions of Hegelianism, especially in cultural history, where Hegel's own thought originated: I have mentioned Cassirer and Brunschvicg. Having in our day lived through a fundamental revolution in physical theory, we have come to view science, even its best-founded branches, like physics, historically, as an institutionalized form of know-how by which a culture understands itself and directs its course. This is the deposit of Hegel modified by evolutionary anthropology, a combination, as it were, of Hegel, Darwin, and Franz Boas.

Dewey's lecture of 1909 emphasized certain specific points:

1) Change is no longer a sign of defect and unreality, but fundamental in all that exists. Knowledge and science can no longer aim at realities lying behind and beyond the processes of nature, but rather at mutual interactions of changing things; not at an Order of Nature, as XVIIth and XVIIIth-century science had aimed, but at events, situations, processes. This shift involved a fundamental temporalizing of all our thinking. For the first time since the abandonment of Aristotle in the XVIIth century for the mathematical order of nature, there was now a "taking time seriously," * * *

2) Thought is no longer concerned with the general and the wholesale, but with the specific and the particular, with the concrete problem. Thinking has become basically pluralistic. The Hegelian temporalism Darwin fundamentally pluralized, and shattered Hegel's own tight monism.

3) Closely allied to these two shifts, is the central emphasis on the experimental temper of mind * * *

4) Finally, there is involved a shift from a concern with the purposes of the Creator to ends and outcomes of natural processes, a shift from "design" to function, from antecedent "final causes,"

in the XVIIIth-century William Paley, Bernardin de Saint-Pierre sense, to specific means-ends relations.

These changes which Dewey signalized fifty years ago are all in what he called our "mode of thinking." But once the hold of the older problem of finding a new religious faith was broken, the employment of this new, genetic, pluralistic, experimental, and functional mode of thinking led to a great change in substantive views. Man's relation to nature was basically altered. He was no longer a fallen angel, but a great ape trying to make good, the last and best-born of nature's children. This alteration effected two great transformations: it transformed man, and it also transformed nature. It transformed nature, for a nature in which man and all his activities have suddenly become "natural" is very different from a nature sharply contrasted with the cardinal features of human life and experience. It also transformed man, altering the whole conception of the nature of human experience.

1. It was Darwin's ideas that generated the new "naturalism" of the XXth century. For among the characteristic features of nature are the various human activities she has uniformly provoked. In seeking to understand man and appraise the world in which we find ourselves, we can hardly afford to neglect the facts that it forces moral choice on men, inspires them to creative works of art, and leads or drives them to religious devotion, even as it stimulates some to scientific inquiry. Man's searching intelligence, his problems of moral choice and obligation, his ideal enterprises of art, science, and religion are all inescapable parts of nature; they are all ways in which man has learned to encounter and cooperate with his world. They all afford evidence of the character of the world in which they take place; their suggestions would have to be included in any transcription of nature that went beyond a diagram to a portrait. Nature must be understood as the kind of world in which they would all have an intelligible place. Inquiry can find out, and has, much about these natural human activities, about their conditions and consequences, about what they do and what they are good for; it has led us to criticise some of the beliefs commonly connected with them. But what inquiry thus finds is an addition to our knowledge, not the truly amazing discovery that they are not, or ought not to be.

The nature in which we live is a world with man in it. It cannot be taken as a world from which man and all his works have been carefully eliminated. Not only would a nature without man not be man's world: it would be a world in which there would be no knowledge, and nothing could be known. We can indeed conceive the world before man appeared in it, but we cannot conceive the world without the possibility that man would there appear, to find in it all he does find.[4] For strive as we may, we can never forget what was to come. All our theories of evolution are inescapably theories of how a world with man in it came to be.

Nor is the nature we live in a world to be known and understood without reference to man. We cannot first work out a scheme for understanding the world to which everything human is irrelevant, and then claim to understand man in terms of that scheme—or man's world. For a world with man in it is a different world from a world defined regardless of man. It is a world in which things occur and are made and found that would not occur without man. And the world in which they occur cannot be understood as being what it is without their occurrence. Man's world cannot be reduced to a world without men—even if we then note man's presence, as something that introduces confusion and threatens to spoil it all, and so try to fit man and all his pursuits into the scheme in which we see the world. We shall not that way see the world. We shall see only those features which everything in the world possesses in common —stars and rocks and amoebae and men—atoms, perhaps, and what we used to call "laws." Man's finding of those common features, in himself as elsewhere, has been of momentous importance, and surely his making of such blueprints is one of his most significant arts. But that is to leave out all the features of the world that have been disclosed by man's presence in it—and all the possibilities revealed by his many other arts.

For all that man does, from birth to death, from walking to thinking, is a genuine co-working with the world. In realizing the world's possibilities, it is a revelation of what those possibilities are. Man's life in all its manifold productions makes clear what the intricate engines his blueprints describe can do, with man to direct them. The world is surely all that man can do in and with it and make out of it; it cannot be less. His doing and his making are a genuine discovery about the world. They are a finding of what the world contains.

A world with man in it contains the richness of human experience. It holds terror and love and thinking and imagination, good and evil and the wrestling with them, knowledge and ignorance and the search for truth, failure, frustration, defeat, beauty and vision and tragedy and comedy, the abyss of despair and the love of God. It has the reflective commentary of the spirit of man on all these wonders, the imaginative expression of what man has felt and suffered and thought and judged, the concentration of it all in

---

4. See Dewey, "The Subject Matter of Metaphysical Inquiry," *Journal of Philosophy*, v. 12 (1915), 337–45. Reprinted in *John Dewey on Experience, Nature, and Freedom*, ed. Richard J. Bernstein (New York, 1960).

words and paint and stone and sound. It has the pursuit of the ideal and the vision of the divine.

All these things are found in a nature with man in it. This is the nature that challenges us to tell how they are found and just how they are there. To be sure, it takes men to find them, even as it takes men to find the equations of physics. Without man's aid a star might well find other things and understand the world differently, or an angel. Stars, however, seem neither to find nor to understand anything. And angels, admirable creatures though they be, have left us no reports of their philosophic attainments. But surely there is no inference that because only men find anything, what they find is not found. The finding is a finding in nature, in cooperation with nature's possibilities.

This is a wisdom about nature that was known to the Greeks. It is the glory of Greek thought, of Plato and of Aristotle, that they took human life and experience as a revelation of what nature can accomplish on the human level. They understand the world as making possible the life of man. It was the theory of biological evolution that a century ago first put man fairly and squarely back into nature again. * * *

By common consent, it was the Greeks who looked most soberly and sanely on the natural setting of human life in the universe. They saw it steadily and whole. They managed to keep the best balance between the two contrasting relations in which man stands to the nature in whose midst he lives. On the one hand, man's life is part and parcel of the web of natural processes: he cannot live or act at all except by sharing in the great community of devices by which everything in nature takes place. He is one physical and chemical being among a host of others, inextricably involved in the interplay of nature's mechanisms. On the other hand, man acts in ways so distinct and unique that they are unparalleled by any other natural being. Both facts are important, man's unique ways of acting, and the continuity of the means by which he does so with the mechanisms of other natural processes. The Greeks, almost alone until our day, denied neither, and emphasized both. Again and again men have returned to the great Greek thinkers, to Plato and Aristotle, when they had forgotten one or the other of these essential facts of man's status in nature. * * *

Aristotle worked out the idea of "process," which has come to play so large a part in our new view of nature—of "process" in contrast to the motion from one place to another that mechanics treats of. Aristotle was at heart a biologist. To him the process by which an egg becomes a chicken was a fundamental kind of change. He was convinced that no science of nature's activities has done its job if it fails to explain the way an egg can grow into a chicken, or an acorn into an oak tree. He analysed living processes —what they do, how they function, the way the mechanisms involved in them work; for living processes, he held, reveal most clearly and fully what natural processes in general are like. Motion in place, though fundamental in all change, he took to be a limiting case of these more complex activities.

In contrast, the scientists of the early modern period took motion in place as typical. They won their triumphs in building up the science of dynamics by concentrating, not on the poultry-yard, but on the billiard table. Their blueprint, which read everything in the world as the motion of tiny billiard balls, had extraordinary fertility and power. But is is hardly surprising that it threw little light on the habits of eggs: it left out too much. It took no account of time—the time that is cumulative and progressive and irreversible, and so essential to the success of eggs. It paid no attention to the relations between means and ends, to outcomes and their necessary conditions, to what we call "functional" or "teleological" relations. Eggs have careers in time which demand the right conditions; billiard balls hardly can be said to enjoy careers.

When Darwin led men to take biology seriously once more, they had to reintroduce these functional concepts the physicists had forgotten—means and end, function, teleology, and time. Even when, with Darwin's generation, men interpreted living processes "mechanistically"—that is, when they tried to reduce them to *nothing but* chemical reactions—these reactions still remained the mechanisms by which living processes function. An egg is a chemical process, but it is not a mere chemical process. It is one that is going places—even when, in our world of chance and contingency, it ends up in an omelet and not in a chicken. Though it surely be a chemical process, we cannot understand it adequately without knowing the kind of chicken it has the power to become.

And then the physicists, seeking elements simpler than the "atom," found them cooperating from the start in a complex interrelated system, the "field." Physics has been forced by its new world of radiant energy to introduce very much the same functional relations, the same kind of temporal and systematic structures, the biologists had already been discovering. Gone are the tiny billiard balls; instead we find systematically organized electrical fields. Now the "field" of the physicists is not just like a chicken; but it is a lot more like one than is a billiard game.

As a result of this scientific advance, our present-day philosophies of nature no longer find living processes radically different from other natural processes. Both exhibit a similar type of relation and pattern, and require similar concepts for their understanding. Other natural processes are not so complex and intricate as those of living things; but they are much more so than the ways of billiard balls.

The consequences of this revolution in ideas precipitated by Darwin are far-reaching. First, we no longer ask whether "life" is to be understood in terms of its mechanisms or of its ends. The answer is, both. Means and ends are both seen to be inseparable aspects of natural processes. All processes involve and depend on some "mechanism," and the analysis and discovery of these mechanisms gives us a knowledge of *how* the processes take place. But all processes also involve the *functioning* of those mechanisms, the results they lead to, the outcomes they achieve, the way they cooperate with other natural processes. And only a study of those functionings can give us a knowledge of what these mechanisms *can do*—the results or ends they can effect. There will be no chicken unless the chemical processes of the egg interact with those of the environment. There is no thinking without a brain cooperating with nature. But what eggs—or brains—*can do*, is to be learned only from studying the way they operate. Chemistry will not tell us. Processes involve ends that are reached by means of some mechanism. The two are correlative. And only the Nothing-Butter emphasizes one exclusively, thus raising an issue and starting a fight.

The rediscovery of "process" and what it implies has reminded us of what the Greeks knew, that nature's processes are full of means and ends, of powers and their operations, that is, of functional and teleological relations and values. The very notion of "process" means the achievement of an end. There is, of course, no evidence that ends can ever bring themselves about, or serve as their own mechanisms. But nature is full of ends achieved through natural means and mechanisms.

A second consequence of our new view of nature is that the similarity between the mechanisms involved in all natural processes —including living and human processes—the fact that they are bound up in a community of interaction and can be stated in the same "laws"—is much less surprising. I do not mean that it is less surprising that an egg should become a chicken, or that a brain should think. Neither is what we should expect, before the event. But there is no evidence that nature was designed to meet human expectations. Until we have found how eggs and brains do act, what they manage to produce, we may well be surprised. But when we have found out, we should be surprised if they do not act that way, and we confidently expect them to do so.

What is less surprising, on our new view of nature, is that she should be so economical of means for her profusion of ends. If the simpler processes really follow a pattern very much like that of the most complex, it is not so hard to understand how a very similar type of mechanism can bring them all to pass. We can see how an egg, or a brain, which is itself an intricate and complex electrical system, can serve as the instrument of further complex processes like growing or thinking. But an egg or a brain that was really nothing but tiny billiard balls would offer little hope for our connecting its behavior with the obvious things that eggs and brains can do—little hope for the unification of our knowledge.

Thirdly, the fact that we can extend scientific method indefinitely to new fields becomes more plausible. A method developed to deal with billiard balls, and employing concepts quite adequate for that purpose, will not take you far in treating human life. Indeed, as Kant found, it stops short before the egg. But a method employing functional concepts: means and ends, mechanisms and their operations, systematic organization and vectors, can hope to get somewhere with living processes, and even with complex human activities. Just how it can be extended is no longer an issue to be fought over, but a problem to be worked out in detail.

Finally, nature is once more for us, as for the Greeks, full of implicit ends and ideals, full of "values," just because it is now an affair of processes, of means effecting ends, of things that are "necessary for," "better" and "worse for" other things. It contains so much "natural teleology," in terms of which its various factors can be "evaluated." It takes but a single flower to refute the contention that there are no "values" in nature, no achievement of ends through valuable means. We may even say it is obviously "good for" the planet to go round the sun. Of course, neither the flower nor the planet "finds" it good: only men "find" anything. But surely it does not follow that because only men find anything good or bad, better or worse, what they find is not found. The finding is a genuine cooperation with nature.

It is such a nature our best post-Darwinian knowledge and thought now reveals to us. Within it, there is no longer anything to prevent our working, desperately if we must, upon our pressing human problems. If we fall short, the responsibility is ours.

> The fault, dear Brutus, is not in our stars,
> But in ourselves, that we are underlings.

2. But Darwin's ideas not only transformed nature; they also transformed man. They led men to a new conception of the nature of human experience, and revolutionized that concept of "experience" that has been so fundamental in modern philosophy. With man now one animal, one biological organism among others, his experience became fundamentally that of any animal, an interaction between an organism and its environment. "Experience" ceased to be what it had been ever since Descartes and Newton, something exclusively mechanical, a being hit on the head—or the sense

organs—by Cartesian particles or Newtonian tiny billiard balls, and seeing stars. For the phenomenalists, from David Hume to Ernst Mach, the billiard balls became dubious, and experience was just seeing stars in succession and coexistence. Such a conception of a purely mechanical experience is still to be found unquestioned in conservative empiricists like A. J. Ayer.

After Darwin, for those who listened—and this does not include the British empiricists—experience became fundamentally biological in character, an active process of adjusting to the environment, and in man, of reconstructing the environment of the organism. Even Herbert Spencer had the sense to define experience as "the adjustment of internal to external relations." Such a biological conception was easily fused, with those who had read Hegel, with the Hegelian conception of experience as fundamentally social in character. Then men were back with Aristotle once more, for whom experience, though it always involves a physical mechanism, is primarily biological and social. * * *

Finally, Darwinian ideas led to an egalitarianism of differences and varieties of experience. All kinds and sorts are to be taken into account. All are, at the outset at least, on the same level. Thus of James's varieties of religious experience, none is "best." In ethics, for him, every claim is an obligation. In Dewey, every impulse, demand, and experienced good has a *prima facie* right to recognition in moral deliberation. The task of moral philosophy he sees suggesting such reconstruction of the pattern of living and social arrangements as will give them all the fullest possible fulfilment. Here is fused the Romantic openness to all varieties of experience, the experimental temper of mind, and evolutionary expansiveness—what Spencer called "heterogeneity," and Guyau, "fecundity."

3. The transformation of both nature and man effected by Darwinian ideas came to a head in a theme and an enterprise that has dominated philosophizing for a century: the appeal to experience as an instrument of criticism. This is the one theme that unites all present-day philosophical movements: they are all critical philosophies of experience. * * *

There was a fusion of the critical aims and methods of Romantic idealism and Darwinian thought in the appeals to immediate experience of most of the late XIXth-century and early XXth-century critical philosophies of experience. Nietzsche used his *Lebensphilosophie* to criticize the degenerate culture of the second *Reich*. Bergson used creative evolution to criticize mechanistic "finalism." James used his stream of consciousness to criticize association psychology, and to develop his radical empiricism in general. Dewey used experimental naturalism to criticize the classic tradition and the assumptions of modern philosophy. He appealed to direct experience to reconstruct such reflective experience, to art against theoretical vision, and to the social against the old individualism. Whitehead employed his philosophy of organism to criticize the abstractness and discreteness of Newton and Hume. Husserl resorted to the phenomenology of experience to criticize the psychologism and formalism of the Neo-Kantians, just as Bradley was doing in England. Heidegger and Jaspers have appealed to human *Existenz* to criticize the formalism and "essentialism" of Husserl's phenomenology. The Vienna Circle appealed to immediate observation formulated in protocol sentences to criticize German voluntarism and a-rationalism in general. Wittgenstein appealed to the linguistic usage of ordinary language, as the best clue to normal, undistorted experience, to criticize the logical atomism and reductive analysis he had originally shared with Bertrand Russell.

All these very diverse critical philosophies of experience have a common function. It is to criticize our theories about the world in the light of the world directly encountered: of the world "immediately experienced," say the Americans; of the experienced world "phenomenologically described," say the Continentals; of the world described in "protocol sentences," say the logical positivists; of the world implied in the many ways we use "ordinary language," say the elucidators of the "logical characteristics" of our uses of language.

But it is not merely the function of the appeal to direct experience that is common to all these critical philosophies. What is found through that appeal, as the setting for our reflective experience, for all our theories and systems, is likewise common. The world directly encountered is found, by all these varied methods, to be fundamentally temporal in character, to be specific and plural, a many rather than a neat one, to be capable of inquiry and manipulation in detail, to be subject to experimental reconstruction, and to be fundamentally functional in character, an affair of many specific means-end relations.

Now these are precisely the characters Dewey assigned in 1909 to the "new mode of thinking" initiated by Darwin. Though they speak in very different tongues, the startling agreement in conclusions among the different philosophical movements today seems to indicate that Darwin was right. The way he suggested we look at the world is still, to our best and most critical knowledge, pretty close to what the world is actually like. On the hundredth anniversary of the publication of his *magnum opus*, and hundred and fiftieth anniversary of his birth, could any featherless biped, or indeed any rational animal, claim a better record?

Theology

ANDREW DICKSON WHITE

The Final Effort of Theology (1896) †

* * *

Darwin's *Origin of Species* had come into the theological world like a plough into an ant-hill. Everywhere those thus rudely awakened from their old comfort and repose had swarmed forth angry and confused. Reviews, sermons, books light and heavy, came flying at the new thinker from all sides.

The keynote was struck at once in the *Quarterly Review* by Wilberforce, Bishop of Oxford. He declared that Darwin was guilty of "a tendency to limit God's glory in creation"; that "the principle of natural selection is absolutely incompatible with the word of God"; that it "contradicts the revealed relations of creation to its Creator"; that it is "inconsistent with the fulness of his glory"; that it is "a dishonouring view of Nature"; and that there is "a simpler explanation of the presence of these strange forms among the works of God": that explanation being—"the fall of Adam." Nor did the bishop's efforts end here; at the meeting of the British Association for the Advancement of Science he again disported himself in the tide of popular applause. Referring to the ideas of Darwin, who was absent on account of illness, he congratulated himself in a public speech that he was not descended from a monkey. The reply came from Huxley, who said in substance: "If I had to choose I would prefer to be a descendant of a humble monkey rather than of a man who employs his knowledge and eloquence in misrepresenting those who are wearing out their lives in the search for truth."

This shot reverberated through England, and indeed through other countries.

The utterances of this the most brilliant prelate of the Anglican Church received a sort of antiphonal response from the leaders of

† Andrew Dickson White (1832–1918), scholar-diplomat, was the first president of Cornell University. The text is from his *A History of the Warfare of Science with Theology in Christendom* (New York, 1896).

the English Catholics. In an address before the "Academia," which had been organized to combat "science falsely so called," Cardinal Manning declared his abhorrence of the new view of Nature, and described it as "a brutal philosophy—to wit, there is no God, and the ape is our Adam."

These attacks from such eminent sources set the clerical fashion for several years. One distinguished clerical reviewer, in spite of Darwin's thirty years of quiet labour, and in spite of the powerful summing up of his book, prefaced a diatribe by saying that Darwin "might have been more modest had he given some slight reason for dissenting from the views generally entertained." Another distinguished clergyman, vice-president of a Protestant institute to combat "dangerous" science, declared Darwinism "an attempt to dethrone God." Another critic spoke of persons accepting the Darwinian views as "under the frenzied inspiration of the inhaler of mephitic gas," and of Darwin's argument as "a jungle of fanciful assumption." Another spoke of Darwin's views as suggesting that "God is dead," and declared that Darwin's work "does open violence to everything which the Creator himself has told us in the Scriptures of the methods and results of his work." Still another theological authority asserted: "If the Darwinian theory is true, Genesis is a lie, the whole framework of the book of life falls to pieces, and the revelation of God to man, as we Christians know it, is a delusion and a snare." Another, who had shown excellent qualities as an observing naturalist, declared the Darwinian view "a huge imposture from the beginning."

Echoes came from America. One review, the organ of the most widespread of American religious sects, declared that Darwin was "attempting to befog and to pettifog the whole question"; another denounced Darwin's views as "infidelity"; another, representing the American branch of the Anglican Church, poured contempt over Darwin as "sophistical and illogical," and then plunged into an exceedingly dangerous line of argument in the following words: "If this hypothesis be true, then is the Bible an unbearable fiction; . . . then have Christians for nearly two thousand years been duped by a monstrous lie. . . . Darwin requires us to disbelieve the authoritative word of the Creator." A leading journal representing the same church took pains to show the evolution theory to be as contrary to the explicit declarations of the New Testament as to those of the Old, and said: "If we have all, men and monkeys, oysters and eagles, developed from an original germ, then is St. Paul's grand deliverance—'All flesh is not the same flesh; there is one kind of flesh of men, another of beasts, another of fishes, and another of birds'—untrue."

Another echo came from Australia, where Dr. Perry, Lord Bishop of Melbourne, in a most bitter book on *Science and the Bible,* declared that the obvious object of Chambers, Darwin, and Huxley, is "to produce in their readers a disbelief of the Bible."

Nor was the older branch of the Church to be left behind in this chorus. Bayma, in the *Catholic World,* declared, "Mr. Darwin is, we have reason to believe, the mouthpiece or chief trumpeter of that infidel clique whose well-known object is to do away with all idea of a God."

Worthy of especial note as showing the determination of the theological side at that period was the foundation of sacro-scientific organizations to combat the new ideas. First to be noted is the "Academia," planned by Cardinal Wiseman. In a circular letter the cardinal, usually so moderate and just, sounded an alarm and summed up by saying, "Now it is for the Church, which alone possesses divine certainty and divine discernment, to place itself at once in the front of a movement which threatens even the fragmentary remains of Christian belief in England." The necessary permission was obtained from Rome, the Academia was founded, and the "divine discernment" of the Church was seen in the utterances which came from it, such as those of Cardinal Manning, which every thoughtful Catholic would now desire to recall, and in the diatribes of Dr. Laing, which only aroused laughter on all sides. A similar effort was seen in Protestant quarters; the "Victoria Institute" was created, and perhaps the most noted utterance which ever came from it was the declaration of its vice-president, the Rev. Walter Mitchell, that "Darwinism endeavours to dethrone God." [1]

In France the attack was even more violent. Fabre d'Envieu brought out the heavy artillery of theology, and in a long series of elaborate propositions demonstrated that any other doctrine than that of the fixity and persistence of species is absolutely contrary to

1. For Wilberforce's article, see *Quarterly Review,* July, 1860. For the reply of Huxley to the bishop's speech I have relied on the account given in *Quatrefages,* who had it from Carpenter; a somewhat different version is given in the *Life and Letters of Darwin.* For Cardinal Manning's attack, see *Essays on Religion and Literature,* London, 1865. For the review articles, see the *Quarterly* already cited, and that for July, 1874; also the *North British Review,* May, 1860; also F. O. Morris's letter in the *Record,* reprinted at Glasgow, 1870; also the *Addresses of Rev. Walter Mitchell* before the Victoria Institute, London, 1867; also Rev. B. G.

Johns, *Moses not Darwin, a Sermon,* March 31, 1871. For the earlier American attacks, see *Methodist Quarterly Review,* April, 1871; *The American Church Review,* July and October, 1865, and January, 1866. For the Australian attack, see *Science and the Bible,* by the Right Reverend Charles Perry, D. D., Bishop of Melbourne, London, 1869. For Bayma, see the *Catholic World,* vol. xxvi, p. 782. For the Academia, see *Essays* edited by Cardinal Manning, above cited; and for the Victoria Institute, see *Scientia Scientiarum,* by a member of the Victoria Institute, London, 1865.

Scripture. The Abbé Désorges, a former Professor of Theology, stigmatized Darwin as a "pedant," and evolution as "gloomy"; Monseigneur Ségur, referring to Darwin and his followers, went into hysterics and shrieked: "These infamous doctrines have for their only support the most abject passions. Their father is pride, their mother impurity, their offspring revolutions. They come from hell and return thither, taking with them the gross creatures who blush not to proclaim and accept them."

In Germany the attack, if less declamatory, was no less severe. Catholic theologians vied with Protestants in bitterness. Prof. Michelis declared Darwin's theory "a caricature of creation." Dr. Hagermann asserted that it "turned the Creator out of doors." Dr. Schund insisted that "every idea of the Holy Scriptures, from the first to the last page, stands in diametrical opposition to the Darwinian theory"; and, "if Darwin be right in his view of the development of man out of a brutal condition, then the Bible teaching in regard to man is utterly annihilated." Rougemont in Switzerland called for a crusade against the obnoxious doctrine. Luthardt, Professor of Theology at Leipsic, declared: "The idea of creation belongs to religion and not to natural science; the whole superstructure of personal religion is built upon the doctrine of creation"; and he showed the evolution theory to be in direct contradiction to Holy Writ.

But in 1863 came an event which brought serious confusion to the theological camp: Sir Charles Lyell, the most eminent of living geologists, a man of deeply Christian feeling and of exceedingly cautious temper, who had opposed the evolution theory of Lamarck and declared his adherence to the idea of successive creations, then published his work on the *Antiquity of Man*, and in this and other utterances showed himself a complete though unwilling convert to the fundamental ideas of Darwin. The blow was serious in many ways, and especially so in two—first, as withdrawing all foundation in fact from the scriptural chronology, and secondly, as discrediting the creation theory. The blow was not unexpected; in various review articles against the Darwinian theory there had been appeals to Lyell, at times almost piteous, "not to flinch from the truths he had formerly proclaimed." But Lyell, like the honest man he was, yielded unreservedly to the mass of new proofs arrayed on the side of evolution against that of creation.

At the same time came Huxley's *Man's Place in Nature*, giving new and most cogent arguments in favour of evolution by natural selection.

In 1871 was published Darwin's *Descent of Man*. Its doctrine had been anticipated by critics of his previous books, but it made, none the less, a great stir; again the opposing army trooped forth, though evidently with much less heart than before. A few were very violent. The *Dublin University Magazine*, after the traditional Hibernian fashion, charged Mr. Darwin with seeking "to displace God by the unerring action of vagary," and with being "resolved to hunt God out of the world." But most notable from the side of the older Church was the elaborate answer to Darwin's book by the eminent French Catholic physician, Dr. Constantin James. In his work, *On Darwinism, or the Man-Ape*, published at Paris in 1877, Dr. James not only refuted Darwin scientifically but poured contempt on his book, calling it "a fairy tale," and insisted that a work "so fantastic and so burlesque" was, doubtless, only a huge joke, like Erasmus's *Praise of Folly*, or Montesquieu's *Persian Letters*. The princes of the Church were delighted. The Cardinal Archbishop of Paris assured the author that the book had become his "spiritual reading," and begged him to send a copy to the Pope himself. His Holiness, Pope Pius IX, acknowledged the gift in a remarkable letter. He thanked his dear son, the writer, for the book in which he "refutes so well the aberrations of Darwinism." "A system," His Holiness adds, "which is repugnant at once to history, to the tradition of all peoples, to exact science, to observed facts, and even to Reason herself, would seem to need no refutation, did not alienation from God and the leaning toward materialism, due to depravity, eagerly seek to support in all this tissue of fables. . . ." * * * Wherefore the Pope thanked Dr. James for his book, "so opportune and so perfectly appropriate to the exigencies of our time," and bestowed on him the apostolic benediction. Nor was this brief all. With it there came a second, creating the author an officer of the Papal Order of St. Sylvester. The cardinal archbishop assured the delighted physician that such a double honour of brief and brevet was perhaps unprecedented, and suggested only that in a new edition of his book he should "insist a little more on the relation existing between the narratives of Genesis and the discoveries of modern science, in such fashion as to convince the most incredulous of their perfect agreement." The prelate urged also a more dignified title. The proofs of this new edition were accordingly all submitted to His Eminence, and in 1882 it appeared as *Moses and Darwin: the Man of Genesis compared with the Man-Ape, or Religious Education opposed to Atheistic*. No wonder the cardinal embraced the author, thanking him in the name of science and religion. "We have at last," he declared, "a handbook which we can safely put into the hands of youth."

Scarcely less vigorous were the champions of English Protestant orthodoxy. In an address at Liverpool, Mr. Gladstone remarked: "Upon the grounds of what is termed evolution God is relieved of the labour of creation; in the name of unchangeable laws he is discharged from governing the world"; and, when Herbert Spencer called his attention to the fact that Newton with the doctrine of gravitation and with the science of physical astronomy is open to the same charge, Mr. Gladstone retreated in the *Contemporary Review* under one of his characteristic clouds of words. The Rev. Dr. Coles, in the *British and Foreign Evangelical Review*, declared that the God of evolution is not the Christian's God. Burgon, Dean of Chichester, in a sermon preached before the University of Oxford, pathetically warned the students that "those who refuse to accept the history of the creation of our first parents according to its obvious literal intention, and are for substituting the modern dream of evolution in its place, cause the entire scheme of man's salvation to collapse." Dr. Pusey also came into the fray with most earnest appeals against the new doctrine, and the Rev. Gavin Carlyle was perfervid on the same side. The Society for Promoting Christian Knowledge published a book by the Rev. Mr. Birks, in which the evolution doctrine was declared to be "flatly opposed to the fundamental doctrine of creation." Even the *London Times* admitted a review stigmatizing Darwin's *Descent of Man* as an "utterly unsupported hypothesis," full of "unsubstantiated premises, cursory investigations, and disintegrating speculations," and Darwin himself as "reckless and unscientific." 2 * * *

2. For the French theological opposition to the Darwinian theory, see Pozzy, *La Terre et le Récit Biblique de la Création*, 1874, especially pp. 353, 363; also, Félix Ducane, *Études sur le Transformisme*, 1876, especially pp. 107 to 119. As to Fabre d'Envieu, see especially his Proposition xliii. For the Abbé Désorges, "former Professor of Philosophy and Theology," see his *Erreurs Modernes*, Paris, 1878, pp. 677 and 595 to 598. For Monseigneur Ségur, see his *La Foi devant la Science Moderne*, sixth ed., Paris, 1874, pp. 23, 34, etc. For Herbert Spencer's reply to Mr. Gladstone, see his *Study of Sociology;* for the passage in the *Dublin Review*, see the issue for July, 1871. For the review in the *London Times*, see *Nature* for April 20, 1871. For Gavin Carlyle, see *The Battle of Unbelief*, 1870, pp. 86 and 171. For the attacks by Michelis and Hagermann, see *Natur und Offenbarung*, Münster, 1861 to 1869. For Schund, see his *Darwin's Hypothese und ihr Verhältniss zu Religion und Moral*, Stuttgart, 1869. For Luthardt, see *Fundamental Truths of Christianity*, translated by Sophia Taylor, second ed., Edinburgh, 1869. For Rougemont, see his *L'Homme et le Singe*, Neuchâtel, 1863 (also in German trans.). For Constantin James, see his *Mes Entretiens avec l'Empereur Don Pédro sur le Darwinisme*, Paris, 1888, where the papal briefs are printed in full. For the English attacks on Darwin's *Descent of Man*, see the *Edinburgh Review*, July, 1871, and elsewhere; the *Dublin Review*, July, 1871; the *British and Foreign Evangelical Review*, April, 1886. See also *The Scripture Doctrine of Creation*, by the Rev. T. R. Birks, London, 1873, published by the S. P. C. K. For Dr. Pusey's attack, see his *Unscience, not Science, adverse to Faith*, 1878; also, *Darwin's Life and Letters*, vol. ii, pp. 411, 412.

ASA GRAY

Natural Selection Not Inconsistent with Natural Theology (1860) †

* * * Mr. Darwin has purposely been silent upon the philosophical and theological applications of his theory. This reticence, under the circumstances, argues design, and raises inquiry as to the final cause or reason why. Here, as in higher instances, confident as we are that there is a final cause, we must not be overconfident that we can infer the particular or true one. Perhaps the author is more familiar with natural-historical than with philosophical inquiries, and, not having decided which particular theory about efficient cause is best founded, he meanwhile argues the scientific questions concerned—all that relates to secondary causes—upon purely scientific grounds, as he must do in any case. Perhaps, confident, as he evidently is, that his view will finally be adopted, he may enjoy a sort of satisfaction in hearing it denounced as sheer atheism by the inconsiderate, and afterward, when it takes its place with the nebular hypothesis and the like, see this judgment reversed, as we suppose it would be in such event.

Whatever Mr. Darwin's philosophy may be, or whether he has any, is a matter of no consequence at all, compared with the important questions, whether a theory to account for the origination and diversification of animal and vegetable forms through the operation of secondary causes does or does not exclude design; and whether the establishment by adequate evidence of Darwin's particular theory of diversification through variation and natural selection would essentially alter the present scientific and philosophical grounds for theistic views of Nature. The unqualified affirmative judgment rendered by the two Boston reviewers, evidently able and practised reasoners, "must give us pause." We hesitate to advance our conclusions in opposition to theirs. But, after full and serious consideration, we are constrained to say that, in our opinion, the adoption of a derivative hypothesis, and of Darwin's particular hypothesis, if we understand it, would leave the doctrine of final causes, utility, and special design, just where they were before. * * *

† Asa Gray (1810–1888) was professor of natural history at Harvard University and one of the ablest botanists of the period. His efforts to reconcile natural selection with natural theology were published in leading scientific and literary periodicals in the 1860's and 1870's. This essay appeared as a series of articles in the *Atlantic Monthly* in 1860 and was reprinted as Article III of Gray's collection of essays, *Darwiniana* (1876).

The whole argument in natural theology proceeds upon the ground that the inference for a final cause of the structure of the hand and of the valves in the veins is just as valid now, in individuals produced through natural generation, as it would have been in the case of the first man, supernaturally created. Why not, then, just as good even on the supposition of the descent of men from chimpanzees and gorillas, since those animals possess these same contrivances? Or, to take a more supposable case: If the argument from structure to design is convincing when drawn from a particular animal, say a Newfoundland dog, and is not weakened by the knowledge that this dog came from similar parents, would it be at all weakened if, in tracing his genealogy, it were ascertained that he was a remote descendant of the mastiff or some other breed, or that both these and other breeds came (as is suspected) from some wolf? If not, how is the argument for design in the structure of our particular dog affected by the supposition that his wolfish progenitor came from a post-tertiary wolf, perhaps less unlike an existing one than the dog in question is to some other of the numerous existing races of dogs, and that this post-tertiary came from an equally or more different tertiary wolf? And if the argument from structure to design is not invalidated by our present knowledge that our individual dog was developed from a single organic cell, how is it invalidated by the supposition of an analogous natural descent, through a long line of connected forms, from such a cell, or from some simple animal, existing ages before there were any dogs?

Again, suppose we have two well-known and apparently most decidedly different animals or plants, A and D, both presenting, in their structure and in their adaptations to the conditions of existence, as valid and clear evidence of design as any animal or plant ever presented: suppose we have now discovered two intermediate species, B and C, which make up a series with equable differences from A to D. Is the proof of design or final cause in A and D, whatever it amounted to, at all weakened by the discovery of the intermediate forms? Rather does not the proof extend to the intermediate species, and go to show that all four were equally designed? Suppose, now, the number of intermediate forms to be much increased, and therefore the gradations to be closer yet—as close as those between the various sorts of dogs, or races of men, or of horned cattle: would the evidence of design, as shown in the structure of any of the members of the series, be any weaker than it was in the case of A and D? Whoever contends that it would be, should likewise maintain that the origination of individuals by generation is incompatible with design, or an impossibility in Nature. We might all have confidently thought the latter, antecedently to experience of the fact of reproduction. Let our experience teach us wisdom.

These illustrations makes it clear that the evidence of design from structure and adaptation is furnished *complete* by the individual animal or plant itself, and that our knowledge or our ignorance of the history of its formation or mode of production adds nothing to it and takes nothing away. We infer design from certain arrangements and results; and we have no other way of ascertaining it. Testimony, unless infallible, cannot prove it, and is out of the question here. *Testimony is not the appropriate proof of design: adaptation to purpose is.* Some arrangements in Nature appear to be contrivances, but may leave us in doubt. Many others, of which the eye and the hand are notable examples, compel belief with a force not appreciably short of demonstration. Clearly to settle that such as these must have been designed goes far toward proving that other organs and other seemingly less explicit adaptations in Nature must also have been designed, and clinches our belief, from manifold considerations, that all Nature is a preconcerted arrangement, a manifested design. A strange contradiction would it be to insist that the shape and markings of certain rude pieces of flint, lately found in drift-deposits, prove design, but that nicer and thousand-fold more complex adaptations to use in animals and vegetables do not *a fortiori* argue design.

We could not affirm that the arguments for design in Nature are conclusive to all minds. But we may insist, upon grounds already intimated, that, whatever they were good for before Darwin's book appeared, they are good for now. * * *

It is very easy to assume that, because events in Nature are in one sense accidental, and the operative forces which bring them to pass are themselves blind and unintelligent (physically considered, all forces are), therefore they are undirected, or that he who describes these events as the results of such forces thereby assumes that they are undirected. This is the assumption of the Boston reviewers, and of Mr. Agassiz, who insists that the only alternative to the doctrine, that all organized beings were supernaturally created just as they are, is, that they have arisen *spontaneously* through the *omnipotence of matter.*[1]

As to all this, nothing is easier than to bring out in the conclusion what you introduce in the premises. If you import atheism into your conception of variation and natural selection, you can readily exhibit it in the result. If you do not put it in, perhaps there need be none to come out. * * *

So the real question we come to is as to the way in which we are to conceive intelligent and efficient cause to be exerted, and

1. In *American Journal of Science,* July, 1860, pp. 147–149.

upon what exerted. Are we bound to suppose efficient cause in all cases exerted upon nothing to evoke something into existence—and this thousands of times repeated, when a slight change in the details would make all the difference between successive species? Why may not the new species, or some of them, be designed diversifications of the old?

There are, perhaps, only three views of efficient cause which may claim to be both philosophical and theistic:

1. The view of its exertion at the beginning of time, endowing matter and created things with forces which do the work and produce the phenomena.

2. This same view, with the theory of insulated interpositions, or occasional direct action, engrafted upon it—the view that events and operations in general go on in virtue simply of forces communicated at the first, but that now and then, and only now and then, the Deity puts his hand directly to the work.

3. The theory of the immediate, orderly, and constant, however infinitely diversified, action of the intelligent efficient Cause.

It must be allowed that, while the third is preëminently the Christian view, all three are philosophically compatible with design in Nature. The second is probably the popular conception. Perhaps most thoughtful people oscillate from the middle view toward the first or the third—adopting the first on some occasions, the third on others. Those philosophers who like and expect to settle all mooted questions will take one or the other extreme. The *Examiner* inclines toward, the *North American* reviewer fully adopts, the third view, to the logical extent of maintaining that *"the origin of an individual,* as well as the origin of a species or a genus, can be explained only by the *direct* action of an intelligent creative cause." To silence his critics, this is the line for Mr. Darwin to take; for it at once and completely relieves his scientific theory from every theological objection which his reviewers have urged against it.

At present we suspect that our author prefers the first conception, though he might contend that his hypothesis is compatible with either of the three. That it is also compatible with an atheistic or pantheistic conception of the universe, is an objection which, being shared by all physical, and some ethical or moral science, cannot specially be urged against Darwin's system. As he rejects spontaneous generation, and admits of intervention at the beginning of organic life, and probably in more than one instance, he is not wholly excluded from adopting the middle view, although the interventions he would allow are few and far back. Yet one interposition admits the principle as well as more. Interposition presupposes particular necessity or reason for it, and raises the question, when and how often it may have been necessary. It might be the natural supposition, if we had only one set of species to account for, or if the successive inhabitants of the earth had no other connections or resemblances than those which adaptation to similar conditions, which final causes in the narrower sense, might explain. But if this explanation of organic Nature requires one to "believe that, at innumerable periods in the earth's history, certain elemental atoms have been commanded suddenly to flash into living tissues," and this when the results are seen to be strictly connected and systematic, we cannot wonder that such interventions should at length be considered, not as interpositions or interferences, but rather— to use the reviewer's own language—as "exertions so frequent and beneficent that we come to regard them as the ordinary action of Him who laid the foundation of the earth, and without whom not a sparrow falleth to the ground." [2]

What does the difference between Mr. Darwin and his reviewer now amount to? If we say that according to one view the origination of species is *natural,* according to the other *miraculous,* Mr. Darwin agrees that "what is natural as much requires and presupposes an intelligent mind to render it so—that is, to effect it continually or at stated times—as what is supernatural does to effect it for once." [3] He merely inquires into the form of the miracle, may remind us that all recorded miracles (except the primal creation of matter) were transformations or actions in and upon natural things, and will ask how many times and how frequently may the origination of successive species be repeated before the supernatural merges in the natural.

In short, Darwin maintains that the origination of a species, no less than that of an individual, is natural; the reviewer, that the natural origination of an individual, no less than the origination of a species, requires and presupposes Divine power. A *fortiori,* then, the origination of a variety requires and presupposes Divine power. And so between the scientific hypothesis of the one and the philosophical conception of the other no contrariety remains. And so, concludes the *North American* reviewer, "a proper view of the nature of causation places the vital doctrine of the being and the providence of a God on ground that can never be shaken." [4] A worthy conclusion, and a sufficient answer to the denunciations and arguments of the rest of the article, so far as philosophy and natural theology are concerned. If a writer must needs use his own favorite dogma as a weapon with which to give *coup de grace* to a pernicious theory, he should be careful to seize his edge-tool by the handle, and not by the blade. * * *

2. *North American Review* for April, 1860, p. 506.
3. *Vide* motto from Butler, prefixed to the second edition of Darwin's work.
4. *North American Review, loc. cit.* p. 504.

THOMAS HENRY HUXLEY

The Origin of Species (1860) †

Mr. Darwin's long-standing and well-earned scientific eminence probably renders him indifferent to that social notoriety which passes by the name of success; but if the calm spirit of the philosopher have not yet wholly superseded the ambition and the vanity of the carnal man within him, he must be well satisfied with the results of his venture in publishing the "Origin of Species." Overflowing the narrow bounds of purely scientific circles, the "species question" divides with Italy and the Volunteers the attention of general society. Everybody has read Mr. Darwin's book, or, at least, has given an opinion upon its merits or demerits; pietists, whether lay or ecclesiastic, decry it with the mild railing which sounds so charitable; bigots denounce it with ignorant invective; old ladies of both sexes consider it a decidedly dangerous book, and even savants, who have no better mud to throw, quote antiquated writers to show that its author is no better than an ape himself; while every philosophical thinker hails it as a veritable Whitworth gun in the armoury of liberalism; and all competent naturalists and physiologists, whatever their opinions as to the ultimate fate of the doctrines put forth, acknowledge that the work in which they are embodied is a solid contribution to knowledge and inaugurates a new epoch in natural history.

Nor has the discussion of the subject been restrained within the limits of conversation. When the public is eager and interested, reviewers must minister to its wants; and the genuine *littérateur* is too much in the habit of acquiring his knowledge from the book he judges—as the Abyssinian is said to provide himself with steaks from the ox which carries him—to be withheld from criticism of a profound scientific work by the mere want of the requisite preliminary scientific acquirement; while, on the other hand, the men of science who wish well to the new views, no less than those who dispute their validity, have naturally sought opportunities of expressing their opinions. Hence it is not surprising that almost all the critical journals have noticed Mr. Darwin's work at greater or less length; and so many disquisitions, of every degree of excel-

† Huxley debated the opponents of Darwin not only on his own ground of scientific fact and theory but often in the field of theology as well. The first of the following two essays was published in the *Westminster Review* for April, 1860, and reprinted as Chapter 2 of Huxley's *Darwiniana* (1893). The second essay was published in the *Contemporary Review* for November, 1871, and also reprinted, as Chapter 5, in *Darwiniana*.

lence, from the poor product of ignorance, too often stimulated by prejudice, to the fair and thoughtful essay of the candid student of Nature, have appeared, that it seems an almost hopeless task to attempt to say anything new upon the question.

But it may be doubted if the knowledge and acumen of prejudged scientific opponents, and the subtlety of orthodox special pleaders, have yet exerted their full force in mystifying the real issues of the great controversy which has been set afoot, and whose end is hardly likely to be seen by this generation; so that, at this eleventh hour, and even failing anything new, it may be useful to state afresh that which is true, and to put the fundamental positions advocated by Mr. Darwin in such a form that they may be grasped by those whose special studies lie in other directions. * * *

Indeed history * * * has embalmed for us the speculations upon the origin of living beings, which were among the earliest products of the dawning intellectual activity of man. In those early days positive knowledge was not to be had, but the craving after it needed, at all hazards, to be satisfied, and according to the country, or the turn of thought, of the speculator, the suggestion that all living things arose from the mud of the Nile, from a primeval egg, or from some more anthropomorphic agency, afforded a sufficient resting-place for his curiosity. The myths of Paganism are as dead as Osiris or Zeus, and the man who should revive them, in opposition to the knowledge of our time, would be justly laughed to scorn; but the coeval imaginations current among the rude inhabitants of Palestine, recorded by writers whose very name and age are admitted by every scholar to be unknown, have unfortunately not yet shared their fate, but, even at this day, are regarded by nine-tenths of the civilised world as the authoritative standard of fact and the criterion of the justice of scientific conclusions, in all that relates to the origin of things, and, among them, of species. In this nineteenth century, as at the dawn of modern physical science, the cosmogony of the semi-barbarous Hebrew is the incubus of the philosopher and the opprobrium of the orthodox. Who shall number the patient and earnest seekers after truth, from the days of Galileo until now, whose lives have been embittered and their good name blasted by the mistaken zeal of Bibliolaters? Who shall count the host of weaker men whose sense of truth has been destroyed in the effort to harmonise impossibilities—whose life has been wasted in the attempt to force the generous new wine of Science into the old bottles of Judaism, compelled by the outcry of the same strong party?

It is true that if philosophers have suffered, their cause has been amply avenged. Extinguished theologians lie about the cradle of every science as the strangled snakes beside that of Hercules; and history records that whenever science and orthodoxy have been fairly opposed, the latter has been forced to retire from the lists, bleeding and crushed if not annihilated; scotched, if not slain. But orthodoxy is the Bourbon of the world of thought. It learns not, neither can it forget; and though, at present, bewildered and afraid to move, it is as willing as ever to insist that the first chapter of Genesis contains the beginning and the end of sound science; and to visit, with such petty thunderbolts as its half-paralysed hands can hurl, those who refuse to degrade Nature to the level of primitive Judaism.

Philosophers, on the other hand, have no such aggressive tendencies. With eyes fixed on the noble goal to which "per aspera et ardua" they tend, they may, now and then, be stirred to momentary wrath by the unnecessary obstacles with which the ignorant, or the malicious, encumber, if they cannot bar, the difficult path; but why should their souls be deeply vexed? The majesty of Fact is on their side, and the elemental forces of Nature are working for them. Not a star comes to the meridian at its calculated time but testifies to the justice of their methods—their beliefs are "one with the falling rain and with the growing corn." By doubt they are established, and open inquiry is their bosom friend. Such men have no fear of traditions however venerable, and no respect for them when they become mischievous and obstructive; but they have better than mere antiquarian business in hand, and if dogmas, which ought to be fossil but are not, are not forced upon their notice, they are too happy to treat them as non-existent.

The hypotheses respecting the origin of species which profess to stand upon a scientific basis, and, as such, alone demand serious attention, are of two kinds. The one, the "special creation" hypothesis, presumes every species to have originated from one or more stocks, these not being the result of the modification of any other form of living matter—or arising by natural agencies—but being produced, as such, by a supernatural creative act.

The other, the so-called "transmutation" hypothesis, considers that all existing species are the result of the modification of pre-existing species, and those of their predecessors, by agencies similar to those which at the present day produce varieties and races, and therefore in an altogether natural way; and it is a probable, though not a necessary consequence of this hypothesis, that all living beings have arisen from a single stock. With respect to the origin of this primitive stock, or stocks, the doctrine of the origin of species is obviously not necessarily concerned. The transmutation hypothesis, for example, is perfectly consistent either with the conception of a special creation of the primitive germ, or with the supposition of its having arisen, as a modification of inorganic matter, by natural causes.

The doctrine of special creation owes its existence very largely to the supposed necessity of making science accord with the Hebrew cosmogony; but it is curious to observe that, as the doctrine is at present maintained by men of science, it is as hopelessly inconsistent with the Hebrew view as any other hypothesis.

If there be any result which has come more clearly out of geological investigation than another, it is, that the vast series of extinct animals and plants is not divisible, as it was once supposed to be, into distinct groups, separated by sharply-marked boundaries. There are no great gulfs between epochs and formations—no successive periods marked by the appearance of plants, of water animals, and of land animals, *en masse*. Every year adds to the list of links between what the older geologists supposed to be widely separated epochs: witness the crags linking the drift with older tertiaries; the Maestricht beds linking the tertiaries with the chalk; the St. Cassian beds exhibiting an abundant fauna of mixed mesozoic and palæozoic types, in rocks of an epoch once supposed to be eminently poor in life; witness, lastly, the incessant disputes as to whether a given stratum shall be reckoned devonian or carboniferous, silurian or devonian, cambrian or silurian.

This truth is further illustrated in a most interesting manner by the impartial and highly competent testimony of M. Pictet, from whose calculations of what percentage of the genera of animals, existing in any formation, lived during the preceding formation, it results that in no case is the proportion less than *one-third*, or 33 per cent. It is the triassic formation, or the commencement of the mesozoic epoch, which has received the smallest inheritance from preceding ages. The other formations not uncommonly exhibit 60, 80, or even 94 percent. of genera in common with those whose remains are imbedded in their predecessor. Not only is this true, but the subdivisions of each formation exhibit new species characteristic of, and found only in, them; and, in many cases, as in the lias for example, the separate beds of those subdivisions are distinguished by well-marked and peculiar forms of life. A section, a hundred feet thick, will exhibit, at different heights, a dozen species of ammonite, none of which passes beyond its particular zone of limestone, or clay, into the zone below it or into that above it; so that those who adopt the doctrine of special creation must be prepared to admit, that at intervals of time, corresponding with the thickness of these beds, the Creator thought fit to interfere with the natural course of events for the purpose of making a new ammonite. It is not easy to transplant oneself into the frame of mind of those who can accept such a conclusion as this, on any evidence short of absolute demonstration; and it is difficult to see what is to be gained by so doing, since, as we have said, it is obvious that such a view of the origin of living beings is utterly opposed to the Hebrew cosmogony. Deserving no aid from the powerful arm of Bibliolatry, then, does the received form of the hypothesis of special creation derive any support from science or sound logic? Assuredly not much. The arguments brought forward in its favour all take one form: If species were not supernaturally created, we cannot understand the facts x, or y, or z; we cannot understand the structure of animals or plants, unless we suppose they were contrived for special ends; we cannot understand the structure of the eye, except by supposing it to have been made to see with; we cannot understand instincts, unless we suppose animals to have been miraculously endowed with them.

As a question of dialectics, it must be admitted that this sort of reasoning is not very formidable to those who are not to be frightened by consequences. It is an *argumentum ad ignorantiam*—take this explanation or be ignorant. But suppose we prefer to admit our ignorance rather than adopt a hypothesis at variance with all the teachings of Nature? Or, suppose for a moment we admit the explanation, and then seriously ask ourselves how much the wiser are we; what does the explanation explain? Is it any more than a grandiloquent way of announcing the fact, that we really know nothing about the matter? A phænomenon is explained when it is shown to be a case of some general law of Nature; but the supernatural interposition of the Creator can, by the nature of the case, exemplify no law, and if species have really arisen in this way, it is absurd to attempt to discuss their origin. * * *

THOMAS HENRY HUXLEY

Mr. Darwin's Critics (1871) †

The gradual lapse of time has now separated us by more than a decade from the date of the publication of the "Origin of Species" —and whatever may be thought or said about Mr. Darwin's doctrines, or the manner in which he has propounded them, this much is certain, that, in a dozen years, the "Origin of Species" has worked as complete a revolution in biological science as the "Principia" did in astronomy—and it has done so, because, in the words of

† This essay deals with the following works: A. R. Wallace, *Contributions to the Theory of Natural Selection* (1870); St. George Mivart, F. R. S., *The Gen-* esis *of Species* (2nd ed., 1871); "Darwin's *Descent of Man,*" *Quarterly Review*, July 1871.

Helmholtz, it contains "an essentially new creative thought." [1]

And as time has slipped by, a happy change has come over Mr. Darwin's critics. The mixture of ignorance and insolence which, at first, characterised a large proportion of the attacks with which he was assailed, is no longer the sad distinction of anti-Darwinian criticism. Instead of abusive nonsense, which merely discredited its writers, we read essays, which are, at worst, more or less intelligent and appreciative; while, sometimes, like that which appeared in the "North British Review" for 1867, they have a real and permanent value.

The several publications of Mr. Wallace and Mr. Mivart contain discussions of some of Mr. Darwin's views, which are worthy of particular attention, not only on account of the acknowledged scientific competence of these writers, but because they exhibit an attention to those philosophical questions which underlie all physical science, which is as rare as it is needful. And the same may be said of an article in the "Quarterly Review" for July 1871, the comparison of which with an article in the same Review for July 1860, is perhaps the best evidence which can be brought forward of the change which has taken place in public opinion on "Darwinism." * * *

I may assume, then, that the Quarterly Reviewer and Mr. Mivart admit that there is no necessary opposition between "evolution whether exclusively Darwinian or not," and religion. But then, what do they mean by this last much-abused term? On this point the Quarterly Reviewer is silent. Mr. Mivart, on the contrary, is perfectly explicit, and the whole tenor of his remarks leaves no doubt that by "religion" he means theology; and by theology, that particular variety of the great Proteus, which is expounded by the doctors of the Roman Catholic Church, and held by the members of that religious community to be the sole form of absolute truth and of saving faith.

According to Mr. Mivart, the greatest and most orthodox authorities upon matters of Catholic doctrine agree in distinctly asserting "derivative creation" or evolution; "and thus their teachings harmonise with all that modern science can possibly require" (p. 305).

I confess that this bold assertion interested me more than anything else in Mr. Mivart's book. What little knowledge I possessed of Catholic doctrine, and of the influence exerted by Catholic authority in former times, had not led me to expect that modern science was likely to find a warm welcome within the pale of the greatest and most consistent of theological organisations.

---

1. Helmholtz: *Ueber des Ziel und die Fortschritte der Naturwissenschaft.* Eröffnungsrede für die Naturforscherversammlung zu Innsbruck. 1869.

And my astonishment reached its climax when I found Mr. Mivart citing Father Suarez as his chief witness in favour of the scientific freedom enjoyed by Catholics—the popular repute of that learned theologian and subtle casuist not being such as to make his works a likely place of refuge for liberality of thought. But in these days, when Judas Iscariot and Robespierre, Henry VIII and Catiline, have all been shown to be men of admirable virtue, far in advance of their age, and consequently the victims of vulgar prejudice, it was obviously possible that Jesuit Suarez might be in like case. And, spurred by Mr. Mivart's unhesitating declaration, I hastened to acquaint myself with such of the works of the great Catholic divine as bore upon the question, hoping, not merely to acquaint myself with the true teachings of the infallible Church, and free myself of an unjust prejudice; but, haply, to enable myself, at a pinch, to put some Protestant bibliolater to shame, by the bright example of Catholic freedom from the trammels of verbal inspiration.

I regret to say that my anticipations have been cruelly disappointed. But the extent to which my hopes have been crushed can only be fully appreciated by citing, in the first place, those passages of Mr. Mivart's work by which they were excited. In his introductory chapter I find the following passages:—

"The prevalence of this theory [of evolution] need alarm no one, for it is, without any doubt, perfectly consistent with the strictest and most orthodox Christian [2] theology" (p. 5).

"Mr. Darwin and others may perhaps be excused if they have not devoted much time to the study of Christian philosophy; but they have no right to assume or accept without careful examination, as an unquestioned fact, that in that philosophy there is a necessary antagonism between the two ideas 'creation' and 'evolution,' as applied to organic forms.

"It is notorious and patent to all who choose to seek, that many distinguished Christian thinkers have accepted, and do accept, both ideas, *i.e.* both 'creation' and 'evolution.'" * * *

Mr. Mivart then cites certain passages from St. Augustin, St. Thomas Aquinas, and Cornelius à Lapide, and finally adds:—

As to Suarez, it will be enough to refer to Disp. xv. sec. 2, No. 9, p. 508, t. i. edition Vivés, Paris; also Nos. 13—15. Many other references to the same effect could easily be given, but these may suffice.

It is then evident that ancient and most venerable theological authorities distinctly assert *derivative* creation, and thus their teachings harmonise with all that modern science can possibly require.

2. It should be observed that Mr. Mivart employs the term "Christian" as if it were the equivalent of "Catholic."

It will be observed that Mr. Mivart refers solely to Suarez's fifteenth Disputation, though he adds, "Many other references to the same effect could easily be given." I shall look anxiously for these references in the third edition of the "Genesis of Species." For the present, all I can say is, that I have sought in vain, either in the fifteenth Disputation, or elsewhere, for any passage in Suarez's writings which, in the slightest degree, bears out Mr. Mivart's views as to his opinions.[3]

The title of this fifteenth Disputation is "De causa formali substantiali," and the second section of that Disputation (to which Mr. Mivart refers) is headed, "Quomodo possit forma substantialis fieri in materia et ex materia?"

The problem which Suarez discusses in this place may be popularly stated thus: According to the scholastic philosophy every natural body has two components—the one its "matter" (*materia prima*), the other is "substantial form" (*forma substantialis*). Of these the matter is everywhere the same, the matter of one body being indistinguishable from the matter of any other body. That which differentiates any one natural body from all others is its substantial form, which inheres in the matter of that body, as the human soul inheres in the matter of the frame of man, and is the source of all the activities and other properties of the body. * * *

But Mr. Mivart does not hesitate to push his attempt to harmonise science with Catholic orthodoxy to its utmost limit; and, while assuming that the soul of man "arises from immediate and direct creation," he supposes that his body was "formed at first (as now in each separate individual) by derivative, or secondary creation, through natural laws" (p. 331).

This means, I presume, that an animal, having the corporeal form and bodily powers of man, may have been developed out of some lower form of life by a process of evolution; and that, after this anthropoid animal had existed for a longer or shorter time, God made a soul by direct creation, and put it into the manlike body, which, heretofore, had been devoid of that *anima rationalis*, which is supposed to be man's distinctive character.

This hypothesis is incapable of either proof or disproof, and therefore may be true; but if Suarez is any authority, it is not Catholic doctrine. "Nulla est in homine forma educta de potentia materiæ," [4] is a dictum which is absolutely inconsistent with the doctrine of the natural evolution of any vital manifestation of the human body.

Moreover, if man existed as an animal before he was provided with a rational soul, he must, in accordance with the elementary

3. The edition of Suarez's *Disputationes* from which the following citations are given, is Birckmann's, in two volumes folio, and is dated 1630.

4. Disput. xv. § x. No. 27.

requirements of the philosophy in which Mr. Mivart delights, have possessed a distinct sensitive and vegetative soul, or souls. Hence, when the "breath of life" was breathed into the manlike animal's nostrils, he must have already been a living and feeling creature. But Suarez particularly discusses this point, and not only rejects Mr. Mivart's view, but adopts language of very theological strength regarding it.

"Possent præterea his adjungi argumenta theologica, ut est illud quod sumitur ex illis verbis Genes. 2. *Formavit Deus hominem ex limo terræ et inspiravit in faciem ejus spiraculum vitæ et factus est homo in animam viventem*: ille enim spiritus, quam Deus spiravit, anima rationalis fuit, et PER EADEM FACTUS EST HOMO VIVENS, ET CONSQUENTER, ETIAM SENTIENS.

"Aliud est ex VIII. Synodo Generali quæ est Constantinopolitana IV. can. 11, qui sic habet. *Apparet quosdam in tantum impietatis venisse ut homines duas animas habere dogmatizent: talis igitur impictatis inventores et similes sapientes, cum Vetus et Novum Testamentum omnesque Ecclesiæ patres unam animam rationalem hominem habere asseverent, Sancta et universalis Synodus anathematizat.*" [5]

Moreover, if the animal nature of man was the result of evolution, so must that of woman have been. But the Catholic doctrine, according to Suarez, is that woman was, in the strictest and most literal sense of the words, made out of the rib of man.

"Nihilominus sententia Catholica est, verba illa Scripturæ esse ad literam intelligenda. AC PROINDE VERE, AC REALITER, TULISSE DEUM COSTAM ADAMÆ, ET, EX ILLA, CORPUS EVÆ FORMASSE." [6]

Nor is there any escape in the supposition that some woman existed before Eve, after the fashion of the Lilith of the rabbis; since Suarez qualifies that notion, along with some other Judaic imaginations, as simply "damnabilis." [7]

After the perusal of the "Tractatus de Opere" it is, in fact, impossible to admit that Suarez held any opinion respecting the origin of species, except such as is consistent with the strictest and most literal interpretation of the words of Genesis. For Suarez, it is Catholic doctrine, that the world was made in six natural days. On the first of these days the *materia prima* was made out of nothing, to receive afterwards those "substantial forms" which moulded it into the universe of things; on the third day, the ancestors of all living plants suddenly came into being, full-grown, perfect, and possessed of all the properties which now distinguish them; while, on the fifth and sixth days, the ancestors of all existing animals were simi-

---

5. Disput. xv. "De causa formali substantiali," § x. No. 24.
6. *Tractatus de Opere*, Lib. III. "De

hominis creatione," cap. ii. No. 3.
7. *Ibid*. Lib. III cap. iv. Nos. 8 and 9.

larly caused to exist in their complete and perfect state, by the infusion of their appropriate material substantial forms into the matter which had already been created. Finally, on the sixth day, the *anima rationalis*—that rational and immortal substantial form which is peculiar to man—was created out of nothing, and "breathed into" a mass of matter which, till then, was mere dust of the earth, and so man arose. But the species man was represented by a solitary male individual, until the Creator took out one of his ribs and fashioned it into a female.

This is the view of the "Genesis of Species" held by Suarez to be the only one consistent with Catholic faith: it is because he holds this view to be Catholic that he does not hesitate to declare St. Augustin unsound, and St. Thomas Aquinas guilty of weakness, when the one swerved from this view and the other tolerated the deviation. And, until responsible Catholic authority—say, for example, the Archbishop of Westminster—formally declares that Suarez was wrong, and that Catholic priests are free to teach their flocks that the world was *not* made in six natural days, and that plants and animals were *not* created in their perfect and complete state, but have been evolved by natural processes through long ages from certain germs in which they were potentially contained, I, for one, shall feel bound to believe that the doctrines of Suarez are the only ones which are sanctioned by Infallible Authority, as represented by the Holy Father and the Catholic Church.

I need hardly add that they are as absolutely denied and repudiated by Scientific Authority, as represented by Reason and Fact. * * *

The present antagonism between theology and science does not arise from any assumption by the men of science that all theology must necessarily be excluded from science, but simply because they are unable to allow that reason and morality have two weights and two measures; and that the belief in a proposition, because authority tells you it is true, or because you wish to believe it, which is a high crime and misdemeanour when the subject matter of reasoning is of one kind, becomes under the *alias* of "faith" the greatest of all virtues when the subject matter of reasoning is of another kind.

The Bishop of Brechin said well the other day:—"Liberality in religion—I do not mean tender and generous allowances for the mistakes of others—is only unfaithfulness to truth." [8] And, with the same qualification, I venture to paraphrase the Bishop's dictum: "Ecclesiasticism in science is only unfaithfulness to truth." * * *

8. Charge at the Diocesan Synod of Brechin. *Scotsman,* Sept. 14, 1871.

HERBERT W. SCHNEIDER

The Influence of Darwin and Spencer on American Philosophical Theology (1945) †

Theologians are of two kinds—dogmatic and philosophical. This is true of the orthodox and the liberals alike. The simplest way for dogmatic theology to avoid conflict with the sciences is to keep away from science. Thus many dogmatic theologians, especially orthodox Catholics and liberal Protestants, are willing to accept any scientific discoveries because they cannot possibly endanger religious faith. The Bible, they say, does not teach science and science does not teach religion. Hence they accept Copernican astronomy and Darwinian evolution in so far as they are systems of natural science, but they reserve the right to declare the truth about God and the soul. Though this dogmatic solution is easy and peaceful, it is usually accepted only after a struggle, for it involves considerable self-denial on the part of theologians, and considerable tolerance on the part of scientists. John Fiske, for example, following Darwin's own lead, made this peace with orthodox theism:

> The consistent theist will always occupy an impregnable position in maintaining that the entire series in each and every one of its incidents is an immediate manifestation of the creative action of God. . . . To say that complex organisms were directly created by the Deity is to make an assertion which, however true in a theistic sense, is utterly barren.[1]

A few Protestant theologians like James Woodrow [2] were ready, on their part, to accept these terms of peace, and many liberals, Catholics, and Jews were relatively happy to make peace thus readily and radically. One theologian, President Barnard of Columbia, was willing to surrender ignobly.

> Much as I love truth in the abstract, I love my hope of immortality more. . . . If this, after all, is the best that science can give me, give me, then, I pray, no more science. Let me live on in my

† Journal of the History of Ideas, VI (1945), 3–18. Herbert W. Schneider (b. 1892) is professor emeritus of philosophy at the Claremont Graduate School.
1. John Fiske, Darwinism and Other Essays (Boston, 1885), 7–8.
2. James Woodrow, uncle of Woodrow Wilson, was Perkins Professor of Natural Science in connexion with Revelation, in the Presbyterian Theological Seminary at Columbia, S. C. He made an eloquent and clear exposition of his interpretation of the Bible as "almost certainly" not teaching science, and of his belief in evolution as "mediate creation," in a notable address before the Alumni Association of his Seminary, May 7, 1884. He was dismissed in consequence.

simple ignorance, as my fathers lived before me; and when I shall at length be summoned to my final repose, let me still be able to fold the drapery of my couch about me and lie down to pleasant, even though they be deceitful, dreams.[3]

But the great majority of dogmatic theologians adopted a militant attitude toward evolutionary theory. Many of them failed to suspect serious trouble from Darwinism until the publication of the *Descent of Man* in 1871 and the subsequent growth of genetic psychology. But when the implications of evolutionary theory for the creation and history of man, for the nature and immortality of the soul, and for the authority of the Bible became evident, a bitter struggle ensued, and the theologians gave way very slowly, point by point, and only after waging a hopeless battle against superior forces.

Their usual tactics were to deny that evolution is true science and to regard it as a philosophy of design without a designer. Typical of these tactics are the arguments presented in the works of Augustus Orestes Brownson, the radical and independent Catholic, Charles Hodge of Princeton University, author of *What Is Darwinism?* (1874), Professor Enoch F. Burr of Amherst College, author of *Pater Mundi* (1873), and Professor Andrew P. Peabody of Harvard University, author of *Christianity and Science* (1874). Peabody was especially explicit in pointing out that he felt free to question the truth of evolution precisely because evolution is a speculative theory and not science. The reception of evolution by such dogmatic theologians has been described by Windsor Hall Roberts, Sidney Ratner, and Bert James Loewenberg.[4]

The purpose of this article is to call attention to a different type of theological argument, and an evaluation of evolution by more philosophical theologians. A philosophical theologian is unwilling

3. F. A. P. Barnard, "The Law of Disease," in *College Courant*, XIV, 27.
4. Windsor Hall Roberts, *The Reaction of American Protestant Churches to the Darwinian Philosophy 1860–1900*. Abstract of a dissertation submitted to the Department of History of Chicago University in 1936 (Chicago, 1938). This is by far the most comprehensive treatment of the subject. In addition, see Sidney Ratner, "Evolution and the Rise of the Scientific Spirit in America," *Philosophy of Science*, III (1936), 104–22; and Bert James Loewenberg, "The Controversy over Evolution in New England," *New England Quarterly*, VIII (1935), 232–57; and "Darwinism Comes to America, 1859–1900," *Mississippi Valley Historical Review*, XXVIII (1941), 339–68.

Dr. Roberts analyzes the general theological reaction as follows: an earlier wave of "alarmism," a "Mild group of hesitating compromisers" in the seventies, followed "in the early eighties by a group of enthusiastic evolutionists, lay and clerical, who had been captivated by the Spencerian optimism" (13–14). He attempts an interesting, though probably premature, statement of "theology's final adjustment," which includes an analysis of the literature of the early twentieth century. Roberts' conclusion suggests that "the cosmic process [was] . . . too costly for trusting souls who had been accustomed to sing 'Jesus paid it all.' A dole in the field of soteriology is preferable to work relief. But the ability of Christianity to adapt itself to contemporary thought enabled thousands to remain faithful to its cause who otherwise would have been lost" (44).

to be a religious isolationist and to accept the doctrine that theological truth and scientific truth are independent inquiries into different subject-matters. And a philosophical scientist is unwilling to renounce speculation on matters of religion, morals, and human destiny. They meet on the philosophical battlefield, where neither is at home, but both take high ground. A theologian who has a philosophical conception of the nature and function of his vocation, will represent his system as a *summa* of human wisdom and a reflective commentary on human affairs, including science. He can therefore not be indifferent to science and must continually reinterpret his revelations to bring them into conformity with empirical discovery, for it is important to him that religious revelations be also revelations of truth.

In the America of the nineteenth century there were two chief types of philosophical Christian theology—Presbyterian and Unitarian. I shall describe how the philosophical representatives of these traditions dealt with evolution, and I shall try to explain why the Presbyterians found Darwinism congenial, while the Unitarians were attracted by John Fiske's version of Herbert Spencer.

One of the first theological expounders and adapters of Darwinism in America was James McCosh of Princeton. Before coming to America, as early as 1850, he had written *The Method of the Divine Government*, a work that enjoyed great popularity in Scotland as well as here, going through ten editions. In it he had argued that God has an infinite treasury of spontaneous variations which he introduces into the normal course of events, and which makes his government a combination of law and of "special providences" or "adaptations," as McCosh called them. He also points out how this government by apparently accidental and practically "invisible" variations adds a temporal dimension to Leibniz's version of the perfect chain of being. He criticized Leibniz, Comte, Spencer, and the natural theology of the Enlightenment in general for believing that there is only a general providence or law of progress in the world. He reasserted the Calvinist faith in special providences, in spontaneous or unpredictable acts of God whereby some are elected and other rejected, and restated the argument from design, which was the commonplace of natural theology, to include the gradual achievement of fitness or adaptation in nature by means of numerous "accidental" interferences with the normal course of events. In other words, he located God's design or "method" not in the immediate fitness of organs or mechanisms to perform their functions, but in the general plan by which fitness was achieved through what appears on the surface to be arbitrary selection. When Darwin's *Origin of Species* appeared in 1859, he saw almost at once that his theory of "Divine government" could be identified with the doctrine of natural selection. Why not interpret the variations which Darwin called spontaneous, chance, or accidental differences, and for which he did not pretend to give an explanation, as supernatural choices of an intervening Designer? Natural selection and divine election amounted to the same thing in practice, or, to quote McCosh: "Supernatural design produces natural selection." [5]

McCosh used this Calvinistic version of Darwinism very effectively to criticize the uniformitarianism and mechanism of Spencer and the Positivists. He also emphasized struggle as a basic factor in the divine economy, contrasting the tragic aspects of Calvinism and Darwinism with the superficial optimism of the Spencerians. Those who survive in the "moral struggle" of history are not the heroes of physical power nor of intelligence, but those who have "moral power." * * *

While McCosh was making Darwinian theology at Princeton, Asa Gray was doing a similar work at Harvard. Though he was a botanist by profession and not a theologian, he professed to be an orthodox Christian. He represented himself as "philosophically a convinced theist, and religiously an acceptor of the 'creed commonly called the Nicene,' as the exponent of the Christian faith." [6] * * *

The chief difference between McCosh's and Gray's versions of Darwinism is that Gray emphasized a general providence and Mc-Cosh the special providences. Gray was more critical of the design argument, and defended the doctrine of Providence on the ground that "teleology is equally difficult" in theology and in evolution, but that "without the implication of a superintending wisdom, nothing is made out and nothing credible." [7] * * *

These illustrations must suffice for the present to substantiate my generalization concerning the affiliation of Calvinism and Dar-

5. James McCosh, *The Religious Aspect of Evolution* (New York, 1888), 7. In this connection he quoted with approval from Isaac Taylor's *Natural History of Enthusiasm:* "Those unforeseen accidents which so often control the lot of men, constitute a superstratum in the system of human affairs, wherein peculiarly the Divine providence holds empire for the accomplishment of its special purposes. It is from this hidden and inexhaustible mine of chances, as we must call them, that the Governor of the world draws, with unfathomable skill, the materials of his dispensations towards each individual of mankind." Mc-Cosh, *The Method of the Divine Government Physical and Moral* (London, 1874), 164. McCosh continues with the following comment: "If, in contemplating the general order that pervades the world, we seemed to fall in with beautiful figures rectilinear and circular, we feel now, in dealing with these fortuities, that we are ascending to curves of a higher order, and figures of greater complexity; or rather as if we had got an infinitesimal calculus, in which every one thing is infinitely small, but in which the infinite units produce magnitudes and forces infinitely great. The curves . . . form, an instrument unequalled at once for its potency and its pliability, its wide extended range, and the certainty with which it hits the point at which it aims." *Loc. cit.*

6. George Frederick Wright, "The Debt of the Church to Asa Gray," *Bibliotheca Sacra*, XLV (1888), 523, quoting Gray's *Darwiniana* (1876), p. vi.

7. *Ibid.*, 525, quoting Gray's *Darwiniana.*

winism in America. Note that Darwinism was used to support the ideas of supernatural selection and design, revelation, transcendent deity, moral struggle, and social conflict.

A very different version of theological evolutionism arose among the Unitarians, an optimistic conception of progressive salvation through immanent design, evolutionary love, a faith in the natural growth of intelligence, virtue, and peace. The Darwinian theologies were theocentric; these liberalistic versions were humanistic.

Even in these liberal circles Spencer's philosophy was, of course, criticized and condemned as too materialistic and agnostic. But it was nevertheless taken seriously, and in the modified form preached by Fiske, the Spencerian conception of evolution was readily detached from his materialism, hedonism, and agnosticism, and was adapted to liberal theology and to the transcendentalist heritage.

One of the first whole-hearted preachers of this type of evolution was Minot J. Savage (1841–1918), Unitarian minister in Boston and New York, who in 1876 published *The Religion of Evolution.* Savage did not interpret natural selection as *laissez faire* and pointed out that "human selection" is also natural; however, he did present the natural progress of evolution as an alternative to "proposed 'short-cuts' " "that lead to nowhere in particular." [8] Among the short-cuts criticized by him from this evolutionary point of view are Communism, the Single Tax, Tolstoy's ideal country, industrial coöperation, state socialism or nationalism, and any schemes that attempt to build perfect cities of "imperfect bricks." * * *

By the turn of the century the liberal theologians had split into two divergent trends. Those whose chief interest was in preaching the gospel cut loose from Spencer entirely and also from biology, expounding a Christian version of moral evolution. Henry Ward Beecher's *Evolution and Religion* was obviously an exploitation of evolutionary concepts for evangelical purposes; there was scarcely a pretext in him of being scientific. His successor at Plymouth Church, Brooklyn, Lyman Abbott, was a more genuine evolutionist, since he believed in the evolution of revelation, the evolution of immortality, the evolution of anything; but he paid little or no attention to biological evolution, except to dismiss it politely. * * *

Abbott began with the usual criticism of Spencer, but he added to it a very significant and penetrating critique of Kant and of transcendental idealism. Thus freed of both strains in his burdensome past, he announced a new theory of "Universal Realistic Evolution," based on the doctrine of the Universal Organism or Person.

8. Minot J. Savage, "The Effects of Evolution on the Coming Civilization," *Evolution. Popular Lectures and Dis-* *cussions before the Brooklyn Ethical Association* (Boston, 1889), 376.

He formulated briefly, but clearly, the doctrines which have subsequently come to be known as emergent evolutionism and the theory of organic structures. He invented the term "objective relativism" and also developed a theory of realistic empiricism, similar to that of H. Shadworth Hodgson. In short, he opened up the field, or, to bring the metaphor up-to-date, "softened" the ground for much of the most important work in recent American philosophy. But he was destined to be a forgotten man, because his philosophy was too tightly constructed as a monistic theology to be welcome to the freer thought that came after William James, and his theology was too pantheistic to serve as a basis for worship. * * *

When Abbott decided, in 1867, to leave the Unitarian ministry, he sought advice from his friend Chauncey Wright, a scientist whose chief interest was to reconcile the two dominant scientific methods of his time, the empiricism and utilitarianism of John Stuart Mill, and the evolutionism of Darwin. He hoped to do thoroughly what Spencer was doing superficially. He typifies the completely secularized, non-theological interest in evolution. He regarded evolutionary science as an empirical, experimental procedure dealing with specific problems. His own particular interest in this field was to apply Darwinian method to the question of the origin and function of consciousness. If he could discover the particular organic utility of consciousness and thus lay the foundation of "psychozoölogy," he thought he might both round out the work of Darwin and put an end to much useless philosophy and metaphysics. He was as "pure" a scientist as one is apt to find, but he loved conversation with his more philosophical friends, especially Charles Peirce and William James, and through them exercised a notable influence on American philosophy. He failed, however, to interest either of his friends in the reconciliation of empiricism and Darwinism. Peirce had his own idealistic version of "evolutionary love," and James was more impressed by Darwin's emphasis on spontaneity and struggle. * * *

I have now distinguished four philosophical attitudes on the question of evolutionary theology:

1) the complete separation of revelation and science accepted by conservative scientists and evangelical clergy.

2) the justification of revealed theology and supernatural election by a theological version of Darwinian natural selection.

3) the justification of liberal or rationalistic theology by a theological version of the Spencerian doctrine of progressive adaptation and the evanescence of evil.

4) the restriction of evolutionary theory to specific scientific problems, the restriction of religion to practical problems, and the separation of philosophy from both.

The first position was philosophically expressed by Asa Gray, and the last by Chauncey Wright. The second and the third, however, are culturally the more important positions in American thought. The second, which I have labelled "Calvinist," is directly related to the philosophy of William James, whose conception of evolution was Darwinian and of theology, supernaturalist. The third, which I have labelled "Unitarian," is well represented by Charles Peirce, whose philosophy of evolutionary love, the process whereby the universe gradually becomes more orderly, was a more sophisticated formulation than Fiske's of the faith in natural progress through the growth of mind.

ROBERT W. GLEASON

A Note on Theology and Evolution (1960) †

The controversies over evolution that excited the nineteenth century and the beginning of the twentieth century have to a certain extent disappeared from theological literature. While the origin of man and the question of his parents will always be a matter of vital interest, present-day theologians are far more moderate in their claims than were their predecessors. Similarly, modern scientists seem to be more content to remain within the area of their respective fields with their appropriate probabilities and certitudes than were some of their forerunners.[1] At one time in theology a certain fundamentalism seemed to be popular. What is known today as concordism, that is, the effort to treat the Bible as though its apparently literal expressions were teaching facts of science, no longer finds favor with exegetes or theologians.[2] Nonetheless, the teaching body of the Church, the official *magisterium*,

† From Walter J. Ong, S.J., ed., *Darwin's Vision and Christian Perspectives* (New York, 1960), pp. 104–113. Robert W. Gleason (b. 1917) is professor of theology at Fordham University.

1. For a balanced evaluation in English of both anthropological and theological data on human evolution, F. Ewing's "Human Evolution—1956," *Anthropological Quarterly*, Oct., 1956, pp. 91–139, should be consulted. In addition to this and to the other works cited in the notes to the present study, the following publications may prove helpful to further study of the theological implications of evolution: F. Ceuppens, *Genèse I–III* (Paris: Desclée, 1945); *Gregorianum*, XXIX (1948), 342–527 (a symposium); A. M. Henry, *God and His Creation* (Chicago: Fides, 1955); A. Jones, *Unless Some Man Show Me* (New York: Sheed and Ward, 1957); V. Marcozzi, *Evoluzione o creazione* (Milan, 1948); P. M. Perier, *Le transformisme, l'origine de l'homme et le dogme catholique* (Paris: Beauchesne, 1938); B. de Solanges, "Christianity and Evolution," *Cross Currents*, I (1951), 26–37; T. Steinbuchel, *Die Abstammung des Menschen* (Frankfurt, 1951); B. Vawter, *A Path Through Genesis* (New York: Sheed and Ward, 1957); C. Vollert, "Human Evolution and Theological Implications," *Proceedings, American Catholic Theological Society*, 1951, pp. 122–45.
2. Cf. E. Arbez, "Genesis I–XI and Prehistory," *American Ecclesiastical Review*, CXXIII (1950), 82–83. Cf. ibid., pp. 86–87.

still exercises vigilance over the writings of theologians where these touch the origins of man and especially his derivation from a single pair.

It is evident today that the Sacred Books of other Semitic cultures, the Egyptian, the Sumerian, the Assyrian, bear remarkable similarity to the Bible in many details, while they are wholly different in the affirmations they conceal beneath their imagery. Today we realize that theological opportunism is of very little apologetic value. Moreover, exegetes are willing to recognize certain facets of biblical interpretation which seemed foreign to nineteenth-century thought. In the first chapter of Genesis, the section which causes most problems for the theologian interested in evolution, there are undoubtedly images, expressions and elements of popular folklore common to other cultures besides that of the Israelites. It is no longer popular to consider all these elements as having been dictated by God.[3] Again, there are two different accounts of the creation of man in this chapter of Genesis and the author of the first account is evidently a very different personality from the author of the second. While all theologians agree that history is expressed in the assertions of Genesis, nevertheless today they admit that it is a peculiar type of history whose rules are still partly unknown to us. There are certain definite ways of telling a story, certain idioms which are peculiar to the Semitic language and which do not correspond to any of our categories of Greco-Roman history or of modern literary forms. Modern archaeological research is enabling us to come much closer to the original meaning of Genesis and in doing so, some of the barriers to a modern form of evolution are being removed for the theologian.[4]

The first narrative of the creation and especially of the account of the creation of man probably does not go back to the actual date of Moses, that is, to the thirteenth or the fifteenth century before Christ but is rather a sort of theological résumé of Mosaic tradition. It is a popular account of the creation of man, adapted to the memory of the oriental people and yet, it is not popular in the sense that it is as imaged as the second creation account. To understand this we must realize that the human author whom God chooses as an instrument of His message works within the secular framework of his own time. He shares the so-called scientific notions of his contemporaries based upon personal observation and experience. The sacred author communicates a divine thought to us, through the medium of scientific notions which are a part of the mental culture of his own time. He is, after all, attempting to

3. Cf. C. Hauret, *Beginnings; Genesis and Modern Science* (Dubuque: Priory Press, 1955), p. 16.
4. Ewing, "Human Evolution—1956," *Anthrop. Qtrly.*, Oct., 1956, pp. 123–27. Cf. E. Boné, "L'homme: genèse et cheminement," *Nouvelle Revue Théologique*, 1947, p. 389.

express things in terms in which his readers can understand him. It is possible that the scientific notions of the author of Genesis are erroneous, drawn as they are from contemporary science but it is not these notions that he is affirming or implying. It is not the intention of Sacred Scripture to teach us cosmogony. It preserves neutrality before various hypotheses concerning the original development of life and mankind in this world.

With regard to the question of the evolution of the human body, the problem which most intrigues Catholic scholars, the air has been considerably cleared since the nineteenth century.[5] Numerous Catholic scholars are prepared today to admit a form of theistic transformism or evolution. Exegetes and theologians are today more concerned with observing the demands which theology places upon itself as a science and with pointing out the demands which scientific evolutionary theories should place upon themselves as sciences. The origin of the human body by way of evolution does not appear improbable today. Many anthropologists believe that there is some genetic and physical connection between man and lower animals. This is at least a working hypothesis which the theologian must treat as such, and within the framework of his own science determine how much validity can be granted to it.[6] Although Scripture says that God formed Adam from the dust of the earth, it may well be that the dust refers rather to organic matter oriented by God through a long process. We no longer feel it necessary to hold that God formed the body of man immediately and directly from inorganic matter. It is true that some years ago many theologians viewed such transformism with anything but favor, since transformism was so frequently anti-theistic in its implications and connected with many other theories scarcely calculated to please Catholic thinkers. The conclusions of scientists which are debatable should be controlled by their own science and conclusions of theology should also be controlled by its scientific methods. The certain should be distinguished from the probable and the possible, and the unchanging affirmations of Scriptures should be distinguished from the interpretations of exegetes and from the images used by the first writer. From the first creation account we can derive the fact that man owes his existence to a special intervention on the part of God. But we are unable to decide with certainty *from the text* when this intervention of God took place, whether it took place upon organic or inorganic matter and how many human beings were in question. It is not easy either to decide *from the text* of the first creation account whether Adam

5. Cf. Achille Cardinal Liénart, "Science and the Bible," *The Commonweal*, June 24, 1949, pp. 265–67.

6. Cf. W. Hauber, "Evolution and Catholic Thought," *American Ecclesiastical Review*, CVI (1942), 161–64.

and Eve were a single couple or many primitive couples.[7]

The second account clarifies many of the questions which were left unclear from the first account. In the first account the author told of the origin of the universe in terms of a science of his day, and in the second account the author pictured the creation of man according to his own ideas of what man is. The second account portrays a Creator molding clay as a potter and breathing life into it. These are images that were traditional to Israelite culture, and in fact, in other texts of Babylonian literature we see similar stories recounted. Egyptian folklore has its god Khnum who created man, modeling him upon a potter's wheel. Other folklores tell us of goddesses modeling men and women from clay. What the sacred author is insisting upon is the fact that at the origin of man, the creator God is seen and that He stands at the origin of both man's body and soul. Man is the master of his own destiny, and, gifted with intelligence and will, he resembles God Himself. There is a very special poetic setting set forth by the author in order to show us that man and only man caused God to intervene in a special fashion in his creation.[8]

The nature of the divine intervention in the formation of Adam's body is not entirely clear. We know that man is a being endowed with freedom of choice and intellectual processes and as such must have an immaterial soul directly created by God. Is it possible that the divine intervention consisted merely in the vivification by an immortal soul of previously organically organized matter? That the human soul is due to a special intervention of God in the form of creation is irreversible Catholic teaching. As a spiritual substance, this human soul comes directly from the hands of God who creates it in each individual case. Is it possible that the sacred author is simply expressing this reality of the joining of the spiritual soul to organic matter by his image of God breathing into matter? In order to obtain some kind of a picture of the divine intervention by which the human body was formed, we do not have to resort to the primitive ideas condemned by Augustine which envision God molding earth to the form of a human body and then breathing into that earth a human soul.

It is perfectly acceptable to maintain that God created man's body directly from inorganic matter and by an act of his will caused that matter to be animated by the spiritual soul. However, some modern theologians, approaching the text with much more knowledge of paleontological discoveries, feel that it is also possible to

7. Cf. P. Chaine, *Le Livre de la Genèse* (Paris: Cerf, 1948), p. 46; also M. Gruenthaner, "Evolution and the Scriptures," *Catholic Biblical Quarterly*, XIII (1951), 21–27, for the scriptural evidence against polygenism.

8. Hauret, *op. cit.*, p. 94. Cf. Gruenthaner, "Evolution . . . ," *Cath. Bib. Qtrly.*, XIII (1951), 24–26, on the nature of the intervention.

interpret the text as saying that God drew the human body from an animal organism which was transformed so as to receive a human soul. It is possible that this transformation occurred before the infusion of the human soul, so that God retouched, as it were, an animal organism and the animal became a living person upon the infusion of the divinely created soul. Thus the body of man may actually have been enjoying some animal or subhuman life when God infused the spiritual soul into it. If we accept the fact that the human came into being at the end of a series of sudden mutations directed to this end by the Creator God, then these changes reveal God's Providence throughout. At a certain point, the animal organism in question may have been sufficiently perfected so that it was ready for the last touches preceding the infusion of the human soul. But we must not conceive this perfection as though it *required* the infusion of a human soul from purely immanent intramundane processes. Rather, the mutations which prepared for the soul would be directed by God and His special action throughout.

Whatever theory one holds, one must always accept the fact that the creation of man is peculiar in several senses. The creation of his soul is due directly to the creative act of God, and his body itself is formed by a peculiar intervention of the Most High. Whether this intervention consists in the transformation of purely inorganic matter, or in a divine alteration of an animal organism, or in the elevation of subhuman activities in order to prepare and dispose for the reception of the soul, we must in any event maintain that the man Adam arose, *body and soul*, from a special intervention on the part of God. By reason of his intellectual nature, man is directly related to his Creator and requires this intervention of God, which is expressed in the text by the act of God breathing life into him. Whether this be reorganization of a pre-existing animal organism, whether it be the transformation of the dust of the earth in a literal sense, or whether it be by the infusion of the human soul, the sacred text does not explicitly say. However, we can be sure that the hypotheses of the purely animal origin of man is excluded. Man is in no sense a child of an animal.[9] Pius XII in the encyclical *Humani Generis* has said that the Church does not forbid research and discussion by men of theology and science with regard to the doctrine of evolution in so far as this doctrine inquires into the origin of the human body as coming from pre-existing living matter. But the Catholic Faith obliges us to hold that all human souls are immediately created by God. With modesty and moderation the expert may submit his reasons on

9. M. Flick "L'Origine del corpo del primo uomo," *Gregorianum*, 1948, p. 366.

one side or the other with regard to mitigated, theistic transformism.

We cannot accept the theory that the transformation from one
species to another took place as a result of causes purely immanent. But we can accept a theory of transformism in which a
special intervention of God takes place. In no supposition may we
admit that any animal body demanded the creation of the human
soul. For there is an essential difference between matter and spirit.
It can indeed be said that God, Who directed evolution precisely
to man as to an end, owes it to Himself to create a man by the
infusion of the human soul but that this is not due to any internal
exigency on the part of organic matter no matter how highly organized. It is preferable to say that an animal body evolved and
was slowly formed under the direction of God to that point where
it was suitable for the infusion of the spiritual soul. In this case,
the soul as the form of the body, by its own information of the
animal body profoundly transforms the body into which it is inserted and thus constitutes that body genuinely human. There is
no great difference whether one says that the spiritual form
created the last disposition within the matter by informing it
under the influence of God as the efficient cause or whether one
says that God Himself, logically prior, produced certain ultimate
dispositions in organic matter to proximately dispose this animal
body to be the material cause of a human composite. In both cases
it is evident that God, by infusing the spiritual soul, disposes this
organic matter so that it should become human matter. In the first
opinion a body of a brute is adorned with a human soul and
thus becomes human. In the second opinion, it becomes human
after having been an animal but close to the human. In the second
opinion, which is preferable, the whole man, body and soul, is
clearly formed by the immediate operation of God. The organic
matter, which is the material cause, would in this opinion have
been previously animal. In the classical opinion it has been considered inorganic matter. But in both cases, matter does not become
the matter of man through its innate forces but through the direct
intervention of God.

Man, even with regard to his body, arises by a special intervention of God inasmuch as the infusion of a human soul induces a
specifically human organization of the body, whether this humani-
zation is conceived as rationally prior to the infusion of the soul or
concomitant with it through that mutual and reciprocal causality
by which the ultimate disposition for the reception of the form is
affected by the presence of the form itself. It does not appear to
us, from theological sources, that there is any contradiction between
such theory and what the Catholic theologian is obliged to hold.

Man is still essentially different from the brute, and body and soul are still formed by the immediate intervention of God.

Not every species of transformism can be admitted. Materialistic transformism, which explains the body of man by immanent intramundane forces of evolution prescinding from the activity of God, cannot be accepted by the theologian. However, if the theologian accepts the doctrine of the peculiar intervention of God in regard to the formation not only of the soul of man but also of his body, we do not see that he is in any difficulty from any magisterial text. The theories of moderate transformism could, it seems, be modestly proposed until such a moment as theology and science arrive at fuller clarity.

There is no doubt that many elements in the Genesis recital are also figurative. Among the symbolic elements may perhaps be considered the formation of man from the slime of the earth, the Garden of Paradise, the trees, the leading of the animals to man that he might give them their names, the formation of Eve from the rib of Adam, the serpent, the splendid sword, and the tunics of leaves.

As regards the formation of Eve, it is perhaps possible to interpret the text as implying formation of Eve from some part of Adam's body, or as implying that Adam is the exemplary cause of Eve, thus intimating the equality of human nature in Adam and Eve. We do not assert that this interpretation is the genuine interpretation of the formation of Eve, but we merely state negatively, that it is not evident that the narrative of Sacred Scripture forbids this interpretation. Thus Eve would be presented as the equal of Adam according to her human nature, an equality which is the basis for monogamy, but subordinate to him within the household.

The Genesis narrative obviously supposes the essential unity of the human race. The term used in describing the creation of Eve, namely, "rib" or "side," is certainly one of the most obscure words in Genesis. Man and woman form a unity, each enjoys a common nature superior to the nature of animals, each complements the other and is meant for the other. The author certainly teaches in this story of Eve the spiritual nature of womanhood and her root equality with man, and the fact that the two form a moral person according to God's design. Woman possesses the identical human nature as man and this truth is strongly underscored in the relation of her creation. It seems legitimate to suggest modestly that what is underscored here are these religious truths and that an interpretation of Adam as an exemplary cause is not forbidden. The Biblical Commission has formally stated that Eve was drawn in some way from Adam. From whatever aspect we look upon the problem, the idea that God took an animal and transformed it is somewhat artificial with respect to Eve. The furthest that we can go in suggesting a solution to this problem is that Adam was at least the exemplary cause of Eve in so far as her body and her nature were fashioned after his. The exact manner in which her body is formed is uncertain from the text, nor has tradition clarified it with any certainty.

The doctrine of the origin of all men from one pair seems to be so intimately involved with other dogmatic truths, such as the dogma of original sin, that all Catholics must hold it.[10] "No Catholic can hold that after Adam there existed on this earth true men who did not take their origin through natural generation from him as from the first parent of all, or that Adam is merely a symbol for a number of first parents. For it is unintelligible how such an opinion can be squared with what the sources of revealed truth and the documents of the Magisterium of the Church teach on original sin, which proceeds from sin actually committed by an individual Adam, and which, passed on to all by way of generation, is in everyone as his own." [11]

10. V. Marcozzi, "Poligenesi ed evoluzione nelle origini dell'uomo," *Gregorianum*, 1948, p. 390. Cf. also H. Lennerz, "Quid theologo dicendum de polygenismo," *Gregorianum*, 1948, pp. 81–98.

11. This translation is taken from p. 43 of *The Encyclical "Humani Generis" with a Commentary* [by] A. C. Cotter, S.J. (2d ed.; Weston, Mass.: Weston College Press, 1952), which gives the text of this 1950 papal encyclical in the original Latin with an English translation opposite. The Latin original here runs as follows: "Cum vero de alia coniecturali opinione agitur, videlicet de polygenismo quem vocant, tum Ec-clesiae filii eiusmodi libertate minime fruuntur. Non enim christifideles eam sententiam amplecti possunt quam qui retinent, asseverant vel post Adam hisce in terris veros homines exstitisse qui non ab eodem prouti omnium proto-parente naturali generatione originem duxerint, vel Adam significare multitu-dinem quamdam protoparentum; cum nequaquam appareat quomodo huiusmo-di sententia componi queat cum iis quae fontes revelatae veritatis et acta Magisterii Ecclesiae proponunt de peccato originali, quod procedit ex peccato vere commisso ab uno Adamo, quodque generatione in omnes transfusum, inest unicuique proprium." *Ibid.*, p. 42.

Evolutionary Mysticism: Teilhard de Chardin

PIERRE TEILHARD DE CHARDIN

The Phenomenon of Man (1955) †

Preface

If this book is to be properly understood, it must be read not as a work on metaphysics, still less as a sort of theological essay, but purely and simply as a scientific treatise. The title itself indicates that. This book deals with man *solely* as a phenomenon; but it also deals with the *whole* phenomenon of man.

In the first place, it deals with man *solely* as a phenomenon. The pages which follow do not attempt to give an explanation of the world, but only an introduction to such an explanation. Put quite simply, what I have tried to do is this; I have chosen man as the centre, and around him I have tried to establish a coherent order between antecedents and consequences. I have not tried to discover a system of ontological and casual relations between the elements of the universe, but only an experimental law of recurrence which would express their successive appearance in time. * * *

But this book also deals with the *whole* phenomenon of man. Without contradicting what I have just said (however much it may appear to do so) it is this aspect which might possibly make my suggestions *look* like a philosophy. * * *

† Pierre Teilhard de Chardin (1881–1955), French priest and paleontologist, was banned from France for many years by his religious superiors because of the unorthodoxy of his thinking on human evolution. *The Phenomenon of Man*, representing the culmination of this thought, was written in 1938 but not permitted publication until 1955, after Teilhard's death. The present selections are from the Preface and from Book 4, Chapter 2, of the 1961 American edition.

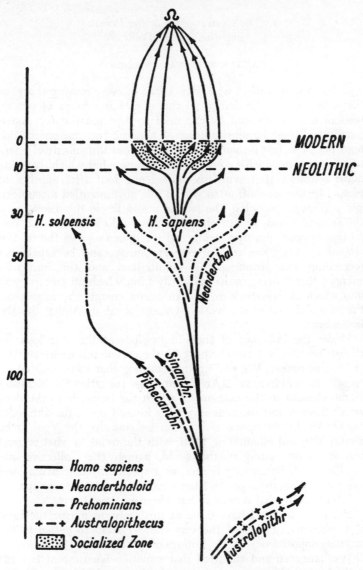

The development of the Human Layer. The figures on the left indicate thousands of years. They are a minimum estimate and should probably be at least doubled. The hypothetical zone of convergence on the point Omega is obviously not to scale. By analogy with other living layers, its duration should certainly run into millions of years.

1. The Convergence of the Person
and the Omega Point

A. THE PERSONAL UNIVERSE

Unlike the primitives who gave a face to every moving thing, or the early Greeks who deified all the aspects and forces of nature, modern man is obsessed by the need to depersonalise (or impersonalise) all that he most admires. There are two reasons for this tendency. The first is *analysis*, that marvellous instrument of scientific research to which we owe all our advances but which, breaking down synthesis after synthesis, allows one soul after another to escape, leaving us confronted with a pile of dismantled machinery, and evanescent particles. The second reason lies in the discovery of the sidereal world, so vast that it seems to do away with all proportion between our own being and the dimensions of the cosmos around us. Only one reality seems to survive and be capable of succeeding and spanning the infinitesimal and the immense: energy—that floating, universal entity from which all emerges and into which all falls back as into an ocean; energy, the new spirit; the new god. So, at the world's Omega, as at its Alpha, lies the Impersonal.

Under the influence of such impressions as these, it looks as though we have lost both respect for the person and understanding of his true nature. We end up by admitting that to be pivoted on oneself, to be able to say 'I,' is the privilege (or rather the blemish) of the element in the measure to which the latter closes the door on all the rest and succeeds in setting himself up at the antipodes of the All. In the opposite direction we conceive the 'ego' to be diminishing and eliminating itself, with the trend to what is most real and most lasting in the world, namely the Collective and the Universal. Personality is seen as a specifically corpuscular and ephemeral property; a prison from which we must try to escape.

Intellectually, that is more or less where we stand today.

Yet if we try, as I have done in this essay, to pursue the logic and coherence of facts to the very end, we seem to be led to the precisely opposite view by the notions of space-time and evolution.

We have seen and admitted that evolution is an ascent towards consciousness. That is no longer contested even by the most materialistic, or at all events by the most agnostic of humanitarians. Therefore it should culminate forwards in some sort of supreme consciousness. But must not that consciousness, if it is to be supreme, contain in the highest degree what is the perfection of our consciousness—the illuminating involution of the being upon itself? * * *

All our difficulties and repulsions as regards the opposition between the All and the Person would be dissipated if only we understood that, by structure, the noosphere [1] (and more generally the world) represent a whole that is not only closed but also *centred*. Because it contains and engenders consciousness, space-time is necessarily *of a convergent nature*. Accordingly its enormous layers, followed in the right direction, must somewhere ahead become involuted to a point which we might call *Omega*, which fuses and consumes them integrally in itself. * * *

Seen from this point of view, the universe, without losing any of its immensity and thus without suffering any anthropomorphism, begins to take shape: henceforward to think it, undergo it and make it act, it is *beyond* our souls that we must look, *not the other way round*. In the perspective of a noogenesis, time and space become truly humanised—or rather super-humanised. Far from being mutually exclusive, the Universal and Personal (that is to say the 'centred') grow in the same direction and culminate simultaneously in each other.

It is therefore a mistake to look for the extension of our being or of the noosphere in the Impersonal. The Future-Universal could not be anything else but the Hyper-Personal—at the Omega Point.

B. THE PERSONALISING UNIVERSE

Personalisation. It is by this eternal deepening of consciousness upon itself that we have characterised the particular destiny of the element that has become fully itself by crossing the threshold of reflection—and there, as regards the fate of individual human beings—we brought our inquiry to a provisional halt. *Personalisation:* the same type of progress reappears here, but this time it defines the collective future of totalised grains of thought. There is an identical function for the element as for the sum of the elements brought together in a synthesis. * * *

* * * It would be mistaken to represent Omega to ourselves simply as a centre born of the fusion of elements which it collects, or annihilating them in itself. By its structure Omega, in its ultimate principle, can only be a *distinct Centre radiating at the core of a system of centres*; a grouping in which personalisation of the All and personalisations of the elements reach their maximum, simultaneously and without merging, under the influence of a supremely autonomous focus of union.[2] That is the only picture which emerges when we try to apply the notion of collectivity with

---

1. For an explanation of this and other words of Teilhard's coining, see the Huxley commentary which follows [Editor].

2. It is for this central focus, necessarily autonomous, that we shall henceforward reserve the expression 'Omega Point.'

remorseless logic to a granular whole of thoughts.

And at this point we begin to see the motives for the fervour and the impotence which accompany every egoistic solution of life. Egoism, whether person or racial, is quite rightly excited by the idea of the element ascending through faithfulness to life, to the extremes of the incommunicable and the exclusive that it holds within it. It *feels* right. Its only mistake, but a fatal one, is *to confuse individuality with personality*. In trying to separate itself as much as possible from others, the element individualises itself; but in doing so it becomes retrograde and seeks to drag the world backwards towards plurality and into matter. In fact it diminishes itself and loses itself. To be fully ourselves it is in the opposite direction, in the direction of convergence with all the rest, that we must advance—towards the 'other.' * * *

* * * Thus, amongst the various forms of psychic inter-activity animating the noosphere, the energies we must identify, harness and develop before all others are those of an 'intercentric' nature, if we want to give effective help to the progress of evolution in ourselves.

Which brings us to the problem of love.

2. *Love as Energy*

We are accustomed to consider (and with what a refinement of analysis!) only the sentimental face of love, the joy and miseries it causes us. It is in its natural dynamism and its evolutionary significance that I shall be dealing with it here, with a view to determining the ultimate phases of the phenomenon of man.

Considered in its full biological reality, love—that is to say the affinity of being with being—is not peculiar to man. It is a general property of all life and as such it embraces, in its varieties and degress, all the forms successively adopted by organised matter. * * * Driven by the forces of love, the fragments of the world seek each other so that the world may come to being. This is no metaphor; and it is much more than poetry. Whether as a force or a curvature, the universal gravity of bodies, so striking to us, is merely the reverse or shadow of that which really moves nature. To perceive cosmic energy 'at the fount' we must, if there is a *within* of things, go down into the internal or radial zone of spiritual attractions.

Love in all its subtleties is nothing more, and nothing less, than the more or less direct trace marked on the heart of the element by the psychical convergence of the universe upon itself.

This, if I am not mistaken, is the ray of light which will help us to see more clearly around us. * * *

We are often inclined to think that we have exhausted the various natural forms of love with a man's love for his wife, his children, his friends and to a certain extent for his country. Yet precisely the most fundamental form of passion is missing from this list, the one which, under the pressure of an involuting universe, precipitates the elements one upon the other in the Whole—cosmic affinity and hence cosmic direction. A universal love is not only psychologically possible; it is the only complete and final way in which we are able to love.

But, with this point made, how are we to explain the appearance all around of us of mounting repulsion and hatred? If such a strong potentiality is besieging us from within and urging us to union, what is it waiting for to pass from potentiality to action? Just this, no doubt that we should overcome the 'anti-personalist' complex which paralyses us, and make up our minds to accept the possibility, indeed the reality, of some *source* of love and *object* of love at the summit of the world above our heads. So long as it absorbs or appears to absorb the person, the collectivity kills the love that is trying to come to birth. As such the collectivity is essentially un-lovable. That is where philanthropic systems break down. Common sense is right. It is impossible to give oneself to anonymous number. But if the universe ahead of us assumes a face and a heart, and so to speak personifies itself,[3] then in the atmosphere created by this focus the elemental attraction will immediately blossom. Then, no doubt, under the heightened pressure of an infolding world, the formidable energies of attraction, still dormant between human molecules, will burst forth. * * *

3. *The Attributes of the Omega Point*

After allowing itself to be captivated in excess by the charms of analysis to the extent of falling into illusion, modern thought is at last getting acclimatised once more to the idea of the creative value of synthesis in the evolutionary sense. It is beginning to see that there is definitely *more* in the molecule than in the atom, *more* in the cell than in the molecule, *more* in society than in the individual, and *more* in mathematical construction than in calcula-tions and theorems. We are now inclined to admit that at each further degree of combination *something* which is irreducible to isolated elements *emerges* in a new order. And with this admis-sion, consciousness, life and thought are on the threshold of acquir-ing a right to existence in terms of science. But science is nevertheless still far from recognizing that this *something* has a particular value of independence and solidity. For, born of an in-credible concourse of chances on a precariously assembled edifice,

3. Not, of course, by becoming a per-son, but by charging itself at the very heart of its development with the dom-inating and unifying influence of a focus of personal energies and attrac-tions.

and failing to create any measurable increase of energy by their advent, are not these 'creatures of synthesis,' from the point of view of experiment, the most beautiful as well as the most fragile of things? How could they anticipate or survive the ephemeral union of particles on which their souls have alighted? So in the end, in spite of a half-hearted conversion to spiritual order, it is still on the *elementary* side—that is, towards matter infinitely diluted—that physics and biology look to find the eternal and the Great Stability.

In conformity with this state of mind the idea that some Soul of souls should be developing at the summit of the world is not as strange as might be thought from the present-day views of human reason. After all, is there any other way in which our thought can generalise the Principle of Emergence? [4] At the same time, as this Soul coincides with a supremely improbable coincidence of the totality of elements and causes, it remains understood or implied that it could not form itself save at an extremely distant future and in a total dependence on the reversible laws of energy.

Yet it is precisely from these two restrictions (fragility and distance), both incompatible to my mind with the nature and function of Omega, that we want to rid ourselves—and this for two positive reasons, one of love, the other of survival.

First of all the *reason of Love*. Expressed in terms of internal energy, the cosmic function of Omega consists in initiating and maintaining within its radius the unanimity of the world's 'reflective' particles. But how could it exercise this action were it not in some sort loving and lovable *at this very moment?* Love, I said, dies in contact with the impersonal and the anonymous. With equal infallibility it becomes impoverished with remoteness in space—and still more, much more, with difference in time. For love to be possible there must be co-existence. Accordingly, however marvellous its foreseen figure, Omega could never even so much as equilibrate the play of human attractions and repulsions if it did not act with equal force, that is to say with the same stuff of proximity. With love, as with every other sort of energy, it is within the existing datum that the lines of force must at every instant be enclosed. Neither an ideal centre, nor a potential centre could possibly suffice. A present and real noosphere goes with a real and present centre. To be supremely attractive, Omega must be supremely present. * * *

In Omega we have in the first place the principle we needed to explain both the persistent march of things toward greater consciousness, and the paradoxical solidity of what is most fragile. Contrary to the appearances still admitted by physics, the Great Stability is not at the bottom in the infra-elementary sphere, but

4. See the quotation from J. B. S. Haldane in footnote p. 57.

at the top in the ultra-synthetic sphere. It is thus entirely by its tangential envelope that the world goes on dissipating itself in a chance way into matter. By its radial nucleus it finds its shape and its natural consistency in gravitating against the tide of probability towards a divine focus of mind which draws it onward.

Thus something in the cosmos escapes from entropy, and does so more and more.

During immense periods in the course of evolution, the radial, obscurely stirred up by the action of the *Prime Mover ahead,* was only able to express itself, in diffuse aggregates, in animal consciousness. And at that stage, not being able, above them, to attach themselves to a support whose order of simplicity was greater than their own, the nuclei were hardly formed before they began to disaggregate. But as soon as, through reflection, a type of unity appeared no longer closed or even centred, but punctiform, the sublime physics of centres came into play. When they became centres, and therefore persons, the elements could at last begin to react, directly as such, to the personalising action of the centre of centres. When consciousness broke through the critical surface of hominisation, it really passed from divergence to convergence and changed, so to speak, both hemisphere and pole. Below that critical 'equator' lay the relapse into multiplicity; above it, the plunge into growing and irreversible unification. Once formed, a reflective centre can no longer change except by involution upon itself. To outward appearance, admittedly, man becomes corrupted just like any animal. But here and there we find an inverse function of the phenomenon. By death, in the animal, the radial is reabsorbed into the tangential, while in man it escapes and is liberated from it. So we come to escape from entropy by turning back to Omega: the *hominisation* of death itself.

Thus from the grains of thought forming the veritable and indestructible atoms of its stuff, the universe—a well-defined universe in the outcome—goes on building itself above our heads in the inverse direction of matter which vanishes. The universe is a collector and conservator, not of mechanical energy, as we supposed, but of persons. All round us, one by one, like a continual exhalation, 'souls' break away, carrying upwards their incommunicable load of consciousness. One by one, yet not in isolation. Since, for each of them, by the very nature of Omega, there can only be one possible point of definitive emersion—that point at which, under the synthesising action of personalising union, the noosphere (furling its elements upon themselves as it too furls upon itself) will reach collectively its point of convergence—at the 'end of the world.'

Three Scientists' Views of Teilhard

SIR JULIAN HUXLEY

Introduction to *The Phenomenon of Man* (1958) †

The Phenomenon of Man is a very remarkable work by a very remarkable human being. Père Teilhard de Chardin was at the same time a Jesuit Father and a distinguished palaeontologist. In *The Phenomenon of Man* he has effected a threefold synthesis—of the material and physical world with the world of mind and spirit; of the past with the future; and of variety with unity, the many with the one. He achieves this by examining every fact and every subject of his investigation *sub specie evolutionis*, with reference to its development in time and to its evolutionary position. Conversely, he is able to envisage the whole of knowable reality not as a static mechanism but as a process. In consequence, he is driven to search for human significance in relation to the trends of that enduring and comprehensive process; the measure of his stature is that he so largely succeeded in the search. * * *

Père Teilhard starts from the position that mankind in its totality is a phenomenon to be described and analysed like any other phenomenon: it and all its manifestations, including human history and human values, are proper objects for scientific study.

His second and perhaps most fundamental point is the absolute necessity of adopting an evolutionary point of view. Though for certain limited purposes it may be useful to think of phenomena as isolated statically in time, they are in point of fact never static: they are always processes or parts of processes. The different branches of science combine to demonstrate that the universe in its entirety must be regarded as one gigantic process, a process of becoming, of attaining new levels of existence and organization, which can properly be called a genesis or an evolution. For this reason, he uses words like *noogenesis*, to mean the gradual evolution of mind or mental properties, and repeatedly stresses that we should no longer speak of a cosmology but of a *cosmogenesis*. Similarly, he likes to use a pregnant term like *hominisation* to denote the process by which the original proto-human stock became

† This selection is from Huxley's Introduction to the English translation of *The Phenomenon of Man*.

466

(and is still becoming) more truly human, the process by which potential man realized more and more of his possibilities. Indeed, he extends this evolutionary terminology by employing terms like *ultra-hominisation* to denote the deducible future stage of the process in which man will have so far transcended himself as to demand some new appellation.

With this approach he is rightly and indeed inevitably driven to the conclusion that, since evolutionary phenomena (of course including the phenomenon known as man) are processes, they can never be evaluated or even adequately described solely or mainly in terms of their origins: they must be defined by their direction, their inherent possibilities (including of course also their limitations), and their deducible future trends. He quotes with approval Nietzsche's view that man is unfinished and must be surpassed or completed; and proceeds to deduce the steps needed for his completion.

Père Teilhard was keenly aware of the importance of vivid and arresting terminology. Thus in 1925 he coined the term *noosphere* to denote the sphere of mind, as opposed to, or rather superposed on, the biosphere or sphere of life, and acting as a transforming agency promoting hominisation (or as I would put it, progressive psychosocial evolution). He may perhaps be criticized for not defining the term more explicitly. By *noosphere* did he intend simply the total pattern of thinking organisms (i.e. human beings) and their activity, including the patterns of their interrelations: or did he intend the special environment of man, the systems of organized thought and its products in which men move and have their being, as fish swim and reproduce in rivers and the sea? [1] Perhaps it might have been better to restrict *noosphere* to the first-named sense, and to use something like *noosystem* for the second. But certainly *noosphere* is a valuable and thought-provoking word.

He usually uses *convergence* to denote the tendency of mankind, during its evolution, to superpose centripetal on centrifugal trends, so as to prevent centrifugal differentiation from leading to fragmentation, and eventually to incorporate the results of differentiation in an organized and unified pattern. Human convergence was first manifested on the genetic or biological level: after *Homo sapiens* began to differentiate into distinct races (or *subspecies*, in more scientific terminology) migration and intermarriage prevented the pioneers from going further, and led to increasing interbreed-

---

1. In *Le Phénomène Humain* (p. 201) he refers to the *noosphere* as a new layer or membrane on the earth's surface, a 'thinking layer' superposed on the living layer of the *biosphere* and the lifeless layer of inorganic material, the *lithosphere*. But in his earlier formulation of 1925, in *La Vision du Passé* (p. 92), he calls it 'une sphère de la réflexion, de l'invention consciente, de l'union sentie des âmes.'

ing between all human variants. As a result, man is the only success-ful type which has remained as a single interbreeding group of species, and has not radiated out into a number of biologically separated assemblages (like the birds, with about 8,500 species, or the insects with over half a million).

Cultural differentiation set in later, producing a number of psy-chosocial units with different cultures. However, these 'interthink-ing groups,' as one writer has called them, are never so sharply separated as are biological species; and with time, the process known to anthropologists as cultural diffusion, facilitated by migration and improved communications, led to an accelerating counter-process of cultural convergence, and so towards the union of the whole hu-man species into a single interthinking group based on a single self-developing framework of thought (or noosystem).

In parenthesis, Père Teilhard showed himself aware of the dan-ger that this tendency might destroy the valuable results of cultural diversification, and lead to drab uniformity instead of to a rich and potent pattern of variety-in-unity. However, perhaps because he was (rightly) so deeply concerned with establishing a global unifica-tion of human awareness as a necessary prerequisite for any real future progress of mankind, and perhaps also because he was by nature and inclination more interested in rational and scientific thought than in the arts, he did not discuss the evolutionary value of cultural variety in any detail, but contented himself by maintain-ing that East and West are culturally complementary, and that both are needed for the further synthesis and unification of world thought.

Before passing to the full implications of human convergence, I must deal with Père Teilhard's valuable but rather difficult con-cept of *complexification*. This concept includes, as I understand it, the genesis of increasingly elaborate organization during cosmogene-sis, as manifested in the passage from subatomic units to atoms, from atoms to inorganic and later to organic molecules, thence to the first subcellular living units or self-replicating assemblages of molecules, and then to cells, to multicellular individuals, to ce-phalized metazoa with brains, to primitive man, and now to civi-lized societies.

But it involves something more. He speaks of complexification as an all-pervading tendency, involving the universe in all its parts in an *enroulement organique sur soi-même*, or by an alterna-tive metaphor, as a *reploiement sur soi-même*. He thus envisages the world-stuff as being 'rolled up' or 'folded in' upon itself, both locally and in its entirety, and adds that the process is accompanied by an increase of energetic 'tension' in the resultant 'corpuscular' organizations, or individualized constructions of increased organizational complexity. For want of a better English phrase, I shall use *convergent integration* to define the operation of this process of self-complexification. * * *

Père Teilhard, extrapolating from the past into the future, envisaged the process of human convergence as tending to a final state,[2] which he called 'point *Omega*,' as opposed to the *Alpha* of elementary material particles and their energies. If I understand him aright, he considers that two factors are co-operating to promote this further complexification of the noosphere. One is the increase of knowledge about the universe at large, from the galaxies and stars to human societies and individuals. The other is the increase of psychosocial pressure on the surface of our planet. The result of the one is that the noosphere incorporates ever more facts of the cosmos, including the facts of its general direction and its trends in time, so as to become more truly a microcosm, which (like all incorporated knowledge) is both a mirror and a directive agency. The result of the other is the increased unification and the increased intensity of the system of human thought. The combined result, according to Père Teilhard, will be the attainment of point Omega, where the noosphere will be intensely unified and will have achieved a 'hyperpersonal' organisation.

Here his thought is not fully clear to me. Sometimes he seems to equate this future hyperpersonal psychosocial organisation with an emergent Divinity: at one place, for instance, he speaks of the trend as a *Christogenesis;* and elsewhere he appears not to be guarding himself sufficiently against the dangers of personifying the nonpersonal elements of reality. Sometimes, too, he seems to envisage as desirable the merging of individual human variety in this new unity. Though many scientists may, as I do, find it impossible to follow him all the way in his gallant attempt to reconcile the supernatural elements in Christianity with the facts and implications of evolution, this in no way detracts from the positive value of his naturalistic general approach. * * *

Once he had grasped and faced the fact of man as an evolutionary phenomenon, the way was open towards a new and comprehensive system of thought. It remained to draw the fullest conclusions from this central concept of man as the spearhead of evolution on earth, and to follow out the implications of this approach in as many fields as possible. The biologist may perhaps consider that in *The Phenomenon of Man* he paid insufficient attention to genetics

2. Presumably, in designating this state as Omega, he believed that it was a truly final condition. It might have been better to think of it merely as a novel state or mode of organization, beyond which the human imagination cannot at present pierce, though perhaps the strange facts of extra-sensory perception unearthed by the infant science of parapsychology may give us a clue as to a possible more ultimate state.

and the possibilities and limitations of natural selection,[3] the theologian that his treatment of the problems of sin and suffering was inadequate or at least unorthodox, the social scientist that he failed to take sufficient account of the facts of political and social history. But he saw that what was needed at the moment was a broad sweep and a comprehensive treatment. This was what he essayed in *The Phenomenon of Man*. In my view he achieved a remarkable success, and opened up vast territories of thought to further exploration and detailed mapping. * * *

GEORGE GAYLORD SIMPSON

Evolutionary Theology: The New Mysticism (1964) †

* * * The conflict between science and religion has a single and simple cause. It is the designation as religiously canonical of any conception of the material world open to scientific investigation. That is a basis for conflict even when religion and science happen to agree as to the material facts. The religious canon (if normally designated as such) demands absolute acceptance not subject to test or revision. Science necessarily rejects certainty and predicates acceptance on objective testing and the possibility of continual revision. As a matter of fact, most of the dogmatic religions have exhibited a perverse talent for taking the wrong side on the most important concepts of the material universe, from the structure of the solar system to the origin of man. The result has been constant turmoil for many centuries, and the turmoil will continue as long as religious canons prejudge scientific questions. * * *

I am no theologian, natural or otherwise, and I am unwilling to pose as one. Here I am also not directly or primarily concerned with the conflict between science and religion, but with a peculiar, related interaction of the two. The path of religious intuition or of mystic communion need not have conscious connection with the material world, and indeed this is one of several ways in which the conflict with science can be successfully resolved. However, for some scientists there has seemed to be such a connection, and then some reconciliation or fusion of the two conceptual schemes has been sought. The relationships envisioned vary greatly. For Julian Huxley (*Religion Without Revelation*) theology itself be-

3. Though in his Institute for Human Studies he envisaged a section of Eugenics.
† This selection is from Chapter 11 of Simpson's *This View of Life* (New York, 1964). George Gaylord Simpson (b. 1902) is Alexander Agassiz Professor of Vertebrate Paleontology in the Museum of Comparative Zoology, Harvard University, and Professor of Geology in the School of Earth Sciences, University of Arizona.

comes a subject for scientific investigation and religious emotion
is a psychological fact centering on direct experience of sacredness
in the universe. For Teilhard de Chardin the mystic conviction is
overwhelming and primary; it is the premise for all interpretation
and overrides any consideration of objective science. Huxley and
Teilhard could hardly differ more as regards theories of evolution,
attitudes toward science, and conclusions as to theology, but they
both have proposed systems in which, in quite different ways and
proportions, science and mysticism are involved.

It is that phenomenon that I shall discuss in the present chapter.
This will be done mainly by reference to the works of three biologists whom I would call new mystics: Pierre Lecomte du Noüy,
Edmund W. Sinnott, and P. Teilhard de Chardin. They are nearly
alone, or at the least have been most eloquent, in expression of varieties of evolutionary theology or theological evolution. All three are
both finalists and vitalists of sorts and so those minority schools,
given short shrift elsewhere in this book, will have some notice.
All agree with other finalists and vitalists that a naturalistic theory
of evolution has not been and cannot be achieved. All make appeals
to the supernatural, in these three cases to different forms of
dogmatic Christianity, and all advocate concepts or theories of
evolution in which the approaches of science and religion are confused. With varying degrees of overtness, all make some claims
that their religious conclusions are derived from scientific premises
and interpretations. That aspect has led in some instances to popularity among those piously concerned but not cognizant of the actual
issues or capable of judging the theories. * * *

One of Teilhard's fundamental propositions is that all phenomena must be considered as developing dynamically, that is, in an
evolutionary manner, in space-time. "It [i.e., evolution] is a general condition to which all theories, all hypotheses, all systems
must bow and which they must satisfy henceforward if they are to
be thinkable and true." On this basis, unimpeachable in itself, he
reviews briefly the evolution of the cosmos and at greater length
that of organisms and of man. He is not concerned with details but
with the broadest features of the story as it moves onward.
These are traced in a style often delightfully poetic but sometimes
syntactically overcomplex and often obscurely metaphorical. The
whole process, from dissociated atoms to man, is seen as a gradual
progress with two revolutionary turning points among others of
less importance: first, and early, the achievement of cellular organization; second, and late, the emergence of true man. Much of
the intervening story is envisioned in terms of the succession and
frequently the replacement of what Teilhard usually called
"*nappes,*" a term difficult to translate that is rendered as "layers"

or "grades" in the English version. The *nappe* phenomenon involves the expansion or radiation of groups that had reached new structural and adaptive levels, and it has been extensively discussed by other evolutionists in those or similar terms.

Teilhard's book is not, however, strictly or even mainly concerned with describing the factual course of evolution. That is "the *without*" of things, and the author is concerned rather with "the *within.*" The within is another term for consciousness (the French *"conscience,"* another word without a really precise English equivalent), which in turn implies spontaneity and includes every kind of "psychism." Consciousness, in this sense, is stated to be a completely general characteristic of matter, whether in an individual atom or in man, although in the atom it is less organized and less evident. The origin of the cell was critical because it involved a "psychic mutation" introducing a change in the nature of the state of universal consciousness. The origin of man was again critical because at this stage consciousness became self-consciousness, reflection or thought. Now this as yet highest stage of consciousness begins a concentration or involution that will eventually bring it into complete unity, although without loss of personality in that collective hyper-personal. Then the consciousness of the universe, which will have evolved through man, will become eternally concentrated at the "Omega point," free from the perishable planets and material trammels. The whole process is intended; it is the *purpose* of evolution, planned by the God Who is also the Omega into which consciousness is finally to be concentrated. Mystical Christianity is to be the path or the vehicle to ecstatic union with Omega.

Teilhard's first sentence in *The Phenomenon of Man* is as follows:

> If this book is to be properly understood, it must be read not as a work on metaphysics, still less as a sort of theological essay, but purely and simply as a scientific treatise.

In the last chapter (before the epilogue, the postscript, and the appendix) he wrote:

> Man will only continue to work and to research so long as he is prompted by a passionate interest. Now this interest is entirely dependent on the conviction, strictly undemonstrable to science, that the universe has a direction and that it could—indeed, if we are faithful, it should—result in some sort of irreversible perfection. Hence comes belief in progress.

But the direction of evolution toward an irreversible perfection is the whole theme, and not merely a philosophical appendage, of the book. Hence we have a book submitted purely as a scientific treatise and yet devoted to a thesis admittedly undemonstrable scientifically. (The word here translated as "belief" is *"foi,"* and the context makes it unmistakable that religious faith is meant.) The anomaly is partly explained by the fact that in this particular manuscript Teilhard did avoid explicit discussion of certain points in dogmatic theology. The origin and fate of the individual soul, Adam and Eve and original sin, and the divinity of Christ, for instance, are all alluded to or allowed for, but only briefly and in veiled terms. In addition the discussion begins as a sort of mystical science and only gradually, almost imperceptibly, becomes mystical religion. Identification of Omega with God is evident from the beginning to anyone already familiar with Teilhard's thought, but in this book it is not made explicit until the epilogue. In others of Teilhard's works, lacking the pretense of being scientific treatises, Omega is discussed in frankly theological mystical terms.

The sense in which Teilhard's science, and not alone his theology, must be called mystical may be illustrated from an early passage in *The Phenomenon of Man* (Chapter II) that introduces concepts crucially used throughout all that follows. First he makes a distinction between material energy and spiritual energy, and points out that material energy, for instance that derived from bread, is not closely correlated either in intensity or in variety with spiritual energy, for instance that exhibited by human thought. But surely both of these can be described and at least conceivably may be explained in material terms. A reasonable mechanical analogy is provided by a television set, in which the activity and multiplicity of the pictures are not well correlated with the intensity and uniformity of the power in wires and tubes. One could speak of "picture energy" as distinct from "electron energy," but it would be evident that "energy" is not even roughly comparable in the two senses and that the metaphorical terminology obscures rather than promotes understanding of the phenomena. And surely it is further obfuscation when Teilhard goes on to explain:

> We shall assume that, essentially, all energy [i.e., both material and spiritual energy] is physical in nature; but add that in each particular element this fundamental energy is divided into two distinct components: A *tangential energy* which links the element with all others of the same order (that is to say of the same complexity and the same centricity) as itself in the universe; and a *radial energy* which draws it towards ever greater complexity and centricity—in other words forwards.

Alas! That is no better than double talk, from the statement that something *defined* as spiritual is nevertheless *assumed* to be physical onward through the whole discussion.

As to the mechanism of evolution, obviously a, or indeed *the*, crucial point of the scientific part of the inquiry, Teilhard accepted both Darwinism and Neo-Lamarckism as partial factors. He called

Darwinism evolution by chance (although natural selection is the only objectively established antichance evolutionary factor) and therefore considered the nonchance Neo-Lamarckian factors more important (although, as he knew, most biologists consider them not merely unimportant but nonexistent). However, he maintained that these and all proposed material mechanisms of evolution are related only to various details of the process. The basic over-all pattern and also the essentially directional elements in its various lineages he ascribed to orthogenesis.

Orthogenesis was variously defined by Teilhard as the "law of controlled complication" which acts "in a predetermined direction," as "definite orientation regularizing the effects of chance in the play of heredity," as "the manifest property of living matter to form a system in which 'terms *succeed each other* experimentally, following the constantly increasing values of centro-complexity,' " or as "*directed* transformation (to whatever degree and under whatever influence 'the direction' may be manifested)." The last definition, which is from a brief manuscript written just before Teilhard's death, is broad enough to include the effects of natural selection, but that was certainly not intended, because Teilhard repeatedly contrasted selection with orthogenesis and indeed usually treated them as complete opposites. Similar imprecision or contradiction in definition is one of the constant problems in the study of the Teilhardian canon.

Indeed these and other usages of the term "orthogenesis" in Teilhard's work seem at first sight to have no explanatory meaning whatever but to be tautological or circular. History is inherently unrepeatable, so that any segment of a historical sequence (such as that of organic evolution) begins with one state and ends with another. It therefore necessarily has a direction of change, and if orthogenesis is merely that direction, it explains nothing and only applies a Greek term to what is obvious without the term. However, when Teilhard says that the direction is "pre-determined" and that there is only one direction—toward greater "centro-complexity," toward Omega, ultimately toward God—then the statement is still not explanatory and is obviously not science, but it is no longer trivial.

Now it is easy enough to show that, although evolution is directional as a historical process must always be, it is multidirectional; when all directions are taken into account, it is erratic and opportunistic. Obviously, since man exists, from primordial cell to man was one of the directions, or rather a variety of them in succession, for there was no such sequence *in a straight line* and therefore literally orthogenetic. Teilhard was well aware of the consensus to that effect, but he brushed it aside and refused to grapple with it in terms of the detailed evidence.

Here we come to the real crux of the whole problem: Which are the premises and which the conclusions? One may start from material evidence and from interpretive probabilities established by tests of hypotheses, that is, from science. Despite the objections of some philosophers and theologians, it is then legitimate to proceed logically from these premises to conclusions regarding the nature of man, of life, or of the universe, even if these conclusions go beyond the realm of science in the strictest sense, and that is not only legitimate but also necessary if science is to have value beyond serving as a base for technology. On the other hand, one may start from premises of pure faith, nonmaterial and nontestable, therefore non-scientific, and proceed to conclusions in the same field of the nature of the material cosmos. It cannot be argued that this approach from metaphysical or religious premises is *ipso facto* illegitimate. It is, however, proper to insist that its conclusions should not be presented as scientific, and that when they are materially testable they should be submitted to that scientific discipline. Gradual recognition of that necessity has been evident in the historical change in the relationships between science and religion.

Teilhard's major premises are in fact religious and, except for the conclusion that evolution has indeed occurred, his conclusions about evolution derive from those premises and not from scientific premises. One cannot object to the piety or mysticism of *The Phenomenon of Man*, but one can object to its initial claim to be a scientific treatise and to the arrangement that puts its real premises briefly, in part obscurely, as a sort of appendage after the conclusions drawn from them. That this really is an inversion of the logic involved is evident from the whole body of Teilhard's philosophical writings and also from the statements, or admissions, made toward the end of this book. A passage indicating that the main thesis of the book is a matter of faith and not scientifically demonstrable has already been quoted. Elsewhere in Teilhard's work there is abundant testimony that his premises were always in Christian faith and especially in his own mystical vision.

That is evident, too, in the complex concept of Omega that is the key to Teilhard's personal religious system. He explained on various occasions that the concept is necessary in order to keep mankind on its job of self-improvement and in order to evade distasteful thoughts of aimlessness and eventual death—worthy but certainly not scientific premises. The following passage from another of his manuscripts may additionally represent this contribution of Teilhard's, also essential in *The Phenomenon of Man* but there even less clear:

> In order to resolve the internal conflict that opposes the innate evanescence of the planets against the necessary irreversibility developed on their surface by planetized life, it is not enough to

draw a veil or to recoil. It is a case for radical exorcism of the specter of Death from our horizon.

Very well, is it not that which permits us to form the idea (a corollary, as we have seen, of the mechanism of planetization) that there exists ahead of, or rather at the heart of, the universe, extrapolated along its axis of complexity, a divine center of convergence. Let us call it, to prejudge nothing and to emphasize its synthesizing and personalizing function, the *Omega point*. Let us suppose that from this universal center, this Omega point, there are continuously emitted rays perceptible only, up to now, by those whom we call "mystic souls." Let us further imagine that as mystical sensitivity or permeability increases with planetization, the perception of Omega comes to be more widespread, so that the earth is heated psychically while growing colder physically. Then does it not become conceivable that humanity at the end of its involution and totalization within itself may reach a critical point of maturation at the end of which, leaving behind earth and stars to return slowly to the vanishing mass of primordial energy, it will detach itself psychically from the planet in order to rejoin the Omega point, the only irreversible essence of things?

(Translated by me from an essay written in 1945, published in *L'Avenir de L'Homme*, Paris: Editions de Seuil, 1959, pp. 155–156.)

That is mysticism at its purest (if not exactly simplest), without vestige of either premise or conclusion in the realm of science. Teilhard's beliefs as to the course and the causes of evolution are not scientifically acceptable, because they are not in truth based on scientific premises and because to the moderate extent that they are subject to scientific tests they fail those tests. Teilhard's mystic vision is not thereby invalidated, because it does not in truth derive from his beliefs on evolution—quite the contrary. There is no possible way of validating or of testing Teilhard's mystic vision of Omega. Any assurance about it must itself be an unsupported act of mystic faith. * * *

P. B. MEDAWAR

Review of *The Phenomenon of Man* (1961) †

Everything does not happen continuously at any one moment in the universe. Neither does everything happen everywhere in it. There are no summits without abysses.

† *Mind*, LXX (1961), 99–106. P.B. Medawar (b. 1915), Nobel laureate in physiology and medicine, is director of the National Institute for Medical Research, London.

When the end of the world is mentioned, the idea that leaps into our minds is always one of catastrophe.

Life was born and propagates itself on the earth as a solitary pulsation.

In the last analysis the best guarantee that a thing should happen is that it appears to us as vitally necessary.

This little bouquet of aphorisms, each one thought sufficiently important by its author to deserve a paragraph to itself, is taken from Père Teilhard's *The Phenomenon of Man*. It is a book widely held to be of the utmost profundity and significance; it created something like a sensation upon its publication a few years ago in France, and some reviewers hereabouts have called it the Book of the Year—one, the Book of the Century. Yet the greater part of it, I shall show, is nonsense, tricked out by a variety of tedious metaphysical conceits, and its author can be excused of dishonesty only on the grounds that before deceiving others he has taken great pains to deceive himself. *The Phenomenon of Man* cannot be read without a feeling of suffocation, a gasping and flailing around for sense. There is an argument in it, to be sure—a feeble argument, abominably expressed—and this I shall expound in due course; but consider first the style, because it is the style that creates the illusion of content, and which is in some part the cause as well as merely the symptom of Teilhard's alarming apocalyptic seizures.

The Phenomenon of Man stands square in the tradition of *Naturphilosophie*, a philosophical indoor pastime of German origin which does not seem even by accident (though there is a great deal of it) to have contributed anything of permanent value to the storehouse of human thought. French is not a language that lends itself naturally to the opaque and ponderous idiom of nature-philosophy, and Teilhard has accordingly resorted to the use of that tipsy, euphoric prose-poetry which is one of the more tiresome manifestations of the French spirit. It is of the nature of reproduction that progeny should outnumber parents, and of Mendelian heredity that the inborn endowments of the parents should be variously recombined and reassorted among their offspring, so enlarging the population's candidature for evolutionary change. Teilhard puts the matter thus: it is one of his more lucid passages, and Mr. Wall's translation, here as almost everywhere else, captures the spirit and sense of the original.

> Reproduction doubles the mother cell. Thus, by a mechanism which is the inverse of chemical disintegration, *it multiplies without crumbling*. At the same time, however, it transforms what was only intended to be prolonged. Closed in on itself, the living element reaches more or less quickly a state of immobility. It becomes stuck and coagulated in its evolution. Then by the act of

reproduction it regains the faculty for inner re-adjustment and consequently takes on a new appearance and direction. The process is one of pluralization in form as well as in number. The elemental ripple of life that emerges from each individual unit does not spread outwards in a monotonous circle formed of individual units exactly like itself. It is diffracted and becomes iridescent, with an indefinite scale of variegated tonalities. The living unit is a centre of irresistible multiplication, and *ipso facto* an equally irresistible focus of diversification.

In no sense other than an utterly trivial one is reproduction the inverse of chemical disintegration. It is a misunderstanding of genetics to suppose that reproduction is only "intended" to make facsimiles, for parasexual processes of genetical exchange are to be found in the simplest living things. There seems to be some confusion between the versatility of a population and the adaptability of an individual. But errors of fact or judgement of this kind are to be found throughout, and are not my immediate concern; notice instead the use of adjectives of excess (misuse, rather, for genetic diversity is not indefinite nor multiplication irresistible). Teilhard is for ever shouting at us: things or affairs are, in alphabetical order, astounding, colossal, endless, enormous, fantastic, giddy, hyper-immense, implacable, indefinite, inexhaustible, inextricable, infinite, infinitesimal, innumerable, irresistible, measureless, mega-monstrous, mysterious, prodigious, relentless, super-, ultra-, unbelievable, unbridled, or unparalleled. When something is described as merely *huge* we feel let down. After this softening-up process we are ready to take delivery of the neologisms: biota, noosphere, hominization, complexification. There is much else in the literary idiom of nature-philosophy: *nothing-buttery*, for example, always part of the minor symptomatology of the bogus. "Love in all its subtleties is nothing more, and nothing less, than the more or less direct trace marked on the heart of the element by the psychical convergence of the universe upon itself." "Man discovers that he is *nothing else than evolution become conscious of itself*," and evolution is "nothing else than the continual growth of . . . 'psychic' or 'radial' energy". Again, "the Christogenesis of St. Paul and St. John is nothing else and nothing less than the extension . . . of that noogenesis in which cosmogenesis . . . culminates." It would have been a great disappointment to me if Vibration did not somewhere make itself felt, for all scientistic mystics either vibrate in person or find themselves resonant with cosmic vibrations; but I am happy to say that on page 266 Teilhard will be found to do so.

These are trivialities, revealing though they are, and perhaps I make too much of them. The evolutionary origins of consciousness are indeed distant and obscure, and perhaps so trite a thought does need this kind of dressing to make it palatable: "refracted rearwards along the course of evolution, consciousness displays itself qualitatively as a spectrum of shifting hints whose lower terms are lost in the night." (The roman type is mine.) What is much more serious is the fact that Teilhard habitually and systematically cheats with words. His work, he has assured us, is to be read, not as a metaphysical system, but "purely and simply as a scientific treatise" executed with "remorseless" or "inescapable" logic; yet he uses in metaphor words like energy, tension, force, impetus, and dimension *as if* they retained the weight and thrust of their special scientific usages. Consciousness, for example, is a matter upon which Teilhard has been said to have illuminating views. For the most part consciousness is treated as a manifestation of energy, though this does not help us very much because the word 'energy' is itself debauched; but elsewhere we learn that consciousness is a dimension, something with mass, something corpuscular and particulate which can exist in various degrees of concentration, being sometimes infinitely diffuse. In his lay capacity Teilhard, a naturalist, practised a comparatively humble and unexacting kind of science, but he must have known better than to play such tricks as these. On page 60 we read: "The simplest form of protoplasm is already a substance of unheard-of complexity. This complexity increases in geometrical progression as we pass from the protozoon higher and higher up the scale of the metazoa. And so it is for the whole of the remainder always and everywhere." Later we are told that the "*nascent* cellular world shows itself to be already infinitely complex". This seems to leave little room for improvement. In any event complexity (a subject on which Teilhard has a great deal to say) is not measureable in those scalar quantities to which the concept of a geometrical progression applies.

In spite of all the obstacles that Teilhard perhaps wisely puts in our way, it is possible to discern a train of thought in *The Phenomenon of Man*. It is founded upon the belief that the fundamental process or motion in the entire universe is *evolution*, and evolution is "a general condition to which all theories, all hypotheses, all systems must bow . . . a light illuminating all facts, a curve that all lines must follow". This being so, it follows that "nothing could ever burst forth as final across the different thresholds successively traversed by evolution . . . which has not already existed in an obscure and primordial way" (again my romans). Nothing is wholly new: there is always some primordium or anlage or rudiment or archetype of whatever exists or has existed. Love, for example— "that is to say, the affinity of being with being"—is to be found in some form throughout the organic world, and even at a "prodigiously rudimentary level", for if there were no such affinity between atoms when they unite into molecules it would be "physically impossible for love to appear higher up, with us, in 'hominized form". But above all consciousness is not new, for this would contradict the evolutionary axiom; on the contrary, we are "logically forced to assume the existence in rudimentary form . . . of some sort of psyche in every corpuscle", even in molecules; "by the very fact of the individualization of our planet, a certain mass of elementary consciousness was originally emprisoned in the matter of earth".

What form does this elementary consciousness take? Scientists have not been able to spot it, for they are shallow superficial fellows, unable to see into the inwardness of things—"up to now, has science ever troubled to look at the world other than from *without?*" Consciousness is an interiority of matter, an "inner fact that everywhere duplicates the 'material' external face, which alone is commonly considered by science". To grasp the nature of the within of things we must understand that energy is of two kinds: the 'tangential', which is energy as scientists use that word, and a radial energy (a term used interchangeably with spiritual or psychic energy) of which consciousness is treated sometimes as the equivalent, sometimes as the manifestation, and sometimes as the consequence (there is no knowing what Teilhard intends). Radial energy appears to be a measure of, or that which conduces towards, complexity or degree or arrangement; thus "spiritual energy, by its very nature, increases in 'radial' value . . . in step with the increasing chemical complexity of the elements of which it represents the inner lining". It confers *centricity*, and "the increase of the synthetic state of matter involves . . . an increase of consciousness".

We are now therefore in a position to understand what evolution is (is nothing but). Evolution is "the continual growth of . . . 'psychic' or 'radial' energy, in the course of duration, beneath and within the mechanical energy I called 'tangential' "; evolution, then, is "an ascent towards consciousness". It follows that evolution must have a "precise *orientation* and a privileged *axis*" at the topmost pole of which lies Man, born "a direct lineal descendant from a total effort of life".

Let us fill in the intermediate stages. Teilhard, with a penetrating insight that Sir Julian Huxley singles out for special praise, discerns that consciousness in the everyday sense is somehow associated with the possession of nervous systems and brains ("we have every reason to think that in animals too a certain inwardness exists, approximately proportional to the development of their brains"). The direction of evolution must therefore be towards cerebralization, *i.e.* towards becoming brainer. "Among the infinite modalities in which the complication of life is dispersed," he tells us, "the differentiation of nervous tissue stands out . . . as a significant transformation. *It provides a direction;* and by its consequences *it proves that evolution has a direction.*" All else is equivocal and insignificant; in the process of becoming brainier we find "the very essence of complexity, of essential metamorphosis". And if we study the evolution of living things, organic evolution, we shall find that in every one of its lines, except only in those in which it does not occur, evolution is an evolution towards increasing complexity of the nervous system and cerebralization. Plants don't count, to be sure (because "in the vegetable kingdom we are unable to follow along a nervous system the evolution of a psychism obviously remaining diffuse") and the contemplation of insects provokes a certain shuffling of the feet (p. 153); but primates are "a phylum of *pure and direct cerebralization*" and among them "evolution went straight to work on the brain, neglecting everything else". Here is Teilhard's description of noogenesis, the birth of higher consciousness among the primates, and of the noosphere in which that higher consciousness is deployed:

> By the end of the Tertiary era, the psychical temperature in the cellular world had been rising for more than 500 million years. . . . When the anthropoid, so to speak, had been brought 'mentally' to boiling point some further calories were added. . . . No more was needed for the whole inner equilibrium to be upset. . . . By a tiny 'tangential' increase, the 'radial' was turned back on itself and so to speak took an infinite leap forward. Outwardly, almost nothing in the organs had changed. But in depth, a great revolution had taken place: consciousness was now leaping and boiling in a space of super-sensory relationships and representations. . . .

The analogy, it should be explained, is with the vaporization of water when it is brought to boiling point, and the image of hot vapour remains when all else is forgotten.

I do not propose to criticize the fatuous argument I have just outlined; here, to expound is to expose. What Teilhard seems to be trying to say is that evolution is often (he says always) accompanied by an increase of orderliness or internal coherence or degree of integration. In what sense is the fertilized egg that develops into an adult human being 'higher' than, say, a bacterial cell? In the sense that it contains richer and more complicated genetical instructions for the execution of those processes that together constitute development. Thus Teilhard's radial, spiritual or psychic energy may be equated to 'information' or 'information content' in the sense that has been made reasonably precise by modern communications engineers. To equate it to consciousness, or to regard degree of consciousness as a measure of information content, is one of the silly little metaphysical conceits I mentioned in an earlier paragraph. Teilhard's belief, enthusiastically shared by Sir Julian Huxley, that evolution flouts or foils the second law of thermodynamics is based on a confusion of thought; and the idea that evolution has a main track or privileged axis is unsupported by scientific evidence.

Teilhard is widely believed to have rejected the modern Mendelian-Darwinian theory of evolution or to have demonstrated its inadequacy. Certainly he imports a ghost, the entelechy of *élan vital* of an earlier terminology, into the Mendelian machine; but he seems to accept the idea that evolution is probationary and exploratory and mediated through a selective process, a "groping", a billionfold trial and error"; "far be it from me", he declares, "to deny its importance". Unhappily Teilhard has no grasp of the real weakness of modern evolutionary theory, namely its lack of a complete theory of variation, of the origin of *candidature* for evolution. It is not enough to say that 'mutation' is ultimately the source of all genetical diversity, for that is merely to give the phenomenon a name: mutation is so defined. What we want, and are very slowly beginning to get, is a comprehensive theory of the forms in which new genetical information comes into being. It may, as I have hinted elsewhere, turn out to be of the nature of nucleic acids and the chromosomal apparatus that they tend spontaneously to proffer genetical variants—genetical solutions of the problem of remaining alive—which are more complex and more elaborate than the immediate occasion calls for; but to construe this 'complexification' as a manifestation of consciousness is a wilful abuse of words.

Teilhard's metaphysical argument begins where the scientific argument leaves off, and the gist of it is extremely simple. Inasmuch as evolution is the fundamental motion of the entire universe, an ascent along a privileged and necessary pathway towards consciousness, so it follows that our present consciousness must "culminate forwards in some sort of supreme consciousness". In expounding this thesis, Teilhard becomes more and more confused and excited and finally almost hysterical. The Supreme Consciousness, which apparently assimilates to itself all our personal consciousness, is, or is embodied in, "Omega" or the Omega-point; in Omega "the movement of synthesis culminates". Now Omega is "already in existence and operative at the very core of the thinking mass", so if we have our wits about us we should at this moment be able to detect Omega as "some excess of personal, extra-human energy", the more detailed contemplation of which will disclose the Great Presence. Although already in existence, Omega is added to progressively: "All round us, one by one, like a continual exhalation, 'souls' break away, carrying upwards their incommunicable load of consciousness", and so we end up with "a harmonized collectivity of consciousnesses equivalent to a sort of super-consciousness".

Teilhard devotes some little thought to the apparently insuperable problem of how to reconcile the persistence of individual consciousnesses with their assimilation to Omega. But the problem yields to the application of "remorseless logic". The individual particles of consciousness do not join up any old how, but only centre to centre, thanks to the mediation of Love; Omega, then, "in its ultimate principle, can only be a distinct Centre radiating at the core of a system of centres", and the final state of the world is one in which "unity coincides with a paroxysm of harmonized complexity". And so our hero escapes from his appalling predicament: with one bound, Jack was free.

Although elsewhere Teilhard has dared to write an equation so explicit as "Evolution = Rise of Consciousness" he does not go so far as to write "Omega = God"; but in the course of some obscure pious rant he does tell us that God, like Omega, is a "Centre of centres", and in one place he refers to "God-Omega".

How have people come to be taken in by *The Phenomenon of Man?* We must not underestimate the size of the market for works of this kind, for philosophy-fiction. Just as compulsory primary education created a market catered for by cheap dailies and weeklies, so the spread of secondary and latterly of tertiary education has created a large population of people, often with well developed literary and scholarly tastes, who have been educated far beyond their capacity to undertake analytical thought. It is through their eyes that we must attempt to see the attractions of Teilhard, which I shall jot down in the order in which they come to mind.

1. *The Phenomenon of Man* is anti-scientific in temper (scientists are shown up as shallow folk skating about on the surface of things), and, as if that were not recommendation enough, it was written by a scientist, a fact which seems to give it particular authority and weight. Laymen firmly believe that scientists are one species of person. They are not to know that the different branches of science require very different aptitudes and degrees of skill for their prosecution. Teilhard practised an intellectually unexacting kind of science in which he achieved a moderate proficiency. He has no grasp of what makes a logical argument or of what makes for proof. He does not even preserve the common decencies of scientific writing, though his book is professedly a scientific treatise.

2. It is written in an all but totally unintelligible style, and this is construed as *prima facie* evidence of profundity. (At present this applies only to works of French authorship; in later Victorian

and Edwardian times the same deference was thought due to Germans, with equally little reason.) It is because Teilhard has such wonderful *deep* thoughts that he's so difficult to follow—really it's beyond my poor brain but doesn't that just *show* how profound and important it must be?

3. It declares that Man is in a sorry state, the victim of a "fundamental anguish of being", "a malady of space-time", a sickness of "cosmic gravity". The Predicament of Man is all the rage now that people have sufficient leisure and are sufficiently well fed to contemplate it, and many a tidy little literary reputation has been built upon exploiting it; anybody nowadays who dared to suggest that the plight of man might not be wholly desperate would get a sharp rap over the knuckles in any literary weekly. Teilhard not only diagnoses in everyone the fashionable disease but propounds a remedy for it—yet a remedy so obscure and so remote from the possibility of application that it is not likely to deprive any practitioner of a living.

4. *The Phenomenon of Man* was introduced to the English-speaking world by Sir Julian Huxley, which seemed to give it a scientific benediction. Unlike myself, Sir Julian finds Teilhard in possession of a "rigorous sense of values", one who "always endeavoured to think concretely". He was speculative, to be sure, but his speculation was "always disciplined by logic". The only common ground between us is that Huxley, too, finds Teilhard somewhat difficult to follow ("If I understood him aright", p. 16 and again p. 18; "here his thought is not fully clear to me", p. 19, etc.). But then it does not seem to me that Huxley expounds Teilhard's argument; his Introduction does little more than to call attention to parallels between Teilhard's thinking and his own. Chief among these is the cosmic significance attached to a suitably generalized conception of evolution—a conception so diluted or attenuated in the course of being generalized as to cover all events or phenomena that are not immobile in time (pp. 12, 13). In particular, Huxley applauds the, in my opinion, superficial and ill thought out view that the so-called 'psycho-social evolution' of mankind and the genetical evolution of living organisms generally are two episodes of a continuous integral process (though separated by a "critical point", whatever that may mean). Yet for all this Huxley finds it impossible to follow Teilhard "all the way in his gallant attempt to reconcile the supernatural elements in Christianity with the facts and implications of evolution". But, bless my soul, this reconciliation is just what Teilhard's book is *about*! And so, it seems to me, Huxley contrives to enrage all parties—those who have some concern for rigorous analytical thought, and those who see in Teilhard's work the elements of a profound spiritual revelation.

I have read and studied *The Phenomenon of Man* with real distress, even with despair. Instead of wringing our hands over the Human Predicament, we should attend to those parts of it which are wholly remediable, above all to the gullibility which makes it possible for people to be taken in by such a bag of tricks as this. If it were an innocent, passive gullibility it would be excusable; but all too clearly, alas, it is an active willingness to be deceived.

PART V

Darwin and Society

A struggle is inevitable and it is a question of the survival of the fittest.

—Andrew Carnegie, 1900

The fortunes of railroad companies are determined by the law of the survival of the fittest.

—James J. Hill, 1910

The growth of a large business is merely the survival of the fittest.

—John D. Rockefeller, c. 1900

God gave me my money.

—John D. Rockefeller, 1915

History warns us * * * that it is the customary fate of new truths to begin as heresies and to end as superstitions. * * *

—Thomas Henry Huxley, 1880

Competition and Cooperation

RICHARD HOFSTADTER

The Vogue of Spencer (1955) †

As it seems to me, we have in Herbert Spencer not only the profoundest thinker of our time, but the most capacious and most powerful intellect of all time. Aristotle and his master were no more beyond the pygmies who preceded them than he is beyond Aristotle. Kant, Hegel, Fichte, and Schelling are gropers in the dark by the side of him. In all the history of science, there is but one name which can be compared to his, and that is Newton's * * *

—F. A. P. Barnard

I am an ultra and thoroughgoing American. I believe there is great work to be done here for civilization. What we want are ideas—large, organizing ideas—and I believe there is no other man whose thoughts are so valuable for our needs as yours are.
—Edward Livingston Youmans to Herbert Spencer

I

"The peculiar condition of American society," wrote Henry Ward Beecher to Herbert Spencer in 1866, "has made your writings far more fruitful and quickening here than in Europe." [1] Why Americans were disposed to open their minds to Spencer, Beecher did not say; but there is much to substantiate his words. Spencer's philosophy was admirably suited to the American scene. It was scientific in derivation and comprehensive in scope. It had a reassuring theory of progress based upon biology and physics. It was large enough to be all things to all men, broad enough to satisfy agnostics like Robert Ingersoll and theists like Fiske and Beecher. It offered a comprehensive world-view, uniting under one generalization everything in nature from protozoa to politics. Satisfying the desire of "advanced thinkers" for a world-system to replace the shattered Mosaic cosmogony, it soon gave Spencer a public influence that transcended Darwin's. Moreover it was not a technical creed for professionals. Presented in language that tyros in philosophy could understand,[2] it made Spencer the metaphysician

† From Chapter 2 of Hofstadter's *Social Darwinism in American Thought* (Boston, 1955). Richard Hofstadter (b. 1916) is professor of history at Columbia University.

1. David Duncan, *The Life and Letters of Herbert Spencer* (London, 1908), p. 128.
2. Spencer, wrote William James, "is the philosopher whom those who have no other philosopher can appreciate." *Memories and Studies*, p. 126.

of the homemade intellectual, and the prophet of the cracker-barrel agnostic. Although its influence far outstripped its merits, the Spencerian system serves students of the American mind as a fossil specimen from which the intellectual body of the period may be reconstructed. Oliver Wendell Holmes hardly exaggerated when he expressed his doubt that "any writer of English except Darwin has done so much to affect our whole way of thinking about the universe." [3] * * *

II

Herbert Spencer and his philosophy were products of English industrialism. It was appropriate that this spokesman of the new era should have trained to be a civil engineer, and that the scientific components of his thought—the conservation of energy and the idea of evolution—should have been indirectly derived from earlier observations in hydrotechnics and population theory. Spencer's was a system conceived in and dedicated to an age of steel and steam engines, competition, exploitation, and struggle. * * *

The aim of Spencer's synthesis was to join in one coherent structure the latest findings of physics and biology. While the idea of natural selection had been taking form in the mind of Darwin, the work of a series of investigators in thermodynamics had also yielded an illuminating generalization. Joule, Mayer, Helmholtz, Kelvin, and others had been exploring the relations between heat and energy, and had brought forth the principle of the conservation of energy which Helmholtz enunciated most clearly in his *Die Erhaltung der Kraft* (1847). The concept won general acceptance along with natural selection, and the convergence of the two discoveries upon the nineteenth-century mind was chiefly responsible for the enormous growth in the prestige of the natural sciences. Science, it was believed, had now drawn the last line in its picture of a self-contained universe, in which matter and energy were never destroyed but constantly changing form, whose varieties of organic life were integral, intelligible products of the universal economy. Previous philosophies paled into obsolescence much as pre-Newtonian philosophies had done in the eighteenth century. The transition to naturalism was marked by an efflorescence of mechanistic world-systems, whose trend is suggested by the names of Edward Büchner, Jacob Moleschott, Wilhelm Ostwald, Ernst Haeckel, and Herbert Spencer. Among these new thinkers, Spencer most resembled the eighteenth-century philosophers in his attempt to apply the implications of science to social thought and action.

3. M. De Wolfe Howe, ed., *Holmes-Pollock Letters* (Cambridge, 1941), I, 57–58. "Spencer," wrote Parrington, "laid out the broad highway over which American thought traveled in the later years of the century." *Main Currents in American Thought*, III, 198.

The conservation of energy—which Spencer preferred to call "the persistence of force"—was the starting point of his deductive system. The persistence of force, manifested in the forms of matter and motion, is the stuff of human inquiry, the material with which philosophy must build. Everywhere in the universe man observes the incessant redistribution of matter and motion, rhythmically apportioned between evolution and dissolution. Evolution is the progressive integration of matter, accompanied by dissipation of motion; dissolution is the disorganization of matter accompanied by the absorption of motion. The life process is essentially evolutionary, embodying a continuous change from incoherent homogeneity, illustrated by the lowly protozoa, to coherent heterogeneity, manifested in man and the higher animals.[4]

From the persistence of force, Spencer inferred that anything which is homogeneous is inherently unstable, since the different effects of persistent force upon its various parts must cause differences to arise in their future development.[5] Thus the homogeneous will inevitably develop into the heterogeneous. Here is the key to universal evolution. This progress from homogeneity to heterogeneity—in the formation of the earth from a nebular mass, in the evolution of higher, complex species from lower and simpler ones, in the embryological development of the individual from a uniform mass of cells, in the growth of the human mind, and in the progress of human societies—is the principle at work in everything man can know.[6]

The final result of this process, in an animal organism or society, is the achievement of a state of equilibrium—a process Spencer called "equilibration." The ultimate attainment of equilibration is inevitable, because the evolutionary process cannot go on forever in the direction of increasing heterogeneity. "Evolution has an impassable limit."[7] Here the pattern of universal rhythm comes into play: dissolution follows evolution, disintegration follows integration. In an organism this phase is represented by death and decay, built in society by the establishment of a stable, harmonious, completely adapted state, in which "evolution can end only in the establishment of the greatest perfection and the most complete happiness."[8]

This imposing positivistic edifice might have been totally unacceptable in America, had it not also been bound up with an important concession to religion in the form of Spencer's doctrine of

4. In the words of the original definition, "Evolution is an integration of matter and concomitant dissipation of motion; during which the matter passes from an indefinite, incoherent homogeneity to a definite, coherent heterogeneity; and during which the retained motion undergoes a parallel transformation." *First Principles* (4th Amer. ed., 1900), p. 407.
5. "The Instability of the Homogeneous," *ibid.*, Part II, chap. xix.
6. *Ibid.*, pp. 340–71.
7. *Ibid.*, p. 496.
8. *Ibid.*, p. 530.

the Unknowable. The great question of the day was whether religion and science could be reconciled. Spencer gave not only the desired affirmative answer, but also an assurance for all future ages that, whatever science might learn about the world, the true sphere of religion—worship of the Unknowable—is by its very nature inviolable.[9] * * *

III

Spencer's supposition that a general law of evolution could be formulated led him to apply the biologic scheme of evolution to society. The principles of social structure and change, if the generalizations of his system were valid, must be the same as those of the universe at large. In applying evolution to society, Spencer, and after him the social Darwinists, were doing poetic justice to its origins. The "survival of the fittest" was a biological generalization of the cruel processes which reflective observers saw at work in early nineteenth-century society, and Darwinism was a derivative of political economy. The miserable social conditions of the early industrial revolution had provided the data for Malthus' *Essay on The Principle of Population*, and Malthus' observations had been the matrix of natural-selection theory. The stamp of its social origin was evident in Darwinian theory. "Over the whole of English Darwinism," Nietzsche once observed, "there hovers something of the odor of humble people in need and in straits." [1]

Spencer's theory of social selection, also written under the stimulus of Malthus, arose out of his concern with population problems. In two famous articles that appeared in 1852, six years before Darwin and Wallace jointly published sketches of their theory, Spencer had set forth the view that the pressure of subsistence upon population must have a beneficial effect upon the human race. This pressure had been the immediate cause of progress from the earliest human times. By placing a premium upon skill, intelligence, self-control, and the power to adapt through technological innovation, it had stimulated human advancement and selected the best of each generation for survival.

Because he did not extend his generalization to the whole animal world, as Darwin did, Spencer failed to reap the full harvest of his insight, although he coined the expression "survival of the fittest." [2] He was more concerned with mental than physical evolution, and accepted Lamarck's theory that the inheritance of acquired characteristics is a means by which species can originate.

9. *Ibid.*, pp. 99, 103–4.
1. Quoted from *The Joyful Wisdom*, in Crane Brinton, *Nietzsche* (Cambridge, 1941), p. 147.
2. "A Theory of Population, Deduced from the General Law of Animal Fer-

tility," *Westminster Review*, LVII (1852), 468–501, esp. 499–500; "The Development Hypothesis," reprinted in *Essays* (New York, 1907), I, 1–7; see *Autobiography*, 450–51.

This doctrine confirmed his evolutionary optimism. For if mental as well as physical characteristics could be inherited, the intellectual powers of the race would become cumulatively greater, and over several generations the ideal man would finally be developed. Spencer never discarded his Lamarckism, even when scientific opinion turned overwhelmingly against it.[3]

Spencer would have been the last to deny the primacy of ethical and political considerations in the formulation of his thought. "My ultimate purpose, lying behind all proximate purposes," he wrote in the preface to his *Data of Ethics*, "has been that of finding for the principles of right and wrong in conduct at large, a scientific basis." It is not surprising that he began his literary career with a book on ethics rather than metaphysics. His first work, *Social Statics* (1850), was an attempt to strengthen laissez faire with the imperatives of biology; it was intended as an attack upon Benthamism, especially the Benthamite stress upon the positive role of legislation in social reform. Although he consented to Jeremy Bentham's ultimate standard of value—the greatest happiness of the greatest number—Spencer discarded other phases of utilitarian ethics. He called for a return to natural rights, setting up as an ethical standard the right of every man to do as he pleases, subject only to the condition that he does not infringe upon the equal rights of others. In such a scheme, the sole function of the state is negative—to insure that such freedom is not curbed.

Fundamental to all ethical progress, Spencer believed, is the adaptation of human character to the conditions of life. The root of all evil is the "non-adaptation of constitution to conditions." Because the process of adaptation, founded in the very nature of the organism, is constantly at work, evil tends to disappear. While the moral constitution of the human race is still ridden with vestiges of man's original predatory life which demanded brutal self-assertion, adaptation assures that he will ultimately develop a new moral constitution fitted to the needs of civilized life. Human perfection is not only possible but inevitable:

> The ultimate development of the ideal man is logically certain —as certain as any conclusion in which we place the most implicit faith; for instance that all men will die. . . . Progress, therefore, is not an accident, but a necessity. Instead of civilization being artificial, it is a part of nature; all of a piece with the development of the embryo or the unfolding of a flower.[4]

Despite its radicalism on incidental themes—the injustice of private land ownership, the rights of women and children, and a peculiar Spencerian "right to ignore the state" which was dropped from his later writings—the main trend of Spencer's book was

3. See the controversy with Weismann   4. *Social Statics*, pp. 79–80.
in Duncan, *op. cit.*, pp. 342–52.

ultra-conservative. His categorical repudiation of state interference with the "natural," unimpeded growth of society led him to oppose all state aid to the poor. They were unfit, he said, and should be eliminated. "The whole effort of nature is to get rid of such, to clear the world of them, and make room for better." Nature is as insistent upon fitness of mental character as she is upon physical character, "and radical defects are as much causes of death in the one case as in the other." He who loses his life because of his stupidity, vice, or idleness is in the same class as the victims of weak viscera or malformed limbs. Under nature's laws all alike are put on trial. "If they are sufficiently complete to live, they *do* live, and it is well they should live. If they are not sufficiently complete to live, they die, and it is best they should die." [5]

Spencer deplored not only poor laws, but also state-supported education, sanitary supervision other than the suppression of nuisances, regulation of housing conditions, and even state protection of the ignorant from medical quacks.[6] He likewise opposed tariffs, state banking, and government postal systems. Here was a categorical answer to Bentham.

In Spencer's later writings social selection was less prominent, although it never disappeared. The precise degree to which Spencer based his sociology upon biology was never a matter of common agreement, and the inconsistencies and ambiguities of his system gave rise to a host of Spencer exegesists, among whom the most tireless and sympathetic was Spencer himself.[7] Accused of brutality in his application of biological concepts to social principles, Spencer was compelled to insist over and over again that he was not opposed to voluntary private charity to the unfit, since it had an elevating effect on the character of the donors and hastened the development of altruism; he opposed only compulsory poor laws and other state measures.[8]

Spencer's social theory was more fully developed in the *Synthetic Philosophy*. In *The Principles of Sociology* there is a long exposition of the organic interpretation of society, in which Spencer traces the parallels between the growth, differentiation, and integration of society and of animal bodies.[9] Although the purposes of a social organism are different from those of an animal organism,

5. *Ibid.*, pp. 414–15.
6. *Ibid.*, pp. 325–444.
7. In an article on "The Relations of Biology, Psychology, and Sociology," *Popular Science*, L (1896), 163–71, Spencer defended himself against the then-common charge that his sociology had been too dependent upon biology, and argued that he had always made ample use of psychology too. In a defense of his ethical writings he also argued that he had not apotheosized the struggle for existence. "Evolutionary Ethics," *ibid.*, LII (1898), 497–502.
8. Duncan, *op. cit.*, p. 366.
9. "A Society Is an Organism," *The Principles of Sociology* (3rd ed., New York, 1925), Part II, chap. ii. For an excellent critique of Spencer's organismic theory see J. Rumney, *op. cit.*, chap. ii.

he maintained that there is no difference in their laws of organization.[1] Among societies as among organisms, there is a struggle for existence. * * *

In *The Study of Sociology*, first published in the United States in 1872–73 in serial form by the *Popular Science Monthly* and incorporated in the International Scientific Series, Spencer outlined his conception of the practical value of social science. Written to show the desirability of a naturalistic social science and to defend sociology from the criticisms of theologians and indeterminists, the book had a notable influence on the rise of sociology in the United States.[2] Spencer was animated by the desire to foster a science of society that would puncture the illusions of legislative reformers who, he believed, generally operated on the assumption that social causes and effects are simple and easily calculable, and that projects to relieve distress and remedy ills will always have the anticipated effect. A science of sociology, by teaching men to think of social causation scientifically, would awaken them to the enormous complexity of the social organism, and put an end to hasty legislative panaceas.[3] Fortified by the Darwinian conception of gradual modification over long stretches of time, Spencer ridiculed schemes for quick social transformation.

The great task of sociology, as Spencer envisioned it, is to chart "the normal course of social evolution," to show how it will be affected by any given policy, and to condemn all types of behavior that interfere with it.[4] Social science is a practical instrument in a negative sense. Its purpose is not to guide the conscious control of societal evolution, but rather to show that such control is an absolute impossibility, and that the best that organized knowledge can do is to teach men to submit more readily to the dynamic factors in progress. Spencer referred to the function of a true theory of society as a lubricant but not a motive power in progress: it can grease the wheels and prevent friction but cannot keep the engine moving.[5] "There cannot be more good done," he said, "than that

1. Spencer was not consistent in carrying out his theory of the social organism. As Ernest Barker has pointed out, he was unable to overcome the antagonism between his individualistic ethics and his organic conception of society. Barker, *Political Thought in England,* pp. 85–132. From his individualistic bias Spencer seems to have derived the atomistic idea, most clearly expressed in *Social Statics* and *The Study of Sociology,* that a society is but the sum of its individual members and takes its character from the aggregate of their characters (*Social Statics,* pp. 28–29; *The Study of Sociology,* pp. 48–51). In *The Principles of So-*ciology, however, Spencer says that there arises in the social organism "a life of the whole quite unlike the lives of the units, though it is a life produced by them" (3rd ed., I, 457). A similar dualism can be found in his ethical criteria, which are sometimes determined by the impersonal requirements of evolution and sometimes by personal hedonism. Cf. A. K. Rogers, *English and American Philosophy Since 1800,* pp. 154–57.

2. Cooley, *op. cit.,* pp. 129–45.
3. *The Study of Sociology,* chap. i.
4. *Ibid.,* pp. 70–71.
5. Duncan, *op. cit.,* p. 367.

of letting social progress go on unhindered; yet an immensity of mischief may be done in the way of disturbing, and distorting and repressing, by policies carried out in pursuit of erroneous conceptions." [6] Any adequate theory of society, Spencer concluded, will recognize the "general truths" of biology and will refrain from violating the selection principle by "the artificial preservation of those least able to take care of themselves." [7]

IV

With its rapid expansion, its exploitative methods, its desperate competition, and its peremptory rejection of failure, post-bellum America was like a vast human caricature of the Darwinian struggle for existence and survival of the fittest. Successful business entrepreneurs apparently accepted almost by instinct the Darwinian terminology which seemed to portray the conditions of their existence.[8] Businessmen are not commonly articulate social philosophers, but a rough reconstruction of their social outlook shows how congenial to their thinking were the plausible analogies of social selection, and how welcome was the expansive evolutionary optimism of the Spencerian system. In a nation permeated with the gospel of progress, the incentive of pecuniary success appealed even to many persons whose ethical horizons were considerably broader than those of business enterprise. "I perceive clearly," wrote Walt Whitman in *Democratic Vistas*, "that the extreme business energy, and this almost maniacal appetite for wealth prevalent in the United States, are parts of amelioration and progress, indispensably needed to prepare the very results I demand. My theory includes riches, and the getting of riches . . . " No doubt there were many to applaud the assertion of the railroad executive Chauncey Depew that the guests at the great dinners and public banquets of New York City represented the survival of the fittest of the thousands who came there in search of fame, fortune, or power, and that it was "superior ability, foresight, and adapta-

6. Spencer, *op. cit.*, pp. 401–2.
7. *Ibid.*, pp. 343–46.
8. "It would be strange," wrote a sociologist in 1896, "if the 'captain of the industry' did not sometimes manifest a militant spirit, for he has risen from the ranks largely because he was a better fighter than most of us. Competitive commercial life is not a flowery bed of ease, but a battle field where the 'struggle for existence' is defining the industrially 'fittest to survive.' In this country the great prizes are not found in Congress, in literature, in law, in medicine, but in industry. The successful man is praised and honored for his success. The social rewards of business prosperity, in power, in praise, and luxury, are so great as to entice men of the greatest intellectual faculties. Men of splendid abilities find in the career of a manufacturer or merchant an opportunity for the most intense energy. The very perils of the situation have a fascination for adventurous and inventive spirits. In this fierce, though voiceless contest, a peculiar type of manhood is developed, characterized by vitality, energy, concentration, skill in combining numerous forces for an end, and great foresight into the consequence of social events." C. R. Henderson, "Business Men and Social Theorists," *American Journal of Sociology*, I (1896), 385–86.

bility" that brought them successfully through the fierce competitions of the metropolis.[9] James J. Hill, another railroad magnate, in an essay defending business consolidation, argued that "the fortunes of railroad companies are determined by the law of the survival of the fittest," and implied that the absorption of smaller by larger roads represents the industrial analogy of the victory of the strong.[1] And John D. Rockefeller, speaking from an intimate acquaintance with the methods of competition, declared in a Sunday-school address:

> The growth of a large business is merely a survival of the fittest. . . . The American Beauty rose can be produced in the splendor and fragrance which bring cheer to its beholder only by sacrificing the early buds which grow up around it. This is not an evil tendency in business. It is merely the working-out of a law of nature and a law of God.[2]

The most prominent of the disciples of Spencer was Andrew Carnegie, who sought out the philosopher, became his intimate friend, and showered him with favors. In his autobiography, Carnegie told how troubled and perplexed he had been over the collapse of Christian theology, until he took the trouble to read Darwin and Spencer.

> I remember that light came as in a flood and all was clear. Not only had I got rid of theology and the supernatural, but I had found the truth of evolution. "All is well since all grows better," became my motto, my true source of comfort. Man was not created with an instinct for his own degradation, but from the lower he had risen to the higher forms. Nor is there any conceivable end to his march to perfection. His face is turned to the light; he stands in the sun and looks upward.[3]

* * *

Conservatism and Spencer's philosophy walked hand in hand. The doctrine of selection and the biological apology for laissez faire, preached in Spencer's formal sociological writings and in a series of shorter essays, satisfied the desire of the select for a scientific rationale. Spencer's plea for absolute freedom of individual enterprise was a large philosophical statement of the constitutional ban upon interference with liberty and property without due process of law. Spencer was advancing within a cosmic framework the same general political philosophy which under the Supreme Court's exegesis of the Fourteenth Amendment served so brilliantly to turn back the tide of state reform. It was this convergence of Spencer's philosophy with the Court's interpretation of due proc-

9. *My Memories of Eighty Years* (New York, 1922), pp. 383–84.
1. *Highways of Progress* (New York, 1910), p. 126; cf. also p. 137.

2. Quoted in William J. Ghent, *Our Benevolent Feudalism*, p. 29.
3. *Autobiography of Andrew Carnegie* (Boston, 1920), p. 327.

ess which finally inspired Mr. Justice Holmes (himself an admirer of Spencer) to protest that "the fourteenth Amendment does not enact Mr. Herbert Spencer's Social Statics." [4] The social views of Spencer's popularizers were likewise conservative. Youmans took time from his promotion of science to attack the eight-hour strikers in 1872. Labor, he urged in characteristic Spencerian vein, must "accept the spirit of civilization, which is pacific, constructive, controlled by reason, and slowly ameliorating and progressive. Coercive and violent measures which aim at great and sudden advantages are sure to prove illusory." He suggested that, if people were taught the elements of political economy and social science in the course of their education, such mistakes might be avoided.[5] Youmans attacked the newly founded American Social Science Association for devoting itself to unscientific reform measures instead of a "strict and passionless study of society from a scientific point of view." Until the laws of social behavior are known, he declared, reform is blind; the Association might do better to recognize a sphere of natural, self-adjusting activity, with which government intervention usually wreaks havoc.[6] There was precious little scope for meliorist activities in the outlook of one who believed with Youmans that science shows "that we are born well, or born badly, and that whoever is ushered into existence at the bottom of the scale can never rise to the top because the weight of the universe is upon him." [7]

Acceptance of the Spencerian philosophy brought with it a paralysis of the will to reform. One day, some years after the publication of *Progress and Poverty*, Youmans in Henry George's presence denounced with great fervor the political corruption of New York and the selfishness of the rich in ignoring or promoting it when they found it profitable to do so. "What do you propose to do about it?" George asked. Youmans replied, "Nothing! You and I can do nothing at all. It's all a matter of evolution. We can only wait for evolution. Perhaps in four or five thousand years evolution may have carried men beyond this state of things." [8]

4. Lochner v. New York, 198 U.S. 45 (1905).
5. Youmans, "The Recent Strike," *Popular Science Monthly*, III (1872), 623–24. See also R. G. Eccles, "The Labor Question," *ibid.*, XI (1877), 606–11; *Appleton's Journal*, N. S., V (1878), 473–75.
6. "The Social Science Association," *Popular Science Monthly*, V (1874), 267–69. See also *ibid.*, VII (1875), 365–67.
7. "On the Scientific Study of Human Nature," reprinted in Fiske, *op. cit.*, p. 482. For other statements of the conservative Spencerian viewpoint, see Erastus B. Bigelow, "The Relations of

Capital and Labor," *Atlantic Monthly*, XLII (1878), 475–87; G. F. Parsons, "The Labor Question," *ibid.*, LVIII (1886), 97–113. Also "Editor's Table," *Appleton's Journal*, N. S., V (1878), 473–75.
8. Henry George, *A Perplexed Philosopher*, pp. 163–64 n. Fiske shared Youman's conservatism, but was less alarmed at the menace of radicalism to the American future. See Fiske, *op. cit.*, pp. 381–82n. For the social outlook of an American thinker thoroughly influenced by Spencer, see Henry Holt, *The Civic Relations* (Boston, 1907), and *Garrulities of an Octogenarian Editor*, pp. 374–88.

Spencer's doctrines were imported into the Republic long after individualism had become a national tradition. Yet in the expansive age of our industrial culture he became the spokesman of that tradition, and his contribution materially swelled the stream of individualism if it did not change its course. If Spencer's abiding impact on American thought seems impalpable to later generations, it is perhaps only because it has been so thoroughly absorbed.[9] His language has become a standard feature of the folklore of individualism. "You can't make the world all planned and soft," says the businessman of Middletown. "The strongest and best survive—that's the law of nature after all—always has been and always will be."[1]

ANDREW CARNEGIE

The Gospel of Wealth (1900) †

* * * The price which society pays for the law of competition, like the price it pays for cheap comforts and luxuries, is also great; but the advantages of this law are also greater still than its cost—for it is to this law that we owe our wonderful material development, which brings improved conditions in its train. But, whether the law be benign or not, we must say of it, as we say of the change in the conditions of men to which we have referred: It is here, we cannot evade it; no substitutes for it have been found; and while the law may be sometimes hard for the individual, it is best for the race, because it insures the survival of the fittest in every department. We accept and welcome, therefore, as conditions to which we must accommodate ourselves, great inequality of environment; the concentration of business, industrial and commercial, in the hands of a few; and the law of competition between these, as being not only beneficial, but essential to the future progress of the race. * * *

Objections to the foundations upon which society is based are not in order, because the condition of the race is better with these than it has been with any other which has been tried. Of the effect of any new substitutes proposed we cannot be sure. The Socialist or Anarchist who seeks to overturn present conditions is to be regarded as attacking the foundation upon which civilization

9. See Thomas C. Cochran, "The Faith of Our Fathers," *Frontiers of Democracy*, VI (1939), 17–19.
1. Robert S. and Helen M. Lynd, *Middletown in Transition* (New York, 1937), p. 500.
† From Chapter 2 of Carnegie's *The Gospel of Wealth and Other Timely Essays* (New York, 1900). Andrew Carnegie (1835–1919), American industrialist and philanthropist, wrote extensively on business and social problems.

itself rests, for civilization took its start from the day when the capable, industrious workman said to his incompetent and lazy fellow, "If thou dost not sow, thou shalt not reap," and thus ended primitive Communism by separating the drones from the bees. One who studies this subject will soon be brought face to face with the conclusion that upon the sacredness of property civilization itself depends—the right of the laborer to his hundred dollars in the savings-bank, and equally the legal right of the millionaire to his millions. Every man must be allowed "to sit under his own vine and fig-tree, with none to make afraid," if human society is to advance, or even to remain so far advanced as it is. To those who propose to substitute Communism for this intense Individualism, the answer therefore is: The race has tried that. All progress from that barbarous day to the present time has resulted from its displacement. Not evil, but good, has come to the race from the accumulation of wealth by those who have had the ability and energy to produce it. But even if we admit for a moment that it might be better for the race to discard its present foundation, Individualism,—that it is a nobler ideal that man should labor, not for himself alone, but in and for a brotherhood of his fellows, and share with them all in common, realizing Swedenborg's idea of heaven, where, as he says, the angels derive their happiness, not from laboring for self, but for each other,—even admit all this, and a sufficient answer is, This is not evolution, but revolution. It necessitates the changing of human nature itself—a work of eons, even if it were good to change it, which we cannot know.

It is not practicable in our day or in our age. Even if desirable theoretically, it belongs to another and long-succeeding sociological stratum. Our duty is with what is practicable now—with the next step possible in our day and generation. It is criminal to waste our energies in endeavoring to uproot, when all we can profitably accomplish is to bend the universal tree of humanity a little in the direction most favorable to the production of good fruit under existing circumstances. We might as well urge the destruction of the highest existing type of man because he failed to reach our ideal as to favor the destruction of Individualism, Private Property, the Law of Accumulation of Wealth, and the Law of Competition; for these are the highest result of human experience, the soil in which society, so far, has produced the best fruit. Unequally or unjustly, perhaps, as these laws sometimes operate, and imperfect as they appear to the Idealist, they are, nevertheless, like the highest type of man, the best and most valuable of all that humanity has yet accomplished.

We start, then, with a condition of affairs under which the best interests of the race are promoted, but which inevitably gives wealth to the few. Thus far, accepting conditions as they exist, the situation can be surveyed and pronounced good. The question then arises,—and if the foregoing be correct, it is the only question with which we have to deal,—What is the proper mode of administering wealth after the laws upon which civilization is founded have thrown it into the hands of the few? And it is of this great question that I believe I offer the true solution. It will be understood that fortunes are here spoken of, not moderate sums saved by many years of effort, the returns from which are required for the comfortable maintenance and education of families. This is not wealth, but only competence, which it should be the aim of all to acquire, and which it is for the best interests of society should be acquired.

There are but three modes in which surplus wealth can be disposed of. It can be left to the families of the decedents; or it can be bequeathed for public purposes; or, finally, it can be administered by its possessors during their lives. Under the first and second modes most of the wealth of the world that has reached the few has hitherto been applied. Let us in turn consider each of these modes. The first is the most injudicious. In monarchical countries, the estates and the greatest portion of the wealth are left to the first son, that the vanity of the parent may be gratified by the thought that his name and title are to descend unimpaired to succeeding generations. The condition of this class in Europe to-day teaches the failure of such hopes or ambitions. The successors have become impoverished through their follies, or from the fall in the value of land. Even in Great Britain the strict law of entail has been found inadequate to maintain an hereditary class. Its soil is rapidly passing into the hands of the stranger. Under republican institutions the division of property among the children is much fairer; but the question which forces itself upon thoughtful men in all lands is, Why should men leave great fortunes to their children? If this is done from affection, is it not misguided affection? Observation teaches that, generally speaking, it is not well for the children that they should be so burdened. Neither is it well for the State. Beyond providing for the wife and daughters moderate sources of income, and very moderate allowances indeed, if any, for the sons, men may well hesitate; for it is no longer questionable that great sums bequeathed often work more for the injury than for the good of the recipients. Wise men will soon conclude that, for the best interests of the members of their families, and of the State, such bequests are an improper use of their means.

It is not suggested that men who have failed to educate their sons to earn a livelihood shall cast them adrift in poverty. If any man has seen fit to rear his sons with a view to their living idle lives, or, what is highly commendable, has instilled in them the sentiment that they are in a position to labor for public ends without reference to pecuniary considerations, then, of course, the duty of the parent is to see that such are provided for in moderation. There are instances of millionaires' sons unspoiled by wealth, who, being rich, still perform great services to the community. Such are the very salt of the earth, as valuable as, unfortunately, they are rare. It is not the exception, however, but the rule, that men must regard; and, looking at the usual result of enormous sums conferred upon legatees, the thoughtful man must shortly say, "I would as soon leave to my son a curse as the almighty dollar," and admit to himself that it is not the welfare of the children, but family pride, which inspires these legacies.

As to the second mode, that of leaving wealth at death for public uses, it may be said that this is only a means for the disposal of wealth, provided a man is content to wait until he is dead before he becomes of much good in the world. Knowledge of the results of legacies bequeathed is not calculated to inspire the brightest hopes of much posthumous good being accomplished by them. The cases are not few in which the real object sought by the testator is not attained, nor are they few in which his real wishes are thwarted. In many cases the bequests are so used as to become only monuments of his folly. It is well to remember that it requires the exercise of not less ability than that which acquires it, to use wealth so as to be really beneficial to the community. Besides this, it may be said that no man is to be extolled for doing what he cannot help doing, nor is he to be thanked by the community to which he only leaves wealth at death. Men who leave vast sums in this way may fairly be thought men who would not have left it at all had they been able to take it with them. The memories of such cannot be held in grateful remembrance, for there is no grace in their gifts. It is not to be wondered at that such bequests seem so generally to lack the blessing.

The growing disposition to tax more and more heavily large estates left at death is a cheering indication of the growth of a salutary change in public opinion. The State of Pennsylvania now takes—subject to some exceptions—one tenth of the property left by its citizens. The budget presented in the British Parliament the other day proposes to increase the death duties; and, most significant of all, the new tax is to be a graduated one. Of all forms of taxation this seems the wisest. Men who continue hoarding great sums all their lives, the proper use of which for public ends would work good to the community from which it chiefly came, should be made to feel that the community, in the form of the State, cannot thus be deprived of its proper share. By taxing estates heavily at death the State marks its condemnation of the selfish millionaire's unworthy life.

It is desirable that nations should go much further in this direction. Indeed, it is difficult to set bounds to the share of a rich man's estate which should go at his death to the public through the agency of the State, and by all means such taxes should be graduated, beginning at nothing upon moderate sums to dependents, and increasing rapidly as the amounts swell, until of the millionaire's hoard, as of Shylock's, at least

> The other half
> Comes to the privy coffer of the State.

This policy would work powerfully to induce the rich man to attend to the administration of wealth during his life, which is the end that society should always have in view, as being by far the most fruitful for the people. Nor need it be feared that this policy would sap the root of enterprise and render men less anxious to accumulate, for, to the class whose ambition it is to leave great fortunes and to be talked about after their death, it will attract even more attention, and, indeed, be a somewhat nobler ambition, to have enormous sums paid over to the State from their fortunes.

There remains, then, only one mode of using great fortunes; but in this we have the true antidote for the temporary unequal distribution of wealth, the reconciliation of the rich and the poor—a reign of harmony, another ideal, differing, indeed, from that of the Communist in requiring only the further evolution of existing conditions, not the total overthrow of our civilization. It is founded upon the present most intense Individualism, and the race is prepared to put it in practice by degrees whenever it pleases. Under its sway we shall have an ideal State, in which the surplus wealth of the few will become, in the best sense, the property of the many, because administered for the common good; and this wealth, passing through the hands of the few, can be made a much more potent force for the elevation of our race than if distributed in small sums to the people themselves. Even the poorest can be made to see this, and to agree that great sums gathered by some of their fellow-citizens and spent for public purposes, from which the masses reap the principal benefit, are more valuable to them than if scattered among themselves in trifling amounts through the course of many years. * * *

This, then, is held to be the duty of the man of wealth: To set an example of modest, unostentatious living, shunning display or extravagance; to provide moderately for the legitimate wants of those dependent upon him; and, after doing so, to consider all surplus revenues which come to him simply as trust funds, which he is called upon to administer, and strictly bound as a matter of duty to administer in the manner which, in his judgment, is best calculated to produce the most beneficial results for the community—the man of wealth thus becoming the mere trustee and agent for his poorer brethren, bringing to their service his superior wisdom, experience, and ability to administer, doing for them better than they would or could do for themselves. * * *

* * * It were better for mankind that the millions of the rich were thrown into the sea than so spent as to encourage the slothful, the drunken, the unworthy. Of every thousand dollars spent in so-called charity to-day, it is probable that nine hundred and fifty dollars is unwisely spent—so spent, indeed, as to produce the very evils which it hopes to mitigate or cure. A well-known writer of philosophic books admitted the other day that he had given a quarter of a dollar to a man who approached him as he was coming to visit the house of his friend. He knew nothing of the habits of this beggar, knew not the use that would be made of this money, although he had every reason to suspect that it would be spent improperly. This man professed to be a disciple of Herbert Spencer; yet the quarter-dollar given that night will probably work more injury than all the money will do good which its thoughtless donor will ever be able to give in true charity. He only gratified his own feelings, saved himself from annoyance—and this was probably one of the most selfish and very worst actions of his life, for in all respects he is most worthy.

In bestowing charity, the main consideration should be to help those who will help themselves; to provide part of the means by which those who desire to improve may do so; to give those who desire to rise the aids by which they may rise; to assist, but rarely or never to do all. Neither the individual nor the race is improved by almsgiving. Those worthy of assistance, except in rare cases, seldom require assistance. * * *

Time was when the words concerning the rich man entering the kingdom of heaven were regarded as a hard saying. To-day, when all questions are probed to the bottom and the standards of faith receive the most liberal interpretations, the startling verse has been relegated to the rear, to await the next kindly revision as one of those things which cannot be quite understood, but which, meanwhile, it is carefully to be noted, are not to be understood literally. But is it so very improbable that the next stage of thought is to restore the doctrine in all its pristine purity and force, as being in perfect harmony with sound ideas upon the subject of wealth and poverty, the rich and the poor, and the contrasts everywhere seen and deplored? In Christ's day, it is evident, reformers were against the wealthy. It is none the less evident that we are fast recurring to that position to-day; and there will be nothing to surprise the student of sociological development if society should soon approve the text which has caused so much anxiety: "It is easier for a camel to enter the eye of a needle than for a rich man to enter the kingdom of heaven." Even if the needle were the small casement at the gates, the words betoken serious difficulty for the rich. It will be but a step for the theologian from the doctrine that he who dies rich dies disgraced, to that which brings upon the man punishment or deprivation hereafter.

The gospel of wealth but echoes Christ's words. It calls upon the millionaire to sell all that he hath and give it in the highest and best form to the poor by administering his estate himself for the good of his fellows, before he is called upon to lie down and rest upon the bosom of Mother Earth. So doing, he will approach his end no longer the ignoble hoarder of useless millions; poor, very poor indeed, in money, but rich, very rich, twenty times a millionaire still, in the affection, gratitude, and admiration of his fellow-men, and—sweeter far—soothed and sustained by the still, small voice within, which, whispering, tells him that, because he has lived, perhaps one small part of the great world has been bettered just a little. This much is sure: against such riches as these no bar will be found at the gates of Paradise.

WALTER BAGEHOT

The Use of Conflict (1869) †

I

'The difference between progression and stationary inaction,' says one of our greatest living writers, 'is one of the great secrets which science has yet to penetrate.' I am sure I do not pretend that I can completely penetrate it; but it undoubtedly seems to me that the problem is on the verge of solution, and that scientific successes in kindred fields by analogy suggest some principles which wholly remove many of its difficulties, and indicate the sort of way in which those which remain may hereafter be removed too.

But what is the problem? Common English, I might perhaps say common civilised thought, ignores it. Our habitual instructors, our ordinary conversation, our inevitable and ineradicable prejudices tend to make us think that 'Progress' is the normal fact in human

† Walter Bagehot (1826–1877), English economist and critic, applied the theory of evolution to the study of primitive societies in *Physics and Politics* (1869), of which the present excerpt is from Chapter 2.

society, the fact which we should expect to see, the fact which we should be surprised if we did not see. But history refutes this. The ancients had no conception of progress; they did not so much as reject the idea; they did not even entertain the idea. Oriental nations are just the same now. Since history began they have always been what they are. Savages, again, do not improve; they hardly seem to have the basis on which to build, much less the material to put up anything worth having. Only a few nations, and those of European origin, advance; and yet these think—seem irresistibly compelled to think—such advance to be inevitable, natural, and eternal. Why then is this great contrast? * * *

* * * Three laws, or approximate laws, may, I think, be laid down, with only one of which I can deal in this paper, but all three of which it will be best to state, that it may be seen what I am aiming at.

First. In every particular state of the world, those nations which are strongest tend to prevail over the others; and in certain marked peculiarities the strongest tend to be the best.

Secondly. Within every particular nation the type or types of character then and there most attractive tend to prevail; and the most attractive, though with exceptions, is what we call the best character.

Thirdly. Neither of these competitions is in most historic conditions intensified by extrinsic forces, but in some conditions, such as those now prevailing in the most influential part of the world, both are so intensified.

These are the sort of doctrines with which, under the name of 'natural selection' in physical science, we have become familiar; and as every great scientific conception tends to advance its boundaries and to be of use in solving problems not thought of when it was started, so here, what was put forward for mere animal history may, with a change of form, but an identical essence, be applied to human history.

At first some objection was raised to the principle of 'natural selection' in physical science upon religious grounds; it was to be expected that so active an idea and so large a shifting of thought would seem to imperil much which men valued. But in this, as in other cases, the objection is, I think, passing away; the new principle is more and more seen to be fatal to mere outworks of religion, not to religion itself. At all events, to the sort of application here made of it, which only amounts to searching out and following up an analogy suggested by it, there is plainly no objection. Everyone now admits that human history is guided by certain laws, and all that is here aimed at is to indicate, in a more or less distinct way, an infinitesimally small portion of such laws. * * *

Particular consequences may be dubious, but as to the main fact there is no doubt: the military strength of man has been growing from the earliest time known to our history, straight on till now. And we must not look at times known by written records only; we must travel back to older ages, known to us only by what lawyers call *real* evidence—the evidence of things. Before history began, there was at least as much progress in the military art as there has been since. The Roman legionaries or Homeric Greeks were about as superior to the men of the shell mounds and the flint implements as we are superior to them. There has been a constant acquisition of military strength by man since we know anything of him, either by the documents he has composed or the indications he has left.

The cause of this military growth is very plain. The strongest nation has always been conquering the weaker; sometimes even subduing it, but always prevailing over it. Every intellectual gain, so to speak, that a nation possessed was in the earliest times made use of—was *invested* and taken out—in war; all else perished. Each nation tried constantly to be the stronger, and so made or copied the best weapons; by conscious and unconscious imitation each nation formed a type of character suitable to war and conquest. Conquest improved mankind by the intermixture of strengths; the armed truce, which was then called peace, improved them by the competition of training and the consequent creation of new power. Since the long-headed men first drove the short-headed men out of the best land in Europe, all European history has been the history of the superposition of the more military races over the less military—of the efforts, sometimes successful, sometimes unsuccessful, of each race to get more military; and so the art of war has constantly improved.

But why is one nation stronger than another? In the answer to that, I believe, lies the key to the principal progress of early civilisation, and to some of the progress of all civilisation. The answer is that there are very many advantages—some small and some great—every one of which tends to make the nation which has it superior to the nation which has it not; that many of these advantages can be imparted to subjugated races, or imitated by competing races; and that, though some of these advantages may be perishable or inimitable, yet, on the whole, the energy of civilisation grows by the coalescence of strengths and by the competition of strengths.

II

* * * The true scientific method is to explain the past by the present—what we see by what we do not see. We can only comprehend why so many nations have not varied, when we see how hateful variation is; how everybody turns against it; how not only the conservatives of speculation try to root it out, but the very innovators invent most rigid machines for crushing the 'monstrosities and anomalies'—the new forms, out of which, by competition and trial, the best is to be selected for the future. The point I am bringing out is simple:—one most important pre-requisite of a prevailing nation is that it should have passed out of the first stage of civilisation into the second stage—out of the stage where permanence is most wanted into that where variability is most wanted; and you cannot comprehend why progress is slow till you see how hard the most obstinate tendencies of human nature make that step to mankind.

Of course the nation we are supposing must keep the virtues of its first stage as it passes into the after stage, else it will be trodden out; it will have lost the savage virtues in getting the beginning of the civilised virtues; and the savage virtues which tend to war are the daily bread of human nature. Carlyle said, in his graphic way, 'The ultimate question between every two human beings is, "Can I kill thee, or canst thou kill me?"' History is strewn with the wrecks of nations which have gained a little progressiveness at the cost of a great deal of hard manliness, and have thus prepared themselves for destruction as soon as the movements of the world gave a chance for it. But these nations have come out of the 'pre-economic stage' too soon; they have been put to learn while yet only too apt to unlearn. Such cases do not vitiate, they confirm, the principle—that a nation which has just gained variability without losing legality has a singular likelihood to be a prevalent nation. * * *

It may be objected that this principle is like saying that men walk when they do walk, and sit when they do sit. The problem is, why do men progress? And the answer suggested seems to be, that they progress when they have a certain sufficient amount of variability in their nature. This seems to be the old style of explanation by occult qualities. It seems like saying that opium sends men to sleep because it has a soporific virtue, and bread feeds because it has an alimentary quality. But the explanation is not so absurd. It says: 'The beginning of civilisation is marked by an intense legality; that legality is the very condition of its existence, the bond which ties it together; but that legality—that tendency to impose a settled customary yoke upon all men and all actions—if it goes on, kills out the variability implanted by nature, and makes different men and different ages facsimiles of other men and other ages, as we see them so often. Progress is only possible in those happy cases where the force of legality has gone far enough to bind the nation together, but not far enough to kill out all varieties and destroy nature's perpetual tendency to change.' The point of the solution is not the invention of an imaginary agency, but an assignment of comparative magnitude to two known agencies. * * *

III

* * * But how far are the strongest nations really the best nations? how far is excellence in war a criterion of other excellence? I cannot answer this now fully, but three or four considerations are very plain. War, as I have said, nourishes the 'preliminary' virtues, and this is almost as much as to say that there are virtues which it does not nourish. All which may be called 'grace' as well as virtue it does not nourish; humanity, charity, a nice sense of the rights of others, it certainly does not foster. The insensibility to human suffering, which is so striking a fact in the world as it stood when history first reveals it, is doubtless due to the warlike origin of the old civilisation. * * *
Very like this is the contempt for physical weakness and for women which marks early society too. The non-combatant population is sure to fare ill during the ages of combat. But these defects, too, are cured or lessened; women have now marvellous means of winning their way in the world; and mind without muscle has far greater force than muscle without mind. * * *
What has been said is enough, I hope, to bring out that there are many qualities and many institutions of the most various sort which give nations an advantage in military competition; that most of these and most warlike qualities tend principally to good; that the constant winning of these favoured competitors is the particular mode by which the best qualities wanted in elementary civilisation are propagated and preserved.

JOHN LOUIS O'SULLIVAN

Manifest Destiny (1885) †

We have seen how desirable it is that self-governing groups of men should be enabled to work together in permanent harmony and on a great scale. In this kind of political integration the work of civilization very largely consists. We have seen how in its most

† *Harper's New Monthly Magazine*, LXX (1885), 578–590. John Louis O'Sullivan (1813–1895), journalist and diplomat, coined the term "manifest destiny" in 1845; after 1859, evolution served as a convenient sanction for this imperialistic doctrine.

primitive form political society is made up of small self-governing groups that are perpetually at war with one another. Now the process of change which we call civilization means quite a number of things, but there is no doubt that it means primarily the gradual substitution of a state of peace for a state of war. This change is the condition precedent for all the other kinds of improvement that are connoted by such a term as "civilization." Manifestly the development of industry is largely dependent upon the cessation or restriction of warfare; and furthermore, as the industrial phase of civilization slowly supplants the military phase, men's characters undergo, though very slowly, a corresponding change. Men become less inclined to destroy life or to inflict pain; or to use the popular terminology, which happens to coincide precisely with that of the doctrine of evolution, they become less *brutal* and more *humane*. Obviously, then, the primary phase of the process called civilization is the general diminution of warfare. But we have seen that a general diminution of warfare is rendered possible only by the union of small political groups into larger groups that are kept together by community of interests, and that can adjust their mutual relations by legal discussion, without coming to blows. * * * At the dawn of history we see a few brilliant points of civilization surrounded on every side by a midnight blackness of barbarism. In order that the pacific community may be able to go on doing its work it must be strong enough and warlike enough to overcome its barbaric neighbors, who have no notion whatever of keeping peace. This is another of the seeming paradoxes of the history of civilization, that for a very long time the possibility of peace can be guaranteed only through war. Obviously the permanent peace of the world can be secured only through the gradual concentration of the preponderant military strength into the hands of the most pacific communities. * * *

In the United States of America a century hence we shall therefore doubtless have a political aggregation immeasurably surpassing in power and in dimensions any empire that has as yet existed. But we must now consider for a moment the probable future career of the English race in other parts of the world. The colonization of North America by Englishmen had its direct effects upon the eastern as well as upon the western side of the Atlantic. The immense growth of the commercial and naval strength of England between the time of Cromwell and the time of the elder Pitt was intimately connected with the colonization of North America and the establishment of plantations in the West Indies.

These circumstances reacted powerfully upon the material development of England, multiplying manifold the dimensions of her foreign trade, increasing proportionately her commercial marine, and giving her in the eighteenth century the dominion over the seas. Endowed with this maritime supremacy, she has with an unerring instinct proceeded to seize upon the keys of empire in all parts of the world—Gibraltar, Malta, the Isthmus of Suez, Aden, Ceylon, the coasts of Australia, island after island in the Pacific— every station, in short, that commands the pathways of maritime commerce, or guards the approaches to the barbarous countries which she is beginning to regard as in some way her natural heritage. Any well-filled album of postage stamps is an eloquent commentary on this maritime supremacy of England. It is enough to turn one's head to look over her colonial blue-books. The natural outcome of all this overflowing vitality it is not difficult to foresee. No one can carefully watch what is going on in Africa to-day without recognizing it as the same sort of thing which was going on in North America in the seventeenth century; and it can not fail to bring forth similar results in course of time. Here is a vast country, rich in beautiful scenery, and in resources of timber and minerals, with a salubrious climate and fertile soil, with great navigable rivers and inland lakes, which will not much longer be left in control of tawny lions and long-eared elephants, and negro fetich-worshippers. Already five flourishing English states have been established in the south, besides the settlements on the Gold Coast, and those at Aden commanding the Red Sea. English explorers work their way with infinite hardship through its untravelled wilds, and track the courses of the Congo and the Nile as their forefathers tracked the Potomac and the Hudson. The work of LaSalle and Smith is finding its counterpart in the labors of Baker and Livingstone. Who can doubt that within two or three centuries the African continent will be occupied by a mighty nation of English descent, and covered with populous cities and flourishing farms, with railroads and telegraphs and free schools and other devices of civilization as yet undreamed of? * * *

It is not necessary to dwell upon such considerations as these. It is enough to point to the general conclusion that the work which the English race began when it colonized North America is destined to go on until every land on the earth's surface that is not already the seat of an old civilization shall become English in its language, in its religion, in its political habits and traditions, and to a predominant extent in the blood of its people. The day is at hand when four-fifths of the human race will trace its pedigree to English forefathers, as four-fifths of the white people in the United States trace their pedigree to-day. The race thus spread over both hemispheres, and from the rising to the setting sun, will not fail to keep that sovereignty of the sea and that commercial supremacy which it began to acquire when England first stretched its arm across the Atlantic to the shores of Virginia and Massachusetts. The language spoken by these great communities will not be sundered into dialects like the language of the ancient Romans, but perpetual intercommunication and the universal habit of reading and writing will preserve its integrity, and the world's business will be transacted by English-speaking people to so great an extent that whatever language any man may have learned in his infancy, he will find it necessary sooner or later to learn to express his thoughts in English. And in this way it is by no means improbable that, as Jacob Grimm long since predicted, the language of Shakespeare will ultimately become the language of mankind. * * *

* * * As this process goes on, it may, after many more ages of political experience, become apparent that there is really no reason, in the nature of things, why the whole of mankind should not constitute politically one huge federation, each little group managing its local affairs in entire independence, but relegating all questions of international interest to the decision of one central tribunal supported by the public opinion of the entire human race. I believe that the time will come when such a state of things will exist upon the earth, when it will be possible (with our friends of the Paris dinner party) to speak of the United States as stretching from pole to pole, or with Tennyson to celebrate the "parliament of man and the federation of the world." Indeed, only when such a state of things has begun to be realized can civilization, as sharply demarcated from barbarism, be said to have fairly begun. Only then can the world be said to have become truly Christian. Many ages of toil and doubt and perplexity will no doubt pass by before such a desideratum is reached. Meanwhile it is pleasant to feel that the dispassionate contemplation of great masses of historical facts goes far toward confirming our faith in this ultimate triumph of good over evil. Our survey began with pictures of horrid slaughter and desolation; it ends with the picture of a world covered with cheerful homesteads, blessed with a Sabbath of perpetual peace.

THEODORE ROOSEVELT

Biological Analogies in History (1910) †

* * * He who would fully treat of man must know at least something of biology, of the science that treats of living, breathing

---

† The Romanes lecture for 1910; published in *History as Literature*, Vol. XXVI of *The Works of Theodore Roosevelt* (New York, 1913), pp. 39–93.

Theodore Roosevelt (1858–1919), twenty-sixth President of the United States, was an avid naturalist and a widely-read historian.

things; and especially of that science of evolution which is insep-
arably connected with the great name of Darwin. Of course, there is
no exact parallelism between the birth, growth, and death of
species in the animal world and the birth, growth, and death of societies in the world of man. Yet there is a certain parallelism. There
are strange analogies; it may be that there are homologies. * * *

As in biology, so in human history, a new form may result from
the specialization of a long-existing, and hitherto very slowly changing, generalized or non-specialized form; as, for instance, occurs
when a barbaric race from a variety of causes suddenly develops a
more complex cultivation and civilization. This is what occurred,
for instance, in western Europe during the centuries of the Teutonic and, later, the Scandinavian ethnic overflows from the north.
All the modern countries of western Europe are descended from
the states created by these northern invaders. When first created
they would be called "new" or "young" states in the sense that part
or all of the people composing them were descended from races
that hitherto had not been civilized, and that therefore, for the first
time, entered on the career of civilized communities. In the southern part of western Europe the new states thus formed consisted
in bulk of the inhabitants already in the land under the Roman
Empire; and it was here that the new kingdoms first took shape.
Through a reflex action their influence then extended back into the
cold forests from which the invaders had come, and Germany and
Scandinavia witnessed the rise of communities with essentially the
same civilization as their southern neighbors; though in those communities, unlike the southern communities, there was no infusion
of new blood, so that the new civilized nations which gradually
developed were composed entirely of members of the same races
which in the same regions had for ages lived the life of a slowly
changing barbarism. The same was true of the Slavs and the Slavo-
nized Finns of eastern Europe, when an infiltration of Scandinavian
leaders from the north, and an infiltration of Byzantine culture
from the south, joined to produce the changes which have gradually, out of the little Slav communities of the forest and the steppe,
formed the mighty Russian Empire of to-day.

Again, the new form may represent merely a splitting off from a
long-established, highly developed, and specialized nation. In this
case the nation is usually spoken of as a "young," and is correctly
spoken of as a "new," nation; but the term should always be used
with a clear sense of the difference between what is described in
such case, and what is described by the same term in speaking of a
civilized nation just developed from barbarism. Carthage and Syra-
cuse were new cities compared to Tyre and Corinth; but the Greek
or Phœnician race was in every sense of the word as old in the new

city as in the old city. So, nowadays, Victoria or Manitoba is a new community compared with England or Scotland; but the ancestral type of civilization and culture is as old in one case as in the other. I of course do not mean for a moment that great changes are not produced by the mere fact that the old civilized race is suddenly placed in surroundings where it has again to go through the work of taming the wilderness, a work finished many centuries before in the original home of the race; I merely mean that the ancestral history is the same in each case. * * *

A like wide diversity in fact may be covered in the statement that a civilization has "died out." The nationality and culture of the wonderful city-builders of the lower Mesopotamian Plain have completely disappeared, and, though doubtless certain influences dating therefrom are still at work, they are in such changed and hidden form as to be unrecognizable. But the disappearance of the Roman Empire was of no such character. There was complete change, far-reaching transformation, and at one period a violent dislocation; but it would not be correct to speak either of the blood or the culture of Old Rome as extinct. We are not yet in a position to dogmatize as to the permanence of evanescence of the various strains of blood that go to make up every civilized nationality; but it is reasonably certain that the blood of the old Roman still flows through the veins of the modern Italian; and though there has been much intermixture, from many different foreign sources—from foreign conquerors and from foreign slaves—yet it is probable that the Italian type of to-day finds its dominant ancestral type in the ancient Latin. As for the culture, the civilization of Rome, this is even more true. It has suffered a complete transformation, partly by natural growth, partly by absorption of totally alien elements, such as a Semitic religion, and certain Teutonic governmental and social customs; but the process was not one of extinction, but one of growth and transformation, both from within and by the accretion of outside elements. * * *

Why do great artificial empires, whose citizens are knit by a bond of speech and culture much more than by a bond of blood, show periods of extraordinary growth, and again of sudden or lingering decay? In some cases we can answer readily enough; in other cases we can not as yet even guess what the proper answer should be. If in any such case the centrifugal forces overcome the centripetal, the nation will of course fly to pieces, and the reason for its failure to become a dominant force is patent to every one. The minute that the spirit which finds its healthy development in local self-government, and is the antidote to the dangers of an extreme centralization, develops into mere particularism, into inability to combine effectively for achievement of a common end, then it is hopeless to expect great results. Poland and certain republics of the Western Hemisphere are the standard examples of failure of this kind; and the United States would have ranked with them, and her name would have become a byword of derision, if the forces of union had not triumphed in the Civil War. So, the growth of soft luxury after it has reached a certain point becomes a national danger patent to all. Again, it needs but little of the vision of a seer to foretell what must happen in any community if the average woman ceases to become the mother of a family of healthy children, if the average man loses the will and the power to work up to old age and to fight whenever the need arises. If the homely commonplace virtues die out, if strength of character vanishes in graceful self-indulgence, if the virile qualities atrophy, then the nation has lost what no material prosperity can offset.

But there are plenty of other phenomena wholly or partially inexplicable. It is easy to see why Rome trended downward when great slave-tilled farms spread over what had once been a countryside of peasant proprietors, when greed and luxury and sensuality are like acids into the fibre of the upper classes, while the mass of the citizens grew to depend not upon their own exertions, but upon the state, for their pleasures and their very livelihood. But this does not explain why the forward movement stopped at different times, so far as different matters were concerned; at one time as regards literature, at another time as regards architecture, at another time as regards city-building. There is nothing mysterious about Rome's dissolution at the time of the barbarian invasions; apart from the impoverishment and depopulation of the empire, its fall would be quite sufficiently explained by the mere fact that the average citizen had lost the fighting edge—an essential even under a despotism, and therefore far more essential in free, self-governing communities, such as those of the English-speaking peoples of today. The mystery is rather that out of the chaos and corruption of Roman society during the last days of the oligarchic republic, there should have sprung an empire able to hold things with reasonable steadiness for three or four centuries. * * *

The phenomena of national growth and decay, both of those which can and those which can not be explained, have been peculiarly in evidence during the four centuries that have gone by since the discovery of America and the rounding of the Cape of Good Hope. These have been the four centuries of by far the most intense and constantly accelerating rapidity of movement and development that the world has yet seen. The movement has covered all the fields of human activity. It has witnessed an altogether unexampled spread of civilized mankind over the world, as well as an altogether unexampled advance in man's dominion over nature; and this together with a literary and artistic activity to be matched in but one previous epoch. This period of extension and development has been that of one race, the so-called white race, or, to speak more accurately, the group of peoples living in Europe, who undoubtedly have a certain kinship of blood, who profess the Christian religion, and trace back their culture to Greece and Rome.

The memories of men are short, and it is easy to forget how brief is this period of unquestioned supremacy of the so-called white race. It is but a thing of yesterday. During the thousand years which went before the opening of this era of European supremacy, the attitude of Asia and Africa, of Hun and Mongol, Turk and Tartar, Arab and Moor, had on the whole been that of successful aggression against Europe. More than a century went by after the voyages of Columbus before the mastery in war began to pass from the Asiatic to the European. During that time Europe produced no generals or conquerors able to stand comparison with Selim and Solyman, Baber and Akbar. Then the European advance gathered momentum; until at the present time peoples of European blood hold dominion over all America and Australia and the islands of the sea, over most of Africa, and the major half of Asia. Much of this world conquest is merely political, and such a conquest is always likely in the long run to vanish. But very much of it represents not a merely political, but an ethnic conquest; the intrusive people having either exterminated or driven out the conquered peoples, or else having imposed upon them its tongue, law, culture, and religion, together with a strain of its blood. During this period substantially all of the world achievements worth remembering are to be credited to the people of European descent. * * *

Every modern civilized nation has many and terrible problems to solve within its own borders, problems that arise not merely from juxtaposition of poverty and riches, but especially from the self-consciousness of both poverty and riches. Each nation must deal with these matters in its own fashion, and yet the spirit in which the problem is approached must ever be fundamentally the same. It must be a spirit of broad humanity, of brotherly kindness, of acceptance of responsibility, one for each and each for all, and at the same time a spirit as remote as the poles from every form of weakness and sentimentality. As in war to pardon the coward is to do cruel wrong to the brave man whose life his cowardice jeopardizes, so in civil affairs it is revolting to every principle of justice to give to the lazy, the vicious, or even the feeble or dull-witted a reward which is really the robbery of what braver, wiser, abler men have earned. The only effective way to help any man is to help him to help himself; and the worst lesson to teach him is that he can be permanently helped at the expense of some one else. True liberty shows itself to best advantage in protecting the rights of others, and especially of minorities. Privilege should not be tolerated because it is to the advantage of a minority; nor yet because it is to the advantage of a majority. No doctrinaire theories of vested rights or freedom of contract can stand in the way of our cutting out abuses from the body politic. Just as little can we afford to follow the doctrinaires of an impossible—and incidentally of a highly undesirable—social revolution which, in destroying individual rights—including property rights—and the family, would destroy the two chief agents in the advance of mankind, and the two chief reasons why either the advance or the preservation of mankind is worth while. It is an evil and a dreadful thing to be callous to sorrow and suffering and blind to our duty to do all things possible for the betterment of social conditions. But it is an unspeakably foolish thing to strive for this betterment by means so destructive that they would leave no social conditions to better. In dealing with all these social problems, with the intimate relations of the family, with wealth in private use and business use, with labor, with poverty, the one prime necessity is to remember that, though hardness of heart is a great evil, it is no greater an evil than softness of head. * * *

No hard-and-fast rule can be drawn as applying to all alien races, because they differ from one another far more widely than some of them differ from us. But there are one or two rules which must not be forgotten. In the long run there can be no justification for one race managing or controlling another unless the management and control are exercised in the interest and for the benefit of that other race. This is what our peoples have in the main done, and must continue in the future in even greater degree to do, in India, Egypt, and the Philippines alike. In the next place, as regards every race, everywhere, at home or abroad, we can not afford to deviate from the great rule of righteousness which bids us treat each man on his worth as a man. He must not be sentimentally favored because he belongs to a given race; he must not be given immunity in wrong-doing or permitted to cumber the ground, or given other privileges which would be denied to the vicious and unfit among ourselves. On the other hand, where he acts in a way which would entitle him to respect and reward if he was one of our own stock, he is just as entitled to that respect and reward if he comes of another stock, even though that other stock produces a much smaller proportion of men of his type that does our own. This has nothing to do with social intermingling, with what is called social equality. It has to do merely with the question of doing to each man and each woman that elementary justice which will permit him or her to gain from life the reward which should always accompany thrift, sobriety, self-control, respect for the rights of others, and hard and intelligent work to a given end. To more than such just treatment no man is entitled, and less than such just treatment no man should receive.

The other type of duty is the international duty, the duty owed by one nation to another. I hold that the laws of morality which should govern individuals in their dealings one with the other, are just as binding concerning nations in their dealings one with the other. The application of the moral law must be different in the two cases, because in one case it has, and in the other it has not, the sanction of a civil law with force behind it. The individual can depend for his rights upon the courts, which themselves derive their force from the police power of the state. The nation can depend upon nothing of the kind; and therefore, as things are now, it is the highest duty of the most advanced and freest peoples to keep themselves in such a state of readiness as to forbid to any barbarism or despotism the hope of arresting the progress of the world by striking down the nations that lead in that progress. It would be foolish indeed to pay heed to the unwise persons who desire disarmament to be begun by the very peoples who, of all others, should not be left helpless before any possible foe. But we must reprobate quite as strongly both the leaders and the peoples who practise, or encourage, or condone, aggression and iniquity by the strong at the expense of the weak. We should tolerate lawlessness and wickedness neither by the weak nor by the strong; and both weak and strong we should in return treat with scrupulous fairness. The foreign policy of a great and self-respecting country should be conducted on exactly the same plane of honor, for insistence upon one's own rights and of respect for the rights of others, that marks the conduct of a brave and honorable man when dealing with his fellows. Permit me to support this statement out of my own experience. For nearly eight years I was the head of a great nation, and charged especially with the conduct of its foreign policy; and during those years I took no action with reference to any other people on the face of the earth that I would not have felt justified in taking as an individual in dealing with other individuals.

I believe that we of the great civilized nations of to-day have a right to feel that long careers of achievement lie before our several countries. To each of us is vouchsafed the honorable privilege of doing his part, however small, in that work. Let us strive hardily for success, even if by so doing we risk failure, spurning the poorer souls of small endeavor, who know neither failure or success. Let us hope that our own blood shall continue in the land, that our children and children's children to endless generations shall arise to take our places and play a mighty and dominant part in the world. But whether this be denied or granted by the years we shall not see, let at least the satisfaction be ours that we have carried onward the lighted torch in our own day and generation. If we do this, then, as our eyes close, and we go out into the darkness, and others' hands grasp the torch, at least we can say that our part has been borne well and valiantly.

PETER KROPOTKIN

Mutual Aid (1902) †

Introduction

Two aspects of animal life impressed me most during the journeys which I made in my youth in Eastern Siberia and Northern Manchuria. One of them was the extreme severity of the struggle for existence which most species of animals have to carry on against an inclement Nature; the enormous destruction of life which periodically results from natural agencies; and the consequent paucity of life over the vast territory which fell under my observation. And the other was, that even in those few spots where animal life teemed in abundance, I failed to find—although I was eagerly looking for it—that bitter struggle for the means of existence, *among animals belonging to the same species*, which was considered by most Darwinists (though not always by Darwin himself) as the dominant characteristic of struggle for life, and the main factor of evolution.

The terrible snow-storms which sweep over the northern portion of Eurasia in the later part of the winter, and the glazed frost that often follows them; the frosts and the snow-storms which return every year in the second half of May, when the trees are already in full blossom and insect life swarms everywhere; the early frosts and, occasionally, the heavy snowfalls in July and August, which suddenly destroy myriads of insects, as well as the second broods of the birds in the prairies; the torrential rains, due to the monsoons, which fall in more temperate regions in August and September—resulting in inundations on a scale which is only known in America and in Eastern Asia, and swamping, on the plateaus, areas as wide as European States; and finally, the heavy snowfalls, early in October, which eventually render a territory as

† Peter Kropotkin (1842–1921) was a Russian prince who spent much of his mature life in anarchist-nihilist activities. As a young man, however, he held a variety of military and diplomatic posts in Siberia and led geographical survey expeditions in Manchuria, where he observed some of the phenomena he described in *Mutual Aid*. The present selections are from the Introduction and the first two chapters.

520 · *Peter Kropotkin*

large as France and Germany, absolutely impracticable for ruminants, and destroy them by the thousand—these were the conditions under which I saw animal life struggling in Northern Asia. They made me realize at an early date the overwhelming importance in Nature of what Darwin described as "the natural checks to overmultiplication," in comparison to the struggle between individuals of the same species for the means of subsistence, which may go on here and there, to some limited extent, but never attains the importance of the former. Paucity of life, under-population—not overpopulation—being the distinctive feature of that immense part of the globe which we name Northern Asia, I conceived since then serious doubts—which subsequent study has only confirmed—as to the reality of that fearful competition for food and life within each species, which was an article of faith with most Darwinists, and, consequently, as to the dominant part which this sort of competition was supposed to play in the evolution of new species.

On the other hand, wherever I saw animal life in abundance, as, for instance, on the lakes where scores of species and millions of individuals came together to rear their progeny; in the colonies of rodents; in the migrations of birds which took place at that time on a truly American scale along the Usuri; and especially in a migration of fallow-deer which I witnessed on the Amur, and during which scores of thousands of these intelligent animals came together from an immense territory, flying before the coming deep snow, in order to cross the Amur where it is narrowest—in all these scenes of animal life which passed before my eyes, I saw Mutual Aid and Mutual Support carried on to an extent which made me suspect in it a feature of the greatest importance for the maintenance of life, the preservation of each species, and its further evolution.

And finally, I saw among the semi-wild cattle and horses in Transbaikalia, among the wild ruminants everywhere, the squirrels, and so on, that when animals have to struggle against scarcity of food, in consequence of one of the above-mentioned causes, the whole of that portion of the species which is affected by the calamity, comes out of the ordeal so much impoverished in vigour and health, that *no progressive evolution of the species can be based upon such periods of keen competition.*

Consequently, when my attention was drawn, later on, to the relations between Darwinism and Sociology, I could agree with none of the works and pamphlets that had been written upon this important subject. They all endeavoured to prove that Man, owing to his higher intelligence and knowledge, *may* mitigate the harshness of the struggle for life between men; but they all recognized at the same time that the struggle for the means of existence, of every animal against all its congeners, and of every man against all other men, was "a law of Nature." This view, however, I could not accept, because I was persuaded that to admit a pitiless inner war for life within each species, and to see in that war a condition of progress, was to admit something which not only had not yet been proved, but also lacked confirmation from direct observation.

On the contrary, a lecture "On the Law of Mutual Aid," which was delivered at a Russian Congress of Naturalists, in January 1880, by the well-known zoologist, Professor Kessler, the then Dean of the St. Petersburg University, struck me as throwing a new light on the whole subject. Kessler's idea was, that besides the *law of Mutual Struggle* there is in Nature *the law of Mutual Aid*, which, for the success of the struggle for life, and especially for the progressive evolution of the species, is far more important than the law of mutual contest. This suggestion—which was, in reality, nothing but a further development of the ideas expressed by Darwin himself in *The Descent of Man*—seemed to me so correct and of so great an importance, that since I became acquainted with it (in 1883) I began to collect materials for further developing the idea. * * *

* * * To reduce animal sociability to *love* and *sympathy* means to reduce its generality and its importance, just as human ethics based upon love and personal sympathy only have contributed to narrow the comprehension of the moral feeling as a whole. It is not love to my neighbour—whom I often do not know at all—which induces me to seize a pail of water and to rush towards his house when I see it on fire; it is a far wider, even though more vague feeling or instinct of human solidarity and sociability which moves me. So it is also with animals. It is not love, and not even sympathy (understood in its proper sense) which induces a herd of ruminants or of horses to form a ring in order to resist an attack of wolves; not love which induces wolves to form a pack for hunting; not love which induces kittens or lambs to play, or a dozen of species of young birds to spend their days together in the autumn; and it is neither love nor personal sympathy which induces many thousand fallow-deer scattered over a territory as large as France to form into a score of separate herds, all marching towards a given spot, in order to cross there a river. It is a feeling infinitely wider than love or personal sympathy—an instinct that has been slowly developed among animals and men in the course of an extremely long evolution, and which has taught animals and men alike the force they can borrow from the practice of mutual aid and support, and the joys they can find in social life.

The importance of this distinction will be easily appreciated by the student of animal psychology, and the more so by the student of human ethics. Love, sympathy and self-sacrifice certainly play an immense part in the progressive development of our moral feelings. But it is not love and not even sympathy upon which Society is based in mankind. It is the conscience—be it only at the stage of an instinct—of human solidarity. It is the unconscious recognition of the force that is borrowed by each man from the practice of mutual aid; of the close dependency of every one's happiness upon the happiness of all; and of the sense of justice, or equity, which brings the individual to consider the rights of every other individual as equal to his own. Upon this broad and necessary foundation the still higher moral feelings are developed. * * *

After having discussed the importance of mutual aid in various classes of animals, I was evidently bound to discuss the importance of the same factor in the evolution of Man. This was the more necessary as there are a number of evolutionists who may not refuse to admit the importance of mutual aid among animals, but who, like Herbert Spencer, will refuse to admit it for Man. For primitive Man—they maintain—war of each against all was *the* law of life. * * *

Chapter I

MUTUAL AID AMONG ANIMALS

The conception of struggle for existence as a factor of evolution, introduced into science by Darwin and Wallace, has permitted us to embrace an immensely-wide range of phenomena in one single generalization, which soon became the very basis of our philosophical, biological, and sociological speculations. An immense variety of facts:—adaptations of function and structure of organic beings to their surroundings; physiological and anatomical evolution; intellectual progress, and moral development itself, which we formerly used to explain by so many different causes, were embodied by Darwin in one general conception. We understood them as continued endeavours—as a struggle against adverse circumstances—for such a development of individuals, races, species and societies, as would result in the greatest possible fulness, variety, and intensity of life. It may be that at the outset Darwin himself was not fully aware of the generality of the factor which he first invoked for explaining one series only of facts relative to the accumulation of individual variations in incipient species. But he foresaw that the term which he was introducing into science would lose its philosophical and its only true meaning if it were to be used in its narrow sense only—that of a struggle between separate individuals for the sheer means of existence. And at the very beginning of his memorable work he insisted upon the term being taken in its "large and metaphorical sense including dependence of one being on another, and including (which is more important) not only the life of the individual, but success in leaving progeny." [1]

While he himself was chiefly using the term in its narrow sense for his own special purpose, he warned his followers against committing the error (which he seems once to have committed himself) of overrating its narrow meaning. In *The Descent of Man* he gave some powerful pages to illustrate its proper, wide sense. He pointed out how, in numberless animal societies, the struggle between separate individuals for the means of existence disappears, how *struggle* is replaced by *co-operation*, and how that substitution results in the development of intellectual and moral faculties which secure to the species the best conditions for survival. He intimated that in such cases the fittest are not the physically strongest, nor the cunningest, but those who learn to combine so as mutually to support each other, strong and weak alike, for the welfare of the community. "Those communities," he wrote, "which included the greatest number of the most sympathetic members would flourish best, and rear the greatest number of offspring" (2nd edit., p. 163). The term, which originated from the narrow Malthusian conception of competition between each and all, thus lost its narrowness in the mind of one who knew Nature.

Unhappily, these remarks, which might have become the basis of most fruitful researches, were overshadowed by the masses of facts gathered for the purpose of illustrating the consequences of a real competition for life. Besides, Darwin never attempted to submit to a closer investigation the relative importance of the two aspects under which the struggle for existence appears in the animal world, and he never wrote the work he proposed to write upon the natural checks to over-multiplication, although that work would have been the crucial test for appreciating the real purport of individual struggle. Nay, on the very pages just mentioned, amidst data disproving the narrow Malthusian conception of struggle, the old Malthusian leaven reappeared—namely, in Darwin's remarks as to the alleged inconveniences of maintaining the "weak in mind and body" in our civilized societies (ch. v.). As if thousands of weak-bodied and infirm poets, scientists, inventors, and reformers, together with other thousands of so-called "fools" and "weak-minded enthusiasts," were not the most precious weapons used by humanity in its struggle for existence by intellectual and moral arms, which Darwin himself emphasized in those same chapters of *Descent of Man*.

It happened with Darwin's theory as it always happens with theories having any bearing upon human relations. Instead of

1. *Origin of Species,* chap. iii.

widening it according to his own hints, his followers narrowed it still more. And while Herbert Spencer, starting on independent but closely-allied lines, attempted to widen the inquiry into that great question, "Who are the fittest?" especially in the appendix to the third edition of the *Data of Ethics*, the numberless followers of Darwin reduced the notion of struggle for existence to its narrowest limits. They came to conceive the animal world as a world of perpetual struggle among half-starved individuals, thirsting for one another's blood. They made modern literature resound with the war-cry of *woe to the vanquished*, as if it were the last word of modern biology. They raised the "pitiless" struggle for personal advantages to the height of a biological principle which man must submit to as well, under the menace of otherwise succumbing in a world based upon mutual extermination. Leaving aside the economists who know of natural science but a few words borrowed from second-hand vulgarizers, we must recognize that even the most authorized exponents of Darwin's views did their best to maintain those false ideas. In fact, if we take Huxley, who certainly is considered as one of the ablest exponents of the theory of evolution, were we not taught by him, in a paper on the 'Struggle for Existence and its Bearing upon Man,' that,

> "from the point of view of the moralist, the animal world is on about the same level as a gladiators' show. The creatures are fairly well treated, and set to fight; whereby the strongest, the swiftest, and the cunningest live to fight another day. The spectator has no need to turn his thumb down, as no quarter is given."

Or, further down in the same article, did he not tell us that, as among animals, so among primitive men,

> "the weakest and stupidest went to the wall, while the toughest and shrewdest, those who were best fitted to cope with their circumstances, but not the best in another way, survived. Life was a continuous free fight, and beyond the limited and temporary relations of the family, the Hobbesian war of each against all was the normal state of existence." [2]

In how far this view of nature is supported by fact, will be seen from the evidence which will be here submitted to the reader as regards the animal world, and as regards primitive man. But it may be remarked at once that Huxley's view of nature had as little claim to be taken as a scientific deduction as the opposite view of Rousseau, who saw in nature but love, peace, and harmony destroyed by the accession of man. In fact, the first walk in the forest, the first observation upon any animal society, or even the perusal of any serious work dealing with animal life (D'Orbigny's, Audubon's, Le Vaillant's, no matter which), cannot but set the

2. *Nineteenth Century*, Feb. 1888, p.165.

naturalist thinking about the part taken by social life in the life of animals, and prevent him from seeing in Nature nothing but a field of slaughter, just as this would prevent him from seeing in Nature nothing but harmony and peace. Rousseau had committed the error of excluding the beak-and-claw fight from his thoughts; and Huxley committed the opposite error; but neither Rousseau's optimism nor Huxley's pessimism can be accepted as an impartial interpretation of nature.

As soon as we study animals—not in laboratories and museums only, but in the forest and the prairie, in the steppe and the mountains—we at once perceive that though there is an immense amount of warfare and extermination going on amidst various species, and especially amidst various classes of animals, there is, at the same time, as much, or perhaps even more, of mutual support, mutual aid, and mutual defence amidst animals belonging to the same species or, at least, to the same society. Sociability is as much a law of nature as mutual struggle. Of course it would be extremely difficult to estimate, however roughly, the relative numerical importance of both these series of facts. But if we resort to an indirect test, and ask Nature: "Who are the fittest: those who are continually at war with each other, or those who support one another?" we at once see that those animals which acquire habits of mutual aid are undoubtedly the fittest. They have more chances to survive, and they attain, in their respective classes, the highest development of intelligence and bodily organization. If the numberless facts which can be brought forward to support this view are taken into account, we may safely say that mutual aid is as much a law of animal life as mutual struggle, but that, as a factor of evolution, it most probably has a far greater importance, inasmuch as it favours the development of such habits and characters as insure the maintenance and further development of the species, together with the greatest amount of welfare and enjoyment of life for the individual, with the least waste of energy. * * *

If we knew no other facts from animal life than what we know about the ants and the termites, we already might safely conclude that mutual aid (which leads to mutual confidence, the first condition for courage) and individual initiative (the first condition for intellectual progress) are two factors infinitely more important than mutual struggle in the evolution of the animal kingdom. In fact, the ant thrives without having any of the "protective" features which cannot be dispensed with by animals living an isolated life. Its colour renders it conspicuous to its enemies, and the lofty nests of many species are conspicuous in the meadows and forests. It is not protected by a hard carapace, and its stinging apparatus, however dangerous when hundreds of stings are plunged into the flesh of an animal, is not of a great value for individual defence; while the eggs and larvæ of the ants are a dainty for a great number of the inhabitants of the forests. And yet the ants, in their thousands, are not much destroyed by the birds, not even by the ant-eaters, and they are dreaded by most stronger insects. When Forel emptied a bagful of ants in a meadow, he saw that "the crickets ran away, abandoning their holes to be sacked by the ants; the grasshoppers and the crickets fled in all directions; the spiders and the beetles abandoned their prey in order not to become prey themselves;" even the nests of the wasps were taken by the ants, after a battle during which many ants perished for the safety of the commonwealth. Even the swiftest insects cannot escape, and Forel often saw butterflies, gnats, flies, and so on, surprised and killed by the ants. Their force is in mutual support and mutual confidence. And if the ant—apart from the still higher developed termites—stands at the very top of the whole class of insects for its intellectual capacities; if its courage is only equalled by the most courageous vertebrates; and if its brain—to use Darwin's words—"is one of the most marvellous atoms of matter in the world, perhaps more so than the brain of man," is it not due to the fact that mutual aid has entirely taken the place of mutual struggle in the communities of ants? * * *

Chapter II

MUTUAL AID AMONG ANIMALS (CONTINUED)

* * * I have to say yet a few words about the societies of monkeys, which acquire an additional interest from their being the link which will bring us to the societies of primitive men.

It is hardly needful to say that those mammals, which stand at the very top of the animal world and most approach man by their structure and intelligence, are eminently sociable. Evidently we must be prepared to meet with all varieties of character and habits in so great a division of the animal kingdom which includes hundreds of species. But, all things considered, it must be said that sociability, action in common, mutual protection, and a high development of those feelings which are the necessary outcome of social life, are characteristic of most monkeys and apes. From the smallest species to the biggest ones, sociability is a rule to which we know but a few exceptions. The nocturnal apes prefer isolated life; the capuchins (*Cebus capucinus*), the monos, and the howling monkeys live but in small families; and the orang-outans have never been seen by A. R. Wallace otherwise than either solitary or in very small groups of three or four individuals, while the gorillas seem never to join in bands. But all the remainder of the monkey tribe—the chimpanzees, the sajous, the sakis, the mandrills, the baboons, and so on—are sociable in the highest degree. They live in great bands, and even join with other species than their own. Most of them become quite unhappy when solitary. The cries of distress of each one of the band immediately bring together the whole of the band, and they boldly repulse the attacks of most carnivores and birds of prey. Even eagles do not dare attack them. They plunder our fields always in bands—the old ones taking care for the safety of the commonwealth. The little tee tees, whose childish sweet faces so much struck Humboldt, embrace and protect one another when it rains, rolling their tails over the necks of their shivering comrades. Several species display the greatest solicitude for their wounded, and do not abandon a wounded comrade during a retreat till they have ascertained that it is dead and that they are helpless to restore it to life. Thus James Forbes narrated in his *Oriental Memoirs* a fact of such resistance in reclaiming from his hunting party the dead body of a female monkey that one fully understands why "the witnesses of this extraordinary scene resolved never again to fire at one of the monkey race." [1] In some species several individuals will combine to overturn a stone in order to search for ants' eggs under it. The hamadryas not only post sentries, but have been seen making a chain for the transmission of the spoil to a safe place; and their courage is well known. Brehm's description of the regular fight which his caravan had to sustain before the hamadryas would let it resume its journey in the valley of the Mensa, in Abyssinia, has become classical.[2] The playfulness of the tailed apes and the mutual attachment which reigns in the families of chimpanzees also are familiar to the general reader. And if we find among the highest apes two species, the orang-outan and the gorilla, which are not sociable, we must remember that both—limited as they are to very small areas, the one in the heart of Africa, and the other in the two islands of Borneo and Sumatra—have all the appearance of being the last remnants of formerly much more numerous species. The gorilla at least seems to have been sociable in olden times, if the apes mentioned in the *Periplus* really were gorillas.

We thus see, even from the above brief review, that life in societies is no exception in the animal world; it is the rule, the law of Nature, and it reaches its fullest development with the higher vertebrates. Those species which live solitary, or in small families only, are relatively few, and their numbers are limited. Nay, it appears very probable that, apart from a few exceptions, those birds and mammals which are not gregarious now, were living in societies

1. Romanes's *Animal Intelligence*, p. 472.
2. Brehm, i. 82; Darwin's *Descent of* *Man*, ch. iii. The Kozloff expedition of 1899–1901 have also had to sustain in Northern Thibet a similar fight.

before man multiplied on the earth and waged a permanent war against them, or destroyed the sources from which they formerly derived food. "On ne s'associe pas pour mourir," was the sound remark of Espinas; and Houzeau, who knew the animal world of some parts of America when it was not yet affected by man, wrote to the same effect.

Association is found in the animal world at all degrees of evolution; and, according to the grand idea of Herbert Spencer, so brilliantly developed in Perrier's *Colonies Animales,* colonies are at the very origin of evolution in the animal kingdom. But, in proportion as we ascend the scale of evolution, we see association growing more and more conscious. It loses its purely physical character, it ceases to be simply instinctive, it becomes reasoned. With the higher vertebrates it is periodical, or is resorted to for the satisfaction of a given want—propagation of the species, migration, hunting, or mutual defence. It even becomes occasional, when birds associate against a robber, or mammals combine, under the pressure of exceptional circumstances, to emigrate. In this last case, it becomes a voluntary deviation from habitual moods of life. The combination sometimes appears in two or more degrees—the family first, then the group, and finally the association of groups, habitually scattered, but uniting in case of need, as we saw it with the bisons and other ruminants. It also takes higher forms, guaranteeing more independence to the individual without depriving it of the benefits of social life. With most rodents the individual has its own dwelling, which it can retire to when it prefers being left alone; but the dwellings are laid out in villages and cities, so as to guarantee to all inhabitants the benefits and joys of social life. And finally, in several species, such as rats, marmots, hares, etc., sociable life is maintained notwithstanding the quarrelsome or otherwise egotistic inclinations of the isolated individual. Thus it is not imposed, as is the case with ants and bees, by the very physiological structure of the individuals; it is cultivated for the benefits of mutual aid, or for the sake of its pleasures. * * *

EDWARD ALSWORTH ROSS

Sin and Society (1907) †

The sinful heart is ever the same, but sin changes its quality as society develops. Modern sin takes its character from the mutualism of our time. Under our present manner of living, how many of

† From *Sin and Society* (Boston, 1907), *passim.* Edward Alsworth Ross (1866– 1951) was a prolific writer on sociological subjects.

my vital interests I must intrust to others! Nowadays the water
main is my well, the trolley car my carriage, the banker's safe my
old stocking, the policeman's billy my fist. My own eyes and nose
and judgment defer to the inspector of food, or drugs, or gas, or
factories, or tenements, or insurance companies. I rely upon others
to look after my drains, invest my savings, nurse my sick, and teach
my children. I let the meat trust butcher my pig, the oil trust
mould my candles, the sugar trust boil my sorghum, the coal trust
chop my wood, the barb wire company split my rails.

But this spread-out manner of life lays snares for the weak and
opens doors to the wicked. Interdependence puts us, as it were, at
one another's mercy, and so ushers in a multitude of new forms of
wrong-doing. The practice of mutualism has always worked this
way. Most sin is preying, and every new social relation begets its
cannibalism. No one will "make the ephah small" or "falsify the
balances" until there is buying and selling, "withhold the pledge"
until there is loaning, "keep back the hire of the laborers" until
there is a wage system, "justify the wicked for a reward" until men
submit their disputes to a judge. The rise of the state makes possible counterfeiting, smuggling, peculation, and treason. Commerce
tempts the pirate, the forger, and the embezzler. Every new fiduci-
ary relation is a fresh opportunity for breach of trust. To-day the
factory system makes it possible to work children to death on the
double-quick, speculative building gives the jerry-builder his
chance, long-range investment spawns the get-rich-quick concern,
and the trust movement opens the door to the bubble pro-
moter. * * *

Modern Sin Is Not Superficially Repulsive

To-day the sacrifice of life incidental to quick success rarely calls
for the actual spilling of blood. How decent are the pale slayings
of the quack, the adulterator, and the purveyor of polluted water,
compared with the red slayings of the vulgar bandit or assassin!
Even if there is blood-letting, the long-range, tentacular nature of
modern homicide eliminates all personal collision. What an abyss
between the knife-play of brawlers and the law-defying neglect to
fence dangerous machinery in a mill, or to furnish cars with safety
couplers! * * * Unlike the old-time villain, the latter-day male-
factor does not wear a slouch hat and a comforter, breathe forth
curses and an odor of gin, go about his nefarious work with clenched
teeth and an evil scowl. In the supreme moment his lineaments
are not distorted with rage, or lust, or malevolence. One misses
the dramatic setting, the time-honored insignia of turpitude. Fa-
gin and Bill Sykes and Simon Legree are vanishing types. Gamester,
murderer, body-snatcher, and kidnapper may appeal to a Hogarth,

but what challenge finds his pencil in the countenance of the boodler, the savings-bank wrecker, or the ballot-box stuffer? Among our criminals of greed, one begins to meet the "grand style" of the great criminals of ambition, Macbeth or Richard III. The modern high-power dealer of woe wears immaculate linen, carries a silk hat and a lighted cigar, sins with a calm countenance and a serene soul, leagues or months from the evil he causes. Upon his gentlemanly presence the eventual blood and tears do not obtrude themselves.

This is why good, kindly men let the wheels of commerce and of industry redden and redden, rather than pare or lose their dividend. This is why our railroads yearly injure one employee in twenty-six, and we look in vain for that promised "day of the Lord" that "will make a man more precious than fine gold."

Modern Sins Are Impersonal

The convenant breaker, the suborned witness, the corrupt judge, the oppressor of the fatherless,—the old-fashioned sinner, in short, —knows his victim, must hearken, perhaps, to bitter upbraidings. But the tropical belt of sin we are sweeping into is largely impersonal. Our iniquity is wireless, and we know not whose withers are wrung by it. The hurt passes into that vague mass, the "public," and is there lost to view. * * *

Secure in his quilted armor of lawyer-spun sophistries, the criminaloid promulgates an ethics which the public hails as a disinterested contribution to the philosophy of conduct. He invokes a pseudo-Darwinism to sanction the revival of outlawed and by-gone tactics of struggle. Ideals of fellowship and peace are "unscientific." To win the game with the aid of a sleeveful of aces proves one's fitness to survive. A sack of spoil is Nature's patent of nobility. A fortune is a personal attribute, as truly creditable as a straight back or a symmetrical face. Poverty, like the misshapen ear of the degenerate, proves inferiority. The wholesale fleecer of trusting, workaday people is a "Napoleon," a "superman." Labor defending its daily bread must, of course, obey the law; but "business," especially the "big proposition," may free itself of such trammels in the name of a "higher law." The censurers of the criminaloid are "pin-headed disturbers" who would imitate him if they had the chance or the brains. * * *

If the laws guarding the interests of one class are enforced, while the counter-balancing statutes protecting another class lie dormant, or if a law is enforced downward but not upward, or if Justice wields a sword on the poor but a lath on the rich and influential, the cheated class fiercely resolves to capture the state and to govern ruthlessly in its own interests. But, imbued with this vengeful spirit, government soon becomes the engine rather than the arbiter of conflicting interests, and the state sense perishes in the flame of class hate. This is why it may be more imperative to cut out alike Pinkertons and sluggers, to put down impartially corporation law-breaking and mob violence, than to enforce the ordinances for the "red light" district. * * *

* * * In Pennsylvania the law-abiding disposition was so weakened by the Standard Oil Company's example that a man who tapped a pipe-line and stole Standard oil for two years was found innocent by jurors who had heard him plead guilty. In California the Southern Pacific Railroad Company brought law into such contempt that the train robbers, Evans and Sontag, were befriended by nearly the whole local population. In certain Rocky Mountain states mine operators and miners have both well-nigh lost the state sense, and reach for a judgeship or a sheriffalty as unhesitatingly as in a fight one would reach for a crowbar. Thus breach of law begets counter-breach. * * *

The truth is, on the plane of our inherited institutions government might be so administered in the public-welfare spirit, that three fourths of the subversive sentiment existing would vanish. But the policy of "Score while you're in!" plays into the hands of the radicals who tell the workingman "there is no halfway house between capitalism and collectivism." "Our innings!" cries Big Business exultantly, and with fifty-year franchise laws, iniquitous tariff schedules, excessive railway-mail charges, grabbing of public mineral lands, corrupt sale of canals and gas plants, fake meat inspection, Niagara grabs, and the cynical denial of protection to labor, it plunges ahead, inviting the day when the cry will ring out, "To your tents, O Israel!" Every tampering with the simple logical rules of the game on the theory that if you take care of business business will take care of the general welfare, or if you take care of the capitalist, the capitalist will take care of the workingman, adds to those who think the game itself so hopelessly bad that there is no use in trying to make it fair. * * *

Those who put their faith in a transfigured individualism should make haste to clean the hull of the old ship for the coming great battle with the opponents of private capital and individual initiative. Certainly many of the villainies and oppressions that befoul it are no more a part of individualism than are the barnacles and trailing weed a part of the vessel. Moreover, if they are to put up a good fight for the ship, it behooves them to rid it of the buccaneers, wreckers, and shanghaiers that now impudently claim the shelter of its flag, and by their sinister presence compromise the efforts of its legitimate defenders. * * *

Unless Rules be Enforced, the Moral Plane Will Not Be Lifted
Simply by Adding to the Number of Righteous Men

Many spiritual leaders imagine that the Kingdom of Heaven comes simply by regenerating souls, that as man after man turns his face upward society is duly uplifted. It would follow that the quiet work [of] individuals does not need to be supplemented by the recourse to law or public opinion, and that the Puritan's endeavor to *establish righteousness* is superfluous.

This may have been true before competition became lord of life, but now that the few lead off while the rest must follow suit, much depends on giving the lead to the good man rather than the bad man. You may add to the number of good men, but, without enforced rules, it will be impossible for them to stay in the higher posts and callings. For the social trend denies most men a free hand. More and more the chief vocations come under the baton of competition, so that one may not maintain one's self in them at all unless one feels at liberty to do as his rivals are permitted to do. Those in the same line must move in lock step, and the pace is set by the meanest man who is allowed to continue in the business. The department store that pays its girls living wages and closes at six can hardly live in the same town with one that pays four dollars a week and closes at nine. If the price of glass jars is fixed by the manufacturer who overdrives little boys, every competitor must, unless he possesses some offsetting advantage, conform to this practice. Leave the business he may, change it he cannot. If one dealer in foods successfully adulterates, his fellows must follow suit or else seek their patrons among the few who prefer a brand because it is dear. * * *

* * * There are already enough granite men to man the high posts; but, till the ways be cleared for them, they accumulate on the lower levels where, having no free hand, they feel no moral responsibility. By themselves they can get no foothold at the strategic points where conditions are made, where the weal or woe of thousands is determined. Without aid they cannot maintain themselves in these competitive fields. It is, therefore, the first duty of society *to establish the righteous by lifting the plane of competition.*

Pure food laws mean an open door for honest men in the purveying business. An efficient state insurance department means a chance for the "old-fashioned" manager. A stricter ethical code for the legal profession would enable certain briefless lawyers to forge to the front. Child-labor restriction is a godsend to the humane manufacturer. * * *

Other Social Responses to Darwinism

The Scopes Trial (1925) †

GEN. STEWART—[*Reading:*] State of Tennessee, County of Rhea. Circuit Court. July Special Term, 1925.

The grand jurors for the state aforesaid, being duly summoned, elected, empanelled, sworn, and charged to inquire for the body of the county aforesaid, upon their oaths present:

That John Thomas Scopes, heretofore on the 24th day of April, 1925, in the county aforesaid, then and there, unlawfully did willfully teach in the public schools of Rhea County, Tennessee, which said public schools are supported in part and in whole by the public school fund of the state, a certain theory and theories that deny the story of the divine creation of man as taught in the Bible, and did teach instead thereof that man has descended from a lower order of animals, he, the said John Thomas Scopes, being at the time, and prior thereto, a teacher in the public schools of Rhea County, Tennessee, aforesaid, against the peace and dignity of the State.

THE COURT—What is your plea, gentlemen?

* * *

† In 1925, the Tennessee legislature passed the "Butler Act," forbidding the teaching of evolution in the public schools of that state. In May, John Thomas Scopes, a science teacher at Dayton High School, consented to be the defendant in a court test of the law. He was arrested and indicted by a grand jury and stood trial on July 10–21, 1925. Defended by the American Civil Liberties Union, Scopes was represented by (among others) the noted trial lawyer Clarence Darrow; the prosecution was assisted by William Jennings Bryan, thrice-defeated presidential candidate. These men broadened the case from an investigation of a simple issue of law to a forum for the debate of a highly controversial issue: whether science (particularly evolution) and religion (particularly fundamentalism) could coexist.

In the wake of excitement following the Scopes trial, there was a nation-wide flurry of anti-evolutionary activity, led by fundamentalist religious groups.

In 1926 and 1927, laws similar to the Butler Act were passed by the legislatures of Mississippi and Arkansas, and these, together with the Butler Act, survived, though almost wholly unenforced, until very recently. The Butler Act was finally repealed in 1967, and in 1968 the United States Supreme Court declared the Arkansas law unconstitutional—thus in effect nullifying the last remaining anti-evolutionary law, which is still formally in effect in Mississippi. (See also the following article.)

The present text is from the official stenographic transcript of the trial: *State of Tennessee* vs. *John Thomas Scopes,* Nos. 5231 and 5232, in the Circuit Court of Rhea County, Tennessee. Besides Scopes, Darrow, and Bryan, others mentioned in the transcript are Attorney General A.T. Stewart, counsel for the state, and John R. Neal, Dudley Field Malone, and Arthur Garfield Hays, all counsel for the defendant.

MR. NEAL—[*Reading:*] The defendant moves the court to quash the indictment in this case for the following reasons:

First—(A) Because the act which is the basis of the indictment, and which the defendant is charged with violating, is unconstitutional and void in that it violates * * * Section 3, Article I of the constitution of Tennessee:

> Section 3. Right of Worship Free—That all men have a natural and indefeasible right to worship Almighty God according to the dictates of his own conscience; that no man can of right, be compelled to attend, erect or support any place of worship, or to maintain any minister against his consent; that no human authority can, in any case whatever, control or interfere with the rights of conscience; and that no preference shall ever be given, by law, to any religious establishment or mode of worship.

* * *

GEN. STEWART—The next one, and the one which Dr. Neal referred to as one of the most important ones, Section 3, Article I, still of the constitution, the right of free worship. * * *

If your Honor please, this law is as far removed from that interference with the provision in the constitution as it is from any other that is not even cited. This does not interfere with the religious worship—it does not even approach interference with religious worship. * * *

MR. DARROW— * * * The part we claim is that last clause, "no preference shall ever be given, by law, to any religious establishment or mode of worship."

GEN. STEWART—Yes, that "no preference shall ever be given, by law, to any religious establishment or mode of worship." Then, how could that interfere, Mr. Darrow?

MR. DARROW—That is the part we claim is affected.

GEN. STEWART—In what wise?

MR. DARROW—Giving preference to the Bible.

* * *

GEN. STEWART— * * * There is as little in that as in any of the rest. If your Honor please, the St. James Version of the Bible is the recognized one in this section of the country. The laws of the land recognize the Bible; the laws of the land recognize the law of God and Christianity as a part of the common law.

MR. MALONE—Mr. Attorney General, may I ask a question?

GEN. STEWART—Certainly.

MR. MALONE—Does the law of the land or the law of the state of Tennessee recognize the Bible as part of a course in biology or science?

GEN. STEWART—I do not think the law of the land recognizes them as confusing one another in any particular.

* * *

GEN STEWART— * * * The question involved here is, to my mind, the question of the exercise of the police power.

MR. NEAL—It does not mention the Bible?

GEN. STEWART—Yes, it mentions the Bible. The legislature, according to our laws, in my opinion, would have the right to preclude the teaching of geography. That is—

MR. NEAL—Does not it prefer the Bible to the Koran?

GEN. STEWART—It does not mention the Koran.

MR. MALONE—Does not it prefer the Bible to the Koran?

GEN. STEWART—We are not living in a heathen country.

MR. MALONE—Will you answer my question? Does not it prefer the Bible to the Koran?

GEN. STEWART—We are not living in a heathen country, so how could it prefer the Bible to the Koran? * * *

MR. MALONE— * * * I would say to base a theory set forth in any version of the Bible to be taught in the public school is an invasion of the rights of the citizen, whether exercised by the police power or by the legislature.

GEN. STEWART—Because it imposes a religious opinion?

MR. MALONE—Because it imposes a religious opinion, yes. What I mean is this: If there be in the state of Tennessee a single child or young man or young woman in your school who is a Jew, to impose upon any course of science a particular view of creation from the Bible is interfering, from our point of view, with his civil rights under our theory of the case. That is our contention.

* * *

MR. DARROW— * * * This case we have to argue is a case at law, and hard as it is for me to bring my mind to conceive it, almost impossible as it is to put my mind back into the sixteenth century, I am going to argue it as if it was serious, and as if it was a death struggle between two civilizations.

* * * We have been informed that the legislature has the right to prescribe the course of study in the public schools. Within reason, they no doubt have, no doubt. They could not prescribe it, I am inclined to think, under your constitution, if it omitted arithmetic and geography and writing, neither under the rest of the constitution, if it shall remain in force in the State, could they prescribe it if the course of study was only to teach religion, because several hundred years ago, when our people believed in freedom, and when no man felt so sure of their own sophistry that they were willing to send a man to jail who who did not believe them, the people of Tennessee adopted a constitution, and they made it broad and plain, and said that the people of Tennessee would always enjoy religious freedom in its broadest terms; so, I assume, that no legislature could fix a course of study which violated that. * * *

I remember, long ago, Mr. Bancroft wrote this sentence, which is true: "That it is all right to preserve freedom in constitutions, but when the spirit of freedom has fled from the hearts of the people, then its matter is easily sacrificed under law." And so it is, unless there is left enough of the spirit of freedom in the state of Tennessee, and in the United States, there is not a single line of any constitution that can withstand bigotry and ignorance when it seeks to destroy the rights of the individual; and bigotry and ignorance are ever active. Here, we find today as brazen and as bold an attempt to destroy learning as was ever made in the Middle Ages, and the only difference is we have not provided that they shall be burned at the stake, but there is time for that, your Honor; we have to approach these things gradually.

Now, let us see what we claim with reference to this law. If this proceeding, both in form and substance, can prevail in this court, then your Honor, no law—no matter how foolish, wicked, ambiguous, or ancient, but can come back to Tennessee. All the guarantees go for nothing. All of the past has gone, will be forgotten, if this can succeed. * * *

The statute should be comprehensible. It should not be written in Chinese anyway. It should be in passing English, as you say, so that common, human beings would understand what it meant, and so a man would know whether he is liable to go to jail when he is teaching, not so ambiguous as to be a snare or a trap to get someone who does not agree with you. If should be plain, simple and easy. Does this statute state what you shall teach and what you shall not? Oh, no! Oh, no! Not at all. Does it say you cannot teach the earth is round, because Genesis says it is flat? No. Does it say you cannot teach that the earth is millions of ages old, because the account in Genesis makes it less than six thousand years old? Oh, no. It doesn't state that. If it did you could understand it. It says you shan't teach any theory of the origin of man that is contrary to the divine theory contained in the Bible.

Now let us pass up the word "divine"! No legislature is strong enough in any state in the Union to characterize and pick any book as being divine. Let us take it as it is. What is the Bible? * * * The Bible is not one book. The Bible is made up of sixty-six books written over a period of about one thousand years, some of them very early and some of them comparatively late. It is a book primarily of religion and morals. It is not a book of science. Never was and was never meant to be. Under it there is nothing prescribed that would tell you how to build a railroad or a steamboat or to make anything that would advance civilization. It is not a textbook or a text on chemistry. It is not big enough to be. It is not a book on geology; they knew nothing about it. It is not a work on evolution; that is a mystery. It is not a work on astronomy. The man who looked out at the universe and studied the heavens had no thought but that the earth was the center of the universe. But we know better than that. We know that the sun is the center of the solar system. And that there are an infinity of other systems around about us. They thought the sun went around the earth and gave us light and gave us night. We know better. We know the earth turns on its axis to produce days and nights. They thought the earth was 4,004 years before the Christian Era. We know better. They told it the best they knew. And while suns may change all you may learn of chemistry, geometry and mathematics, there are no doubt certain primitive, elemental instincts in the organs of man that remain the same; he finds out what he can and yearns to know more and supplements his knowledge with hope and faith.

That is the province of religion and I haven't the slightest fault to find with it. Not the slightest in the world. One has one thought and one another, and instead of fighting each other as in the past, they should support and help each other. Let's see now. Can your Honor tell what is given as the origin of man as shown in the Bible? Is there any human being who can tell us? There are two conflicting accounts in the first two chapters. There are scattered all through it various acts and ideas, but to pass that up for the sake of argument, no teacher in any school in the state of Tennessee can know that he is violating a law, but must test every one of its doctrines by the Bible, must he not? You cannot say two times two equals four or make a man an educated man if evolution is forbidden. It does not specify what you cannot teach, but says you cannot teach anything that conflicts with the Bible. Then just imagine making it a criminal code that is so uncertain and impossible that every man must be sure that he has read everything in the Bible and not only read it but understands it, or he might violate the criminal code. Who is the chief mogul that can tell us what the Bible means? He or they should write a book and make it plain and distinct, so we would know. Let us look at it. There are in America at least five hundred different sects or churches, all of which quarrel with each other and the importance and nonimportance of certain things or the construction of certain passages. All along the line they do not agree among themselves and cannot agree among themselves. They never have and probably never will. There is a great division between the Catholics and the Protestants. There is such a disagreement that my client, who is a school-teacher, not only must know the subject he is teaching, but he must know everything about the Bible in reference to evolution. And he must be sure that he expresses it right or else some fellow will come along here, more ignorant perhaps than he, and say, "You made a bad guess and I think you have committed a crime." No criminal statute can rest that way. * * *

It cannot stand a minute in this court on any theory than that it is a criminal act, simply because they say it contravenes the teaching of Moses, without telling us what those teachings are. Now, if this is the subject of a criminal act, then it cannot make a criminal out of a teacher in the public schools and leave a man free to teach it in a private school. It cannot make it criminal for a teacher in the public schools to teach evolution, and for the same man to stand among the hustings and teach it. It cannot make it a criminal act for this teacher to teach evolution and permit books upon evolution to be sold in every store in the state of Tennessee and to permit the newspapers from foreign cities to bring into your peaceful community the horrible utterances of evolution. Oh, no, nothing like that. If the state of Tennessee has any force in this day of Fundamentalism, in this day when religious bigotry and hatred is being kindled all over our land, see what can be done. * * *

* * * Ignorance and fanaticism is ever busy and needs feeding. Always it is feeding and gloating for more. Today it is the public school teachers, tomorrow the private. The next day the preachers and the lecturers, the magazines, the books, the newspapers. After a while, your Honor, it is the setting of man against man and creed against creed, until with flying banners and beating drums we are marching backward to the glorious ages of the sixteenth century, when bigots lighted fagots to burn the men who dared to bring any intelligence and enlightenment and culture to the human mind. * * *

MR. BRYAN—Little Howard Morgan—and, your Honor, that boy is going to make a great lawyer someday. I didn't realize it until I saw how a 14-year-old boy understood the subject so much better than a distinguished lawyer who attempted to quiz him. The little boy understood what he was talking about and, to my surprise, the attorneys didn't seem to catch the significance of the theory of evolution and the thought—and I'm sure he wouldn't have said it if he hadn't had thought it—he thought that little boy was talking about the individuals coming up from one cell. That wouldn't be evolution—that is growth, and one trouble about evolution is that it has been used in so many different ways that people are confused about it. * * *

Tell me that the parents of this day have not any right to declare that children are not to be taught this doctrine? Shall not be taken down from the high plane upon which God put man? Shall be detached from the throne of God and be compelled to link their ancestors with the jungle; tell that to these children? Why, my friends, if they believe it, they go back to scoff at the religion of their parents! And the parents have a right to say that no teacher paid by their money shall rob their children of faith in God and send them back to their homes, skeptical, infidels, or agnostics, or atheists!

This doctrine that they want taught, this doctrine that they would force upon the schools, where they will not let the Bible be read—why, up in the state of New York they are now trying to keep the schools from adjourning for one hour in the afternoon, not that any teacher shall teach them the Bible, but that the children may go to the churches to which they belong and there have instruction in the Word. And they are refusing to let the school do that. These lawyers who are trying to force Darwinism and evolution on your children do not go back to protect the children of New York in their right to even have religion taught to them outside of the schoolroom, and they want to bring their experts in here. * * *

Now, my friends, I want you to know that they not only have no proof, but they cannot find the beginning. I suppose this distinguished scholar who came here shamed them all by his number of degrees. He did not shame me, for I have more than he has, but I can understand how my friends felt when he un-rolled degree after degree. Did he tell you where life began? Did he tell you that back of all these that there was a God? Not a word about it. Did he tell you how life began? Not a word, and not one of them can tell you how life began. The atheists say it came some way without a God; the agnostics say it came in some way, they know not whether with a God or not. And the Christian evolutionists say we came away back there somewhere, but they do not know how far back—they do not give you the beginning—not that gentleman that tried to qualify as an expert; he did not tell you whether it began with God or how. No, they take up life as a mystery that nobody can explain, and they want you to let them commence there and ask no questions. They want to come in with their little padded up evolution that commences with nothing and ends nowhere. They do not dare to tell you that it began with God and . . . ended with God. They come here with this bunch of stuff that they call evolution, that they tell you that everybody believes in, but do not know that every-body knows as a fact, and nobody can tell how it came, and they do not explain the great riddle of the universe—they do not deal with the problems of life—they do not teach the great science of how to live—and yet they would undermine the faith of these little children in that God who stands back of everything and whose promise we have that we shall live with Him forever bye and bye. They shut God out of the world. They do not talk about God. Darwin says the beginning of all things is a mystery unsolvable by us. He does not pretend to say how these things started. * * *

And your Honor asked me whether it has anything to do with the principle of the virgin birth. Yes, because this principle of evolution disputes the miracle; there is no place for the miracle in this train of evolution, and the Old Testament and the New are filled with miracles, and if this doctrine is true, this logic elim-inates every mystery in the Old Testament and the New, and eliminates everything supernatural; and that means they eliminate the virgin birth—that means that they eliminate the resur-rection of the body—that means that they eliminate the doc-trine of atonement. And they believe man has been rising all the time, that man never fell; that when the Savior came there was not any reason for His coming; there was no reason why He should not go as soon as He could, that He was born of Joseph or some other correspondent, and that He lies in his grave. And when the Christians of this state have tied their hands and said, "We will not take advantage of our power to teach religion to our children, by teachers paid by us," these people come in from the outside of the state and force upon the people of this state and upon the children of the taxpayers of this state a doctrine that refutes not only their belief in God, but their belief in a Savior and belief in heaven, and takes from them every moral standard that the Bible gives us. * * *

Your Honor, we first pointed out that we do not need any experts in science. . . . And, when it comes to Bible experts, every member of the jury is as good an expert on the Bible as any man that they could bring, or that we could bring. The one beauty about the Word of God is, it does not take an expert to understand it. They have translated that Bible into five hundred languages; they have carried it into nations where but few can read a word, or write, to people who never saw a book, who never read, and yet can understand that Bible, and they can accept the salvation that the Bible offers, and they can know more about that book by accepting Jesus and feeling in their hearts the sense of their sins forgiven than all of the skeptical outside Bible experts that could come in here to talk to the people of Tennessee about the construction that they place upon the Bible, that is foreign to the construction that the people here place upon it.

* * *

MR. HAYS—The Defense desires to call Mr. Bryan as a witness, and, of course, since the only question here is whether Mr. Scopes taught what these children said he taught, we recognize what Mr. Bryan says as a witness would not be very valuable. We think there are other questions involved, and we should want to take Mr. Bryan's testimony for the purposes of our record, even if your Honor thinks it is not admissible in general, so we wish to call him now.

* * *

THE COURT—Mr. Bryan, you are not objecting to going on the stand?

MR. BRYAN—Not at all.

THE COURT—Do you want Mr. Bryan sworn?

MR. DARROW—No.

MR. BRYAN—I can make affirmation; I can say, "So help me God, I will tell the truth."

MR. DARROW—No, I take it you will tell the truth, Mr. Bryan.

Q [MR. DARROW]—You have given considerable study to the Bible, haven't you, Mr. Bryan?

A [MR. BRYAN]—Yes, sir, I have tried to.

* * *

Q—Do you claim that everything in the Bible should be literally interpreted?

A—I believe everything in the Bible should be accepted as it is given there; some of the Bible is given illustratively. For instance: "Ye are the salt of the earth." I would not insist that man was actually salt, or that he had flesh of salt, but it is used in the sense of salt as saving God's people.

Q—But when you read that Jonah swallowed the whale—or that the whale swallowed Jonah—excuse me please—how do you literally interpret that?

A—When I read that a big fish swallowed Jonah—it does not say whale.

Q—Doesn't it? Are you sure?

A—That is my recollection of it. A big fish, and I believe it; and I believe in a God who can make a whale and can make a man and make both do what He pleases.

Q—Mr. Bryan, doesn't the New Testament say a whale?

A—I am not sure. My impression is that it says fish; but it does not make so much difference; I merely called your attention to where it says fish—it does not say whale.

Q—But in the New Testament it says whale, doesn't it?

A—That may be true; I cannot remember in my own mind what I read about it.

Q—Now, you say, the big fish swallowed Jonah, and he there remained how long? three days? and then he spewed him upon the land. You believe that the big fish was made to swallow Jonah?

A—I am not prepared to say that; the Bible merely says it was done.

Q—You don't know whether it was the ordinary run of fish, or made for that purpose?

A—You may guess; you evolutionists guess.

Q—But when we do guess, we have a sense to guess right.

A—But do not do it often.

Q—You are not prepared to say whether that fish was made especially to swallow a man or not?

A—The Bible doesn't say, so I am not prepared to say.

Q—You don't know whether that was fixed up specially for the purpose?

A—No, the Bible doesn't say.

Q—But you do believe He made them—that He made such a fish and that it was big enough to swallow Jonah?

A—Yes, sir. Let me add: one miracle is just as easy to believe as another.

Q—It is for me.

A—It is for me.

Q—Just as hard?

A—It is hard to believe for you, but easy for me. A miracle is a thing performed beyond what man can perform. What you get beyond what man can do, you get within the realm of miracles; and it is just as easy to believe the miracle of Jonah as any other miracle in the Bible.

Q—Perfectly easy to believe that Jonah swallowed the whale?

A—If the Bible said so; the Bible doesn't make as extreme statements as evolutionists do.

MR. DARROW—That may be a question, Mr. Bryan, about some of those you have known.

A—The only thing is, you have a definition of fact that includes imagination.

Q—And you have a definition that excludes everything but imagination.

GEN. STEWART—I object to that as argumentative.

THE WITNESS—You—

MR. DARROW—The witness must not argue with me, either.

Q—Do you consider the story of Jonah and the whale a miracle?

A—I think it is.

Q—Do you believe Joshua made the sun stand still?

A—I believe what the Bible says. I suppose you mean that the earth stood still?

Q—I don't know. I am talking about the Bible now.

A—I accept the Bible absolutely.

Q—The Bible says Joshua commanded the sun to stand still for the purpose of lengthening the day, doesn't it? and you believe it?

A—I do.

Q—Do you believe at that time the entire sun went around the earth?

A—No, I believe that the earth goes around the sun.

Q—Do you believe that men who wrote it thought that the day could be lengthened or that the sun could be stopped?

A—I don't know what they thought.

Q—You don't know?

A—I think they wrote the fact without expressing their own thoughts.

* * *

MR. DARROW—Have you an opinion as to whether—whoever wrote the book, I believe it is, Joshua, the Book of Joshua, thought the sun went around the earth or not?

A—I believe that he was inspired.

MR. DARROW—Can you answer my question?

A—When you let me finish the statement.

Q—It is a simple question, but finish it.

THE WITNESS—You cannot measure the length of my answer by the length of your question.

[*Laughter in the courtyard.*]

MR. DARROW—No, except that the answer be longer.

[*Laughter in the courtyard.*]

A—I believe that the Bible is inspired, an inspired author, whether one who wrote as he was directed to write understood the things he was writing about, I don't know.

Q—Whoever inspired it? Do you think whoever inspired it believed that the sun went around the earth?

A—I believe it was inspired by the Almighty, and He may have used language that could be understood at that time.

Q—Was—

THE WITNESS—Instead of using language that could not be understood until Mr. Darrow was born.

[*Laughter and applause in the courtyard.*]

* * *

Q—You believe the story of the flood to be a literal interpretation?

A—Yes, sir.

Q—When was that flood?

A—I would not attempt to fix the date. The date is fixed, as suggested this morning.

Q—About 4004 B.C.?

A—That has been the estimate of a man that is accepted today. I would not say it is accurate.

* * *

MR. DARROW—How long ago was the flood, Mr. Bryan?

* * *

THE WITNESS—Oh, I would put the estimate where it is, because I have no reason to vary it. But I would have to look at it to give you the exact date.

Q—I would, too. Do you remember what book the account is in?

A—Genesis.

MR. HAYES—Is that the one in evidence?

MR. NEAL—That will have it; that is the King James Version.

MR. DARROW—The one in evidence has it.

THE WITNESS—It is given here, as 2348 years B.C.

Q—Well, 2348 years B.C. You believe that all the living things that were not contained in the ark were destroyed.

A—I think the fish may have lived.

Q—Outside of the fish?

A—I cannot say.

Q—You cannot say?

A—No, I accept that just as it is; I have no proof to the contrary.

Q—I am asking you whether you believe?

A—I do.

Q—That all living things outside of the fish were destroyed?

A—What I say about the fish is merely a matter of humor.

Q—I understand.

* * *

Q—Don't you know that the ancient civilizations of China are 6,000 or 7,000 years old, at the very least?

A—No; but they would not run back beyond the creation, according to the Bible, 6,000 years.

Q—You don't know how old they are, is that right?

A—I don't know how old they are, but probably you do. [*Laughter in the courtyard.*] I think you would give preference to anybody who opposed the Bible, and I give the preference to the Bible.

Q—I see. Well, you are welcome to your opinion. Have you any idea how old the Egyptian civilization is?

A—No.

Q—Do you know of any record in the world, outside of the story of the Bible, which conforms to any statement that it is 4,200 years ago or thereabouts that all life was wiped off the face of the earth?

A—I think they have found records.

Q—Do you know of any?

A—Records reciting the flood, but I am not an authority on the subject.

Q—Now, Mr. Bryan, will you say if you know of any record, or have ever heard of any records, that describe that a flood existed 4,200 years ago, or about that time, which wiped all life off the earth?

A—The recollection of what I have read on that subject is not distinct enough to say whether the records attempted to fix a time, but I have seen in the discoveries of archaeologists where they have found records that described the flood.

Q—Mr. Bryan, don't you know that there are many old religions that describe the flood?

A—No, I don't know.

Q—You know there are others besides the Jewish?

A—I don't know whether these are the record of any other religion or refer to this flood.

Q—Don't you ever examine religion so far to know that?

A—Outside of the Bible?

Q—Yes.

A—No; I have not examined to know that, generally.

Q—You have never examined any other religions?

A—Yes, sir.

Q—Have you ever read anything about the origins of religions?

A—Not a great deal.

Q—You have never examined any other religion?

A—Yes, sir.

Q—And you don't know whether any other religion ever gave a similar account of the destruction of the earth by the flood?

A—The Christian religion has satisfied me, and I have never felt it necessary to look up some competing religions.

* * *

HERMANN J. MULLER

One Hundred Years Without Darwinism Are Enough (1959) †

One hundred years ago Charles Darwin, in what was undoubtedly the greatest scientific book of all time, presented the evidence that

† *The Humanist,* XIX (1959), 139–149. Hermann J. Muller (1890–1967), geneticist and Nobel laureate in phy-siology and medicine, was Distinguished Service Professor of Zoology at Indiana University.

he had gathered and developed during the previous twenty years for the theory of evolution by natural selection. His treatment was so unprecedented, so comprehensive, and so masterly as first to stagger and then to convince all whose minds were mobile enough to follow his arguments adequately. Since that time, the whole matter has been subjected to the most copious and exacting criticism, and to ever more searching exploration and testing. The result has been that this revolutionary view of life now stands as one of the most firmly established generalizations of science and that far more is now understood about the manner by which evolution operates than was even imagined a century ago.

It ill befits the American people, four generations after Darwin published his epochal discovery, to turn their backs on it, to pretend that it is unimportant or uncertain, to adopt euphemistic expressions to hide and soften its impact, to teach it only as one alternative theory, to leave it for advanced courses in universities, where the multitudes cannot encounter it, or, if it is dealt with at all in a school biology course, to present it as unobtrusively and near the end of the course as possible, so that the student will fail to appreciate how every other feature and principle found in living things is in reality an outgrowth of its universal operation. The failure of our people to take evolution seriously can be traced to the slighting of the subject in our schools, although, of course, beneath this neglect there lurks a still deeper cause: our domination by antiquated religious traditions. Here, however, we shall deal mainly with the educational aspects of this matter.

Spiritual Significance of the Evolutionary Outlook

We need, in these decisive days of world tension, when free men will stand or fall according to how fully they recognize and act upon the most honest views of the truth that they can glean, to execute a complete about-face in this critical area. We dare not leave it to the Soviets alone to offer to their rising generation the inspiration that is to be gained from the wonderful world view opened up by Darwin and other Western biologists. This view, founded so solidly upon the discoveries of modern science, is, when fully understood and incorporated into men's personalities, the source of the profoundest idealism and hope. It should lend us support in our struggle for a freer world, for it shows how the most essential properties of living things have led to their perpetual reaching out, self-transformation, and, for some of them, progression, and conquest of the rest of nature, until from a slimy scum they have stood erect, become aware of themselves, evolved social feelings and moral principles, and striven toward the stars. It shows that this great process is still at work and that we can carry it further. But, analyzing the manner of operation of these forces, and noting the millions of species that have fallen by the way, this view of things also points to the practical dangers, and leads us to seek ways of avoiding the pitfalls and the insidious deflections of course that would otherwise cause disaster again.

Boys and girls in grade and high school are by no means too young for such lessons. * * *

* * * The text called *Modern Biology*, which is said to be that most widely used in high schools throughout the country, fails to contain the word evolution in the index or anywhere else. It does, however, in its next-to-the-last chapter have a moderately acceptable discussion of evolution, without using the word. This treatment, unfortunately, comes at too late a point to allow consideration of all other parts of biology as manifestations of evolution. Moreover, the words *racial development* are given, in italics, as the term by which this principle of nature is known! What better expression could be devised for veiling from one's view the awe-inspiring pattern by which primeval life progressively and divergently flowered out into all kinds of living beings, including ourselves!

Is it not clear that, if this imposing view of the course taken by living things is as true as all our criteria demonstrate it to be, we have no right to mince words about it, and sneakily to prevent our children from learning even the term by which this grandest principle in nature is properly known? * * *

A study published in 1942 by the Commission on the Teaching of Biology of the Union of American Biological Societies [1] under our beloved Dr. Oscar Riddle showed that even then fewer than half of the high school teachers of biology taught evolution as the principle underlying the development of all living things. There has been little or no improvement since that time. It was found in that study that some of those who failed to teach evolution did so because they themselves had not been well enough educated to recognize the truth of it. However, more of the teachers had been browbeaten by the dread that the teaching of this subject would arouse the opposition of administrators or of the public. With the passage of time, this ostrich policy has become, if anything, even more firmly fixed, despite the fact, or rather, because of the fact, that this field is so pregnant in its implications for everyone. Thus do we fail our youth.

Yet during all this time the subject itself has moved forward.

1. *The Teaching of Biology in Secondary Schools of the United States: A Report of Results from a Questionnaire,* by O. Riddle (editor), F. L. Fitzpatrick, H. B. Glass, B. C. Gruenberg, D. F. Miller and F. W. Sinnott, sponsored and published by The Committee on the Teaching of Biology of the Union of American Biological Societies, 76 pp. (1942).

Although it has become abundantly clear that the Darwinian principle of the natural selection of randomly occurring variation lies at the basis of all evolution, much more is now known of what, in turn, in the make-up of living things, lies behind this principle and gives rise to it. Much more is also known about evolution's progress, stagnation, or retrogression. Moreover, much of the essence of these facts is simple enough and important enough to be taught to youngsters. This being the case, it is their prerogative to have the opportunity to learn it. Evolution teaching must not stop with Darwin, Mendel, deVries, and a mere smattering of chromosome patter. Like knowledge of the meaning and implications of atomic energy or rocket operations, this subject must be brought up to date for the rising generation.

The history of living things, and its interpretation, can be made a fascinating story that will give our young people a strong sense of the meaning of life, not only for plants and animals in general, but for mankind in particular, and for them themselves. In fact, this has already been done in a number of college texts on biology, notably in George Gaylord Simpson's recent text called *Life*. This book has such clarity and impact that it is being used successfully even in some high school classes. Moreover, there are some otherwise very good high school texts that by no means ignore the issue. But what is most needed in this line are interesting texts which are primarily directed toward youngsters of high school or even grade school age, and which consistently attribute all the appurtenances of living things to the one integrating framework of evolution. We have no more right to starve the masses of our youth intellectually and emotionally because of the objections of the uninformed than we have a right to allow people to keep their children from being vaccinated and thus to endanger the whole community physically. * * *

I believe that it would in many ways be a grievous step backward if the Soviet system, with its authoritarianism and its perversion of biological as well as social progress, were to win out in the struggle for the minds, spirits and bodies of men. We have in our own ways of life much more inspiring possibilities, if we will grant them adequate opportunities for development in the hearts of our younger generation. At present we do not. Our youth are now being allowed to fall into the decadence of the commercialized hoopla that is carried to them over television and radio, in stadia and other public gatherings, and they are being encouraged in their rush to exploit privately and capriciously the opportunities of their high-powered automobiles and their increased allowances. In place of these distractions, they can and must be brought to realize the far richer fulfillment that is afforded them when they orient themselves to the modern view of the greatness of the world and of their own potentialities as revealed by modern science. Such orientation implies that they must learn to enjoy participation in the great co-operative enterprises of humanity as a whole: in men's conquests over outer nature and over their own discordant, outdated pettinesses and provincialisms, and in the never-ending work of improving their own inner beings. And as a primary basis for this re-orientation, let the eyes of our youth be opened wide to the great struggles and victories of their forebears throughout billions of years. Let them discern in this the promise that, by common effort and the use of reason and good will, we can hereafter telescope what would in the past have been a thousand years of progress into every single year of our own times.

For beings who have been endowed by evolution with the social and moral natures of men, individual freedom soon turns into caprice, disillusionment, and decadence unless the individual sees himself as an integral part of a greater whole, working with others in the pursuit of the higher freedoms of his community. In our modern age with its shrinkage of distances, this community now means the whole of mankind. This is the deepest lesson that the study of evolution, especially in its human aspects, can bring to the individual. We may well challenge the Soviets, with their doctrines of the economic man and of the universal class struggle, to offer anything that could be as inspiriting to youths or that could give so firm a sense of purpose and of direction to men's lives.

The Task Confronting Us in Biological Education

But it will take a big determined effort on our part to bring these lessons home to everyone. They must be started with the little child. He must be shown in pictures from the beginning the magnificent panorama of evolution, with its fascinating successions and diversifications of plants and animals as they took over more and more of the environment and fitted in among each other like the parts of a vast picture puzzle. He must be brought to understand the daily efforts of the individual creatures whereby these advances and sometimes retrogressions came about, and he must be taught its lessons explicitly. Always his questioning and his raising of objections must be solicited, so that he can see that this and the other conclusions of science are not arbitrary doctrines imposed by any authority but have been arrived at by the most careful testing and criticism as well as with the help of imaginative flights. He should also be taught to see that the development of our understanding of this great movement of nature is not complete but is open for everyone's participation. Finally, he should learn to participate in the decisions concerning this development.

We are not fulfilling our manifest obligation in teaching biology unless we open up these vistas to the child and also help him to delve into representative details of them. Here, then, we have both a glorious opportunity and a grave responsibility, such as no teachers have ever faced before.

Each teacher can do his bit by pulling individually in this direction as far as he practically can, but this is far from enough. Our country has virtually stood still in this area for the whole century since Darwin and Wallace's discovery, not because individual teachers failed to see the light but, for the most part, because they felt the pressure of ignorance too strong against them. This difficulty can be met, in part, by the practical measure of banding together, as has been done in the formation of our local and national associations of teachers, and of then having the members of these groups make common cause with one another and work collectively on this matter, so as better to protect each other and better to serve the community. Teachers may not expect to be treated otherwise than as underlings if they fail to stand by one another for the right to teach the tested truth.

The teachers' groups should also actively sponsor work on more modern courses, curricula, and textbooks, and then give the fruits of this labor their collective approval. For these purposes the most up-to-date and efficient techniques are imperative if the new teaching is to succeed. Most needed now in this area are recorded lessons. These should show vividly in pictures, photography, animated diagrams, and suitable commentary, followed of course by classroom discussions, the story of living things and the marvelous processes at work in the heart of them whereby the outer changes come about.

Let us, for example, make use of the wonderful moving pictures recently taken at the Brookhaven National Laboratory that show, in nontechnical fashion, how the core of the hereditary material reproduces itself, and how this notable discovery was arrived at. Let us also incorporate in our elementary biology courses the striking movies of cell division recently made by the Polish biologist, Bajer. But these are only starters. The whole complex must be woven together and integrated so as to bring the real world of life, as we moderns see it, home to the multitudes of boys and girls who are so dependent upon us. Such recorded demonstrations, circulated from central offices, will not be so easily dismissed as heresy by the local community, and in time both parents and pupils will feel cheated if lessons as celebrated as these would become have not been presented in their own schools.

The Challenge to Teachers and Scientists

This by no means implies that teachers may, in their own teaching, sit back and wait until ideal recorded courses have been prepared and distributed. The work of reconstruction of our biology teaching should go on at all levels. The most immediate need is for the preparation and adoption of high-quality texts that give evolution its due axial position and deal with it outspokenly and adequately. The author of the text that I criticized previously has informed me that if he had insisted on this policy, his book would have been rejected by the publishers. A representative of the publishers has next asserted that the fault was not theirs, since if they had been on the level with the children (an expression not used by him!) the book would have been rejected in Southern states in which the teaching of evolution is still illegal and by many textbook commissions and school boards in other parts of the United States as well. In short, that the publishers could not have afforded to publish the book under any other conditions. So the passing of the buck will go (*whose buck?*) until the vicious circle is broken somewhere by means of determined, concerted action.

Of course the publishers will make less profit if they have to publish two or three different texts instead of one that can be sold to all their customers. But if it were true, as claimed, that they actually could not afford to sell the text that is now most commonly used if its sale were cut in half, then we might ask how the publishers of the texts now less popular manage to continue publishing, and how it is possible for texts to be published at all in countries like Holland or Sweden, where the total sale of a text in the given language must be only a small fraction of that which our own texts would have if they were restricted to the more enlightened areas. These considerations show that it would be quite possible even today to publish meritorious high school texts in biology without losing money on them, although, of course, the profits would be lower than if their sales were universal. Are we then to allow the urge for profits to keep our children and, through them, all our people benighted and a hundred years out of date in their world view? Can we afford to let the profit system destroy us? Here is where intervention by government, by the general public, and by the professional groups most concerned—those of educators and scientists—is in order to break the vicious circle. Or do we think democracy means that the bulk of the people should be given only the knowledge that is sanctioned by the most ignorant?

If teachers, scientists, and as many of the public as are aware of the situation would stand together in insisting that American children be taught the lessons of our own age in this time of world crisis, it might not be long before the demand for adequate texts and courses would be so widespread that the present antiquated and evasive texts would be rejected by an even larger fraction of our country than that fraction which now rejects texts teaching the truth. Then the publishers would begin to find their profits in the other pocket and would have to pay more regard to educational honesty. They would then have to drop the complacency that holds: "If only we don't stir up trouble by making an issue of it, the reform will come about gradually and naturally within another ten years." I have already waited for more than fifty years to see this policy succeed, but our schools today seem even further behind contemporary knowledge in their treatment of evolution than they were half a century ago, and it is clear that another ten years at the same rate will only get us into worse arrears. It is up to all of us, then, together to take the bull by the horns.

Both educators and the public in this country profess to believe, with Jefferson, that education should be for everyone. Most people, moreover, are opposed to the doctrine, widely held by the intellectuals and nobility in Renaissance Europe, that although the elite are entitled to dally with advanced ideas, the masses should continue, for the good of the existing social structure, to be indoctrinated wholly with the ancient superstitions. If we, in this dangerous atomic age, reject so ignoble and undemocratic a view of human nature, then let us create for ourselves in the year 1959 an opportunity of displaying our own appreciation of this theory of evolution, which forms the core of the life science that we *should* be teaching. This epochal theory, that has until now been kept so veiled from most of our people, is surely the most stirring and significant discovery that man has ever made.

CONWAY ZIRKLE

Death of a Science in Russia (1949) †

Darwinism

Late in 1859 Charles Darwin published *The Origin of Species by Means of Natural Selection: or, the Preservation of Favored Races in the Struggle for Life.* Here he established the theory of evolution on a scientific basis and, as a result, evolution was often

† From Zirkle's *Death of a Science in Russia* (Philadelphia, 1949), *passim.* Conway Zirkle (b. 1895) is Emeritus Professor of Botany at the University of Pennsylvania.

called "Darwinism," a usage now archaic in biological circles. Darwinism has also been used to designate Darwin's explanation of evolution and, in this sense, is synonymous with natural selection. This second usage is also disappearing, primarily because our knowledge of the workings of natural selection has increased so greatly during the last fifty years that it is more accurate now not to label it with Darwin's name but to reserve the term for natural selection as it was understood at the time of Darwin. In Russia, however, Darwinism includes both the above meanings, and in addition all other beliefs and hypotheses which Darwin accepted. It is thus a complex of many doctrines. It is self-consistent, for Darwin was a reasonable man; and it is harmonious with the scientific knowledge of the middle nineteenth century, for Darwin kept himself well informed. When Darwin accepted Lamarck's inheritance of acquired characters, Lamarckism became a part of Darwinism, according to this Russian usage. * * *

Mendelism

Mendelian genetics, accepted by the biologists of the world since the beginning of the twentieth century, was officially rejected by Russia in August 1948. In the Russian press it has been consistently attacked and misrepresented. In fact, the Mendelism described in the following *Pravda* articles bears so little resemblance to the science taught in the universities of the world (including those in Russia until 1948 . . .) that it is necessary to describe it here so that the half-truths and complete falsehoods can be recognized when they are encountered later. Mendelism is labeled formalistic, impracticable, sterile, idealistic, reactionary, anti-democratic, and by any other adjective which is now used in a derogatory sense in the land of the Soviets. * * *

The practical application of Mendel's discovery to agricultural problems was immediately apparent. If genes could maintain their identity in hybrids, it became relatively simple to combine useful traits which had hitherto existed only in different races and varieties. All that was needed was to cross the stocks and select the progeny which had the proper combination of genes. These combinations could be reproduced indefinitely, and new races and varieties made to order. Excellent accounts of this application of genetics to improving food plants and domestic animals are in the United States Department of Agriculture *Yearbooks* for 1936 and 1937 (a total of 2,685 pages).

The most spectacular application of genetics to increasing our food supply was the creation of hybrid corn. Indian corn turned out to be an exceptionally favorable plant for the study of Mendelian factors, and today we know more about its genes than we do about those of any other plant. Thirty-five years ago G. H. Shull, E. M. East, and a little later D. F. Jones, East's student, worked out the genetic principles involved in the increased yield of hybrid corn. By 1920 heterosis (the name coined by Shull for hybrid vigor) appeared as a heading in the textbooks of genetics. In the twenty years following, the U. S. Department of Agriculture, state experiment stations, and seed companies developed different strains suitable for different regions, and today, by planting hybrid corn, the yield in the United States is increased by nearly half a billion bushels annually.[1]

In the papers translated from *Pravda*, Mendelism is pictured as a formalistic, academic game which occupies the time of scientists who could spend their energies more profitably by working to improve the food supply of the people. It is true that organisms most suited for genetic investigation are often without economic importance. It was a fortunate accident, however, that many crop plants furnished excellent experimental material so that important advances in pure and applied science occurred together. New and higher-yielding varieties, relatively immune to the common plant diseases, appear every year. Practically all the crops now grown in the United States consist of varieties which have been synthesized by the Mendelians.

Attention should also be called to the fact that the denunciation of genetics by the Communists is never accompanied by data of any kind.

Vernalization

"Vernalization" is the English equivalent of the hard-to-pronounce "iarovization." As originally used, the term referred to treatments of germinated seeds which altered the direction of their subsequent growth. It has been extended to include also treatments which break the rest periods of seeds so that by speeding up their germination less time is needed between seeding and harvesting. Many seeds will not grow when they are first shed. Some, which are shed in the fall and germinate in the spring, have to be subjected to the cold of winter before they will sprout. By shortening the growth period it becomes possible to grow crops farther north where the limiting factor is the length of time between the last killing frost in spring and the first killing frost in autumn. The effective means used to secure this desired end is to soak the seeds in water and then chill them until the water about the seeds is

1. Richard Crabb, *The Hybrid Corn Makers*. New Brunswick, 1947. I. Bernard Cohen, *Science, Servant of Man*. Boston, 1948.

frozen.[2] This is particularly effective with wheat.

There is no logical connection between vernalization and genetics. The topic is included here because Lysenko, the spearhead of the group who destroyed genetics in Russia, rose to eminence in this field and, to protect himself, has had to claim that the effects of vernalization are inherited. In Russia he is also credited with discovering the principles of vernalization and inventing the technique of accomplishing it (see below). This is his claim to greatness: by vernalization he "changes" winter wheat to spring wheat and accomplishes other transformations.

Lysenko's first contribution on the subject was published in 1928 (Azerbaijan Plant Breeding Station *Bulletin* #3, English Summary). Ten years earlier, however, G. Gassner (*Zeit. Bot.* 10:417–80. 1918) had both used the methods and recorded the results. Actually vernalization was old hat. It was well understood in the United States before the Civil War and is not a twentieth-century Russian discovery. * * *

As an agricultural practice in the United States, however, vernalization was soon abandoned as obsolete. The same results were obtained better and without the trouble by breeding varieties of wheat which did not need it. These new races were obtained by the well-tested method of selection, sometimes with and sometimes without previous hybridization. Today about 360 races of wheat are grown in our country, so that there are forms suited to each ecological condition.[3] * * *

The Lysenko Controversy

A Congress of Genetics, Plant and Animal Breeding, attended by about 1400 members, assembled in Leningrad in 1929 under the presidency of Vavilov. Among 348 papers read at this Congress, a fairly interesting but in no way revolutionary study on the physiology of cereals had as its junior author one T. D. Lysenko. A few years later the name of Lysenko was destined to become familiar not only to biologists but to newspaper readers throughout the USSR. He was hailed as the discoverer of vernalization, a process whereby winter wheat can be influenced to produce a crop if sown in the spring. The phenomenon of vernalization had been discovered in the United States years before Lysenko gave it a name; but Lysenko certainly proved himself a master of the art of modern publicity. He claimed, or it was claimed for him, that vernalization inaugurated a new era in Soviet agriculture, permit-

2. The reader is referred to the following works: H. H. McKinney, "Vernalization and the Growth-Phase Concept," *Botanical Review* 6:25–48. 1940. A. E. Murneek and R. O. Whyte, "Vernalization and Photoperiodism," *Lotsya*, Vol. I. Waltham, Mass., 1948. 3. U. S. Dept. of Agriculture *Technical Bulletin*, No. 795, 1942.

ting, among other things, the culture of cereal crops much farther north than was formerly possible. The vernalization bandwagon was highly popular some ten to fifteen years ago, but it is perhaps significant that little has been heard about practical applications of vernalization in the USSR or anywhere else in recent years.

Vavilov welcomed Lysenko's debut; although his published praises of Lysenko sound a bit hollow, he urged facilities for testing Lysenko's ideas. Lysenko was, however, interested in much bigger stakes. Sometime in the early nineteen-thirties, Lysenko formed an alliance with I. I. Prezent. Prezent was neither a biologist nor an agriculturist, but a specialist in the philosophy of dialectical materialism; he was also a highly effective polemical speaker and writer, and a possessor of a cultural refinement conspicuously lacking in Lysenko. In 1935 and 1936, Lysenko, Prezent, and their followers struck. In a stream of magazine and newspaper articles and speeches, they declared genetics to be inconsistent with dialectical materialism and with Darwinism as they construed the latter, and to be, in fact, tainted with fascism and with Nazi race theories. Furthermore, they contended, Vavilov's basing the work of plant and animal improvement on genetic principles had caused inexcusable delays in the successful outcome of this improvement work. Vastly more spectacular, and anyway vastly more rapid, practical attainments would come if only Vavilov's mismanagement and the suspect "Mendelian-Morganian" genetics were supplanted by Lysenko's patriotic leadership and the incorruptibly dialectico-Darwinistic approach.

In 1935 it was a deadly serious matter to be accused of having slowed down the development of agricultural production in USSR. To consider these charges a new Congress on genetics and agriculture was convened in Moscow in 1936, presided over by A. I. Muralov, a high governmental dignitary. The published transactions of this Congress make painful reading. There were Lysenko and Prezent with a well-organized group of followers, pleading, cajoling, and threatening. Several geneticists, among them H. J. Muller, the visiting American, vainly tried to stem the tide against genetics. The least inspiring sight was that of some competent scientists who attempted to sit on the fence or who made unctuous speeches praising both factions. Vavilov himself made two speeches in defense of modern genetics and agricultural science. To judge from the published texts, those speeches lacked Vavilov's customary forcefulness and optimism, as though he felt that the issue had already been decided against him. And indeed, the 1936 genetics Congress turned on the whole against Vavilov, just as the one held in 1929 gave him his greatest triumph.

This rejection of sound scientific principles of established practical value, in favor of a witchcraft supported only by artful propaganda and by big promises, seems utterly incomprehensible. The subversion and demolition of the work on plant improvement organized so successfully and on such a vast scale by Vavilov undoubtedly caused a setback in the development of agriculture in the USSR. Since, even with the energy of another Vavilov, such an organization could not be restored overnight, this blunder has harmed, and will continue to hamstring this development for some time to come. * * *

Downfall and Exile

In August 1939, the Seventh International Congress of Genetics was held at Edinburgh, Scotland, and Vavilov was invited to become its President, thus receiving the highest honor which the consensus of opinion of the world's geneticists can bestow. He accepted the invitation. But less than a month before the Congress was to open, came a letter, signed by Vavilov, which stated that "Soviet geneticists and plant and animal breeders do not consider it possible to take part in the Congress," because the latter was to be held outside the USSR. Few if any members of the Congress had any illusions as to whether Vavilov was a free agent when signing this letter. Matters were moving rapidly toward a denouement. In October 1939, a "Conference on Genetics and Selection" was held in Moscow, at which the problems thrashed out at the 1936 meeting were gone over again, with Lysenko, Prezent, and others greatly expanding their claims as to the theoretical soundness and practical efficacy of their "Darwinism." Vavilov, interrupted and heckled from the floor, delivered what was probably the weakest speech in his life, his attitude being almost entirely defensive, although he courageously reasserted the soundness of the basic principles of genetics. He evidently was already a broken man.

After the 1939 Genetics Conference, a shroud of silence envelops Vavilov. The closing chapter can be reconstructed only from unofficial, fragmentary, but apparently reliable information. Vavilov was arrested, probably in 1940. Part of the time during the winter 1941–1942, he was a prisoner in a concentration camp at Saratov (ironically, it was at the University of Saratov that he held his first post under the new revolutionary regime), and whence he was transported to Siberia. His destination was Magadan, on the Sea of Okhotsk, the capital of a rich gold-bearing region, but a place of sinister reputation, because of its deadly climate and even worse because it was built and operated by forced labor. According to some information, Vavilov was put to work on breeding varieties of vegetables capable of growing in Magadan's climate, but this information is not certain. The release, through death, probably came in late 1942. No mention of N. I. Vavilov's name can be found in the list of living and recently deceased members published by the Academy of Sciences of USSR in connection with its 220-year jubilee celebrated in 1945. * * *

Academician T. D. Lysenko

CONCLUDING REMARKS [4] ON THE REPORT OF THE SITUATION IN BIOLOGICAL SCIENCE

Comrades! Before proceeding to the concluding remarks, I consider it my duty to declare the following.

I have been asked in one of the memoranda as to the attitude of the Central Committee concerning my paper. I answer: the Central Committee of the Party has examined my report and approved it. (*Tremendous applause, passing into an ovation. All rise*)

[*Pravda* (August 8) *describes the scene as follows: "This communication by the President aroused general enthusiasm in the members of the session. As if moved by a single impulse, all those present arose from their seats and started a stormy, prolonged ovation in honor of the Central Committee of the Lenin-Stalin Party, in honor of the wise leader and teacher of the Soviet people, the greatest scientist of our era, Comrade Stalin."*]

I proceed now to an account of some of the results of our session.

The supporters of the so-called chromosome theory of heredity who have appeared here denied that they are Weismannists and almost called themselves opponents of Weismann. At the same time it has been clearly shown in my report, and in the many appearances of the representatives of the Michurinist movement, that Weismannism and the chromosome theory of heredity are one and the same thing. Foreign Mendelists-Morganists do not conceal it in the least. In the report I quoted passages from articles by Morgan and Castle, published in 1945. In these articles it is directly stated that the basis of the chromosome theory of heredity is the so-called doctrine of Weismann. Weismannism (and this is idealism in biology) is any idea on heredity recognizing the division of a living body into two principally different substances: the ordinary living body, apparently not possessing heredity but subject to changes and transformations, i.e., to development, and the specific hereditary substance, apparently independent of the living body and not subject to development in relation to the conditions of life of the ordinary body, called a soma. This is indisputable. None of the attempts of the defenders of the chromosome theory of heredity (whether they attended the session or not) to give their theory a

4. At the close of the Session of the V.I. Lenin Academy of Agricultural   Science, Aug. 7, 1948 [Editor].

materialistic appearance change the essentially idealistic character of this theory. (*Applause*)

The Michurinist movement in biology is materialistic because it does not separate the characteristic of heredity from the living body and the conditions of its life. Without heredity there is no living body, without the living body there is no heredity. The living body and its conditions of life are indissoluble. Should the organism be deprived of its conditions of life, it becomes extinct as a living body. According to the Morganists, heredity is detached and isolated from the mortal living body or, in their terminology, from the soma.[5]

Out of our differences with Weismannism, significant in principle, arises the divergence on the important historical problem of the inheritance of acquired characteristics both by plants and animals. Michurinists proceed from the possibility and necessity of the inheritance of acquired characteristics. Voluminous factual material, demonstrated at the present session by its participants, again completely confirms this position.[6] * * *

"Gene" mutations arise, according to the theory of Mendelism-Morganism, by chance. Chromosome mutations likewise appear by chance. The direction of the mutation process as a result of this is also by chance. Proceeding from these fictitious accidents, Morganists construct their experiments on chance selection of the means of influence on the organism, the so-called muta-genic substances, assuming that by this they will influence their fictitious hereditary substance and hope to obtain by chance that which may be accidentally useful.

According to Morganism, the divergence of the so-called material and paternal chromosomes during the reduction division is likewise subject to pure chance. Fertilization, according to Morganism, does not proceed selectively, but on a principle of chance meeting of the sex cells. Hence, the segregation of characteristics in the hybrid offspring is likewise by chance, and so forth.

In accordance with this type of "science," the development of an organism is not accomplished on the principle of selectivity of conditions of life from the surrounding external environment, but again on the principle of perception of substances received from outside by chance. * * *

Such sciences as physics and chemistry have freed themselves from chance. That is why they became exact sciences.

Animate nature was developed and is developed on a foundation of the most strict and inherent rules. Organisms and species are

5. This misstatement is repeated consistently.
6. In all the fifty-six papers given at the sessions, not a single specific fact was cited to prove the inheritance of acquired characters. Lysenko consistently confuses grandiose claims with scientific proof. He seems to be completely ignorant as to what is demanded of a scientific experiment.

developed on a foundation of their natural and intrinsic needs.

By getting rid of Mendelism-Morganism-Weismannism from our science we banish chance out of biological science. (*Applause*)

We must keep in mind clearly that science is the enemy of chance. (*Tremendous applause*)* * *

Fatherly interest is shown by the Party and the Government for the strengthening and development of the Michurinist movement in our science, and for the elimination of all impediments on the road to its further flourishing. This obliges us to develop the work for the fulfillment of the order of the Soviet people in equipping even more widely and deeply collective and state farms with advanced scientific theory.

We must earnestly place science and theory at the service of the people to increase the fertility of the fields and productivity of animals and to increase the productive efficiency of collective and state farms at an even more rapid tempo.

I call upon all academicians, scientific workers, agronomists, and zoötechnicians to exert all their efforts to close unity with the leaders of socialistic agriculture for the fulfillment of these great and noble tasks. (*Applause*)

Progressive biological science is indebted to humanity's geniuses —*Lenin* and *Stalin—that like a golden fund the doctrine of I. V. Michurin has been added to the treasury of our knowledge, to science.* (*Applause*)

Long live Michurin's doctrine, the doctrine of the transformation of animate nature to the benefit of the Soviet people! (*Applause*)

Long live the party of Lenin-Stalin, which revealed Michurin to the world (*applause*) and which created in our country all the conditions for the flourishing of advanced materialistic biology. (*Applause*)

Glory to the great friend and coryphaeus of science, to our leader and teacher Comrade Stalin!

(*All rise and applaud for a long time*)

* * *

George Zhdanov

LETTER TO THE CENTRAL COMMITTEE OF THE COMMUNIST PARTY
OF THE SOVIET UNION (BOLSHEVIK): TO COMRADE STALIN
(FROM PRAVDA, AUGUST 7, 1948)

[The following letter contains George Zhdanov's confession of his most serious error in supporting Mendelian genetics. It was dated July 10, 1948, but was not published until August 7, the day the Session of the Lenin Academy came to an end. How beautifully its publication was timed is shown by its obvious effect upon Zhukovski and Alikhanyan who recanted on the very day it appeared. George Zhdanov was the son of Col. Gen. Andrei A. Zhdanov, a member of the Central Committee, whose sudden death was announced on September 1. According to Nicolaevsky,[7] the first symptom of General Zhdanov's eclipse by Malenkov was the fact that his son was forced to make this recantation. It is interesting to note that his confession of error in a technical scientific field is addressed to Stalin himself.]

Appearing at a seminar of lecturers with a paper on the debatable questions of modern Darwinism, I undoubtedly committed a whole series of grave mistakes.

1. The very presentation of this paper was a mistake. I clearly underestimated my new position as a worker within the apparatus of the Central Committee, underestimated my responsibility, and failed to take into consideration that my appearance will be thought of as an official point of view of the Central Committee. Here was expressed that "university habit," when I made known my viewpoints in any scientific controversy without meditation. Therefore, when I was invited to give a paper at a seminar of lecturers, I decided to express my deliberations there with the reservation that this is "a personal point of view," so that my appearance would not obligate anyone to anything. There is no doubt that this was "professorial" in its poor judgment and not the Party position.

2. The fundamental error in the report itself was its bearing on a reconciliation of conflicting ideas in biology.

Representatives of formal genetics began to appear from the very first day of my work in the department of science with complaints that new varieties of useful plants (buckwheat, koksaghyz, geranium, hemp, citrus fruit) produced by them and possessing improved qualities are not being introduced into production and are meeting opposition from the followers of Academician Lysenko. * * *

3. My sharp and public criticism of Academician Lysenko was an error. Academician Lysenko is now the recognized leader of the Michurin influence in biology; he defended Michurin and his doctrine from the atttacks of bourgeois geneticists; he personally contributed much to science and practice in our economy. Taking all this into consideration, a criticism of Lysenko, of his individual deficiencies, ought to be conducted so that it would not weaken but strengthen the positions of the Michurinists. * * *

4. Lenin frequently said that a recognition of the necessity of any phenomenon conceals within itself the risk of falling into objectivism. To a definite extent, I likewise did not escape this danger. * * *

Such are my mistakes as I understand them.

7. Boris I. Nicolaevsky, "Palace Revolution in the Kremlin," *New Leader* 32: (12):8. March 19, 1949.

I consider it my duty to assure you, Comrade Stalin, and through your person the Central Committee of the Communist Party of the Soviet Union (Bolsheviks), that I have been and remain an ardent Michurinist. My mistakes result from my insufficient discrimination of the history of the problem and that I built an incorrect front of struggle for the Michurin doctrine. All of this was due to inexperience and immaturity. I will correct my mistakes with deeds.

GEORGE ZHDANOV

July 10, 1948

A. R. Zhebrak's Recantation

TO THE EDITORIAL OFFICE OF PRAVDA
(FROM PRAVDA, AUGUST 15, 1948)

Please publish the following text of my declaration:

As long as both courses in Soviet genetics were recognized by our Party and the controversies concerning these courses were considered as creative discussions of the theoretical problems of modern science, furthering the search for truth through controversy, I persistently defended my views which differed on particular questions with the views of Academician Lysenko. Now, however, since it has become clear to me that the fundamental aspects of Michurin's direction in Soviet genetics are approved by the Central Committee of the All-Union Communist Party (Bolsheviks), then I, as a member of the Party, do not consider it possible for me to retain those views which are recognized as erroneous by the Central Committee of our Party. * * *

I think that my experimental works in the alteration of cultivated plants, generalized on the foundation of Timiryazev's and Michurin's theory, will add their mite to the development of Soviet biological science.

PROFESSOR A. R. ZHEBRAK

August 9, 1948

Praesidium of the Academy of Sciences, USSR

LETTER TO STALIN
(FOUR-COLUMN SPREAD IN PRAVDA, AUGUST 27)

To Comrade I. V. Stalin
Dear Iosif Vissarionovich:

The general meeting of the Praesidium of the Academy of Sciences, USSR, dedicated to the consideration of the question concerning the status and problems of biological science in the Academy of Sciences, USSR, greets you, our beloved leader and teacher, with cordial Bolshevist greetings and gratitude for the interest and aid which you daily show Soviet science and Soviet scientists. Soviet science is indebted to you for its great achievements; you have always directed the development of science in the interests of the people. You have always helped and are helping us to overcome reactionary teachings, hostile to the people, and to protect advanced Soviet science from the danger of its estrangement from the people and from practical work. * * *

The Praesidium of the Academy of Sciences, USSR, and the Bureau of the Division of Biological Sciences made a grave error in giving support to the Mendelist-Morganist movement to the detriment of progressive Michurinist teaching. The Praesidium of the Academy of Sciences inadequately directed the biological institutes of the Academy of Sciences and retained opponents of Michurinist teaching in guiding positions. As a result, the scientific institutes of the Division of Biological Sciences contributed very little to the solution of the practical problems of socialist construction.

The Praesidium of the Academy of Sciences promises you, dear Iosif Vissarinovich, and through you, our Party and Government, determinedly to rectify the errors we permitted, to reorganize the work of the Division of Biological Sciences and its institutes, and to develop biological science in a true materialistic Michurinist direction.

The Academy of Sciences will take all necessary measures in order to give Michurinist biological science full development in biological institutes, journals, and publishing activity. The biological institutes of the Academy of Sciences are revising the programs of their scientific investigations in order to bring closer the works of the institutes to the needs of the country's national economy. Work on the theoretical generalization of the achievements of Michurinist biology, and exposure of the reactionary "theory" of the Weismannists-Morganists, will occupy the official position in the plans of the biological institutes.

We promise you, Comrade Stalin, in the name of the great objectives of our people, in the name of Communism's victory, to take the leading position in the struggle against idealistic, reactionary teachings, and to clear all paths for an unhindered development of progressive Soviet science.

PRAESIDIUM OF THE ACADEMY OF SCIENCES, USSR

Resignation of Professor H. J. Muller
from the Academy of Sciences, USSR

[The following letter, dated September 24, 1948, was sent by H. J. Muller, of Indiana University, Nobel Prize winner and past president of the Genetics Society of America, to the President, the

Secretary, and the Membership of the Academy of Sciences of the USSR:]

In February 1933 the Academy of Sciences of the USSR sent me a diploma, signed by its venerable President, Karpinsky, and its Secretary, Volgin, stating that I had been elected a "Corresponding Member." In accepting this election, I realized that it was a signal honor, inasmuch as your Academy had a long and most distinguished tradition of scientific achievement and integrity, and was still maintaining its high standards and, in fact, greatly expanding its valuable work. Although for nearly a decade I have not been sent your publications, I must presume that I am still on your rolls, since I have received no information to the contrary.

The deep esteem in which I have held your organization in the past makes it the more painful to me to inform you that I now find it necessary to sever completely my connection with you. The occasion for my doing so is the recently reported series of actions of your Praesidium in dropping, presumably for their adherence to genetics, such notable scientists as your most eminent physiologist, Orbeli, and your most eminent student of morphogenesis, Schmalhausen, in abolishing the Laboratory of Cytogenetics of your most eminent remaining geneticist, Dubinin, in announcing your support of the charlatan, Lysenko, whom some years ago you had stooped to take into your membership, and in repudiating, at his insistence, the principles of genetics. These disgraceful actions show clearly that the leaders of your Academy are no longer conducting themselves as scientists, but are misusing their positions to destroy science for narrow political purposes, even as did many of those who posed as scientists in Germany under the domination of the Nazis. In both cases the attempt was made to set up a politically directed "science," separated from that of the world in general, in contravention of the fact that true science can know no national boundaries but, as emphasized at the recent meeting of the American Association for the Advancement of Science, is built up by the combined efforts of conscientiously and objectively working investigators the world over.

In Germany too it was the field of genetics, that of my own specialization, which was subjected to the greatest perversion, as I pointed out in publications and lectures gotten out both shortly before and during several years after the Nazi coup. And in the USSR the prescientific obscurantism of Lysenko, supported by the so-called "dialectical materialism" represented by Prezent, with their faith in the inheritance of acquired characters, must lead inevitably, and indeed by the admission of some of their adherents, to the same dangerous Fascistic conclusion as that of the Nazis: that the economically less advanced peoples and classes of the world have become actually inferior in their heredity. The Nazis would have the allegedly lower genetic status a cause, while the Lysenkoists

would have it an effect, of the lower opportunity of the less fortunate groups for mental and physical development, but in either
case a vicious circle is arrived at, which objective geneticists do not
concede. Objective geneticists, on the contrary, having established
the existence of a separate material of heredity, which is not influenced in any corresponding way by modifications of the phenotype,
or bodily characteristics of organisms, recognize the fallacy of judging the hereditary endowments either of individuals or of whole
groups simply by outward appearances. Especially is this the case
when, as with human mental traits, there are very variable environmental influences, such as differences in tradition, education, nutrition, etc., which have pronounced and systematic effects upon
the development of these characters.

In truth, genetics is so fundamental and so central to all fields
of biological science, and even of social science and philosophy,
that the excision of its established principles from the body of science as a whole cannot but result in the eventual debilitation and
falsification of our understanding of things in general. Even the
physical sciences must in the end be adversely affected by the admission of the naïve and archaic mysticism of Lysenko, Prezent, and
their group into the vacuum left by the removal of genetics, for
processes must then be invoked which are contradictory to the
workings of matter.

Under the circumstances above set forth, no self-respecting scientist, and more especially no geneticist, if he still retains his freedom of choice, can consent to have his name appear on your list.
For this reason I hereby renounce my membership in your Academy. I do so, however, with the ardent hope that I may yet live to
see the day when your Academy can begin to resume its place
among truly scientific bodies.

The importance of the matters here at issue—including that of
the authoritarian control of science by politicians—is in my opinion
so profound that I am making this letter public.[8]

HERMANN J. MULLER

The Guidance of Human Evolution (1960) †

Even though natural selection has been the great guiding principle that has brought us and all other higher organisms to their

8. As Julian Huxley points out (above, p. 339): "Although orthodox genetics is now once more permitted [in the Soviet Union], some official encourage- ment is given to an uneasy mixture of Mendelism and Michurinism" [Editor]. † From Sol Tax, ed., *Evolution after Darwin* (Chicago, 1960), II, 423–461.

present estate, every responsible student of evolution knows that natural selection is too opportunistic and shortsighted to be trusted to give an advantageous long-term result for any single group of organisms. Mankind constitutes one of those relatively rare, fabulously lucky lines whose ancestors did happen to win out—else we would not be here—while the incalculably vast majority of species sooner or later vanished—that is, there are no living descendants now. Of all the species existing at any one time, only a relatively few ever function as conveyors of germ plasm that is to continue indefinitely, but most of these few branch and rebranch to more than compensate for the far greater number that are lost. Do we have reasons for believing that our species belongs in that very limited category that is to continue into the geologically distant future? * * *

Results of the Continuation of Present Practices

On the average, the counterpressure of selection, consisting in the elimination of individuals with excess detrimental genes, almost exactly equals the pressure of mutation in producing these genes. There is evidence from more than one direction that, in man, at least one person in five, or 20 per cent, carries a detrimental gene which arose in the immediately preceding generation and that, therefore, this same proportion—one in five—is, typically, prevented by genetic defects from surviving to maturity or (if surviving) from reproducing. This equilibrium holds only when a population is living under conditions that have long prevailed. Modern techniques are so efficacious that, used to the full, they might today (as judged by recent statistics on deaths and births) be able to save for life and for a virtually normal rate of reproduction some nine-tenths of the otherwise genetically doomed 20 per cent. Assuming this to be the case, there would in the next generation be 18 per cent who carried along those defects that would have failed to be transmitted in the primitive or equilibrium population, plus another 20 per cent (partly overlapping the 18 per cent) who had the most recently arisen defects. At this rate, if the effectiveness of the techniques did not diminish as their job grew, there would, after about eight generations, or 240 years, be an accumulation of about 100 "genetic deaths" (scattered over many future generations) per 100 persons then living, in addition to the regular "load of mutations" that any population would ordinarily carry. It can be estimated (on the supposition that human mutation rates are like those in mice) that this amount of increase in the load is about the same as would be brought about by an acute exposure of all the parents of one generation to 200 r of gamma radiation, a situation similar to that at Hiroshima, or by a chronic, low-dose-rate exposure of each of the eight generations to 100 r. * * *

Let us next suppose that this sparing of genetic deaths by the aid of technology were to continue indefinitely at the assumed rate, a rate at which a genetic defect, on the average, subjects a person to only a tenth as much risk as it would if he were living under primitive conditions. Eventually, after some tens of thousands of years, a new equilibrium would be reached at which the load of mutations would be about ten times as large as at present. Thus as many extinctions as mutations would again be occurring. If we are to keep to our previously chosen figure for mutations, there would be one extinction for every five individuals, or 20 per cent. The frequency of genetic deaths would therewith return to the level which it had in primitive times and would be far above that now prevailing, in spite of all technological efforts. At the same time, the average individual of that time, carrying ten times today's genetic load, would, if tested under primitive conditions, be found to be no longer subject to a risk of extinction of only 20 per cent, but to one of 200 per cent. This means that he would carry twice as much defect as would suffice to eliminate him. Man would thereby have become entirely dependent on the techniques of his higher civilization. Yet, even with these techniques, he would be subject to as high an incidence of genetic misfortunes as had afflicted him in primitive times. That is, his weaknesses would have caught up with him. * * *

Long before such an "advanced" stage of the genetic cul-de-sac was reached, however, this medical utopia would probably be subjected to such great strains as to throw men back toward more primitive ways of life. Many would find themselves incapable of such ways. To be sure, the difficulty then would in a sense be "self-rectifying." But so late and forced a rectification would be likely to cause the loss of much that had previously been gained. * * *

A favorite cliché with those who do not understand this situation is the statement that, by definition, natural selection must always be acting and must always be favoring the fitter. This statement overlooks the fact that the degree of genetically occasioned difference in reproductive rate—that is, the intensity of selection—can be far less in some situations than in others. But the major point disregarded here is that what is fitter in the immediate acts of life is not always fitter for a group or a species as a whole in the long run. In such a case the group is running a race toward debasement and sometimes toward extinction, in this respect following the great majority of species of the past. In the case of man, the trick factor in this connection is a very unusual one: culture. Although culture did serve to sharpen salutary types of human selection in the past, as we have seen, it has now reached a point at which its very efficiency, when not yet involving foresight in regard to genetics, has placed upon society the burden of supporting almost indiscriminately the ever increasing genetic failings of its members.

If, in accordance with the above cliché, we define fitness in the narrow (but erroneous) sense, by the criterion of leaving a larger number of immediate offspring, then, of course, later generations of man must, by definition, by increasingly fit. Yet this type of fitness is no longer the same as fitness in regard to the qualities conducive to the well-being and survival of mankind in general. In fact, it seems not unlikely that in regard to the human faculties of the highest group importance—such as those needed for integrated understanding, foresight, scrupulousness, humility, regard for others, and self-sacrifice—cultural conditions today may be conducive to an actually lower rate of reproduction on the part of their possessors than of those with the opposite attributes. * * *

The Protection of Our Genetic Heritage

The crux of the problem is the interference with salutary types of selection in man that has arisen incidentally as a by-product of the widespread and increased effectiveness of mutual aid when it utilizes the tools supplied by science. What means can be used to protect our genetic heritage from this paradoxical situation? Occasional reactionary voices are to be heard calling upon us to reduce our mutual aid in the name of "rugged individualism," "private enterprise," or the like, and others are asking for a moratorium on science and even for a return to a fancied golden age.

However, it has been exactly the combination of intelligence with co-operative behavior that has made culture possible and raised men above beasts, and these propensities brook no stopping point. The enormous advances opening to men in consequence of the further extension of science (representing intelligence) and of a world-wide social organization (representing mutual aid) so utterly overshadow, in their potential effects within the next few hundred years, the damage that may be done in that period to men's genetic constitution that none but the unbalanced would consider now giving up, for genetic reasons, the march of civilization. * * *

What is most needed in this area of living is an extension of the feeling of social responsibility to the field of reproduction: an increasing recognition that the chief objective in bringing children into the world is not the glorification of the parents or ancestors by the mere act of having children but the well-being of the children themselves and, through them, of subsequent generations in general. When people come to realize that in some measure their gifts, as well as their failings and difficulties—physical, intellectual, and temperamental—have genetic bases and that social approval or disapproval will be accorded them if they take these matters into account in deciding how much of a family to beget, a big step forward will have been taken in the motivation of human reproduction.

It can become an accepted and valued practice to seek advice, though not dictation, in these matters, even as it is today in matters of individual health. Although no one enjoys admitting his faults, he can learn to take pride in exercising humility and ordering the most important of his biological functions—reproduction—in such ways as to win the approbation of himself and his fellows. This is, to be sure, a higher type of mutual aid, a superior moral code, than exists at present, but it can be just around the corner for people who from early youth have had the facts of genetics and evolution made vivid to them and who have been imbued with a strong sense of their participation in the attainment of human well-being. * * *

Two developments of our present period are powerful positive influences toward the needed change in motivation. One is the sudden realization of the damaging effects of radiation on heredity. This, by reason of having been made a political football, has done more to arouse the public and its leaders to the fact that our genetic constitution requires protection than all the propaganda that eugenicists have ever put forth. Characteristically, the danger has been greatly exaggerated in some quarters, for ulterior purposes quite unconnected rationally with the matter at issue, and has been just as unjustifiably dismissed or played down in other quarters, where there were other axes to grind. Nevertheless, the over-all effect of the controversy has been highly educational and has helped to make people far more genetics-conscious than they ever were before. It so happens that this same radiation problem is one of the *proper* faces of the ax which is here being ground. Thus it is fitting to take advantage of the receptivity created by political circumstances to awaken the public to the more general need for a reformation of attitudes toward reproduction.

The other relevant development of our time is the menace of overpopulation. Even publicists are at last becoming alarmed at the smothering of cultural advance and the disaster to democratic institutions that it can being about in a generation or two if unchecked. An absolute check will require not only that birth-control techniques be made available but also that large masses of people execute an about-face in their attitudes toward having children. They must recognize that to have or not to have children, and how many, should be determined primarily by the interests of the children themselves—that is, of the next and subsequent generations. If this change in outlook is effected—as it must be sooner or later—it is a relatively short step to the realization that the inborn equipment of the children also counts mightily in their well-being and opportunity for happiness. * * *

More Distant Prospects

Evolution in the past has been for the most part a matter of millions of years. In this larger view, what we have been discussing is but a matter of today—the step we are just about to take. So great are the present psychological impediments to this step, arising out of our traditions, that we have not had time to consider the enormous vistas beyond.

The rapid upgrading of our general intelligence must be accompanied and co-ordinated as closely as possible with a corresponding effort to infuse into the genetic basis of our moral natures the springs of stronger, more genuine fellow feeling. At the same time, especially interested groups will see to it that diverse abilities and proclivities of specific types will here and there be multiplied, both those of a more purely intellectual nature and those making possible more far-reaching and poignant appreciation of the varied kinds of experiences that life may offer. As all these genetic resources of mankind grow richer, they will increasingly be combined to give more of the population many of their benefits at once. Observation shows that these faculties are not antagonistic but rather mutually enhancing. Finally, increasing attention can be paid to what is called the physical side: bettering the genetic foundations of health, vigor, and longevity; reducing the need for sleep; bringing the induction of sedation and stimulation under better voluntary control; and increasing physical tolerances and aptitudes in general. * * *

There are sure to be powerful attempts to pull in diverse directions, in genetic just as in other matters, but we need not be afraid of this. The diversities will tend to enrich the genetic background, increasing the resources available for recombination. These partial attempts can then be judged by their fruits, and these fruits, where sound, will be added to our bounty.

It seems highly unlikely that, in a world-wide society at an advanced level of culture and technology, founded on the recognition of universal brotherhood, such diversities would proceed so far and for so long as again to split humanity on this shrunken planet into semi-isolated groups and that these groups would thenceforth undergo increasing divergence from one another. It is because man is potentially master of all trades that he has succeeded. And if his culture is to continue to evolve indefinitely, he must retain this essential plasticity and with it the feeling that all men are, at bottom, of his own kind.

Through billions of years of blind mutations, pressing against the shifting walls of their environment, microbes finally emerged as men. We are no longer blind; at least, we are *beginning* to be conscious of what has happened and of what may happen. From now on, evolution is what we make it, provided that we choose the true and the good. Otherwise, we shall sink back into oblivion. If we hold fast to our ideal, then evolution will become, for the first time, a conscious process. Increasingly conscious, it can proceed at a pace far outdistancing that achieved by trial and error—and in ever greater assurance, animation, and enthusiasm. That will be the highest form of freedom that man, or life, can have.

PART VI

Darwin and the Literary Mind

Evolution ever climbing after some ideal good,
And reversion ever dragging Evolution in the mud.

—Alfred Tennyson, 1886

Vous savez * * * ce que c'est que le mot et que l'idée d'*Evolution* * * * que, depuis une vingtaine d'années, ils ont envahi, l'une après l'autre, pour les transformer ou les renouveler, toutes les provinces de l'érudition et de la science * * * puisque nous savons ce que l'histoire naturelle générale, ce que l'histoire, ce que le philosophie en ont déja tiré de profit, je voudrais examiner si l'histoire littéraire et la critique ne pourraient pas aussi l'utiliser à leur tour.

—Ferdinand Brunetière, 1898

The theater is much older than the doctrine of evolution, but its one faith, asseverated again and again for every age and every year, is a faith in evolution, in the reaching and the climb of man toward distant goals, glimpsed but never seen, perhaps never achieved, or achieved only to be passed impatiently on the way to a more distant horizon.

—Maxwell Anderson, 1947

DONALD FLEMING

Charles Darwin, the Anaesthetic Man (1961) †

Here are three voices from Victorian England.

"What do I know of tastes and fancies? What escape have I had from problems that could be demonstrated, and realities that could be grasped? If I had been stone blind; if I had groped my way by my sense of touch, and had been free, while I knew the shapes and surfaces of things, to exercise my fancy somewhat, in regard to them; I should have been a million times wiser, happier, more loving, more contented, more innocent and human in all good respects, than I am with the eyes I have."—"I never knew you were unhappy."—"I always knew it."

I became persuaded, that my love of mankind, and of excellence for its own sake, had worn itself out. For I now saw, what I had always before received with incredulity—that the habit of analysis has a tendency to wear away the feelings. I was left stranded at the commencement of my voyage, with a well-equipped ship and a rudder, but no sail. The fountains of vanity and ambition seemed to have dried up within me, as completely as those of benevolence. I frequently asked myself if I could go on living.

I have tried lately to read Shakespeare, and found it so intolerably dull that it nauseated me. I have also almost lost my taste for pictures or music. I am glad you were at the 'Messiah,' but I dare say I should find my soul too dried up to appreciate it; and then I should feel very flat, for it is a horrid bore to feel as I constantly do, that I am a withered leaf for every subject except Science. The loss of these tastes is a loss of happiness. My mind seems to have become a kind of machine for grinding general laws out of large collections of facts. It sometimes makes me hate Science.

The first speaker is Louisa in Dickens' *Hard Times* of 1854.[1] The second is John Stuart Mill in his *Autobiography* of 1873, describing a crisis that he passed through in the winter of 1826–27.[2] The third is Charles Darwin in a letter of 1868 and his autobiography of 1876.[3] Most historians would say that Dickens is

---

† *Victorian Studies*, IV (1961), 219–236. Donald Fleming (b. 1923) is professor of history at Harvard University.
1. Conflated and abbreviated from Bk. I, ch. xv, and Bk II, ch. xii. The most stimulating analysis of *Hard Times*, by which I have been greatly influenced, is by F. R. Leavis in *The Great Tradition* (London, 1948).
2. Conflated, abbreviated, and rearranged from *Autobiography*, ed. John J. Coss (New York, 1924), pp. 96–99.
3. Conflated, abbreviated, and rearranged from Francis Darwin, ed., *The Life and Letters of Charles Darwin* (London, 1887), III, 92; and *The Autobiography of Charles Darwin*, 1809–1882, ed. Nora Barlow (London, 1958), pp. 138–139.

validated by Mill and Darwin. One might argue instead that recollections of the inner life have to be validated by art in their representative historical character. One thing is certain, when the same theme reverberates upon itself from life to art and back again, the historian had better pay attention.

The common predicament of the fictional Louisa and the real Mill and Darwin may be described as the dissociation of knowledge and sensibility; fact and affect. They know but cannot feel and are afraid to feel and fearful of not feeling—joyless, parched, and worn-out. I am tired, says the young Louisa, "I have been tired a long time" (Bk. I, ch. iii). Louisa's state of exhaustion is the product of her father Thomas Gradgrind's fact-system of education. "Facts alone are wanted in life. Plant nothing else, and root out everything else" (Bk. I, ch. i). Over against the Gradgrinds of Coketown Dickens put the orphan circus-girl Sissy Jupe, lamentably brought up on the "destructive nonsense" of A *Thousand and One Nights* and other fairy tales and predictably unable to see why she cannot have flowers on carpets for the fancy of it, where they would get crushed if real and if not real have no business being there. " 'They wouldn't crush or wither, if you please, Sir. They would be pictures of what was very pretty and pleasant, and I would fancy—' 'Ay, ay, ay. But you mustn't fancy' " (Bk. I, ch. ii). Sissy is an emblem of the circus acrobats from whom she came, with their emotional abundance and immediacy of feeling and their power of taking up easy attitudes and dispensing ease to others—artists who stacked themselves up in pyramids to lift the people of Coketown clean out of the Flood of Facts. The Gradgrinds are Utilitarians, Political Economists, Statisticians; in Dickens's terrible figure, dustmen raising clouds of dust to stifle feeling. The circus people are human beings fulfilling the human condition. In the end only Sissy Jupe can nurse Louisa into humanness.

John Stuart Mill was dusty from the cradle. He was a product of the same philosophy of education that Dickens satirized in *Hard Times*, Benthamite Utilitarianism (*Autobiography*, pp. 27–36). James Mill, the father, was a man of more spacious views than Thomas Gradgrind; and more than this, he had a not merely ideal but felt aversion from pain and suffering. Religion to him was intolerable as postulating an omnipotent and benevolent god as the ground of such evil. He was, his son thought, a man of deep feelings who could not imagine they would be in short supply with anybody else. Education was needed as a bridle upon them and could never lack for a mount to rein in. For this reason it did not occur to him to make good in his education of his son the characteristic Benthamite undervaluation of poetry and imagination. Bentham himself had said, notoriously, that "all poetry is misrepresentation," to which the younger Mill enters the odd demurrer that the old man did not really mean that *poetry* was misrepresentation but merely anything at all that was "more oratorical in its character than a sum in arithmetic" (*Autobiography*, p. 78). Which clears that up. John Stuart Mill as a boy actually did read some poetry—including Pope's *Essay on Man*—but he was like his preceptors in not being able to connect this with the real business of life, to beat abuses over the head with facts. So the boy grew up, speculatively benevolent to all mankind but mainly speculative, and headed straight for deadness of heart.

When the doldrums had come and withered him up and he had no wind to puff his sails, he tried to find help in Byron, but that was no good—"Harold and Manfred had the same burden on them which I had" (*Autobiography*, p. 103). The true medicine was Wordsworth, who dealt in "states of feeling, and of thought coloured by feeling, under the excitement of beauty"—"they seemed to be the very culture of the feelings, which I was in quest of" (*Autobiography*, p. 104). The lesson that Wordsworth drove home to Mill about the necessity of poetry and art as "instruments of human culture," the best means to cultivation of the "passive susceptibilities," he tried to pass on in turn to other Utilitarians, most notably the young Radical politician J. A. Roebuck, already a lover of music, painting, and Byronic poetry, but like the rest unable to see that these things had any value as "aids in the formation of character" (*Autobiography*, pp. 105–107). Cultivation of the feelings through the imagination, Roebuck told him, was "only cultivating illusions." Mill thought that underneath, Roebuck was like his own father, endowed with "quick and strong sensibilities" but "more susceptible to the painful sympathies than to the pleasurable" and seeking to deaden his feelings rather than stir them up. If what John Stuart Mill had to say in praise of poetry could give offense to Utilitarians, his mature view on the role of music would have been more alarming still: it surpassed all other arts in "exciting enthusiasm; in winding up to a high pitch those feelings of an elevated kind which are already in the character, but to which this excitement gives a glow and a fervour, which, though transitory at its utmost height, is precious for sustaining them at other times" (*Autobiography*, p. 101). This exaltation of irresponsible excitement was like ushering an obscene force out of nightmares into the hard clear daytime of Benthamism—a fund of free-floating emotional energy, unexpended and unspoken-for, mere dangerous potentiality declining to be trussed up and handed over to any determinate end. The cure that Wordsworth had commenced, Mill's only love Helen Taylor completed—a Shelley among women in feeling, he said, a veritable Mill in liberation from superstition, as he might have added, and one integral being, who gave proof that Mill to be a whole man would not have to give up his father's warfare upon religion and all other forms of acquiescence in the evil of the world.

I

Louisa Gradgrind and John Stuart Mill after many vain attempts passed through the door of feeling into life. Charles Darwin traced the opposite course from a carefree youth to a desiccated old age when many doors that gave upon the world of art and feeling had slammed upon him (Darwin, *Autobiography*). From the time of his mother's death when he was only eight, the young Darwin had his whole being in the immense shadow of his father—340 pounds the last time they dared to weigh him, with an almost Johnsonian force of personality to match—but the latter never tried to mold him to order or sought to impose his own conviction that religious belief was unworthy of an intelligent man. Darwin as a young man responded to this permissive environment by displaying a catholic enthusiasm for life. His chief pleasure, indeed passion, was hunting, and he got plenty of it in, the anthem in King's Chapel made him shiver with delight, he loved Raphael and Sebastian del Piombo, Handel's *Messiah* and Maria Malibran, Shakespeare and Milton, Wordsworth and Coleridge, and fine scenery into the bargin. He was bored by long stretches of his education but was always permitted to move on to something else and some other prospective career. He began by preparing to be a physician like his father, but between the tedium of the lectures and the horror of operations before chloroform, of which the memory hounded him "for many a long year," he decided to call it a bad job, and Dr. Darwin acquiesced. He himself avoided being present at surgery and could not bear the sight of blood. Their next idea was the clergy, which would never have been the father's choice for himself but anything sooner than an idle sporting life, and the son thought it would be all right if he got a country living with a continual round of hunting and natural history, punctuated by a few sermons. Dogma was no problem. All 39 Articles went down smoothly. It never struck him at the time, he later wrote, "how illogical it was to say that I believed in what I could not understand and what is in fact unintelligible." That was later. On the great voyage of the *Beagle*, Darwin passed among his shipmates for naïvely religious and given to crediting the letter of the Bible in a way that was already old-fashioned. If this was mere habit, he several times in the course of the expedition felt an experiential influx of "the sublime"—"the higher feelings of wonder, admiration, and devotion," which bore irresistible testimony to God and the immortality of the soul (*Autobiography*, p. 91). Once he stood upon the summit of the Andes and surveyed the magnificent prospect all around and felt "as if his nerves had become fiddle-strings, and had all taken to rapidly vibrating" (*Life and Letters*, III, 54). But he felt "most sublime" of all in the rain-forests of Brazil, corresponding to the jungle red in tooth and claw of the homekeeping Tennyson but to Darwin on the spot a source of incommunicable delight, more gorgeous even than the land-scapes of Claude Lorrain—his own comparison. Under the spell of the sublime Darwin did not see the jungle as an arena of combat to be shunned by sensitive men but as an occasion for rejoicing and deep assent to the universe. The thing that made him cringe was the uneven contest between slaves and their masters. "The remem-brance," his son says, "of screams, or other sounds heard in Brazil, where he was powerless to interfere with what he believed to be the torture of a slave, haunted him for years, especially at night" (*Life and Letters*, III, 200). With these deep echoes resounding through his spirit and the queer fauna of oceanic islands teasing his brain, Darwin returned to England in 1836. In the course of the next two years he thought a good deal about religion, found that he could less and less imagine any evidence that would persuade him of the truth of Christianity, and came to think that even if true it was a "damnable doctrine" for condemning to eternal punishment un-believers like his father and elder brother (*Autobiography*, pp. 86–87). In theory, and more or less in practice, this left open the question whether Darwin might still be able to salvage some kind of theism from the ruins of his now exploded orthodoxy. He had al-ready gone far enough in unconventionality to make his father ad-vise him to keep any future wife in the dark.

It was pertinent advice. In the same period when he began to find revealed religion wanting, Darwin was also canvassing in the ab-stract whether to get married or not. One credit item for getting married ran that a wife would be something to play with and better than a dog anyhow. Marriage it was, but marriage to a common-place woman, deeply though not illiberally religious; no Helen Tay-lor to energize and set him free and add her strength to his own. It is clear that in the midst of her tender care for him, Emma Darwin was not above administering the most loving possible pinpricks on the subject of religion; for Darwin did not take his father's advice but told her everything. One gets the impression that she was al-ways checking herself bravely on the verge of lamenting her hus-band's unregenerate state and professing not quite to believe that he really wasn't religious and she of course was just a poor muddle-headed little woman and he mustn't mind her but had he thought of *this* argument for religion (*Autobiography*, pp. 235–238). He says, in point of fact, in his autobiography of 1876, that on the whole he did still believe in a sort of God, though not the God of the Christians, when he wrote the *Origin of Species* (*Autobiography*, p. 93). Total unbelief did not come till later.

This progression from naive faith to abandonment of religion was one of the ground-notes of his private experience, always with the added dimension of flying in the face of his wife's desires for him. They were undergoing divergent evolution. The other ground-note was his estrangement from the arts. The history of this, not the fact itself but the stages by which it was accomplished, is difficult to pin down. Darwin says in his autobiography that "up to the age of 30," which would bring him to the year of his marriage, "or beyond," he loved poetry and specifically Milton, Gray, Byron, Wordsworth, Coleridge, Shelley, and Shakespeare (p. 138). Now for many years he had not been able to "endure" a line of poetry and Shakespeare least of all. His old taste for pictures and music had equally deserted him. "Music generally sets me thinking too energetically on what I have been at work on, instead of giving me pleasure" (p. 138). The only art works that meant anything to him in his prime were novels read aloud by his womenfolk and stipulated to have happy endings, dear lovable women in them, and no aftertaste. Of these he says with characteristic precision of speech that they were a "wonderful relief" to him (pp. 138–139). He took novels as a sedative to put his jangling nerves and churning thoughts to sleep. Great novels making great demands he did not relish. As his contemporary George Eliot went on making her tragic vision more intense and her art more powerful, she continually declined in Darwin's favor (*Life and Letters*, II, 305; III, 40).

With this falling away from great art, Darwin associated a general loss of power to feel intensely. He had experienced a decline in his fondness for fine scenery, which he says in 1876 has lasted longer than any other source of aesthetic gratification but "does not cause me the exquisite delight which it formerly did" (*Autobiography*, p. 138). Worse still, he thought he had lost the power of loving friends deeply. "Whilst I was young and strong I was capable of very warm attachments, but of late years, though I still have very friendly feelings towards many persons, I have lost the power of becoming deeply attached to anyone, not even so deeply to my good and dear friends Hooker and Huxley, as I should formerly have been" (*Autobiography*, p. 115). He took no pleasure in this stripping bare of his personality, so that the thinking machine cast off the flesh that clothed it. "The loss of these tastes is a loss of happiness, and may possibly be injurious to the intellect, and more probably to the moral character, by enfeebling the emotional part of our nature."

II

Why did Darwin experience this atrophy of the aesthetic instincts? At least once he implied that he saw himself as Blake and Wordsworth might have seen him, murdering to dissect, a type of the analytical man who set the atomizing vision of science above the integrating vision of art. "At last I fell fast asleep on the grass, and awoke with a chorus of birds singing around me, and squirrels running up the trees, and some woodpeckers laughing, and it was as pleasant and rural a scene as ever I saw, and I did not care one penny how any of the beasts or birds had been formed" (*Life and Letters*, II, 114). This was written on the only kind of vacation from science that he ever permitted himself, an occasional short visit to a hydropathic establishment to repair the "horrid state" of his stomach induced by steady work. Once he was out from under the burden of science, he could see nature whole again and recover the posture of Wordsworth. But he always buckled his burden back on and headed for the dark tunnel of ratiocination that blotted out the light of common day. He was ratifying out of his own experience the teaching of the poets, Wordsworth, Blake, and Keats, but not Shelley, that a man could not run with them and see as they did and be a scientist too—unweave the rainbow and still expect the heart to leap up at the sight. It was an antinomy that John Stuart Mill declined to be impaled upon. He knew, he said, that clouds are "vapour of water, subject to all the laws of vapours in a state of suspension," but he knew equally that they were objects of beauty lit up by the sun, not either-or but both together (*Autobiography*, p. 107).

The healing and integral nature that Mill submitted to but Darwin put from himself dwelt in the domesticated landscapes of England. As a young man Darwin had gone voyaging on the *Beagle* into some of the most untamed landscapes in the world—from the bleak arid plains of Patagonia, too dour for human comfort, to the "great wild, untidy, luxuriant hothouse" of the Brazilian forest, which overshot the mark in the opposite direction.[4] These landscapes from another world—he so describes them, as the nearest thing to visiting another planet—Darwin could never put out of mind. They stood for a quite determinate thing in his life-history: his most powerful experience of "the sublime." This old category, rendered classic by Longinus and refurbished in the eighteenth century by numerous hands, including Edmund Burke, is the most common piece of aesthetic terminology in Darwin's writings from

4. *Journal of Researches into the Geology and Natural History of the various* countries visited by *H.M.S. Beagle* (London, 1839), pp. 590, 604.

youth into age.[5] He was still puzzling over the exact signification
of it and simultaneously throwing it about with abandon in the
1870's. The two things in his experience which had the most
power to trigger an access of sublimity were scenic grandeur, as in
mountains and forests, and great music, always epitomized for him
by the *Messiah*. "I felt glad I was alone," he said, on top of the
Andes, "it was like watching a thunderstorm, or hearing a chorus of
the Messiah in full orchestra" (*Beagle*, p. 394). What did the
Hallelujah Chorus and the view from the Andes have in common?
What did Darwin mean by "the sublime"? He never did give a
straightforward definition, but one thing is clear. The sublime was
associated by Darwin with an upwelling from the depths of the
spirit that appeared to set reason aside and prevail over it. This, at
any rate, was in keeping with Longinus' formula that the sublime is
above and beyond the mere "persuasive"—compelling assent by
no logical sequence of propositions but by immediate conviction.
No wonder Darwin's sublime encompassed powerful incitements to
religion. Sublime scenery as he witnessed it on his voyage around
the world induced in him reverence, devotion, and worship. Great
art by association with scenic grandeur, scenic grandeur with religion, and all three with the sublime, became part of a single
universe of experience. "The state of mind," he says, "which grand
scenes formerly excited in me, and which was intimately connected
with a belief in God, did not essentially differ from that which is
often called the sense of sublimity" and brings to mind "the powerful though vague and similar feelings excited by music" (*Autobiography*, pp. 91–92). And again: music arouses the feelings of
tenderness and love "which readily pass into devotion."[6] The mature Darwin moved away from art because he was continually
moving away from religion.

The mainspring of Darwin's aversion from religion is unmistakable. He saw in religion what James and John Stuart Mill saw, assent
to the evil of the world and acquiescence in it. To understand the
form in which Darwin chiefly apprehended evil, it is necessary to
juxtapose the peculiarities of his personal situation with the character of the age he lived in. As a boy he was encouraged by his
father's example to hate the sight of blood and the practice of
bleeding. As a medical student in Edinburgh, he had felt a "vivid"
distress in walking the wards and rushed away in horror from
blundering operations. From soon after his marriage till his death
more than forty years later, he was a chronic sufferer from head-
aches, nausea, and stomach upsets. He had always been sensitive to

5. On the concept of the sublime, see
Marjorie Hope Nicolson, *Mountain
Gloom and Mountain Glory* (Ithaca,
N.Y., 1959).
6. *The Descent of Man* (London,
1871), II, 335.

pain. Now he came to live with it as an evil immediately perceived from within. It was all the more an evil for the monumental circumscription of pain that was going forward in Darwin's own lifetime. This took the double form of efforts at the mitigation or removal of pain and the pursuit of new occasions for sympathy with it. Darwin witnessed the introduction of anaesthesia and modern narcotics, the abolition of slavery and serfdom in the Western world, and the birth of organized movements for kindness to animals and children. The "blessed discovery" of chloroform, by which he had out five "grinders" at one time and hardly felt a thing, made him very happy for his children's sake (*Life and Letters*, I, 385). On the evils of slavery, always linked in his mind with the screams heard in Brazil and for ever after in his own nightmares, he was absolutely intransigent. Affection for Asa Gray did not keep him from saying plainly that people in England would never see anything to choose between North and South till the Northern cause was indissolubly bound up with abolition; and the only harsh words he is ever known to have addressed to any of his children were spoken to a son who appeared to be apologizing for the brutal conduct of the infamous Governor Eyre in Jamaica (*Life and Letters*, II, 377; III, 52–53). He was almost equally incensed about cruelty to animals, now first looming up as an unpardonable offense against civilization.

His concern for animals effected a powerful conjunction between the assault on pain and the accomplishment of Darwin's life-work. The discovery in animals of a whole new realm of objects to be felt for, sentimentalized over, and safeguarded from harm was a fundamental, and may have been a necessary, part of the environment in which the doctrine of evolution was established. It was no accident that Darwin lived in an age when Sir Edwin Landseer and Rosa Bonheur were among the most widely admired painters and the organized movement for kindness to animals got under way. It was no accident either that the people portrayed by his contemporary Dickens in *Hard Times* as having found the secret of being fully human were circus performers living on easy terms of companionability with learned dogs and horses and actually constituting with them a single economic and social unit. Darwin and all England with him, and a good deal of the rest of the civilized world besides, were conditioned as never before to accept their kinship with animals. The strategy of a man like Bishop Wilberforce, who tried to undermine the doctrine of evolution by seizing upon the postulated link to animals, could hardly have been more inept. The great apes no doubt were not very widely kept or loved in England, and it would have been better if Darwin had been able to say that men were descended from horses or dogs or better still the Monarch of the Glen, but the general idea of welcoming man's poor relations into the fold of human sympathies had already prevailed. When Darwin sprang from his carriage and fiercely berated a stranger for beating a horse, he was enacting one of the principal reasons for his inevitable triumph over his critics (*Life and Letters,* II, 200).

Not surprisingly, he took an equivocal position on the one matter where the current was superficially flowing in the other direction from the awakening of tenderness: the mushrooming recourse to vivisection by scientific investigators. Darwin did not deny that, properly guarded against abuse, it had an essential role to play in physiology. That did not change the fact that the practice made him personally "sick with horror" and he could not speak too harshly of men who engaged in it out of a "mere damnable and detestable curiosity" (*Life and Letters,* II, 200–201). As a result of these profoundly divided feelings, he initially lent his countenance to the disastrous view that moderate restraints upon vivisection by Parliament would be desirable, only to find that the restraints actually imposed (in 1876) were not moderate and not desirable. Yet even in retreat from his earlier position that legislation could do some good and no harm, he was motivated by his aversion from pain. Vivisection, humanely managed by the conscience of the investigator, would have to be tolerated precisely because it might produce new "remedies for pain and disease" in men and animals alike. He would sanction even pain to put pain to flight.

The raw sensitivity to pain which made Darwin a man of his age, and the fellow-feeling with animals which helped to make him the great vindicator of evolution, afford a clue to his alienation from the best literature of his time, symbolized in his not-so-joking remark that there ought to be a law against novels with unhappy endings. The power which great tragic novels have to raise a storm in the spirit that can never be laid again—their permanent heightening of sensitivity—he could not bear but sought instead for a dampening of consciousness by literature that left no trace behind; ephemeral and conducive to repose. He was in the position of James Mill and J. A. Roebuck, who felt so deeply that they could not imagine that others would experience a dearth of feeling and for themselves wished rather to hold it in check. In the circumstances Darwin could not possibly enter into the younger Mill's vindication of art as an emotional stimulus to the unfeeling. Darwin was trying to cut down on his emotional intake; and according to his own testimony, had considerable success in weaning himself from the rich diet of his youth and learning to feel more dimly. His turning away from art was both a means to this success and a token of it. It was a token as well of the fires within him that he was conscious of having to bank down.

Intense feeling was undesirable in Darwin's own experience as exacerbating his already keen sensitivities. It was or could be undesirable in a cosmic view as well. Therein lay a tremendous ambiguity at the very heart of Darwin's position. Natural selection itself proceeds by pain, suffering, frustration, and unfulfillment— the whole gamut that failure of promise encompasses. Any good that comes *of* it, comes *by* evil. Darwin could not deny, in fact he had to insist, that failure was stalking the world and performing grim labors. If the grim labors were to slacken or failure not to take its toll, natural selection would be by so much impeded. Darwin points in the *Descent of Man* to many dysgenic factors in civilized life by which those who would otherwise go under in the struggle for survival and procreation are kept afloat by the rest, often at the direct expense of the latter: exemption of the physically inferior from warfare, with conscription of the strongest young men to die in battle and leave few or no heirs behind them; public assistance to the poor; organized solicitude for the "imbecile" and "maimed"; and universal extension of medical benefits, so that to take only one example, thousands of people who would have succumbed to smallpox by reason of their weak constitutions have been spared to become fathers of the race.[7] Except for the policy on conscription, which is partly pragmatic as well as compassionate, all of these dysgenic factors arise out of tenderness for the weak. The implication is clear that tenderness has become a clog upon evolution. It was not always thus. Darwin in the *Descent of Man* can be seen looking wistfully back to some indistinct but shining age in the past, a moment of poise between two extremes, when men had learned to value social solidarity but had not yet confused this with tenderness for what he calls "the imbecile, the maimed, and other useless members of society" (*Descent of Man*, I, 103). One catches a momentary glimpse of Darwin's Wagnerian or Carlylean self peeping shyly out from under his invalid's cloak, where such things are often most at home, and yearning for the brave old forest days when the world was bathed in a stern but golden light and men were faithful to comrades, obedient to leaders, and strangers to pity. Good actions were those requiring "selfsacrifice, self-command, and the power of endurance" to further the ends of the tribe rather than the happiness of the individual members (*Descent of Man*, I, 95). Darwin hints that the light that shone in other days might come again if men would take as their object, not the furtherance of individual happiness, but the promotion of the "general good," defined as "the means by which the greatest possible number of individuals can be reared in full vigour

---

7. *Descent of Man*, 2d ed. (London, 1874), cited from 2-volume edition (London, 1888), I, 206–207. The entire argument, except for conscription, in 1st ed. (London, 1871), I, 167– 170. Unless otherwise indicated references will be to the latter edition.

and health, with all their faculties perfect, under the conditions to which they are exposed" (*Descent of Man*, I, 98). But, he adds, rather delightfully, such a procedure might "perhaps require some limitation on account of political ethics."

III

Darwin remained in his central being a deeply sensitive man, shrinking back from the spectacle of pain in other creatures, and wishing to offer some alleviation. What could this consistently be for the great proponent of natural selection? One answer was to refrain from positive acts of cruelty oneself and try to get others to refrain. More profoundly, Darwin's answer consisted in his repudiation of religion. This is the animus behind his unflagging iterest in the theological interpretation of his doctrines. If natural selection were to be construed, as his great friend Asa Gray in America urged, as God's instrument of continuous creation, then there was an overmastering Will in the world that pain and evil should exist, if only to some further end. They were not mere existents, they were existents willed from on high. This to the shrinking and wincing Darwin was an intolerable conception of the universe, shared by all religions alike. People kept telling him that to conjoin belief in God with belief in natural selection merely went to deepen their faith and enlarge the consolations of religion.[8] To him, a God that dwelt in natural selection would be the worst of all possible Gods. For the proprietor of the universe to have to seek for a mere preponderance of good over evil in the world that he made, which was the best that could be said for any progress attained by natural selection, was monstrous in Darwin's eyes. He did not want a God that had to proceed by Benthamite calculus and either did not know how or did not care enough to decree uncontaminated good. In a sense, he belonged, with the Mills, to a class of God-deniers who were yearning after a better God than God. How high their standard was in these matters can be judged from the fact that Darwin thought there was a decided over-balance of happiness as against misery among sentient beings. He expressly says that the world is on the whole a good world—for "if all the individuals of any species were habitually to suffer to an extreme degree they would neglect to propagate their kind," but we have no evidence of this (*Autobiography*, pp. 88–90). Yet much intermittent suffering does occur; and this is sufficient in Darwin's opinion to condemn the idea of an "intelligent first cause" beyond any appeal to the admittedly greater quantity of habitual happiness. Moreover, he says that even if we are willing (as he was not) to accept the traditional

8. See, e.g., Mrs. Boole to Darwin, ca. 1867; *Life and Letters*, III, 63--65.

Christian view that all evils suffered by men can be discounted as opportunities for spiritual improvement, the pain experienced by animals would remain an unanswerable reproach to any deity that presided over it: "the number of men in the world is as nothing compared with that of all other sentient beings, and these often suffer greatly without any moral improvement. A being so powerful and so full of knowledge as a God who could create the universe, is to our finite minds omnipotent and omniscient, and it revolts our understanding to suppose that his benevolence is not unbounded, for what advantage can there be in the sufferings of millions of the lower animals throughout almost endless time?" (*Autobiography*, p. 90). After God was discarded by Darwin, the suffering of the world remained undiminished; but he rightly intuited that modern man would rather have senseless suffering than suffering warranted to be intelligible because willed from on high. Darwin gave to his fellow men the best though terrible gift and comfort that he could devise: the assurance that the evil of the world was like the world itself, brute and ungrounded and ready to be stamped by each man with his own meaning and no other.

Here Darwin was sitting in judgment upon the tradition of natural theology, which sought to confer upon the universe the character of a work of art from the hand of the Great Artist; and more than this, sought to lend a common affective tone, a unifying vision of beauty, harmony, and fostering influences, to the universal landscape, so that all partial evils were lost in a greater good. This impulse to make a willed unity of disparate elements, to fuse parts into an emotional whole, is almost diagnostic for the artist's temperament. Natural selection was precisely the denial of nature as a planned work of art and an effort to dissipate the pleasing affective tone that natural theologians tried to lend it. It would be tempting to say that Darwin turned against works of art because he had determined to smash the greatest of all. At some deep level this may have operated; but we are on safer ground if, while recognizing the profound consonance between his revulsion from art and his repudiation of natural theology, we emphasize Darwin's resolve not to be an accomplice in the evil of the world by assenting to God's dominion.

We are brought round again to Darwin's experience of the sublime and the triple conjunction in this thought of scenic grandeur, music, and religion: all standing in common for the uncontrollable motions in the spirit and cutting adrift from reason which Darwin associated with the intimations of divinity which came to him in the Brazilian forest. He had to believe for his own comfort and the comfort of others that the instruction of the sublime in behalf of religion was false. Just so, the surges of feeling that music could arouse were capable of arming men for battle, but equally without any real bearing upon the right and reason of their cause. The dominion of art, as of religion, is the dominion of the irrational. The association can be documented from both ends of Darwin's career. At twenty-nine, he spoke of getting up close to a painting and being laid open by the "peculiar smell," presumably varnish, to the "old irrational ideas" that "thrilled across me" as an undergraduate in the Fitzwilliam Museum at Cambridge.[9] Thirty-six years later, in a moment of deep revelation in the *Descent of Man*, he touched in immediate succession upon the gusts of emotion that whip through a crowd of African Negroes, the excited chattering of monkeys, and the "sensations and ideas" aroused in modern man by music, which appear "from their vagueness, yet depth, like mental reversions to the emotions and thoughts of a long-past age."[1] Communion with primitive man and subhuman relatives of man and reversion through music to the dawn of history—it is an evocation in time and place of all occasions where feeling may be expected to prevail over reason or not even encounter any reason to put to rout. Response to music, like response to religion, does not give true evidence of anything except a will toward illusion. Music "arouses dormant sentiments of which we had not conceived the possibility, and do not know the meaning; or, as Richter says, tells us of things we have not seen and shall not see."[2] We are here in the general vicinity of Bentham's dictum that art is lies and has the power to certify lies and make them pass for truth. It was among the most terrible indictments that a man like Darwin could imagine, whose most distinctive quality was an instinct for truth-telling which has hardly ever been surpassed—has there ever been another scientist who included in his great book all the arguments against it that he could think of? He could only be true to himself by resisting the access of illusion wherever it tried to creep in.

In his resolve to be one of the great Truth-Bearers, Darwin strove to perfect himself as a fact-and-dust man, more abundant in learning and insight, more generous in spirit, and more divided than Thomas Gradgrind, but endeavoring to stand for the same thing and indeed opening out cosmic vistas for application of the Gradgrind philosophy. To deal, not in apt caricatures upon historical men, but in real men of heroic stature, Darwin was a kind of successor to the seventeenth-century Puritans with their terror of the imagination. To those who would resist the wiles, the Puritans held

9. Entry of 12 Aug. 1838 in the unpublished Notebook 'M' in Cambridge University Library. I owe this quotation to the kindness of Dr. Sydney Smith of St. Catharine's College, Cambridge.
1. *Descent of Man* (London, 1888),

II, 364–365. Negroes omitted in 1st ed.; relevant passage, II, 336.
2. *Descent of Man* (London, 1871), II, 336; the entire passage, including the quotation from Richter, quoted from Herbert Spencer. Cf. fn. 3 below.

out in compensation the prospect of a sober and godly life. Redemption they could not promise. So too with Darwin. In repelling illusion, he was taking the only compassion upon his fellow-men that he could contrive and bestowing upon them the best though somber good that their situation permitted. The chief lie of lying religion for him was that evil could have been inflicted from on high instead of simply occurring. If, by access to the sublime, he should assent to this lie, his act of charity to mankind for uncovering the harsh necessity of natural selection would fall to the ground. Love of mankind and love of the truth combined with fear of religion to make Darwin suspicious of art, a type of the anaesthetic man, both in the literal sense of "not feeling" and in the derivative sense of taking steps to repress the pain that he was capable of feeling.

IV

His own anaesthetic state was mirrored forth in his scientific view of the world. As he had cut art out of his own life, so he left it out of his evolutionary scheme for mankind in the *Descent of Man.* In his only direct confrontation with Herbert Spencer, they took diametrically opposite views on the cosmic role of music. Spencer held that music followed speech in the evolutionary sequence as an "idealized language of emotion" and has been continually reacting upon ordinary language in the form of vocal modulation to produce a kind of running "commentary of the emotions upon the propositions of the intellect." [3] Men not only understand each other, they *feel* for each other to the extent that this language of emotions is perfected. Spencer looks to the day when perfection will be attained. We may expect, he says, that the language of feelings will ultimately enable men to partake "completely" of one another's emotions. It is a prospect of universal good-will born of music and fed by music. For Darwin the role of music in the history of the world has long since been outworn.[4] He held, in direct contradiction to Spencer, that music preceded speech and gave birth to it. Once this occurred, music had outlived its cosmic function except as a means of courtship among birds. In the life of men, music is now a mere epiphenomenon, a froth on the surface of life: "neither the enjoyment nor the capacity of producing musical notes are faculties of the least direct use to man in reference to his ordinary habits of life" (*Descent of Man*, II, 333). He even went on to say that this useless attribute "must be ranked among the most mysterious" with which man is endowed. Here, in his eagerness to put

3. Herbert Spencer, "The Origin and Function of Music" (1857); in *Essays, Scientific, Political, and Speculative* (New York, 1891), II, 419, 422.

4. *Descent of Man* (London, 1888), II, 355–367; slightly amended from 1st ed., II, 330–337.

down the pretensions of music, Darwin was underestimating the power of his own teaching. He had supplied a perfectly plausible account of the *emergence* of poetry, singing, dancing, and love of ornamentation, as rooted in sexual selection. He had even assigned to music in the distant past the tremendous cosmic function of generating language. What he had failed to do was to suggest of what use the fine arts might be in the present and for the long future; why in their "mysterious" way they should stubbornly endure and grow more potent instead of shrivelling up into rudimentary organs like the appendix.

Historical circumstances conspired to make Darwin's great refusal of significance to the arts less glaring. He died in 1882, before the major works of prehistoric sculpture and painting had been authenticated. Though engraved pieces of bone were being uncovered by Edouard Lartet from the early 1860's forward, Sir Charles Lyell in his *Antiquity of Man* of 1863 always meant by "work of art" an artifact; and the incredible cave paintings of Altamira, though actually discovered at the end of the '70's, were not given a clean bill of authenticity by the principal skeptic till 1902. Darwin did refer in the second and last edition of the *Descent* in 1874 to the discovery by Lartet of two flutes made of bone, but these did not have the power to project artistic expression into the very center of prehistoric life as the great mural paintings did.[5] If one could imagine a slight speeding up in the history of archaeology—which is probably excluded by the fact that the cave paintings required for their acceptance at true value precisely the steeping of an entire generation in Darwinism—Darwin would have been confronted with a grave spiritual crisis. If driven to it, he would not have been at a loss to imagine a cosmic function for art. That was the trouble. He had a solution all too ready at hand but one that would have been intolerable to him as a human being. The iron band that clamped art, sublimity, and religion together in his own experience would have meant that the obvious way to build art into his system would be to assign a powerful role to religion as a constructive force in the development of mankind. Despite one or two equivocal tributes to religion as the mainstay of morality but also superstition, the last thing that Darwin wanted to do was to attribute any lasting evolutionary significance to it.

John Stuart Mill, if he had been charged with drawing up an evolutionary scheme, would not have lain under the same inhibition. For him the arts energized indeterminately, they did not confine him to a single channel and that unwelcome, or make him "recreant" to his prior commitments, but infused these with emotional gratification without in any way pitching him into the arms

5. *Descent of Man* (London, 1888), II, 362.

of religion (*Autobiography*, p. 101). He was not turned about in his course but sped rejoicing on his way. That was part of what Dickens had been trying to say about Louisa Gradgrind. By openness to works and endeavors of the imagination, she would have been "wiser, happier, more loving, more contented, more innocent and human" and persuaded that life was "worth the pain and trouble of a contest." But even at the end of the book, when she had begun to be human, she continued to lead the same domestic life as before. She did not find a new calling but new courage and zest to prosecute the old. Significantly, Dickens nowhere attributes to her any yearning after religion or ultimate conversion to it. The instrument of her redemption, Sissy Jupe, is like Mill's Helen Taylor in not even proffering solicitations to conversion.

Darwin was menaced by conversion from within and without. That was the irreducible difference between him and his wife, with her discreet endeavors at bringing him around and silent dissent from his deepening unbelief; and that, above all, was the menace of art. *He* would be turned about by art, manacled to religion, and diverted from his role in history. For the humane import of the doctrine of evolution through natural selection was to lop off the Godhead and show how biological order could be generated without a divine fiat. He could only keep upon his course and be the fit author of his own revolution by burking the evolutionary significance of the arts.

It was an omission that has never been fully repaired. Only one voice since Darwin has spoken with comparable force to the biological situation of man; and though Sigmund Freud took ample account of the arts as a fundamental human activity, he failed equally with Darwin to attribute to them any desirable function in evolution. With some qualifications, he tended to regard the arts as a strategy of concealment by which men attempted to evade the truth about their own nature, to wrap it up in symbols. If Freud had believed with Eugene O'Neill and others in the healing and saving power of illusion, he might have seen in this an aid to survival and increment of fitness. On the contrary, he regarded art as being in this character regressive, a means of turning away from reality to the pleasure principle. It was his own office to make men behold the truth about themselves in its naked aspect with a steady and unflinching regard; and health of mind lay in the scrutiny. Freud could not correct the bias in Darwin. They were at one in their mistrust of the arts as fostering illusion. As their common heirs, we still lack a universally compelling vision of science and art as reenforcing each other and flourishing together, not as truth locked in battle with illusion but as clarity of intellect joined to warmth of feeling.

A. DWIGHT CULLER

The Darwinian Revolution and Literary Form (1968) †

I

What is the form of the Darwinian explanation? In order to answer this we need to inquire as to the central problem which Darwin was attempting to explain. If we were to judge simply by the title of his book, we would have to say that it was the problem of species, whether species are fixed or mutable or, to put it in philosophic terms, whether they are real or simply convenient fictions of the systematic naturalist. Clearly this is an important problem for Darwin, for it is only when species are regarded in this latter point of view that the fact of evolution or development will appear; but it is also clear—and was so to Darwin—that there is another problem which is logically prior to that of species, namely, the problem of the apparently purposive adaptation of individuals to their environment. * * * Species, one might say, are the biological equivalent of the Aristotelian formal cause, but they are made necessary by the supposition of a final cause. Or, to employ Biblical language, if God created living things, then it is natural that he should have created them "after their kind," that is, in accordance with his plan or idea of them; but the real question is whether he created them at all.

Darwin's theory of evolution by natural selection, then, while presenting the mechanism whereby species have been modified, is initially concerned with the explanation of why individuals should be adapted. As such it may be considered a reply to the famous argument from design elaborated by William Paley. It is not simply that Darwin studied Paley at Cambridge and, without bothering himself about the correctness of his premises, greatly admired the lucidity of his prose, but rather that Paley's *Natural Theology* is so much the classic statement of the orthodox argument from design that Darwin would almost have to be considered as answering it whether he would or no. Of course, Paley was not primarily concerned with Darwin's problem. His concern was simply to formulate an argument for the existence of God. But in the course of doing this he also gave an explanation of those very adaptations in nature which were Darwin's problem. This explanation was that organisms are so wonderfully adapted to their environment and organs

† From George Levine and William Madden, eds., *The Art of Victorian Prose* (New York, 1968), pp. 224–246.

A. Dwight Culler (b. 1917) is professor of English at Yale University.

to their function because they were so contrived by an intelligent mind. They were designed *to be* adapted, formed by God so that they would function as they do. This is, of course, at once the simplest and the most complex answer that can be given to this problem—the simplest because it is the most natural thing in the world for human beings to attribute to nature their own intelligent purposive habits of mind, but also the most complex because it requires a separate purposive act for each separate adaptation. Indeed, one may say that it is no explanation at all, being merely a repetition in religious or idealistic terms of the phenomenon to be explained. And yet, being no more than that, it cannot be disproved.

Darwin was not able to disprove it, but he was able to stand it on its head. He said in effect, let's turn this thing upside down, or round about, and look at it from the other end. Perhaps these adaptations are not an end foreseen by an intelligent mind but the chance result of a random process. It is certainly true that individuals of any species vary slightly among themselves. It is also true that such is the struggle for existence among natural forms that not all these individuals can survive to maturity and reproduce themselves. If there are any whose variations give them an advantage, however slight, in the struggle for existence, these will be the ones to survive. Then, if their variations are inherited and if they continue to be advantageous, they will gradually accumulate so as not merely to modify the species but also to adapt it more perfectly to its environment or to continue its adaptation to a changing environment. This is the Darwinian explanation, and it is evident what Darwin has done in proposing it. He has explained adaptations not as an end foreseen by an intelligent mind but as the result of an unintelligent process. He has abandoned the teleological explanation, which looks to the future, for a genetic explanation, which looks to the past. He has appealed not to the formal and final causes of Aristotle but to the material and efficient causes instead. He has given us a new conception of natural law, not as (in capital letters) an antecedent Force or Power which produces harmony in the natural world, but (in small letters) a mere statistical description or formulation of what does in fact take place. Where Paley has taken intelligence to be the cause and adaptation the result, Darwin had shown that adaptation was the cause and survival the result—survival of those fittest to survive.

This dramatic reversal of orthodox thinking is what I take to be the heart of the Darwinian revolution. It is a new manner of conceiving, a new way of looking at things, and it had the impact that it did because, validated in the world of nature, it turned out to be true. * * *

II

Whenever I give to graduate students, as I sometimes do, the problem of Darwin's influence on *Erewhon*, I like to find a student who is just naïve enough to go wrong initially but also keen enough not to persist in his error but to find out the truth for himself. Initially he will head straight for the final sections of the work, "The Book of the Machines" (originally called "Darwin Among the Machines") and "The Rights of Animals and Vegetables," for these are full of evolutionary materials. The former presents the extravagant hypothesis that machines are developing so rapidly that they are actually evolving into a higher kind of life and will soon supplant the human race; and the latter tells of an ancient Erewhonian prophet who preached that animals are so nearly akin to man that to eat animal food is a kind of cannibalism, and also of his even more zealous successor who held that vegetables are so nearly akin to animals that to eat them is also a kind of cannibalism, both of these gentlemen being so successful in enforcing their views that the human race very nearly died of starvation. In both episodes the biological argument is extensive and technical, but when my graduate student comes to examine the meaning of the argument he of course discovers that it has nothing to do with Darwinism. The former episode, although using Darwinian materials, is really a satire on modern technology and also on the process of reasoning by analogy as exemplified in Joseph Butler's *Analogy of Religion, Natural and Revealed*. And the latter episode, although again using elaborate biological materials, is a satire on the Old and New Testament asceticism and also on the a priori mode of treating human problems exemplified in Paine, Godwin, and the "rights of man" school. Thus, if my graduate student is not to be out of a subject, or to have a very thin one, he must look elsewhere for his influence.

I will not claim that he always finds it, at least in quite the way I would desire, but he is usually clear that it lies somewhere not in the substance but in the total feeling and structure of the book. *Erewhon* resulted, we know, from the great double emancipation which Butler experienced when in 1859 he went to New Zealand as a sheep-farmer, thus escaping from the oppressive religiosity of England and his clerical father, and simultaneously read the *Origin of Species*. He tells us that his first night on shipboard was the first time in his life that he omitted to say his prayers, and that it was as if a great weight, like a dead albatross, fell from around his neck. A short time later, when he read the *Origin*, he exclaimed, "If this be true, then Christianity is false," and essentially this was his comment upon his new country. Looking about him at the tanned, healthy faces of the New Zealanders, not pasty as in England or cramped by guilt and Evangelical hypocrisy—at people who did not hesitate to admit that they were in a fever over making money —he felt that he really was in the antipodes. In respect to England he was upside down, or England was upside down in respect to him, and he instinctively embodied his upside-down view in a device which I can only call the Darwinian reversal.

It will be remembered that Butler's hero enters Erewhon by means of a mountain pass in which he encounters ten gigantic statues which loom balefully through the mist and moan with an inhuman malevolence. These statues are evidently to be associated with the Ten Commandments, the horrible "thou-shalt-nots" of the Christian religion, which feed upon human suffering, and the suggestion is that in order to reach the sunny land of Erewhon we must travel back across history into the pre-Mosaic era. Once there we find a land which, although not consistently represented, is most frequently conceived simply as England backwards. This is symbolized, perhaps too obviously, by the fact that the names of the principal Erewhonians are English names spelled backwards or with their syllables reversed, and that Erewhon itself, of course, is "Nowhere" (the English for Utopia) spelled as nearly backwards as euphony will permit. It is quite wrong, I think, to say that Erewhon is an anagram of "Nowhere." It is "Nowhere" backwards with a single concession to pronounceability.

The reversed names, however, are little more than a symbol of the reversal of situation which Butler makes the basis of his satiric technique. The two most famous such situations are those of the Musical Banks and the extraordinary treatment of crime and disease. In the former the roles of bank and church are exchanged, and in the latter criminals are treated medically whereas sick men are punished. In neither reversal, we should notice, does the technique quite fit the matter which Butler has it in hand to say. The bank-church reversal, for instance, is really only one-half of a reversal, for whereas the church is represented as a bank (although one dealing in a very fraudulent spiritual coin), the bank is not represented as a church. One can imagine such an episode, in which the worshippers would kneel down before an altar which had all the aspects of a teller's cage, but for Butler to have done this would be to have satirized the very position which he wished to sustain, namely, that the worship of money is one of our healthiest habits of mind and ought to be indulged in more frankly. Then, when we turn to the other episode, we discover that that is a complete reversal but that both sides of it curiously mean the same thing. On the one hand, we see Mr. Nosnibor, who is suffering from a bad fit of embezzlement, being visited by his friends and the family straightener, who inquire solicitously about the state of his morals. And on the other hand, we see the narrator innocently mentioning to the jailor's daughter that he has a bad cold and being bewildered to see her flounce out of the room as if he had made an indecent proposal. Obviously, both of these episodes illustrate the same idea, only the one by a positive and the other by a negative example. Negatively, we are told that it is no more foolish to be angry with a man for having a bad cold, which he can't help, than it is to be angry with him for having bad intentions, which presumably he can't help either; and positively, we are told that it is quite as sensible to try to cure a man of embezzling as it is to cure him of tuberculosis. That Butler should have reversed his situation, but not his idea, is illuminating, and it prepares us for many other reversals which he employs. When he wishes to satirize the belief in a life after death, he instinctively does it by attributing to the Erewhonians a belief in a life before birth; and when he wants to satirize the parent-child relation, he explains that in Erewhon children "have" parents instead of parents having children, with all the unholy consequences which that idea entails. These, he says, are examples of those extraordinary "perversions of thought" [1] which characterize the Erewhonians, a people so impish and mischievous that they speak not of the "seven deadly sins" but of the "seven deadly virtues," and their text of Alexander Pope (or should one call him Pope Alexander?) has become so corrupt that it reads not, "And those who came to scoff remained to pray," but, "Those who came to pray remained to scoff." [2] A good deal of Butler's wit is of this kind, both in Erewhon and The Way of All Flesh, simply the impish, mischievous reversal of some commonplace or proverb in order to see, as he says, if it is not really one of "those cant half-truths of which the other half is as true or truer." [3] Doubtless most of these were of his father's manufacture, but if so, it was the Origin which gave Butler the courage to play Darwin to his father's Paley and, if not exactly to turn him upside down, at least to reverse his collar and see if he did not look a little more human in that guise. * * *

IV

* * * As the only thing essential to the Darwinian explanation is also its form, this suggests that if we are to look further for Darwin's influence we may find it in the aesthetic movement and the

1. *Erewhon*, Modern Library edition, p. 71.
2. *Letters between Samuel Butler and Miss E. M. A. Savage*, London, 1935, p. 22.
3. Samuel Butler, *Further Extracts from the Notebooks*, ed. A. T. Bartholomew, London, 1934, p. 294.

related "nonsense" literature—in writers like Lewis Carroll, Pater, and Wilde. * * *

It is very difficult to say what *Alice in Wonderland* means, and I do not wish to deny either the psychological interpretation or that which sees in the various episodes allusions to contemporary events. Indeed, both are quite consonant with my view which is simply that in *Alice* we are taken down through a rabbit-hole into a world which is quite as strange and preposterous as that of *Erewhon*. Like Erewhon it has some elements of a backwards world, although this idea is more fully developed in *Through the Looking Glass*. But in general, it is an adult world of rigid, anti-natural manners as seen through the essentially sane and kindly eyes of a child. The pompous moralistic poems, which some devil in Alice prompts her to parody, the travesties of justice and of a tea-party, of education and religion, are all brought down to earth either by their own inherent absurdity or by the relativistic and destructive devices of the book. For Alice's frequent changes in size, which make her now a child to the animals' adulthood, and now an adult to their childishness, not only emphasize the relativism of all these manners and morals but also emphasize on what basis of physical force society is founded. For when at the end of the book Alice sweeps away the cards in disgust, she does what any child would like to do in an England so constituted. But primarily these things are swept away by their own inherent absurdity, for the final basis of Carroll's nonsense is the fact that in the mathematical, logical, and linguistic sciences we have disciplines which can move, in perfect consistency with their own rules, from premises which are not unreasonable to conclusions which are insane in terms of the real world. For whereas the real world consists of certain facts or values which are fixed, the purely formal worlds of mathematics, logic, and language do not. Darwin's world is such a world of biological forms. Here there is no basis for saying that a man is "better" than a champanzee or a deer than a wolf. It is only that different forms come into existence and are validated by their own survival. Obviously, such a system is vastly reductive. In Darwin it is reductive by submitting biological design to a world of flux, in Carroll by submitting the fixities of an ethical society to the whimsies of mathematics, logic, and linguistic play. Thus, I do not say that *Alice in Wonderland* is a part of the post-Darwinian world because it contains evolutionary materials (as in abundance it does) nor despite the fact that its author is known to have detested Darwin (as he certainly did), rather because, like Darwin, he subjects the rigidities of an ethical, social, and religious world to the fresh natural vision of a child and to the destructive analysis of formal chance.

Alice was published in 1865, Pater's *Renaissance* in 1873. The famous Conclusion to the latter work is anomalous (for an aesthetic study) in that it takes its departure from the latest conclusions of modern science. We are told, says Pater, that both our outward physical life and our inward mental life are but the momentary concurrence of atoms which come into being only to pass away again. Thus, all is flux, and what we call the fixities of ethics, philosophy, and religion are merely the forms of thought thrown up by the history of culture and fossilized into realities. To them both art and science are opposed. They are opposed in that they want any form which succeeds simply by virtue of its form to be recognized. The artist does not wish aesthetic forms to be burdened by a didactic content any more than the biologist wishes evolutionary forms to be ranked on an anthropomorphic scale. Neither does he wish the individual work of art to be bound by conceptions of genre, which are the "species" of the aesthetic world. As Pater sees it, art has evolved in the sense of freeing itself from matter. Specifically, it has evolved from architecture, which is a kind of dinosaur emerging from the primeval mud of its practical functions; to sculpture, which is still bound by intractable materials; to bas-relief, which is emergent and therefore suggestive; to painting, poetry, and music. "All art aspires to the condition of music" in the sense that it aspires to pure form, but once any degree of formal perfection has been reached then it is impossible to prefer one school to another. "All periods, types, schools of taste, are in themselves equal," [4] and the task of the critic is not to assign works to schools (that would be the old-fashioned biology of Linnæus), rather to discriminate the unique quality which differentiates one work of art from another. Thus, of preference Pater chooses transitional figures or intermediate forms—the early French stories which mingle the sweetness of the Middle Ages with the strength of the Renaissance, the Pico della Mirandolas who hover between paganism and Christianity, the Botticellis whose middle world takes no sides in conflicts but makes the great refusals, the minor, poetic medium of a painter-sculptor like Michelangelo, the bas-reliefs of Della Robbia, the strange mixture of artist and scientist in Leonardo, and so on. There are, of course, elements of stability in Pater, especially in the Winckelmann essay, and it would be wrong not to notice that much of his effort was to disengage himself from flux. Still, what struck his contemporaries about him was that he set art over against morality, philosophy, and religion and that he did so in conjunction with science. The basis of their association was, of course, the relativism, the atomism, the materialism of both fields—ultimately

4. Walter Pater, *The Renaissance,* London, 1893, p. xii. Cf. Morse Peckham's suggestive remarks on Darwin and Pater in "Darwinism and Darwinisticism," pp. 385–392, above.

their dependence upon sensation. "There is no such thing as a moral or an immoral book," said Wilde. "Books are well written, or badly written. That is all." [5] "There is no such thing as a moral or an immoral organism," Darwin might have said. "Organisms are well adapted, or badly adapted. That is all." * * *

At this point I have come to the end of my subject, but, in the manner of my subject, I would now like to do an about-face and say that I do not think that ultimately the Darwinian technique is susceptible of very profound or satisfying literary exploitation. The reason for this is essentially the same as that which limits the possibilities of the Freudian technique, namely, as Charles Lamb said, that the "poet dreams being awake." [6] Paraphrasing him we might say, the "poet attacks design with design." It is inconceivable that he could be against design itself. He may be against old designs, antiquated designs, ugly designs, stupid designs, but he cannot for very long be against design itself. * * *

* * * It is obvious that the Darwinian-Wildean reversal means something only against the background of a world that is sufficiently firm and established to be reversed. When all is flux, the reversal cannot be distinguished from any other position, and one thing is quite as meaningless as another.

It is the recognition of this fact which leads, in the second generation of all these movements I have described, not to a reversal of the reversals but to a subtle falling away or gravitating back into the older world of design. And yet it is not the same world: it is a world with the same values but reinterpreted in some form more acceptable to the modern spirit. Thus Shaw and Butler turned away from Darwin because, as they said, he "banished mind from the universe," but they did not turn back to Paley. They combined Genesis with geology in Creative Evolution. And the neo-Malthusians, agreeing with their master that there is no principle whereby the population is perpetually kept down to the level of the means of subsistence, nevertheless saw in birth-control the means of creating that principle for themselves. Finally, John Stuart Mill did a comparable thing in respect to Bentham. Raised a Benthamite, he nevertheless reinterpreted the Utilitarian philosophy in a way absolutely at variance with his master's principles, even to the point of reasserting those absolute values which Bentham had been at such pains to deny. It is a great puzzle as to how Mill, the author of a textbook on logic, could have done so illogical a thing, but the truth is that this whole Darwinian-Benthamite-Malthusian view is so antithetic to the purposive cast of the human mind that it is very

5. Oscar Wilde, *The Picture of Dorian Gray*, Preface.

6. "The Sanity of True Genius," *The Last Essays of Elia*.

difficult to keep it firmly in focus. And when we come to express it, then we discover that language, as an instrument of the human intelligence, is simply not adapted to express unintelligence. This, I believe, is why Paley got away for so long with his argument that "design implies a Designer," for people did not see that the word *design* begs the question. Of course if there is design in nature, there must be a designer, but this is the very question, whether there is. And yet any word that Paley might have used would have similarly begged the question. And conversely, when Darwin came to express the idea of undesign, he found that he could hardly talk about his subject without employing expressions such as "Natural Selection," which, as he noted, imply the very opposite of what he was trying to prove, namely, that there is no such thing as Nature and that it doesn't select. But if Darwin had trouble in a scientific treatise, what would a poet do? I suggest that we get our answer in Hardy's "Hap," where the poet is trying to assert that the world is not governed by design, not even by malignant design, but purely by chance. Unfortunately, being a poet, he personifies chance. He calls it "Crass Casualty" or "dicing Time"; in other words, he makes it into a gambler with the normal purpose of a gambler, namely, to win. In this way both the character of language and the conditions of artistic representation have militated against the accurate expression of the Darwinian world-view.

Nevertheless, when that view is taken in conjunction with Paley, as I believe it was in the nineteenth century, then we have a dramatic encounter or confrontation which *is* perfectly intelligible—is indeed replete with meaning—and so is capable of varied and successful literary exploitation.

LIONEL STEVENSON

Darwin among the Poets (1932) †

* * *

What the Poets Thought of Darwinism

In its simplest terms, the result of the evolutionary theory was the supplanting of the idea of permanence by the idea of relativity. Of course, the change had been imminent ever since science began

† From Chapter 1 of Stevenson's *Darwin among the Poets* (New York, 1963; first published 1932). Lionel Stevenson (b. 1902) is James B. Duke Professor of English at Duke University.

to investigate the universe; but so long as the doctrines of orthodox religion were formally respected, most people rested secure. All the evil in the world was attributed to the original sin by which man had forfeited his primal perfection. One had only to live according to the precepts of religion and one could be confident of eternal happiness. Good or wicked deeds would be suitably rewarded or punished in the next world, and self-denial in earthly desires led to compensation by heavenly luxuries. On this solid basis of accepted fact, men established their view of life in which the human race was the pivot of the universe. When microscope and telescope began to reveal infinities surpassing the powers of imagination, man for a time tried to accept them as showing that God had been all the more generous in providing a wonderland for human occupancy; but more and more he became aware of his own insignificance, bounded by inefficient senses and "moving about in worlds not realized." And then the evolutionary theory completed the disruption of the old order. The definite act of creation was replaced by indeterminately long natural processes; the intelligent controlling deity succumbed to blind forces functioning mechanically. Since man was of one essence with the beasts, how could he have an immortal soul, destined for reward or punishment? Human life became a mysterious and melancholy thing, a brief struggle of consciousness against overwhelming and irrational external forces. Mankind appeared as an incidental and fortuitous episode in the age-long history of the stars.

This was the vast shift in human values which gradually revealed itself to the poets. Tennyson, a keen amateur of science, began to perceive the problem about 1830; he recognized the immediate necessity of adapting the idea of God to keep pace with the new outlook. *In Memoriam*, written between 1833 and 1850, is a discussion of the doubts and difficulties involved, an exaltation of human intuition as transcending rational science, and—on that basis—a definition of God as a loving being who directs evolution toward beneficent ends. The other leading poet of the time, Browning, with less attention to scientific arguments, also preached a God of Love, and aligned himself with evolution by finding in human imperfection a promise of development still to come.

The appearance of the Darwinian theory made the problem acute. One of the most painful elements to the poetic mind was the revelation of cruelty in nature. The ruthless struggle for survival, the wasteful fecundity that entailed inevitable destruction, went counter to the belief in beneficence which had colored all previous poetry about nature. If any god existed, he could not be endowed with both omnipotence and benevolence—one or other atribute must be discarded. And if no god existed, nature was but a vast machine indifferent to the sufferings of living beings. Tennyson had to be content with the unsatisfactory conclusion that the world is as yet in the "red dawn" which will eventually develop into a golden noon. Browning dismissed the dilemma more summarily by declaring that suffering and dissatisfaction are necessary concomitants of progress: "Irks care the cropfull bird, frets doubt the mawcrammed beast?" Both Tennyson and Browning were convinced that progress was primarily a matter of the soul, in which earthly life was but an episode.

There were other poets who could not convince themselves of this encouraging possibility. In particular, Matthew Arnold and his friend Arthur Hugh Clough perceived the depressing aspect, and their work was colored with a melancholy fatalistic mood. In *Dover Beach* and *Stanzas in Memory of the Author of Obermann* Arnold spoke regretfully of the loss of faith which left the human spirit unsheltered and oppressed; he looked back to the period when Christianity was unquestioningly accepted, as to a golden age of security and happiness which was irrevocably fled. The fullest expression of his opinions is to be seen in *Empedocles on Etna* (1852) —it is significant that he took the first evolutionist as a mouthpiece to express the fatalism of the nineteenth-century rationalists. He preaches acquiescent endurance of fate and self-reliant defiance of weakness. After surveying the decay of orthodox belief in a benevolent deity who has prearranged man's happiness, he declares that man is conditioned by environment and heredity; his life is but a trivial repetition of an endless recurrent process; he deceives himself with illusions about life, while the world moves on indifferently. Nature has no special regard for humankind:

> Nature, with equal mind,
> Sees all her sons at play;
> Sees man control the wind,
> The wind sweep man away;
> Allows the proudly riding and the founder'd bark.

Whether a man be good or evil, he is similarly the prey to fate; but instead of facing his lot fairly, "to fight as best he can," he has invented supernatural forces, finding it easier to suffer when he can rail at God and Fate for his ills. If any invisible power exists at all, it must be essentially identical with the phenomena and forces of nature, and therefore cannot be omnipotent:

> All things the world which fill
> Of but one stuff are spun,
> That we who rail are still
> With what we rail at, one;
> One with the o'erlabour'd power that through the breadth and
>   length

Of earth, and air, and sea,
In men, and plants, and stones,
Hath toil perpetually,
And travails, pants, and moans;
Fain would do all things well, but sometimes fails in strength.

This immanent life-force, creating and sustaining all nature with incomplete success, is the only God and Fate that can be rationally conceived, "this only *is*—is everywhere"; but man insisted on originating a more personal power to blame for his suffering. The next step of the anthropomorphic process comes when man believes that the gods, whom he first created to curse, are beneficent and will "perfect what man vainly tries." As man comes to realize his insignificance, he tends to impute to God the omniscience which he lacks in himself; but Empedocles scorns the argument as illogical. He sees the dream of immortality as a cowardly pretext by which men comfort themselves in the disappointments of life, and he declares that the only true and certain bliss is in making the most of what earthly life offers:

Is it so small a thing
To have enjoy'd the sun. . . .

That we must fain a bliss
Of doubtful future date,
And, while we dream on this,
Lose all our present state,
And relegate to worlds yet distant our repose?

In closing, Empedocles counsels a temperate happiness, neither despair because the orthodox faith is discountenanced by reason nor extravagant hope, but a determination to make the best of life.

This poem expresses all that was abhorrent to Tennyson and Browning. Its materialistic disbelief in a beneficent God and an immortal life, its fatalistic hedonism, are typical of what the new generation was deducing from the evolutionary theory. In Arnold an innate ethical tendency fostered the austere creed of defying fate's blows; but other poets were more blatantly materialistic. In the very year of *The Origin of Species*, Edward Fitzgerald published his version of the *Rubáiyát*. Although the poem did not refer directly to modern science, it won its popularity because it voiced exactly the pessimistic hedonism that so many people drew from evolution. Since an after-life was uncertain, and since man was powerless to overcome the blind fate in which he was enmeshed, life seemed to offer nothing better than self-indulgence.

Fitzgerald displayed this mood as world-weary and disillusioned; Swinburne, a few years later, endowed it with more virility. He combined it with praises of the Greek pantheon, and derived immense glee from his assaults upon the anthropocentric Christian god and the orthodox morality. However, he was not always the epicurean. His most significant evolutionary poems are the *Hymn of Man* and *Hertha*, in which a new creed is shaped—a pantheistic creed in which the human race is deified as the highest manifestation of nature. In the *Hymn of Man* he arraigns the orthodox creed for its selfishness:

> Therefore the God that ye made you is grievous, and gives not aid,
> Because it is but for your sake that the God of your making is made.
> Thou and I and he are not gods made man for a span,
> But God, if a God there be, is the substance of men, which is man.
> Our lives are as pulses or pores of his manifold body and breath;
> As waves of his sea on the shores where birth is the beacon of death.

He goes on to elaborate this concept of a god who is the sum total of mankind, "A God with the world inwound whose clay to his footsole clings." The evolutionary source of such an idea is obvious: man, as the final result of the creative process, is the most perfect embodiment of the life-force; the only spiritual element in the universe is that which has developed within the human species; and religion should be service to the cause of the race's further development rather than the selfish hope of individual salvation. It is true, Swinburne admits, that man is physically helpless and vulnerable, a servant of Change, but the spirit can overcome the cruel blind forces which hinder him. Man has made himself chains and blinded himself by creating an external god, thereby incurring the evils of dogma and priestcraft. As a result, man has suffered dread and doubt and contrition, has delayed his progress, and only now awakens to the tyranny he suffered. Man's mind has conquered space and comprehended the law of the universe; though the individual perish, the race is immortal:

> Men perish, but Man shall endure; lives die, but the life is not dead.
> He hath sight of the secrets of season, the roots of the years and the fruits,
> His soul is at one with the reason of things that is sap to the roots.
> He can hear in their changes a sound as the conscience of consonant spheres.
> He can see through the years flowing round him the law lying under the years.

Exulting that man is free from superstition, Swinburne proclaims that the anthropomorphic God is dead, and the poem closes with "the love-song of earth": "Glory to man in the highest! for Man is the master of things."

This is the positivist "religion of humanity" imbued with the fervor of a fanatic. Translated into analytic prose, it is unmistakably derived from scientific rationalism; but Swinburne's abundant emotion and imagery endow it with prophetic extravagance. *Hertha* is in the same mood, using the Teutonic earth-goddess as a symbol of the primordial force whence all life flows:

> I am that which began;
>> Out of me the years roll;
> Out of me God and man;
>> I am equal and whole;
> God changes, and man, and the form of them bodily; I am the
>> soul.
>
> First life on my sources
>> First drifted and swam;
> Out of me are the forces
>> That save it or damn;
> Out of me man and woman, and wild-beast and bird; before
>> God was, I am.

The poem goes on to illustrate the ubiquity of the force, after the usual mystical manner. Then we are told that men are reaching "the morning of manhood" and casting off "the Gods of their fashion"; being responsible for all things, it was this life-spirit that "set the shadow called God in your skies to give light," but now man is evolving beyond it. As component parts of the great life-tree, men are immortal; but the gods are worms in the bark, and perish. The great process of growth, going on eternally, is the sole "guerdon" of existence. Man's part is to further this growth by independence: "the lives of my children made perfect with freedom of soul were my fruits." Man need not pray to Hertha, he need only be free. The parasitic God that man made is stricken, and truth and love prevail. Man is at one with the universal spirit that brought him forth.

Inspired by precisely the same fact, Arnold and Swinburne reacted in diametrically opposite manners. In the discarding of orthodox faith, Arnold saw uncertainty, futility, and loss of confidence in supernatural protection; Swinburne saw progress, emancipation, and escape from fear of supernatural vengeance. Science had set the mind free in the vastitudes of space; Arnold felt that it revealed man's impotence, and Swinburne that it revealed his omnipotence. Both conclusions, being based on materialistic assumptions, were unsatisfactory to Tennyson and Browning, who clung to belief in God and immortality.

In the foregoing poems of Arnold and Swinburne may be found seminally most of the ideas which were expanded by the next important poets of the evolutionary theme, George Meredith and Thomas Hardy. As in the case of Arnold and Swinburne, the two poets, owing to temperamental differences, move from identical premises to incompatible conclusions. Both saw that the old supernaturalism was inadequate to explain evolution, and both saw that some metaphysical system of explanation was necessary. Meredith agreed with Arnold that the orthodox God was a product of man's selfish desire for an external power to blame or entreat; Hardy agreed with Swinburne that the orthodox God was defunct. To replace him, they both undertook to develop a system out of the evolutionary theory itself. Meredith accepted the idea of *Hertha*, that the cause of the human race is the highest thing in life, and that in the survival of the race the individual finds his immortality. Being essentially a nature poet, Meredith believed in an indwelling power in nature which made for progress, with man's assistance. Hardy accepted the idea of *Empedocles on Etna*, that if there is an invisible power it is a blind and limited one which cannot successfully carry out its designs. Being essentially a poet of fatalism, Hardy believed that progress was an illusion and that the primal force was merely a ceaseless craving for change in manifestation, unconscious of direction. Thus the two moods of Arnold and Swinburne, loosely labeled "pessimism" and "optimism," are reproduced in Hardy and Meredith.

By the nineties the period of evolutionary excitement in English poetry was at an end. Tennyson's late poems expressed a pantheistic creed in which the fact of evolution was accepted, with the corollary that its cruelties would be recompensed in a future spiritual development, and that progress was directed by God. Browning had died in his belief that the onward struggle was the greatest thing in this life and would continue in the next. Arnold had long abandoned poetry, and Swinburne had gradually modified the violence of his opinions until they practically vanished. Meredith and Hardy had given definite form to their systems in which the evolutionary theory was fundamental, and were merely elaborating them. The younger poets either adopted the Tennysonian pantheism or took the evolutionary principle for granted as an accepted phenomenon needing no discussion. The great shift in poetic outlook had been accomplished, and the poets were free to go back to some of the other topics of poetry which had been virtually neglected for a season. The mantle of prophecy and exegesis was laid aside, and the confraternity rather ostentatiously returned to the cultivation of its garden.

Thus the assimilating of the evolutionary idea appears as one of the chief currents of poetic thought during the Victorian era. Nowhere else, probably, can be found a more interesting illustration of the connection between poetic thought and contemporaneous developments in other spheres. * * *

JOHN ADDINGTON SYMONDS

On the Application of Evolutionary Principles to Art and Literature (1890) †

I

It is a common habit to speak of Darwinism and the Evolutionary philosophy as though they were identical. This is a mistake. Yet, when we consider the luminous results and decisive impact of Darwin's discoveries, the mistake is neither unnatural nor inexcusable. It has, however, the disadvantage of fastening our minds on biological problems, as though these alone were capable of an evolutionary solution. Other issues involved in the philosophy are thrust into the background.

Evolution implies belief in cosmic unity, in the development of the universe on one consistent plan. It implies the rejection of miraculous interferences, abrupt leaps and bounds in Nature. The Evolutionist feels sure that if he could trace the present back through all its stages to the period of origins, the process whereby that incalculably distant past has advanced to this present would be found a gradual unbroken chain of sequences. For him, the genius of a Newton or a Shakespeare is the ultimate known product of elemental matter shaped by energies and forces. * * *

Evolution, in its largest sense, may be defined as the passage of all things, inorganic and organic, by the action of inevitable law, from simplicity to complexity, from an undifferentiated to a differentiated condition of their common stock of primary elements. We have accepted the evolutionary theory for geology, or the history of the earth's crust. We have accepted it for biology, or the history of life upon this planet. The next question is how we can apply it to the history of the human mind in social institutions, religions, morality, literature, art, language. To this question the first answer must be: certainly not in the same way as that in which we have applied it to the history of the earth's crust, and to the history of vegetable and animal life. The subject-matter is different. Nothing can be gained by transferring the language of biological

† Symonds (1840–1893), English historian and literary critic, is best known for his seven-volume history, *The Renaissance in Italy*. The present exerpt is from Chapter 2 of the first volume of Symonds' *Essays Speculative and Suggestive* (London, 1890).

science to the study of mental products. Nothing can be gained by attempting to treat successive stages of society and successive modes of thought as though they were geological strata. In like manner, nothing is gained by transferring the method of geology to biology, and *vice versâ*. Inorganic and organic matter being still disconnected in our thought, each requires its own species of analysis, a different system of investigation, and a separate nomenclature. Yet biology and geology have this in common, that both are evolutionary sciences. The question now is whether mind, which is a function of the most highly organised animals, can be treated upon the principles which are recognised in those two sciences. * * *

These observations are intended to introduce certain mental phenomena which invite an evolutionary explanation. The cases I mean to discuss have this point in common: A certain type of literature or art manifests itself, apparently by casual occurrence, in a nation at a given epoch. If favourable conditions for its development are granted, it runs a well-defined course, in which every stage is connected with preceding and succeeding stages by no merely accidental link; and when all the resources of the type have been exhausted, it comes to a natural end, and nothing but *débris* is left of it. Such types suggest the analogy of organic growth. If the analogy be not fancifully strained, it may be helpful in keeping our attention fixed upon the salient features of the phenomenon in question. This, to put the matter briefly, is the development of a complex artistic structure out of elements existing in national character, which structure is only completed by the action of successive generations and individual men of genius, all of whom in their turns are compelled to contribute either to the formation of the rudimentary type, or to its perfection, or to its decline and final dissolution.[1]

II

Criticism has hitherto neglected the real issues of what is meant by development in art and literature. We are indeed familiar with phrases like "rise and decline," "flourishing period," "infancy of art." But the inevitable progression from the embryo, through ascending stages of growth to maturity, and from maturity by declining stages to decrepitude and dissolution, has not been sufficiently insisted on. * * *

1. The type so produced might have been compared to a nation's thought projected in art—to such a thought as becomes a poem in a single man's work—but which can find expression only through a hundred workers. It differs, however, from any particular work of art in this, that it does not manifest itself as a simple whole. It describes a curve of ascent and descent before it is accomplished.

We have no means at present of stating precisely how or at what moment the germ of a specific type of art is generated in a nation. It often appears that the first impulse toward creativeness is some deep and serious emotion, some religious enthusiasm, or profound stirring of national consciousness. To transmute this impulse into the sphere of art taxes the energies of the first generation of artists, and the form appears to emerge spontaneously from the spirit of the nation as a whole. Unless we knew that nothing is accidental we should be tempted to say that the form of the Attic drama in Greece, the form of the Shakespearian drama in England, was settled by chance. One thing, meanwhile, is certain. The germ, however generated, is bound to expand; the form, however determined, controls the genius which seeks expression through its medium. In the earliest stages of expansion the artist becomes half a prophet, and "sows with the whole sack," in the plenitude of superabundant inspiration. After the original passion for the ideas to be embodied in art has somewhat subsided, when the form is fixed, and its capacities can be serenely measured, but before the glow and fire of enthusiasm have faded out, there comes a second period. In this period art is studied more for art's sake, but the generative potency of the first founders is by no means exhausted. For a while, at this moment, the artist is priest, prophet, hierophant, and charmer all in one. More conscious of the laws of beauty, more anxious about the exponent form than his predecessors were, he makes some sacrifice of the idea in order to meet the requirements of style. But he does not forget that beauty by itself is insufficient to a great and perfect work, nor has he lost his interest in the cardinal conceptions which vitalise a nation's most significant expression of its soul through art. During the first and second stages which I have indicated, the people turns out, through its interpreters, poets and artists, a number of masterpieces—the earlier of them rough-hewn, archaic, cyclopean, pregnant with symbolism, rich in anticipation—the later, exquisite in their combination of full thought and spiritual intensity with techncial perfection, with grace, with the qualities of free and elevated beauty appropriate to the elaborated type. But now the initial impulse is declining; the cycle of animating ideas has been exhausted; the taste of the people has been educated, and its spirit has been manifested in definite forms, which serve as ideal mirrors to the race of its own qualities, and bring it to a knowledge of itself. Conceptions which had all the magic of novelty for the grandparents, become the intellectual patrimony of the grandchildren. It is impossible to return upon the past; the vigour of those former makers may survive in their successors, but their inspiration has taken shape for ever in their works. And that shape abides, fixed in the habits of the nation. The type cannot be changed, because the type grew itself out of the very nature of the people, who are still existent. What then remains for the third generation of artists? They have either to reproduce their models, and this is what true genius will not submit to, and what the public refuses to accept from it; or else they have to extract new motives from the perfected type, at the risk of impairing its strength and beauty, with the certainty of disintegrating its spiritual unity. The latter course is always chosen, inevitably, as we now believe, and by no merely wilful whim of individual craftsmen. Nay, the very artists who begin to decompose the type and to degrade it, and the public who applaud their ingenuity, and dote with love upon their variations from the primal theme, are alike unconscious that the decadence has already arrived. This, too, is inevitable and natural, because life is by no means exhausted when maturity is past, and the type still contains a wealth of parts to be eliminated. Less deeply interested in the great ideas by which they have been educated, and of which they are in no sense the creators, incapable of competing on the same ground with their elders, the artists of this third period are forced to go afield for striking situations, to strain sentiment and pathos, to accentuate realism, to subordinate the harmony of the whole to the melody of details, to sink the prophet in the artist, the hierophant in the charmer. There yet remains another stage of decadence, when even these resources latent in the perfect type have been exhausted. Then formality and affectation succeed to spontaneous and genial handling; technical skill declines; the meaning of the type, projected from the nation's heart and soul in its origin, comes to be forgotten. Art has fulfilled the round of its existence in that specific manifestation, and sinks into the dotage of decrepitude, the sleep of winter.

III

A familiar example shall first be chosen from the history of English literature. It is what we know as the Elizabethan Drama, a type of art which completed its evolution in little more than half a century. When Miracle-plays, which England possessed in common with other European nations, though in a form specific to herself, had been developed to the utmost, certain episodes from the semi-epical dramatic cycle detached themselves from the unwieldy mass. Comedy found its germ in those lighter scenes which had always been conceded to the popular appetite for entertainment. Realistic drama emerged from the story of the woman taken in adultery, and from the biography of Magdalen. The History-play had its origin in subsidiary pieces adapted from the Apocrypha, of which the "Story of Godly Queen Esther" may serve as an example.

At this point the allegorical elements implicit in the Mediæval Miracle assumed a leading part in the disintegration of the ancient structure. Moralities paved the way for the dramatic analysis of character, which took a more definite shape in Heywood's Interludes. Minor comic and realistic motives, already detached in the subordinate scenes which enlivened the Miracle, coalesced with this psychological form of the nascent drama. Independent plays, partly historical, partly tragic, on subjects connected with Biblical history, such as *King Darius* and *Cambyses*, were prepared for separate presentation. At the same time, two principal personages of the Miracle, Herod and the Devil, extended their influence throughout the transitional phase upon which the theatre then entered.

We are able by the help of documents, to set forth the opportunities for secular dramatic representation to which the custom of Miracle-playing led. Stages were erected in the yards of inns. The halls of abbeys and great houses welcomed companies of strolling actors. At last theatres for the public arose in the suburbs of London; they were simple wooden structures, partly open to the air. The small scale and the beggarly equipment of these theatres need to be insisted on, since the peculiar form of the English Drama depended in no small measure on these external circumstances.

Resuming the points already mentioned, we find that episodical farces, histories, and tragic pieces, together with the specialised allegories called Moralities and Interludes, usurped upon the colossal stationary fabric of the Miracle. Miracle-plays continued to be represented at stated intervals. But a new dramatic type had come into existence. To this we give the name of the Romantic Drama. In its beginnings, as its origin appeared to be casual, this type was undecided and received but little attention from the cultivated classes. Yet it was destined to survive many perils, to realise itself, and to pass with astonishing speed to fixity in Marlowe, to perfection in Shakespeare, to over-ripeness in Beaumont and Fletcher, to decadence in Davenant.

Here we have to turn aside and notice the influences of the new learning and the Italian Renaissance, as these were felt in England. Cultivated scholars and the court, critics like Sidney, men of letters like the authors of "Gorboduc" and the "Misfortunes of Arthur" threw the weight of their precepts and their practice into the scale against the popular type of drama, which was as yet only in its stage of infancy. For a while it seemed as though the pseudoclassical principles of the Italian stage, derived mainly from Seneca and the Roman comic poets, might be imposed upon our theatre. But the shoot of the Romantic Drama, which had risen spontaneously from the crumbling masses of the Mediæval Miracle, possessed the vigour and assimilative faculty of expansive life. A group of lettered poets, including Greene, Peele, Nash, Lodge, and Kyd, took part precisely at this juncture with the vulgar. They lent their talents to the improvement of the type, which had already gained the affections of the English people. They systematised the amorphous matter of farce, history, and fable under the form of a regular play, with an action divided into five acts. They introduced classical learning and conceited diction. But they did not alter the radically Romantic character of the type. Some features, including the part of the Vice, which were otiose survivals from the Miracle and the Morality, dropped out at this stage of evolution.

Marlowe, joining this band of cultured playwrights, who had already turned the scale against the "courtly makers," next claims our whole attention. Marlowe ennobled the rough material of the Romantic Drama and made it fit to rank with the Classical Drama of Athens in her glory. This he achieved by raising dramatic blank verse to a higher power, and by his keen sense of what is serious and impassioned in art. Without altering the type, he adopted so much from humanism as it was capable of assimilating. In his hands the thing became an instrument of power and beauty.

Shakespeare was content to use the form refined and fixed by Marlowe. He developed it fully in all its parts, according to its own capacities. There is no process but one of gradual progression discernible between the few examples of the earlier Romantic Drama we possess, and *Macbeth* or *Measure for Measure*. The germ has simply grown and effloresced.

At the side of Shakespeare stands Ben Jonson, in whom we observe an interesting example of the literary hybrid. Jonson did not succeed in freeing himself altogether from the influences of his race and age. His plays belong in large measure to the Romantic type. Yet his humanistic training warped him to such an extent that he stood outside the circle of his compeers, protesting in theory and in practice against the genius of Romantic Drama.

After this point, it remains to notice how the dramatic form, fixed by Marlow and perfected by Shakespeare, begins to break up. It has realised itself and reached completion. What followed was a stage of gradual disintegration. Motives suggested by the supreme masters were elaborated in their details by men like Webster, Tourneur, Ford. We trace an effort to extract its last capabilities from the type. The complex is reduced to its constituents, and these are handled separately. Poetry runs over into eloquence and rhetoric in the work of Fletcher and his kind, who display a lack of artistic conscientiousness nowhere hitherto observable. Plays are made by pattern, as in the case of Massinger and Shirley. A new generation, without creative force, continue the tradition of their predecessors by exaggeration of motives, isolation of elements, facile and conscious imitation.

Soon this stage of decadence leads to one of decrepitude. The incoherences of Davenant, Crowne, and Wilson, illuminated here and there by flashes of the old fire, prove that those elements of weakness which the Romantic Drama contained in its infancy, but which were controlled by strenuous force in the periods of adolescence and maturity, have reasserted themselves in its senility. To advance further, to save the type from ruin, was impossible. The Romantic Drama had been played out. All its changes had been rung; the last drop of its vital sap had been exhausted. Even if the Puritans had refrained from ostracising actors, the Elizabethan theatre could not have been continued.

Such, to indicate the outlines of this subject rapidly, is the history of the rise, progress, decline, and dissolution of what we call Elizabethan Drama. The Evolutionist differs from previous students mainly in this, that he regards the totality of the phenomena presented as something necessitated by conditions to which the prime agents in the process, Marlowe and even Shakespeare, were subordinated. For him, this type of art exhibits qualities analogous to those of an organic complex undergoing successive phases of germination, expansion, efflorescence, and decay, which were independent of the volition of the men who effected them. To him the interest of Sackville and Norton, of Hughes and Sidney, of Jonson and his followers, consists in this: that they were unable, by thwarting or counteracting its development, to arrest its course, or to import nutriment from alien sources into the structure which it was bound to evolve from embryonic elements. When everything which the embryo contained had been used up in the formation of structure, it came to an end. * * *

PHILIP APPLEMAN

Darwin and Pater's Critical Dilemma (1959) †

I

Pater had gone up to Oxford in 1859, the "year of earthquake"; as it turned out, all of Pater's undergraduate years were shockers: Lyell's damage to Genesis had long since been done, of course, but now Colenso attacked the whole of the literalist's Pentateuch,

† From "Darwin, Pater, and a Crisis in Criticism," in Philip Appleman, William A. Madden, and Michael Wolff, eds., *1859: Entering an Age of Crisis* (Bloomington, Ind., 1959), pp. 81–85.

and the "Seven Against Christ" caused desperate concern among the old guard for the sacrosanctity of all of the Scriptures. The most severe tremor of Pater's undergraduate years, however, was caused by the publication of Darwin's *Origin of Species,* for it simultaneously particularized and universalized nineteenth-century predilections for relativism. Even without the *Origin,* relativism would of course have had a brisk sale in the nineteenth-century marketplace of ideas, but given the *Origin,* competitors were the more relentlessly crushed. Pater, at Queen's, discussed Darwin with his fellow students,[1] with results that were soon to be evident in his thinking and writing.

Pater's first published essay was a discussion of Coleridge (1866); it is clearly the work of a man impressed with the *Origin of Species.*

Modern thought is distinguished from ancient by its cultivation of the "relative" spirit in place of the "absolute." Ancient philosophy sought to arrest every object in an eternal outline, to fix thought in a necessary formula, and the varieties of life in a classification by "kinds," or *genera.* To the modern spirit nothing is, or can be rightly known, except relatively and under conditions. *The philosophical conception of the relative has been developed in modern times through the influence of the sciences of observation. Those sciences reveal types of life evanescing into each other by inexpressible refinements of change.*[2]

Pater had "buried himself in" the philosophy of Heraclitus, Plato, and Hegel at Queen's,[3] but this passage is nonetheless outright empiricism,[4] and the empiricism, furthermore, of a man who has pondered his Darwin.

"It is no vague scholastic abstraction that will satisfy the speculative instinct in our modern minds," Pater went on. "Who would change the colour or curve of a rose-leaf for that . . . colourless, formless, intangible being Plato put so high?"[5] What this attitude means for criticism is clear enough. Pater the post-Darwinian wanted to examine "not the truth of eternal outlines ascertained once for all, but a world of fine gradations and subtly linked conditions, shifting intricately as we ourselves change . . ."[6] It is the duty of the critic, then, "by a constant clearing of the organs of observation and perfecting of analysis, to make what we can of these."[7] (Later in life, Pater put it this way: "In Dante's minuteness of touch there was in fact something of that art of miniature

1. Thomas Wright, *The Life of Walter Pater* (1907), I, 174, 203.
2. *Appreciations,* p. 66; latter italics mine. This and all quotations from Pater are from the Library Edition (1910).
3. Wright, I, 170.
4. "Confidence in the particular alone . . . hardly began to be exploited in European thought until the advent, in the seventeenth century, of Baconian experimentalism and especially of British empirical psychology" (Walter Jackson Bate, *From Classic to Romantic* [Cambridge, Mass., 1949], p. 93).
5. *Appreciations,* p. 68.
6. *Appreciations,* p. 68.
7. *Appreciations,* p. 68.

painting . . . Our own delight in it, the welcome we give to minute detail of that kind, uncompromising 'realists' as we needs must be, connects itself with the empirical character of our science, our philosophical faith in the concrete, the particular." [8])

Seven years after the "Coleridge" essay, in the Preface to Pater's first volume, *Studies in the History of the Renaissance*, the full meaning of this empirical, evolutionary view of art is made specific: "Beauty," he said there, "like all other qualities presented to human experience, is relative . . ." [9] This constitutes the challenge for the post-Darwinian critic: once it is admitted that one's perceptions and judgments are relative, beauty itself, which is a "quality presented to human experience," must become relative. The task of the critic, then, is accordingly limited, restricted to subjective statements about particular objects. "To define beauty, not in the most abstract, but in the most concrete terms possible, to find not its universal formula, but the formula which expresses most adequately this or that special manifestation of it, is the aim of the true student of aesthetics." [1] This is the underlying assumption, Pater implies, the starting point, for all post-Darwinian criticism, and he takes his stand firmly upon it: "To regard all things and principles of things as inconstant modes or fashions has more and more become the tendency of modern thought." [2] In an evolutionary world, he proposed that men are obliged to live by "impressions, unstable, flickering, inconsistent, which burn and are extinguished with our consciousness of them." [3] So that life is, indeed, only a "series of moments"; "to a single sharp impression, with a sense in it, a relic more or less fleeting, of such moments gone by, what is real in our life fines itself down. It is with this movement, with the passage and dissolution of impressions, images, sensations, that analysis leaves off . . ." [4]

Anyone even slightly familiar with Pater's work knows that this line of thought will lead to the much-quoted passage on the critic's temperament:

> What is this song or picture, this engaging personality presented in life or in a book, to *me*? What effect does it really produce on me? Does it give me pleasure? and if so, what sort or degree of pleasure? How is my nature modified by its presence, and under its influence? . . . What is important . . . is not that the critic should possess a correct abstract definition of beauty for the intellect, but a certain kind of temperament, the power of being deeply moved by the presence of beautiful objects . . . [5]

8. Introduction to Charles Lancelot Shadwell, *The Purgatory of Dante Alighieri* (1892), p. xviii.
9. *Renaissance*, p. vii.
1. *Renaissance*, pp. vii–viii.

2. *Renaissance*, p. 233.
3. *Renaissance*, p. 235.
4. *Renaissance*, p. 236.
5. *Renaissance*, pp. viii, x.

This is a part—the flamboyant part—of Pater's critical thought; as such it frequently finds its way—along with those other heady clichés of Pater scholarship, the "Mona Lisa" passage and the remarks on burning with a hard, gemlike flame—into textbooks and anthologies. * * * But the part is not the whole, and it seems to me unfortunate to cut Pater thus to a limiting "impressionist" pattern, for in so doing he is denied both his true complexity and the relevance his critical thought could have for our own time.

Pater was more than an impressionist: he was also, and frequently, a historical critic. And just as the *Origin of Species* was an important shaping influence upon Pater's impressionism, so his historicism was also (paradoxically) substantially shaped by Darwin's great work. The word "evolution" was frequently on Pater's tongue: he wrote of the historical "evolution" of the most disparate things—of the state, of the human spirit, of grace, of fictional character, of drama and other works of literature, of sculpture, and of architecture.[6] Pater saw himself as a student of process, of a changing, developing world. He called himself at one time a "student of *origins*" and spoke of the "stages" of art and poetry.[7] In his first book he had asserted that "There is . . . an element of change in art; criticism must never for a moment forget that 'the artist is the child of his time' ";[8] and in a late essay he pointed out the necessity of placing a document "as far as possible in the group of conditions, intellectual, social, material, amid which it was actually produced if we would really understand it."[9] Although Hegel inspires this comment, and Heraclitus automatically comes to his mind, Pater indicates that there is also—and powerfully—in the background "Darwin and Darwinism, for which 'type' itself properly *is* not but is only always *becoming*." "And the Darwinian theory," he goes on, "well! every month is adding to its evidence. Nay, *the idea of development . . . is at last invading one by one, as the secret of their explanation, all the products of mind . . .*"[1] Thus Pater from first to last maintained a conscious linkage between the force of the evolutionary idea and the necessity for the historical approach.

This general evolutionary-historicism underlies Pater's historical criticism in particular, and those scholars who have recognized this complexity in Pater's criticism [2] have sometimes seen it as one term

---

6. *Renaissance*, p. 223; *Appreciations*, p. 153; *Guardian*, p. 55; *Appreciations*, pp. 187, 203; *Renaissance*, p. 157; *Miscellaneous*, pp. 138–139.
7. *Greek Studies*, p. 111.
8. *Renaissance*, p. 199.
9. *Plato and Platonism*, p. 9.
1. *Plato and Platonism*, pp. 19–20;

latter italics mine.
2. See, *e.g.*, Ruth C. Child, "Is Walter Pater an Impressionistic Critic?" *PMLA*, LIII (1938), 1172–1185, and René Wellek's balanced estimate, "Walter Pater's Literary Theory and Criticism," *Victorian Studies*, I (1957–58), 29–46.

in a basic dualism that required metaphor to describe adequately. Sir Maurice Bowra, seeing in Pater both the "aesthete" and the "thinker," put this dualism in terms of "a friend of Circe" on the one hand, and "his bulldog breed" on the other;[3] and Lord David Cecil pointed to Pater's "apple green tie" and his contrasting "broadcloth" as symbolic of the same dualism.[4]

The "friend of Circe" and the "apple green tie" in Pater represent his much-publicized tendency toward aestheticism and impressionism. The "bulldog," the "broadcloath" side of Pater is what anthologists and historians have not given full credit to: that is, his historicism. Recently the very existence of Pater's historical criticism has been, in fact, denied: "During the latter part of the 19th century," says one history of literary criticism, "the aesthetic movement . . . took a contemplative, static view of individual art works and so was antihistorical."[5] For Pater this comment could hardly be more wrong. He recognized that historicism was the characteristic method of his time, and he thought this quite proper. "Nothing man has projected from himself is really intelligible," he said, "except at its own date, and from its proper point of view in the never-resting 'secular process'." And again: "Every intellectual product must be judged from the point of view of the age and the people in which it was produced."[6]

Thus Pater could speak of the poetry of Homer as the product, "the almost mechanical transcript of a time, naturally, intrinsically, poetic, a time in which one could hardly have spoken at all without ideal effect,"[7] and he could call Ronsard's poems "a kind of epitome of his age."[8] Pater spoke of the style of an age, the spirit of an age, and the temperament of an age, and pointed out how these affect the art of their times.[9] His particular criticism of certain earlier scholars was that they were not historically minded: "They lacked the very rudiments of the historical sense, which, by an imaginative act, throws itself back into a world unlike one's own, and estimates every intellectual creation in its connexion with the age from which it proceeded. They had no idea of development, of the differences of ages, of the process by which our race has been 'educated'."[1]

Walter Pater, then, represents a critical dilemma, a dilemma fostered by his empiricism in general and his awareness of Darwin

3. "Walter Pater" in *Inspiration and Poetry* (1955); Bowra's metaphor is borrowed from Paul Bourget whom he quotes as having described Pater as "ami de Circé transformé en dogue" (p. 199).
4. *Walter Pater: The Scholar-Artist* (Cambridge, England, 1955), *passim*.
5. W. K. Wimsatt, Jr., and Cleanth Brooks, *Literary Criticism* (New York, 1957), p. 541.
6. *Renaissance*, pp. 33–34.
7. *Marius the Epicurean*, I, 101.
8. *Renaissance*, p. 166.
9. *Appreciations*, p. 261; *Renaissance*, pp. xiv–xv.
1. *Renaissance*, p. 34.

in particular. The horns of the dilemma are his impressionism and his historicism, each of which, to be consistent, requires the exclusion of the other. For if one undertakes to be an "impressionistic" critic, to ask, "What is this work of art to *me*?" then one has in fact forbidden oneself to assume also the mantle of historicism and say, "Every intellectual product must be judged from the point of view of the age and people in which it was produced." Faced with the dilemma of having to give up the one or the other, however, Pater could not choose. I propose that this indecision was a natural result of his Darwinian conditioning and that this is, as I hope to show, a significant fact. But I propose also * * * that this indecision was actually a saving grace for Pater's criticism * * *

III

* * * That Pater's criticism was "personal" needs no further comment. Yet his aim was always to find the "formula" of an author's work—an example of the way in which the "objective" frequently tempered the "subjective" in his criticism. Pater's dilemma, I have proposed, involved the logical incompatibility of his impressionism and his historicism; yet curiously, Pater sometimes profited by this dilemma. His success is apparent in many of his most valued essays, but the abstract method which underlay this success is nowhere so obvious in his published work as it is in an unpublished draft of a letter to him from "Michael Field" (ellipses indicate cancelled readings):

> we enjoy the lectures & care to follow you as you become the contemporary of Plato . . . Your . . . historical criticism is in deep . . . accord with our newly-awakened interest in the Present—as the point where life flashes into meaning & . . . an attempt to seize the vitality of its own present in any moment of the past . . .[2]

Clearly this is an expansion of what Pater meant when he spoke of the "historical sense" which "by an imaginative act, throws itself back into a world unlike one's own." * * *

In our time awareness of the "reality of the past as past" is inevitably conditioned by Darwin's revolutionary proposals of 1859. Loren Eiseley's recent book, *Darwin's Century* (New York, 1958), makes this point more convincingly, I think, than it has heretofore been made:

> In Darwin's century . . . the unique and unreturning nature of the past began early to evince itself. . . . Without anyone's be-

2. Bodleian Library, MS Eng. letters, d. 120, fol. 9. Quoted by permission of Mr. D. Sturge Moore.

ing able to say just why, the struggle for existence which people had been examining for a century or more was suddenly seen by a few people almost simultaneously to be a creative mechanism. Basically—and this reached great intensity after Darwin—man was adjusting himself, not just to time in unlimited quantities, but rather *to complete historicity, to the emergence of the endlessly new.* His philosophy was to include, henceforth, cosmic as well as organic novelty. It is not enough to say that man had come into possession of time, or even of eternity. These he had possessed before in other cultures, but never with this particular conception of on-goingness. *To see and to recreate the past, to observe how it has come to mold the present, one must possess the knowledge that all things are new under the sun* and that they are flowing in the direction of time's arrow never to return upon their course —that time is noncyclic, unreturning, and creative.[3]

A critic must be constantly aware of both his responsibility to history and the promise of history when considering an aesthetic product, or his attention to other, more "intrinsic" matters will yield less than it might. This proposition was as much the case before 1859 as it is in 1959; but I hope my exploration of Pater's critical dilemma has helped to establish that since the philosophical revolution of the *Origin of Species,* our recognition of the problem has been made both more inescapable and more auspicious. From simple beginnings, Darwin wrote in concluding the *Origin,* "endless forms most beautiful and wonderful have been, and are being evolved." This concept, so commonplace in 1959, is what broke upon the world-mind of 1859 with such shock and such revelation; it was one of the reasons Pater's criticism became neither a vapid impressionism nor just one more variety of nineteenth-century historicism. Pater's "attempt to seize the vitality of its own present in any moment of the past"—as "Michael Field" put it— is the critic's response to the *Origin,* just as its counter-statement represents Darwin's scientific, descriptive awareness translated into the evaluative terms of Pater's scholar-criticism: "there is something verily worth having, and a just equivalent for something else lost, in the mere effect of time . . ."[4]

There is a fusing agent in the theory of evolution, a welding power that blends present with past in causal and meaningful relationships and forces us to be more aware of the multiplicity and yet the interrelation of all sorts of experience. The post-Darwinian critic simply does not have the option of being "either" isolated and personal "or" historical and traditional; nor may he stack the one on the other like building blocks. If any metaphor will do at

3. Eiseley, pp. 330–331; latter italics   4. *Miscellaneous Essays,* p. 117.
mine.

618 · *Joseph Wood Krutch*

all, it is what Eiseley calls Darwin's "sweeping vision" of all forms of life: we are "all melted together." [5] The responsible critic must keep past and present, tradition and texture, history and imagery "melted together," for it is not any one of these alone, but all of them at once, which make the power and richness, the value, of the work of art.

JOSEPH WOOD KRUTCH

The Tragic Fallacy (1929) †

* * * Three centuries lay between the promulgation of the Copernican theory and the publication of the *Origin of Species,* but in sixty-odd years which have elapsed since that latter event the blows have fallen with a rapidity which left no interval for recovery. The structures which are variously known as mythology, religion, and philosophy, and which are alike in that each has as its function the interpretation of experience in terms which have human values, have collapsed under the force of successive attacks and shown themselves utterly incapable of assimilating the new stores of experience which have been dumped upon the world. With increasing completeness science maps out the pattern of nature, but the latter has no relation to the pattern of human needs and feelings.

Consider, for example, the plight of ethics. Historical criticism having destroyed what used to be called by people of learning and intelligence "Christian Evidences," and biology having shown how unlikely it is that man is the recipient of any transcendental knowledge, there remains no foundation in authority for ideas of right and wrong; and if, on the other hand, we turn to the traditions of the human race, anthropology is ready to prove that no consistent human tradition has ever existed. Custom has furnished the only basis which ethics have ever had, and there is no conceivable human action which custom has not at one time justified and at another condemned. Standards are imaginary things, and yet it is extremely doubtful if man can live well, either spiritually or physically, without the belief that they are somehow real. Without them society lapses into anarchy and the individual becomes aware of an intolerable disharmony between himself and the universe. Instinctively and emotionally he is an ethical animal. No known race is so low in the scale of civilization that it has not attributed a moral

---

5. Eiseley, p. 352. DeBeer in his edition of the Notebooks reads "netted" for "melted"; see above, p. 78, n. 4.
† From Chapters 1 and 5 of Krutch's

The Modern Temper (New York, 1929). Joseph Wood Krutch (b. 1893) is a naturalist and literary critic.

order to the world, because no known race is so little human as not to suppose a moral order so innately desirable as to have an inevitable existence. It is man's most fundamental myth, and life seems meaningless to him without it. Yet, as that systematized and cumulative experience which is called science displaces one after another the myths which have been generated by need, it grows more and more likely that he must remain an ethical animal in a universe which contains no ethical element. * * *

And yet, nevertheless, the idea of nobility is inseparable from the idea of tragedy, which cannot exist without it. If tragedy is not the imitation or even the modified representation of noble actions it is certainly a representation of actions *considered* as noble, and herein lies its essential nature, since no man can conceive it unless he is capable of believing in the greatness and importance of man. Its action is usually, if not always, calamitous, because it is only in calamity that the human spirit has the opportunity to reveal itself triumphant over the outward universe which fails to conquer it; but this calamity in tragedy is only a means to an end and the essential thing which distinguishes real tragedy from those distressing modern works sometimes called by its name is the fact that it is in the former alone that the artist has found himself capable of considering and of making us consider that his people and his actions have that amplitude and importance which make them noble. Tragedy arises then when, as in Periclean Greece or Elizabethan England, a people fully aware of the calamities of life is nevertheless serenely confident of the greatness of man, whose mighty passions and supreme fortitude are revealed when one of these calamities overtakes him.

To those who mistakenly think of it as something gloomy or depressing, who are incapable of recognizing the elation which its celebration of human greatness inspires, and who, therefore, confuse it with things merely miserable or pathetic, it must be a paradox that the happiest, most vigorous, and most confident ages which the world has ever known—the Periclean and the Elizabethan —should be exactly those which created and which most relished the mightiest tragedies; but the paradox is, of course, resolved by the fact that tragedy is essentially an expression, not of despair, but of the triumph over despair and of confidence in the value of human life. If Shakespeare himself ever had that "dark period" which his critics and biographers have imagined for him, it was at least no darkness like that bleak and arid despair which sometimes settles over modern spirits. In the midst of it he created both the elemental grandeur of Othello and the pensive majesty of Hamlet and, holding them up to his contemporaries, he said in the words of his own Miranda, "Oh, rare new world that hath *such* creatures in it." * * *

It is, indeed, only at a certain stage in the development of the realistic intelligence of a people that the tragic faith can exist. A naïver people may have, as the ancient men of the north had, a body of legends which are essentially tragic, or it may have only (and need only) its happy and childlike mythology which arrives inevitably at its happy end, where the only ones who suffer "deserve" to do so and in which, therefore, life is represented as directly and easily acceptable. A too sophisticated society on the other hand—one which, like ours, has outgrown not merely the simple optimism of the child but also that vigorous, one might almost say adolescent, faith in the nobility of man which marks a Sophocles or a Shakespeare, has neither fairy tales to assure it that all is always right in the end nor tragedies to make it believe that it rises superior in soul to the outward calamities which befall it.

Distrusting its thought, despising its passions, realizing its impotent unimportance in the universe, it can tell itself no stories except those which make it still more acutely aware of its trivial miseries. When its heroes (sad misnomer for the pitiful creatures who people contemporary fiction) are struck down it is not, like Oedipus, by the gods that they are struck but only, like Oswald Alving, by syphilis, for they know that the gods, even if they existed, would not trouble with them, and they cannot attribute to themselves in art an importance in which they do not believe. Their so-called tragedies do not and cannot end with one of those splendid calamities which in Shakespeare seem to reverberate through the universe, because they cannot believe that the universe trembles when their love is, like Romeo's, cut off or when the place where they (small as they are) have gathered up their trivial treasure is, like Othello's sanctuary, defiled. Instead, mean misery piles on mean misery, petty misfortune follows petty misfortune, and despair becomes intolerable because it is no longer even significant or important. * * *

HERBERT J. MULLER

Modern Tragedy (1956) †

* * * In *The Experimental Novel* Zola argued that the novelist should give fiction the validity of a scientific experiment by operating objectively on his characters in a given situation, just as

† From Chapter 6 of *The Spirit of Tragedy* (New York, 1956). Herbert J. Muller (b. 1905) is Distinguished Professor of English at Indiana University.

scientists operated in the laboratory. Although we need not take this theory seriously, the early naturalists did adopt the method of close, impersonal observation and analysis—"the modern method," as Zola proclaimed—and with it the mechanistic, deterministic doctrine of nineteenth-century science. Habitually they demonstrated that men were victims of their heredity and environment.

The theory of naturalism is plainly disastrous for tragedy. If man is merely a creature of brute compulsion, in no sense a free, responsible agent, his story can have no dignity or ideal significance of any sort. It is not clear why the naturalists should have had such a passion for telling this story. But as their passion suggests, their practice was often inconsistent and impure. The mixed consequences of naturalism may be illustrated by two playwrights—August Strindberg and Gerhardt Hauptmann. * * *

* * * Strindberg describes Miss Julia as a type of "man-hating half-woman" that may have existed in all ages, but has now come to the fore and begun to make a noise. In other plays, notably *The Father* and *The Dance of Death*, the battle of the sexes is still more desperate and elemental; man and wife fight to the death. Strindberg conceived this as Darwinian tragedy. To those who complained that it was too cruel and heartless he replied: "I find the joy of life in its violent and cruel struggles." A milder and perhaps fairer statement of his credo is this: "The true naturalism is that which seeks out those points in life where the great conflicts occur, which loves to see that which cannot be seen every day, rejoices in the battle of elemental powers, whether they be called love or hatred, revolt or sociability; which cares not whether a subject be beautiful or ugly, if only it is great." It was presumably the "greatness" of his conflicts that led Shaw to call Strindberg "the only genuinely Shakespearean modern dramatist."

For his distinctive purposes Strindberg originated a brilliant, if un-Shakespearean technique. Its essence is a fierce concentration. He reduced his cast to a minimum, usually three or four characters. He not only observed the unities but sought ideally a continuous action, without act intermissions. He confined himself to a single set on an almost bare stage, with the fewest possible props; in *The Father* he needed only a lamp and a strait jacket. Especially in this play he achieved a terrific intensity. In general, there is no denying the genius of Strindberg, and the unique power of his naturalistic drama. * * *

But we do not have a great tragic dramatist. Strindberg's naturalistic drama is the clearest illustration of Krutch's dismal thesis. The neurotic Miss Julia is much too mean to be a tragic figure; at most she stirs some pity—more than Strindberg intended, if we take him at his own word—in her utter bafflement. The heroes of his other tragedies are generally stronger, or at least fiercer, but no more admirable. They fight the battle of the sexes with an insane violence and mercilessness. Their madness is not, as with Hamlet and Lear, the result of their tragic experience—it is the mainspring of the tragedy. Though they illustrate the pathological extremes to which men are liable, the hell men can make of life, they are much too abnormal to represent the tragic fate of Man. * * *

At least the naturalists did not simply degrade man. Generally they tended to widen sympathies, create new values in literature. If the tragedy of low life has limited significance, high tragedy may also limit our awareness by accustoming us to an exalted realm where is enacted not the story of Man but of the heroic few. "As for our grand sorrows," remarked a simple woman in Santayana's *The Last Puritan*, "they are a parcel of our common humanity, like funerals; and the Lord designs them for our good to wean our hearts from this sad world. . . . And it's almost a pleasure to grieve, all hung in weeds, like a weeping willow. But the price of eggs, Mr. Oliver, the price of eggs!" Another reason why tragedy gives us pleasure is that it makes us forget the price of eggs, delivers us from all the petty, nagging, humiliating cares that we can never escape in life. No doubt this is all to the good, since we can count on having enough cares. But as Karl Jaspers observed in *Tragedy Is Not Enough*, the glamour of tragedy may obscure the appalling realities of human misery: the hopeless, helpless misery that the masses of men have always known; misery without greatness, without dignity, without any decent meaning whatever; misery that seems more intolerable because men have always tolerated it. We have no right to demand of artists that they treat such misery. As we value the tragic spirit and its essential humanity, we have no right either to condemn the naturalists who did treat it. * * *

Meanwhile most men in the West, including Christians, are still committed on principle as well as in practice to the humanistic belief in the value of life on earth, and of human enterprise to improve this life. They cannot accept the traditional Eastern wisdom of passivity, resignation, or renunciation, nor the traditional Christian view that the whole meaning and value of life derive from the life to come. They may agree with Reinhold Niebuhr that free reason, imagination, creativity—man's distinctive gifts and the source of his highest achievements—are also the source of all evil, which is therefore ineradicable; but like him they do not propose to cut the costs by discouraging the exercise of these gifts. In the democracies most are still committed, more specifically, to a belief in the values of freedom and individuality, the right of a man to a mind and a life of his own. And these distinctively Western be-

liefs, which gave rise to the tragic spirit, make it all the more relevant in a time of crisis.

To me, the tragic sense is the deepest sense of our humanity,
and therefore spiritual enough. But all men may profit from it,
whatever their faith. It is certainly valid as far as it goes, or this
life goes. It sizes up the very reasons for religious faith, the awful
realities that men must face up to if their faith is to be firm, mature, and responsible. It also makes for sensitiveness to the tragic
excesses of all faiths, the inevitable corruptions of all ideals—in
the West, more particularly, to the rugged, irresponsible individualism that has battened on the ideal of freedom, and the bigotry
and self-righteousness that have flourished in the name of Jesus. It
may deepen the sense of community that has been one end of
religion. The tragic writer may most nearly realize the ideal mission
of the artist stated by Joseph Conrad:

> He speaks to our capacity for delight and wonder, to the sense
> of mystery surrounding our lives; to our sense of pity, and beauty,
> and pain; to the latent feeling of fellowship with all creation—and
> to the subtle but invincible conviction of solidarity that knits
> together the loneliness of innumerable hearts, to the solidarity
> in dreams, in joy, in sorrow, in aspirations, in illusions, in hope,
> in fear, which binds men to each other, which binds together all
> humanity—the dead to the living and the living to the unborn.

For the many who are unable to believe that man was specially
created in the image of God, and guaranteed that his earthly history will be consummated in eternity, herein may be the most available means—beyond animal faith—to spiritual acceptance and
order, in a society that has lost its simple faith in progress but
nevertheless remains committed to the belief that "something
ought to be done" about all our problems, and can be. The tragic
spirit can promote a saving irony, in the perception of the naïve or
absurd aspects of this belief; a spirit of compassion, through the
knowledge of irremediable evils and insoluble dilemmas; and a
spirit of reverence, for the idealism that keeps seeking truth, goodness, and beauty even though human ideals are not everlasting. It is
proof of the dignity of man, which remains a basic tenet of Western
democracy. It is now perhaps the strongest proof because of the
very realism, in modern thought and art, that has commonly led to
a devaluation of man and nature.

At its best, the realistic spirit is itself a value, and a source of
further values. It has meant tough-mindedness, the courage and
honesty to admit that we really do not know all that we would
like to know, and that most men have passionately claimed to
know. In modern science it has meant the admission that our most

positive, reliable knowledge of the physical universe is approximate, tentative, hypothetical, and that we cannot know the final, absolute truth about it: a respect for both fact and mystery that gives a pathetic air to the religious thinkers who have leaped to the odd conclusion that this admission of ultimate uncertainty proves the certainty of religious truth. In literature, realism as a technique has often meant superficiality, meagerness, fragmentariness, confusion; but as a controlling attitude it has also toughened the tragic faith. From Ibsen to Sartre, as from Hardy to Malraux, many writers have not only reasserted the dignity of the human spirit but proved its strength by holding fast in uncertainty, or even in the conviction that there is no power not ourselves making for righteousness. Although they cannot readily create heroes with the stature and symbolical significance of the ancient heroes, they may exhibit or exemplify a humbler, more difficult kind of heroism that may be more significant for our living purposes. They no longer leave the worst enemy in the rear.

All this necessarily falls far short of any promise of salvation, and so brings us back to "reality." The spirit of tragedy can never deliver us from tragedy. It cannot take the place of religion. Even in literature it cannot give us the kind of exaltation that some critics now soar to under the spell of Myth. In *The Timeless Theme*, for instance, Colin Still argues that the Living Art of all humanity, like all "authentic" myth and true religion, has "but one essential theme, namely: the Fall of the human Soul and the means of its Redemption." In irony one may remark that he proves his thesis by the easy expedient of dismissing art that lacks this theme as not authentic or living (even though it happens to have lived for a thousand years or so), and that he makes it still easier by asserting that this timeless truth can be grasped only by the Spirit, which most scholars and critics lack. In reverence one should acknowledge that this has in fact been a major theme in Western literature, and that it is the most inspiring theme to many men of good will. In truthfulness one must add that tragedy has had no such uniform, timeless theme, beyond the realities of suffering and death. Modern tragedy is particularly deficient in Spirit; it seldom exhibits or promises Redemption. At most it may help to redeem us from fear or despair, or from the vanity of cheap hopes.

I can conclude on no more exalted note than a verse of Thomas Hardy: "If way to the Better there be, it exacts a full look at the Worst." Come the worst, the survivors of atomic war—if any—will have little stomach for tragedy. Come the better, in something like One World, there will still be sufficient reason for pity and terror, and many more men to experience it with more intensity. The East is now stirring with the willful Western spirit, demanding more of the goods of this world. Tragedy might at last become a universal form, and redeem all the critics who have written so solemnly about its universal and eternal truths. But if so, it will be because the rest of the world has taken a fuller look at the worst, and is no longer resigned to the eternal verities, no longer content to surrender to the will of its gods.

PART VII

Epilogue

PHILIP APPLEMAN

Darwin: On Changing the Mind

"Thought makes the whole
dignity of man."
—Pascal

I

Pascal's remark strikes us immediately as right; nevertheless, its very simplicity, out of context, tends to put us on our guard. Can "thought" be as unexceptionable as all that? Might thought also be man's peculiar blemish? ("Man is, among many other things, the mistaken animal, the foolish animal," writes evolutionist G. G. Simpson. "Other species doubtless have much more limited ideas about the world, but what ideas they do have are much less likely to be wrong. . . . White cats do not denigrate black, and dogs do not ask Baal, Jehovah, or other Semitic gods to perform miracles for them." [1]) To what extent is our "thinking" something we can properly call our own, and to what extent is it merely an unconscious reflection of various conditions in our environment? For we think—and we are aware that we think—within an intimidating maze of events and persuasions.

To be fair to Charles Darwin's originality of mind, we must see him boarding H.M.S. *Beagle* young, amateurish in science, a believer in Genesis. We should picture him carrying in his small library Lyell's new work, the *Principles of Geology*, but warned against its heresies by his respected master, Henslow. We must remember that he carried, too, the lessons of a close study of Paley's *Natural Theology*. ("I do not think I hardly ever admired a book more than Paley's," he was to write in his autobiography; "I could almost formerly have said it by heart.") And it was of course Paley more than any other man who had already convinced a whole generation of readers that in the Deity's neatly constructed universe, "the marks of *design* are too strong to be gotten over."

Darwin also carried in his mental baggage the teachings of the distinguished Dr. William Whewell ("Next to Sir J. Mackintosh . . . the best converser on grave subjects to whom I ever listened"). And by an ironic trick of history, it was during the five years of the *Beagle's* voyage that the British citadel of scientific respectability, the Royal Society, was administering the publication of the Bridgewater Treatises, a series of books by notable scientists and moralists commissioned specifically to illustrate "the power, wisdom, and goodness of God as manifested in the Creation"—so, while Darwin

1. George Gaylord Simpson, *This View of Life* (New York, 1964), p. viii.

was examining reptiles and fossils on the east coast of Brazil, the grave Dr. Whewell, eminent mathematician and mineralogist, was writing for his Treatise: "If there be, in the administration of the universe, intelligence and benevolence, superintendence and foresight, grounds for love and hope, such qualities may be expected to appear in the constitution and combination of those fundamental regulations by which the course of nature is brought about, and made to be what it is." [2]

It is an awesome distance from that kind of reasoning to the conclusion of the *Origin of Species*: "Thus, from the war of nature, from famine and death, the most exalted object which we are capable of conceiving, namely, the production of the higher animals, directly follows"; and Darwin—cautious, skeptical, compulsively industrious, distrustful of his own talents and never daring to suspect himself of genius—Darwin did not make the voyage in a day.

It was not enough for Darwin that he was pre-eminently an empiricist: that for five years in exotic locales he had explored river beds and coral reefs; hiked pampas and climbed mountains; recorded stratifications of rocks and soil; examined the earth with lens, compass, clinometer, penknife, blowpipe, and acids; discovered fossils of conifers and shellfish, megatherium and mastodon; collected flowers, birds, insects, and reptiles. It was not enough that he was a subtle theorist, pondering the elevation and subsidence of volcanic strata, the causes of the earthquakes he experienced, the formation of coral reefs, and the relation of one species of ground sloth to another. Nor was it even enough that the maturing Darwin, widely respected as a naturalist after the *Beagle* voyage, should have come home to spend two decades in the dogged pursuit of a hypothesis: examining the many breeds of domestic pigeons, the skeletons of rabbits, the wings of ducks, the variations in ten thousand specimens of barnacles; keeping notebooks on "transmutation"; discussing the species problem with close scientific friends; and finally, twenty years after debarking for the last time from the *Beagle*, daring to begin to write his great book on "Natural Selection."

All this was not enough for Darwin, because he understood clearly the strength of conventional scientific opinion on the fixity of species. Lamarck's experience had been an object-lesson: he had challenged this conventional opinion, and his arguments had been systematically attacked by the French scientific establishment and discredited by Lyell. The author of *Vestiges of the Natural History of Creation*, that notorious evolutionary publication of 1844, had

2. William Whewell, *Astronomy and General Physics Considered with Reference to Natural Theology* (London, 1833), pp. 4–5.

chosen discretion rather than valor, remaining anonymous. And other scientists, philosophers, and writers (including Darwin's own poetic grandfather) had speculated about the transmutation of species, but their work was never enough, either; it was always too hypothetical, too desultory, too superficial, too limited, too abstract, or too obscure to threaten in any serious way the established Truth of the fixity of species.

So, on June 18, 1858, after five years in the field, twenty years of patient observation and cautious speculation, and two years of busy writing on the manuscript of "Natural Selection," Darwin was still not ready to publish his challenge to prevailing opinion. On that day, however, he received the momentous letter from Alfred Russel Wallace describing Wallace's own recent discovery of the principle of natural selection. Darwin immediately wrote to Lyell: "Your words have come true with a vengeance—that I should be forestalled." But his dismay was temporary: his friends Lyell and Hooker arranged a joint presentation of short papers by both Wallace and Darwin at the Linnean Society in July, 1858, so the names of Darwin and Wallace are permanently linked as co-discoverers of the principle of natural selection. Wallace, however, was always modest about his contribution, since compared to Darwin's it was, as he said, as two weeks are to twenty years.

Darwin then went on, thanks to Wallace's unintentional prompting, and finished an "abstract" of his work: in March, 1859, he completed the *Origin*. It was published on November 24 of that year, and Darwin, tired and sickly, waited for the response.

II

The circumstances which have most influence on the happiness of mankind, the changes of manners and morals, the transition of communities from poverty to wealth, from knowledge to ignorance, from ferocity to humanity—these are, for the most part, noiseless revolutions. Their progress is rarely indicated by what historians are pleased to call important events. They are not achieved by armies, or enacted by senates. They are sanctified by no treaties, and recorded in no archives. They are carried on in every school, in every church, behind ten thousand counters, at ten thousand firesides.

—Thomas Babington Macaulay [3]

Macaulay died in 1859, but he had already written this appropriate epigraph for that eventful year back in 1828, when he was twenty-eight and at the beginning of a brilliant public career; when the aging Malthus, with six more years to live, had seen his portentous *Essay on Population* through the six editions of his lifetime; when Alfred Russel Wallace was a boy of five; and when Darwin was nineteen, "wasting" his time at Cambridge, collecting beetles

3. Thomas Babington Macaulay, "History," *The Works of Lord Macaulay* (London, 1873), V, 156.

and being "charmed" by Paley's logic. But it is not quite accurate to call the Darwinian revolution simply "noiseless." No cannon were fired, true (though Shaw later blamed World War I on "Neo-Darwinism in politics"), but there were enough broadsides of another sort to satisfy even the belligerent bishop-eater Thomas Henry Huxley, who wrote in 1859, "We are in the midst of a gigantic movement, greater than that which preceded and produced the Reformation."

Macaulay was full of admiration for the scientific revolution he was witnessing in the early nineteenth century, and in this, as in so many things, he typified his age. For him as for others, then and now, "science" meant only partly empiricism, a method of looking at data. More immediately, more tangibly, "science" meant the secondary results of that method: the products of technology. During the long reign of Queen Victoria, "science" transformed many of the conditions of people's lives. The first railroad was built in England in 1825, when Victoria was a little girl; before that, the maximum speed of land travel was—for up-to-date Englishmen as it had been for Caesars and Pharaohs—the speed of the horse. But before the Queen and Empress died, almost all of Britain's now existing railroads had been built: "science" had begun that liberation of man from animal muscle, that acceleration toward inconceivable velocities which is so characteristic of our own age and is still as impressive to us as it was to the Victorians.

Impressive: "science" was *doing* things, making things *work*. The practical, empirical, positivistic British temperament was fascinated. While Victoria occupied the throne, transatlantic steamship service was begun; power-driven machines revolutionized industry; the telegraph became a practical instrument and the telephone was developed; the electric lamp and the automobile were produced. Eight years before the *Origin*, the Victorians celebrated Progress at the first world's fair, in the fabulous Crystal Palace, where Macaulay felt as reverent as at St. Peter's. "Science" was making things happen; it could predict their occurence; its success precluded doubt. It seemed to many, at the time, final and unambiguous. One could depend on it. That was the context of attitudes which curiously eluded the perceptive Matthew Arnold: "I cannot understand why all you scientific people make such a fuss about Darwin. Why it's all in Lucretius." Of course it was. It was "in" Hegel, too, and "in" Erasmus Darwin. But, as a biographer of Darwin's has pointed out, "No divination of poetry or philosophy can anticipate the knowledge that comes from dissecting barnacles and observing fossil armadillos and studying the methods of pigeon-breeders. . . . A conjecture—even a fortunate one by a Lucretius about evolution—is quite idle until some Darwin breathes life into it." [4]

"Theology," wrote Dr. Pusey, "precipitates nothing." Apropos of Erasmus Darwin's evolutionism, compare Auden: "Poetry makes nothing happen." One may object that both theology and poetry do indeed "make things happen" in terms of human values and behavior; but science compels rational assent. And since Copernicus shunted man off from the center of the universe to a minor planet of a fifth-rate star, no scientific discovery had been so staggering to the popular mind as Darwin's. One could not simultaneously accept his evidence and the plain words of Genesis; no reconcilement was possible, T. H. Huxley insisted, "between free thought and traditional authority. One or the other will have to succumb."

What was at stake was nothing less than a world-view. Bishop Ussher had calculated that man was created at 9:00 A.M. on October 23 in the year 4004 B.C.; and Paley had proved that the whole creation was wonderfully and intricately designed by a rational Creator. But natural selection was a prodigiously time-consuming process, in which six thousand years are as a single sunset; and it was the reverse of rational: it was fortuitous. Darwin's universe ended up looking much the same as Paley's (as of course it had to); but both its past and its process were new, revolutionary, heretical —and persuasive.

Persuasive because "science" was persuasive, evolution became a watchword to the late Victorians. By the end of the century, hardly a field of thought remained unfertilized by the "new" concept. Historians had begun looking at the past as "a living organism"; legal theorists studied the law as a developing social institution; critics examined the evolution of literary types; anthropologists and sociologists invoked "natural selection" in their studies of social forms; apologists for the wealthy showed how the poor are the "unfit" and how Progress, under the leadership of the "fit," was inevitable; novelists "observed" their creatures as they evolved in an "empirical" way; and poets hymned a creative life-force. Half a century after the publication of the *Origin*, evolution, which in 1800 had been a word used mostly in rather narrow and technical scientific senses, seemed capable of explaining anything. The titles of grave volumes of the period are symptomatic: *The Evolution of Morality* (1878), *The Evolution of Religion* (1894), *The Evolution of Modern Money* (1901), *The Evolution of Immortality* (1901), *The Evolution of the Soul* (1904).

In 1857, the naturalist Philip Gosse could still write:

> I assume that each organism which the Creator educed was stamped with an indelible specific character, which made it

4. Henshaw Ward, *Charles Darwin: The Man and His Warfare* (Indianapolis, 1927), pp. 25, 27.

what it was, and distinguished it from everything else, however near or like. I assume that such character has been, and is, indelible and immutable; that the characters which distinguish species now, were as definite at the first instant of their creation as now, and are as distinct now as they were then. If any choose to maintain . . . that species were gradually brought to their present maturity from humbler forms, he is welcome to his hypothesis, but I have nothing to do with it. . . . I believe . . . there is a large preponderance of the men of science . . . who will be at one with me here.[5]

And Gosse was right about that last point; respectable scientists who believed in the transmutation of species in 1857 were almost as rare as believers in the transmutation of lead into gold. After all, Gosse's world of 1857 was the only world a sane man, scientist or otherwise, could desire. As far as the biologists were concerned, it was a dependable world—the classical world, still, of fixed definitions. "To Aristotle," Herbert J. Muller writes, "definition was not merely a verbal process or a useful tool of thought; it was the essence of knowledge. It was the cognitive grasp of the eternal essences of Nature, a fixed, necessary form of knowing because an expression of the fixed, necessary forms of Being." [6]

Into that satisfied and satisfying universe, the quiet, kindly, unassuming Charles Darwin had dropped a bomb.

III

There is a well-known nineteenth-century epigram which proposes that it is the fate of all great scientific discoveries to pass through three stages: in the first stage, people say, "It's absurd"; in the second, "It's contrary to the Bible"; and in the third, "Oh, we've known *that* all along." Evolution passed through all three stages during Darwin's own lifetime, so that in his last revision of the *Origin* he could write:

As a record of a former state of things, I have retained in the foregoing paragraphs, and elsewhere, several sentences which imply that naturalists believe in the separate creation of species; and I have been much censured for having thus expressed myself. But undoubtedly this was the general belief when the first edition of the present work appeared. I formerly spoke to very many naturalists on the subject of evolution, and never once met with any sympathetic agreement. It is probable that some did then believe in evolution, but they were either silent, or expressed themselves so ambiguously that it was not easy to understand

5. Philip Gosse, *Omphalos* (London, 1857), pp. 111–112. It should perhaps be added that although Gosse was a respectable naturalist, he was a laughing-stock as a self-appointed reconciler of Genesis and geology.
6. Herbert J. Muller, *Science and Criticism* (New Haven, 1943), p. 21.

their meaning. Now things are wholly changed, and almost every naturalist admits the great principle of evolution.[7]

Scientific revolutions depend upon (among other things) the perceptiveness and the industriousness—and sometimes the aggressiveness—of their protagonists. Darwin had had the perception to discover natural selection and the industriousness to fill hundreds of pages with minutely observed facts and close reasoning; friends, upon demand, supplied the aggressiveness; and the world was changed: converted, in a very few years, from an almost total belief in the permanence of species to an almost total belief (among the educated) in the transmutation of species. This in itself was a monumental conversion, but the "Darwinian revolution" implies much more.

It implies, for instance, a transformation of attitudes, of outlook, on the part of other scientists. Since 1859 it has been necessary to think in post-Darwinian terms in order to understand the drift of modern paleontology, comparative anatomy, genetics, ecology, embryology, taxonomy—and in fact virtually all branches of botany and zoology. The "Darwinian revolution" goes well beyond science and scientists, however. It implies a basic change in ways of looking at all ideas, all phenomena. Relativity and flux were not nineteenth-century inventions, of course, but there was an imperiousness about nineteenth-century relativism that was new—new precisely because of the impressiveness of nineteenth-century "science" in general. To the conservative-minded, the terrifying thing about the implications of Darwinism was that nothing was sacrosanct: evolution became not only the science of sciences—worse still, it became the philosophy of philosophies. For those least prepared for change, the impact of all this was shattering. Seventy years after the publication of the *Origin*, Joseph Wood Krutch surveyed the wreckage in his book *The Modern Temper*:

> Three centuries lay between the promulgation of the Copernican theory and the publication of the *Origin of Species,* but in sixty-odd years which have elapsed since that latter event the blows have fallen with a rapidity which left no interval for recovery. The structures which are variously known as mythology, religion, and philosophy, and which are alike in that each has as its function the interpretation of experience in terms which have human values, have collapsed under the force of successive attacks and shown themselves utterly incapable of assimilating the new stores of experience which have been dumped upon the world. With increasing completeness science maps out the pattern of nature, but the latter has no relation to the pattern of human needs and feelings.[8]

7. Charles Darwin, *The Origin of Species* (New York, 1958), p. 445.

8. Joseph Wood Krutch, *The Modern Temper* (New York, 1929), p. 12.

"Mythology, religion, and philosophy" did not succumb without a struggle; counterattacks from the faithful were swift and fierce. Priests, parsons, and bishops defended not only their own faith but also "true Baconian induction," in the pages of the quarterly and theological reviews, where scientific "experts" could flourish in protective anonymity. "The theory of evolution," wrote a truculent contributor to the *Catholic World*, "has no scientific character, is irreconcilable with the conclusions of natural history, and has no ground to stand upon except the worn-out fallacies of a perverted logic. To call it 'hypothesis' is therefore to do it an honor which it does not deserve. A pile of rubbish is not a palace, and a heap of blunders is not a hypothesis." [9] The aging Anglican sage, Dr. Pusey, sternly repudiated Darwin: "Never probably was any system built upon so many 'perhaps,' 'probably,' 'possibly,' 'it may be,' 'it seems to be,' 'most likely,' 'it must be,' 'it requires but a slight stretch of imagination to conceive,' as that mythological account of the origin of all which has life, and, at last of ourselves, which is now being every where or widely acknowledged by unscientific minds as if it were axiomatic truth; some of whose adherents claim that it will revolutionise every other science." [1] And Pope Pius IX, writing to a French anti-Darwinian author, was thoroughly contemptuous:

> We have received with pleasure, dear son, the work in which you refute so well the aberrations of Darwinism. A system which is repudiated by history, by the traditions of all peoples, by exact science, by the observation of facts, and even by reason itself, would seem to have no need at all of refutation, if alienation from God and the penchant for materialism, both stemming from corruption, were not avidly searching for support in this fabric of fables. . . . But the corruption of this century, the guile of the depraved, the danger of oversimplification demand that such dreamings, absurd as they are, since they wear the mask of science, be refuted by true science.[2]

It need hardly be said that this rather novel concern of theologians for "true science" was not wholly disinterested. Theologians worried because they saw, perhaps more clearly than others, the philosophical implications of post-Darwinian thought. It was not just that Darwin had complicated the reading of Genesis; or even that he had furnished impressive scientific authority for the nineteenth-century habit of thinking in terms of wholes and continuities rather than in discrete parts and rigidities; or that the evolutionary

9. "Dr. Draper and Evolution," *Catholic World*, XXVI (1878), 775.
1. Edward Bouverie Pusey, *Un-Science, Not Science, Adverse to Faith* (London, 1879), p. 32.

2. Quoted in Constantin James, *L'Hypnotisme expliqué et Mes Entretiens avec S. M. l'Empereur Don Pédro sur le Darwinisme* (Paris, 1888), pp. 84–85; translation by the editor.

orientation stressed context and complexity—though all of these influences could be bothersome when used by "materialists." The worst threat of all was that Darwin's universe operated not by Design but by natural selection, a self-regulating mechanism. ("Paley's divine watchmaker was unemployed," Gavin de Beer writes, "because the wonderful property of organisms is that they make and mar themselves.") Natural selection pictured the world in a constant process of change, but without any apparent prior intention of going anywhere in particular or of becoming anything in particular.

That was a devastating proposition to the conventional theologian—more so, perhaps, than the Copernican theory had been, because it struck so close to home. Natural selection therefore seemed, to many, hopelessly negative, fraught with blasphemy and conducive of despair. Science, with all of its impressiveness of fact and achievement, was moving in on theologians and philosophers, *taking over*: constantly enlarging the domain of fact and consequently reducing the domain of speculation. Given objective knowledge, people tend (it was already clear) to give up the guessing-games of ignorance—conjecture about which of the "humors" is overbalanced in a person whose blood pressure is abnormal; or whether or not Adam and Eve had navels; or what influence the planets have on our destinies. So it *made a difference* to philosophers and theologians that man not only evolved, but evolved by natural selection rather than by a vital force or cosmic urge of some sort. Darwinism seemed uncompromisingly non-teleological, non-vitalist, and non-finalist, and that basic fact could not help but affect the work of philosophers. "Once man was swept into the evolutionary orbit," Bert James Loewenberg has written, "a revolution in Western thought was initiated. Man was seen to be a part of nature, and nature was seen to be a part of man. The Darwinian revolution was not a revolution in science alone; it was a revolution in man's conception of himself and in man's conception of all his works." [3]

Of course, philosophers and theologians had always seen man as a "part of nature," but as a much grander part: as the crowning achievement of God's universe, a little below the angels. It was the Darwinian demotion of man from that lofty station that not only caused tremors among the professional thinkers but also rattled quite ordinary men on the street. Krutch describes the debilitating effects of this: "When [man's] instinctive faith in that correspondence between the outer and the inner world fades, his grasp upon the faith that sustained him fades also, and Love or Tragedy or what not ceases to be the reality which it was because he

3. Bert James Loewenberg, ed., *Charles Darwin: Evolution and Natural Selection* (Boston, 1959), p. 21.

is never strong enough in his own insignificant self to stand alone in a universe which snubs him with its indifference." [4] Those charged with protecting man from his own weakness repeatedly denounced the new heresy. Pope Pius IX wrote, apropos of Darwinism: "Pride, having rejected the Creator of all things and proclaimed man independent, wishing him to be his own king, his own priest, and his own God, pride having come this far by all these madnesses of its own contriving, then reduces this same man to the level of the dumb animals, perhaps even to raw matter, thus unintentionally confirming the divine word: *When pride cometh, then cometh shame.*" [5]

A century ago the faithful still trusted this kind of righteous indignation; but it gradually became apparent that wishful thinking would no longer serve. With the passing of decades, the tone of the theologians had to be modified and the strategies of philosophers altered: direct opposition to Darwin (in all but the most remote backwaters) gradually made way for accommodation. The first edition of the *Catholic Encyclopedia* (1909), for instance, still clung to the older attitude, saying of natural selection that "As a theory, it is scientifically inadequate," and adding, "The third signification of the term *Darwinism* arose from the application of the theory of selection to man, which is likewise impossible of acceptance." [6] By 1967, however, the *New Catholic Encyclopedia* was looking at these things differently: "Today, with a much better understanding of both the theological sources of the Judeo-Christian revelation and of evolutionary theory, the compatibility of God's creative and directive action is more easily comprehended . . . the solution of the basic difficulties [with Darwinism] was soon found to lie in Biblical research and scholarship and not in the rejection of the new theory. . . . In his encyclical *Humani generis* [1950], Pope Pius XII [asserted] that general evolution, even of the body of man (and woman), should be professionally studied by both anthropologist and theologian." [7]

"Present-day theologians," says a recent Catholic commentator, "are far more moderate in their claims than were their predecessors." [8]

The activities of science, relentlessly pushing back the margins of the unknown, have in effect been forcing the concept of "God" into a perpetual retreat into the still-unknown, and it is in this condition that "God" has frequently come to have meaning for

4. Krutch, p. 136.
5. James, p. 84; translation by the editor.
6. *Catholic Encyclopedia* (New York, 1909), V, 655.
7. *New Catholic Encyclopedia* (New York, 1967), V, 693.
8. Robert W. Gleason, "A Note on Theology and Evolution," in Walter J. Ong, S.J., ed., *Darwin's Vision and Christian Perspectives* (New York, 1960), p. 104.

modern man. The final retreat is of course into the strongholds of the Infinite and the Eternal, and with the scientists' continuing success in exploring the littleness and vastness of the finite, one may assume that, for any practical purpose, that final retreat has long since occurred. The implications of all this have led some men to a renewed humanism: to the proposition that evolutionary man, cut off from theological presumption, might still have sufficient reason to exist—even to respect himself—simply as man. At the beginning of this century, Bertrand Russell wrote:

> That Man is the product of causes which had no prevision of the end they were achieving; that his origin, his growth, his hopes and fears, his loves and his beliefs, are but the outcome of accidental collocations of atoms; that no fire, no heroism, no intensity of thought and feeling, can preserve an individual life beyond the grave; that all the labours of the ages, all the devotion, all the inspiration, all the noonday brightness of human genius, are destined to extinction in the vast death of the solar system, and that the whole temple of Man's achievement must inevitably be buried beneath the debris of a universe in ruins—all these things, if not quite beyond dispute, are yet so nearly certain, that no philosophy which rejects them can hope to stand. Only within the scaffolding of these truths, only on the firm foundation of unyielding despair, can the soul's habitation henceforth be safely built.[9]

It is possible to argue that there has been, in consequence of the retreat of "God," a genuine spiritual gain. To discuss "God" in terms of the Unknown seems to some contemporary thinkers (as indeed it did to Herbert Spencer) a more dignified and tenable procedure than to carry on that discussion in terms of oak trees or thunderbolts or man's image. The possible attitudes toward this "Unknown" are various: they can be put in terms of release and new potentiality, as in Bertrand Russell's further comment, "It is well to exalt the dignity of Man, by freeing him as far as possible from the tyranny of non-human Power"; or of guarded optimism, like Julian Huxley's, seeing man as Vicar of Evolution on Earth, a conscious directing factor in his own progress toward an unknown destiny; or of a kind of ecstasy, like Albert Einstein's, in "rapturous amazement" at the harmony of nature. But in any case, men now seem able to view the human condition not in terms of a fall from grace to degradation but rather as the reverse—as a long struggle to escape from mere animalism, red in tooth and claw, and to establish upon man himself—upon his own best knowledge of himself—a tenable ethical ground.

Scientists have rarely been simple materialists, after all. It is im-

9. Bertrand Russell, *Mysticism and Logic* (New York, 1957), pp. 45–46.

portant to scientists, as scientists, to restrict their investigations to the knowable; but they have not often contended that the results of their researches were the summation of all Truth, or that one should act as though the world were purely deterministic. Moreover, some scientists, like T. H. Huxley and his grandson, Julian Huxley, have been consistently interested in the relationship between science (particularly evolution) and ethics. Their conclusions have been hopeful, not pessimistic, and one may cite, as illustrative examples, both T. H. Huxley's belief that "there lies within [man] a fund of energy, operating intelligently and so far akin to that which pervades the universe, that it is competent to influence and modify the cosmic process" and Julian Huxley's insistence that "in so far as the mechanism of evolution ceases to be blind and automatic and becomes conscious, ethics can be injected into the evolutionary process. Before man that process was merely amoral. After his emergence onto life's stage it became possible to introduce faith, courage, love of truth, goodness—in a word moral purpose —into evolution." [1] So it is not after all strange, or even unusual, to hear the very scientists who remind man of his cosmic littleness at the same time assuring him of his individual dignity in terms which, if not so dogmatic as those of the theologians, are nevertheless heartening.

The point is worth stressing partly because non-scientists have at times in the past tended to disparage science as an amoral or even an immoral study. Erasmus Darwin, Charles's grandfather, once declined to discuss one of his botanical books because, he said, "some Ladies have intimated to me, that the Loves of the Plants are described in too glowing colours." If science had any relation to ethics at all, it was often held to be that of a lowly subordinate. Zoology, for instance, as a recent commentator has noted, was taken to be a mere handmaiden of ethics:

> Animals were studied not to observe their actual characteristics but to find moral examples in their nature or behavior. Topsell's *Historie of Foure-footed Beastes*, a popular book on animals published in 1607, avowed its purpose to be the leading of men to "heavenly meditations upon earthly creatures" and was particularly recommended for Sunday reading.
>
> In such works morality naturally took precedence over accuracy. Many "impossible falsities," said Sir Thomas Browne, "do notwithstanding include wholesome moralities, and such as expiate the trespass of their absurdities." [2]

Today the shoe is pretty snugly on the other foot; few moralists would now be willing to propagate error on the ground that it

1. Julian Huxley and T. H. Huxley, *Touchstone for Ethics* (New York and London, 1947), p. 135.

2. Bergen Evans, *The Natural History of Nonsense* (New York, 1958), p. 29.

contained a "wholesome morality"—would tend, in fact, to doubt that a really wholesome morality could be the product of palpable falsehoods. Some scientists have gone further than this and argued that a scientifically accurate view of the world is the best basis for ethics. "Duty arises from our potential control over the course of events," Whitehead proposed; "where attainable knowledge could have changed the issue, ignorance has the guilt of vice." This is a momentous principle, and one to which scientists are, I believe, more generally alert than are other people. C. H. Waddington, the English zoologist, has shown how scientific awareness can broaden our sense of moral responsibility. "Our ethical notions," he writes,

> are fundamentally based on a system of individual responsibility for individual acts. The principle of statistical correlation be-tween two sets of events, although accepted in scientific practice, is not usually felt to be ethically completely valid. If a man hits a baby on the head with a hammer, we prosecute him for cruelty or murder; but if he sells dirty milk and the infant sickness or death rate goes up, we merely fine him for contravening the health laws. And the ethical point is taken even less seriously when the responsibility, as well as the results of the crime, falls on a statistical assemblage. The whole community of England and Wales kills 8,000 babies a year by failing to bring its infant mortality rate down to the level reached by Oslo as early as 1931, which would be perfectly feasible; but few people seem to think this is a crime.[3]

Those who persist in seeing scientists as "materialists" and non-scientists as "humanists" will no doubt have difficulty accepting all this, but one must hope that such naïveté must now be getting rare. There is grandeur, Darwin insisted, in his scientific view of the world, for, he said, it ennobled man. Man has risen, he added later, "to the very summit of the organic scale; and the fact of his having thus risen, instead of having been aboriginally placed there, may give him hopes for a still higher destiny in the distant future."[4]

IV

As some of the foregoing suggests, the moment one transplants the discussion of evolution from the field of science to the fields of philosophy or ethics or theology, one has to recognize that the discussion has probably become analogical rather than straightfor-wardly analytical, "Darwinistic" rather than Darwinian. ("Darwin-

3. C.H. Waddington, *The Scientific At-titude* (London, 1948), p. 31.
4. See the concluding paragraphs of the *Origin of Species* and *The Descent of Man*.

ism," writes Morse Peckham, "is a scientific theory about the origin of biological species from pre-existent species. . . . Darwinisticism can be an evolutionary metaphysic about the nature of reality and the universe. It can be an economic theory, or a moral theory, or an aesthetic theory, or a psychological theory." [5]) Darwin's propositions, like many other bright and fashionable ideas before and since, caught people's imaginations; and many thinkers picked up the new concepts and exploited them as analogies (or apologies) in their own fields of work, often less in the hope of being led to new perceptions by the analogies than with the intention of reinforcing old positions or of scoring debater's points with them. Whitehead reflected on the dangers of this indiscriminate and tendentious use of Darwinistic ideas. "The last words of science," he wrote, "appeared to be Struggle for Existence and Natural Selection. Darwin's own writings are for all time a model of refusal to go beyond the direct evidence, and of careful retention of every hypothesis. But those virtues were not so conspicuous in his followers, and still less in his camp-followers." [6]

We see this tendency perhaps most clearly in the application of a Darwinistic pattern to society itself. The publication of the *Origin* and the American Civil War were almost coincident, and in the years following those two traumatic events, the United States was industrializing very rapidly. The late nineteenth century became the pre-eminent period in our history of the Rugged Individualist, the Robber Baron, the Captain of Industry, the accumulators of great wealth. It was also a period of sweatshops, of union-busting, of goon squads and strike-breaking massacres, of a dollar a day for workingmen, of tenements without sanitation, of widespread malnutrition.

It was not simple, in a "Christian society," to reconcile such contradictions. The economic establishment had, since the beginnings of the industrial revolution, been casting about for sanctions, for justifications. Manchester political economy had been a powerful sanction for the establishment, emphasizing as it did the necessity for untrammelled individual enterprise, the automatic enlightenment of self-interest, and the "iron" laws of economics. ("There is no more possibility of defeating the operation of these laws," Carnegie once said, "than there is of thwarting the laws of nature which determine the humidity of the atmosphere or the revolution of the earth upon its axis." [7]) Curiously enough, there were religious sanctions, too, for had not material things always been corrupting to man, and was it not therefore self-evident that the

5. Morse Peckham, "Darwinism and Darwinisticism," *Victorian Studies*, III (1959), 32.
6. Alfred North Whitehead, *Science and the Modern World* (New York, 1925), p. 158.
7. Andrew Carnegie, *The Empire of Business* (London, 1902), p. 67.

lower classes had to be kept poor to be kept virtuous—and, para-doxically, could not the virtuous and industrious among the poor expect to be rewarded, even in this world? ("He that gets all he can honestly," Ben Franklin had declared, "and saves all he gets will certainly become rich, if that Being who governs the world, to whom all should look for a blessing on their endeavors, doth not, in His wise providence, otherwise determine." To which a railroad president added, a century later: "The rights and interests of the laboring man will be protected and cared for by the Christian men to whom God has given control of the property rights of the country." [8]

And always, in the nineteenth century, there was that court of last resort, the sanction of Progress, in whose name all contradic-tions were resolved—or ignored.

But in natural selection the economic establishment found a mas-sive sanction which gathered into one grand synthesis all of the previous ones and added to them its own profound, "scientific" prestige. Natural selection and the struggle for existence lent authority to laissez-faire economics (the state, said Herbert Spen-cer, should refrain from action calculated to interfere with the struggle for existence in the industrial field [9]); absorbed the older religious sanctions (the "laws" of natural selection, said one econ-omist, were "merely God's regular methods of expressing his choice and approval" [1]); and seemed to make Progress inevitable (evolu-tion, said Spencer, "can end only in the establishment of the greatest perfection and the most complete happiness"; "Progress," he said, "is not an accident, but a necessity" [2]).

Among American economists, the most thoroughgoing advocate of these views was William Graham Sumner, whose reading of Spencer in the early 1870's convinced him that Spencer was right in seeing the world as "a harsh, exacting nature, enforcing a bitter struggle for the meager goods available to humankind. To him the laws of individual and social existence were simple and rigorous. Rewards and punishments are meted out with impartial justice. Property, the enjoyment of family life, health, social preference go to the fit, while poverty, disease, and starvation are the lot of the unfit." And thus "the millionaires are a product of natural selec-tion, acting on the whole body of men to pick out those who can meet the requirement of certain work to be done." [3] This is con-

8. Quoted in Matthew Josephson, *The Robber Barons* (New York, 1934), p. 299.
9. Edward S. Corwin, "The Impact of the Idea of Evolution on the Amer-ican Political and Constitutional Tradi-tion," in Stow Persons, ed., *Evolution-ary Thought in America* (New Haven, 1950), p. 186.

1. Thomas Nixon Carver, quoted in Richard Hofstadter, *Social Darwinism in American Thought* (Boston, 1955), p. 40.
2. Hofstadter, p. 40.
3. See Maurice R. Davis, ed., *Sumner Today* (New Haven, 1940), p. 92, and Hofstadter, p. 58.

servative "social Darwinism" in a nutshell. (I put the phrase in quotation marks to indicate its spuriousness: Darwin should not, of course, be held responsible for this—or any other—brand of Darwinisticism.)

The Captains of Industry were quick to pick up this Darwinistic vocabulary. "The growth of a large business," said John D. Rockefeller (speaking to a Sunday-school class), "is merely a survival of the fittest. . . . The American Beauty rose can be produced in the splendor and fragrance which bring cheer to the beholder only by sacrificing the early buds which grow up around it. This is not an evil tendency in business. It is merely the working-out of a law of nature and of God." [4] Similarly, James J. Hill held that "the fortunes of railroad companies are determined by the law of the survival of the fittest." [5] And Carnegie once warned his lieutenants, upon his break with the Steel Pool, that "a struggle is inevitable and it is a question of the survival of the fittest." [6]

Carnegie was the most introspective and easily the most articulate of the Rugged Individualists. He was strongly attracted to Spencer's theories, and his own speech and writings became full of Spencer's phraseology. He quickly adopted Spencer's easy optimism about progress; he believed firmly that the "fit" who survived in the struggle were the "best," and that these men would lead the rest to certain progress. "The exceptional man in every department," he said, "must be permitted and encouraged to develop his unusual powers, tastes, and ambitions in accordance with the laws which prevail in everything that lives or grows. The 'survival of the fittest' means that the exceptional plants, animals, and men which have the needed 'variations' from the common standard, are the fructifying forces which leaven the whole." [7]

But there were all sorts of anomalies in this use of the evolutionary sanctions: anomalies of language, for instance. To scientists, the word "natural" meant simply "the way things occur in nature"; but used by the apologists for "social Darwinism," it always implied "the way things ought to be." "Survival" was similarly converted into a term of generalized approbation—so persistently that William James was prompted to object: "The entire modern deification of survival *per se*, survival returning to itself, survival naked and abstract, with the denial of any substantive excellence in *what* survives, except the capacity for more survival still, is surely the strangest intellectual stopping-place ever proposed by one man to another." [8] The most abused of all of the evolutionary terms, how-

4. Quoted in Robert E. L. Faris, "Evolution and American Sociology," in Persons, p. 163.
5. James J. Hill, quoted in Hofstadter, p. 45.
6. Josephson, p. 420.
7. Andrew Carnegie, *Problems of Today* (New York, 1933), p. 125.
8. Quoted in Hofstadter, p. 201.

ever, was the word "fit." Spencer and Sumner insisted that the wealthy must be the "fit," for obvious reasons, and conversely, that the poor must be the "unfit," since the latter were, as Spencer held, the "stupid, vicious, or idle," or, to use Sumner's words, the "negligent, shiftless, inefficient, silly, and imprudent." The fallacies of this terminology are obvious and have often been objected to. T. H. Huxley insisted that the biologically "fittest" were by no means always the "highest" order of creatures, and G. G. Simpson has pointed out that, inchoately in Darwin and definitely for neo-Darwinians, "fittest" means simply: leaving the most descendants over a number of generations. Lester Ward, from a less biological, more moralistic point of view, observed that Sumner's definition of the "fit" was based on the "fundamental error that the favors of this world are distributed entirely according to merit." [9]

Another anomaly in the way the conservative "social Darwinists" used Darwinistic analogies was in their tendency to apply them selectively. Capitalistic theory required a "struggle for existence" among competing economic organizations; in practice, however, those very Rugged Individualists who appealed to the competitive Darwinistic analogy against social reforms often tried to thwart its effects upon themselves. They secured the passage of tariffs to protect their individualism from foreign competition, for instance, and tried hard to eliminate all domestic production struggles. Rockefeller, for one, seemed "convinced that the competitive system . . . was a mistake," that "it was a crime against order, efficiency, economy"; and he came to the characteristic conclusion that "it could be eliminated only by abolishing all rivals." [1] Even Carnegie, "individualist" that he proclaimed himself, nevertheless operated a working monopoly in steel. Walter Lippmann has commented wryly that "most men have shown in their behavior that they wished to impose free capitalism on others and to escape it themselves." [2]

It stands as at least a qualified tribute to the humanity of human beings that many people simply would not accept the callousness of conservative "social Darwinism," however much it attempted to justify itself by the appeal to "scientific" prestige. Richard Tawney once argued that one sees the true character of a social philosophy most clearly in "the way it regards the misfortunes of those of its members who fall by the way." [3] Those who fell by the way in late nineteenth-century America were assured by the conservative apologists that this was their "natural" lot, that "science" proved that they were the unavoidable by-products of a beneficent Struggle

9. Quoted in Hofstadter, p. 79.
1. John T. Flynn, *God's Gold* (New York, 1932), p. 221.
2. Walter Lippmann, *The Method of*

Freedom (New York, 1934), p. 25.
3. Richard Tawney, *Religion and the Rise of Capitalism* (New York, 1926), p. 247.

for Existence, without which there could be no Progress; but meanwhile, men with less emotional investment in maintaining the economic status quo were questioning whether the implications of evolution were really as somberly deterministic as the conservatives made out. As early as the 1870's some zoologists had been investigating the implications of cooperation, as well as competition, in the natural world, and in 1902 Peter Kropotkin was to publish his *Mutual Aid*, revealing that he had

> failed to find—although I was eagerly looking for it—that bitter struggle for the means of existence, *among animals belonging to the same species*, which was considered by most Darwinists (though not always by Darwin himself) as the dominant characteristic of struggle for life, and the main factor of evolution. . . . On the other hand, wherever I saw animal life in abundance . . . I saw Mutual Aid and Mutual Support carried on to an extent which made me suspect in it a feature of the greatest importance for the maintenance of life, the preservation of each species, and its further evolution.[4]

And he generalized, from this pattern, that

> it is not love and not even sympathy upon which Society is based in mankind. It is the conscience—be it only at the stage of an instinct—of human solidarity. It is the unconscious recognition of the force that is borrowed by each man from the practice of mutual aid; of the close dependency of every one's happiness upon the happiness of all; and of the sense of justice, or equity, which brings the individual to consider the rights of every other individual as equal to his own. Upon this broad and necessary foundation the still higher moral feelings are developed.[5]

Thomas Henry Huxley had already made the famous distinction, in his Romanes lecture of 1893, that "the ethical progress of society depends, not on imitating the cosmic process, still less in running away from it, but in combating it." [6] "Social progress," he said, "means a checking of the cosmic process at every step and the substitution for it of another, which may be called the ethical process; the end of which is not the survival of those who may happen to be the fittest, in respect of the whole of the conditions which obtain, but of those who are ethically the best." [7]

By the end of the century, then, there were developing some serious demurrers to narrowly conservative Darwinistic social thought. Some naturalists were broadening the evolutionary view of life to show that nature was not always and simply competitive. And some social and ethical thinkers were attempting to demonstrate

4. Peter Kropotkin, *Mutual Aid* (London, 1902), pp. vii–ix.
5. Kropotkin, pp. xiii–xiv.
6. *Touchstone for Ethics*, p. 92.
7. *Touchstone for Ethics*, p. 91.

that even though ruthless competition does exist in nature, it is not therefore necessarily a proper pattern for human behavior.

V

Discussions of Darwinism and Darwinisticism inevitably return to the *impressiveness* of science, its ineluctable ability to demonstrate, to convince, its power to change the conditions and directions of our lives. Literary men, heirs to thousands of years of a general cultural hegemony, have not always welcomed the intrusion of this new power into their lives. The Victorian author George Gissing once wrote:

> I hate and fear "science" because of my conviction that for long to come if not forever, it will be the remorseless enemy of mankind. I see it destroying all simplicity and gentleness of life, all beauty of the world; I see it restoring barbarism under the mask of civilization; I see it darkening men's minds and hardening their hearts; I see it bringing a time of vast conflicts, which will pale into insignificance "the thousand wars of old," and, as likely as not, will whelm all the laborious advances of mankind in blood-drenched chaos.[8]

Writers' responses to Darwin in particular were often hostile. In novel, story, and poem, frontal attacks and attacks by innuendo and ridicule appeared regularly throughout the last decades of the nineteenth century. But thoughtful writers were at the same time busy assimilating the evolutionary doctrine into their work. Some had been using evolution before 1859: Tennyson was proud of having discussed evolution in his verse not only before the *Origin of Species* but even before the *Vestiges of Creation*. Browning, too, had mentioned evolutionary ideas prior to 1859, and both poets continued to write about the subject, off and on, for the rest of their lives. After 1859, however, evolution cropped up everywhere: in the novels of Bulwer-Lytton, Charles Reade, Mrs. Humphry Ward, Gissing, and Charles Kingsley and in scores of satires and romances, evolution was cited, discussed, and absorbed.

The most distinguished propagators of evolution to the late-Victorian reading public were George Meredith, Thomas Hardy, and A. C. Swinburne, and (in a rather different way and somewhat later) Samuel Butler, H. G. Wells, and George Bernard Shaw. The first three (despite Hardy's gloom) tended to see the outcome of man's tribulations, in a world that is red in tooth and claw, as true progress. Meredith built a "philosophy of earth" around this belief, even though at times he, like Tennyson, only faintly trusted the

8. George Gissing, *The Private Papers of Henry Ryecroft*, Chapter 18.

larger hope that somehow, eventually, good would be the final goal of ill. Equally familiar is the story of how Butler, Wells, and Shaw all turned consciously away from Darwin and toward a Neo-Lamarckian version of evolution. The Lamarckian thesis was more attractive to them than Darwin's natural selection because it seemed more "optimistic"—it allowed more easily a teleological interpretation, a hope that somehow a Purpose did guide our steps aright.

Some writers needed this kind of reassurance; others did not. The influence of Darwinistic thinking upon late-nineteenth-century naturalism is too well known to need recounting here, but it might be recorded that the naturalists saw themselves as tough-minded students of the nature of evolutionary man, observers of his environmental influences, of the objective facts of life. Darwin had revealed man's true corporeal history, and the naturalistic writers pursued this record of the flesh with the intensity of devoted researchers. "Given a strong man and an unsatisfied woman," Zola proposed to "seek in them the beast, to see nothing but the beast . . ."

Less familiar is the story of those professional students of the arts in England, France, Germany, and America who saw and explained the arts in terms of Darwinian analogies. John Addington Symonds, like Walter Bagehot, Sir Leslie Stephen, and others, analyzed what he considered to be the inevitable aesthetic consequences of Darwinian thought. First of all, he said, evolution means that "all things in the universe exist in process." One must not attempt, then, to discuss a work of art without reference to its antecedents. This, Symonds believed, would revitalize aesthetic history and criticism. Second, evolution involves the principle of uniformity: "It implies the rejection of miraculous interferences, abrupt leaps and bounds in Nature." Finally, evolution implies the principle of increasing complexity, or "the passage of all things, inorganic and organic, by the action of inevitable law, from simplicity to complexity." [9]

Symonds became so engrossed with the concept of evolution that he could hardly write on any subject without pointing out that it had gone through a process of development. He was particularly impressed with the image of the growth cycle and the similarity of the growth of an art to the growth of an organism; he saw all arts as developing through three stages, corresponding to physical youth, maturity, and decline. This sort of "evolutionary" perspective, he said,

> lent the charm of biography or narrative to what had previously seemed so dull and lifeless—the history of art or letters. Illumi-

9. John Addington Symonds, *Essays Speculative and Suggestive* (London, 1890), I, 8, 42–43.

nated by this idea, every stage in the progress of culture acquired significance. The origins and incunabula of art, viewed in their relation to its further growth, ceased to have a merely antiquarian interest. Periods of decadence were explicable and intelligible on the principle that every organism, expanding from the germ, passing through adolescence to maturity, is bound at last to exhaust its motive force and perish by exaggerating qualities implicit in the mature type.[1]

Thus his particular application of the evolutionary idea, Symonds thought, could be valuable to criticism in many ways. It would be especially helpful in estimating the significance of lesser works of art, whether these were works of primitives or of decadents. But by illuminating the lesser works, one should also see the greater ones in more accurate perspective.

Symonds clung to his organic analogy because it served as evidence for what he called the "law of sequence" in art. By seeing all artistic change in terms of what he held to be "inevitable" progressions, he could pronounce upon the evolution of the arts with an air of finality, and seem to arrive at scientific certainty in his criticism. Symonds believed it was the purpose of the critic to judge, to evaluate; but his analogical uses of the evolutionary theory did not, in fact, provide a sound basis for judgment; his use of "process" and the "growth cycle" were only speciously scientific. This does not mean that Symonds was never an effective critic, but his best criticism was conducted on principles other than evolutionary.

Explicit adaptations of evolutionary notions into the practice and study of the arts were characteristic of the late nineteenth century, but have been far less so of the twentieth. In part at least this is because the nineteenth century had to go through the difficult process of changing its mind, of adapting itself to evolution; the twentieth century simply accepts it. Evolution has become one of those topics so well founded as not really to be exciting to educated people any more, and consequently direct references to evolution in literature are almost as rare as direct references to the laws of gravity. The indirect influence of evolution on our literature has, on the other hand, been tremendous. Whitehead once proposed, in a much-repeated statement, that students of the history of ideas should not look for those ideas which are under constant discussion in any age, but instead should look for those basic assumptions which are so fundamental to a man's way of thinking that he does not even realize he is assuming them. Evolution has by now become such an unconscious assumption in our society.

One of the supposed literary effects of Darwinian assumptions has already been mentioned: Joseph Wood Krutch (among others)

1. *Essays Speculative and Suggestive*, I, 11.

has maintained that Darwin's ideas have eroded human values and therefore destroyed high tragedy in our century. "With increasing completeness," Krutch wrote in *The Modern Temper*, "science maps out the pattern of nature, but the latter has no relation to the pattern of human needs and feelings." This fact, Krutch said, precludes tragedy because "the Tragic Fallacy depends ultimately upon the assumption which man so readily makes that something outside his own being . . . confirms him in his feeling that his passions and his opinions are important. . . . We can no longer tell tales of noble men because we do not believe that noble men exist." [2]

Looking about us from the perspective of the last third of the twentieth century, we can recognize the symptoms of Krutch's diagnosis. Nevertheless, the case as he states it can hardly be the whole story. For one thing, we ought to consider the negative instances. If Darwin destroyed twentieth-century tragedy, who then was responsible for the palpable failure of early nineteenth-century tragedy, or for the failure of eighteenth-century tragedy? In fact, the occurrence of high tragedy has always been far rarer than its nonoccurrence; to expect every age to produce a Sophocles or a Shakespeare is overoptimistic.

For another thing: it is not simply axiomatic that a physically mechanistic world is necessarily a morally valueless one. Those who propose that it is seem to regret that natural selection is an automatic process, that it acts independently of teleological considerations, and that it, together with Mendelian genetics, makes such a satisfactory explanation of organic evolution; and they sometimes attempt to ignore all this and postulate instead some sort of "will" or "preference" or "emergent evolution." Since Darwin, however, reasonable men have simply had to abandon naturalistic teleology—one cannot, any more, look to nature for revealing patterns of goal-directed process. Or, to put it another way, goal-direction in nature must now be divorced from final causes or preternatural factors. However, as John Herman Randall, Jr., has pointed out,

> nature is once more for us, as for the Greeks, full of *implicit* ends and ideals, full of "values," just because it is now an affair of processes, of means effecting ends, of things that are "necessary for," "better" and "worse for" other things. It contains so much "natural teleology," in terms of which its various factors can be "evaluated." It takes but a single flower to refute the contention that there are no "values" in nature, no achievement of ends through valuable means. We may even say it is obviously "good for" the planet to go round the sun. Of course, neither the flower nor the planet "finds" it good: only men "find" anything. But

2. Krutch, pp. 12, 136–137.

surely it does not follow that because only men find anything good or bad, better or worse, what they find is not found. The finding is a genuine cooperation with nature.

It is such a nature our best post-Darwinian knowledge and thought now reveal to us.[3]

I would propose not that Darwinism has killed human values and therefore great and tragic art in our time, but something nearer the reverse: that since Darwin, we have been forced, in art as in life, to mature to finiteness. I mean maturing as human beings not simply by realizing that there are no usable absolutes for man—for that mere realization is still a kind of adolescence—but by accepting one's finiteness and learning to live with it with some degree of sanity and integrity.

Oedipus and Lear are not great tragic heroes simply because they stand in relation to the gods as flies to wanton boys, after all, but because of their own impressive human characters. And man has not stopped defending his uniqueness. If he is unique because of a certain type of brain rather than some supernatural prerogative, and if he has chosen a perhaps disagreeable scientific fact in preference to a pretty illusion, the case is nevertheless the same: man's uniqueness, his dignity, remain important to him. Twentieth-century literature taken as a whole—despite absurdity, disillusion, black humor, anti-heroism, existential angst, and cosmic nausea—remains a human-centered, human-valued literature. We need not look for the tragic spirit only in drama. The greatest of the modern writers in all genres—Lawrence, Joyce, Faulkner, Camus, Hemingway, Yeats, Frost, Pirandello, Brecht, Beckett—have kept aspiring man as at least the implied focus of their work, so that even when he reads as a gray failure, we must take him to be the ghostly negative of an implicity positive picture.

Looking back at a million years of man's struggle to be human, at his errant and painful attempts to be a special kind of animal— the animal who thinks, the animal who creates—it seems to me that despite his shortcomings, we must remain man's admirer. "Thought makes the whole dignity of man." Yes. Despite its simplicity, despite our sad reflections on the inadequacy of our thinking, on its stunted and twisted travesties in history and our daily lives, we must end by agreeing with Pascal. *Homo* is unique and valuable precisely because he is *sapiens*. He is worth keeping because, given his remarkable past, we may continue to hope that he has, as Darwin surmised, "a still higher destiny in the future."

3. John Herman Randall, Jr., "The ophy," *Journal of the History of Ideas,* Changing Impact of Darwin on Philos XXII (1961), 458–459.

Selected Readings

The number of books and articles written about Darwin's work is (to use one of Darwin's favorite words) staggering. This brief listing is meant merely to be suggestive. For more comprehensive guidance, one may examine the various bibliographies cited below.

In order not to be cumbersome, works included elsewhere in this volume (except primary Darwin materials) are not repeated here. Titles available in paperback editions are starred.

I. BIBLIOGRAPHICAL MATERIALS

R. B. Freeman, *The Works of Charles Darwin: An Annotated Bibliographical Handlist* (London, 1965).

See also the annual bibliographies in *Isis* and *Victorian Studies* and extensive listings of scientific contributions in Julian Huxley, *★ Evolution: The Modern Synthesis* (London, 1963) and of sociological contributions in Ashley Montagu, *Darwin: Competition & Cooperation* (New York, 1952). For an extensive discussion of recent studies in various fields, see Bert James Loewenberg, "Darwin and Darwin Studies, 1959–63" *History of Science,* IV (1965), 15–54.

II. BIOGRAPHY

Barlow, Nora, ed., *★ The Autobiography of Charles Darwin, 1809–1882, with Original Omissions Restored* (New York, 1969).

Barlow, Nora, ed., *Darwin and Henslow: The Growth of an Idea; Letters 1831–1860* (London, 1967).

Darwin, Francis, ed., *The Life and Letters of Charles Darwin* (New York, 1959).

Darwin, Francis and A. C. Seward, eds., *More Letters* (London, 1903).

III. DARWIN'S WORK

★ The Structure and Distribution of Coral Reefs . . . (London, 1842).

Journal of Researches into the Natural History and Geology of the Countries Visited during the Voyage of H. M. S. 'Beagle' . . . (London, 1845).

On the Origin of Species by Means of Natural Selection . . . (London, 1859).

The Variation of Animals and Plants under Domestication (London, 1868).

The Descent of Man . . . (London, 1871).

★ The Expression of the Emotions in Man and Animals (London, 1872).

The Formation of Vegetable Mould . . . (London, 1881).

IV. GENERAL OR MISCELLANEOUS STUDIES

Barnett, S. A., ed., *A Century of Darwin* (London, 1958).

★ Eiseley, Loren C., *Darwin's Century* (New York, 1959).

★ Huxley, Julian, *Evolution in Action* (New York, 1953).

Huxley, Thomas Henry, *Darwiniana* (New York, 1893).

Persons, Stow, ed., *Evolutionary Thought in America* (New Haven, 1950).

★ Simpson, George Gaylord, *The Meaning of Evolution* (New Haven, 1949).

Tax, Sol, ed., *Evolution after Darwin* (Chicago, 1960).

V. DARWIN AND SCIENCE

Bateson, W., *Problems of Genetics* (Oxford, 1913).

★ Bell, P. R., ed., *Darwin's Biological Work* (Cambridge, England, 1959).

De Beer, Gavin R., *Embryos and Ancestors* (Oxford, 1940).

DeVries, Hugo, *Species and Varieties* (Chicago and London, 1905).

★ Dobzhansky, Theodosius, *Genetics and the Origin of Species* (New York, 1937).

Fisher, Ronald A., *The Genetical Theory of Natural Selection* (Oxford, 1930).

★ Gray, Asa, *Darwiniana* (New York, 1876).

Mayr, Ernst, *Animal Species and Evolution* (Cambridge, Mass., 1963).

Morgan, T. H., *Evolution and Genetics* (Princeton, 1925).

———, *The Scientific Basis of Evolution* (London, 1932).

Simpson, George Gaylord, *Horses* (New York, 1961).

Wallace, Alfred Russel, *Darwinism* (London and New York, 1889).

653

VI. DARWIN AND PHILOSOPHICAL AND THEOLOGICAL THOUGHT
Bergson, Henri, *Creative Evolution* (London, 1911).
Fiske, John, *Darwinism* (London and New York, 1879).
★ Greene, John C., *Darwin and the Modern World View* (Baton Rouge, 1961).
★ Hardin, Garrett James, *Nature and Man's Fate* (New York, 1959).
★ Medawar, P. B., *The Future of Man* (London, 1960).
Passmore, John, "Darwin's Impact on British Metaphysics," *Victorian Studies*, III (1959), 41–54.
Raphael, D. D., "Darwinism and Ethics," in Barnett, *Darwin's Century* (q.v.).
★ Waddington, C. H., *The Ethical Animal* (London, 1960).

VII. DARWIN AND SOCIETY
Banton, Michael, ed., *Darwinism and the Study of Society* (London and Chicago, 1961).
Burton, D. H., "Theodore Roosevelt's Social Darwinism and Views on Imperialism," *Journal of the History of Ideas*, XXVI (1965), 103–118.
Burrow, J. W., *Evolution and Society* (Cambridge, England, 1966).
Goldman, Irving, "Evolution and Anthropology," *Victorian Studies*, III (1959), 55–75.
Gordon, Scott, "Darwinism and Social Thought," in H. H. J. Nesbitt, ed., *Darwin in Retrospect* (Toronto, 1960).
Huxley, Julian, *Soviet Genetics and World Science* (London, 1949).
MacRae, Donald G., "Darwin and the Social Sciences," in Barnett, *Darwin's Century* (q.v.).
Montagu, Ashley, *Darwin: Competition & Cooperation* (New York, 1952).
Zirkle, Conway, *Evolution, Marxian Biology, and the Social Scene* (Philadelphia, 1959).

VIII. DARWIN AND THE LITERARY MIND
Beach, Joseph Warren, *The Concept of Nature in Nineteenth-Century English Poetry* (New York, 1936).
★ Barzun, Jacques, *Darwin, Marx, Wagner: Critique of a Heritage* (New York, 1941).
★ Bush, Douglas, *Science and English Poetry* (New York, 1950).
Henkin, Leo J., *Darwinism in the English Novel, 1860–1910* (New York, 1940).
★ Hyman, Stanley Edgar, *The Tangled Bank: Darwin, Marx, Frazer and Freud as Imaginative Writers* (New York, 1962).
Irvine, William, "The Influence of Darwin on Literature," *Proceedings of the American Philosophical Society*, CIII (1959), 616–628.
★ Muller, Herbert J., *Science and Critsicism* (New York, 1956).
★ Shaw, George Bernard, *Back to Methuselah* (London, 1921).
Willey Basil, *Darwin and Butler: Two Versions of Evolution* (London, 1960).

Index